THE NEW CHAUCER SOCIETY

Studies in the Age of Chaucer, the yearbook of The New Chaucer Society, is published annually. Each issue contains substantial articles on all aspects of Chaucer and his age, book reviews, and an annotated Chaucer bibliography. Manuscripts should follow the *Chicago Manual of Style,* 16th edition. Unsolicited reviews are not accepted. Authors receive twenty free offprints of articles and ten of reviews. All correspondence regarding manuscript submissions should be directed to the Editor, David Matthews, School of Arts, Languages and Cultures, University of Manchester, Oxford Road, Manchester M13 9PL, United Kingdom. Subscriptions to The New Chaucer Society and information about the Society's activities should be directed to Ruth Evans, Department of English, Saint Louis University, Adorjan Hall 231, 3800 Lindell Blvd., St. Louis, MO 63108–3414. Back issues of the journal may be ordered from University of Notre Dame Press, Chicago Distribution Center, 11030 South Langley Avenue, Chicago, IL 60628; phone: 800-621-2736; fax: 800-621-8476; from outside the United States: phone: 773-702-7000; fax: 773-702-7212.

PUBLICATIONS OF THE NEW CHAUCER SOCIETY

Studies in the Age of Chaucer

Studies in the Age of Chaucer

Volume 34
2012

EDITOR

DAVID MATTHEWS

PUBLISHED ANNUALLY BY THE NEW CHAUCER SOCIETY
SAINT LOUIS UNIVERSITY IN ST. LOUIS

The frontispiece design, showing the Pilgrims at the Tabard Inn, is adapted from the woodcut in Caxton's second edition of the *Canterbury Tales*.

ISBN-10 0-933784-36-8
ISBN-13 978-0-933784-36-9
ISSN 0190-2407

CONTENTS

CONTENTS

REVIEWS

CONTENTS

Studies in the Age of Chaucer

Names of the Beasts: Tracking the *Animot* in Medieval Texts

Carolynn Van Dyke
Lafayette College

> The domination which God gave people over all living creatures is implicit throughout all Bestiaries. Names and their etymology are very important parts of [Bestiary texts]. It is a well-known psychological concept that to give a name to something is a way of controlling it.
>
> —Christopher de Hamel, Introduction, *Book of Beasts*

> On farms where cows were called by name, milk yield was 258 liters higher than on farms where this was not the case (*p* < 0.001).
>
> —Catherine Bertenshaw and Peter Rowlinson, "Exploring Stock Managers' Perceptions of the Human-Animal Relationship"

THE EMERGING FIELD GENERALLY KNOWN AS "animal studies" is vexed by a problem familiar to medievalists: the reference of general names. Among scientists, names for species and genera have been subject to debate and revision at least since Charles Darwin undermined the assumption that organisms can be assigned to stable categories. More fundamentally, many contemporary scholars echo the medieval debate over the most general names, universals, with their challenge to *animal* itself. The most widely cited version of that challenge is central to Jacques Derrida's *L'animal que donc je suis* (2006), edited and translated as *The Animal That Therefore I Am*. Derrida opens the lecture on which the book is based by acknowledging his embarrassment when naked before the gaze of his "little cat," who is, he insists, a truly singular creature, not "the exemplar of a species called 'cat,' even less so of an 'animal' genus or kingdom."[1] *Animal* epitomizes the "general singular" name, he argues, with which we claim "to designate every living thing that is

---

[1] Jacques Derrida, *The Animal That Therefore I Am,* trans. David Wills, ed. Marie-Louise Mallet (New York: Fordham University Press, 2008), 9.

Studies in the Age of Chaucer 34 (2012):1–51

held not to be human." Even to use that name constitutes an "asininity," a "*bêtise.*" Derrida exposes the *bêtise* with the brilliant spotlight of another coinage, *l'animot*—a "chimerical word" signifying that "animal" is not a biological reality.[2] Throughout the book, however, Derrida continues to use "animals" and "the animal." And the many writers who take up his attack on the "general singular" seem similarly unable to dispense with it.[3] Semantic disputes are of course common in academic fields, but animal studies (like its variants, including critical animal studies, human/animal studies, animal cultural studies, and animality studies) may be the only discipline unable to dispense with a self-designation that it finds wrongheaded and even unethical. *Animal* unsettles the field's practitioners as much as the gaze of his cat did Derrida.

Many writers who express this discomfort seem to regard it as both admirable and recent. That is, they imply that earlier thinkers had no scruples about "homogenizing" animals.[4] Derrida "venture[s] to say that never, on the part of any great philosopher from Plato to Heidegger, . . . have I noticed a protestation *based on principle,* . . . against the general singular that is *the animal.*"[5] Medieval thinkers in particular are said to have affirmed a separation of "man" and "beast" ordained when God invited Adam to name the other animals.[6] In the

[2] Ibid., 31–32, 41.

[3] Among those who continue to use *animal* even as they denounce it are Giorgio Agamben, *The Open: Man and Animal,* trans. Kevin Attell (Stanford: Stanford University Press, 2004); Erica Fudge, *Animal* (London: Reaktion, 2002); Leonard Lawlor, *This Is Not Sufficient: An Essay on Animality and Human Nature in Derrida* (New York: Columbia University Press, 2007); Cary Wolfe, *What Is Posthumanism?* (Minneapolis: University of Minnesota Press, 2010); and several contributors to the "Theories and Methodologies: Animal Studies" section of *PMLA* 124.2 (March 2009): 361–575.

[4] I take "homogenization" from Clare Palmer, "Madness and Animality in Michel Foucault's *Madness and Civilization,*" in *Animal Philosophy: Essential Readings in Continental Thought,* ed. Matthew Calarco and Peter Atterton (London and New York: Continuum, 2004), 72–84 (83); in turn, Palmer refers (Calarco and Atterton, *Animal Philosophy,* 209 n. 37) to the "discussion of homogenization and 'hyper-separation'" in Val Plumwood, *Feminism and the Mastery of Nature* (London: Routledge, 1993).

[5] Derrida, *The Animal,* 40.

[6] See, for instance, James J. Sheehan, Introduction to Part 1, *The Boundaries of Humanity: Humans, Animals, Machines,* ed. Sheehan and Morton Sosna (Berkeley and Los Angeles: University of California Press, 1991), 27–35 (28); Harriet Ritvo, "The Animal Connection," in Sheehan and Sosna, *Boundaries of Humanity,* 68–84 (68); Jennifer Ham and Matthew Senior, Introduction, *Animal Acts: Configuring the Human in Western History,* ed. Ham and Senior (New York: Routledge, 1997), 1–7 (4); Joyce E. Salisbury, "Human Beasts and Bestial Humans in the Middle Ages," in Ham and Senior, *Animal Acts,* 9–21 (10) (referring specifically to the era before the twelfth century), and *The Beast Within: Animals in the Middle Ages* (New York: Routledge, 1994), 62; Kelly Oliver, *Animal*

passage with which I open this essay, Christopher de Hamel suggests that medieval writers emphasized the names of animals to reassert human control. Nor did onomastic dominion weaken, according to a common metanarrative, until the modern or even the postmodern era: Darwin and other nineteenth-century scientists undermined the Christian paradigm of "superiority and dominion"; in the twentieth century, philosophers have at last challenged the view maintained "throughout Western civilization" that the animal existed to serve the human.[7] In a pattern familiar to medievalists, the metanarrative casts premodern positivism as the Other of postmodern questioning.

Like most such self-congratulatory stories, the notion that we are only now rattling the semantic cages constructed by premoderns rests on oversimplifications, both historical and theoretical. Naming practices in medieval animal texts are hardly uniform. Derrida is right that medieval writers do not criticize *animal* explicitly, but they certainly scrutinize it. Moreover, some use this term, or *beast,* with destabilizing inconsistency, alternately including and excluding human beings. And many medieval texts name and rename nonhuman creatures dynamically, mixing levels of abstraction to suggest an interplay of generic and singular identity. Thus they demonstrate that naming can signal not control but recognition, even deference.

After sketching some medieval theories of appellation, I will follow animal namings in the encyclopedia of Bartholomaeus Anglicus, the Middle English *Owl and the Nightingale,* Caxton's version of the Reynard cycle, and a remarkable thirteenth-century lyric called "The Names of a Hare in English," finding in most of them complex ways of representing species that avoid linguistic and conceptual *bêtise.*

Singularity in Paradise

Oversimplified descriptions of medieval naming practices often refer to the originary text cited by many medieval writers themselves: Adam's naming of the beasts and fowls in the second chapter of Genesis. The

---

Lessons: How They Teach Us to Be Human (New York: Columbia University Press, 2009), 240.

   [7] The statement about Darwin is in Fudge, *Animal,* 19; the reference to philosophers since 2004 is from Peter Singer, Preface, Calarco and Atterton, *Animal Philosophy,* xi–xii (xi).

significance of that scene depends in part on the first chapter, in which God blesses humankind, bidding them "rule over the fishes of the sea, and the fowls of the air, and all living creatures that move upon the earth" (Douay-Rheims, Gen. 1.28). The second chapter reprises the Creation (in significantly different order), then adds that God "brought [the beasts and birds] to Adam to see what he would call them: for whatsoever Adam called any living creature the same is its name" (Gen. 2.19). The power to name the animals thus appears as an aspect or confirmation of human dominion.

As de Hamel notes, names and etymologies are central to encyclopedias and bestiaries. The authors and compilers of those texts may indeed be seeking psychological control, as de Hamel implies; in any case, their ways of using names also assert epistemological and even ontological mastery. And Derrida's meditations on the general singular illuminate a key element of that mastery. Adducing the essence of a species from its name, many medieval writers claim to delimit the attributes and behavior of an uncountable number of beings at once. Isidore of Seville identifies "castrated" as the defining feature of any cock, presumably because *galli* could designate not just cocks but also the eunuch priests of Cybele. Isidore also writes that the Greeks called the panther Πάν or "all" "because it is the friend of 'all' animals, except the dragon, or because it both rejoices in the society of its own kind and gives back whatever it receives in the same kind."[8] Particular explications may be murky, but the premise is clear: to understand the name is to grasp the species' nature.

But the connection between appellation and hegemony in the Genesis story is complicated by visual images of the biblical text. If natural historians summarize or invoke the naming scene, graphic artists recreate it, often and richly. Sometimes their images do convey human mastery—through the animals' submissive postures, for instance, or perhaps through their "stand[ing] before Adam raising a front hoof or a paw."[9] But illustrators necessarily represent the creatures as acting for themselves as well, submitting or deferring voluntarily. And while we might debate the degree to which such submission is truly voluntary,

[8] Isidore, *The Etymologies of Isidore of Seville,* trans. Stephen A. Barney et al. (Cambridge: Cambridge University Press, 2006), XII.vii.50 and XII.ii.8.

[9] Henry Maguire, "Adam and the Animals: Allegory and the Literal Sense in Early Christian Art," *Studies on Art and Archeology in Honor of Ernst Kitzinger on His Seventy-Fifth Birthday,* Dumbarton Oaks Papers 41 (January 1987): 363–73 (366).

the gestures must be read in conjunction with another element of the illustrations: individualization. Necessarily, the beasts and birds strike us not as schematic representatives of their species but as particular creatures, rendered naturalistically but displaying something like personality.[10] Thus individualized through expressive faces and postures, the animals in illustrations of the scene seem less subjects than responsive agents.[11]

The biblical text does not disclose the names that Adam gave the birds and beasts. We might imagine, following the illustrators, that he confronted one or a pair of each type. Perhaps, then, he named them as individuals; perhaps he had no conception of species. The Bible's next reference to animals is the statement that Abel is "shepherd of sheep" (Gen. 4:2). By that point, *ovis* presumably covers and in a sense levels

---

[10] Debra Hassig finds similar indications of individuation and affect in bestiary illustrations, contrasting with the generalized moralizations found in the accompanying texts; perhaps that counterpoint reflects the difference between visual and verbal media. "Beauty in the Beasts: A Study of Medieval Aesthetics," *RES: Anthropology and Aesthetics* 19/20 (1990): 137–61 (151–57).

[11] Typical are the images of Genesis 2:19 available through the ARTstor database (http://www.artres.com/c/htm). For instance, in Lorenzo Maitani's marble relief on the facade of the Duomo di Orvieto from the last quarter of the twelfth century, Adam reaches toward a lion, with whom he exchanges serious but benign gazes, while a ram imitates his gesture with a raised hoof. A fresco in the nave of San Pietro a Valle, Ferentillo, shows Adam reaching down with his right hand toward a canine of some sort while resting his left hand on the head of a smiling ram. The creatures in a thirteenth-century cupola mosaic in the atrium of Saint Mark's Cathedral in Venice are all paired, as they are in a "creation of the living creatures" mosaic in the same installation that shows (as do other illustrations of the same scene) a male and female of each type, but the members of each pair differ in features and expressions. Again Adam rests his hand on the head of one creature, here a lion. He looks, however, not toward the animals but back at God, who extends his open hand toward Adam—perhaps a delegation of power but also a chain of recognitions. A fourth illustration of the Genesis scene, this time from a manuscript—the Ashmole Bestiary—seems to fuse Adam with the scholars who extended his appellations in encyclopedias and bestiaries. A fully clothed Adam sits on an elaborate chair in the upper left of five rectilinear frames, which are separated by bars into what look like rooms in a multistory building with the front wall removed. Groups of beasts occupy the other rooms, some only partly visible as they approach from the right. But the frames seem permeable. In some cases a creature's foot or nose edges over a floor or wall. Adam's foot too crosses into the lower of the frames to his right, and he gestures and gazes toward the rabbit, three beasts, and two birds in the frame above it. He and they appear able to see one another. In some cases, particularly the bottom frame, the animals look at each other or at something they are eating, as if unaware of what occurs above them. Other plates in the Ashmole Bestiary use the same reticulation, particularly those illustrating God's creation of sea creatures and birds and beasts; but the naming scene evokes for me the work of the encyclopedist or bestiarist himself, defining and to some degree confining the creatures while also recognizing their agency and particularity.

all of the beasts under his control. But of course Abel's semantic (and physical) corralling postdates the Fall. As Richard Sorabji observes, the killing and eating of animals also begins after the Fall; indeed, only after the Flood does God classify "omne quod movetur et vivit" (everything that moves and lives) as food for human beings.[12] In the state of innocence, on the other hand, men needed the animals in order "to acquire an experiential knowledge of their natures" [ad experimentalem cognitionem sumendam de naturis eorum]; this is "suggested," Thomas Aquinas writes, by God's having led them to Adam to be named.[13] Presumably experiential knowledge would have begun as Adam (and Eve?) encountered particular creatures.[14] And perhaps an unfallen humanity would have continued to identify animals as individuals, neither wanting nor needing to stamp them with generic templates.

Falling into Species

Like other linguistic practices, collective naming does not simply represent human epistemological control; it doubles back to shape human perception. In particular, it reflects and confirms perceptions of nonhuman creatures, supporting a view that I will call species determinism.

As is commonly known, medieval authorities vigorously debated the extent of human self-determination, but almost no one attributed individual autonomy to other animals. Jan M. Ziolkowski points out that biblical animals act only as "tool[s] of God's will" or "implement[s] in a miracle."[15] Aristotle denied intentional agency (though not volition) to animals, and the Stoics held that animals "can be activated (*energein*), but cannot act (*prattein*)."[16] Similarly, medieval philosophers and theologians held animals to be incapable of intentional choice. Aquinas ac-

[12] Richard Sorabji, *Animal Minds and Human Morals: The Origins of the Western Debate* (Ithaca: Cornell University Press, 1993), 198; citing Genesis 1:26–30, 3:21, 4:3–5, and 8:20–9:4.

[13] Thomas Aquinas, *Summa theologiae,* Blackfriars edition (Latin and English), 61 vols. (New York: McGraw-Hill, 1964–73), vol. 13, 1a. 96, q1.

[14] Of course, Aquinas does not mention Eve in this passage, but he does refer to human beings in the plural. In contrast, Kelly Oliver is right to point out, expanding on Derrida's treatment of the Genesis story, that not only does Adam name the animals only in the second Creation version—in which man and woman are created separately—but he also "names woman *in the same way* that he names the other animals" (*Animal Lessons: How They Teach Us to be Human* [New York: Columbia University Press, 2009], 142–43).

[15] Jan M. Ziolkowski, *Talking Animals: Medieval Latin Beast Poetry, 750–1150* (Philadelphia: University of Pennsylvania Press, 1993), 33.

[16] Sorabji, *Animal Minds and Human Morals,* 108–10, 53.

knowledges that animals seem to choose among alternatives, but he attributes such apparent voluntariness to the "sensitive appetite," not the will. "Once presented by outward sense or imagination," he explains, "the desire is moved without choice to something to which the animal has a natural bent, as flame leaps up when fire is kindled."[17] As Eve Salisbury writes, "medieval philosophers attributed animal action to instinct, and animals (unlike humans) were incapable of acting apart from instinctive behavior."[18]

Crucially, this instinctive, involuntary motivation was thought to operate at the level of species. To support his argument that even "examples of sagacity in animal behaviour" arise from "a natural inclination to carry out the intricate processes planned by supreme art," Aquinas adduces "the fact that all members of the same species display the same pattern of behaviour."[19] Abelard writes that dogs bark "in order to express a precise concept (anger, pain, or bliss)," but not by their own will; "rather, [the dog] acts by another will, which is of a natural order (a kind of 'agent will,' we would say, which is the same for all dogs)."[20] Species determinism even informed canon law: at times "[w]hole species of insects and rodents were excommunicated if they caused damage to crops."[21] Karl Steel suggests that species determinism rested in part on the conviction that animals do not share "the key privilege of the human likeness to God": immortality. "Salvation," Steel points, out, "requires being singled out" rather than "meld[ing] into an undifferentiated mass."[22]

Of course, few would dispute that an animal shares many of its features and habits with its conspecifics. Today's popular commentators echo Aquinas when they tell us what to expect from a (any) dog or cat. Researchers report on the behavior of snakes, prairie voles, the thick-

[17] Aquinas, *ST,* vol. 17, 1a2æ. 13, q2.
[18] Salisbury, *Beast Within,* 5.
[19] Aquinas, *ST,* vol. 17, 1a2æ. 13, q2.
[20] Umberto Eco, Roberto Lambertini, Constantino Marmo, and Andrea Tabarroni, "On Animal Language in the Medieval Classification of Signs," in *On the Medieval Theory of Signs,* ed. Eco and Marmo, Foundations of Semiotics 21 (Amsterdam: Benjamins, 1989), 3–41 (15); citing Peter Abelard, *Dialectica,* I.iii.
[21] Ziolkowski, *Talking Animals,* 33.
[22] Karl Steel, "How to Make a Human," *Exemplaria* 20 (2008): 3–27 (16). The "mass" to which Steel refers here is the threatened amalgamation of humans with other animals, but the encyclopedic text that he analyzes in this article—like others of the genre—treats species categorically, suggesting that nonhuman creatures were not "singled out" between or within their own species.

tailed opossum, and captive white-winged vampire bats, to cite a few recent titles. Studying a species or subspecies as a whole permits the broad, reproducible conclusions fundamental to science. But modern science sometimes joins medieval theology in the degree to which it disregards variations within species. According to Marc Bekoff, mistrust of anecdotal evidence leads many scientists to avoid reporting or even acknowledging individual behavior.[23] Indeed, lab animals are often specially bred for homogeneity.[24] According to the authors of *The Evolution of Animal Communication,* even evolutionary biologists have focused unduly on species, assuming that selection operates at the group rather than the individual level.[25] Phylogeneticists, breeders of experimental animals, and many behavioral researchers posit that "all members of the same species display the same pattern of behaviour."[26]

This concurrence across the centuries further complicates the self-congratulatory story to which I referred earlier, in which enlightened constructivism has replaced medieval positivism. We might conclude that both eras adhere to a strong version of species determinism, viewing animals as instances stamped from Platonic templates. But there is another way to explain the concurrence, one that I intend now to pursue: in neither era does this orthodox paradigm dominate completely and continuously. Creatures did not undergo one cataclysmic fall into species. They have been plunged repeatedly, by human discourse and human acts, into collectively determined categories; but they climb back.

In our era, some scientists challenge the assumption that behavior and evolutionary development are to be considered only on the level of species or subspecies. Bekoff and others have published longitudinal

---

[23] Marc Bekoff, *The Emotional Lives of Animals: A Leading Scientist Explores Animal Joy, Sorrow, and Empathy—and Why They Matter* (Novato, Calif.: New World Library, 2007), 119–20.

[24] Mary T. Phillips, "Proper Names and the Social Construction of Biography: The Negative Case of Laboratory Animals," *Qualitative Sociology* 17.2 (1994): 119–42 (130); Jackson Laboratory, "The Importance of Understanding Substrains in the Genomic Age: The Jackson Laboratory," *JAX NOTES* 491 (Fall 2003), http://jaxmice.jax.org/jaxnotes/archive/491a.html; Canadian Council on Animal Care, "Guide to the Care and Use of Experimental Animals Volume 1–Chapter VII," *CCAC Programs,* 1993, http://www.ccac.ca/en/CCAC_Programs/Guidelines_Policies/GUIDES/ENGLISH/V1_93/CHAP/CHVII.HTM.

[25] William A. Searcy and Stephen Nowicki, *The Evolution of Animal Communication: Reliability and Deception in Signaling Systems* (Princeton: Princeton University Press, 2005), 219.

[26] Aquinas, *ST,* 1a2æ. 13, q2 (cited above).

studies of individual animals—chimpanzees, gorillas, and one famous parrot. Some academic researchers study "animal personality" not just across but within species.[27] In developmental biology, William Searcy and Stephen Nowicki are not alone in contesting the emphasis on group selection. As I suggested earlier, Darwin's work undermined the essentialist view of species, leading to fundamental questions about taxonomy. Reviewing many such challenges, some researchers refer to a "cognitive revolution" or "paradigm shift," one that they acknowledge to be neither complete nor uncontested.[28]

As far as I know, no medieval investigations of animals herald a cognitive revolution; but dissent from species determinism emerges in various ways, some limited and some systematic. The limited challenges appear in both expository and fictional genres. It is hardly surprising that pragmatic texts such as hunting manuals acknowledge variations within species. The fourteenth-century *Master of Game* traces those differences to the same causes that influence human beings:

Some [deer] goeth better and are better running and fly better than some, as other beasts do, and some be more cunning and more wily than others, as it is with men, for some be wiser than others. And it cometh to them of the good kind of their father and mother, and of good getting (breeding) and of good nurture and from being born in good constellations, and in good signs of heaven and that (is the case) with men and all other beasts.[29]

The hunter must take these varying traits into account, responding as he would to an agent little more predictable than he is himself. But

[27] Oliver John et al., "Animal Personality," Department of Psychology, University of Texas, December 20, 2009, http://homepage.psy.utexas.edu/homepage/faculty/gosling/animal_personality.htm; Charles Locurto, "Individual Differences and Animal Personality," *Comparative Cognition & Behavior Reviews* 2 (2007), http://psyc.queensu.ca/ccbr/Vol2/Locurto.html. The parrot to which I refer is the subject of Irene Maxine Pepperberg's research, reported most fully in *The Alex Studies: Cognitive and Communicative Abilities of Grey Parrots* (Cambridge, Mass.: Harvard University Press, 1999).

[28] Searcy and Nowicki, *Evolution of Animal Communication,* 25. A useful summary of issues in taxonomy is provided by Marc Ereshefsky, "Species," *The Stanford Encyclopedia of Philosophy* (Spring 2010 edition), ed. Edward N. Zalta, http://plato.stanford.edu/archives/spr2010/entries/species/, section 5. For references to a cognitive revolution in animal science, see, for instance, Pepperberg, *The Alex Studies,* 2; Charles Siebert, "Watching Whales Watching Us," *New York Times Magazine,* July 10, 2009, sec. MM; and Bekoff, *Emotional Lives,* xviii.

[29] Edward of Norwich, *The Master of Game: The Oldest English Book on Hunting,* ed. William A. Baillie-Grohman and F. Baillie-Grohman (London: Chatto & Windus, 1909), 30; parenthetical interpolations in edition. Here Edward closely follows his

there is no evidence that the operational attribution of individual self-determination challenged the orthodox position on species determinism. Much the same can be said of individualized animals in narrative fiction. Romances, religious legends, beast epics, and fables often depict specific creatures that make choices based on particular motives. But most such narratives turn on supernatural causation; in many, the creatures are heavily and consistently anthropomorphized. Once again, species determination and representations of individual agency failed to intersect.

Nonetheless, in many animal texts they do intersect—neither through generalizations about animals nor through fictional narration but through a more widespread semiotic practice: naming. Some non-fictional and fictional texts that represent the acts of animals equivocate in referring to them. "The owl" or "the fox" might be an individual creature, or a species, or a hypothetical creature meant to epitomize the species. An ostensibly individual name may turn out to be stereotypical, even generic. A few remarkable texts foreground such slippages, compounding possibilities in a productive but self-deconstructing way. To varying degrees, unstable namings convey, paradoxically, a powerful and credible sense of animals as self-determining agents.

Ways of Naming

Questions about naming—the relation between name and referent, the differences between proper and common or "improper" names, the ways in which names' referents could be extended or restricted, the status of verbs as names, and so on—were central to medieval grammar, semantics, and logic. Particularly relevant to naturalist and literary texts is the complex and changing discussion of appellation. For Abelard, *appellatio* differed from another form of naming, *significatio,* in that a noun "appellates" things of which it is true but "signifies" a property of whatever it appellates.[30] Later writers continued to use "appellation" primarily in the first way, for deictic reference, but differences arose over the range of reference. Both William of Sherwood and Roger Bacon defined appellation narrowly as "the present correct application of a term." Presum-

---

source text: compare Gaston Phébus, *Livre de chasse,* ed. Gunnar Tilander, *Cynegetica* XVIII (Karlshamn: E. G. Johanssons Boktrycker, 1971), 1.58–59.

[30] Martin M. Tweedale, "Abelard and the Culmination of the Old Logic," in *The Cambridge History of Later Medieval Philosophy: From the Rediscovery of Aristotle to the Disintegration of Scholasticism, 1100–1600,* ed. Norman Kretzmann, Anthony Kenny, and Jan Pinborg (Cambridge: Cambridge University Press, 1984), 143–57 (149).

ably, if Adam did intend to name only those individual creatures facing him, he was appellating them in this strict sense. But William of Sherwood stipulates that an appellation "may be [either] 'ampliated' or 'restricted' within the proposition for some reason, e.g., because of the past or future tense of the verb of that proposition, or as a result of the use of such words as 'potest' ('can') which ampliate the appellation to include merely possible individuals."[31] So Adam might have been conferring "lion" not just on a beast in his part of the garden but on unseen, even unborn, conspecifics. Indeed, writes L. M. de Rijk, "The anonymous *Fallacie Parvipontane* says that the appellative noun was invented in order to bring together all things denoted by it (its *appellata*) under one and the same name. However, which *appellata* are actually referred to in a proposition depends upon the verb of that proposition."[32] Adam left us no propositions in which he may have used his animal names, but of course later writers did. Their verbs—and other "ampliating" or "restricting" words—can determine whether a given name designates perceptible individuals or "all things denoted by it."

Animals play a significant role in medieval discussions of such questions. Problems in semantics and ontology are often illustrated with names of species or with the hypernym *animal,* and occasionally with stereotypical animal names such as *Brunellus* (for a donkey).[33] That may be because such terms illustrate problems of appellation especially clearly. Out of context, *animal* and species-names refer ambiguously to particulars and to groups, or even to properties—"the animal in him," "don't be a rat."

In context—particularly in literary texts—we can see those philosophical ambiguities in operation. To trace their operations, I propose a rough taxonomy of the ways of naming animals in medieval encyclopedias, bestiaries, and narratives. The five practices that I will identify overlap, particularly in use, but their prototypical uses differ in ways that carry contrasting ontological implications.

[31] L. M. de Rijk, "The Origins of the Theory of the Property of Terms," in Kretzmann, Kenny, and Pinborg, *Cambridge History,* 161–73 (165). On Bacon's agreement, see (in the same volume) Alain de Libera, "The Oxford and Paris Traditions in Logic," 174–87 (180).

[32] De Rijk, "Origins of the Theory," 165.

[33] For instance, "every man is an animal" (as the first term in a paradigmatic syllogism) goes back at least to Aristotle and recurs throughout Western and Arabic commentaries. Later in this section of my text, I cite philosophers' references to species and individual names.

I begin by positing two extremes, one maximally general and the other maximally particular.

(1) **Generic:** Names of species often encompass innumerable past, present, and potential individuals. Insisting on the particularity of his "little cat," Derrida acknowledges that we commonly take *cat* to designate "the exemplar of a species called 'cat,'" or even "an 'animal' genus or kingdom."[34] In English, the most generic appellations for animals are governed by the definite article. *The*-plus-noun is not always generic, of course: "the book" normally refers to one particular book. Acknowledging that such constructions can be generic, however, one philosopher of language cites animal examples: "the whale is a mammal"; "the dog is a loyal friend."[35] What distinguishes those phrases as generic is that they govern predicates, in the simple present, that indicate recurring acts and habitual states: "The viper (*vipera*) is so named because it 'spawns through force' (*vi parere*)," writes Isidore of Seville; according to Bartholomaeus Anglicus, in John Trevisa's translation, "the owle . . . is always iholde with slouþe, and is feble to flee" [gravi semper detenta pigritia, debilis est ad volandum].[36]

(2) **Proper:** In sharp contrast, some animals in romance and legend bear individualizing names, appropriate to their distinctive roles, including their ability to recognize individual human beings. The hound in the Middle English *Sir Tryamour,* named "Trewe-love," "[h]alpe his maystyr and be hym stode. / Byttyrly he can byte."[37] Such appellations can be called proper names—that is, noun phrases that "can occur with markers of definiteness."[38] Among those markers are the deictic modifier (here, "*his* hound so gode") and preterite or other perfective verbs ("helped," "stood"). Both subject and verb are thus singular. Trewe-love is no less an individual agent than are the human characters in *Sir Trya-*

---

[34] Derrida, *The Animal,* 9.

[35] Peter Ludlow, "Descriptions," *Stanford Encyclopedia of Philosophy* (Winter 2010 edition), ed. Edward N. Zalta, http://plato.stanford.edu/archives/win2010/entries/descriptions/, section 9.

[36] Isidore, *Etymologies,* XII.iv.10; John Trevisa, *On the Properties of Things: John Trevisa's Translation of Bartholomaeus Anglicus De Proprietatibus Rerum, A Critical Text,* gen. ed. Maurice Charles Seymour, 3 vols. (Oxford: Clarendon Press, 1975–88), XII.vi; Bartholomaeus Angelicus [*sic*], *De rerum proprietatibus* (1601; rpt. Frankfurt: Minerva, 1964), XII.v.

[37] *Sir Tryamour,* in *Four Middle English Romances,* ed. Harriet Hudson, 2nd ed. (Kalamazoo: Medieval Institute Publications, 2006), 313–15.

[38] Sam Cumming, "Names," *Stanford Encyclopedia of Philosophy* (Spring 2009 edition), ed. Edward N. Zalta, http://plato.stanford.edu/archives/spr2009/entries/names/, section 1.

mour; indeed, shortly after the passage that I cited above, the French version of the dog's name will be given to the newborn (human) hero.[39]

Somewhere between those poles are two uses of the generic with more complex implications. If pluralized, generic names can avoid categorical homogenization: "vipers" or "owls" allows for individual differences. Nonetheless, a text can still represent such groups categorically, as when Bartholomaeus writes that hounds "haueþ oþere propretees þat beeþ nought ful goode; for houndes haueþ contynual bolysme, þat is 'immoderate appetit.'"[40] Thus plural species names can either acknowledge or obviate individuality. Similarly flexible is a fourth method: indefinite singular generics, marked with an indefinite article in languages that lexicalize indefiniteness. Sometimes these names govern habitual verbs, equating the individual with the species—"A hare [being chased] shall last well four miles or less"[41]—but a creature initially identified as "a hare" might also enter a particular, if fictitious, time and place, becoming no less distinctive than an unnamed man or woman in a naturalistic novel. Thus Trewe-love's temporal and spatial localization would make him an individual agent even if he had been introduced as "a hound" rather than with a proper name. Singular generics can also be individualized by demonstrative and possessive determiners. Commenting in the fourteenth century on Aristotle's *De anima,* John Buridan called appellations such as "this man" "the most proper singular term[s]" because they "must point to one united existent present object"; the same would surely apply to "this hound" or "Derrida's cat."[42]

---

[39] Trewe-love's acts might seem as generic as those of Isidore's dog (*Etymologies* XII.25); encyclopedists and natural historians commonly attribute fidelity even past death to dogs as a species. The editor of *Sir Tryamour* notes also that both "Trewe-love" as a dog's name and "Tryamour" as a human name occur in other romances (Hudson, ed., *Sir Tryamour,* 191 nn. 313 and 452). But a long series of narrative details confirms the individualization of this faithful hound. Equally important, human characters in romance also behave in accordance with stereotypes. The locus of agency is determined not by analogues but by the syntax, deictic or generic, of a particular narrative.

[40] Trevisa, *On the Properties,* XVIII.xxvii; closely following Bartholomaeus, *De rerum proprietatibus,* XXVIII.xxvi.

[41] Edward of Norwich, *Master of Game,* 15.

[42] Buridan's statement is quoted in E. Jennifer Ashworth, "Medieval Theories of Singular Terms," *Stanford Encyclopedia of Philosophy* (Fall 2008 edition), ed. Edward N. Zalta, http://plato.stanford.edu/archives/fall2008/entries/singular-terms-medieval/, section 9. I must acknowledge, however, that Buridan would probably not regard "this hound" as a "proper singular" equivalent to "this man." According to Ashworth, singularity for Buridan requires continuous identity through time, something possessed in the fullest sense only by God. "Man" is a proper singular in a more limited sense because his soul is also continuous through time. Animals, human bodies, and rivers display only the

Finally, a common variation on the proper name itself can be called a fifth method, one that moves from deictic *appellatio* back toward descriptive *significatio*. Among the proper nouns applied to medieval literary animals, "Trewe-love" is unusually individualizing. More often, names that are grammatically "proper"—not governed by determiners, capitalized in modern editions—were closely tied to entire species, semantically or by convention. French cats in at least two texts were *Tiberz;* translating one of those texts, Chaucer substitutes "Gibbe," a "common English name for a tomcat."[43] The *Middle English Dictionary* cites two texts in addition to Chaucer's *Nun's Priest's Tale* in which dogs are named "Talbot." "Scot" was "apparently a common name for a horse," and "Brok ('badger') was commonly used for gray farm animals."[44] In beast epics, a wolf was often Isegrim, a bear Bruin, and the fox so predictably Reynard that the name could take the indefinite article. Thus conventionalized, proper names can be little more individualizing than are generic ones: successive cats might be "Gibbe," and the *Oxford English Dictionary* attests that by the sixteenth century, a woman behaving like a male cat could be said to be "play[ing] the gib."

That history epitomizes the referential malleability of animal names: "Gib" might be male or female, human or feline, categorical or particular. Such alternatives do not amount to anarchy; names imply degrees of individuation. By default, proper nouns "represent," in the words of Claude Lévi-Strauss, "the *quanta of signification* below which one no longer does anything but point." They lie on the margin of a "general system of classification," opposite, I would argue, the upper margins occupied by generics like *fox* and ultimately *animal*. As Lévi-Strauss demonstrates, cultures largely determine the degree to which a lexeme is *"perceived as* a proper name,"[45] and a particular written text can particularize a species name or render a proper noun common. The importance of forms of appellation lies in their openness to reinterpretation.

Many medieval writers exploit that openness, alternately confirming

---

continuity of diverse parts succeeding one another (Ashworth, "Medieval Theories of Singular Terms," section 10).

[43] *The Romaunt of the Rose,* in *The Riverside Chaucer,* gen. ed. Larry D. Benson (Boston: Houghton Mifflin, 1987), 6204, and Alfred David, Explanatory Notes, in *Riverside Chaucer,* 1113 n. 6204.

[44] Janette Richardson, Explanatory Notes for *The Miller's Tale,* in *Riverside Chaucer,* 876 n. 1543.

[45] Claude Lévi-Strauss, *The Savage Mind* (Chicago: University of Chicago Press, 1966), 215; my emphasis in the phrase quoted last.

and undermining the expectations raised by names. I turn now to four texts that appellate, to powerful effect, the equivocal agency of the non-human.

Tracking the *Animot*

The Gendered Generic

Þilke þat beþ in oon forme in general kynde haþ oon general name in kynde, as man is animal and hors is animal, and so of oþer bestes.[46]

John Trevisa's translation of *De proprietatibus rerum* of Bartholomaeus Anglicus provided medieval English writers with a vernacular version of *"the* standard medieval encyclopedia."[47] Bartholomaeus, a Franciscan born around 1200, maintained many practices of earlier medieval encyclopedists. The first of his nineteen volumes "treteth of God and of his names and nownes þat he is inempned by, touchinge beynge and persone oþir effect, doynge, and propirte."[48] Names and etymologies continue to be central in the lengthy volume dealing with animals. Even when he passes from "generalle" to "special" discussion, Bartholomaeus opens each segment with a generic name governing habitual predicates: "The asse hatte *asinus* and haþ þat name of *sedendo* 'sittynge' as it were a beste to sitte vpon. . . . And is a malencolik beste þat is colde and druye and is þerfore kyndeliche heuy, slowh, and lustiles" (XVIII.viii). He shares with Isidore of Seville (one of his major sources) and with bestiarists the kind of naming practice that homogenizes members of a category.

But Bartholomaeus's encyclopedia also presented English readers with slippages in that naming practice. The *Oxford English Dictionary* cites the passage that I quote above as the earliest English use of "ani-

[46] Trevisa, *On the Properties,* XIX.cxvi.

[47] A. S. G. Edwards, "Bartholomaeus Anglicus' *De Proprietatibus Rerum* and Medieval English Literature," *Archiv für das Studium der neueren Sprachen und Literaturen* 222 (1985): 121–28 (121).

[48] Trevisa, *On the Properties,* Prohemium. Trevisa uses both "names" and "nownes" for "nominibus divinis" in *De rerum proprietatibus.* Unless otherwise noted, future references to Trevisa's translation will be to this edition and will be documented in the text by book and chapter number. Where I cite only Trevisa, I have judged his translation faithful to Bartholomaeus's Latin as represented in the 1601 printing of *De rerum proprietatibus* cited above. Trevisa's "actual copy-text is not known to survive" (Seymour, Introduction to Trevisa, *On the Properties,* vol. 1, xii).

mal"; perhaps because the term was unfamiliar, Trevisa paraphrases it in a previous section of the text: "a best."[49] But the English term does not cover the same range as the Latin. A few lines later, Trevisa will use *best* to translate *bestia* in reference to a particular kind of animal, one that contrasts with "men" rather than including human beings as does Bartholomaeus's *animal* (XVIII.1). That awkwardness epitomizes a problem that appears throughout the text: the unstable reference of names for animals in both—if not in all—languages.

Some anomalies appear even in a list of chapter titles in *De proprietatibus rerum.* One involves the placement of birds: Bartholomaeus describes thirty-eight kinds of flying creatures in his twelfth book, *De avibus,* but the eighteenth book incorporates birds under animals. The duplication may reflect two methods of organization, one hypotactic and the other paratactic. The second mention (in Book XVIII) locates birds in a familiar hierarchy, with *animal* embracing successively smaller subcategories. The earlier treatment, the book entirely devoted to birds, immediately follows *De aere et eius passionibus,* the book on air, weather, and wind. Birds belong here by contiguity rather than subcategory: birds and fowls "pertain," as Bartholomaeus puts it, to the height, beauty, and ornamentation of the air (XII.i).

Contiguity trumps hierarchy in another way as well, this one more accidental: like his contemporary Vincent of Beauvais, Bartholomaeus arranges species not in larger families, as does Isidore—grouping lion, tiger, panther, and leopard—but "by the ordre of a. b. c." (XVIII.ii). Thus in Book XVIII, six chapters on large mammals (*ariete* through *asino*) are followed by a long one on serpents, a shorter one on the adder, a chapter each on spiders and bees, then *De boue* (the ox), and so on. The structure gives the reader access to any species directly rather than through a larger category.

In fact, the alphabetized sequence defies categorization. The *f* section begins with *fauni,* which (along with *satiri*) are "wonderlich yschape wiþ likenesse and schappe of men" [bestiæ monstrosæ, effigiem quidem hominis habentes].[50] The fauns are not the only legendary creatures intercalated with ordinary animals. Even more anomalous is the next entry: *De femina,* treating females in general but with ample reference to women and girls. Next come chapters on the *fetans* (fertile—or preg-

---

[49] *OED* Online (March 2011), s.v. "animal. n."

[50] Trevisa, *On the Properties,* XVIII.xlviii; Bartholomaeus, *De rerum proprietatibus,* XVIII. xlvi.

nant—creatures of any species) and the fetus. And the chapter on the ox is immediately followed by *De bubulco*, "[a]n oxeherde" (XVIII.xiv). A human occupational group is structurally equivalent to an animal species, a legendary one, a gender, and a cross-species developmental stage. Individuals included under any category could belong to others— the ox-herd is also an adult human male—and the categories themselves are not controlled by a logical hierarchy.

In fact, two of the largest categories of *De proprietatibus rerum*—*animal* and *homo*—are ambiguously ordered. After treating God and the angels in books I and II, Bartholomaeus devotes five books to human beings (books III through VII). Although we might expect animals to follow, the next nine books treat inanimate things, with birds included in the book on the air and fish treated in "De proprietatibus aque" (books XII and XIII). Animals get their due in Book XVIII, exceeded in length only by its predecessor, on the plants. The animals may in fact get more than their due here, for they now include creatures treated earlier—not just birds but also mankind. "Dicitur autem animal," Bartholomaeus explains, "omne quod consistit ex carne & spiritu vitæ animatum, sive sit aereum, ut volitalia, sive aquaticum, ut natatilia, sive terrenum, sicut sunt agrestia & gressibilia, scilicet homines, reptilia, bestiæ & iumenta" [And all is called "animal" that consists of flesh and the animating spirit of life, whether aerial or flying, or aquatic or swimming, or land-based, as are wild and tractable [creatures], men, crawling things, beasts, and beasts of burden].[51] To appellate man as a type of animal was of course traditional; following Isidore and echoing other patristic writers, Bartholomaeus defines man in Book III as *animal deiforme*.[52] In itself, that name positions humankind at the intersection of a superior and an inferior category, precisely the hierarchy implied in the early books of the *De proprietatibus rerum*. But the eighteenth book proposes an alternative ontology, with man as subcategory or cognate of animal.

Bartholomaeus may have been influenced in this regard by sources other than Isidore and Augustine, particularly Aristotle and the Islamic philosopher Ibn Sina (Avicenna). Although Aristotle classifies animals on a hierarchical *scala naturae* (*Historia animalium* VIII.i), he also includes human beings under a binary distinction between animals with and without blood (*Historia animalium* I.iv), just as Bartholomaeus makes

---

[51] Bartholomaeus, *De rerum proprietatibus,* XVIII.Proem (my translation).
[52] Ibid., III.i; Trevisa, *On the Properties,* III.i.

men one subdivision of *animal.* Aristotle and Avicenna also treat animals topically by system, feature, or part, rather than by species, often including man along with other species in elaborating a given topic. Bartholomaeus follows them in the lengthy first section of Book XVIII. He cites Avicenna for the observation that some beasts have parts in common, as man and horse do with flesh and sinews. He notes later that some animals whose lips are full and equal drink by sucking, "as man, hors, cow, and mule and oþre suche." Similarly, some animals increase or decrease in marrow and blood at different times, "as it is openliche yknowe in schellefissh of þe see and in mannes brayne"—and perhaps, Bartholomaeus adds, in the brain of any animal.[53]

Use of Greek and non-Western sources has been cited as an innovation of *De proprietatibus rerum.*[54] If, as I am suggesting, those sources prompted Bartholomaeus to mix top-down taxonomy with metonymic associations and lateral comparisons, they thereby influenced his representation of animals. When "the horse" or "the ox" parallels "female" and "ox-herd," and when mules or shellfish share physiological and even behavioral features with humans, the creatures do not seem determined solely by species.

Aristotle and Avicenna evidently influenced Bartholomaeus to loosen the rigidity of generic naming in a more overt way as well: through narration. Encyclopedias and bestiaries commonly include brief narratives, but the agents remain generic thanks to minimal detail and habitual predicates. Thus Isidore writes that when lions walk, "their tail brushes away their tracks, so that a hunter cannot find them. When they bear their cubs, the cub is said to sleep for three days and nights, and then after that the roaring or growling of the father, making the den shake, as it were, is said to wake the sleeping cub."[55] Bartholomaeus spins longer and less categorical stories. Many chapters provide alternate

---

[53] Bartholomaeus, *De rerum proprietatibus,* XVIII.Proem; Trevisa, *On the Properties,* XVIII.i. For the last observation, Bartholomaeus again cites Aristotle, but the statement in question comes from *De proprietatibus elementorum,* one of several texts incorrectly attributed to Aristotle (see the Index of Authorities in the third volume of Trevisa, *On the Properties,* 316).

[54] For instance, Lynn Tarte Ramey, "Monstrous Alterity in Early Modern Travel Accounts: Lessons from the Ambiguous Medieval Discourse on Humanness," *L'Esprit créateur* 48.1 (2008): 81–95 (86); and Eva Albrecht, Excursus to "The Organization of Vincent of Beauvais' *Speculum maius* and of Some Other Latin Encyclopedias," *Medieval Hebrew Encyclopedias of Science and Philosophy: Proceedings of the Bar-Ilan University Conference,* ed. Steven Harvey (New York: Springer, 2000), 58–74 (65–67).

[55] Isidore, *Etymologies,* XII.ii.5.

accounts of various members of a species; many attribute the actions of a creature to internal motivations. For instance, the generic opening of *De asino* is followed by several colorful anecdotes. Bartholomaeus cites both Avicenna and Aristotle for the observation that the ass is loathsome to small birds that nest in bushes and briars ("minutis avibus . . . est exosus") because he eats and abrades their nesting material. The vicious assaults then launched by sparrows might be regarded as instinctive defenses of territory, but that is not the case with the next instance of hostility. For unspecified reasons, the raven—not a small bird that nests in bushes and briars—also "hateþ ful moche þe asse," again as per Aristotle and Avicenna, and seeks opportunities to peck out his eyes.[56] The use of "hateþ" and "odit" here might be called anthropomorphic, but some ethologists would regard such terms as the most parsimonious representation of observed behavior.[57] In any case, the narrative crosses species boundaries, lifting sparrows and asses alike out of categorical determinism.

In another section, Bartholomaeus provides a more benign version of creaturely habits:

And whenne he findeþ mete he [the rooster] clepiþ his wifes togedres with a certeyn voys and spareþ his owne mete to fede þerwiþ his wifes. And settiþ next to him on rooste þe henne þat is most fatte and tendre and loueþ hire best and desireþ most to haue hire presence.

In the morning, Bartholomaeus continues, the rooster lays his side next to the favored hen's, and "bi certeyne tokenes and beckes" he "woweþ and prayeþ hire to tredinge" [per quosdam nutus ipsam ad sui copulam allicit & invitat].[58] The behavior of this cock may be ampliated to all and only those creatures driven by a generic "agent will," but Bartholomaeus represents him with subjective terms applicable to many species and with details that evoke individual intent. Indeed, the passage seems to have engendered one of the most distinctive protagonists in medieval literature. Chaucer's *Nun's Priest's Tale* adheres closely enough to Bartholomaeus's text to convince several scholars of direct influence.[59] Trevisa's

[56] Bartholomaeus, *De rerum proprietatibus*, XVIII.vii; Trevisa, *On the Properties*, XVIII. viii.

[57] See, for example, Bekoff, *Emotional Lives*, 121–23.

[58] Bartholomaeus, *De rerum proprietatibus*, XII.xvi; Trevisa, *On the Properties*, XII.xvii.

[59] Edwards, "Bartholomaeus Anglicus' *De Proprietatibus Rerum* and Medieval English Literature," 126; and compare Chaucer, *Nun's Priest's Tale*, in *Riverside Chaucer*, VII.2865–76, 3167–83.

translation may have supplied a particular hint: in the passage just quoted, Trevisa elaborates on his initial translation of *quosdam nutus* with "as it were loue tacchis." Whether or not Chaucer used Trevisa, Chauntecleer demonstrates that Bartholomaeus has moved his *Gallus* very close to a creature with whom many readers identify, one with enough free will—indeed, willfulness—to ignore his sound generic instincts.

Species-Climbing Specimens

"Veir!" fet il, "veirs est dist en engleis: *Stroke oule and schrape oule and evere is oule oule.*"

["You're right," he said. "It's true what the English say: *Stroke an owl or scrape an owl but always an owl's an owl.*"][60]

> Ich habbe bile stif & stronge
> & gode cliuers scharp & longe:
> So hit bicumeþ to hauekes cunne.
> Hit is min hiȝte, hit is mi wunne,
> þat ich me draȝe to mine cunde.
> Ne mai me no man þareuore schende.

[I've got a hard, strong beak and long, sharp claws, as is fitting for a member of the hawkish clan. It is my joy and my delight to associate myself with those who are of my kind. Nobody can reproach me for that.][61]

The speaker in the second of these epigraphs might, if real, have taken serious issue with her portrayal in *De proprietatibus rerum.* According to Bartholomaeus, *bubo,* the owl, resembles hawks only in its feathers and bill. It lacks the "boldnesse and vertue" of other predators, being sloth-

---

[60] From Nicolas Bozon (Anglo-Norman, fl. c. 1320), *Contes moralisés,* ed. Lucy Toulmin-Smith and Paul Meyer (Paris, 1889), 23; as reprinted and translated in Neil Cartlidge, ed., *The Owl and the Nightingale: Text and Translation* (Exeter: University of Exeter Press, 2001), 100. My excerpt comes from an anecdote cited by Cartlidge as an analogue for lines 101–38 in *The Owl and the Nightingale.* "Il" in the passage is a hawk whose nest has been fouled by owlets.

[61] Cartlidge, *The Owl and the Nightingale,* 269–74. Future references to the *Owl and the Nightingale* will be documented in the text by line number (underlining in his edition indicates additions to the base text, London, British Library, MS Cotton Caligula A.ix). All will be to this edition and translation, except that I provide my own translation of the following passages: 129–30; 969–70; 1099; 1788; 1794.

ful and feeble in flight; moreover, the owl signifies destruction and death, eats excrement, and is hated by other birds.[62] The self-satisfied owl in *The Owl and the Nightingale* (dated by its recent editor around the middle of the thirteenth century) will have none of that. Just before the excerpt that I quote, her antagonist has paraphrased the anecdote from which my first quotation is taken, concluding that no good can come from the "ungood one that comes from a foul breed" (129–30). In response, the Owl not merely admits but rejoices that she acts according to her *cunde,* a kind that, she alleges, the Nightingale has seriously misrepresented.

The Owl and the Nightingale names its protagonists in a formally straightforward way. Never receiving individual names or characterizations, the birds begin as specimens, "[a]n hule and one niȝtingale" whose "grete tale" the speaker heard in an out-of-the-way valley (1–4). Both the determiners and the preterite verbs establish the species names as singular generics. But the early confrontation over the Owl's *cunde* typifies three complications. First, the names will often function as fully generic rather than individual, appellating the species as a whole. Second, those generic references will be made not by a human commentator but by the birds themselves. Just as the Owl defends her species in the passage quoted above, the Nightingale will later reject or reinterpret generic slanders recorded in other texts (e.g., 1043–110, 1347–77). Used that way, the categorical terms actually combat categorical homogenization: the birds claim the right to define their species. Derrida might applaud these beasts' attack on semantic *bêtise.* Of course, they can make such an attack only with capabilities that they ought not, as members of their species, to possess. That constitutes the third and most serious complication in the protagonists' identities. The weakness in their claims to define their *cunde* is not simply their fictitiousness: in other texts, notably Chaucer's, fictional female characters persuasively model a real woman's sovereignty over her category.[63] The problem is, rather, their relationship to their real correlatives, who cannot verbally assert anything at all. The birds' deployment of their own species names raises a fundamental question about the species—indeed, the biological kingdom—to which they belong.

[62] Trevisa, *On the Properties,* XII.vi.

[63] Many writers have analyzed texts in which—to cite Susan Crane's phrase—female characters "[respeak] and remanipulat[e] familiar gender paradigms" (*Gender and Romance in Chaucer's Canterbury Tales* [Princeton: Princeton University Press, 1994], 55).

That question has shaped scholarly response to *The Owl and the Nightingale*. In one way or another, any reader must deal with the birds' use of human discourse. Most critics take one of two opposing approaches, but I have found none who can keep them separate. On the one hand, many early analyses and some recent ones focus on the discourse itself, treating its avian origin as a convention without significance. That is, the birds are ventriloquists, to adapt Jill Mann's term,[64] for a debate whose antagonists have been variously identified as human individuals, professional groups, nationalities, attitudes, institutions, rhetorical or musical styles, ethical or ideological stances, legal or judicial practices, or philosophical positions. More recently, on the other hand, many commentators note that the diversity of those discourse-centered readings undermines any one of them.[65] Thus these writers focus on the birds themselves, creatures that the poet "endows . . . with a creatural realism that makes them not icons but ornithological specimens."[66] Not just the bodies but also the attitudes of the birds are, writes Neil Cartlidge, "too specific and too irreducibly avian for the contrast between them to constitute any kind of statement about life in general."[67]

Neither approach avoids awkward confrontations with its alternative, backtrackings often registered by inconclusive references to fictionality or comic incongruity. Thus Tamara A. Goeglein, who reads the poem through John of Salisbury's treatment of the "universals problem," ends by conceding that the issue "is given a comic turn when we recall that this particular owl is actually a literary fiction."[68] Goeglein does not specify where this "comic turn" leaves the philosophical argument. Beginning from the avian side, Mann finds it "impossible to say that the Owl and the Nightingale represent anything other than themselves" but adds that the "playful yoking of animal nature and human verbiage is a way of expressing a serious point about the function of rhetoric in

---

[64] Jill Mann, *From Aesop to Reynard: Beast Literature in Medieval Britain* (Oxford: Oxford University Press, 2009), 168.

[65] That the disparity of readings undermines any one of them is suggested by Thomas Honegger, *From Phoenix to Chauntecleer: Medieval English Animal Poetry* (Tübingen: Francke Verlag, 1996), 115–16; Cartlidge, Introduction, *Owl and the Nightingale*, xvi–xvii; and Wendy A. Matlock, "Law and Violence in *The Owl and the Nightingale*," *JEGP* 109 (2010): 446–67 (446–47).

[66] Mann, *From Aesop to Reynard*, 169.

[67] Cartlidge, Introduction, *Owl and the Nightingale*, xvii.

[68] Tamara A. Goeglein, "The Problem of Monsters and Universals in 'The Owl and the Nightingale' and John of Salisbury's 'Metalogicon,'" *JEGP* 94 (1995): 190–206 (205).

human life."[69] Mann says little, however, about that serious point or its connection to the self-representing birds. And Cartlidge ends his bird-centered reading with a major concession: the poem's "collapsing of the distinction between human reason and animal instinct is only made possible by a fiction—that birds might talk—but it is nevertheless slightly disquieting, as well as comical."[70] "Comical" forestalls an explanation of what he finds "disquieting," and "fiction"—here as elsewhere—seems to dismiss altogether the significance of the birds as birds. Might the debate have been essentially the same if voiced by two plants, or two men?

Goeglein expands her point about fictionality with a statement that suggests a resolution of the interpretive impasse. As a "literary fiction," she writes, the Owl is what the Nightingale calls her: an *unwiȝt* (literally "un-creature").[71] *Wiȝt* and its derivatives appear often in *The Owl and the Nightingale,* and their meaning telescopes in the same way as that of "beast" in *De proprietatibus rerum.* In fact, the referential focus of *wiȝt* is even more unstable: while "beast" sometimes embraces and sometimes excludes human beings, *wiȝt* refers at various times to an animal, to a human being, or indeterminately to either. In branding the Owl *unwiȝt* for singing only at night and in lamentation (217–20), the Nightingale might mean that her opponent acts unlike all other birds, or unlike all other creatures, or, as her ensuing paraphrase suggests, contrary to human norms (235–38). The poem juggles those levels of reference. We might say, paraphrasing Luce Irigaray, that the Owl—like the Nightingale, and like its readers—is a *wiȝt* that is not one.[72]

In neither Irigaray's usage nor my own does "not one" equate with "nonexistent." The birds fit no single taxonomic or ontological template, but they represent two kinds of extratextual reality: biological and intersubjective.

The poem is certainly grounded in avian behavior. The Nightingale's initial "speech" is simply her song, which seems better to the narrator than pipe or harp music (19–24). When she shifts to English words, it is to berate the Owl because the proximity of the latter—a predator,

[69] Mann, *From Aesop to Reynard,* 190.
[70] Cartlidge, Introduction, *Owl and the Nightingale,* xxxvii–xxxviii.
[71] Goeglein, "Problem of Monsters," 205–6.
[72] I refer to Luce Irigaray, *This Sex Which Is Not One,* trans. Catherine Porter and Carolyn Burke (Ithaca: Cornell University Press, 1985); originally published as *Ce sexe qui n'en est pas un,* 1977. Of "woman," Irigaray writes, "She resists all adequate definition. Further, she has no 'proper' name" (26).

after all—interrupts her singing (25–36). The nocturnal Owl waits until evening to respond that she too sings, though not with "twittering," and that the Nightingale's habitual insults could someday end "ʒif ich þe holde on mine uote" (41–54) [if I got a hold of you in my foot]. Their antagonism is of long standing, and it is entirely indigenous. The Nightingale goes on to insult the Owl by listing what owls— particularly of the species *Strix aluco*—do in fact look like, sound like, and eat.[73] Thomas Honegger adds the important observation that "the debate is not only carried on by birds, but it is primarily about birds"; thus the subject matter upsets readers' expectations that animal debaters must be transparent vehicles for human concerns.[74] As I will argue later, the denouement of the debate resembles the outcome of many natural confrontations between predator and potential prey. This is not ventriloquism, unless the poet is the dummy;[75] it is a verbalized ornithological face-off.

It does not follow that we can easily read the poem as burlesque, a mere bird-brawl tricked forth as a debate. The debate achieves another kind of credibility: rhetorical persuasiveness. The birds voice their genuinely avian interests in finely crafted, pungent octosyllabic couplets. Editing the poem in 1922, J. W. H. Atkins called its characters "birds with the minds that human beings would possess, could we imagine them transformed, for the time being, into birds."[76] Notwithstanding Atkins's nervous conditionals, he reveals that at least one reader *has*— "for the time being"—imagined himself into the minds of the birds. I do not mean that readers experience life as an owl or a nightingale: these word-birds are not quite literary versions of *Luscinia* and *Strix aluco*. Rather, the birds co-opt the reader's subjectivity. The poem draws us into the perspective of agents that are credibly avian but also intentional, self-aware, and partly self-determining—in short, a perspective both within and beyond species determination. That will turn out to be a subject-position not limited to birds.

[73] Royal Society for the Protection of Birds, "The RSPB: Tawny Owl," October 2, 2010, http://www.rspb.org.uk/wildlife/birdguide/name/t/tawnyowl/index.aspx.

[74] Honegger, *From Phoenix to Chauntecleer,* 121, 115.

[75] Jill Mann similarly contests readings that regard the birds as channels for human discourse: "If this is ventriloquism, then the ventriloquist is giving his dummies their own voice" (*From Aesop to Reynard,* 171). I would go further: initially, the poet is the channel for avian voices.

[76] John William Hey Atkins, ed., *Owl and the Nightingale* (Cambridge: Cambridge University Press, 1922), lxxix.

A key expressive strategy of these *unwi ʒt* subjects is name-calling. As Mann observes, "the Owl and the Nightingale are at once individuals and generic representatives."[77] But her "are" is insufficiently transitive: the birds cast themselves and each other as generic representatives, but with revealing slippages. In a passage to which I have already referred, for instance, the Nightingale places her opponent, improbably, into an anecdote from "some years ago": "You," she claims, "crept in [to a falcon's nest] one day, and laid in there your own nasty egg"; eventually the falcon detected the alien chick because it had fouled the nest (101–26). The Owl does not respond by distinguishing herself from the owl of the story; on the contrary, she embraces their common identity, voicing the celebration of Owl Pride that I quoted earlier (272–73). Later she will subject her opponent to a similar vicarious slander when she localizes an exemplum about a nightingale. "Once you sang near a certain bedroom—I know well where!" she begins (1049–50). This identification of anecdote with addressee is not merely improbable but impossible, since the story ends with the nightingale's death: having induced a lady to commit adultery, the Owl reports, the bird was captured, convicted, and "torn apart by wild horses" (1050–62). But the Nightingale voices no objection to being coindexed with a dead bird. Instead, she objects (strenuously though not credibly) to the Owl's incomplete version of the story. I sang out of compassion for the lady, she insists, and good King Henry had the husband banished and fined for killing that little bird; so the whole story "was wurþsipe al mine kunne" (brought honor to all my kind; 1083–99). Like the Owl, the Nightingale accepts categorical appellation but contests the category's signification. In flagrant but somewhat charming self-contradiction, she proclaims that the law of that species compels her to aspire above it: "Hit is mi riʒt, hit is my laʒe, / þat to þe hexst ich me draʒe" (969–70) [It is my right, it is my law, that I draw myself toward whatever is superior].

That the birds object to being defined generically would be enough to make *The Owl and the Nightingale* richly comic. What makes the poem brilliant is that they do the same thing to each other and occasionally to themselves—inconsistently, and out of self-interest. Their feathers and beaks protect the reader only weakly from recognizing those tactics.

---

[77] Mann, *From Aesop to Reynard,* 177; for an earlier observation to the same effect, she cites E. J. Dobson, "A New Edition of 'The Owl and the Nightingale,'" *N&Q* 206 (1961): 373–78, 405–11, and 444–48 (410).

If we remember that we inhabit bodies that can be variably appellated as subjects of species determinism or as autonomous selves, we may acknowledge that we too affirm or deny individual autonomy depending on our interests of the moment. We may admit, for instance, that although we equate ourselves with the authoritative "Nicholas of Guilford," the properly named but never-located adjudicator of the poem's debate, we sometimes take refuge in versions of species determinism, attributing individual acts (our own or others') to the nature of "man." Or woman. Or human animality—or, conversely, to a higher agency.

"Man" and "woman" are in fact the terms that dominate the last half of *The Owl and the Nightingale.* The debaters devote far less attention to specifically avian topics; instead, they declaim on sin and redemption, justifications for adultery, the weaknesses of women, and the validity of astrology. Readers can be excused for concluding that here, at any rate, the birds are merely conventional devices for exploring human issues. In fact, however, no single issue emerges clearly, and the speakers cannot be aligned consistently with opposing positions on any issue. Instead, the issue is alignment itself—the ways of naming, and thus judging, creaturely behavior.

The debate's reorientation begins when the Nightingale adopts a new strategy: defense by cross-species association. From the outset, both birds have occasionally described their own habits and traits interchangeably with human proverbs and lore about other species. Now, in response to the Owl's charge that nightingales do nothing but sing and thus promote sensuality, the Nightingale equates her own singing at some length with liturgical music. Just like priests in church, she declares, she sings to remind men that their destiny is heavenly bliss, "þar euer is song & murȝþe iliche" (713–42). The Owl astutely attacks the cross-species analogy: nobody mistakes your "pipinge" for a priest's singing, she sneers (901–2). But she also challenges the Nightingale's premise about church music, alleging that men have even greater need for calls to repentance, conveyed in sounds of "longinge" like her own (837–86).

Many scholars read past the feathered vehicles and regard the passage as a debate about styles of preaching, prophecy, music, or poetry.[78] But a larger consideration underlies this and the other hermeneutical tactics

---

[78] See Kathryn Hume's summary and critique of such interpretations (proposed by, among others, G. R. Owst and J. W. H. Atkins) in *"The Owl and the Nightingale": The Poem and Its Critics* (Toronto: University of Toronto Press, 1975), 53–60.

that the birds deploy. The debate can reference human practices only on the basis of correspondences whose fundamental validity we should recognize. Granted that the Nightingale is indeed no priest, her "pipinge" contrasts with owl-hoots much as liturgical or rhetorical styles do with each other. And, more important, the birds associate their generic songs with those contrasting styles for the same reason that groups of practitioners contest each other's musicology, poetics, or homiletics: self-interest. Their cross-species affiliations exhibit, to borrow again from J. W. H. Atkins, the mentality "that human beings would possess, could we imagine them transformed, for the time being, into birds"[79]—here, the "mentality" of special pleading.

Following the musical debate, the cross-species alignments become increasingly ambitious but remain poised between objective credibility and self-interest. The Nightingale first claims, and claims to trump, human regional identity. Returning to the Owl's charge that she never ventures to cold, waste areas where people most need her joyous singing, she asserts that people in such areas live like "wild animals" (995–1012). Not only do they eat raw food and wear pelts, but they are irredeemable: a missionary from Rome could no more reform them than he could teach a boar to use shield and spear (1009–24). Representing herself as a rational agent choosing to avoid an instinctively driven subspecies of humanity, the Nightingale closely mimics human regional and categorical prejudices. Perhaps members of all species assert autonomy partly by constructing categories for others.

Both birds then affiliate with a larger and even more contested human category: women. Here their self-identifications correspond with human categorizations not just in being self-serving but also in lacking coherence. The Nightingale defends her stereotypic association with eroticism by exonerating women's sexual behavior in a series of inconsistent ways: first as the natural order, then as fleshly frailty that leads some women to "[go] outside the nest for [their] breeding" (1385–86), next as youthful experimentation that can be remedied by marriage (1423–32). The last extenuation leads to a vehement denunciation of the unfaithful wives whom she earlier excused, and finally to an odd diatribe on the folly of male adulterers (1467–1510). Reflexively, the Owl then champions unfaithful wives because husbands often neglect them for unworthy rivals; for good measure, she curses jealous husbands

[79] Atkins, *Owl and the Nightingale*, lxxix.

who lock up their wives (1511–62). In themselves, these arguments have dubious moral or analytical weight. Equally doubtful is the arguments' function as self-defense. The birds choose sides like unprincipled tacticians rather than advocates for any species, ideology, or social category. Because their imitation of human disputation also invokes natural territorialism, it does not amount to complete anthropomorphism—or gynomorphism, as Christopher Cannon suggests.[80] The birds are represented here not as people but as cross-species egos, intent on self-assertion.

If the debate ended here, it would suggest a reductive vision of creaturely behavior. The birds are displaying the individuality associated with proper names—as Cartlidge writes, readers respond to them as "characters"[81]—but in the process they give singularity itself a bad name: selfishness. But the last two exchanges produce a fuller resolution.

The first involves a new form of name-calling, flattering self-metaphorization. In response to the charge that everyone hates her because her calls portend calamity, the Owl reinterprets the connection between hooting and disaster as testimony to her prodigious wisdom (1175–1232). On one level this is hubristic self-anthropomorphism, but readers may be reminded that encyclopedias and bestiaries explain the owl's cries as warnings of ill fortune, the kind of signal God intends for our benefit.[82] Indeed, the Owl adds that her foresight does not cause the misfortunes against which she tries to warn people; everything happens through God's will (1233–56). Her humble concession is a tacit claim to ulterior importance. Deferring to the supreme supernatural agent, she positions herself as God's instrument. She returns quickly to grandiloquent bragging, but she will claim Christian instrumentality more

---

[80] Christopher Cannon, *The Grounds of English Literature* (Oxford: Oxford University Press, 2004). Pointing out that the poet stresses the birds' grammatical gender to an extent unusual at this stage in the development of Early Middle English, Cannon argues that they are "represented as women" (129)—that is, in the marked, female position. But I take that as another instance of cross-species congruence rather than as gynomorphism: these are female birds, not women. As Mann observes, "the animals cannot at one and the same time *represent* humans and argue about their usefulness *to* humans" (*From Aesop to Reynard*, 189–90).

[81] Cartlidge, Introduction, *Owl and the Nightingale*, xix.

[82] Isidore, *Etymologies*, XII.38; Trevisa, *On the Properties*, XII.vi. On the providential role of birds, in particular their calls, see *The Medieval Book of Birds: Hugh of Fouilloy's Aviarium*, ed. Willene B. Clark (Binghamton, N.Y.: Medieval & Renaissance Texts & Studies, 1992), 226–27.

powerfully in two subsequent self-characterizations. The first leverages human subjectivity with particular effectiveness. To counter the Nightingale's self-identification with lust-tormented young girls, the Owl claims that her own plaintive songs commiserate with more deserving victims—abused and lonely wives; but she supports the claim not with disputation but by voicing, in the poem's most lyric passage, the suffering of someone whose beloved husband is absent for blameless reasons:

> Haueþ daies kare & niʒtes wake;
> An swuþe longe hire is þe hwile,
> An ech steape hire þunþ a mile.
> Hwanne oþre slepeþ hire abute,
> Ich one lust þar wiʒþute
> An wot of hire sore mode,
> An singe a niʒt for hire gode,
> An mine gode song for hire þinge
> Ich turne sundel to murnige.
> Of hire seorhe ich bere sume:
> Forþan ich am hire wel welcume. (1590–1600)

[She has anxiety by day and sleeplessness by night. For her, the time seems to go very slowly and every step he [her voyaging husband] takes seems like a mile. When everyone else is fast asleep around her, I alone am listening outside and I fully appreciate her anguish. I sing at night for her benefit and, on her account, I give my song a little touch of mournfulness. I bear some of her sorrow and that's why she welcomes me.]

The poet evokes human grief simultaneously with the real habits of owls—their mournful singing at night in lonely places—and thus represents the Owl as an instrument of cross-species compassion. He goes on to align her with an even higher form of selflessness. Returning to the charge that human beings despise her, the Owl acknowledges that people stone and mutilate her and then hang her up to scare off magpies and crows. But thereby, she says, "ich do heom god / An for heom ich chadde mi blod. / Ich do heom god mid mine deaþe" (1615–17) [I do them good when I shed my blood for them. I do them good when I die]. In itself, this is true. And the startling analogy with Christ's sacrifice gains some credibility because it remains implicit. The analogy is the poet's half-serious gift, probably modeled on Christological interpretations of other creatures in bestiaries but grounded in the treatment of real owls.[83] The poet reinscribes the dead bird as pan-generic savior.

As if to confirm that the poet's gift was only half-serious, the Owl herself uses the scarecrow argument not to redeem but to attack. Unlike my species, she tells the Nightingale, yours serves no purpose; I don't know to what purpose you even produce young—"liues ne deaþes ne deþ hit god" (1618–34) [dead or alive it'll never do any good]. Thus she enacts opposing conceptions of creaturely behavior: on the one hand, redemptive self-sacrifice; on the other, an invitation to species-suicide. Saint and predator meet in one interspecies body. It is a standoff more significant than the forensic stalemate toward which the debate seems to be heading.

Both deadlocks, forensic and ontological, are resolved in a surprising but natural way. The final reconfiguration of creaturely identity begins with a regression toward the level of predator and prey. The Nightingale, either missing or dismissing the point of the scarecrow defense, proclaims that by acknowledging that humans persecute her, the Owl has lost the "game" (1635–52). She sings so jubilantly that other songbirds flock to the site. The Owl scoffs at their jeers, reminding them of the superior fighting strength of her own kind, particularly the hawks (1673–88). The debaters are initiating what ornithologists call a mobbing, "the assemblage of individuals around a potentially dangerous predator."[84] Mobbings can involve various species, including fish, but are particularly common between birds of prey and songbirds. They rarely include physical attack; rather, they proceed with threatening gestures and vocalizations, intended perhaps to preclude mutually damaging violence.[85] They are, in short, hostile rhetorical confrontations— like the one we have just followed.[86]

---

[83] For medieval references to the use of owls' bodies as scarecrows, see Cartlidge, *Owl and the Nightingale,* 91–92 n. 1623–30. In bestiaries and some encyclopedias, the lion, the pelican, and the vulture are among the creatures said to imitate Christ, sometimes through behavior attested only in legends and sometimes via strained explications. Hugh of Fouilly figures the *Nycticorax*—night heron or owl—as Christ by reading *in bono* the bird's nocturnal habits as avoidance of vainglory (Clark, *Medieval Book of Birds,* 172–75).

[84] Wallace J. Dominey, "Mobbing in Colonially Nesting Fishes, Especially the Bluegill, *Lepomis macrochirus,*" *Copeia* 1983, 4 (1983): 1086–88 (1087).

[85] Paul Ehrlich, David Dobkin, and Darryl Wheye, "Mobbing," Birds of Stanford, 1988, http://www.stanford.edu/group/stanfordbirds/text/essays/Mobbing.html.

[86] For a provocative discussion of pan-species rhetoric, see George A. Kennedy, "A Hoot in the Dark: The Evolution of General Rhetoric," *Philosophy and Rhetoric* 25 (1992): 1–21.

Mobbings generally do not end with victories and defeats; this verbal one certainly does not. Like ornithological *flytings*, the debate has arisen not from contrary propositions (not even "nightingales are better" versus "owls are better") but from conflicting interests. It has placed the nature of those interests under playful but intense scrutiny. As they abandon physical threats, the birds renew their agreement to submit to "riht dom" (1692), but what they seek is not a verdict on some charge or issue. It is a more generic—and more personal—kind of vindication. They, and we, seek a *voir dit* on themselves.

That verdict is of course the poem itself, which ends by sentencing creatures to a mutual recognition of singularity. The mobbing has brought in more birds who express interests. Leading them is "the Wren"—introduced with the definite article, as if she embodies a species, but soon revealed as a remarkable *unwiȝt*. She was bred in the forest but educated among mankind and may speak wherever she wants to, even before the king. Recalling that the single word *regulus* could itself mean "little king" and "wren" (and could even refer to a poisonous serpent),[87] we may suspect the poet of engaging in Derridean wordplay. Fittingly, this polyspecies *animot* mediates among the other agents. She voices the king's (her own?) objection to any breach of peace and urges the birds to seek judgment forthwith. The Nightingale accedes—of her own free will, she insists—and reminds the Owl that they have agreed to be judged by Master Nicholas (1739–49). The poem ends before the birds locate this individual. By sad coincidence, scholars have also failed to identify him definitively; moreover, the Wren laments that bishops and others who "of his nome / Habbeþ ihert" have not adequately recognized him (1760–63). They could learn much from his wise words and writings, she adds (1755–68).

If Nicholas is the poet, as most believe, he may be equating his situation with that of owls and nightingales: people know his name but do not listen to his voice. But he has earned the Wren's praise for his wisdom by ending his own silence and the birds' at once. In a poem that appellates other creatures as intentional agents, he inscribes his own singular though multireferential name. And whether or not he is Nicho-

---

[87] "Wren" is attested around 1290: R. E. Latham, *Revised Medieval Latin Word-List from British and Irish Sources* (London: British Academy / Oxford University Press, 1965), s.v. "regula." Citing Isidore, Bartholomaeus translates "cockatrice" as *basiliscus* in Greek and *regulus* in Latin, the latter because "he is king of serpentes" (Trevisa, *On the Properties*, XVIII.xvi).

las, the poet has amplified his voice by conveying the voices of birds. In turn, the birds agree to transmit their voices through each other. When the Nightingale asks who will relay their speeches to Nicholas, the Owl affirms that she herself can repeat each of their words, in order. She then adds a crucial proviso: "An ȝef þe þincþ that ich misrempe / þu stond aȝein & do me crempe" (1787–88) [But if it seems to you that I go astray, stand up and hold me back]. Mobbing becomes mutually beneficial détente; name-calling turns into antiphonal storytelling. The poem's last line—"Her nis na more of þis spelle" (1794) [Here is no more of this story]—is pleasantly ironic, for there has been plenty already: a rich comedy of cross-species subjectivity, generated by the ontological expansions and contractions of "an owl and one nightingale" (4).

Proper Appropriation

The name that was gyuen to him / abydeth alway stylle wyth hym / he hath lefte many of his crafte in this world.[88]

. . . þe der þat nomon nedar nemnen.[89]
[The animal that nobody dares name.]

The Owl and the Nightingale contravenes a natural assumption that texts relying on categorical animal names will not do justice to what Derrida calls the "heterogeneous multiplicity of the living."[90] I turn now to the complementary assumption, equally natural, that proper names automatically individualize their referents. Grammatically proper nouns often individualize, of course, but they can also produce categorical misrepresentations.

In popular understanding, a proper name indexes a unique referent but has no meaning in itself. Philosophers and semioticians complicate that understanding, pointing out that proper names can be pluralized ("are there any female Shakespeares?") and are used of hypothetical referents ("Homer did not exist"). Thus proper names serve a second, descriptive function, beyond the indexical one: they designate features of

---

[88] William Caxton, *The History of Reynard the Fox,* ed. N. F. Blake, EETS 263 (London: Oxford University Press, 1970), 110, lines 8–9.
[89] A. S. C. Ross, "The Middle English Poem on the Names of a Hare" [edition and commentary], *Proceedings of the Leeds Philosophical and Literary Society, Literary and Historical Section* 3.6 (1935): 347–77 (351, line 54).
[90] Derrida, *The Animal,* 31.

the referent ("Homer" equals "blind bard believed to have composed the *Iliad*"). They share that second function with common nouns, including the names of species when used to appellate specific referents. The indexical function, by contrast, is served paradigmatically by the names of individual human beings. Indeed, in Western culture, we privilege that function by avoiding human names with clear descriptive associations. Mary has her name not because she shares some feature with other Marys but because her family has thus confirmed her individuality. Of course, a few general features attach to such names—gender and linguistic affiliation, for instance—and biographical features soon accumulate (the Johnsons' first daughter, born in a certain hospital, longer than most newborns), but those associations are incidental to the designation of uniqueness. Even characteristic-based nicknames (Blondie, Shorty) deindividualize only partially, usually in a teasing way.

By contrast, many names given to individual animals do not privilege the indexing function over descriptive associations. "Blackie," "Champion," and "Buttercup" not only characterize their referents, like human nicknames; in addition, as I have already noted, many proper names for animals are associated by convention with a particular species, even when they lack obvious descriptive meanings ("Ned," "Rex," "Polly"). Some conventional names slide toward common status ("a chauntecleer," "eight reynards"). If medieval people generally avoided using the same names for human beings and for animals, as Robert Bartlett reports, a key distinction between the two sets may have been that only the latter denoted or connoted species-wide features.[91]

Those onomastic distinctions figure prominently in the beast epic, not least through their manipulation. "It has been suggested," writes N. F. Blake, "that the medieval beast epic came into being when the animals of the earlier fables were given {historically} human names."[92] Like other writers, Blake locates the transition in the mid-twelfth-century *Ysengrimus,* which expands widely circulated stories of the fox and wolf. The names, he writes, "fall into two broad categories": "sim-

---

[91] Robert Bartlett, *England Under the Norman and Angevin Kings, 1075–1225* (Oxford: Clarendon Press, 2000), 668. See also Keith Vivian Thomas, *Man and the Natural World: Changing Attitudes in England, 1500–1800* (New York: Pantheon Books, 1983), 114. Westerners now use unique, nondescriptive names for their companion animals, but those are advisedly exceptional: the grammatically proper "Maggie" or "Mrs. Dalloway" is semiotically *im*proper for a dog or cat. We seem to be acknowledging, perhaps with self-directed irony, our appropriation of the animals to quasi-human status.

[92] Caxton, *History,* ed. Blake, Introduction, xi.

ple human names" such as Reynard and Isegrim, and those that "imply the character or a particular characteristic of the animal in question."[93] What Blake does not note is that both kinds, but particularly the former, were followed habitually with a species sobriquet: "Reynard the Fox," "Isegrim the Wolf." A generic name apposites for an indexical one; that is, the characters are appellated both as humans would be and as animals normally are. In fables, in contrast, the one-named "fox" remains a generic hybrid—a typical fox aside from its ability to verbalize behavior that it shares with certain human beings. But the double names in the beast epic distinguish the human and nonhuman components enough to reveal the tension in their union.

The impossible conjunction epitomizes the powerful but peculiar agency of the characters thus named. As often noted, characters in beast epics are mostly inhuman physically but have human biographies (fraudulent monastic vows, visits to Rome or Jerusalem) and human desires (gold and silver, ornate combs), not to mention multilingual competency. But the split is even more pervasive. Even their bodies are inconsistently named: in Caxton's translation of Middle Dutch Reynard stories, Chauntecleer smites together "his handes and his fetheris," while two of his hens have limbs with which they can carry lighted tapers upright; later, Reynard is advised to soak his tail in urine and "smyte the wulf therewyth in his berde."[94] More conspicuously impossible are the interbreedings. That Reynard raped Isegrim's "wife," as the wolf claims (7/6–24; 9/16–23; 89/3–20), might represent natural though deviant behavior, though a union of fox and wolf would be infertile. But the imagination fails to account for Reynard's allospecific nephews: not just Isegrim but also a badger (his "suster sone"; 8/29), a bear, and an ape.

We may well *try* to imagine how a fox could be a badger's uncle, though. Although the text presupposes the possibility of such kinships just as *The Owl and the Nightingale* presupposes that birdsong can become Middle English, the effect is entirely different. In the earlier text, the birds' speech and attitudes were congruent with the behavior and even the physiology of nightingales and owls. Nothing in natural science explains a fox's rape of a wolf, much less a candlelit procession of hens

---

[93] Ibid., xi. Blake cites *Ysengrimus* as the transition point on xvi.

[94] Caxton, *History,* ed. Blake, 10, lines 21–27, and 97, lines 7–8. Future references will be to this edition and will be documented in the text by page and line number, separated by a solidus.

to the inscribed marble tomb of one of their "sisters" (10/21–28). The personages of *Reynard the Fox* are mutants: nonhuman bodies onto which human consciousness, kinship relations, and a few appendages have been unsuccessfully grafted.

Moreover, some of the species-mixing is difficult to pass over as conventional anthropomorphization. Bodies metamorphose within the narrative, sometimes in ghoulish ways. Pretending to undertake a redemptive pilgrimage, Reynard convinces the Lion king and queen to let him take "as moche of the beres skyn vpon his ridge [back] as a foote longe and a foot brode for to make hym therof a scryppe" (43/11–13). They agree that he will also need "foure stronge shoon," two from Isegrim and the others from the latter's wife—who has little need for good shoes because "she gooth but lytil out / but abydeth alway at home" (43/14–23). It isn't clear how Reynard will wear the "shoes," but we witness their removal from the Wolf's feet, pulled off from claws to sinews; "ye sawe neuer foule that men rosted laye so stylle / as Isegrym dyde / when his shoes were haled of / he styred not / and yet his feet bledde" (43/34–36). Comparably brutal is the remedy later devised by the king: to let the Bear and wolves use the "tabart" of Bellyn the Ram to replace their own skin (50/22–26, 51/13–14). The physiological incongruity heightens the characters' appropriations of each other's bodies.

Mutant beings exert their own fascination, as witness the long-standing popularity of fantasy and tales of marvels. At one point Reynard locates his own narrative in an alternative universal history like that of science fiction: "I shal saye the trouthe / lyke as myn elders haue alway don / syth the tyme that we fyrst vnderstode reson" (90/31–32). But beast epics also exert a deeper appeal. Their mutant personages attract us through a common mechanism of comedy: a balancing of the preposterous and the recognizably mundane. The Lion king's cruelty, physically monstrous but superbly articulate, is all too human. That may again recall the polygeneric protagonists of *The Owl and the Nightingale.* But the conjuncture of species in the beast epic is less balanced. If the Owl and Nightingale have the minds that we ourselves might possess, the Lion, Fox, and Wolf have the kind of mind that we attribute to some of our fellow humans—perhaps those whom we simultaneously despise and admire. Their mutant singularity illuminates not the fundamental shape of creaturely behavior but the distortions of a particular kind of human agency, one prone to ruthless appropriation. And it represents that kind of human behavior by appropriating the identities of nonhumans.

Two passages in Caxton's *Reynard* exemplify both kinds of appropriation, behavioral and semiotic. The first passage completes a triad of episodes in which Reynard has exploited other beasts by pretending not to know what members of their species eat. When Bruin the Bear comes to conduct him to the king's court, Reynard complains of sickness from eating too much honey. He feigns surprise when Bruin eagerly praises that food but offers to share his source—which turns out to be a bee-tree that Reynard knows to have been wedged open by a carpenter. As Bruin begins to eat, Reynard releases the wedge. The king next commands Tybert the Cat to summon Reynard. The Fox agrees to go but apologizes as they leave his "castle" that the only road-food he can offer is honey. When the Cat predictably declines, venturing that he would prefer a mouse, Reynard again feigns surprise at such dietary habits but proposes that Tybert visit the mouse-infested barn of a priest—where, he knows, Tybert will spring a trap set to stop Reynard himself from stealing hens (19/25–23/31).

The last installment of the triad begins when Reynard finally allows himself to be led to the court, primarily, one suspects, to exhibit his verbal wiles at the expense of Noble the Lion himself. During his devious self-exoneration, the Fox complains that Isegrim has cheated him of a share of calves and sheep but adds, in an ostensibly generous aside, that he doesn't mind the loss because he has "so grette scatte [treasure] and good of syluer and of gold that seuen waynes [wagons] shold not conne carye it away" (34/9–11). The king takes the bait. Burning with "desyre and couetyse," he demands to know where the riches are (34/12–14), and Reynard's execution is indefinitely postponed. The catachresis—lions do not crave silver and gold—resembles the earlier identification of wolf-paws as shoes, but this one lacks physical enactment. Here, the misfiguration can be resolved hermeneutically. Among the major characters, the king has been the most simply appellated. Since his introduction as "lyon the noble kynge of all beestis" (6/26), he has been referred to as the king, named by position rather than by proper name plus species. That position might pertain to human and non-human social structures alike: Noble could be imagined as human ruler or most powerful carnivore. In this episode, his gold-lust splits the two possible referents, pointing toward a man—but, crucially, one who acts inappropriately bestial. Reynard tempts Noble with treasure in the same way that he lured the bear with honey; thus the text reappellates the cupidity of human nobles (even kings) as an "animal" appetite. The denatured lion becomes a signifier for human carnality.

The second parable of appropriation uses animal figuration similarly but against a different human target: clerics deluded by intellectual pride. During a long self-styled "confession," Reynard says that he once agreed to ask a mare to sell her fat foal to the nearly starved Isegrim. According to Reynard, she refused to take money for the foal but added that her terms for a trade were written under her back foot. Reynard says that he reported this to Isegrim, claiming (falsely) that he himself could not read. The Wolf fell into the trap set by both mare and Fox. Boasting that he knew four languages, had studied at Oxford, was licensed in canon and civil law, and could thus read whatever "ony man can deuyse" as perfectly as his own name, Isegrim went to "read" the mare's terms—and, predictably, took a nearly fatal blow from her newly shod hoof (58/10–59/21). Reynard recalls having taunted the bleeding Wolf by asking if the writing was in prose or rhyme. Alas, Isegrim replied, I thought those six nails in her shoe were letters (59/26–35). The catachresis here is sharper than in the earlier episode: lions and kings might be commonly blinded by appetite, but there is no lupine equivalent of erudite stupidity. Reynard delivers a *sentence* that locates the episode's significance in the human world: "it is true that I long syth haue redde and herde / that the beste clerkes / ben not the wysest men / the laye peple otherwhyle wexe wyse" (59/38–60/1). That formulation *almost* renominates Isegrim (and presumably Reynard) as human. The "Fox" and "Wolf" parts of their names still matter, but only as signifiers of deviant human behavior, comparable to the king's bestiality. The nonhuman component gives a particular force to human-directed satire. Isegrim's extratextual correlative is not simply a foolish cleric; he is a cleric who has fooled himself into believing that he is not fundamentally a wolf. Indeed, in masking his predatory instincts, the wolfish clerk has forgone the innate survival skills that we attribute to nonhuman predators.

Nor are clerics the only target. Behind a scrim of feigned ignorance, Reynard outflanks Isegrim's linguistic skills: not only can Reynard read (59/38), not only does he know rhetorical terms (59/27–28), but he can use his knowledge to manipulate others. Perhaps he represents fraudulent monastic populism. Or he may be a self-mocking figure for the human author, since he not only moralizes the episode but also re-counts—or invents—the action.

In any case, beginning with this passage, human targets proliferate while the animal vehicles lose differentiation. Norman Blake notes that shortly before the mare's-hoof episode, the text that Caxton is translating changes mode. According to Blake, the first part of the Middle Dutch *Hystorie van Reynaert die Vos* functions primarily as parody; the second part recapitulates and expands events but renders them as didactic satire, often directed at particular locales and individuals.[95] In inset fables and anecdotes, the characters allude to corrupt clerics and rulers, sometimes particular ones notorious for greed and fraud, and to the pope and his close associates.[96] A consequence of the change that Blake does not discuss is that we lose track of who is voicing those digressions; the characters are disembodied vehicles for satiric attacks on human targets. Even when they return to attacking each other, they do so with decreasing reference to their own nominal species. They also report—or misreport—the main action itself. As Paul Wackers points out, readers have no way to distinguish (fictional) truth from the self-interested accounts by Reynard, Isegrim, Grymart, and Rukenawe. "Reality is always being manipulated," Wackers writes, "and if it is not by one person it is by another."[97]

Wackers's "person" represents a choice among various problematic names for all the agents in beast-epic. Blake calls them "personages"; I have mostly used "characters," a word whose semantic range also includes human linguistic artifacts, comparable to Derrida's *animots*. As Wackers's generalization implies, in the last part of the *Historie* the characters become interchangeable except as competing egos. They differ by what we can indeed call "personality," but nothing marks their monologues as the products of fox, badger, or ape. That they are nominally nonhuman matters a great deal, but it signifies not specifically—not by species—but as an undifferentiated whole. It constitutes the amoral impulse toward survival and self-aggrandizement that we often call animality. The characters make sense as human beings who are comically improper.

---

[95] Caxton, *History,* ed. Blake, Introduction, xix–xx.

[96] Ibid., 60/27–62/7, 66/9–19, 66/31–67/6; see also Blake's note 64/21 on page 131.

[97] Paul Wackers, "Words and Deeds in the Middle Dutch Reynaert Stories," in *Medieval Dutch Literature in Its European Context,* ed. Erik Kooper (Cambridge: Cambridge University Press, 1994), 131–47 (141–44, and 144).

That semiosis appears most clearly when it is occasionally interrupted. Like its sources, Caxton's *Reynard* climaxes in a battle between Reynard and Isegrim that briefly recasts the beasts as fully integrated hybrids rather than mutants. They fight *as* fox and wolf, vividly represented, even as they continue to speak and think. Rukenawe prepares her "nephew" as if he were indeed a fox with a human brain: she advises him to shave and oil his body, to minimize his opponent's handholds by flattening his ears and tucking his tail between his legs, and to drink enough that he will be able to soak his tail in urine. The urine-soaked tail, with which Reynard will indeed blind Isegrim, would remind readers of the way foxes mark their territory. Similarly grounded in nature are the Wolf's size advantage, the rivalry of the two species, and even Reynard's wiliness, attested in the folklore and hunting texts of many cultures. Even the ritualized proceedings (formal expressions of defiance, initial postures, angry vocalizations, feints) correspond to behaviors noted by ethologists.[98] Perhaps most crucial is that the motives expressed in the characters' human language are also grounded in nature—that is, in trans-species behavior. Single combat for physical dominance and even survival, balanced between rule-governed ceremony and unprincipled brutality, is a form of "animality" not just accepted but celebrated among men. As Blake observes, the episode parodies combat in courtly romances.[99] Parody distorts, as he also notes, but its success depends on generic—and here, genetic—congruence. Here, that is, the parts of Reynard's name appellate him synergistically. With good reason, Blake concludes that "the battle exemplifies all that is best in the Reynard story."

By contrast, it does not typify the *History of Reynard the Fox*. As soon as Reynard wins, parody yields to satire, a mode that bends the beasts back toward human figuration. Concomitantly, the action also returns to exploitation. Reynard's victory attracts hordes of previously unmentioned characters who proclaim kinship and demand a share of the spoils. Had the Fox actually slain the Wolf, this opportunism might mimic nonhuman scavenging. Instead, the text points again toward humans who behave inappropriately like animals (or like denigrated *ani-*

---

[98] See, for instance, Bekoff, *Emotional Lives,* 97–98, and Gregory Bateson's account of behaviors (Bateson calls them metamessages) through which animals differentiate threats from play. Bateson, "A Theory of Play and Fantasy," 1954; rpt. *Steps to an Ecology of Mind* (New York: Ballantine Books, 1972), 170–93 (179–81).

[99] Caxton, *History,* ed. Blake, Introduction, 138 n. 98/13.

mots). The narrator breaks his customary silence with an anthropocentric moralization ("Thus fareth the world now. who that is riche and hye on the wheel. he hath many kynnesmen and frendes"; 105/21–22). Reynard himself then appellates his kinsmen as two species: he compares them to dogs fighting over a bone but also calls them extortioners who, when "made lordes," act worse than greedy dogs (106/18–107/36). With superlative irony, he contrasts these "false extorcionners" with himself, boasting that no man can say "that I haue don otherwyse than a *trewe man* ought to doo / *Alleway the foxe* / *shal a byde the foxe*" (107/31, 108/3–7; emphasis added).

The last clause is true because it is false—because, that is, it is not really about foxes. When the Owl embraces her species in a similar way—"It is my joy and my delight to associate myself with those who are of my kind"—she refers to the nesting and predatory behavior that are indeed proper to her *cunde*.[100] And throughout that poem, she remains both generic owl and individual voice. In contrast, Caxton, like his source, gives us a fox that splits himself between true man and inveterate fox. The narrator later echoes Reynard's oxymoronic tautology with an important difference. Indirectly explaining how fox, badger, wolf, ape, and hangers-on of other species can be kin, he writes, "The name that was gyuen to hym / abydeth alway stylle wyth hym / he hath lefte many of his crafte in this world. . . . Ther is in the world moche seed left of the foxe" (110/8–15). Reynard is right that "the Fox" will remain unchanged—but only as the name that those who call themselves human give each other. And the narrator is right that this fox has left "much seed" in the world. Reynard, his allospecific relatives, and his human progeny all descend from the name with which we appropriate the nonhuman, of whatever species: *bêtise*.

In my focus on the characters with individual-plus-species names, I have neglected a large supporting cast who contribute to the richness of Reynard's fictional world. There are, for instance, human characters with categorical or individual names: "the preest of the chirche," "[t]he prestis wyf Iulok" (16/18–20). There are also nonhuman characters designated only by species—the mare that clobbers Isegrim, for instance, and the ferret, mouse, and squirrel who claim kinship with the victorious Reynard (105/17). Finally, one somewhat important character acts,

[100] Cartlidge, *Owl and the Nightingale,* lines 272–73.

and is named, in accordance with his species stereotype: Cuwart the Hare, Reynard's principal victim. "Cuwart" is only marginally proper, a Middle English and Old French common noun; it reifies the generic temerity that the Hare consistently enacts.[101] Cuwart exemplifies the anonymous and powerless of all species: when Reynard's victims vainly accuse the Fox of Cuwart's death, the narrator remarks that it "wente with hem as it ofte doth the feblest hath the worst" (30/30–31). If Reynard and his kin point toward "animalized" humans, sometimes particular ones, Cuwart's only extratextual referent is the nameless mortal creature.

It is thus particularly notable that a hare receives the most successful proper-naming of a nonhuman animal that I have found in the literature of any era. Bodleian MS Digby 86, a late thirteenth-century manuscript, includes a sixty-three-line Middle English poem headed, in French, "the names of a hare in English."[102] The poem's speaker avers that any man meeting the hare will never "be the better" unless he puts down whatever rod or bow he is carrying and says a prayer "in þe worshipe of þe hare."

The *oreisoun* offered by way of example consists of seventy-seven names, the majority of them *hapax legomena*.[103] Morphologically, the names span and even expand the naming practices I have discussed. The title and the closing section appellate a single member of the species—*vn leure,* addressed directly as "sire hare." In contrast, the first line uses the collective generic, "the hare"; the names themselves similarly begin with the definite article and lack verbs that might particularize their reference. Among the names are one or two species stereotypes, notably *couart.* But far more are sobriquets that would, if capitalized, resemble *Sir Tryamour*'s properly named *Trewe-love:* "stele-awai," "wint-swifft," "liȝtt-fot." Four names—*bouchart, goibert, turpin,* and *wimount*—were otherwise used as human proper names. In his 1935 edition and commentary, A. S. C. Ross writes that at least two of those individual human names had become categorical pejoratives.[104] If so, in applying

---

[101] Cuwart is in fact the only character slain by Reynard, and almost the only one that dies in the *History*. Reynard "confesses" to having killed Dame Sharpebek the Raven, but that happens (if it does) off-stage. Before the story opens, he has apparently killed Coppen the Hen. Assuming that the hen's name originated in the French *Roman de Renart* as *Couppée*—a reference to what Reynard did to her head—all of these proper names are characterizations rather than simply indices.

[102] Ross, "Middle English Poem," 350.

[103] Ibid., 350, lines 1–9, and 348–49 n. 3.

[104] Ibid., 353.

them to an individual animal, the poet reversed the process by which *gib* was first generalized to all housecats and then used for a promiscuous woman. Most remarkably, some names are morphologically human but semantically appropriate to the hare. Ross notes that *deubert, swikebert, scotewine,* and perhaps the fifteen names ending in *–art* employ "well-known endings of [human] proper names" such as *Edwin, Godwin, Albert,* and *Osbert.*[105] Here the suffixes are grafted onto roots that somehow characterize hares: "dew," "traitor," "scot" meaning "hare," "frisk" in *skikart,* and so forth.

Most of the names blend species appellations with tokens of individuality much more closely than do the proper-plus-generic names in the *History of Reynard the Fox.* They can justly be called proper—or appropriate—to their referent, which is, like all creatures, at once singular and generic. Of course, we expect individuals to bear a single proper name, or perhaps a few, whereas these names tumble forth in apparently inexhaustible number, perhaps suggesting an obsessive use of Adam's prerogative to control by naming. That the poem serves, rather, to recognize a hare, if not exactly to show it "worshipe" (line 9), follows from its onomastic tour de force. The namings posit, simultaneously, three realms of reference: hares, human perceptions, and the act of naming itself. It is in acknowledging those three standpoints, each limited, that the names become comprehensively apt.

Of the seventy-seven names, most "derive," in Margaret Laing's words, "from observed natural behaviour of the hare." Modifying Ross's five-part categorization, Laing sorts all seventy-seven names into six categories, noting that they "follow no particular order in the poem, although similar types do sometimes seem to cluster."[106] Ross and Laing list a few terms that simply mean "hare" (*hare, scot, scotewine*). For the others, I propose two large categories. The first includes forty-eight terms that Ross groups together because they "indicat[e] points in connection with the hare of a fairly obvious nature." These appellate physical characteristics, behavior, and habitat: "short-animal," "long-eared," "white-bellied," "side-looker," "nibbler," "fast-traveler," "jumper," "hopper-in-the-dew," "sitter-in-the-bracken," "grass-biter," "kale-hart," "cat-of-the-woods." Ross lists fifteen others that refer to "points

[105] Ibid., 353 and 353 n2.
[106] Margaret Laing, "Notes on Oxford, Bodleian Library, MS Digby 86, *The Names of a Hare in English,*" *MÆ* 67 (1998): 201–11 (202).

in connection with the hare which are not altogether obvious,"[107] but most of them also reflect "observed natural behaviour," as Ross indicates in annotating particular lines. For instance, *"þe go-mit-lombe"* probably refers to reports of hares' "concealing their scent when hunted by mingling with a flock of sheep"; *"þe hert wiþ þe leþerene hornes"* may testify to a disease in which "warty excrescences, often exactly like a pair of horns," grow on the head of an otherwise healthy hare.[108] Several of Ross's notes cite details in Edward of Norwich's *Master of Game*, whose references to the hare as a ruminant may also confirm one of Ross's proposed translations of *momelart*, "mumbler (of food)."[109] The cascade of evocative coinages sends the reader (and the annotator) repeatedly back to naturalists' accounts of the hare. Each epithet implies a fresh act of perception; some seem to catch a hare in action, the way Bartholomaeus's short narratives particularize the raven and the cock.

As naturalistic observations, the perceptions are often highly subjective. The second large group of appropriate names is, somewhat paradoxically, those that we impose: several dozen names conveying human judgments on the hare. Among these are the two that Ross categorizes, tendentiously enough, as indicating "moral characteristics" of "a fairly obvious nature": *couart* and *babbart*, the latter a *hapax legomenon*, which he also translates "coward." He also lists six "general terms of abuse," three of which apparently referred earlier to disreputable men (*turpin, bouchart, goibert;* also *srewart* "scoundrel," *choumbe* "numbskull," and *chiche* "niggard"). Perhaps he should have included among the abusive terms *soillart* "filthy beast" and *frendlese* "friendless"; in contrast, he might have balanced those with the more positive *brodlokere, liȝtt-fot, wint-swifft, tirart* "fast traveler," and *coue-arise* "get-up-quickly." Finally, at least four terms from Ross's other categories convey human reactions not attributively but directly: the hare is *þe der þat alle men scornes, euelelmet, make-fare* "cause-to-travel," and *þe der þat no-mon nedar nemnen.*[110]

However arbitrary they may seem to modern readers, those responses are as fully grounded in natural history as the names in my first category—grounded in the natural history, that is, of human beings. Medie-

[107] Ross, "Middle English Poem," 354.
[108] Ibid., 368 n. 45 and 369 n. 51.
[109] Ibid., 358 n. 18; see Edward of Norwich, *Master of Game*, 181, and Appendix, 221.
[110] Ross, "Middle English Poem," 353–55.

val texts record unstable but powerful reactions to hares. By contrast, a hare is the paradigmatic prey for humans and foxes alike, a role dramatized in *Reynard* and objectified in the contemptuous quasi-generic name *couart*. Bartholomaeus reports that the hare is "fereful, and fighteþ nouȝt" and is "feble of sight" (XVIII.lxviii). But hunting texts express respect for hares' ability to run long distances and to deceive pursuers.[111] The hare, writes Edward of Norwich in *Master of Game,* is "king of all venery" as well as "the most marvellous beast that is," in part because of its unusual digestive habits.[112] Particularly marvelous was the creature's alleged sexual ambiguity. Beginning with Pliny, writers report that hares are bisexual or can change sex.[113]

Whatever their basis, those reactions indicate ambivalence about a small, apparently defenseless herbivore with surprising resilience and unusual physiology. Representations of its behavior could flip-flop: in some folktales, the hare takes the place of the fox as duplicitous victimizer, even as cross-species rapist.[114] That a hare crossing one's path brought bad luck is the pretext for "Names of a Hare." That belief persisted into the 1880s, when William George Black opened an essay for *The Folk-Lore Journal* by "admit[ting] that the hare is regarded as an 'uncanny' animal."[115]

Freud, who attributed the feeling of the uncanny to the return of the repressed, might have recognized the narrator's advice: to put down one's defenses ("be it staf, be hit bouwe") and talk. In this case, the talk is not about but *to* the uncanny agent. And that speech act constitutes a third, vital realm of reference in "Names of a Hare."

Appellation here takes much of its significance from its rhetorical and prosodic form. "Names of a Hare" differs in both those ways from the other texts that I have considered. It is, first, a sustained first-person

---

[111] See Edward of Norwich, *Master of Game,* 14–16.

[112] Ibid., 181; see the editors' note on 221.

[113] E.g., Trevisa, *On the Properties,* XVIII.lxviii, and Edward of Norwich, *Master of Game,* 14 n. 1 and 181.

[114] Essays by Kenneth Varty and Elina Suomela-Härmä show that a hare takes the place of a fox or wolf, as aggressive trickster, in some oral analogues to the Reynard stories. See Kenneth Varty, "The Fox and the Wolf in the Well: The Metamorphoses of a Comic Motif," in *Reynard the Fox: Social Engagement and Cultural Metamorphoses in the Beast Epic from the Middle Ages to the Present,* ed. Varty (New York: Berghahn Books, 2000), 245–56 (252–56); and Elina Suomela-Härmä, "The Fox and the Hare: An Odd Couple," in Varty, *Reynard the Fox,* 257–67 (263–67).

[115] William George Black, "The Hare in Folk-Lore," *The Folk-Lore Journal* 1.3 (March 1883): 84–90 (84). See also John Andrew Boyle, "The Hare in Myth and Reality: A Review Article," *Folklore* 84 (Winter 1973): 313–26 (315).

address to a creature. More precisely, the speaker addresses a hypothetical human listener confronting a hare, but the address puts words into that speaker's mouth. Indeed, because the initial speaker addresses any person confronting any hare, he could become that inner speaker. The addressee's ambiguity, simultaneously an indefinite "anyone" and a present "I," resembles appellations like "the cock" or "the hare," which can also be either general or singular. Addressing an indefinite number of hearers, the poem is as much an exhortation to name as a catalogue of names.

It is also a virtuoso performance. As I hope to demonstrate in the following paragraphs, the poem's prosody merits explication on the basis of its formal craft alone. Its strong but varied rhythms suit the movements of an alternately wind-swift, lurking, scuttling, leaping ground-sitter. More fundamentally, the prosodic momentum deflects a reader's attention from individual names, engaging us in the act of naming itself.

The poem opens with five couplets in predominantly trochaic tetrameter:

> Þe mon þat þe hare Imet,
> Ne shal him neuere be þe bet,
> Bote if he lei doun on londe
> Þat he bereþ in his honde,
> (Be hit staf, be hit bouwe),
> And blesce him wiþ his helbowe.
> And mid wel goed devosioun
> He shal saien on oreisoun
> In þe worshipe of þe hare;
> Þenne mai he wel fare.[116]

[Things will never go well for the man who meets the hare unless he lays down on the ground what he carries in his hands (whether it be rod or bow) and blesses himself with his elbow, and with utmost devotion he shall say a prayer, in honor of the hare; then he may fare well.]

The last ten lines match those opening ones in meter and rhyme scheme. But between these formally unremarkable passages, the forty-three lines

[116] Ross, "Middle English Poem," 350–51, lines 1–10. Future references to "The Names of a Hare in English" will be from the edition on pages 350–51 of Ross's article and will be documented in the text by line number.

of names make masterful use of the form now associated with John Skelton: short, isochronous lines, nearly all two-stress, often with a caesura, in sporadic runs of strong rhyme sounds.

Although most textbooks now call Skeltonics "irregular" and "rough," in this case the changes in line length and rhyme sound are carefully controlled. There are, first, nine lines with two stressed syllables each, all ending in the unstressed suffix -art:

> Þe hare, þe scotart,
> Þe bigge, þe bouchart,
> Þe scotewine, þe skikart,
> Þe turpin, þe tirart,
> Þe wei-betere, þe ballart,
> Þe gobidich, þe soillart,
> Þe wimount, þe babbart,
> Þe stele-awai, þe momelart,
> Þe euelelmet, þe babbart . . .[117]

The first four of these are essentially pairs of amphibrachs (x / x // x / x), but the number of unstressed syllables after the first stress gradually increases from one in lines 11 and 12 to three in lines 18 and 19. A reader who respects the two-beat isochrony will speed up to accommodate the extra unstresses, but the acceleration is orderly because the expansion proceeds in line-pairs identical in length. The momentum slows in line 20, which drops from six unstressed syllables to three. The change is subtly underlined by a shift in rhyme sound to –ert, maintained for three lines that again accelerate somewhat: "Þe scot, þe deubert, / Þe gras-bitere, þe goibert, / Þe late-at-hom, þe swikebert . . ." (20–22). Two triplets follow: three lines that rhyme on –cat and three on –kere (23–28). The first five of those lines are metrically consistent ("Þe frendlese, þe wodecat, / Þe brodlokere, þe bromcat . . ."), but line 28 decreases to five syllables, with, exceptionally, only one medial slack: "And eke the roulekere."

After this pause, acceleration resumes through ten lines rhyming on –ere, with an expansion to six unstressed syllables (29–30). Then a couplet with long lines, rhyming in –ille or –ulle, precedes a major shift to four short-line couplets—possibly monometer, in contrast to the rest of the poem—of somewhat ominous content:

---

[117] Lines 11–19. For translations of these terms, see the preceding paragraphs.

> þe coue-arise,
> þe make-agrise,
> þe wite-wombe,
> þe go-mit-lombe. (42–45)

Next are five lines that resemble the first sequence of Skeltonics in meter and in rhyming on –art (46–50; compare 11–19). The last of these lines breaks the nearly universal anaphora on "the" to announce that the hare's "hei nome is srewart" (scoundrel). Only four lines now remain before the closing frame. The first three are long enough to be read with three stresses, and their syntax changes from simple to recursive noun phrases: "þe hert wiþ þe leþerene hornes, / þe der þa woneþ in þe cornes, / þe der þat alle men scornes" (51–53). And the fourth line stands out both in form and in content. The sole nonrhyming line in the poem, it disavows everything that has gone before: "þe der þat nomon nedar nemnen" (54).

That no man dares name the hare probably alludes to one of the ancient taboos that Ross and Laing mention.[118] Thus the poem may be imputing to hares a potency that annuls the ontological and psychological control that we assert by naming. By contrast, having just flouted any such prohibition seventy-six times, the speaker may be mocking both the taboo and the hare itself. In fact, neither extreme is tenable. The poem has neither cowered before the hare nor submerged it under human nominations. The names have, rather, defined deftly but glimpsingly both a recognizable creature and its impact on our own minds. All the while, the names, in their inventiveness and inventedness (many names are, as per the *Oxford English Dictionary,* "alleged" names of the hare), proclaim themselves as tentative and conditional. Perhaps no man should dare to appellate the categorical hare, but we may all "be þe bet" if we honor creaturely particularities with fresh verbal inventions.

The poem's final naming is its most contingent. The speaker has assured his unnamed human listener, perhaps himself, that after saying "al þis," he will have diminished the hare's agency and reclaimed his own: "þenne is þe hare miȝtte alaid. / þenne miȝtt þu wenden forþ, / Est and west and souþ and norþ . . ."; 55–57). He then addresses the hare in his own right:

> Haue nou godnedai, sire hare!
> God þe lete so wel fare,

---

[118] Ross, "Middle English Poem," 355; Laing, "Notes," 202.

> þat þou come to me ded,
> Oþer in ciue, oþer in bred! Amen. (61–64)

[Have now good day, sir hare! God let you fare so well that you will come to me dead, either in stew or in pastry. Amen.]

The cheerful farewell brings a particular hare into the speaker's own present, only to dismiss it into his future. There the speaker proposes to greet the returning creature with a terminal appellation: as food. It may seem that the elaborate naming exercise boils down (so to speak) to control in its most primal form. But the poem folds back into its beginning: upon encountering any hare, the speaker would incur his own adjuration to drop his weapons and recite "on oreisoun" like this one. Thus he defers the grasping (and eating) indefinitely, releasing the hare that he confronts into its singular mortality, pursued by properly endless namings.

Naming Matters

Nonacademic journalists and commentators gave unusual attention to a 2009 research report entitled "Exploring Stock Managers' Perceptions of the Human-Animal Relationship on Dairy Farms and an Association with Milk Production." Particularly prominent in headlines and summaries was the finding excerpted in my second epigraph to this essay: that dairy farmers who gave their cows names, as they did on 46 percent of the farms surveyed, realized greater milk production than those who did not.[119] Most commentators turned the observed correlation into a causal claim that they reported flippantly or dismissively. "Will Bessie make more milk if you call her by name? British ag specialists say she will," reported the blogger for *Scientific American*.[120] A trade publication, *Neuromarketing*, included the causal claim in its "Weird News" column and noted, as did many other reports, that the work had won the satirical "Ig Nobel" prize.[121] The mockery was somewhat off-target. The increase in milk production had been modest, about 3.4 percent per lactation, and

---

[119] Catherine Bertenshaw and Peter Rowlinson, "Exploring Stock Managers' Perceptions of the Human-Animal Relationship on Dairy Farms and an Association with Milk Production," *Anthrozoös* 22 (2009): 59–69 (62).

[120] Jordan Lite, "News Blog: Cows with Names Make More Milk," *Scientific American Blog,* January 28, 2009, http://www.scientificamerican.com/blog/post.cfm?id = cows-with-names-make-more-milk-2009–01–28.

[121] Roger Dooley, "Weird News: Cow Names Matter," *Neuromarketing: Where Brain Science and Marketing Meet,* October 2, 2009, http://www.neurosciencemarketing.com/blog/articles/weird-news-cow-names-matter.htm.

the scientists mentioned naming practices only incidentally in their analysis of farmers' attitudes and behavior toward cows. That is, Catherine Bertenshaw and Peter Rowlinson did not argue that individual names in themselves affected the cows.

But their study, and the subsequent reaction, demonstrated that names did matter, in two indirect ways. For the cows, naming marked a broader set of practices that the researchers summarized as "human attention to the individual animal," and those practices improved the cows' health.[122] To some commentators, however, the very idea that naming matters mattered in a negative way: they inflated or even invented such a claim in order to belittle it. Perhaps we both anticipate and resist a mandate to appellate animals—at least, animals other than pets—as individuals.[123]

Naming matters in equally complex ways in laboratories. In a three-year study of twenty-three biomedical and behavioral labs, Mary T. Phillips found that scientists seldom give individual names to animals used in research.[124] Like the dairy study, Phillips's work elicited strong human responses. Many researchers dismissed the idea of individual names for laboratory animals as patently inappropriate, even silly. Some reacted defensively, misinterpreting her questions as advocacy— somewhat the way commentators projected a brief for naming into the findings of Bertenshaw and Rowlinson. And some lab supervisors greatly exaggerated their use of individual names, "apparently on the assumption," Phillips reports, "that I would take [individual naming] as evidence that they cared about their animals."[125] Evidently animal studies is not the only discipline whose practitioners are uneasy over the semantic homogenizing of our fellow creatures.

I cite those nonliterary studies in part because my topic is not narrowly literary. Nonhuman creatures matter, to themselves but also to human beings. The names that we give to other animals reflect and affect our perceptions of them, which may in turn shape the ways we

[122] Bertenshaw and Rowlinson, "Exploring Stock Managers' Perceptions," 59.

[123] Differences in naming practices are one reason Erica Fudge offers for suggesting that in a real sense, pets are not "animals" (*Animal*, 27–34).

[124] Phillips, "Proper Names and the Social Construction of Biography," 124. See also Marc Bekoff, "Should Scientists Bond with the Animals Who They Use? Why Not?: Book Review of Davis & Balfour on Human-Animal-Bond," *Psycoloquy* 4.37 (1993), http://www.cogsci.ecs.soton.ac.uk/cgi/psyc/newpsy?4.37; and Thomas L. Wolfe, "Introduction: Environmental Enrichment," *Enrichment Strategies for Laboratory Animals, ILAR Journal* 46.2 (2005), http://dels-old.nas.edu/ilar_n/ilarjournal/46_2/html/v4602wolfle.shtml.

[125] Phillips, "Proper Names and the Social Construction of Biography," 125.

treat them. One worker interviewed by Phillips indicated that to name his research subjects might make it impossible to kill them in the course of research.[126] Phillips proposes no particular correlation between naming and treatment, nor will I. But certain parallels between literary and extraliterary practices can clarify the prior correlation: between naming and perception. By way of conclusion, then, I return to the problem of general names for nonhuman animals.

What I earlier called the default operation of general names obtains in labs and on farms as well as in literature: in contrast to proper nouns, species names promote collective representation. Just as the panther is categorically "friend to all," the members of *Rattus norvegicus* are presumed to be interchangeable, whereas Isegrim and Bessie should be individuals. Equally important, however, those default associations commonly weaken or even fail in practice. Narratives, for instance, particularize the bearers of collective names: Phillips summarizes a highly personalized biography that a science journalist constructed for a laboratory rat known only by number;[127] centuries earlier, as I have argued, Bartholomaeus turned the etymologically homogeneous ass and rooster into protagonists in intermorphic anecdotes, and "an owl and one nightingale" distinguished themselves by articulating their categorial identities. Conversely, proper names can obscure animals' identities. Some researchers studied by Phillips did name their animals, for instance, but the names alluded to well-known scientists or to students' romantic rivals; naming thus "had less to do with recognizing the animal's individuality than . . . with poking fun at [a human] namesake"[128]—a more directed version of the use of "Reynard," "Isegrym," and "Rukenake" to impute animality to certain clerics or counselors. In neither the lab workers' joke nor the beast epic's satire does the animal's meaning depend on its species. Such practices "deindividuate," to use Phillips's term, not by aggregating creatures into species but by bypassing species altogether.

Those outcomes should counter categorical objections to categorical names. Species names do not preclude a full representation of animals' identity as individuals; they mediate it. Phillips even suggests—inadvertently—that the "general singular" itself, by which we "corral

---

[126] Ibid., 132–33.
[127] Ibid., 136–37; referring to Robert Kanigel, "Specimen No. 1913: A Rat's Brief Life in the Service of Science," in *The Sciences* (NYAS), January/February 1987, 30–37.
[128] Phillips, "Proper Names and the Social Construction of Biography," 133.

the heterogeneous multiplicity of the living," need not constitute what Derrida calls *bêtise*.[129] Phillips reports that scientists commonly refer to experimental subjects "merely as the 'animal,'" not even " 'rat,' or 'monkey.'" Like Derrida, she regards that habit as the epitome of deindividuation. One of her two examples supports a different view, however. Addressing a rat recovering from anesthesia, an experimenter asked, "Are you light, animal?"[130] A neuroscientist colleague of mine explains that the question "would mean that the effects of the anesthesia had almost worn off and the animal may start experiencing pain."[131] Thus the researcher may have been acknowledging the rat's dual identity—as a paradigmatically generic lab specimen and as a fellow creature whose experience he understands. He or she gave "animal" a second name, the singular "you." Thereby he modeled, on a small scale, the same escape from the *animal* trap that some medieval texts perform at length. The path can begin at any point on the naming continuum, but it does not rest at one point. It travels from the categorical concept to the finely observed particular and back again, exhibiting toward its referent both cognitive appropriation and agnostic deference.

I have no doubt that the author of "Names of a Hare" did eat hare stew. But in his little *oreisoun,* he engages in what Derrida calls metonymic "eating well": an assimilation of the other that involves "*addressing oneself to the other*" while also "absolutely limiting understanding itself."[132] The poet addresses the hare with compelling and relentless immediacy, naming it so comprehensively as to disclose the limits of comprehension. So too *The Owl and the Nightingale* appellates its speakers in a full range of convincing but insufficient ways—as natural specimens, interspecies hybrids, metaphors, and self-defining subjects. Both overdetermined and indeterminate, the animal Others in both poems enact the interchange of species determinism and singular freedom that is the condition proper to any *animot,* be it owl, nightingale, woman, or man.

---

[129] Derrida, *The Animal,* 31.

[130] Phillips, "Proper Names and the Social Construction of Biography," 138.

[131] Lisa A. Gabel, e-mail to author, January 17, 2011.

[132] Jacques Derrida, " 'Eating Well,' or the Calculation of the Subject," in *Points . . . : Interviews, 1974–1994,* ed. Elisabeth Weber, trans. Peggy Kamuf et al. (Stanford: Stanford University Press, 1995), 255–87 (283); emphasis in original.

Calling: Langland, Gower, and Chaucer on Saint Paul

Isabel Davis
Birkbeck, University of London

T
HIS ARTICLE IS ABOUT CALLING in late medieval literature, an idea that was most thoroughly installed in Christian doctrine by Saint Paul. Unsurprisingly, the Pauline imprint on late medieval writing is marked, but, in contrast, the notion of calling has not been much attended to by medievalists.[1] I shall use William Langland's *Piers Plowman,* John Gower's *Vox clamantis,* and Geoffrey Chaucer's *House of Fame* and *Wife of Bath's Prologue* and *Tale* in order to show not only an extensive engagement with the theory of calling in the work of three key late medieval English writers but also to demonstrate what was at stake in that engagement. A Pauline turn in recent Continental philosophy has acknowledged and endorsed a significant theological residue within Marxist thinking; in particular, it has rewritten Paul's doctrine of calling to describe the relationship between individual and Law as intersubjective. In this article, I will use Louis Althusser's recasting of Paul's calling as "interpellation," which has, in turn, been influential in theories of the Event (*l'événement*) and most notably, recently, those of Alain Badiou.[2] I

I would like to thank Richard Rowland for his careful reading of this essay and trenchant comments, as well as two anonymous readers for *SAC*. Research was generously funded by a Leverhulme Fellowship.

[1] Russell A. Peck, "Biblical Interpretation: St. Paul and *The Canterbury Tales,*" in *Chaucer and Scriptural Tradition,* ed. David Lyle Jeffrey (Ottawa: University of Ottawa, 1984), 143–70, stresses the pervasiveness of Pauline reference in the *Canterbury Tales* as a whole, especially in relation to literary theory, but does not treat the topic of calling in particular. The following have considered the importance of Paul to *Piers Plowman,* but also have not focused on calling: R. James Goldstein, "'Why calle ye hym Crist, siþen Iewes called hym Iesus?' The Disavowal of Jewish Identification in *Piers Plowman* B Text," *Exemplaria* 13 (2001): 215–51 (226–29); and Nicolette Zeeman, *"Piers Plowman" and the Medieval Discourse of Desire* (Cambridge: Cambridge University Press, 2006), e.g., 1.

[2] Alain Badiou, *Saint Paul: The Foundation of Universalism,* trans. Ray Brassier (Stanford: Stanford University Press, 2003). For discussions about the relationships between, respectively, Badiou and Althusser, and Marxism and Saint Paul, see Slavoj Žižek, "Paul

shall also look at Giorgio Agamben's commentary on the Pauline epistles, which he wrote as a response, and partial corrective, to that turn.
I do this because this theoretical work explicitly exposes the political
mechanics of calling as it was written by Saint Paul and taken into key
medieval texts.

While the self-evidence of Pauline philosophy in medieval writing
may have deterred some medievalists from studying it, the centrality of
calling to studies of the Protestant reform movement, since Max Weber's *The Protestant Ethic and the Spirit of Capitalism,* has perhaps discour-
aged others. Weber, looking for the theologies that underpinned
modernity, considered the modern sense of calling (*Beruf,* in German)—of a secular profession—to have been fathered in Martin Luther's German Bible and fostered by the soteriology of John Calvin.[3]
This thesis has encouraged some historians of early modernity wrongly
to imagine that anterior understandings of vocation, and even those of
Paul himself, are "not yet," that is, limited, immature, or monologic.[4]
Christiane Frey has also raised doubts about Weber's "secularization
narrative," which caricatures and dismisses medieval thinking on calling.[5] In this essay I will consider some of the complex pre-Lutheran
thinking on calling that Frey acknowledges but that it is not her main
aim to consider. Medieval debates about vocation were different from
those formulated in the sixteenth century but nonetheless offer sophisticated and radical ways of thinking about the politics of Christian subjectivity, which, I will show, are complete in themselves, although trained
on the different problems of their own times. Agamben argues that
Weber understood Luther's lexical choice of *Beruf* for Saint Paul's *klēsis*
as having produced a new regard for secular occupation and the lived

---

and the Truth Event," in *Paul's New Moment: Continental Philosophy and the Future of Christian Theology,* ed. John Milbank, Slavoj Žižek, and Creston Davis (Grand Rapids, Mich.: Brazos Press, 2010), 74–99 (88); Giorgio Agamben, *The Time That Remains: A Commentary on the Letter to the Romans,* trans. Patricia Dailey (Stanford: Stanford University Press, 2005), e.g., 29–42.

[3] Max Weber, *The Protestant Ethic and the Spirit of Capitalism and Other Writings,* ed. and trans. Peter Baehr and Gordon C. Wells (London: Penguin, 2002), 28–35. The inadequacy of the "hermeneutic revolution" proposed by D. W. Robertson has also perhaps inhibited consideration of Christian doctrine in medieval literature. For a typical disavowal of Robertson's thesis and the quotation here, see Nicholas Watson, "Chaucer's Public Christianity," *Religion and Literature* 37 (2005): 99–114 (99).

[4] See, for example, Paul Marshall, *A Kind of Life Imposed on Man: Vocation and Social Order from Tyndale to Locke* (Toronto: University of Toronto Press, 1996), 21, and the telling repetition of "merely" in a description of pre-Lutheran assessments of calling.

[5] Christiane Frey, "κλῆσις/Beruf: Luther, Weber, Agamben," *New German Critique* 105 (2008): 35–56 (46–47).

life, because Weber overstated Pauline indifference to the mundane.[6] Agamben rereads 1 Corinthians 7:20 to reassert Paul's interest in the social world:

Klēsis indicates the particular transformation that every juridical status and worldly condition undergoes because of, and only because of, its relation to the messianic event. It is therefore not a matter of eschatological indifference but of change, almost an internal shifting of each and every single worldly condition by virtue of being "called." For Paul, the *ekklēsia*, the messianic community, is literally all *klēseis*, all messianic vocations. The messianic vocation does not, however, have any specific content; it is nothing but the repetition of those same factical or juridical conditions *in which* or *as which* we are called. Inasmuch as *klēsis* describes this immobile dialectic, this movement *sur place*, it can be taken for both the factical condition and the juridical status that signifies "vocation" [here Agamben refers to Jerome's rendering of *klēsis* in his Latin translation of the epistle] as much as it does *Beruf*.[7]

Although Paul portends the deactivation of social categories at the End of Days, he also recommends adherence to them in the time that remains. Far from dismissing human forms of organization, the messianic event encourages a retroactive and iterative connectedness to worldly conditions, even as it hollows them out. This interest in the world also motivates later medieval engagements with Pauline theory. The "immobile dialectic" that Agamben finds in Paul's theory of vocation was staged in medieval literature as a legal property relation: God is seised of all juridical conditions, and people or institutions enjoy and use those conditions only as his tenants or stewards. Within this theory of calling, instead of earthly names and estates being naturalized, fixed, and God-given or, alternatively, alien and anathema to God, God temporarily suffers imperfect human "callings" at the same time that he issues his own call. Thus, although human and divine "callings" are not identical, they are also not necessarily distinguishable and in fact often coincide; as such, the characters within these poems, and sometimes the poems themselves, do not always disambiguate them.

Weber argued for a sharp division within medieval society between the contemplative life of the cloister, which qualified as a vocation, and life outside of it, which did not. Only with Protestantism did he think

---

[6] Here I do not agree with Frey (ibid., 50) that Agamben adopts the same "distinctions" as Weber in relation to Paul's "indifference." Agamben demonstrates an attachment to the world in the Pauline epistles themselves, as well as within Franciscan thought, and therefore before Luther's translation. *The Time That Remains*, 22–23, 27.

[7] Agamben, *The Time That Remains*, 22–23.

secular everyday labor was made part of a life that was pleasing to God.[8] However, in medieval society, a concept of calling was reserved neither for monastics specifically nor even for religious lives more broadly. Although pre-Reformation ethics undoubtedly hung upon the division between *praecepta* and *consilia* and on the hierarchies of conduct that division produced, this served to amplify, rather than minimize, insecurities about the spiritual value of lay living.[9] Furthermore, the ethics that applied to religious lives were not hermetic; as Mary C. Erler has pithily said of the relation between the cloister and the world: "[T]he passage of monastic spirituality into lay possession is one of the great narratives of the later Middle Ages."[10] As I shall show here, while debates about *dominium* (possession) and *usus* (use) were most fervent in and around the Franciscan movement from the end of the thirteenth century, and were further inflamed by Wycliffite rigorism a century later, the implications of these debates extended to the ethics that applied to ordinary, active, and lay lives.[11] This cultural translation gave a new urgency not so much to the question (which had always preoccupied the religious orders) of whether people could meet the desiderata of perfect, apostolic imitation, but rather to the evaluation of the soteriological prospects of those who did not but were also not required to by rule. I shall also consider, as some of these poems do, the status of marriage as an appendage to the debate about Church property because, in a culture attended by a celibate priesthood, marriage was similarly involved in the question of lay "mediocrity" (to use a term deployed by Nicholas Watson in a study of the *Canterbury Tales*).[12]

It is true that pre-Reformation discussions of calling consider a number of different aspects of social condition and do not consistently sepa-

---

[8] Weber, *The Protestant Ethic*, 29, and see the overstatements in Marshall, *A Kind of Life*, 22; and Gary D. Badcock, *The Way of Life: A Theology of Christian Vocation* (Grand Rapids, Mich.: Wm. B. Eerdmans, 1998), 25.

[9] On *praecepta/consilia*, see Weber, *The Protestant Ethic*, 29.

[10] Mary C. Erler, review of *Lay Piety and Religious Discipline in Middle English Literature*, by Nicole R. Rice, *SAC* 32 (2010): 462–65 (462).

[11] There is a vast literature on the poverty debates of the thirteenth and fourteenth centuries and their passage into late medieval literature. See, for example, James Doyne Dawson, "Richard FitzRalph and the Fourteenth-Century Poverty Controversies," *JEH* 34 (1983): 315–44; Lawrence Clopper, *Songes of Rechelesnesse: Langland and the Franciscans* (Ann Arbor: University of Michigan Press, 1997), 27–28.

[12] Watson, "Chaucer's Public Christianity," e.g., 101. However, see also the response to Watson in R. James Goldstein, "Future Perfect: The Augustinian Theology of Perfection and the *Canterbury Tales*," *SAC* 29 (2007): 87–140, esp. 88–89. Goldstein argues against the notion that Chaucer "abandoned the Augustinian model of lay perfection."

rate out socioeconomic status from ethno-religious, gender, age, and marital identities. The crucial statement on calling in the Pauline epistles is often thought to be 1 Corinthians 7, which, similarly, did not chiefly focus on socioeconomic identities. In that text, Paul answered a query about marriage—should the Corinthians stay married on conversion to a religion that preferred celibacy—but he did so by cross-referencing the social distinctions produced in practices of slavery and circumcision: between freeman and bondman, Jew and gentile, respectively. His answer, for the married as for the bonded and the non-Jewish, was "Ech man in what clepyng he is clepid, in that dwelle he."[13] Correspondingly, medieval writers considered many different aspects of personhood to be equivalent callings, equally relevant to the ethical problems posed by the Christic event.[14] The late medieval notion of calling was broader than the one that succeeded it and a set of associations focused on the voice and naming, hailing, and response will be the subject of the first three sections of this essay. That said, the fourteenth century, marked by demographic crises and peasant insurrection, was a crucible within which concepts of labor and estate identity were being vigorously reformed. A concept of calling, and the postevental ethics that attended it, was being powerfully mobilized against ideologies of blood and heredity, which had traditionally claimed a perfect correspondence between civil and natural law (as the instantiation of divine commandment). In contrast, the idea of calling maintained an agnosticism about that relation. In the fourth part of this essay, I shall consider the state of affairs in the messianic vocation, or New Law, as it is described in these texts: as an "immobile dialectic" between human and divine callings. The theory of calling did not deny nature, or break earthly settlements but, instead, circumvented them with an alternative understanding of the confection of the social self.

As well as defining calling for their own times and in advance of the

---

[13] 1 Cor. 7:20; I cite the Wycliffite English translation because it is most closely contemporary to the texts I discuss here, and another witness to the Middle English terminology under consideration, although these authors undoubtedly encountered scripture in Jerome's Latin Vulgate translation. *The Holy Bible, Containing the Old and New Testaments, in the Earliest English Versions made from the Latin Vulgate by John Wycliffe and his Followers*, ed. Josiah Forshall and Frederic Madden, 4 vols. (Oxford: Oxford University Press, 1850). All scriptural quotations will be from this edition and will be cited hereafter in the text.

[14] For another discussion of the event, in late medieval literature, although one that is trained upon the idea of Fortune, see J. Allan Mitchell, *Ethics and Eventfulness in Middle English Literature* (New York: Palgrave Macmillan, 2009), 2.

Protestant revolution, I shall show that these texts also departed from what had gone before. For example, the popular and influential *Elucidarium* of Honorius of Autun (c. 1098) is pessimistic about the expectation that those in various lay estates, engaged in the sinful theaters of war and the market, might have for their salvation. An English translation, from the end of the fourteenth century, not only elides this gloomy prediction but goes further, including a new statement which insists that people are "callid" to Holy Church in their several estates or "manners," and reclaiming knighthood in particular.[15] The point here is not that people in the eleventh or twelfth centuries could not imagine or argue for lay salvation but rather that, by the end of the fourteenth century, where such pessimistic estimations were found, one way to resist them was to resort to a notion of calling, which incorporated worldliness into the messianic life. In the conclusion to this essay I shall develop a contrast between the idea of vocation in late medieval writing and Alain of Lille's more hygienic account of the New Law in his *Anticlaudianus* (c. 1182), arguing for the particular importance of calling for theologies of selfhood in the late fourteenth century.

Calling: Hailing and Naming

The word *klēsis* was rendered in Jerome's Vulgate Bible as *vocatio,* which was accordingly translated (in 1 Cor. 7:20, for example) with the Middle English *clepen:* "Ech man in what clepyng he is clepid, in that dwelle he." *Clepen* and its synonyms, *callen* and *hoten,* all carry two senses: of being named and of being hailed. Calling, the idea that people are summoned in and to their social places or roles, locates the instigation for subjective identity outside the individual. In this respect, it challenges ideologies of blood, finding social condition to be lodged in naming practices and noise, which have always been suspected of vacancy. However, the exteriorization of social identity that is calling does not make that designation *necessarily* unreliable. Instead, it establishes subjectivity as, in Althusser's terms, interpellated:

[15] Honorius Augustodunensis, *Elucidarium sive dialogus de summa totius Christianae theologiae,* in J.-P. Migne, ed., *Patrologiae cursus completus. . .* vol. 172 (Paris, 1854), cols. 1148B–1148C. The English translation is found in a Wycliffite miscellany: Cambridge, St. John's College MS G25, and is printed in Friedrich Schmitt, ed., *Die mittelenglische Version des Elucidariums des Honorius Augustodunensis* (Burghausen: W. Trinkl, 1909), 31.

I shall then suggest that ideology "acts" or "functions" in such a way that it "recruits" subjects among the individuals . . . by that very precise operation which I have called *interpellation* or hailing, and which can be imagined along the lines of the most commonplace everyday police (or other) hailing: "Hey, you there!"

Assuming that the theoretical scene I have imagined takes place in the street, the hailed individual will turn round. By this mere one-hundred-and-eighty-degree physical conversion, he becomes a *subject.* Why? Because he has recognized that the hail was "really" addressed to him, and that "it was *really him* who was hailed" (and not someone else).[16]

Althusser's policeman might equally, he acknowledges, be a Christian God and God's call produces an answering recognition from the Christian subject: "that they really do occupy the place it [i.e., religious ideology] designates for them as theirs in the world, a fixed residence: 'It really is me, I am here, a worker, a boss or a soldier!' in this vale of tears."[17] Names and labels may be externally assigned, rather than being natural, but they are stabilized, and made proper, by the individual subject's recognition of and faith in the authority that thus addresses them. The allusion to the "vale of tears" comes from Psalm 83:7, in which the narrator's soul longs for and calls to heaven from "the place that he sette." It also recalls the *Salve Regina* breviary anthem that hails the Virgin Mary. The individual is not only hailed but responds with a duplicate call that acknowledges her "place." In this allusion, Althusser registers interpellation as a mirror-structure—in his characteristic recourse to Jacques Lacan—an antiphonal that mutually conceives and corroborates both the subject and the Law. The idea of interpellation was a version of and indeed derived from a reading of Paul's concept of calling. Paul, after all, was literally called by name *en route* to Damascus: "Saul, Saul what pursuest thou me?" (Acts 9:4). "Who art thou, Lord?" Paul asks in return and his answer is another proper name: "Jhesu of Nazareth" (Acts 9:5). The recognition with which Paul responds to the call—falling to the ground and using the honorific, "Lord"—confirms him as "one called up," that is, part of the ecclesia and witness to the messianic event.

---

[16] Louis Althusser, "Ideology and Ideological State Apparatuses," in *Lenin and Philosophy and Other Essays,* trans. Ben Brewster (London: New Left Books, 1971), 121–73 (162–63).

[17] Ibid., 178.

Such calls are heard in Middle English literature, although not always so unequivocally. The central conceit of Gower's *Vox clamantis* is that it relates the words of a calling voice, which channels other calls the narrator hears. This idea is encapsulated in the title, which comes from the gospel descriptions of the ministry of John the Baptist (e.g., Matt. 3:3) where it realizes Isaiah's prophecy (Isa. 40:3) that the messiah would be prefigured by "the voice of one crying in the wilderness." Just as the voice of the Baptist heralds the Word, Gower claims that his being called precedes his writing of the *Vox*. The first book of *Vox clamantis,* much of which was appended after the rest of the poem was written, develops the theme of calling in multiple and noisy ways.[18] Indeed the poem, and especially its first book, is made up of a cacophony of competing calls whose origins are shifting and indistinct. This emphasis is established early, in the first lines:

> Contigit vt quarto Ricardi regis in anno,
> Dum clamat mensem Iunius esse suum,
> Luna polum linquens sub humo sua lumina condit,
> Sponsus et Aurore Lucifer ortus erat . . .

[It happened in the fourth year of King Richard, when June claims the month as its own, that the moon, leaving the heavens, hid its rays under the earth, and Lucifer the betrothed arose at Dawn.][19]

This opening uses the verb *clamare* (literally, to cry or call) somewhat unnaturally to establish the theme of competing claims. The word *clamat* makes June a claimant, only, to the month as its property.

The rest of the book's first chapter comprises an Ovidian celebration of a previous time in which the only voices were those of the birds (I.1.91–108); but those are not straightforwardly pleasant, being a "dis-

---

[18] The early version of *Vox clamantis* began with what is now the prologue and first chapter of Book I and then continued with what is now the prologue to Book II, which was numbered as Book I, Chapter 2. What are now chapters 2–21, in the first book, are later interpolations. This is how the poem appears, for example, in Bodleian Library, Oxford, Bodleian Library, MS Laud 719; see its description in the introduction to John Gower, *The Complete Works of John Gower. Volume 4: The Latin Works*, ed. G. C. Macaulay (Oxford: Clarendon Press, 1902), lxvii–lxviii.

[19] Gower, *The Latin Works*, Book I, Chapter 4, 1–4. Hereafter cited by book, chapter, and line number in the text. The English translation is from: John Gower, *The Major Latin Works of John Gower: The Voice of One Crying and the Tripartite Chronicle*, trans. Eric W. Stockton (Seattle: University of Washington Press, 1962), 51. Hereafter cited by page number in the text.

cordia concors" (harmonious discord), a harmony complicated, then, by its variety. Then the voices in the poem become more contemporary and particularized as Gower's nightmarish vision of the peasants' revolt displaces the birds' song with unmistakeably hostile and dissonant noise: "Ecce rudis clangor, sonus altus, fedaque rixa, / Vox ita terribilis non fuit vlla prius" (I.11.815–16) [Behold the loud din, the wild clangor, the savage brawling—no sound (more properly voice) was ever so terrible before (68)]. The peasant voices first take on the quality of animal noises, but they then transmute into the roaring of monsters, in conscious allusion to Ovid's *Metamorphoses*. In a much-quoted passage, the peasantry are described calling and collecting together: "Watte vocat, cui Thomme venit" (I.11.783) [Wat calls, Tom comes to him (67)]. The narrator flees, taking refuge onboard a ship, but the calls follow him, migrating into the winds and the sea and the roaring of a sea creature; these are supplemented by the crying of the terrified sailors who have given him passage. However, among these earthly voices he hears others: the inner voice of Wisdom and also another, from an external, celestial source. Wisdom identifies a divine call even in the wrathful voices that have terrorized him: "Quo deus offensus te reparando vocat" (I.16.1548) [Because God is displeased, He is calling you to redemption (83)]. Finally the celestial voice calls him to write and to preserve these heterogeneous, inner, outer, low, high, mundane, and otherworldly calls as the *Vox clamantis*.

The narrator of William Langland's *Piers Plowman* also receives, but continually postpones answering, his call. Here, in a particularly sonorous part of Langland's poem, is one of the damascene moments to which Will only partially responds:

> Treuth trompede tho and song *Te deum laudamus*
> And thenne lutede Loue in a loude note:
> *Ecce quam bonum et quam iocundum, etc.*
> Til the day dawed thes damoyseles caroled
> That men rang to the resureccioun, and riht with that Y wakede
> And calde Kitte my wyf and Calote my douhter:
> "Arise and go reuerense godes resureccioun,
> And crepe to the croes on knees and kusse hit for a iewel
> And rihtfollokest a relyk, noon richore on erthe. . . ."[20]

[20] William Langland, *Piers Plowman: A New Annotated Edition of the C-Text,* ed. Derek Pearsall (Exeter: University of Exeter Press, 2008), XX.467–75. Hereafter this text will be cited by passus and line number in the text. I use the C-text because of the

In this passage, Langland produces a momentary intersection between three different planes of his narrative: the dream-vision story about how the daughters of God are reconciled; the waking life and the story of the narrator in his own historical time at a particular moment of the *Temporale* (Easter); and the universal story of the resurrection, which is the messianic event or call. Will, and through him his family, are called to church, to the Church, and into the ecclesia, in a metaphysical sense. The new unity between the Daughters of God authorizes their calling of others and the words that Love sings, from Psalm 132, make that call to unity explicit. The sounds in this excerpt are ambiguous: they could be those of instruments—a trumpet, a lute, and bells—or of voices that take on the character of those instruments.[21] Truth's trumpeting is, as it is elsewhere in medieval symbolism and on scriptural authority, especially associated with the resurrection.[22] Truth's calling echoes the final call to the elect, which, as Jesus is reported as prophesying in Matthew's gospel, will be both vocal and sounded on the trumpet: "And he schal sende hise aungels with a trumpe, and a greet vois; and thei schulen gedere hise chosun fro foure wyndis, fro the hiȝest thingis of heuenes to the endis of hem" (24:31). This ambiguity between voices and instruments blurs the relation between ordinary noise—the church bells on Easter morning—and the divine voice. On hearing these dream sounds, Will is spurred to call his family to "reuerense godes resureccioun." The resurrection is inserted here in the segue between dream and waking life (the two instances of the word "resureccioun" are separated by the act of waking), and is unlocated either temporally or spatially, allowing it to happen at a number of locations and moments at once. Calling effects in Will a miniature resurrection as he finds an uncharacteristic energy and resolve, seen in his issuing of firm instructions to his family: "Arise and go reuerense godes resureccioun," a line

---

"autobiographical" passage in Passus V, which is unavailable in other versions of the poem, although many of the other passages considered here are also present in the B-text.

[21] Calling, according to the so-called John Ball letters, is also performed as a collation of human and instrumental agency. The text addresses the rebels: John Ball "haþ rungen ȝoure belle." These letters are reproduced in Steven Justice, *Writing and Rebellion: England in 1381* (Berkeley and Los Angeles: University of California Press, 1994), 14.

[22] On the trumpet and the resurrection, see Bruce W. Holsinger, *Music, Body, and Desire in Medieval Culture: Hildegard of Bingen to Chaucer* (Stanford: Stanford University Press, 2001), 94.

in which ordinary and spiritual revivification are thrown to either end. He thus operates as a conduit, passing the call onto his family. Will mediates the call of Truth's trumpet to Kitte and Calote, in the same way that Gower's narrator passes on the call that he has heard to his reader by writing *Vox clamantis*. Furthermore, just as it does for Will, calling revives Gower's narrator: "Et iam deficiens sic ad sua verba re-uixi" (I.19.1899) [And just on the point of failing, I revived at its words (i.e., the words of the celestial voice) (90)], and the verb *revivere*, which is used here, literally, to live again, is the same that is used of Christ's resurrection in Jerome's translation of Romans 14:9.

Will calls his family in two ways: he both summons and names them. Moreover, he names them doubly: by their proper names, "Kitte" and "Calote," and by their social roles, "wyf" and "douhter." Yet there is a critical suspicion that, to contemporary audiences, the purported proper names here, "Kitte" and "Calote," may have meant something similar to "wife" and "daughter," respectively.[23] Thus the dreamer gives them names that are hardly proper to them, but that are the descriptions that happen to apply to them when they are called. In their vacuity, these personal names defer to callings. Kitte's and Calote's callings are given added fragility because they are given them by Will, an all-too-fallible representative of human society, and they are relative to him as husband and father. In the Middle Ages, Emily Steiner reminds us, names were more provisional than they are today. A system of fixed naming was not universally available in the later Middle Ages: "humbler people were less likely to be designated fixed surnames, or even bynames, than those of higher station," and such people may sometimes have gone by an occupational or locative name, rather than a patronymic; as a result, their names were highly dependent upon context. She describes Gower and Langland, in particular, intervening in the "inevitable—and pro-ductive—gap" between description and identification in traditions of plebeian naming.[24] Steiner and Anne Middleton, too, have understood Middle English literary interventions into questions of naming as self-

[23] Tauno F. Mustanoja, "The Suggestive Use of Christian Names in Middle English Poetry," in *Medieval Literature and Folklore Studies: Essays in Honor of Francis Lee Utley,* ed. Jerome Mandel and Bruce A. Rosenberg (New Brunswick: Rutgers University Press, 1970), 51–76 (72–73).

[24] Emily Steiner, "Naming and Allegory in Late Medieval England," *JEGP* 106 (2007): 248–75 (251–54).

conscious negotiations of legal instruments designed to regulate "proprietary relations" in what Middleton has described as a "pervasive fourteenth-century crisis of the proper."[25]

These preoccupations are on display in the most famous Middle English discussion of the contest between blood and conduct, in Chaucer's *Wife of Bath's Tale*. In a digressive aside, the old lady asks whether *gentillesse* is natural—as heat is to fire—or "a strange thyng to thy persone":

> "But, for ye speken of swich gentillesse
> As is descended out of old richesse,
> That therfore sholden ye *be* gentil men,
> Swich arrogance is nat worth an hen.
> Looke who that is moost vertuous alway,
> Pryvee and apert, and moost entendeth ay
> To *do* the gentil dedes that he kan;
> Taak hym for the grettest gentil man.
> Crist wole we *clayme* of hym oure gentillesse,
> Nat of oure eldres for hire old richesse.
> For thogh they yeve us al hir heritage,
> For which we *clayme* to been of heigh parage,
> Yet may they nat biquethe for no thyng
> To noon of us hir vertuous lyvyng,
> That made hem gentil men *ycalled* be,
> And bad us folwen hem in swich degree.
> "Wel kan the wise poete of Florence,
> That highte Dant, speken in this sentence.
> Lo, in swich maner rym is Dantes tale:
> 'Ful selde up riseth by his branches smale
> Prowesse of man, for God, of his goodnesse,
> Wole that of hym we *clayme* oure gentillesse';
> For of oure eldres may we no thyng *clayme*
> But temporel thyng, that man may hurt and mayme. . . ."[26]

[25] Anne Middleton, "William Langland's 'Kynde Name': Authorial Signature and Social Identity in Late Fourteenth-Century England," in *Literary Practice and Social Change in Britain, 1380–1530,* ed. Lee Patterson (Berkeley and Los Angeles: University of California Press, 1990), 15–82 (18, 62); see also Steiner, "Naming and Allegory," 255.

[26] Geoffrey Chaucer, *The Riverside Chaucer,* gen. ed. Larry D. Benson (Oxford: Oxford University Press, 1988), III.1161, 1109–32; my emphases. All quotations from Chaucer's works will be from this edition and hereafter cited in the text.

The old lady begins with a contrast between being and doing, but shifts into the language of calling, bringing the cognate words, "claim" and "call" (both are rooted in Latin *clamare* and Greek καλέω, *kaleo*, a cognate of *klēsis*), into tension. She berates her young husband for the arrogance that convinces him that he *is* gentle; his *gentillesse* is nothing more than a "clayme." A claim, in both Middle and modern English, must be externally validated—otherwise it exists only in the shifting sands of human language—and his is not. Human claims are all too likely to be false and divisive; the Wycliffite Egerton Sermon, for example, decries the fragmentation of the Church, which ought to be a unitary *ecclesia*, into a multiplicity of sectarian "cleymes."[27] In *The Wife of Bath's Tale,* even the "gentil men" of the past were only "ycalled" gentle and because of their "vertuous lyvyng," rather than anything more intrinsic; the old lady makes her use of the word "ycalled" more pointed by displacing the verb *to be,* here used only as the passive auxiliary, to the end of the line. Property claims upon a blood line might well, the old lady hints, be upended in the Christian communion; she suggests he claim instead through conduct, rather than ownership, that is, through imitation of virtuous examples, and ultimately that of Christ himself.

The word claim has a legal sense and with it the old lady establishes the calling to gentle conduct as an alternative to the law of heritable property. In *Piers Plowman,* Christ also calls people in this legalistic way; referring to the souls he liberates from Hell, he says: "Myne they were and of me; Y may the bet hem *clayme*" (XX.372). In this way, he calls to him human souls that rightly belong to him. Of course, the kind of calling discussed in *The Wife of Bath's Tale* is neither as literal as it was for Paul, say, nor the souls in *Piers Plowman.* As Judith Butler writes, in her commentary on Althusser's theory of interpellation: "If we accept that the scene is exemplary and allegorical, then it never needs to happen for its effectivity to be presumed."[28] In that sense, the call has "always already" happened.[29]

The allegory of interpellation is dramatized in a more explicit way in

---

[27] Anne Hudson, ed., *The Works of a Lollard Preacher: The Sermon "Omnis plantacio," the Tract "Fundamentum aliud nemo potest ponere," and the Tract "De oblacione iugis sacrificii,"* EETS 371 (Oxford: Oxford University Press, 2001), 23–25.

[28] Judith Butler, *The Psychic Life of Power: Theories in Subjection* (Stanford: Stanford University Press, 1997), 106.

[29] On the precocity of messianic presence, see Agamben, *The Time That Remains,* 71.

a passage from Chaucer's *House of Fame,* in a way that anticipates the old lady's lecture.[30] There claimants approach the goddess Fame, seeking her corroboration of their high self-estimations. Kneeling down, they plead:

> "Lady, graunte us now good fame,
> And lat oure werkes han that name
> Now in honour of gentilesse,
> And also God your soule blesse!
> For we han wel deserved hyt,
> Therfore is ryght that we ben quyt."
> "As thryve I," quod she, "ye shal faylle!
> Good werkes shal yow noght availle
> To have of me good fame as now.
> But wite ye what? Y graunte yow
> That ye shal have a shrewed fame,
> And wikkyd loos, and worse name,
> Though ye good loos have wel deserved. . . ."
>
> (1609–21)

Again, the bid-for calling is *gentil(l)esse.* The search for a superlative name through devotion to a goddess of temporal glory produces unreliable results; these claimants, for example, find their names defamed. They are given a name that is either "worse" than the one they had before or "worse" than their good conduct deserves. Other groups of claimants approach Fame with varying degrees of interest in winning a favorable reputation, and their demands are variously met or rebuffed. There is no logic, not even a consistent inversion, to Fame's operations.[31] For example, one group of claimants who request anonymity are bathetically and comically satisfied: " 'I graunte yow alle your askyng,' / Quod she; 'let your werkes be ded' " (1700–1701); another group, with the same request, have their good works reported. The old lady, in *The*

---

[30] This point of similarity has been noted before by J. A. W. Bennett, *Chaucer's Book of Fame: An Exposition of "The House of Fame"* (Oxford: Clarendon Press, 1968), 149, 156. For the poem's explicit allusions to Paul and also to Pauline philosophy as mediated by Dante, see Lawrence Besserman, *Chaucer's Biblical Poetics* (Norman: University of Oklahoma Press, 1998), 173–74.

[31] Helen Cooper, "Poetic Fame," in *Cultural Reformations: Medieval and Renaissance Literary Theory,* ed. Brian Cummings and James Simpson (Oxford: Oxford University Press, 2010), 361–78 (366).

Wife of Bath's Tale, however, recommends a different kind of supplication performed in *imitatio Christi* and a renunciation of all social names.

In her *Prologue* the Wife of Bath says, with a direct quotation from 1 Corinthians 7:20, that she empties out her social designations to embrace a messianic vocation:

> I nyl envye no virginitee.
> Lat hem be breed of pured whete-seed,
> And lat us wyves hoten barly-breed;
> . . . In swich estaat as God hath cleped us
> I wol persevere; I nam nat precius.
> In wyfhod I wol use myn instrument
> As frely as my Makere hath it sent.
>
> (III.142–44, 147–50)

Virgins seem, in the first two lines here, to be securely attached to the analogy of white bread, with the verb "to be." However, Alisoun loosens that attachment with the hortatory subjunctive, "lat hem." Further, she produces a destabilizing pun on bread/bred in the lexical choice of "seed," a word that can apply to human reproduction as well as breadmaking, as it does when Alisoun makes a similar point earlier in the *Prologue:* "if ther were no seed ysowe, / Virginitee, thanne werof sholde it growe?" (71–72). Let them try to breed, she scoffs; because it does not reproduce, virginity therefore cannot *be* intrinsic and inherited. When she turns to the subject of wives, she jettisons the verb "to be" in favor of "hoten" (to be called), resignedly accepting a duff label. Indeed, although Alisoun claims to *be* an "expert" (174) on marriage, and that she *is* "as kynde / As any wyf" (823–24), that does not add up to saying "I *am* a wife" or, more properly given that she is a widow in the time of the *Prologue,* "I was a wife." However, she does say that she is "Venerian," and that her "herte is Marcien" (609–10), naturalizing the instincts that, on Paul's instruction, compel her to marry, but throwing them away from herself with her astrological rationale.[32] The pessimism of "hoten" is undercut, however, by the translation of 1 Corinthians 7:20 a few lines later, in which she pits God's call against these human

---

[32] Furthermore, it has been suggested that these statements are the fifteenth-century additions of a misogynist redactor. Beverley Kennedy, "Contradictory Responses to the Wife of Bath as Evidenced by Fifteenth-Century Manuscript Variants," in *The Canterbury Tales Project: Occasional Papers,* ed. Norman Blake and Peter Robinson, 2 vols. (Oxford: Office for Humanities Communication, 1997), 2:23–39 (29–30).

slurs, embracing her divine calling. "I nam nat precius" also has a double sense: suggesting both that she is not prudish and, because the lexis of material value is so commonly used of sexual purity, that she is defined against virginity as a category.[33] She presents herself as a "subject without identity," scrupulously avoiding a positive identification through the double negative: "I nam nat."[34] In this way, she reproduces the annulments that Paul described in his characterization of the messianic life as one in which:

thei that han wyues, be as thouȝ thei hadden noon; and thei that wepen, as thei wepten not; and thei that ioien, as thei ioieden not; and thei that bien, as thei hadden not; and thei that vsen this world, as thei that vsen not.

(1 Cor. 7:29–31)

Answering: Use and Do Well

Alisoun's resort to the language of use, in the quotation from her *Prologue* above, follows Paul: "Thou seruaunt art clepid, be it no charge to thee; but if thou maist be fre, the rather *vse* thou" (1 Cor. 7:21; see also 29–31 above). Negation and use characterize the messianic vocation; use, writes Agamben in his reading of this part of the epistle,

is the definition Paul gives to messianic life in the form of the *as not*. To live messianically means "to use" *klēsis;* conversely, messianic *klēsis* is something to use, not to possess. . . . Paul contrasts messianic *usus* with *dominium;* thus, to remain in the calling in the form of the *as not* means to not ever make the calling an object of ownership, only of use. The *hōs mē* [i.e., the *as not*] therefore does not only have a negative content; rather, for Paul, this is the only possible *use* of worldly situations. The messianic vocation is not a right, nor does it furnish an identity; rather, it is a generic potentiality that can be used without ever being owned.[35]

The same rhetoric—of use and negation—is on display when the Wife of Bath argues that Christ's virginal example is counsel rather than universal precept:

[33] This can be seen, for example, in the poem *Pearl:* "that precios perle wythouten spotte." J. J. Anderson, ed., *Sir Gawain and the Green Knight, Pearl, Cleanness, Patience* (London: J. M. Dent, 1996), line 36.

[34] Alain Badiou, *Saint Paul,* suggests the "subject without identity" is made available through Pauline philosophy (5).

[35] Agamben, *The Time That Remains,* 26.

He spak to hem that wolde lyve parfitly;
And lordynges, by youre leve, that am nat I.
I wol bistowe the flour of al myn age
In the actes and in fruyt of mariage.

(III.111–14)

Again, Alisoun defines herself through negation, "that am nat I." She also here deploys the language of both use—"bistowe"—and fruit.[36] She does so legalistically; correctly, she is a tenant in, rather than owner of, her own body, enjoying it not by right of freehold, but instead only in usufruct. Further, when Alisoun cites Saint Paul on the marriage debt (III.130–31), she indicates that as well as being subject to God, spouses surrender sovereignty over their bodies to each other, living in each other's debt.

Agamben has noted that the questions of use and property were especially explosive in the controversy over Franciscan poverty, which came to a head in the work and condemnation of Peter Olivi in the 1280s.[37] Olivi argued, in his treaty *Usus pauper,* that the Franciscan vow not only excluded the brothers from the ownership of private property but also restricted them to necessary use.[38] Olivi's opponents agreed that absolute poverty was a desirable ambition, a perfect way of life, but they disagreed that *usus pauperis* was intrinsic to the vow, or that it could be laid down by precept; the ownership of property was clearly proscribed, but the question of its use was open and flexible. David Burr offers this *précis:* "The central point of debate is clear enough, Olivi's opponents argue that any obligations incurred through a vow must be precisely determinable or the vower would be in constant danger of sinning."[39] In spite of the time that had passed up to Chaucer's writing the *Canterbury Tales,* the furor had not dissipated; ethics within the fraternal orders were obviously an ongoing concern. Furthermore, the reforming impulses in Wycliffitism pressed on this same sore point; for Wycliffites, the argument against absolute poverty was a scholastic loophole that

[36] Both the *Oxford English Dictionary* (5a) and the *Middle English Dictionary* (2b) record this example of "bestow," under the sense of "employ" or "apply." Hereafter cited as *OED* and *MED.*

[37] Agamben, *The Time That Remains,* 27.

[38] David Burr, "The Persecution of Peter Olivi," *Transactions of the American Philosophical Society* 66 (1976): 1–98 (15–16); and Clopper, *Songes of Rechelesnesse,* 230–32.

[39] Burr, "The Persecution of Peter Olivi," 16–17.

killed the spirit, while attending to the letter, of the law.[40] Wyclif also distinguished lordship (*dominium*), the right to exercise authority and own property, from use and fruit; God retained lordship, but gave it on loan to those who used it properly and, as such, were in a state of grace.[41] Sinners who held office and property did so without legitimacy. Like the old lady in *The Wife of Bath's Tale,* Wyclif argued that evangelical possession overrode other kinds of possession, both civil and natural; unlike the petitioners in *The House of Fame,* he believed that evangelical possession is the only guarantor of a truly good name, over and above worldly *fama.*[42]

The Spiritual Franciscans and Wycliffites were, of course, at the sharp end of debates around *praecepta* and *consilia,* because of their ambitions to the apostolic life. Antimendicant satire repeatedly pointed to the gap between the vows of the fraternal orders and the conduct of their members, and attacks on the Wycliffite movement complained that a similar hypocrisy undid both the Wycliffite claim to Christlike asceticism and the movement's antifraternal agenda.[43] *The Wife of Bath's Prologue* and *Tale* are implicated in the antifraternalism in the *Canterbury Tales,* and are thus bound up with the question of evangelical vocation in this specific, ecclesiastical application. Her *Tale* begins with a piece of antifraternal satire in a direct attack on the friar, Huberd, in the pilgrim company. Furthermore, Huberd tries to tell his own tale in Alisoun's place, establishing them as rivals, of course, but also as possible substitutes for one another. Indeed Alisoun sounds friarlike in her mock-begging of permission to speak—"If I have licence of this worthy Frere" (III.855)—just as the friars themselves had to apply for preaching licences. When Huberd finally wrests the right to speak from her, he contends that her contribution is inappropriately exegetical (III.1271–77). Unlike other heroines in loathly lady stories, the old lady in *The Wife of Bath's Tale* is not poor because of a hostile spell; rather, as recommended both by Wyclif and the mendicant orders, she chooses to be

[40] Hudson, *Works of a Lollard Preacher,* 266 n. 692–95, and for discussion of the implications of the Franciscan poverty debate for Langland and his age, see Clopper, *Songes of Rechelesnesse,* 27, 63–67.

[41] John Wycliffe, *Tractatus de civili dominio,* ed. Reginald Lane Poole et al., 4 vols. (London: Trübner & Co., 1885), 1: Book I, esp. Chapter I, pages 1–8.

[42] Ibid., I.viii, 53–60.

[43] Anne Hudson, *The Premature Reformation* (Oxford: Clarendon Press, 1988), 345.

poor in apostolic imitation of Christ (III.1179).[44] Yet the ethical implications of such contests did not remain neatly bounded within debates about Church property and poverty, and *The Wife of Bath's Prologue* and *Tale* are not only occluded commentaries on the ethics therein. Indeed, Wyclif is clear in *Civil dominium* that while his main target was the proper governance of the Church, his ideas were also relevant to secular forms of governance and, indeed, "omnes Christiani."[45]

However, if Wyclif reanimated an older, Franciscan discussion, he nonetheless still resisted, or failed to produce, a definitive account of what proper use was. Use was particularly pertinent to the fraternal vow of poverty, a vow that was different from the vows of chastity and obedience because it governed necessities such as food and clothing, things that had to be used. But exactly how *much* they were to be used was difficult to quantify. Because of this difference, the discussion of poverty set a pattern for considering the problem of attaining perfection in secular life. As Alisoun's *Prologue* in particular shows, the notion of *usus* in a secular life was even more contested because there it also came to govern the ethics of sexuality and marriage, those things from which the regular clergy were expressly disqualified.[46] Without the clarity of an outright ban, ethical rules proliferated, but, in their very multiplicity, they failed to prelimit right living. Chaucer's Wife argues, like Olivi's opponents in the poverty debate, that while a virtuous life is self-evidently good, it cannot practicably be upgraded from aspiration to precept: "conseillyng is no comandement" (III.67), she says, repeating the words "counseil" and "comandement" to press home her point (III.73, 82). However, Alisoun goes further, co-opting Paul's account of the suspension and persistence of juridical conditions within the messianic ecclesia, in defense not just of an ordinary lay life but of one lived in admitted laxity.[47]

[44] For the analogues to *The Wife of Bath's Tale*, see John Withrington and P. J. C. Field, "The Wife of Bath's Tale," in *Sources and Analogues of "The Canterbury Tales" II*, ed. Robert M. Correale and Mary Hamel (Cambridge: D. S. Brewer, 2005), 405–48.

[45] Wycliffe, *Tractatus de civili dominio*, 1:I.xi, 75; and on secular governance see, for example: 1:I.xxvi, 185–92; 1:I.xi, 75.

[46] Olivi had taken a similarly rigorist line on marriage, denying that it was a sacrament (although he was later forced to recant) and in any way morally equivalent to a chaste or virginal life. Burr, "The Persecution of Peter Olivi," 12.

[47] Others have discussed the accuracy or partiality of Alisoun's exegesis. Most famously, D. W. Robertson, *A Preface to Chaucer: Studies in Medieval Perspectives* (Princeton: Princeton University Press, 1963), wrote Alisoun off as a misreader of scripture and an unreconstructed representative of the Old Law (321). I argue here that Alisoun has an impressive grasp of the suspended conditions under the New Law. However, I also

Alisoun is not alone. Will, the narrator of *Piers Plowman,* also uses Paul's instruction to the Corinthians in defense of a questionable *habitus.* You "sholde" live, he says: "In eadem vocacione qua vocati estis" [in the calling to which you are called] (V.43a).[48] Armed with this injunction, Will justifies his noncompliance with the demands made by his own Reason and Conscience, demands that are fashioned in the terms of the labor legislation of the second half of the fourteenth century.[49] Instead of helping to bring in the harvest, Will says that he perseveres (to borrow a word from Alisoun of Bath) in the callings in which he was socialized and to which he is now habituated:

> And so Y leue in London and opelond bothe;
> The lomes that Y labore with and lyflode deserue
> Is *pater-noster* and my prymer, *placebo* and *dirige,*
> And my sauter som tyme and my seuene psalmes.
> This Y synge for here soules of suche as me helpeth,
> And tho that fynden me my fode fouchen-saf, Y trowe,
> To be welcome when Y come, other-while in a monthe,
> Now with hym, now with here; on this wyse Y begge
> Withoute bagge or botel but my wombe one.
>
> (V.44–52)

As a defense, this statement is curiously forceless. While these working patterns might be defended as apostolic, instead they are described as

---

cannot agree with Theresa Tinkle, "The Wife of Bath's Marginal Authority," *SAC* 32 (2010): 67–101, when she argues that the insertion of scriptural references into the margins of *Prologue* manuscripts confirms that medieval readers regarded the wife as an unproblematically authoritative exegete (72–73). Identifying the Wife's source text does not indicate that her interpretation of that text was necessarily correct. See also the debate about the status of the most indefensible parts of the *Prologue* between Kennedy, "Contradictory Responses," 30–32, and A. J. Minnis, "The Wisdom of Old Women: Alisoun of Bath as *Auctrice,*" in *Writings on Love in the English Middle Ages,* ed. Helen Cooney (New York: Palgrave Macmillan, 2006), 99–114 (e.g., 106). My view is similar to that of Peck, "Biblical Interpretation," who argues that the Wife of Bath develops a strange rapport with Saint Paul, even in the service of a defense that does not quite look right (158).

[48] Others have considered the relationship between Langland's poem and Franciscan literature and debate. See, for example, Katherine Kerby-Fulton, *Reformist Apocalypticism and Piers Plowman* (Cambridge: Cambridge University Press, 1990), esp. 12, 146. For a consideration of the importance of 1 Corinthians 7:20 to Franciscan poverty controversies, see Clopper, *Songes of Rechelesnesse,* 60–61.

[49] For a discussion of this section and contemporary labor legislation, see, for example, Anne Middleton, "Acts of Vagrancy: The C Version 'Autobiography' and the Statute of 1388," in *Written Work: Langland, Labor, and Authorship,* ed. Steven Justice and

diffuse and dubious: "som tyme," "other-while," "[n]ow with hym, now with here." The word "lomes," and the idea of books as tools, offers clerical work as a parody of manual labor, augmenting by comic contrast the insufficiency of Will's work at a time of labor crisis. Like the Wife of Bath ("I wol use myn instrument"), Will also turns body parts to use, substituting his stomach for a begging bag or bottle. The stomach is contrasted with those other vessels because it guarantees that Will lives on bare necessities, in *usus pauperis,* rather than storing superfluity.[50] Despite the rigorism of his diet and the restraint on his mendicancy, Will cannot defend his lifestyle and regimen with any conviction. In particular, he is demonstrably at odds with his own Conscience, who rebuffs him thus: "Ac it semeth no sad parfitnesse in citees to begge" (V.90); Will, offering no contradiction, instantly concedes: "That is soth," (V.92). Alisoun is also all too willing to admit (but in no hurry to address) the problem of her own (im)*parfitnesse,* and she uses the word *parfit* and its forms many times to describe what she is not. The apostle, she concedes, "spak to hem that wolde lyve *parfitly;* / And lordynges, by youre leve, that am nat I" (III.111–12). Will and Alisoun both indicate a commitment to persevere in shifting states: Will's calling is gyrovague and made of conflicting parts, and Alisoun looks to change and even downgrade her calling as a widow by marrying for the sixth time. In their appeal to Saint Paul, Will and Alisoun publicize the theoretical (im)*parfitnesse* of social subject positions that were widely practiced and tacitly licensed (and might be better defended on that basis). Both narrators describe themselves as committed to im*proper* callings that, accordingly, they do not own.[51]

The English words "perfect" and "im-" or "unperfect" are late medieval coinages. "Perfect" is first recorded in a late thirteenth-century *vita* of Saint Francis in the *South English Legendary,* where it translates Francis's reading of Matthew 19:21.[52] The first extant example of "inperfite" is in the work of Richard Rolle (c. 1340), where it distinguishes the souls who "erre noghte disposed to contemplacyoun of Godd" from the

---

Kathryn Kerby-Fulton (Philadelphia: University of Pennsylvania Press, 1997), 208–317.

[50] On bag-begging, see Wendy Scase, *"Piers Plowman" and the New Anti-Clericalism* (Cambridge: Cambridge University Press, 1989), 137; and Kerby-Fulton, *Reformist Apocalypticism,* 144–45.

[51] Middleton, "Langland's 'Kynde Name,'" has argued that this passage signals Langland's dreamer's *improperness,* displaced from his "kynde" place (58).

[52] See the definitions in the *OED* and *MED.*

"perfite" lives of those who live apostolically.[53] Imperfect souls can expect a "lawere mede" but are nonetheless eligible for salvation: "Þus callis oure Lorde chosen saules," writes Rolle, acknowledging the diversity of those called to the ecclesia. Here the idea of calling is not reserved only for the regular clergy; rather, it is used to imagine positive soteriological fortunes for those whose "imperfect" lives were not explicitly dedicated to apostolic imitation. The possibility of perfection dominated rigorist appeals for the evangelical life, like those of John Wyclif, for example, who argued for it as the only qualification for legitimate *dominium*. Gordon Leff has suggested that Wyclif's theory had a limited impact; it was, he says, "singularly devoid of immediacy" and "reduced to nullity . . . by the impossibility of knowing who was damned and who was saved."[54] Anne Hudson has disagreed, arguing that "even if only God could know the state of grace, man could make a pretty shrewd guess in cases of outrageous behaviour."[55] It is this problem into which the poetry I am investigating here inserts itself, presenting hard cases on which anyone might make a "shrewd guess" but on which God would finally decide. While Nicholas Watson has argued that, in its depiction of some of these hard cases, the *Canterbury Tales* makes an anomalous defense of imperfection or, in his word, "mediocrity," R. James Goldstein has countered that Chaucer never closes the possibility of his pilgrims' renovation *hors texte*. He writes that if Alisoun "were a real person, only God could know with any certitude, Chaucer would doubtless agree, how that story would end."[56] I suggest something in between: that in their admissions of imperfection the narrators in these texts both posit the possibility of their moral renewal—beginning their confession and suggesting their contrition—and, paradoxically, perpetually postpone it. After all, in its earliest sense "imperfect" suggests not a final, defective condition but, rather, a state of incompletion: an "as

[53] Richard Rolle, *The English Prose Treatises of Richard Rolle de Hampole,* ed. George G. Perry, EETS 20 (1866, revised 1921), 46.

[54] Gordon Leff, *Heresy in the Later Middle Ages: The Relation of Orthodoxy to Dissent, c. 1250–c. 1450* (Manchester: Manchester University Press, 1967), 549.

[55] Hudson, *Premature Reformation,* 360.

[56] Watson, "Chaucer's Public Christianity," 104. However, Watson argues that Chaucer presents himself as a "mediocrist", I am not as sure that Chaucer writes *in propria persona*. Conversely, I am also unconvinced by Watson's suggestion that *Piers Plowman* is so doggedly trained on the ideal of perfection that the "mediocrist" habitus is only parodied in that poem. Goldstein, "Future Perfect," 121, 127, counters Watson with a different account of Chaucer's *own* position; again, I do not find that authorial position to be clear in the text.

yet not."[57] "Perfect" and "imperfect" are not, in their first uses, opposites. Alisoun and Will describe themselves in the process of perpetual formation, a process whose end is infinitely deferred. Indeed, they embody the nullity that Leff finds in Wyclif's account of *dominium*.

Failing a perfect imitation of Christ, there were various gradations of good living, established in the Pauline categories of doing well and doing better, which, although permissible, were inferior to the unstated doing best:

> For he that ordeynede stabli in his herte, not hauynge nede, but hauynge power of his wille, and hath demed in his herte this thing, to kepe his virgyn, *doith wel*. Therfore he that ioyneth his virgyn in matrymonye, *doith wel;* and he that ioyneth not, *doith betere*.

> (1 Cor. 7:37–38; my emphasis)

While Alisoun's use of the verb "to be" for the virginal life ("Virginitee *is* greet perfeccion" [105]) implicitly accuses champions of celibacy (like Saint Jerome) of overstating temporal *claims,* she nonetheless concedes that the conduct of the sexually continent is axiomatically better than that of the married.[58] Alisoun is clear that Paul "heeld virginitee / Moore parfit than weddyng in freletee" (91–92). The enjambment in this line throws a special emphasis onto the word "[m]oore," drawing attention to Alisoun's use of Pauline comparatives to calibrate conduct. In this way, she correctly realizes the ethical hierarchies that Saint Paul lays out in relation to sexual status, quoted in the passage above. Indeed, Alisoun mobilizes another comparative adjective from the biblical text partially to defend her compromised choices: "Bet is to be wedded than to brynne" (52; 1 Cor. 7:9). The categories of doing well and better (in the Vulgate translation, *bene* and *melius fecit*) are shored up into distinct ethical categories in the church fathers' writings on marriage and, most pertinently, in relation to the Wife's repertoire of *auctoritas,* Jerome's *Adversus Jovinianum.*[59] Because the notion of *bene fecit* was explicitly

---

[57] According to the *OED,* the English word "perfect" comes from Latin *perfectus*, an adjective derived from the past participle of *perficere* (to accomplish, perform, complete). This is how the words "perfect" and "imperfect," are still understood, for example, in their technical grammatical senses as tenses of completed or continuing action in the past.

[58] Like Chaucer's Wife of Bath, Agamben also regards Jerome as a "shoddy and dubious exegete of Paul." *The Time That Remains,* 85.

[59] See, for example, *Adversus Jovinianum, Patrologiae cursus completus. . .* vol. 23, I, XIII, col. 0232B.

linked to marriage in the Pauline text, it was actively deployed in late medieval marriage-making. Richard Helmholz has identified a number of contested marriage cases brought before the medieval consistory courts in the late fourteenth and early fifteenth centuries that depended on conditions of good conduct. Those conditions deployed the same words that Jerome used both in his translation of and his commentary on Paul's epistle: "si bene facias."[60] Wan-Chuan Kao has connected these conditions to the strange contract that is made between Dorigen and Arveragus in *The Franklin's Tale,* a tale that, in Kao's reading, then turns on the troubling, because unanswerable, question of what good conduct in fact is.[61] Given the uncertain status of such conditions, Helmholz notes, "[W]e should not be surprised that contracts like this . . . ended up as the subject of marriage litigation."[62] Notwithstanding the fictiveness of and flexibility within ideologies of blood, they seemed to offer clearer accounts of social difference than those predicated upon conduct.

In the quotation from Paul's epistle above, the separation of the faculty of "wille" or *voluntas* (in the Vulgate) from the person, the "he" that maintains his virginity, already suggests the psychological allegories of William Langland's *Piers Plowman.* Indeed, it is Langland's poem that most famously poses the question of what Dowel and Dobet actually are. The same issue is also rightly still unsettled in modern Langland studies. The kaleidoscopic answers that the poem's personae and critics deliver draw attention to the absence of clear definitions that made Olivi's *Usus pauper* controversial and brought the *si bene facias* marriage cases to court.[63] Furthermore, whatever else Dowel is in *Piers Plowman,* it is usually connected to marriage, but, contrary to *The Wife of Bath's Prologue,* that is not the exclusive focus. Other contemporary citations of this passage also understand it more broadly. " 'Certes, lady bryght, / We han *don wel* with al our myght' " (1693–94), *claims* one group of

---

[60] R. H. Helmholz, *Marriage Litigation in Medieval England* (Cambridge: Cambridge University Press, 1974), 54–57, brought to my attention by Wan-Chuan Kao, "Conduct Shameful and Unshameful in the *Franklin's Tale,*" *SAC* 34 (2012): 99–139.

[61] Ibid., 100–101.

[62] Helmholz, *Marriage Litigation in Medieval England,* 57.

[63] See, for example, S. S. Hussey, "Langland, Hilton, and the Three Lives," *RES* 7 (1956): 132–50; P. M. Kean, "Justice, Kingship, and the Good Life in the Second Part of *Piers Plowman,*" in *"Piers Plowman": Critical Approaches,* ed. S. S. Hussey (London: Methuen, 1969), 76–110.

petitioners to Fame, in *The House of Fame*, speaking of their conduct more broadly. The endorsement by capricious Fame of disrupted status hierarchies means that doing well does not logically correspond to a calling; some are given a "worse" and others a "better" name than they really deserve (1620, 1667). John Gower's *Vox clamantis* also explores what it means to do well or better as it draws to this Pauline close:

> Corrigit hic *mundum,* qui cor retinet sibi *mundum:*
> Cor magis vnde *regat,* hec sibi scripta *legat.*
> Quod scripsi *plebis* vox est, set et ista *videbis,*
> Quo clamat *populus,* est ibi sepe *deus.*
> Qui bonus est *audit* bona, set peruersus *obaudit,*
> Ad bona set *pronus* audiat ista *bonus.*
> Hec ita scripta *sciat* malus, vt bonus ammodo *fiat,*
> Et bonus hec *querat,* vt meliora *gerat.*
> (VII.25.1467–74; my emphases indicate rhyme words)

[The man who keeps his heart pure sets the world right. Therefore, let him rule his heart, let him read these writings for himself. What I have set down is the voice of the people, but you will also see that where the people call out, God is often there. The man who is good listens to what is good, but the perverse man disregards it. Yet the man prone to what is good should listen to this. Likewise, the bad man should know these writings so that he may presently become good, and the good man should seek them out so that he may do better.]

(287–88)

While it has been thought that this passage alludes to *Piers Plowman,* and while indeed it might, it much more evidently shares with Langland's poem an intertext: Paul's first letter to the Corinthians 7:37–38.[64] The coronary imagery that opens this passage connects it directly to the biblical text, quite without the commitment to Paul's comparatives, in the discussion of what the good should do to do better, which closes it. The recommendation to "doþ wele and ay bettur and bettur" in the so-called John Ball letters might also be connected to Langland's poem less

---

[64] See Stockton, ed., *The Major Latin Works,* 470 n. 5, who suggests Gower might have Langland's vision of Dowel in mind.

directly than is always suggested.[65] In those letters, Dowel cryptically refers to conduct both within a lived calling—as, say, a carter, miller, or ploughman—and within the rebellion itself. For Gower, the Pauline passage is about self-governance (using the verb *gerere* rather than *facere* to supply an extra stress upon right conduct), which he fits into the notion, dominating all his work, of the human as a microcosmic extraction of the whole; self-governance will right the whole world. The internal rhymes and near rhymes in these lines, which are not a feature of the rest of Gower's poem, pick up Paul's semantic parallelism that Jerome preserved in his translation of the epistle, and not least in the phrasal homophony between *bene fecit* and *melius fecit*.[66] The many repetitions of *bonus* insist, with some anxiety, that readers undertake the relentless task of managing their conduct in the badlands beyond clearly mapped precept.

Answering: Kneeling and *Kenosis*

Kitte and Calote are never actually shown creeping to the cross on their knees in Langland's *Piers Plowman,* and Will's instruction to them to do so (which I cited earlier) remains in the uncertain realm of projected ambition. Furthermore, although the narrator is swift to issue instructions to his family, he has no explicit expectations of himself. Indeed, in the next passus, the dreamer notably struggles to achieve the recognition that the call should initiate. In particular, Will is not said to kneel, despite his citing Philippians 2, which instructs that he should:

> Y ful eftesones aslepe and sodeynliche me mette
> That Peres the plouhman was peynted al blody
> And cam in with a cros bifore the comune peple
> And riht lyke in alle lymes to oure lord Iesu.
> And thenne calde Y Conscience to kenne me the sothe:
> "Is this Iesus the ioustare," quod Y, "that Iewes dede to dethe?
> Or hit is Peres the plouhman? who paynted hym so rede?"

---

[65] Dowel in the John Ball letters is discussed in relation to *Piers Plowman,* in Steven Justice, *Writing and Rebellion,* 13, 128–30. See Lawrence Warner, *The Lost History of "Piers Plowman": The Earliest Transmission of Langland's Work* (Philadelphia: University of Pennsylvania Press, 2011), 16, for a doubt about the relationship between the John Ball Letters and Langland's poem.

[66] For a discussion of Paul's use of homophony in this part of the epistle, and Jerome's sensitivity to it, see Agamben, *The Time That Remains,* 85–86.

Quod Consciense and knelede tho, "This aren Peres armes,
His colours and his cote armure; ac he that cometh so blody
Is Crist with his croes, conquerour of cristene."
    "Whi calle ye hym Crist, sennes Iewes callede hym Iesus?
Patriarkes and prophetes profecied bifore
That alle kyn creatures sholde knelen and bowen
Anoon as men nemned the name of god Iesus. . . ."
                                                    (XXI.5–18)

The question of kneeling has been considered in *Piers Plowman* before
and most notably by James F. G. Weldon.[67] Weldon has argued that
the part of the poem from the entry of Longinus in the previous passus,
to the quotation from Philippians 2:10—"Omnia celestia terrestria
flectantur in hoc nomine Iesu" [All things in heaven and earth bow
down at the name of Jesus] (XXI.80a)—constitutes a discrete piece
within the poem, a piece that is dominated by "a pattern of kneeling."
For Weldon, the repeated gesture "signals an act of recognition of
Christ's lordship—the proper response towards his nobility."[68] Recognition, which kneeling would signify, is the proper response to true calling: it acknowledges the direct address and confirms the power of names
to individuate and designate. Yet the dreamer fails to reproduce Longinus's act of recognition, even at the instigation of Conscience, and thus
to complete the process of his interpellation. Although Will kneels elsewhere in the poem (V.106), in this section he might more properly be
described as producing a pattern of *not* kneeling. True to their allegorical
characters, Conscience kneels, but the poem is silent on whether Will
follows suit. The passus continues thus: Conscience kneels and he reiter-
atively describes the kneeling of others at Jesus' birth and resurrection—
angels and magi—and he repeatedly counsels Will to do the same
(XXI.74, 75, 81, 91, 95, 151, 200, 207, 209).
    In contrast, in Gower's *Vox clamantis,* the voice of Wisdom (again
with allegorical fitness) alerts the narrator to the call to redemption and
does achieve his contrition, which is signaled by his kneeling. This call
forces two related recognitions on the part of the narrator: first, that the

[67] James F. G. Weldon, "Gesture of Perception: The Pattern of Kneeling in *Piers
Plowman* B.18–19," *YLS* 3 (1989): 49–66. See also J. A. Burrow, *Gestures and Looks in
Medieval Narrative* (Cambridge: Cambridge University Press, 2002), 22, and Mary Cle-
mente Davlin, "Devotional Postures in *Piers Plowman* B, with an Appendix on Divine
Postures," *ChauR* 42 (2007): 161–79 (163).
[68] Weldon, "Gesture of Perception," 55.

revolt and the storm are divine instruments and, second, that the target of God's displeasure is the narrator himself, who, despite having fled the terrors of revolt, has internalized and carries it within: he *is* the revolt:

> Talia fingebam misero michi fata parari,
> Demeritoque meo rebar adesse malum.
> Sic mecum meditans, tacito sub murmure dixi,
> "Hec modo que pacior propria culpa tulit."
> Non latuit quicquam culparum cordis in antro,
> Quin magis ad mentem singula facta refert:
> Cor michi commemorat scelerum commissa meorum,
> Vt magis exacuat cordis ymago preces.

(I.18.1781–87)

[Wretchedly I pictured the fate contrived for myself, and I judged that misfortune was at hand because of my own unworthiness. Meditating to myself in this way, I said in a low murmur, "My own guilt has brought the things I am now suffering." None of my faults lay hidden in the recesses of my heart, but instead my deeds brought everything to mind. My heart remembered the crimes I had committed, so that the picture in my heart stimulated my prayers.]

(88)

In recognition of his own sinfulness, Gower's narrator evacuates the cavities of his heart. This thorough cardiac examination enables him to hear, on or over the wind, the divine voice to which Wisdom has already alerted him. Once the storm has subsided, after the death of Wat the Jackdaw, the narrator kneels in thanks:

> Tunc ego, deflexis genibus set ad ethera palmis
> Tensis, sic dixi: "Gloria, Criste, tibi!"

(I.19.1931–32)

[Then on bended knee and with hands stretched toward the heavens, I said, "Glory be unto Thee, O Christ!"]

(91)

The narrator's contrition and prayers, which culminate in this act of kneeling, are the turning point around which the whole poem pivots. At this point, the poem reframes its invective as self-scrutiny. His own crying to God and God's answering call produce an antiphonal that emerges from, rather than being antithetical to, the tumult of other calls, which together constitute the revolt. Of course the dream-vision form, in itself and just as it is in *Piers Plowman,* is concerned to obfuscate the boundary between inner and outer, between what is sent from God or from demonic external sources, and what comes from within, the product of moral or humoral corruption.[69] Indeed, it was this aspect of dreams that Chaucer was to satirize, in a direct response to Gower's *Vox clamantis,* in *The Nun's Priest's Tale:* "Swevenes engendren of replecciouns, / And ofte of fume and of complecciouns, / Whan humours been to habundant in a wight" (VII.2923–25).[70]

Like Gower's *Vox clamantis,* Chaucer's *House of Fame* offers another inverted counterpoint to the incomplete structures of interpellation of *Piers Plowman.* Chaucer's poem, too, presents a "pattern of kneeling." It is also interested in the noise of calling and, although the trumpets that blast there are categorically not messianic and make a much more worldly sound, the patterns of kneeling and calling in Chaucer's poem imitate the structures of divine calling; however arbitrary, the estimations of the world will prevail until the End of Days. There are many people in *The House of Fame,* even virtuous people, who are prepared to fall to their knees (1534, 1659, 1705, 1772) and recognize the authority of Fame. The trumpets are those of Eolus, god of wind, signaling the vacuity of temporal ac*claim.* Althusser, considering the dictum of Blaise Pascal, "Kneel down, move your lips in prayer, and you will believe," denies that this is an "inversion or overturning" but argues instead that ideology exists in "material practices governed by a material ritual, which practices exist in the material actions of a subject acting in all consciousness according to his belief."[71] It is not true to say, then, that the petitioners in *The House of Fame* kneel misguidedly: because they kneel, Fame prevails. Not only that, but their faith installs a temporal

---

[69] Although on other sources of blame in the *Vox clamantis,* see Sylvia Federico, *New Troy: Fantasies of Empire in the Late Middle Ages,* Medieval Cultures 36 (Minneapolis: University of Minnesota Press, 2003), 10–11.

[70] See Justice, *Writing and Rebellion,* 214–18, and Helen Barr, *Socioliterary Practice in Late Medieval England* (Oxford: Oxford University Press, 2001), 106–11, for a full discussion of the relationship between Gower's *Vox clamantis* and Chaucer's *Nun's Priest's Tale.*

[71] Althusser, "Ideology," 158–59. This temporal reordering of "Truth-Event" and faith has been most thoroughly thought through by Badiou, *Saint Paul,* 14–15; see also Mitchell, *Ethics and Eventfulness,* 13–14.

regime that sometimes does and sometimes does not coincide with true calling or designation.[72]

In *Piers Plowman,* Will has a different problem: he can neither kneel to nor name the true aspect of his vision. It is Will who cites the Philippians passage (XXI.17–18), but he needs Conscience to call the figure in his vision "Jesus" to enable the recognition that would oblige him to follow its injunction to kneel. Kneeling and acknowledgment of name, of what someone is *called,* are thus intricately bound together. Indeed, in an early fourteenth-century poem by William Shoreham, knowing and kneeling are made commensurate homonyms—"knowe"—in an instruction on how concertedly to acknowledge and honor God.[73] Will is unable to "knowe" because he gets tangled up in the onomastic questions raised in Paul's epistle. Although the scriptural text asserts, as Will does, that kneeling is required at the naming of Jesus, it also indicates that Christ is entitled to other, more prestigious names, but fails to be thoroughly clear about what those names might be.

This lack of clarity in the source text necessitates Will's questioning and Conscience's extrapolation:

> *Ergo* is no name to the name of Iesus
> Ne noen so nedfol to nemnie by nyhte ne by day,
> For alle derke deueles aren drad for to heren hit
> And synfole ben solaced and saued by that name.
> And ye callen hym Crist—for what cause, telleth me.
> Is Crist more of myhte and more worthiore name
> Then Iesu or Iesus, that all oure ioye cam of?"
>   "Thow knowest wel," quod Concience, "and thou kunne resoun,
> That knyht, kyng, conquerour may be o persone.
> To be cald a knyht is fayr, for men shal knele to hym;
> To be cald a kyng is fairor, for he may knyhtes make;
> Ac to be conqueror cald, that cometh of special grace. . . ."
>
>   (XXI.19–30)

The name of Jesus, Will argues, negates other names. The first two lines here hollow those names out with a copious alliteration on "n," which emphasizes the multiple negatives, and the absenting idea of needful-

---

[72] See also Wycliffe, *Tractatus de civili dominio,* 1:I.viii, 53–60.
[73] William Shoreham, *The Poems of William Shoreham,* ed. M. Konrath, EETS 86 (1902), 91.

ness, making them, as in 1 Corinthians 7:29–31, in the form of the *as not*. The messianic name confuses Will: How does it relate to the name Jesus? Conscience responds somewhat inscrutably by filling in the titles that Paul does not supply in Philippians, creating an ascending scale of names with the adjective, "fayr," and its comparative, "fairor" (which also suggests, but does not explicitly state, the superlative, "fairest," for the final name "conqueror"). The use of the comparative still holds out the possibility of another, more perfect name that is left unspoken because true names are above every name. We learn, later in the passus, that these titles—knight, king, and conqueror—are indeed to be applied to Jesus in different phases of his life and ministry, where they are also attached to the names Dowel, Dobet, and, similarly by unspoken implication, Dobest (XXI.48–49, 53, 96–100, 123, 128–29). This hierarchy of names is accompanied by a kenotic "pattern of kneeling": a gestural drama of lowering and rising, of emptying and filling. Throughout Passus XXI, Conscience creates a complex series of ranked designations that are derived from or, he says, especially associated with the meanings of the word Christ, which, he explains, supplement rather than supplant the proper noun Jesus.

"Knight," "king," and "conqueror" are, unlike "Jesus," not proper names but descriptions, titles that come from social ranks or roles, and this may be why the passage above switches from its repetitive use of the word "name" and its cognates, in Will's questions, to a similarly reiterative stress on "callen," in Conscience's evasive answers. Conscience is not yet firmly assigning the callings of knight, king, and conqueror to Christ. He uses the passive construction: "to be cald . . . is." He might also, then, be discussing the priorities of the world. Indeed, he goes on after this passage not to clear up Will's uncertainty about the nature of divinity in his vision but, instead, to discuss social designations and status in the temporal world that have, he says, been upended in the New Law. In this turn toward the human world, Conscience moves his frame of reference, engaging not just with Paul's letter to the Philippians but also with his first letter to the Corinthians. The Philippians passage notes the paradox of Jesus' advancement to his superlative name through his voiding or abasement of self, his *kenosis,* both in the incarnation but also in his ultimate act of nonbeing (submission to death on the cross). In contrast, in the epistle to the Corinthians, Paul describes the similar revolutions (the high being made low and vice versa) that were brought about in the human world with the institution of the new law:

> He that is a seruaunt, and is clepid in the Lord, is a freman of the Lord. Also he that is a freman, and is clepid, is the seruaunt of Crist.
>
> (1 Cor. 7:22)

Langland conveys it thus:

> Ac to be conquerour cald, that cometh of special grace
> And of hardiness of herte and of hendenesse,
> To make lordes of laddes of lond that he wynneth
> And fre men foule thralles that folleweth nat his lawes.
> The Iewes that were gentel men Iesu thei dispisede,
> Bothe his lore and his lawe—now are they lowe cherles . . .
>
> (XXI.30–35)

The shift to ethno-religious categories (that is, Jewishness and non-Jewishness) from categories of social status ("lordes"/"laddes"; "fre men"/"thralles") is motivated by their close association in 1 Corinthians 7:18–22. However, the dichotomy of free and bonded status is much more completely intertwined with that of Jewishness/non-Jewishness in *Piers Plowman* than it is in the letter to the Corinthians. The Jews, in Langland's anti-Semitism, have lost their status, becoming "cherles" where once they were "gentel men." That fusion is managed through a playful use of the word "gentel," which literally here means gentle, in the sense of well born, but also offers a pun on gentile. Langland's "joke" is that the Jews of the past, being once "gentel men," were more like gentiles, that is, the opposite of modern Jews.[74]

These depreciations are the exact inverse of the *kenosis,* the voluntary self-renunciation of Christ, described in the Philippians passage, which effects his paradoxical promotion. In *The Wife of Bath's Tale,* the old lady explicitly compares herself to Christ in his voluntary poverty (1177–79). Like Christ, but unlike women in similar loathly lady stories, Alisoun's

---

[74] According to the *OED,* the word "gentile," to mean non-Jew, was emerging at this moment, in part through the translation of the Latin *gentilis* in the Vulgate bible. "Gentle" and "gentile" are cognates, sharing the same etymological root in Latin *gens* (family, race); indeed, the *MED* records them as the same word.

heroine has a choice, and by first socially lowering herself she is then inversely elevated. The phrase Jerome supplies in the Vulgate translation of Philippians is *ipsum exanivit*. The verb *exanivire* is commonly associated with hydraulics; what the Wycliffite Bible offers as "lowide hym silf" is more literal in the Vulgate: he poured himself out. For Paul, the bowed knee is the gestural articulation of this imitative self-demotion and is necessary to "fele ʒe this thing in ʒou, which also in Crist Jhesu" (Phil. 2:5). *Vox clamantis* also describes its narrator's Christlike evacuation. The kneeling narrator desires to void himself: "vacare volo" (literally, "I wish to be empty" [I.21.2148]).[75] The dreamer's act of kneeling in *Vox clamantis* operates as a synecdoche for the work: vacated and afterward in-filled with the voices of others.

In *Vox clamantis*, this process of vacation and occupation dominates both the compositional form and its narrative arc. One of the most common literary-critical comments on Gower's poem is that it compulsively recycles prior text.[76] Gower himself acknowledges that the *Vox* is made up of the writing of others:

> Doctorum veterum mea carmina fortificando
> Pluribus exemplis scripta fuisse reor.
> Vox clamantis erit nomenque voluminis huius,
> Quod sibi scripta noui verba doloris habet.
>
> (II.Prologue.81–84)

[I acknowledge that my verses have been written with many models and strengthened by learned men of old. And the name of this volume shall be *The Voice of One Crying*, because the work contains a message of the sorrow of today.]
(98)

Stockton's translation here does not draw out the contrast, which is clear in Gower's Latin, between old and new; a more literal rendering might indicate the reformation of old models into "words of new grief." The words, most notably of Ovid but also others, supply Gower's poem with

---

[75] Maura Nolan offers a different, but not incompatible, reading of Gower's "vacare" as leisured. See her "The Poetics of Catastrophe: Ovidian Allusion in Gower's *Vox Clamantis*," in *Medieval Latin and Middle English Literature: Essays in Honour of Jill Mann*, ed. Christopher Cannon and Maura Nolan (Cambridge: D. S. Brewer, 2011), 113–33 (131).

[76] Robert Yeager, "Did Gower Write *Cento*?" in *John Gower: Recent Readings. Papers Presented at the Meetings of the John Gower Society at the International Congress on Medieval Studies, Western Michigan University, 1983–1988*, ed. R. F. Yeager, Studies in Medieval Culture 26 (Kalamazoo: Medieval Institute Publications, 1989), 113–32 (119).

yet more, and more varied, voices.[77] Prior text animates the poem's contemporary grief-ful subjectivity. What is more, these prescribed words make up not only the calls, which the narrator describes hearing, but also the narrator's own vocation. Andrew Galloway, in his study of the poem's citatory practice, has noted the appositeness of the narrator's calling being announced by Wisdom, describing this "visitation" as "a miniature allegory of his learned vocation," which "identifies his learning as the heart of his poetic vocation."[78] Galloway's repetition of the word "vocation" picks up Wisdom's own use of the verb *vocare:* "Quo deus offensus te reparando vocat" (I.16.1548) [Because God is displeased, he is calling you to redemption (83)]. Similarly appropriate is the cryptic form in which the narrator's name is interleaved in his verse:

> Scribentis nomen si queras, ecce loquela
> Sub tribus implicita versibus inde latet.
> (I.Prologue.19–20)

[If you should ask the name of the writer, look, the word lies hidden and entangled in three verses about it.]

(50)

Gower's name is made intrinsic to his verse just as William Langland's name is also an embedded literary signature in *Piers Plowman,* their callings thus literally made out of poetry.[79]

Although critics dislike Gower's ventriloquizing of the rebels' protests as inarticulate braying, barking, and howling, Gower imagines that *he* is the dummy, made to articulate thrown voices. The narrator comes to be identified with the rebellion, which the poem so lividly attacks, through a kenotic occupation of his voice. In his exile, following his flight from the rebellion, the narrator experiences aphasic symptoms; it is as if the voices surrounding and pursuing him have replaced or repressed his own. The narrator's words are constantly hedged around with pianissimo marks, as in the passage I cited earlier "tacito sub murmure dixi" (I.18.1783) [I said in a low murmur (88)], or he loses

---

[77] For discussions of Gower's sources, see Federico, *New Troy,* 10–11; Nolan, "Poetics of Catastrophe," passim.

[78] Andrew Galloway, "Gower in His Most Learned Role and the Peasants' Revolt of 1381," *Mediaevalia* 16 (1993, for 1990): 329–47. Others also refer to Gower's "vocation" and "calling" as a poet: Justice, *Writing and Rebellion,* 209; Federico, *New Troy,* 17.

[79] Middleton, "Langland's 'Kynde Name,'" 37–52, 79–82.

his voice completely, becoming tongue-tied (I.16.1505–14). Sometimes he can speak only in semaphore:

> Brachia porrexi tendens ad lumina solis,
> Et, quod lingua nequit promere, signa ferunt . . .
> (I.16.1471–72)

[Pointing toward the sun's light, I stretched out my arms, and I made signs with them, because of the fact that my tongue could not utter a sound.]

(81)

Because the *Vox* is such a noisy poem, its moments of silence are stark. The narrator's silence is reminiscent of the hush that descends on the crowd addressed by Wat the Jackdaw, who is thus made a spokesman, calling the people together to shout with one voice at his instigation and forming a new diabolic ecclesia (I.9.passim). Like the crowd, Gower's narrator is occupied and operated by the voice of rebellion. Nor is it just his voice that changes; the narrator observes that his body, as if he is a character from Ovid's *Metamorphoses*, also undergoes strange physical changes: "Iam michi subducta facies humana videtur" (I.16.1483) [My human appearance now seemed taken away (82)]; he feels he is becoming a bird, a hare, or a hunted boar (I.16.1390, 1395–96, 1432). Finally, he says his mind "exhorruit equoris instar" (I.16.1475) [shivered like the surface of the sea (81)] and his body becomes limpid (I.16.1488–90). Indeed, it is as if the narrator is like the things from which he flees: transforming into a wild, unreasoning animal and then the sea. The rebellion engulfs him so fully that he incorporates it as a febrile interior complaint that he is unable to vocalize. This interior occupation, the disobedient self, that he acknowledges on his knees, is a guilt that activates his subjective interpellation.[80] Although when he first runs from the rebellion, the narrator presumes himself innocent (I.16.1384), the rest of the poem stresses the need to look inward for the causes of corruption:

> Nescio quis purum se dicet, plebs quia tota
> Clamat iam lesum quemlibet esse statum.
> Culpa quidem lata, non culpa leuis, maculauit
> Tempora cum causis, nos quoque nostra loca . . .
> (III.prologue.17–20)

[80] On guilt and interpellation, see Butler, *The Psychic Life of Power*, e.g. 108.

[No matter who he is, a man will say he is innocent, for the whole population now cries out that every estate is the injured party. Indeed, an extensive guilt, not an insignificant one, has with good reason tainted us, our country, and our times.]

(113)

The verbs that are used at the beginning of this excerpt—*dicet, clamat*—again stress the voice: the vagaries and unsubstantiated *claims* of public opinion that work centrifugally to thrust away blame. The first-person plural pronouns in the last line here bring them back in, advising the reader to look closer to home for the sources (*causis*) of pollution. In this way, Gower's centripetal poem excuses neither narrator nor poet from fault.

The Messianic Vocation

John Gower's *Vox clamantis* has not always attracted a "good press." In particular, it has been disliked for the rebarbative invective against the 1381 rebels in the first book that some critics have argued makes Gower a spokesman for the forces of medieval political repression.[81] Others, like Steven Justice, have suggested that the offensive parts of the poem's first book, being appended later to the rest of the *Vox*, represent Gower's attempt to distance himself from a rebel movement whose reformist demands are uncomfortably close to his own in the "later" books; his reading finds a magnetic attraction and repulsion between the *Vox* and the revolt.[82] My own view is that there is a larger gap than is often recognized between the poet and the narrator and that, while the rising is certainly one of the subjects of the *Vox*, the poem is also about the ethics of social complaint. Indeed, it is part of a larger cultural discussion

[81] See, for example, David Aers, "Representations of the 'Third Estate': Social Conflict and Its Milieu around 1381," *Southern Review* 16 (1983): 335–49 (345–47); see also Barr, *Socioliterary Practice*, 108–11. Despite its subtitle, a similar reading is offered in Eve Salisbury, "Violence and the Sacrificial Poet: Gower, the *Vox*, and the Critics," in *On John Gower: Essays at the Millennium*, ed. R. F. Yeager (Kalamazoo: Western Michigan University Press, 2007), 124–43 (125).

[82] For arguments that, in various ways, find points of contact between the poem's narrator and the 1381 rebels, as they are described in *Vox clamantis*, see Justice, *Writing and Rebellion*, 211, 216; Nolan, "Poetics of Catastrophe," 133; Kim Zarins, "From Head to Foot: Syllabic Play and Metamorphosis in Book I of Gower's *Vox Clamantis*," in *On John Gower*, ed. Yeager, 144–60 (148–49). Judith Ferster, "O Political Gower," *Mediaevalia* 16 (1993 for 1990): 33–53 (esp. 43), has also argued that Gower's position on the third estate is more reflective than Aers accepts.

about the legitimacy of social criticism, a discussion that has a Pauline frame. In their different ways, the texts that concern this essay hold out the possibility of social reform but universally fail to deliver it; whatever improvements are brought by the messianic vocation are neither permanent nor complete. The force of the injunction to *remain* in one's calling, at 1 Corinthians 7:20, was that the New Law was not the total annihilation, but rather the "use and messianic vocation of the old"; the old world was passing, not past.[83] Langland's Christ, speaking in the words of Matthew 5:17, says "Non veni soluere legem, set adimplere" [I have not come to destroy the law, but to fulfill it (XX.395a)].[84] Under the New Law, temporal juridical conditions do not come to an end, nor indeed do people's imperfect practice of them; instead, the ownership of those conditions is transferred to God. Furthermore, God is "recounselide" (as the quotation from the Wycliffite Bible, above, has it) through Christ, to the practice of the world.

While some, like D. W. Robertson, have argued that Chaucer's Wife of Bath is a representative of the unreconstructed Old Law, in fact she is an articulate advocate of the messianic life.[85] This is her encapsulation of what that regime entails:

> But—Lord Crist!—whan that it remembreth me
> Upon my yowthe, and on my jolitee,
> It tikleth me aboute myn herte roote.
> Unto this day it dooth myn herte boote
> That I have had my world as in my tyme.
> But age, allas, that al wole envenyme,
> Hath me biraft my beautee and my pith.
> Lat go. Farewel! The devel go therwith!
> The flour is goon; there is namoore to telle;
> The bren, as I best kan, now moste I selle;
> But yet to be right myrie wol I fonde.
> Now wol I tellen of my fourthe housbonde.
>
> (III.469–80)

[83] Agamben, *The Time That Remains,* 26–27.

[84] For a psychoanalytic reading of the coexistence of the Old and New Law and, through it, Langland's ambivalent identification with Judaism, which also puts guilt at the center of the relationship between subject and Law, see Goldstein, "'Why calle ye hym Crist,'" esp. 222–23.

[85] Robertson, *Preface to Chaucer,* 321; see also Graeme D. Caie, "The Significance of Marginal Glosses in the Earliest Manuscripts of *The Canterbury Tales,*" in *Chaucer and the Scriptural Tradition,* ed. Jeffrey, 75–88 (75).

This statement offers an adaptation of Paul's assertion that, in the messianic now, "For whi the figure of this world passith" (1 Cor. 7:31). In this interlude, Alisoun notes that she has "had"—enjoyed and used up—worldly things and that those things are now passing. She comes to a momentary halt, at the "now," to which she twice refers. There is, it seems, "namoore to telle." "Farewel," "goon," she says, consigning her story hitherto to the past. However, this is not the end of the *Prologue;* such things are passing rather than past, and she manages to contrive another four hundred lines before she advances to her *Tale* proper; more time, in fact, remains. Alisoun ends this digression with a new lease of life in the buoyant "[b]ut yet," disrupting her iambs with an emphatic "[n]ow," in the last line here, as if to herald a new time quite distinct from what has gone before. And yet, resuming where she left off, this "new" time sees her return to the same theme: her fourth marriage.

"Abyde . . . my tale is nat bigonne" (169), she tells the Pardoner, suggesting (through negation) that she might at last advance to the trailed *Tale.* However, instead of progressing as promised, her exchange with the Pardoner ends with his urging her to continue "as ye bigan" (185), sending her back to her starting point. "[T]eche us yonge men of youre praktike" (187), he suggests, resetting her *Prologue* on the theme of experience with which she started, but also enticing her with the desire for young men that postpones her full and final reform. In a grammatical as well as a moral sense, the messianic life is imperfect: ongoing, rather than completed, a state characterized by the tenacity rather than the surrender of old habits. Gower's poem, too, ends with a return to the beginning, both for Gower, who inserts new material into the first book after the rest of the work is in circulation, and for the reader, who is instructed at the end of the work: "hec sibi scripta legat" [read these writings for him (or, in fact, her) self], as if he or she had not already done so.[86] Most obviously the Wife's *Tale* is interested in making old things new and the reformations of her characters look, at first glance, conclusive: the rapist learns his lesson in courtesy and the old, poor, and ugly lady is transformed into a young, high-born

---

[86] Malte Urban, "Past and Present: Gower's Use of Old Books in *Vox Clamantis,*" in *John Gower: Manuscripts, Readers, Contexts,* ed. Malte Urban (Brepols: Turnhout, 2009), 175–96 (179–80), has also made the point about the way that the poem's composition process fits with its inverted temporalities.

beauty.[87] However, the *Tale* is not so easily dissevered from its *Prologue* and its recidivist narrator; Alisoun's own conduct hardly lives up to the moral heart of the *Tale,* about the importance of virtue to shore up a claim to gentility in Christ, and the last lines of her *Tale* retract whatever sentence is to be found there with a prayer said in her own self-interest: "and Jhesu Crist us sende / Housbondes meeke, yonge, and fressh abedde" (1258–59). Indeed, the heroine's transformation, in the *Tale,* gives her an unhampered intimacy, even a companionate marriage with a young man, thus working into the center of Alisoun's most corrupting desires. However, this reiterative weakness does not necessarily damn Alisoun; rather, it characterizes the provisional condition of the messianic life in the shadow of the End.

Similarly in Gower's *Vox clamantis,* fixed things will not stay fixed. The narrator finds refuge from the rebellion on a ship, only for a storm to erupt and a sea monster to threaten both the ship and, most particularly, the narrator himself (I.18, especially 1767). Once the storm has subsided and the jaws of the monster have closed, the narrator gives thanks: like Jonah, he has been saved by God from shipwreck (I.18.1819). He forgets, of course, that Jonah's story does not end with that rescue. Gower's narrator, like Jonah, is then cast away on an island inhabited by sinners (I.20). Like Will's inconclusive resurrection in Passus XX of *Piers Plowman,* Gower's narrator's "ups" are always cancelled by a countervailing "down"; here is an "up":

> Percipiens furias veteri de lege repressas,
> Et noua quod fractum lex reparasset iter,
> . . . Et renouantur eo tempore iura viri.
> Tunc prius ad dominum cordis nouitate reviuens
> Cantica celsithrono laudis honore dedi. . . .
> (I.21.2061–62, 2066–68)

[I perceived that the mad men had been subdued under the law of old and that a new mode of law had repaired the broken course of events . . . and at this time the rights of man were restored. Revived by fresh courage, I first offered canticles of praise to the Lord enthroned with glory on high.]

(94)

[87] The old lady in *The Wife of Bath's Tale* has been read as a figure for the Pauline *vetus homo* by Anne Kernan, "The Archwife and the Eunuch," *ELH* 41 (1974): 1–25 (5); Kernan also offers an interesting riposte to Robertson's reading of Alisoun (10, 16). Peck also sees the transformation in the *Tale* as a Pauline reformation; "Biblical Interpretation," 158.

The idea of law here brings these renovations into Christian time. The revivification of the narrator's heart (*cordis*) is expressed as an assumption of sovereign rights (*iura*) in a way that is reminiscent of the final lines of the book, which urge the reader to do likewise, to govern his or her heart. The claim would be conceited if the rest of the work did not undermine it. The narrator retains vestiges of his previous fear, in his traumatized memory of the storm, just as the peasantry retain an antipathy to their social betters:

> Sic ope diuina Sathane iacet obruta virtus,
> Que tamen indomita rusticitate latet;
> Semper ad interitum nam rusticus insidiatur,
> Si genus ingenuum subdere forte queat.
> (I.21.2097–2100)

[Similarly, Satan's power lay prostrate, overwhelmed by divine might; but nevertheless it lurked in hiding among the ungovernable peasantry. For the peasant always lay in wait to see whether he by chance could bring the noble class to destruction.]

(94–95)

> . . . nec dum tamen inde quietus
> Persto, set absconso singula corde fero.
> (I.21.2137–38)

[For because of them (i.e., his memories), I am not yet at peace, but suffer them all secretly in my heart.]

(95)

In both these passages, the problems of the past persist in the present, despite the installation of the New Law. In Gower's work, the New Law does not, after all, cancel out the Old but makes it provisional and passing. In the second quotation, the suspension of ordinary time is signaled in the use of the word "dum" (until) and also in the enjambment that postpones the verb, "persto," (I persevere/remain constant) until the next line. "Persto" is undone by the negative in the line before, offering a paradox that describes the steadiness of unsteadiness. Instead of persevering in peace, and being psychically repaired, the narrator remains in the state in which he was called: with his heart disordered by fear. Like Chaucer's Wife of Bath and Will in *Piers Plowman,* Gower's persona thus indicates the persistence of his (im)*parfitnesse*.[88] Just as Alisoun defines herself through negation—"that am nat I"—Gower similarly presents the stability of his vocation as radical revocation: "nec . . . [p]ersto." The language of hiding and waiting in ambush in these two passages—"latet," "insidiatur," "absconso," "fero"—forges connections between the residues, even under the New Law, of satanic power, peasant rebellion, and the narrator's inner ferment. The identification between the narrator and the peasants' revolt continues (and is put into cosmological context), even after the revivification produced by divine calling, creating a recidivist cycle rather than the social repair and self-mastery that are at first claimed. In the final line in the first book of *Vox clamantis*, the narrator requests a new situation that looks, by gratuitous repetition, all too similar to the old: "Sit prior et *cura cura* repulsa noua" (I.21.2150) [and let my former care be banished by this new one (95)].[89]

Conclusion

Gower's reversals and continuities in the *Vox clamantis* recall the ending of Alain of Lille's *Anticlaudianus,* a poem that has been compared to Gower's work before and that, although it was written in the twelfth century, holds out an interesting counterpoint to the theologies of selfhood on display in the writing of the later Middle Ages that I have been discussing.[90] This is the close of Alain's poem:

> Jam ratis, euadens Scillam monstrumque Caribdis,
> Ad portum transquilla meat, jam littore gaudet
> Nauita, iam metam cursor tenet, anchora portum.
> Nauta tamen tremebundus adhuc post equoris estum
> Terrenos timet insultus, ne tutus in undis
> Naufragus in terra pereat, ne liuor in illum
> Seuiat aut morsus detractio figat in illo

---

[88] Again, I differ here with Nicholas Watson, who argues that in the *Vox clamantis* Gower projects a "prophetic voice" instead of presenting himself as a "mediocrist," as Chaucer does in the *Canterbury Tales.* "Chaucer's Public Christianity," 104.

[89] For an alternative, and ingenious, reading of "cura cura" in relation to the poem's composition, see Nolan, "Poetics of Catastrophe," 131.

[90] James Simpson, *Sciences and the Self in Medieval Poetry: Alan of Lille's "Anticlaudianus" and John Gower's "Confessio Amantis"* (Cambridge: Cambridge University Press, 1995). As Simpson points out, there is no direct evidence that Gower knew the work, although Chaucer did because he mentions it in *The House of Fame,* 21 n. 38.

Qui iam scribendi studium pondusque laboris
Exhausit, proprio concludens fine laborem.
Si tamen ad presens fundit sua murmura liuor,
Et famam delere cupit laudesque poete
Supplantare nouas, saltem post fata silebit.

[Now the ship, avoiding Scylla and the monster, Charybdis, sails on a calm sea to the harbor. Now the mariner rejoices at the sight of land; now the runner is at the winning post; the anchor is fast in the harbor. However, the mariner, after negotiating the heaving sea, trembles and fears attacks on land: he fears that, though he has been safe asea, he may be shipwrecked and lost ashore, that spite may rage against him or slander sink her teeth in him who, as he brings his work to a fitting conclusion, has drained his energy in writing and borne the burden of toil. If spite pours out her whisperings for the present and wishes to ruin the reputation of the poet and waylay his newly-won honors, at least she will be silent after his death.][91]

Alain's poem tells the story of the remaking of a corrupted world, from which the virtues have been exiled; the virtues are also refugees in the *Vox,* but in Gower's poem there is no remaking. In Alain's text, the reformation of the world is effected, and the virtues restored by the victory in battle of Novus Homo—the New Man described in the pseudo-Pauline Ephesians 4:17—over Alecto, the fury who commands the vices. In contrast, there is no triumphal return for the virtues in Gower's poem. Alain's ending at first confirms a definitive postwar settlement and might have ended there, but instead it offers an envoy, apparently on a different topic: the poet's concerns for his name and the reception of his work. Despite the fact that the narrator's boat has dropped anchor in the harbor and escaped both rough seas and sea monsters, it is still imperiled, adrift and in danger of wrecking. In this way, Alain signals that the perfection achieved in his allegory is yet to be finally realized in the world outside the text. Gower uses the destabilizing idea of authorial name in the envoy, amplifying Alain's false dawn across the whole of his work, making of it a much more dismantling retraction.

[91] Alain de Lille, *Anticlaudianus, texte critique avec une introduction et des tables,* ed. R. Bossuat, Textes philosophiques du moyen âge 1 (Paris: J. Vrin, 1955), Book IX, lines 415–26; Alain of Lille, *Anticlaudianus: or The Good and Perfect Man,* trans. James J. Sheridan (Toronto: Pontifical Institute of Medieval Studies, 1973), 216–17.

James Simpson, in his comparison of Gower's *Confessio Amantis* and Alain's *Anticlaudianus,* understands Gower to be working in a different, Ovidian and Aristotelian "humanism" at odds with Alain's earlier Platonism.[92] He finds the *Confessio Amantis* to be "much less strictly elitist, and rooted much 'lower' down in the soul"; I think that difference from the *Anticlaudianus* also resides in the *Vox.*[93] What is more, an ideological opposition to Alain's works, the *Anticlaudianus* and *De planctu Naturae,* has been discovered in both Chaucer's *House of Fame* and Langland's *Piers Plowman,* by Sarah Powrie and Hugh White, respectively.[94] Simpson, Powrie, and White are thus charting an explicit rethinking, in late medieval writing, of the theology of selfhood as laid out in Alain's influential work. White, for example, has described Langland's poem as a "counterblast" to the Chartrian tradition, for which Alain stands as representative, a tradition that produced a "separatist" account of how God related to "the unsatisfactoriness of the natural realm."[95] Although some critics have discovered similar "separatist" impulses in Gower's *Vox,* in fact he, like Langland, locates sinfulness close to, if not at the heart of both God and the self.[96]

In *Piers Plowman,* the dreamer's depressing survey of Middle Earth is similar to the complaints of nature in *Anticlaudianus* and *De planctu Naturae.* However, in *Piers Plowman,* instead of the narrator's complaints being addressed, they are condemned both by Ymaginatif and by Reason; when Will argues with Reason on the subject, he is thrown out of his inner dream of Middle Earth, punished like a latter-day Adam evicted from paradise (XIII.193–216). According to Langland, God owns his disobedient creation, and he deflects self-righteous attacks on

[92] Simpson, *Sciences and the Self,* 15–21.

[93] Ibid., 16.

[94] Sarah Powrie, "Alan of Lille's *Anticlaudianus* as Intertext in Chaucer's *House of Fame,*" ChauR 44 (2010): 246–67; and Hugh White, *Nature and Salvation in "Piers Plowman"* (Cambridge: D. S. Brewer, 1988), e.g., 66–68.

[95] White, *Nature and Salvation,* 66–68. There is also a seminal and positive reading of failure and sin in Langland's poem in Zeeman, *"Piers Plowman" and the Medieval Discourse of Desire,* esp. 21–22.

[96] For example, Aers, "Representations of the 'Third Estate,'" 346–47, suggests that Gower—whom Aers conflates with the narrator—thinks "God is unequivocally a supporter of the ruling classes" rather than the rebels and thus Aers dubs the work "unreflexive"; a similar confusion of poet and narrator is found in Elizabeth Porter, "Gower's Ethical Microcosm and Political Macrocosm," in *Gower's Confessio Amantis: Responses and Reassessments,* ed. A. J. Minnis (Cambridge: D. S. Brewer, 1983), 135–62: "In the *Vox,* Gower in his self-appointed role as social critic had stood outside the disordered world which his poem surveyed and analysed" (145–46).

it by redirecting them against their source. Gower's narrator already suspects that he is boring people with his invective and, as a result, he becomes increasingly silent: "Non meus vt querat noua sermo quosque fatigat" (I.16.1513) [In order that my talk might not consist of complaint about recent happenings and become burdensome to people (82)], but he is also advised by the celestial voice to stop complaining. The narrator is washed up on an island inhabited by sinners, rather in the way that Jonah is vomited by the whale onto the shores of Nineveh (I.18.1819). Jonah's desire for the punishment of the Ninevites also ricochets: he is taught to tolerate sinful im*parfitnesse.* Likewise, the celestial voice tells the narrator in the *Vox clamantis* to love his new neighbors:

> . . . quia discors
> Insula te cepit, pax vbi raro manet.
> Te minus ergo decet mundanos ferre labores,
> Munera nam mundus nulla quietis habet:
> Si tibi guerra foris pateat, tamen interiori
> Pace, iuuante deo, te pacienter habe.
> . . . Qui silet est firmus, loquitur qui plura repente,
> Probra satis fieri postulat ipse sibi.
> Ocia corpus alunt, corpus quoque pascitur illis,
> Excessusque tui dampna laboris habent:
> Gaudet de modico natura . . .
>
> (I.20.2023–28, 2041–45)

[For a quarrelsome island where peace seldom lasts long has received you. Therefore it is less fitting for you to carry on worldly struggles, for the world holds out no peaceful rewards. If a war lies outside you, with God's help control yourself patiently by the peace within you. . . . He who is silent is strong; he who says a great deal in haste is asking for reproaches to be made against him. Leisure nourishes the body, and the body takes sustenance from it, but excessive toil on your part has an ill effect. Nature rejoices in moderation.]

(93)

Gower imagines his "counterblast" to the Chartrian complaint tradition spatially. The verb *capere* can mean "receive," as in Stockton's translation, but it can also suggest a more hostile capture or military occupation. What is inside and what is out is unclear here. Like Will in *Piers Plowman,* who immoderately takes issue with Reason, Gower's dreamer has complained too much and should look to make peace within himself. Rigorist complaints lodged against the corruptions of human nature are not upheld in either *Piers Plowman* or *Vox clamantis,* because the presumption of natural rights that underpins those complaints—a presumption that was elsewhere used to shore up hereditary privilege—is displaced by a theory of calling.

The comparison with the *Anticlaudianus* points up a commitment, in the work that I have assessed here, to imagine—although perpetually defer—the spiritual recoverability of the imperfect life. Chaucer, Langland, and Gower wield a theory of calling that is different both to what had gone before and also what was to come, from sixteenth-century thinkers. If, unlike Alain of Lille, they fostered the possibility that imperfect callings might not be anathema but instead practiced as kenotic deprecation in imitation of Christ, they nonetheless did not, like later Protestant reformers, focus their theory of calling specifically or exclusively on economic occupation. The wide scope of the late medieval theory of vocation, which, after Weber, has made it look negligible, is its point; calling offered a way to reconsider the prospects of the social subject—and not just the economic agent—in Christian time, and used the undisclosed judgments of God to render human hierarchies provisional and passing. In this theory of calling, there was no contradiction of "kynde," or the God that had instituted it, but rather a challenge to the existence of any clear relationship between arbitrary social designations and the natural or divinely appointed world. Out of such disconnections, these writers assembled a startlingly optimistic impression even of damaged, imperfect subjectivity, with a subtle interpretation of Paul's idea of calling that declared the importance of the secular world as much as the spiritual.

Conduct Shameful and Unshameful in *The Franklin's Tale*

Wan-Chuan Kao
The Graduate Center, CUNY

"Dictus vero Johannes fatetur quod promisit ipsam ducere in uxorem sub hiis verbis, 'Volo te ducere in uxorem si bene facias.'" [The said John admits that he promised to marry the woman with these words: 'I will take you as my wife if you conduct yourself well.']

—*Registrum primum,* Act Book, Ely, 1381

"If I am a bright housewife, I may be ashamed because too much of my work is too exclusively muscular."

—Silvan Tomkins

I N THE MARITAL NEGOTIATION that opens *The Franklin's Tale,* Dorigen and Arveragus premise their marriage on an interlocking set of conduct obligations applying to both sexes. Dorigen, having observed Arveragus's worth, vows to be a "humble trewe wyf" and permits him to possess "swich lordshipe as men han over hir wyves."[1] And Arveragus pledges obedience to Dorigen's will, on the condition that she preserves his "name of soveraynetee, / That wolde he have for shame of his degree" (V.751–52). Each would be wife or husband only if certain behavioral conditions are met: her wifehood is conditioned on his display of *gentillesse,* and his husbandhood on her consent to his name of *soveraynetee.*

The agreement set out here falls, in certain respects, under what R. H. Helmholz has categorized as "conditional marriages." In his an-

---

I am grateful for the generous advice of Glenn Burger, Steven Kruger, Shannon McSheffrey, and the anonymous readers for *SAC.* I would also like to thank Alcuin Blamires for the opportunity to present an early version of this paper at the 2006 congress of the New Chaucer Society, as well as Sylvia Tomasch for her support.

[1] *The Franklin's Tale,* V.758, 742–43. All references are to *The Riverside Chaucer,* gen. ed. Larry D. Benson (Boston: Houghton Mifflin, 1987).

alysis of marriage litigation in late fourteenth- and early fifteenth-century England, Helmholz notes a particular category concerned with disputes over the precise meaning of various conditions stipulated in marriage contracts, especially those involving a woman's conduct. In a 1365 marriage case in York, for example, a man contended that he had agreed to marry a woman "sub bono gestu suo" [under the condition of her good conduct]. In 1381, a man in Ely claimed that he had pledged to a woman, "Volo te ducere in uxorem si bene facias" [I will take you as my wife if you conduct yourself well]. And in a 1417 Norwich case, a man testified that he had promised marriage only if a woman could demonstrate "bonam gestionem" [good conduct]. According to Helmholz, such conditional matrimonial contracts caused real difficulties of legal interpretation. The courts did not possess any useful tradition of precedents to help clarify the ambiguities, nor were they able to establish definitive rulings.[2] The records of the 1381 Ely case, he notes, offer no conclusive ruling or legal clarity.

The origins of medieval theories of conditional marriage have been traced by Bartholomew Timlin to the School of Bologna in the twelfth century.[3] Gratian, the first to speak of giving marriage consent with a condition, picked up Augustine's discussion on the validity of marriage to an infidel on the condition of his or her conversion. John Faventinus contended that marital conditions must not be against canon or civil law. Alexander III (Roland Bandinelli) asserted that marriage engagements are contracts, and he distinguished present consent from future consent. Condition of present consent (*consensus de praesenti sub condicione*), however, was rejected by Huguccio of Pisa, who allowed conditional *sponsalia de sponsalia de futuro* and affirmed that sexual consummation makes marriage unconditional. To Tancred of Bologna, a thirteenth-century Dominican canonist, present consent may be declared with a condition, but the condition must refer to a future event. The theoretical debates also centered on the honorableness of conditions, the verification of which would validate a marriage immediately. By the second decade of the thirteenth century, the doctrine of conditional marriage was met with wide approval by canon lawyers.[4]

[2] These and similar cases are cited in R. H. Helmholz, *Marriage Litigation in Medieval England* (Cambridge: Cambridge University Press, 1974), 47–57.

[3] Bartholomew Thomas Timlin, *Conditional Matrimonial Consent: An Historical Synopsis and Commentary*, Ph.D. diss. (Catholic University of America, 1934), 25–69.

[4] On medieval conditional marriages, see also Shannon McSheffrey, *Marriage, Sex, and Civic Culture in Late Medieval London* (Philadelphia: University of Pennsylvania Press, 2006), 87–97; Helmholz, *Marriage Litigation in Medieval England,* 47–57; Frederik Pedersen, *Marriage Disputes in Medieval England* (London: Hambledon Press, 2000), 28–29,

In a crucial sense, contractual disputes over conditions of female conduct centered on the contested meaning of *si bene facias,* and I want to suggest that a similar semantic difficulty exists in Dorigen and Arveragus's marital contract. What exactly is the sense of shame that Arveragus possesses or of the "name of soveraynetee" that he demands? The idea of shame, rather than eliminating *maistrie* and upholding the Franklin's ideal of "an humble, wys accord" (V.791), reintroduces the question of a power differential into their marriage and constrains the free love to which, purportedly, they subscribe. Shame is therefore integral to Arveragus and Dorigen's marriage because it realizes and measures the efficacy of the conduct condition *si bene facias.* Sovereignty, galvanized by shame, is more than a mere name that preserves public reputation. The alignment of shame and honor with the modern public/private dyad, typified in G. L. Kittredge's reading of the tale as a convincing solution to the marriage debate in the *Canterbury Tales,* does not accurately describe the complex workings of shame within the married estate.[5] Emotions, Ewa Hess and Hennric Jokeit recently have suggested, are "social attention signals directed inward and outward," and knowledge about emotions is both interpretive and productive knowledge because it always involves the possibility of application.[6] Within the emotional economy of *The Franklin's Tale,* shame is a social attention signal that directs the traffic of love, marriage, and *gentillesse.*

In the first section below, I examine the marriage contract between Dorigen and Arveragus within the contexts of companionate marriage and of the household. I argue that their contract does not definitively draw a clear public/private divide or stipulate divergent behaviors for separate spheres along dichotomies of man/woman or courtly love/marriage. Shame, instead of carving out a protected interiority for a post-Enlightenment sense of the liberal self, destabilizes the boundaries of the

---

64–65; Peter Fleming, *Family and Household in Medieval England* (New York: Palgrave, 2001), 47–48; and Ruth Mazo Karras, *Sexuality in Medieval Europe: Doing unto Others* (New York: Routledge, 2005), 70–71. On the frequency of marriage litigations involving conditional contracts, see Helmholz, *Marriage Litigation in Medieval England,* 48. On the legal arbitration clause, see Frederik Pedersen, "Marriage Contracts and the Church Courts of Fourteenth-Century England," in *To Have and to Hold: Marrying and Its Documentation in Western Christendom, 400–1600,* ed. Philip L. Reynolds and John Witte Jr. (Cambridge: Cambridge University Press, 2007), 287–331 (290). And on the bargaining nature of conditional marriages, see Helmholz, "Marriage Contracts in Medieval England," in ibid., 265–66.

[5] G. L. Kittredge, "Chaucer's Discussion of Marriage," *MP* 9.4 (1912): 435–67. Kittredge calls the marriage of Arveragus and Dorigen "a brilliant success" (467).

[6] Ewa Hess and Hennric Jokeit, "Neurocapitalism," trans. Melanie Newton, *Eurozine* (2009): 1–8 (7).

public and private. In the second section, I show that medieval conduct literature is of key importance to understanding Arveragus's deployments of shame. The late medieval middle classes, in their pursuit of wealth and status, embraced a premodern form of emotional capitalism that emphasized affective, immaterial labor. Consequently, the male authors of conduct manuals for wives actively attempt to map distinctions between the public and private onto distinctions between shame and honor, while simultaneously exposing the inherent gender asymmetries in companionate marriage. In the third section, I analyze Dorigen's litany of virtuous women in terms of the technologies of affective literacy prescribed in conduct and devotional literature. By mimicking the devotional programs prescribed for laywomen in texts such as the *journées chrétiennes,* Dorigen defers her shaming and gains access to the virtues of the good wife. Yet the internal incoherence of Dorigen's litany ultimately prevents her from assuming any stable identity. In the concluding section, I theorize that conduct literature upends gender and class distinctions, thereby allowing Dorigen to acquire a queer female masculinity and the Franklin to become an effective but feminized manager of shame. In *The Franklin's Tale,* the affective labor of shame produces conditions of conduct that regulate companionate marriage and the purportedly *fre* selves within the middling household.

Contracting Marriage *Pryvely, Apert*

With its lack of any explicit reference to land or money and its focus only on conditions productive of *gentil* conduct, Arveragus and Dorigen's model of conjugality closely resembles that of companionate marriage. Martha Howell has noted that the late Middle Ages and early modern period gave rise to "a form of conjugality grounded in personal choice, intimacy, and desire rather than . . . in property or more generalized socio-political relations."[7] Socioeconomically, companionate mar-

---

[7] Martha Howell, "The Properties of Marriage in Late Medieval Europe: Commercial Wealth and the Creation of Modern Marriage," in *Love, Marriage, and Family Ties in the Later Middle Ages,* ed. Isabel Davis, Miriam Müller, and Sarah Rees Jones (Turnhout: Brepols, 2003), 17–61 (17). The development of companionate marriage can be traced to the Gregorian Reform in the High Middle Ages that sought to separate celibate clergy from married laity and to reconceptualize the institution of marriage. The twelfth and thirteenth centuries witnessed new ecclesiastical definitions of marriage that stressed the necessity of consent in the creation of the matrimonial bond, that required a public setting for the marriage ceremony, that mandated marriage be indissoluble, and that emphasized the internalized relationship between spouses. By the thirteenth

riage came to be associated with the middle strata during this period.[8] While Arveragus and Dorigen's union might appear more aristocratic than "middling" in nature, as Howell points out, historically it was Europe's elites who first adopted elements of companionate marriage; marriages among English aristocrats were " 'affective' in some sense" and spouses entered marriage with expectations of forming bonds of intimacy.[9] This ideological focus on marital affection is central to the Franklin's valuation of Dorigen and Arveragus's marriage, for he consistently

---

century, marriage had become a sacrament that incorporated the discourse of friendship and that viewed the union as a partnership of equals. And in tandem with the emerging idea of conjugal debt went the desirability of marital affection. But for all its emphasis on the individual, the church also sought to place marriage under greater surveillance by ecclesiastical and civic authorities. Thus the ecclesiastically approved process of marriage begins with a betrothal, a contract undertaken in the future tense, followed by the calling of banns in the parish church. The couple then forms a present-tense contract before the parish priest, prior to a nuptial mass solemnizing their marriage. By the late Middle Ages, however, social practice did not necessarily follow the prescribed steps; present-tense contracts were frequently the first and only step in a marriage contract, thus bypassing the betrothal and the calling of banns. Lawrence Stone, who postulated the rise of "affective individualism" that shaped the modern nuclear household, provided the first full historical study of companionate marriage, in *The Family, Sex, and Marriage in England, 1500–1800* (New York: Harper, 1977). For in-depth historical accounts, see Michael M. Sheehan, *Marriage, Family, and Law in Medieval Europe: Collected Studies,* ed. James K. Farge (Toronto: University of Toronto Press, 1996); James Brundage, *Law, Sex, and Christian Society in Medieval Europe* (Chicago: University of Chicago Press, 1987); Erik Kooper, "Loving the Unequal Equal: Medieval Theologians and Marital Affection," in *The Olde Daunce: Love, Friendship, Sex, and Marriage in the Medieval World,* ed. Robert R. Edwards and Stephen Spector (Albany: State University of New York Press, 1991), 44–56; Neil Cartlidge, *Medieval Marriage: Literary Approaches, 1100–1300* (Woodbridge: Brewer, 1997); Conor McCarthy, *Marriage in Medieval England: Law, Literature, and Practice* (Woodbridge: Boydell Press, 2004); Rüdiger Schnell, "The Discourse on Marriage in the Middle Ages," *Speculum* 73.3 (1998): 771–86; D. L. D'Avray, *Medieval Marriage: Symbolism and Society* (Oxford: Oxford University Press, 2005); and Reynolds and Witte Jr., eds., *To Have and to Hold.*

[8] Howell notes that the modern sense of a "middle class" is anachronistic in the late Middle Ages; it is more accurate to speak of " 'middle classes' or, perhaps better still, of 'middling sorts'—artisans, merchants, professionals, and rural yeomanry, people who often shared little except their common distinction from both landed aristocrats and the peasantry" ("Properties of Marriage," 22). Paul Strohm, in *Social Chaucer* (Cambridge, Mass.: Harvard University Press, 1989), adopts the term "middle strata" from Sylvia Thrupp to describe the middle groups in late medieval English society whose "horizontal" form of sociality, based on more fluid forms of service and remuneration, redefined the older "vertical" model of social relations (1–14); recently, David Gary Shaw has noted that status for the middling groups was "vague, uncertain, [and] changeable," in his *Necessary Conjunctions: The Social Self in Medieval England* (New York: Palgrave, 2005), 90. And within the context of the *Canterbury Tales,* Glenn Burger argues that the middling *gentils* "fail to cohere as a stable, homogeneous group," in *Chaucer's Queer Nation* (Minneapolis: University of Minnesota Press, 2003), 49.

[9] Howell, "The Properties of Marriage," 22, 28.

notes that they "lyveth in blisse and in solas" (V.803), and by the end of the tale, in "sovereyn blisse" (V.1552). Because the production and maintenance of affects are the desired ends of matrimony, conditions of conduct become crucial to the marriage contract. Demands of particular conduct are made of Arveragus and Dorigen precisely "for to lede the moore in blisse hir lyves" (V.744). Hence, conduct within their companionate marriage seeks to uphold the amalgamated ideals of free choice, equality, mutuality, partnership, married friendship, and love. More important, conduct *as* the production of affect is vital to the claims of each character, and implicitly also the Franklin, to gentility.

The Franklin glosses Dorigen and Arveragus's marriage agreement as a utopic fusion of courtly love and marriage: Arveragus will be "Servant in love, and lord in marriage" (V.793), and Dorigen "His lady, certes, and his wyf also" (V.797). But the nature of the condition that Arveragus demands of Dorigen—the name of sovereignty—is more complicated than it appears, for it reflects the interpretative difficulty of *si bene facias*. Kittredge contends that Arveragus, as "an enlightened and chivalric gentleman," requires the name of sovereignty in order to "ensure the happiness of their wedded life."[10] Subsequent critics, working within or against Kittredge's construct of the Marriage Group, have variously read Arveragus's proposition as a generic adaptation of a romance motif in which a low-ranked knight courts a high-born lady, as a reflection of the "Epicurian optimism" of the Franklin's class, as an imaginative extension of ideas of vassalage and lordship, as Arveragus's conformity to traditional hierarchy or to "a non-utopian public's expectations," as an indication of his being a "proper man" within an ideal society, and as Arveragus's defense of his reputation as a knight or as a husband.[11] Underpinning many of these readings is a critical move that

[10] Kittredge, "Chaucer's Discussion of Marriage," 463–64.

[11] Adaptation of romance: John M. Fyler, "Love and Degree in the *Franklin's Tale*," *ChauR* 21.3 (1987): 321–37 (323); "Epicurian optimism": D. W. Robertson Jr., *A Preface to Chaucer: Studies in Medieval Perspectives* (Princeton: Princeton University Press, 1962), 470; extension of vassalage: Strohm, *Social Chaucer*, 105; conformity to traditional hierarchy: A. C. Spearing, introduction to *The Franklin's Tale*, ed. A. C. Spearing (Cambridge: Cambridge University Press, 1966), 36; Derek Pearsall, *The Canterbury Tales* (London: Routledge, 1985), 151; Francine McGregor, "What of Dorigen? Agency and Ambivalence in the *Franklin's Tale*," *ChauR* 31.4 (1997): 365–78 (371); nonutopian public's expectation: David Aers, *Chaucer, Langland, and the Creative Imagination* (London: Routledge, 1980), 63; "proper man": Kathryn Jacobs, "The Marriage Contract of the *Franklin's Tale*: The Remaking of Society," *ChauR* 20.2 (1985): 132–43 (136); knightly reputation: D. S. Brewer, "Honour in Chaucer," *Essays and Studies* n.s. 26 (1973): 1–19 (16); Gerald Morgan, "Experience and the Judgment of Poetry: A Reconsideration of the *Franklin's Tale*," *MÆ* 70.2 (2001): 204–25 (210); Emma Lipton, *Af-*

uncannily reenacts Arveragus's strategy to mask and avoid shame by subsuming it under the cultural ideal of *soveraynetee*. Moreover, Arveragus's prenuptial maneuvers are symptomatic of the Franklin's broader approach to shame throughout the tale, in which he repeatedly invokes the threat of shame only to expose it as a sham that appears to harm no one, thereby converting shame into a preservative of *gentillesse*. Dorigen, faced with the consequences of her rash promise of love to Aurelius, is nonetheless spared the shame of her name and body when he releases her from her vow; and Aurelius, unable to pay the Clerk of Orleans for the illusion he has created, escapes the shaming of his "kyndred" (V.1565) when the Clerk absolves him of his financial obligations. As the Franklin would have it, shame is merely a felicitous route to "gentil dede[s]" (V.1611), and upholds the state of virtues.

Replicating the Franklin's affective strategy, many critics have read the tale's negotiations with shame, exemplified in Arveragus's reverse discourse that transforms shame into the "name of soveraynetee," as self-evident. Arveragus's concern for reputation is therefore interpreted as obvious and natural, as what A. C. Spearing calls an "all-too-human approach to *gentillesse*."[12] In reading shame as a mere impetus toward its own concealment in the tale, recent scholarship has both sidestepped shame and contained it within the privileged ideal of *gentillesse* and its cluster of noble virtues: *trouthe, routhe, curteysie, honour, pacience, pite, frendshipe,* and *franchise*.[13] Yet shame is instrumental to the regulation of *gentil*

---

fections of the Mind: The Politics of Sacramental Marriage in Late Medieval English Literature (Notre Dame: University of Notre Dame Press, 2007), 28; defense of husband's reputation: Elaine Tuttle Hansen, *Chaucer and the Fictions of Gender* (Berkeley and Los Angeles: University of California Press, 1992), 274; McCarthy, *Marriage in Medieval England,* 103; Angela Jane Weisl, *Conquering the Reign of Femeny: Gender and Genre in Chaucer's Romance* (Cambridge: Brewer, 1995), 107; social appearance: Elizabeth Robertson, "Marriage, Mutual Consent, and the Affirmation of the Female Subject in 'The Knight's Tale,' 'The Wife of Bath's Tale,' and 'The Franklin's Tale,'" in *Drama Narrative and Poetry in the Canterbury Tales,* ed. Wendy Harding (Toulouse: Presses universitaires du Mirrail, 2003), 175–93 (189).

[12] Spearing, *The Franklin's Tale,* 36.

[13] For *pacience,* see Jill Mann, "Wife-Swapping in Medieval Literature," *Viator* 32 (2001): 93–112. Mann argues that patience allows for the realization of *gentillesse* and leads to social harmony. For *pite* as a social virtue that sanctifies hierarchy, see Felicity Riddy, "Engendering Pity in the *Franklin's Tale,*" in *Feminist Readings in Middle English Literature: The Wife of Bath and All Her Sect,* ed. Ruth Evans and Lesley Johnson (London: Routledge, 1994), 54–71. For the *frendshipe* model as political and personal ideals in the *Tale,* see Lipton, *Affections of the Mind,* esp. 22–23. And for *trouthe,* see Alison Ganze, "'My trouthe for to holde—allas, allas!': Dorigen and Honor in the *Franklin's Tale,*" *ChauR* 42.3 (2008): 312–29.

conduct, as it is explicitly integrated into the marital contract between Dorigen and Arveragus from the outset. Resisting Spearing's contention that *gentillesse* and shame are "not quite so closely connected as the Franklin feels," I contend that while *gentillesse* remains a central discursive rubric that governs *The Franklin's Tale,* it cannot be understood in isolation, that is, without a fuller engagement with negative affect.[14] Moreover, treating shame as solely "the spur to honourable acts" risks overlooking the material reality of shame as a bodily affect, which both Arveragus and Dorigen experience.[15]

Medieval companionate marriage, while emphasizing bonds of intimacy between partners, demanded that the formation of conjugality follow recognized, if not necessarily publicly performed, formulas and rituals. In *The Franklin's Tale,* the companionate marriage between Arveragus and Dorigen is established through an explicit exchange of vows. After Arveragus swears "Of his free wyl" (V.745), Dorigen professes: "I wol be youre humble trewe wyf" (V.758). The exchange of pledges and consent between Dorigen and Arveragus is here facilitated through spoken words, words that in J. L. Austin's speech-act theory are performative utterances that effect the marriage ceremony. The tale thus enacts late medieval marriage practices in which the speaking of the words of consent created the marriage bond.[16] Dorigen's verbal allusion to the marriage vow suggests that *The Franklin's Tale,* in spite of its pagan setting, actively engages the discourse of Christian marriage in the late Middle Ages. For Dorigen and Arveragus, the performative "I do" brings the possibility of companionate marriage into their married estate more fully than the reversals of hierarchy imagined by courtly love could do. In the vows exchanged between them, the "I do" func-

---

[14] Spearing, *The Franklin's Tale,* 37.

[15] Pearsall, *The Canterbury Tales,* 151.

[16] J. L. Austin, *How to Do Things with Words,* ed. J. O. Urmson and Marina Sbisá, 2nd ed. (Cambridge, Mass.: Harvard University Press, 1962), 14. McSheffrey (*Marriage, Sex, and Civic Culture,* 22), Lipton (*Affections of the Mind,* 29), and McCarthy (*Marriage in Medieval England,* 102) have commented that Dorigen's words resemble late medieval marriage vows. Her vow reflects the medieval notion of mutual consent in the formation of a marriage contract. Peter Lombard, in the twelfth century, distinguished two types of *consensus,* one by words of present consent (*verba de presenti*), as in "accipio te" [I accept you], the other by words of future consent (*verba de futuro*), as in "accipiam te" [I will accept you]. The thirteenth-century synodal statute from Salisbury provided a standard formulation of the marriage vow: "Ego N. accipio te in meam" [I N. accept you as mine]; see *Love, Sex, and Marriage in the Middle Ages: A Sourcebook,* ed. Conor McCarthy (London: Routledge, 2004), 75.

tions proleptically to imagine the prenuptial conditions as already appearing real within their new married estate.[17] And by insisting on his "name of soveraynetee," Arveragus points to the potential threat of shame as a foundational force that makes possible the realization of his and Dorigen's marriage performative in the first place.

But the formation of Dorigen and Arveragus's marriage raises more questions than answers. The Franklin, in fact, presents multiple iterations of the couple's contracting of marriage. Dorigen agrees to take Arveragus as her "housbonde and hir lord" (V.742). Arveragus, as a lover and out of his free will, promises to take no *maistrie* against her will, to show no jealousy, and to obey her will (V.745–50). He then demands the "name of soveraynetee . . . for shame of his degree" (V.751–52). In response, Dorigen pledges to be a good wife and forswears war and strife between them (V.758–59). At the end of his discussion of friendship, love, and *mastrie,* the Franklin notes that Arveragus "suffrance hire bihight" (V.788), and Dorigen vows there would be no "defaute in here" (V.790). However, in all these iterations of the marriage contract, we do not know definitively where the contract took place, if there were witnesses, whether love tokens were exchanged, and despite the virtual absence of Christianity in the tale, whether banns were pronounced, or if the marriage was ever solemnized. The Franklin seems uninterested in the details of the lovers' courtship or the formal steps of the marriage process. Instead, he telescopes the courtship rituals and strips the marriage formation down to the bare minimum requirement for a valid marriage: present consent. Indeed, Dorigen and Arveragus are married because the Franklin calls them "housbonde" and "wyf" (V.805).

Dorigen "pryvely" voices her consent to become Arveragus's wife. But, as Elaine Tuttle Hansen has asked, "Just what is Dorigen 'pryvely' agreeing to, and why 'pryvely'?"[18] On the basis of the word *pryvely,* many critics have read the marriage agreement between Arveragus and Dorigen as comprised of two contracts: one for the masculine public sphere of marriage, in which the husband rules his wife, the other for the feminine private sphere of romance, in which the lady dominates her

---

[17] See *MED,* s.v. "condicioun," 1(a): "A situation or state; circumstances of life or existence"; and 4(a): "A stipulation or proviso; also, an exception, reservation, or qualification."

[18] Hansen, *Chaucer and the Fictions of Gender,* 271.

knight.[19] Such readings are quick to interpret *pryvely* as strictly meaning "privately" in the modern liberal sense of the public/private divide; thus the two contracts are assumed to be secretly formed between Dorigen and Arveragus. However, we cannot with confidence know from the tale whether the couple contracted marriage without witnesses, or if the conditions of conduct stipulated in their contract were known only to themselves. The marriage, though "pryvely" agreed to at least by Dorigen, is not necessarily "secret" or "private."

The Middle English *priveli* and the Old French *privément* certainly carry the sense of "secretly, covertly." However, *priveli* also means "intimately," or "carefully, discreetly." When used in reference to architectural spaces, the Middle English *prive* suggests physical seclusion; but it also can convey the sense of one's being "aware, knowing, informed."[20] The Anglo-Norman *privé*, as an adjective, means both "private" and "intimate"; as a noun, it denotes a "close friend, [an] intimate," or in the legal sense, an interested individual who is party to "an action, contract, [or] conveyance."[21] Intimacy, friendliness, discretion, awareness, and contractual consent are not the same as secrecy or privacy. In the *Ménagier de Paris,* a conduct manual for wives written by an anonymous and presumably male author around 1392–94, the husband-narrator urges his wife to maintain the proper distance with respect to different categories of men: "vous devez estre tresamoureuse et tresprivé de vostre mary par dessus toutes autres creatures vivans, moyennement amour-

---

[19] Spearing, for instance, suggests that while Arveragus promises to be a courtly lover, "this situation will be concealed from the outside world" because of his concern for public reputation (*The Franklin's Tale,* 30); Elizabeth Robertson, similarly, argues that the couple agree to "mutuality in private, and . . . subordination in public" ("Marriage, Mutual Consent, and the Affirmation of the Female Subject," 190); and, more recently, Cathy Hume postulates that the two present "divergent behavior in private and public" ("'The name of soveraynetee': The Private and Public Faces of Marriage in *The Franklin's Tale,*" *SP* 105.3 (2008): 284–303 [286]). See also Mary R. Bowman, "'Half as She Were Mad': Dorigen in the Male World of the *Franklin's Tale,*" *ChauR* 27.3 (1993): 239–51 (245–46); Pearsall, *The Canterbury Tales,* 150–51; David Aers, *Chaucer* (Atlantic Highlands, N.J.: Humanities Press International, 1986), 86; Weisl, *Conquering the Reign of Femeny,* 107, 114; Kathryn Jacobs, *Marriage Contracts from Chaucer to the Renaissance Stage* (Gainesville: University Press of Florida, 2001), 53, 57; Lipton, *Affections of the Mind,* 26–28; David Raybin, "'Wommen, of kynde, desiren libertee': Rereading Dorigen, Rereading Marriage," *ChauR* 27.1 (1992): 65–86 (70, 77); Joseph D. Parry, "Dorigen, Narration, and Coming Home in the *Franklin's Tale,*" *ChauR* 30.3 (1996): 262–93 (282); and McGregor, "What of Dorigen?" 371.

[20] *MED,* s.v. "priveli," 1(a), 2(a), and 2(b). And *MED,* s.v. "prive," 1(d) and 2(e).

[21] *Anglo-Norman Dictionary,* s.v. "privé," (a.1), (s.1), and (s.3). See also the etymology of "privy" in *OED.*

euse et privee de voz bons et parfaiz prochains parans charnelz et les charnelz de vostre mary, et tresestrangement privee de tous autres hommes."[22] Eileen Power, in her 1928 translation, renders *privé* into the English "privy," whereas Arthur Goldhammer, in his 1988 translation, opts for the English "private." Both Power's and Goldhammer's translations occlude the sense of intimacy and closeness in the French original. In contrast, Gina L. Greco and Christine M. Rose have recovered and preserved the affective dimensions of the French *privé* in their recent translation: "Your obligation [is] to be especially loving and intimate with your husband above all other living creatures. Be moderately affectionate and close toward your and your husband's nearest blood relatives, but distant from all other men."[23] Given the semantic complexity and range that *privé* encompasses, it is possible to read Dorigen's "pryvely" as not simply denoting her marriage taking place "privately" or "secretly," but her accepting of Arveragus in an intimate fashion while being fully informed. In other words, "pryvely" could also express the state of Dorigen's affection and her legal consent to enter the marriage contract.

Shannon McSheffrey has recently examined the problematic applications of the modern public/private dyad in critical studies of late medieval marriage practices, especially the unqualified use of terms such as "private," "clandestine," "secret," "illicit," and "extra-ecclesiastical."[24] Central to McSheffrey's critique is Georges Duby's problematic appropriation of the liberal public/private divide in the multivolume series *A History of Private Life,* especially in volume 2, *Revelations of the Medieval World.* Duby theorizes that the economic growth of the eleventh to thirteenth centuries led to a greater awareness of personal property and to a more individualistic, introspective existence. The opposition between the public and private hinges on space, and "the zone of private life is apparently that of domestic space, circumscribed by walls," which

---

[22] *Le ménagier de Paris,* ed. Georgine E. Brereton and Janet M. Ferrier (Oxford: Clarendon Press, 1981), 57.

[23] *The Goodman of Paris,* trans. Eileen Power (London: Routledge, 1928), 107. Arthur Goldhammer's translation is in Georges Duby, *A History of Private Life,* vol. 2, *Revelations of the Medieval World,* trans. Arthur Goldhammer, ed. Philippe Ariès and Georges Duby (Cambridge, Mass.: Belknap Press, 1988), 350. See also *The Good Wife's Guide (Le ménagier de Paris): A Medieval Household Book,* trans. and ed. Gina L. Greco and Christine M. Rose (Ithaca: Cornell University Press, 2009), 94.

[24] Shannon McSheffrey, "Place, Space, and Situation: Public and Private in the Making of Marriage in Late-Medieval London," *Speculum* 79.4 (2004): 960–90.

offers "an inner privacy of the self."[25] But Duby's erasure of the affective register of *privé* and his construction of an enclosed inner self, McSheffrey argues, implicitly naturalize and perpetuate the liberal public/private dyad, as formulated by John Locke and later developed into the ideology of separate spheres in the nineteenth century. Despite his admission that the adoption of modern notions of public and private is anachronistic, Duby nonetheless characterizes medieval "private life" as sexual, feminine, domestic, and familial.[26]

The labeling of medieval marriages contracted outside the church as "private," and hence problematic and disreputable, is therefore both inaccurate and misleading. As historians have shown, the model of separate spheres along gender lines cannot accurately account for the complexity of medieval marriage or that of the household. The home of the middle strata, in particular, was a site not only of domesticity but also of manufacture and trade. In addition to the married couple and their children, servants, apprentices, and guests inhabited the *domus,* all working to "consolidate friendship networks, business contacts or the house-

[25] Duby, *A History of Private Life,* 2:xii, 6–7.

[26] See McSheffrey, "Place, Space, and Situation," 960, 989. Scholarship on John Locke's public/private dyad in modern liberalism is a vast field. Some representative works include Hannah Arendt, "The Public and the Private Realm," in *The Human Condition* (Chicago: University of Chicago Press, 1998), 22–78; Daniela Gobetti, *Private and Public: Individuals, Households, and Body Politic in Locke and Hutcheson* (New York: Routledge, 1992); Jean Bethke Elshtain, *Public Man and Private Woman: Women in Social and Political Thought* (Princeton: Princeton University Press, 1981); Michael McKeon, *The Secret History of Domesticity: Public, Private, and the Division of Knowledge* (Baltimore: Johns Hopkins University Press, 2005); Gerald Turkel, *Dividing Public and Private: Law, Politics, and Social Theory* (Westport, Conn.: Praeger Publishers, 1992); *Philosophical Dimensions of Privacy: An Anthology,* ed. Ferdinand David Schoeman (Cambridge: Cambridge University Press, 1984); Lawrence Eliot Klein, "Gender and the Public/Private Distinction in the Eighteenth Century: Some Questions about Evidence and Analytic Procedure," *Eighteenth-Century Studies* 29.1 (1995): 97–109; Mary B. Walsh, "Locke and Feminism on Private and Public Realms of Activities," *Review of Politics* 57.2 (1995): 251–78; Kristin A. Kelly, "Private Family, Private Individual: John Locke's Distinction between Paternal and Political Power," *Social Theory and Practice* 28.3 (2002): 361–80; and Eric R. Claeys, "The Private Society and the Liberal Public Good in John Locke's Thought," *Social Philosophy and Policy* 25.2 (2008): 201–34. For medievalists' critique of the liberal public/private paradigm, see Felicity Riddy, " 'Burgeis' Domesticity in Late-Medieval England," in *Medieval Domesticity: Home, Housing, and Household in Medieval England,* ed. Maryanne Kowaleski and P. J. P. Goldberg (Cambridge: Cambridge University Press, 2008), 14–17; and Riddy, "Looking Closely: Authority and Intimacy in the Late Medieval Urban Home," in *Gendering the Master Narrative: Women and Power in the Middle Ages,* ed. Mary C. Erler and Maryanne Kowaleski (Ithaca: Cornell University Press, 2003), 212–15.

hold's social standing."[27] Never an exclusively private and enclosed space, the household was engaged in a continuous exchange with the outside world: buying and selling goods, hiring labor, receiving visitors, and negotiating hierarchy and authority.[28] Architecturally, medieval houses had thinner walls, and the boundaries between the interior and exterior spaces were more porous than those of their modern counterparts. Instead of a clear separation between the public and private, a sense of a more permeable boundary predominated. Medieval domesticity, Felicity Riddy observes, did not necessarily depend on the paradigm of a private, domestic feminine sphere and a public, external masculine sphere.[29]

While medieval companionate marriage was intimate and personal, it was never a strictly private affair. Publicity, McSheffrey argues, was "situational as well as spatial," and homes also served as the place of the public exchange of marital consent.[30] In the late Middle Ages, marriages contracted at the home of the prospective wife, her parents, employers, relatives, or friends, were not perceived as secret and disreputable but quasi-public and respectable. In fact, court records show that marriages were frequently contracted in a domestic setting, before a few or even no witnesses. In the Canterbury deposition book of 1411–20, thirty-eight of the forty-one marriages contracted by words of present consent took place at home or in some private place. For example, in a 1372 case before the diocese of York, a witness testified that the marriage in dispute was in fact contracted at a home.[31] In this instance, the witness

[27] P. J. P. Goldberg, "The Fashioning of Bourgeois Domesticity in Later Medieval England: A Material Culture Perspective," in *Medieval Domesticity,* 124–44 (136).

[28] See Christopher Dyer, "Public and Private Lives in the Medieval Household," in *Love, Marriage, and Family Ties,* ed. Davis, Müller, and Rees Jones, 237–39 (237–38). On the ambiguous separation between the public and private in medieval households, see Cordelia Beattie and Anna Maslakovic, "Introduction—Locating the Household: Public, Private, and the Social Construction of Gender and Space," in *The Medieval Household in Christian Europe, c. 850–c. 1550: Managing Power, Wealth, and the Body,* ed. Cordelia Beattie, Anna Maslakovic, and Sarah Rees Jones (Turnhout: Brepols, 2003), 1–8 (2); and Isabel Davis, "Unfamiliar Families: Investigating Marriage and the Family in the Past," in *Love, Marriage, and Family Ties,* ed. Davis, Müller, and Rees Jones, 1–13 (2–3).

[29] Riddy, " 'Burgeis' Domesticity," 17. Riddy notes that the concept of *privata* ("private business") did not have a definitive sense of spatial divide; in fact, fourteenth-century "burgeiseries" in London were in the process of defining where the public/private divide would lie (32).

[30] McSheffrey, "Place, Space, and Situation," 986, 971. Other "domestic" spaces that served as the place for marriage formation included taverns and gardens.

[31] "[The witness says that] one year ago on the feast day of the apostles Philip and James just past, he was present in the house of William Burton [*in domo Willelmi de*

served a quasi-public function at a marriage contract initiated within a household. Even an allegedly "secret" marriage could involve more than the couple in question. In 1269, a certain Cecilia "made all the women who were present swear that they would reveal [her marriage] to no one in that year."[32] While Cecilia thus gave herself and her husband some time to secure her father's permission, the marriage itself was not strictly a clandestine affair. And in *The Wife of Bath's Tale,* though the knight marries the old woman "prively" (III.1080), the marriage is not secret because the royal court already knew of the contract between them; in fact, by making public their private agreement in front of the queen, the old woman forces the knight's compliance.

In *The Franklin's Tale,* Dorigen's consenting to the marriage "pryvely" offers no precise indication of where it takes place. Even if the marriage were contracted in a domestic setting (such as Dorigen's household) or in some secluded space, it is not necessarily a secret marriage. The fact of the marriage is public knowledge in the tale; all of Dorigen's friends, as well as Aurelius, who is "hire neighebour" (V.961), know that she and Arveragus are married. Henry Ansgar Kelly, who notes that the marriage was contracted without explicit witnesses, concedes that "presumably they made their marriage public . . . for they lived together publicly as man and wife."[33] Instead of reading Arveragus and Dorigen's marriage and seemingly secret agreement as two separate contracts for the public and private spheres, it might be more useful to view their marriage as a process that moves through "widening circles of publicity rather than from private to public."[34] Where church and state authorities played an active role in matters of gender and sexuality, McSheffrey concludes, private sexual relationships did not exist.

The critique of the liberal public/private dyad present in Duby's

---

Burton], tanner of York, about the third hour past the ninth, when and where John Beke, saddler, sitting down on a bench of that house [*dicte domus*], called in English 'le Sidebynke,' called the said Marjory to him and said to her, 'Sit with me.' Acquiescing in this, she sat down. John said to her, 'Marjory, do you wish to be my wife?' And she replied, 'I will if you wish.'" English translation in Helmholz, *Marriage Litigation in Medieval England,* 28–29. For discussion of marriage litigation in the Ely register, see Sheehan, *Marriage, Family,* 61. For the Canterbury book, see Helmholz, *Marriage Litigation in Medieval England,* 28.

[32] "ipsa Cecilia fecit omnes mulieres affidare que interfuerunt quod in illo anno nulli demonstrarent" (Helmholz, *Marriage Litigation in Medieval England,* 48.) The translation is Helmholz's.

[33] Henry Ansgar Kelly, *Love and Marriage in the Age of Chaucer* (Ithaca: Cornell University Press, 1975), 91.

[34] McSheffrey, "Place, Space, and Situation," 965–66, 968.

study of medieval domesticity and marriage, I argue, could also be extended to our understanding of shame in the Middle Ages. Many readings of *The Franklin's Tale* have applied the modern paradigm of the public and private not only to the formation of Dorigen and Arveragus's marriage but also to the workings of shame in the tale. Joseph D. Parry, for instance, suggests that Arveragus's insistence on "'lordshipe' is for public show, to avoid the shame of his own noble, knightly status," while *pryvely* he and Dorigen enjoy their respective *libertee*.[35] Parry's reading implicitly coordinates a liberal demarcation—one between publicity and privacy—with shame and shamelessness. The deep entrenchment of the Enlightenment spatial model in modern psychology is evident in many contemporary studies of shame. Psychologist Léon Wurmser, for example, postulates that

[t]here is above all an area of inwardness and interior value that should not be violated by any agent from outside or even by other parts of one's personality. If this area of integrity and self-respect is infringed upon, shame and often violent rage ensue. . . . There is an inner limit covering this intimate area that one does not want to show. Yet there is also an outer limit beyond which one should not expand one's power. The inner limit may be called the "boundary of privacy," the outer limit the "boundary of power expansion." . . . Shame guards the separate, private self with its boundaries and prevents intrusion and merger.[36]

Likewise, Carl Schneider contends that the primary function of shame is the protection of the private sphere from public exposure. Privacy is crucial to the development and maintenance of the inner psyche, which Schneider renders in spatial terms: "Each of us needs some time offstage, a private space, before we are ready to go public. Rehearsal is a process which becomes more sophisticated and differentiated as we mature. . . . The sense of shame protects this process"; shame is a protective covering for the embryonic self.[37] Like Duby, who conceives of the private as

---

[35] Parry, "Dorigen, Narration, and Coming Home in the *Franklin's Tale*," 282.

[36] Léon Wurmser, *The Mask of Shame* (Baltimore: Johns Hopkins University Press, 1981), 62–65.

[37] Carl Schneider, "A Mature Sense of Shame," in *The Many Faces of Shame*, ed. Donald L. Nathanson (New York: Guilford Press, 1987), 201; and his *Shame, Exposure, and Privacy* (New York: W. W. Norton, 1977), xv. Other theorists of shame who replicate the liberal public/private divide include Carroll Ellis Izard, *Human Emotions* (New York: Plenum Press, 1977), 400; Francis J. Broucek, *Shame and the Self* (New York: Guilford Press, 1991), 37; and Mario Jacoby, *Shame and the Origins of Self-Esteem: A Jungian Approach* (New York: Routledge, 1994), 21.

"an enclosure, a protected zone, much like a fortress under siege," both Wurmser's and Schneider's theories of shame depend on the liberal dichotomy of the public and private.[38]

One reason critics of *The Franklin's Tale* have neglected shame is that in dividing Dorigen and Arveragus's marriage contract into separate spheres of proper conduct, they impose the liberal public/private dyad on shame as well. Reflecting Wurmser's and Schneider's notion that shame is a shield covering a private, interior essence, Arveragus's sense of shame thus protects his inner self—his *degree,* however defined. Consequently, the sovereignty he demands is understood to be merely the name of authority. Such a reading is premised on the sense of the Middle English *name* as a "label, pretense."[39] But is Arveragus's name of sovereignty a mere appearance? As the tale bears out, his authority is anything but mere appearance. Benjamin Kilborne, in his discussion of the modern experience of shame, suggests that "the dichotomies between public and private spheres of our lives may be said to depend upon culturally shared illusions of mastery, and these, in turn, upon appearance."[40] The equation of Arveragus's name of sovereignty with mere appearance, therefore, indirectly reproduces the modern public/private divide that Kilborne describes.

While the Franklin uses the word *pryvely,* he never uses *apert,* or the more familiar phrase "privé and apert" to convey the sense of "in private and public."[41] It is true that Dorigen *pryvely* agrees to take Arveragus as her husband and lord. However, when Arveragus proposes to obey her will but keep his name of sovereignty, he does not explicitly frame these conditions in terms of *privé* and *apert.* Critics, such as Kittredge, are too quick to accept the Franklin's gloss of Dorigen and Arveragus's marriage and to align "Servant in love" (V.793) with the private and "lord in mariage" (V.793) with the public. Arveragus might never intend to

---

[38] Duby, *A History of Private Life,* 2:6.

[39] *MED,* s.v. "name," 2(c). See Kittredge, "Chaucer's Discussion of Marriage," 30; Aers, *Chaucer, Langland and the Creative Imagination,* 163; and Priscilla Martin, *Chaucer's Women: Nuns, Wives, and Amazons* (London: Macmillan, 1990), 124.

[40] Benjamin Kilborne, *Disappearing Persons: Shame and Appearance* (Albany: State University of New York Press, 2002), 5.

[41] *The Riverside Chaucer* glosses *apert* as: (1) "plain, clear"; and (2) "open, not secret" (1215). In *The Squire's Tale,* when the falcon grants the tercet her love, she stipulates "upon this condicioun, / That everemoore [her] honour and renoun / Were saved, bothe privee and apert" (V.529–31). And in *The Wife of Bath's Tale,* the old woman asserts that a *gentil* man is he "that is moost vertuous always, / Pryvee and apert" (III.1113–14).

demarcate his "name of soveraynetee" into mutually exclusive spheres, obeying Dorigen's will only *in privé* and demanding his sovereignty only *apert*. Their marriage contract remains difficult and messy. If we must characterize Dorigen and Arveragus's marriage agreement in terms of publicity and privacy, it is at best partially private and partially public, mirroring the permeability of the late medieval household and the married estate. Arveragus never ceases to be Dorigen's husband *in privé*. Instead of a dyad, publicity and privacy form a continuum along which the spouses locate and shift the everyday condition of their married life; never is their marriage at either pole of full publicity or privacy. Only then can we begin to understand what happens later in the tale, when Arveragus orders Dorigen to fulfill her pledge to Aurelius but keep it secret, and why she obeys him without protest.

This is not to suggest that there was no sense of the public and private dimensions of shame in the late Middle Ages. On the contrary, husbands, wives, and lovers deliberately allude to and contest the dividing line of the public and private in order to advance their particular ends in love and marriage.[42] If shame turns on what is brought into the

---

[42] Aristotle classifies shame as a species of fear, and it is associated with the masculine public realm. Unmanliness or cowardice is therefore shameful. Likewise, a man feels ashamed before those he holds in high regard. The classical theory of the public nature of shame remained foundational in medieval understandings of shame. See Aristotle, *The Art of Rhetoric,* trans. H. C. Lawson-Gancred (New York: Penguin Books, 1991), 157–58; and Thomas Aquinas, *Commentary on the Nicomachean Ethics,* trans. C. I. Litzinger, O.P., 2 vols. (Chicago: Regnery, 1964). In the religious realm, there was the diligent attendance at mass and the "public" requirement, after Lateran IV, of confession. But increasingly in the late Middle Ages, more personal and "private" modes of acknowledging the shame of sinfulness became available to the laity. Public images and rituals, reconfigured and appropriated by conduct manuals and spiritual guides, became the bases of private devotion taking place in solitary spaces. In secular terms, chivalry and courtly love work in similar ways. Siegfried Christoph has shown that Arthurian heroes require a sense of modest shame in order to develop their personal ethos, and Stephanie Trigg argues that courtly shame is more often a performance of authority than an actual assault on emotions. The shame a lover feels has a public dimension in the poetry and songs that already exist to express his feelings, and in private he trains himself to focus solely on his beloved. This is exactly what Aurelius engages in before he reveals his love to Dorigen (V.943–50). In both spiritual and secular discourses, the ideal homology between public and private modes of shame works to keep it not really shameful but capable of constituting proper identities. See Christoph, "Honor, Shame and Gender," in *Arthurian Romance and Gender,* ed. Friedrich Wolfzettel (Amsterdam: Rodopi, 1995), 29–32; and Trigg, "'Shamed be . . .': Historicizing Shame in Medieval and Early Modern Courtly Ritual," *Exemplaria* 19.1 (2007): 67–89. We can also look at the fabliaux, in which characters often undergo extreme shaming punishments for their pride or sexual misconduct taking place in private. At the same time, many fabliaux also work to deflect public shame in order to preserve order and social relations. See

public, it also turns on what is brought into the private. It may be helpful to conceive of Dorigen and Arveragus's companionate marriage as a lever: shame is the fulcrum on which the public-private continuum pivots. Depending on where the fulcrum is placed, the lever allows for the multiplication of the individual effort exerted to counteract the force of publicity or privacy, gain personal leverage, and achieve social equilibrium. However, in *The Franklin's Tale,* shame does not function as a proper fulcrum. It is rather the constant shift of the pivot of shame and the concomitant destabilization of the public-private continuum that are at work here. The marriage vows between Arveragus and Dorigen do not confidently establish coherent identities, for the conditions of their union are not yet, if at all, fully realized. In fact, the trajectory of the tale brings about a torsion from the conjugal "I do" to the postnuptial "Shame on you"—a movement away from any stable marriage to a conditional married estate whose dynamics are governed by shame.[43]

The Art of Keeping

Although *The Franklin's Tale* opens as a courtly romance, the genre of conduct literature rapidly comes to dominate our understanding of courtliness in it.[44] Conduct manuals, such as the *Ménagier de Paris* and *The Book of the Knyght of the Towre,* were central to the ethos of the middle

---

Sheila J. Nayar, " 'Thou Art Inexcusable': Deflected Disgrace in the Old French Fabliaux," *Exemplaria* 21.1 (2009): 24–42.

[43] I am indebted to Eve Kosofsky Sedgwick's foundational work on J. L. Austin's exemplary performative "I do" and the queer performative "Shame on you." See Sedgwick's "Queer Performativity: Henry James's *The Art of the Novel,*" *GLQ* 1 (1993): 1–16; and her *Touching Feeling: Affect, Pedagogy, Performativity* (Durham: Duke University Press, 2003), 35–66.

[44] See Kathleen Ashley and Robert L. A. Clark, "Medieval Conduct: Texts, Theories, Practices," introduction to *Medieval Conduct,* ed. Kathleen Ashley and Robert L. A. Clark (Minneapolis: University of Minnesota Press, 2001), ix–xx. Middle English romances, Riddy argues, were always already centered on domesticity and the nuclear family. See Felicity Riddy, "Middle English Romance: Family, Marriage, Intimacy," in *The Cambridge Companion to Medieval Romance,* ed. Roberta L. Krueger (Cambridge: Cambridge University Press, 2000), 235–52; Riddy, "Temporary Virginity and the Everyday Body: *Le Bone Florence of Rome* and Bourgeois Self-Making," in *Pulp Fictions of Medieval England: Essays in Popular Romance,* ed. Nicola McDonald (Manchester: Manchester University Press, 2004), 197–216; and D. Vance Smith, *Arts of Possession: The Middle English Household Imaginary* (Minneapolis: University of Minnesota Press, 2003). Caxton, in many of the introductions to his printed works, advocates romances because they are guides to proper conduct. See N. F. Blake, *Caxton's Own Prose* (London: André Deutsch, 1973), 58, 60, 109.

classes.[45] And despite the popularity of the genre with both sexes, women remain its narrative focus. Kathleen Ashley suggests that as an alternative to the emphasis in romance on noble birth as desirable in marriageable daughters or young wives, conduct literature, aiming at bourgeois readers, seeks to redefine women's desirability through their comportment. Specifically, the good wife's conduct carries significant political and socioeconomic valence, for she is responsible for creating domestic harmony through virtues that can also promote the common good. For the middling sorts, the common good begins with the household and the family that resides within it. Female honor, in a household economy that fuses economic and affective functions, is synonymous with bourgeois family honor. A woman's *bonne renomée* therefore affects not only her reputation but her family's social aspirations as well.[46] In *The Book of the Knyght of the Towre,* the father-author delineates three "prisons" that his daughters would face as wives: "The one pryson was loue the other was dred / and the thyrd shame." He also urges them to seek "the grete worship / whiche cometh of good name and Renomme."[47] Companionate marriage, with its ideological aspiration to noble values, is conceived as primarily a *gentil* discipline.

Medieval conduct literature for young girls and wives has as one of its goals the maintenance of conduct conducive to the affective bond promised, whether explicitly or not in conditional contracts, in the formation of companionate marriage. Yet despite the fact that proper con-

---

[45] The late Middle Ages witnessed changes within the traditional upper classes; the gentry, increasingly distinguished from the nobility, converged with the urban elites. See Riddy, "Middle English Romance," 237; Riddy, "Mother Knows Best: Reading Social Chance in a Courtesy Text," *Speculum* 71.1 (1996): 66–86 (67); and Mark Addison Amos, "Violent Hierarchies: Disciplining Women and Merchant Capitalists in *The Book of the Knyght of the Towre,*" in *Caxton's Trace: Studies in the History of English Printing,* ed. William Kuskin (Notre Dame: University of Notre Dame Press, 2006), 69–100 (90–91). The bourgeois-gentry, in search of self-definition and a code of behavior that would legitimize their growing economic and political powers, were busily appropriating modes of noble display. See Mark Addison Amos, " 'For Manners Make Man': Bourdieu, De Certeau, and the Common Appropriation of Noble Manners in the *Book of Courtesy,*" in *Medieval Conduct,* 23–48 (28–29, 46).

[46] See Kathleen Ashley, "The *Miror des bonnes femmes:* Not for Women Only?" in *Medieval Conduct,* 86–105 (100). For the good wife's conduct and the common good in the French tradition, see Carolyn P. Collette, "Chaucer and the French Tradition Revisited: Philippe de Mézières and the Good Wife," in *Medieval Women: Texts and Contexts in Late Medieval Britain: Essays for Felicity Riddy,* ed. Jocelyn Wogan-Browne, Rosalynn Voaden, Arlyn Diamond, Ann Hutchison, Carol M. Meale, and Lesley Johnson (Turnhout: Brepols, 2000), 151–68 (152–54).

[47] *The Book of the Knyght of the Towre,* trans. William Caxton, ed. M. Y. Offord, EETS s.s. 2 (Oxford: Oxford University Press, 1971), 129, 151.

duct was frequently included as a precondition in late medieval marriage negotiations, historically, marriage contracts did not stipulate the regulation of everyday conduct *during* marriage. Helmholz observes that "neither secular nor spiritual contracts made any provision for regulating the conduct of the man and woman during the course of their marriage. . . . This excludes the trendy modern forms: agreement about who will do the dishes, where the couple will live, how long their vacation will be, and so on."[48] Conduct manuals therefore filled the regulatory vacuum left unattended by conditional matrimonial contracts.

But while the *Ménagier* preaches wifely obedience and diligent management of the household, its male author exhibits an open hostility toward the idea of a regulatory contract for daily conduct within companionate marriage. In one exemplary story, a married couple's constant bickering necessitated the intervention of their friends. And "out of pride, the wife would accept no alternative but, on the one hand, that all of her rights be written down, point by point, with all of the obligations she owed her husband, and, on the other hand, that her husband's rights and obligations to her also be clearly listed."[49] Having done so, the wife then carefully guarded her rights and conducted herself according to her charter (*cedule*). One day, when the husband fell into water and sought his wife's assistance, she insisted that she look into her *cedule* first to see what she should do. Since the *cedule* made no particular mention of the current situation, the wife told her husband that she would do nothing and went on her way. Later, the local lord and his retinue passed by the drowning husband and saved his life. When the lord found out what had happened, he had the wife seized and burned to death.

Ostensibly, the *Ménagier* exemplum shows the deadly consequences of wifely disobedience and of a wife's literal reading of a conduct *cedule*.[50] But more crucially, the story suggests that the idea of a contract for regulating daily behavior between spouses is, on the one hand, com-

---

[48] Helmholz, "Marriage Contracts," 269.

[49] Brereton and Ferrier, *Le ménagier de Paris,* 73–74; *The Good Wife's Guide,* trans. and ed. Greco and Rose, 119.

[50] Greco and Rose read the story as demonstrating the dangers of both conduct contracts and a literal reading of them, constructed by the male author as abuses of contract (*The Good Wife's Guide,* 39). See also Roberta L. Krueger, "Identity Begins at Home: Female Conduct and the Failure of Counsel in *Le ménagier de Paris,*" *Essays in Medieval Studies* 22 (2005): 21–39. Krueger argues that the *cedule* "fails to restore harmony and leads instead to the couple's dissolution" (30).

pletely meaningless and impractical because it simply cannot address every possible scenario in the married life. On the other hand, the exemplum does not wholeheartedly dismiss the necessity of a conduct *cedule* in marriage; rather, what it upholds is a more foundational marital contract formed at the outset of marriage that stipulates the wife's complete obedience to her husband's will in all matters big or small. In fact, the existence of a separate contract that governs the everyday might actually work to undermine the husband's authority.[51] An obedient wife presumably needs no other source of guidance than her husband. The *Ménagier* exemplum, by making a violent mockery of the wife's unsophisticated reading skills, implicitly reaffirms the notion that while the wife needs no conduct *cedule,* she does need a conduct manual, like the *Ménagier de Paris,* that is authored and glossed by men.

In *The Franklin's Tale,* matters of conduct are expressed through social deployments of shame and their effects on reputation. When Dorigen takes Arveragus as her husband, she binds herself to a conditional matrimonial contract in which her conduct is measured primarily by her wifely obedience. It may be objected that the opening lines of the tale stress Arveragus's *obeysaunce* (V.739, 749) and not hers. However, when Dorigen subjects herself to "swich lordshipe as men han over hir wyves" (742–43), she in essence neutralizes his claim to obedience by professing her servile humility in return. For her, obedience coordinates with wifely honor and disobedience with wifely shame. As Aurelius demands that Dorigen fulfill her promise, he disingenuously expresses concern for her honor (V.1331). And Arveragus, fearing the loss of his reputation, commands Dorigen to keep her *trouthe* to Aurelius a secret. He further instructs her to mask her shame by making "no contenance of hevynesse" (V.1485), assuming that, as a good wife, Dorigen will align her will with that of her husband.

Dorigen's shame, moreover, serves as the link between Arveragus and Aurelius. The two men, who never meet in person, are connected through a woman, or more specifically, through the shaming of a woman. Dorigen takes on a mediate function in male competition. That is, in light of the constitutive role played by shame in male honor, the traffic in women between the two male characters—Aurelius, who confronts Dorigen, and Arveragus, who commands her—can be read as a wager between two men to see who has the most control over women,

---

[51] Helmholz, "Marriage Contracts," 269.

and who can best tolerate the threat of shame himself, traffic it most successfully, and thereby become the most *gentil*. The topos of the male wager over the obedience of wives is used by the ménagier several times to illustrate the need of wifely submission. In one account, a group of young husbands at Bar-sur-Aube compete to find "the best and most obedient wife, compliant in all things—orders or interdictions, large or small."[52] By releasing Dorigen from her promise, Aurelius shows Arveragus that he, too, can play the game of shame. The husband, by displaying and symbolically sharing his obedient wife, transforms personal marital relation into collective entertainment.

Surprisingly, Arveragus, perhaps the person most concerned with shame in the tale, never uses the word "shame" himself; he refers to his predicament only as his "woe" (V.1484). It is Aurelius who names Arveragus's action as a deliberate choice to suffer "shame" (V.1528). Yet having renamed Arveragus's "woe," Aurelius immediately appropriates Arveragus's term of suffering for himself: "I have wel levere evere to suffre wo" (V.1531). And as a man who refuses to name shame as shame, is Arveragus rather surprised by the outcome, in which Aurelius also shuns the name of shame by relinquishing his claim on Dorigen? After Dorigen's tearful confession of her rash promise, Arveragus nonchalantly asks her: "Is ther oght elles, Dorigen, but this?" (V.1469). Arveragus's attitude suggests that he, with seemingly greater foreknowledge than Dorigen, has always sensed that no harm would result from her blunder. He confidently proclaims, "It may be wel, paraventure, yet to day" (V.1473). Arveragus's sense of confidence also imbues the Franklin, who precludes any objections from his audience that might deem Arveragus a "lewed man" (V.1494) by predicting a happy ending to his tale and by asking his listeners to suspend their judgment: "Herkneth the tale er ye upon hire crie. / She may have bettre fortune than yow semeth; / And whan that ye han herd the tale, demeth" (V.1496–

---

[52] Brereton and Ferrier, *Le ménagier de Paris*, 8; *The Good Wife's Guide*, trans. and ed. Greco and Rose, 130. In the version of the wager found in *The Book of the Knyght of the Towre*, three drapers bet on who has the most obedient wife (36). See Gaston Paris, "Le cycle de la gageure," *Romania* 32 (1903): 481–551; and Roberta L. Krueger, "Double Jeopardy: The Appropriation of Women in Four Old French Romances of the *Cycle de la gageure*," in *Seeking the Woman in Late Medieval and Renaissance Writing: Essays in Feminist Contextual Criticism*, ed. S. Fisher and J. E. Halley (Knoxville: University of Tennessee Press, 1989), 21–50. For the tradition of the wager motif in medieval and early modern drama, see Lynette R. Muir, "The Wager," in *Love and Conflict in Medieval Drama: The Plays and Their Legacy* (Cambridge: Cambridge University Press, 2007), 102–5.

98). Like Arveragus, the Franklin never uses the word "shame" for himself or his family. When he interrupts the Squire, he admits that he would rather his son "lerne gentillesse aright" (V.694) than possessing "twenty pound worth lond" (V.683). The Franklin may very well be ashamed of his son, and he can face his shame only by masking it under an affected modesty topos.

No one—including the Franklin and his immediate audience—seems surprised by the denouement. In the tale, all utterances of shame are not instances of actual shaming, but acts that forecast yet forestall shame. Aquinas states that a man may lack a feeling of shame "because a disgraceful deed is counted as unlikely or readily avoided."[53] In fact, shaming is frequently a preemptive act that prevents the actualization of shame. The threat of shame is like a promise that no one intends to fulfill: an unfinished doing. As Judith Butler points out, a threat "can be derailed, defused, [and] fail to furnish the act that it threatens."[54] Arveragus's silence on and avoidance of the word "shame" are indicative of his immunity to the negative affect; he appears untouched by shame. This is the leverage he wields. Or so it would seem.

When he calmly tells Dorigen to uphold her words, Arveragus insists that "Trouthe is the hyeste thyng that man may kepe" (V.1479). But immediately, Arveragus "with that word" bursts into tears (V.1480). Although he refuses to register shame as shame, his body nonetheless enters a negative state of affection. The Middle English *kepen* evokes the standard formulation of late medieval marriage vows in which prospective spouses promise "to have and to keep (or hold)" each other.[55] Throughout the tale, the Franklin emphasizes the art of keeping, rather than of losing, and he underscores the mandate to "enduren" woes

[53] "quia non apprehendunt turpitudinem ut possibilem sibi vel quasi non facile vitabilem." Thomas Aquinas, *Summa theologicae*, vol. 43, *Temperance*, trans. John Patrick Reid (New York: McGraw-Hill, 1964), 68; English translation on 69.

[54] Judith Butler, *Excitable Speech: A Poetics of the Performative* (New York: Routledge, 1997), 11.

[55] In the fifteenth-century marital litigation of *Brocher vs. Cardif*, the deposition records: "Et tunc ipse Johannes tenens antedictam Johannam per manum dexteram, secundum informacionem eiusdem Johannis Monk primo dixit eidem sic, *I John take the Johan to my weddid wif, the to loue and kepe, and as a man owght to loue his wife, and therto I pliȝt the my trowth.* Et incontinenter prefata Johanna similiter ad informacionem predicti Johannis Monk dixit antenominato Johanni Brocher, *I Johan take the John to my weddid husbond, the to loue and to kepe as a woman ought to do her husband, and therto I pliȝt the my feith*" (London, Guildhall Library, MS 9065, fol. 23r). I would like to thank Shannon McSheffrey for sharing this with me. See also *MED*, s.v. "kepen," 22(a): "To abide by ... follow ... obey ... adhere to"; also 22(b): "To observe ... to honor ... to follow."

(V.1484), "holden" *trouthes* (V.1513), and "saven" promises (V.1478). Yet paradoxically, to keep shame is also to be pierced by it: when Arveragus confesses that he would "wel levere ystiked for to be" (V.1476) than that Dorigen fail in *trouthe,* he foreshadows his own affective rupture. Desperately avoiding shame, Arveragus ends up keeping it as a bodily affection; his confidence, not his shame per se, is the real sham.[56]

The affective strategy at work in *The Franklin's Tale* is thus not so much preemptive as possessive and preservative. If *kepen* evokes the marital vows between Dorigen and Arveragus, it also denotes affairs of the household. In the late Middle Ages, *kepen* can also mean "to take care of (property), look after (goods), manage (affairs), in the sense of 'kepen hous.'"[57] The word's valence with both conjugality and household conduct forcefully ruptures the protective veil of Arveragus's spurious self-possession. His weeping suggests that late medieval ideologies of conduct serve as an affective technology for both husbands and wives, one that allows them to produce and survey one another's affective capacities. As such, conduct manuals are shame scripts that provide a theory of life; shame becomes what Steve Connor calls "a condition of being, a life-form."[58] Despite his weeping, Arveragus remains committed to his earlier advice to Dorigen that she should "lat slepen that is stille" (V.1472).[59] Here his admonishment evokes a different *kepen,* meaning "to preserve (a quality, state, or condition), keep in a state of being, maintain."[60] For Arveragus, the fulcrum of shame must *keep* social equilibrium undisturbed along the public-private continuum.

---

[56] According to the *OED,* "sham" is of obscure origin, and the word first appeared about 1677. While the *OED* concedes it is "not impossible" that the word is connected to "shame" in northern dialects, the alleged origin is ultimately inconclusive and unsatisfactory.

[57] *MED,* s.v. "kepen," 15(b).

[58] Steve Connor, "The Shame of Being a Man," *Textual Practice* 15.2 (2001): 211–30 (212).

[59] Arveragus's words are proverbial. See Bartlett J. Whiting and Helen W. Whiting, *Proverbs, Sentences, and Proverbial Phrases from English Writing Mainly Before 1500* (Cambridge, Mass.: Harvard University Press, 1968). The medieval proverb, in its basic form, states that "[i]t is not good to wake a sleeping hound (cat)" (296). Arveragus's juxtaposition of Dorigen and the embedded but suppressed animal in the original proverb suggests an uncanny parallel between them. Riddy, commenting on the association between conduct literature and folkloric wisdom, notes the prevalence of "the old-fashioned, home-spun, experiential advice" in the conduct genre ("Mother Knows Best," 78).

[60] *MED,* s.v., "kepen," 13(a). See also *OED,* s.v. "keep," 24: "preserve, maintain, retain, or cause to continue, in some specified condition, state place, position, action, or course . . . in suspense."

Yet immediately after displaying his "glad chiere, in freendly wyse" (V.1467), he threatens Dorigen with death if she ever exposes her, his, or their shame: "I yow forbede, up peyne of deeth" (V.1481). Arveragus's sudden change in affective registers parallels a common rhetorical strategy found in conduct manuals, in which a man's counsel to an errant woman is followed by a threat of violence toward her. In *The Book of the Knyght of the Towre,* the narrator speaks of a wife who had shamed her husband publicly. When the wife refused the husband's command to "be stylle and lowe," he "whiche was wrothe smote her with his fyste to the erthe. And smote her with his foote on the vysage so that he brake her nose."[61] Threat, Greco and Rose point out, is one of the many rhetorical devices—such as exempla, cajolements, and anecdotes—used by the husband to tame his young wife.[62] Although Arveragus stops short of actual violence toward Dorigen, the intended effects of his words are the same.

Keeping shame, in the sense of "keeping watch for" shame, dovetails with the act of "preserving without losing" honor.[63] The affective keeping of sociality, found in conduct literature, can be understood as what Michael Hardt terms affective labor, laboring practices that "produce collective subjectivities, produce sociality, and ultimately produce society itself."[64] Companionate marriage necessitates not simply physical labor that maintains the household, but affective labor that shapes the conjugal subjects within it. Shame, through strenuous keeping, saturates and characterizes the conjugal activities of Arveragus and Dorigen. In the absence of any visible production of material values, their married life is purely a labor of affects. While the Franklin offers no details on the daily workings of their household, he meticulously notes the "joye and blisse" that fill their home (V.1099). And the affective labor of Dorigen and Arveragus resonates with the social life of the bourgeois-gentry, who, being most dependent on movable wealth (in the forms of knowledge, skills, clientele, or expertise), eagerly embrace the rhetoric of love, the construct of conjugal companionship, and the ideal of emotional marital bonds. For these dealers in immaterial capital, affect becomes another form of mobile wealth that they could produce and

[61] *The Book of the Knyght of the Towre,* ed. Offord, 35.

[62] *The Good Wife's Guide,* trans. and ed. Greco and Rose, 13.

[63] *MED,* s.v. "kepen," 12(a): "To preserve (sth.) without loss or change"; and 17(a): "To keep watch for (sb. a hunted animal)."

[64] Michael Hardt, "Affective Labor," *Boundary 2* 26.2 (1999): 89–100 (89).

circulate as the necessary condition for proper conduct and the basis of *gentil* sociality. As the husband in the *Ménagier* reminds his wife, she must be well versed in "bien," "l'onneur," and "service."[65]

Howell argues that for the late medieval middling sorts with movable wealth, companionate marriage answered the question of what sealed their marriage.[66] I would like to suggest that Eva Illouz's recent discussion of the rise of emotional capitalism in modernity is useful in examining the affective workings of companionate marriage in premodern figurations of capitalism. For Illouz, modernity does not necessarily consolidate the Lockean public/private divide but instead brings about the dissolution of the separate spheres. The result is the public performance of the private self, particularly within economic and political realms: "The language of emotionality and that of productive efficiency were becoming increasingly intertwined, each shaping the other."[67] The existence of departments of human resources in the work place, Illouz suggests, demonstrates the interest of capitalism in managing workers' emotions and relations, as well as the assumption that displays of proper emotional attachments would translate into career advancement. The confluence of emotional behavior and economic behavior is especially true for the middle classes. Twentieth-century advice literature, in fact, provides a common vocabulary for the bourgeois self as it negotiates among social relations. If modern psychology has enabled the language and practice of emotional capitalism, then medieval conduct literature, I contend, serves a similar function for the middling sorts. That is, marriage and household conduct are economic behaviors inseparable from affects.

The conditionality of the shame contract between Dorigen and Arveragus, its "if . . . then . . ." temporal logic, implies an affective economy—a traffic in shame—that creates symbolic capital. As Mark Amos observes, being a member of the bourgeois-gentry required both substantial financial investment and a less visible investment in reputation.[68] And it was the men of the middling elites who were most concerned with their *gentil* name. Late medieval conduct literature, os-

---

[65] Brereton and Ferrier, *Le ménagier de Paris,* 2; *The Good Wife's Guide,* trans. and ed. Greco and Rose, 50. For movable wealth, see Howell, "The Properties of Marriage," 30.

[66] Ibid., 52.

[67] Eva Illouz, *Cold Intimacies: The Making of Emotional Capitalism* (Cambridge: Polity Press, 2007), 14.

[68] Amos, "For Manners Make Man," 26.

tensibly meant for women, ideologically catered to men. When describing Arveragus's marital bliss, the Franklin asks: "Who koude telle, but he hadde wedded be, / The joye, the ese, and the prosperitee / That is bitwixe an housbonde and his wyf?" (V.803–5). The male authorial voice of conduct literature, likewise, addresses not only his wife and other women, but other men as well. Forever forward-looking, the old husband in the *Ménagier* is conscious of his young wife's next husband, whom he desires to impress with his wife-training skills. Aurelius himself is a prospective husband who, through his brother, Arveragus and the Clerk of Orleans, participates in the disciplining of Dorigen. It is he whom Arveragus seeks to impress, under the pretense of upholding Dorigen's *trouthe.* What the conduct genre advocates is the art of keeping both personal and collective investment in the affects conducive to companionate marriage and to household management.

A man is never home alone with his wife. There are always other men present, ghostly or bodily, in his household. Arveragus, when he returns to Dorigen, "is comen hoom, and othere worthy men" (V.1089). The marriage between a husband and a wife is never simply a marriage of two. The haunting presence of other men within the nuclear household exposes the porosity of the boundaries between the public and private in late medieval conjugality. As the tale unfolds, the rigidly demarcated identities of servant-lord and lady-wife are impossible to achieve because the public is already embedded within the private, and vice versa. In the *Ménagier* exemplum of the disobedient wife and her conduct *cedule,* the couple initially draws their friends into their squabbles, and the husband later requires the intervention of his lord to save him and to punish his wife.

In spite of the ambiguous borders of the public and private within the married estate, the male authors of conduct literature cling to the Aristotelian theory of a public masculine shame that must be avoided at all cost. When the ménagier instructs his wife on proper devotion to the husband, he articulates what appears to be a model of separate gender spheres: "I entreat you to see that he has clean linen, for that is your domain, while the concerns and troubles of men are those outside affairs that they must handle."[69] The father-narrator of *The Book of the Knyght of the Towre* argues that it is "to a woman gret shame and vylonye to stryue ageynst her husbond be it wrong or right / And in especial to

---

[69] *The Good Wife's Guide,* trans. and ed. Greco and Rose, 138.

before the peple," and that she should divulge her thoughts only when she and her husband are "pryuely and allone."[70] But within the multifunctional medieval household that does not offer clear lines of publicity and privacy, where and when could the couple be truly alone and in private?[71]

I am less interested in the historical inaccuracy of the public/private divide put forth by the male authors of conduct books and more in the fact that theirs is a masculine articulation of gender asymmetries within marriage. Such asymmetries are rooted in the problematic concept of companionate marriage, which conceives of the wife as simultaneously her husband's inferior and his equal partner. The *Ménagier* desires a wife who contractually agrees to her subordination and to her function as the husband's lover, helper, and mate. This incoherence is already evident in Hugh of Saint Victor, who wrote that

since [woman] was given as a companion (*socia*), not a servant or a mistress, she was to be produced not from the highest or from the lowest part but from the middle. . . . She was made from the middle, that she might be proved to have been made for equality of association. Yet in a certain way she was inferior to him, in that she was made from him, so that she might always look to him as to her beginning and cleaving to him indivisibly might not separate herself from that association which ought to have been established reciprocally.[72]

The Franklin's application of the friendship model to Dorigen and Arveragus's marriage is flawed and misleading. The male-friendship paradigm appropriated by medieval theologians for companionate marriage is based on an inherent inequality between friends. For Aristotle, love in friendship is excellent because it is proportionate to one's worth, and "those who are unequal will become friends because they will thus be

[70] *The Book of the Knyght of the Towre*, ed. Offord, 35, 94.
[71] Even the bedchamber is not exactly a private space in the modern sense, for it is where the couple sleeps and where the wife gives birth, engages in devotional practices, and entertains female friends and relations. See Goldberg, "The Fashioning of Bourgeois Domesticity." For the bedchamber as a site of marriage formation, see Helmholz, *Marriage Litigation in Medieval England,* 29; and McSheffrey, "Place, Space, and Situation," 977–78.
[72] Hugh of Saint Victor, *On the Sacraments of the Christina Faith (De sacramentis),* trans. Roy J. Deferrari (Cambridge, Mass: Medieval Academy of America, 1951), 329. Although writing in the twelfth century, Hugh was responsible for setting a particular tone on the sacramentalization of marriage that incorporated the paradoxical differential in power between spouses. For a full discussion of the unequal equality in companionate marriage, see Kooper, "Loving the Unequal Equal," 44–56.

made equal"; Aquinas similarly argues that "when people love one another according to their worth, even those who are of unequal condition can be friends because they are made equal in this way."[73] Arveragus and Dorigen never use any terms of friendship to describe their marriage; that gloss belongs to the Franklin.

Although the Franklin professes that "Love wol not been contreyned by maistrye" (V.764), Arveragus and Dorigen's nuptial agreement already serves as a condition that constrains their love and enforces the inequality between them. Arveragus's concern for public shame marks not simply his narcissistic class aspiration and his attachment to social appearance; it exposes the very ambiguities of companionate marriage—ambiguities stemming from the difficulties of conduct ideals—troubling the period. As articulated in conduct manuals, female honor exists always under threat of slippage into shameful behavior. Ironically, the male authors of conduct literature also bring the threat of female shame dangerously close to masculinity by situating it within the married estate and the conjoined household. Companionate marriage therefore leads to greater risk of mutual contamination of shame for both spouses. What Arveragus discovers is that he cannot keep his honor without keeping Dorigen's shame at the same time.

Wifely Devotee: A Future Dead Person

Once she recognizes the reality of her dilemma, Dorigen identifies her shame primarily in bodily and sexual terms: "yet have I levere to lese / My lif than of my body to have a shame" (V.1360–61). Shame, for medieval women, is an affective experience inseparable from sexuality. Valerie Allen has argued that while shame is "a more widely diffused emotion in medieval male experience, in woman it signifies more purely, retaining its essential mark of sexual lack and exposure."[74] The only viable alternative to losing her wifely chastity and to facing shame, Dorigen believes, is suicide. Feminist readings of Dorigen have tended to

---

[73] Both quotes are from Aquinas, *Commentary*, 740, 743. See Aelred of Rievaulx's discussion of marriage and friendship in *De spirituali amicitia* (c. 1160); English translation in Mary Eugenia Laker, *Spiritual Friendship* (Kalamazoo: Cistercian Publications, 1974). Aelred discusses the friendship model of marriage in which "a superior must be on a plane of equality with an inferior" (115).

[74] Valerie Allen, "Waxing Red: Shame and the Body, Shame and the Soul," in *The Representation of Women's Emotions in Medieval and Early Modern Culture*, ed. Lisa Perfetti (Gainesville: University Press of Florida, 2005), 191–210 (194).

stress the apparent gender difference in *The Franklin's Tale*. Central to this critical tradition of gender difference is the idea of a unique and locatable female voice, subjectivity, or self-expression that seeks to be heard. And closely related to the concern with women's representation is the project of reclaiming female literary characters from the margin. This impulse to uncover the feminine is premised, in some readings, on a model of separate spheres of gender existence and of women's exclusion from the male public space.[75] But rather than seeing Dorigen as consciously carving out an essentialized, biologically based female identity in her lament, it might be more useful to interpret her litany as an instance of what Eve Sedgwick calls a "minoritizing" act.[76] The critical task is not necessarily the unearthing of an identity formed around a timeless essence but the teasing out of how one identity, as opposed to another, assumes a determinative importance in the lives of a minority.

Countering a universalizing discourse of male-inflected shame that regulates the daily life of the household, Dorigen seeks to align affectively her identity with a small, distinct minority of dead women in whose lives the threat of shame remains a persistent structural difficulty. To support her theory, she has no trouble locating virtuous female predecessors: "Hath ther nat many a noble wyf er this, / And many a mayde, yslayn hirself, allas, / Rather than with hir body doon trespas?" (V.1364–66). Through her litany, Dorigen attempts to contain her shame by mapping and inserting herself into a genealogy of exemplary women, thereby constructing her wifely identity within an imagined community across time—a kind of female *translatio studii* instantiated by shame. Critics have traditionally read Dorigen's lament as a rhetorical set-piece and as Chaucer's reworking of his source, Jerome's *Against Jovinian*.[77] But it might also be useful to look to late medieval conduct

---

[75] See Bowman, "'Half as She Were Mad,'" 240; Jacob, "The Marriage Contract," 135; Ann Thompson Lee, "'A Woman True and Fair': Chaucer's Portrayal of Dorigen in the *Franklin's Tale*," *ChauR* 19.2 (1984): 169–78 (169); Parry, "Dorigen, Narration, and Coming Home in the *Franklin's Tale*," 262–93; and Raybin, "Rereading Dorigen," 65–86.

[76] Eve Kosofsky Sedgwick, *Epistemology of the Closet* (Berkeley and Los Angeles: University of California Press, 1990), 1.

[77] As a rhetorical set-piece, see James Sledd, "Dorigen's Complaint," *MP* 45.1 (1947): 36–45; and Pearsall, *Canterbury Tales*, 155. As Chaucer's reworking of his source, Jerome's *Against Jovinian*, see James I. Wimsatt, "The Wife of Bath, the Franklin, and the Rhetoric of St. Jerome," in *A Wyf Ther Was: Essays in Honour of Paule Mertens-Fonck*, ed. Juliette Dor (Liège: Université de Liège, 1992), 275–81; and Warren S. Smith, "Dorigen's Lament and the Resolution of the *Franklin's Tale*," *ChauR* 36.4 (2002): 374–90 (375).

and devotional literature contemporaneous with Chaucer for a different interpretive lens.[78] What is significant here is the didacticism of both genres that seeks to produce and regulate gender roles within the household. The necessary inculcation of proper wifely conduct is not lost on Dorigen; in fact, the pursuit of self-betterment through exemplarity is the central work of her complaint. Immediately after Arveragus's departure for England and prior to her encounter with Aurelius, Dorigen already patterns her behavior after noble wives: "For his absence wepeth she and siketh, / As doon thise noble wyves whan hem liketh" (V.817–18). While Dorigen is of nobler birth than Arveragus, her affective imitation of aristocratic feminine ideals is more "middling" in nature; the Franklin therefore heeds the *Ménagier*'s warning that a wife's superior lineage does not excuse her disdainful behavior. But whereas the old husband in the *Ménagier* takes it upon himself to train his young wife in the hope that she could one day instruct herself, Dorigen quickly becomes her own teacher, household manager, and husband who discipline a misbehaving wife: herself.

Dorigen's impulse toward rhetorical listing mimics the citations of female exempla found in late medieval conduct literature, such as Griselda and Lucretia in the *Ménagier de Paris* or *The Book of the Knyght of the Towre;* her litany is as much an actual speech as a virtual reading of an internalized text of conduct. She cites stories "as the bookes telle" (V.1378), expresses the view that "it is ful greet pitee / To reden" of the death of Cedasus's daughter (V.1428–29), and speaks about how "of Laodomya is writen thus" (V.1446). Beyond recitation, Dorigen also strategically performs her complaint as she weeps, wails, and swoons, "With face pale and with ful sorweful cheere" (V.1353). In so doing, Dorigen engages in what Mark Amsler identifies as affective literacy, a practice of reading in which one develops "emotional, somatic, [and] activity-based relationships with texts."[79] An affective phenomenon, reading (silently or out loud) can be viewed as a form of speech act precisely because of the involvement of the body in an active relationship with the text. At the nexus of reading and utterance, the body

---

[78] See also Mary J. Carruthers, "The *Gentillesse* of Chaucer's Franklin," *Criticism* 23.4 (1981): 283–300; and Hume, "The Private and Public Faces of Marriage in *The Franklin's Tale*," 284–303. Neither Carruthers nor Hume analyzes Dorigen's litany in the context of conduct literature.

[79] Mark Amsler, "Affective Literacy: Gestures of Reading in the Later Middle Ages," *Essays in Medieval Studies* 18 (2001): 83–110 (83).

performs the text, for "there is what is said, and then there is a kind of saying that the bodily 'instrument' of the utterance performs."[80] While he primarily analyzes real or imagined reading scenes in which the materiality of texts is central to the reader's affective experience, Amsler asserts that affective literacy need not necessarily involve bodily contact with a physical book or manuscript. Margery Kempe, for example, is a self-proclaimed illiterate who recites her narrative out loud, weeps, faints, and moans; yet hers is a text that she remembers and not the one she touches or sees. For Amsler, Kempe's affective literacy is "located *in* her desire to textualize her spiritual story and *on* her own responsive body, rather than in her physical contact with texts themselves."[81] In *The Franklin's Tale,* it is unclear if Dorigen is physically holding a text as she laments. Dorigen's affective literacy is therefore akin to that of Margery Kempe; lacking any direct contact with a conduct book, Dorigen still marks its presence in her desire and on her body. Her litany is an act of affective labor that consciously engages with its own performative potential. Shame, as is voiced through her, becomes tangible and emotive.

In crucial ways, Dorigen's affective engagement with shame resembles the instructions for proper confession found in late medieval conduct manuals. In *The Book of the Knyght of the Towre,* Mary Magdalene's shameful weeping for her sins is praised as the exemplary attitude for the confessant, for "the shame that men haue to telle [sins] / is to them a grete part of their indulgence & god whiche seeth the humylyte & the repentaunce moueth hym self to pyte & eslargyssheth his misericorde."[82] Dorigen's affective state also mirrors closely the kind of "private" devotional program prescribed for laywomen, such as the one found in the 1408 *journée chrétienne* written by an anonymous clerical author and included in Bibliothèque de l'Arsenal MS 2176.[83] Here the male narrator

---

[80] Butler, *Excitable Speech,* 11.

[81] Amsler, "Affective Literacy," 95–96.

[82] *The Book of the Knyght of the Towre,* ed. Offord, 132.

[83] *La journée chrétienne* ("The Christian Day") is a term coined by Geneviève Hasenohr to describe a particular genre of conduct texts composed in French and Italian from the mid-thirteenth century to the early sixteenth century that seeks to project a quasi-monastic form of religious devotion onto the daily activities of the laity, especially those of lay wives. See Hasenohr, "La vie quotidienne de la femme vue par l'Eglise: L'enseignement des 'journées chrétiennes' de la fin du Moyen-Age," in *Frau und spätmittelalterlicher Alltag* (Vienna: Verlag der Österreichischen Akademie der Wissenschaften, 1988), 19–101; Robert L. A. Clark, "Constructing the Female Subject in Late Medieval Devotion," in *Medieval Conduct,* 160–82; and Glenn Burger, "Labouring to Make the Good Wife

urges a female devotee, at midnight after a day of labor, to seek an isolated place where she may display signs of her sweet devotion to God, such as "bitter cries, plaints, and laments interrupted by many humble sighs, prostrations, and kneeling, eyes moist, face changing and damp, now red, now pale."[84] Private devotion—including prayer, confession, and reading—transforms the solitary devotee into both actor and audience in the sight of God. Dorigen, trapped at home and confiding her dilemma in no one (V.1351), creates a self-imposed isolation and affective program not dissimilar to the devotional solitude of the female devotee advocated in the 1408 *journée*.[85]

There are of course important differences between Dorigen's litany and medieval devotional literature; her litany is not an instance of lay piety in the strict sense. While Dorigen is busily constructing her sense of self and its place within an imagined community through affective performance, there is neither a Christian God nor Christ the spiritual spouse to whom she prays. Yet I contend that Dorigen's lament is not only a readerly but also a devotional engagement. The real object of her secular devotion, in fact, is shame itself, not Fortune. Hers is not time sanctified but time ashamed. In her affective engagement with shame are techniques of lay devotion—isolation, recitation, and affection—that she deploys in order to make sense of her predicament. Even pagan wives depicted in conduct books sometimes behave uncannily like pious Christian women. Lucretia, in the *Ménagier de Paris,* is pictured as sitting "within the innermost chambers of her house . . . alone and apart . . .

Good in the *journées chrétiennes* and *Le ménagier de Paris,*" *Florilegium* 23.1 (2006): 19–40. For books of hours, see *Time Sanctified: The Book of Hours in Medieval Art and Life,* ed. Roger S. Wieck (New York: George Braziller, 1988).

[84] "les ameres clameurs, plainctes et complainctes entrerompuez par fors souspirs, les prostracions et agenoillemens d'umilité, les yeux moulliez, la face muante ou suante, maintenant rouge, maintenant pale." French in Hasenohr, "La vie quotidienne," 44–45; English translation in Clark, "Constructing the Female Subject in Late Medieval Devotion," 175–76.

[85] In the *Ménagier de Paris,* the young wife is urged to select a private and solitary place within the church; and in the evening at home, she is advised to withdraw herself "from all worldly thoughts, and find a private, solitary place and remain there . . . thinking only of hearing Mass early the next morning" (*The Good Wife's Guide,* trans. and ed. Greco and Rose, 60). Often the only place of real or imagined privacy available to the good wife is her bedchamber, which becomes sanctified through private devotion. See Diana Webb, "Domestic Space and Devotion in the Middle Ages," in *Defining the Holy: Sacred Space in Medieval and Early Modern Europe,* ed. Andrew Spicer and Sarah Hamilton (Burlington, Vt.: Ashgate, 2005), 27–47.

holding her book devoutly and with bowed head saying her hours humbly and piously."[86] If the *journées chrétiennes* foreground the superiority of the good wife's immaterial labor, Dorigen's litany, devoid of an explicitly Christian framework, emphasizes affective labor—one that is ethical if not spiritual in nature—as the work par excellence of the good wife. Not a narrative defect, the pagan setting of the *Tale* has the powerful effect of accentuating the affective nature of companionate marriage, in which shame and honor are forms of cultural capital that facilitate particular social ends. *The Franklin's Tale* is an instance of the bourgeois devotion if not to God then to an emerging affect-based economy.

The public performance of private suffering, Illouz suggests, is key to the therapeutic work of self-realization and social recognition in emotional capitalism.[87] Dorigen's litany, though performed in solitude, is not exactly a "private" or personal act. Rather, she is manipulating shame as a fulcrum to pivot the public-private continuum in ways that would grant her personal leverage and counteract the force of male surveillance of female conduct. That is, Dorigen is actively invoking noble women's avoidance of shame in solitude in order that her sense of honor be "publicly" demonstrated and acknowledged. Devotional performance, Jessica Brantley observes, is "an individual and private activity that nonetheless draws upon communal and public ones."[88] Although personal acts of piety might be performed in solitary spaces, they are rooted in the traditional prestige associated with collective devotion practiced within monastic communities. To engage in private devotion is to seek membership in the community of the faithful. Lay devotional programs, produced by the clergy for the middling sorts, are simultaneously universal and individual, public and private.[89] The good wife's spiritual labor, like her secular work, accrues social capital in the forms

---

[86] *The Good Wife's Guide,* trans. and ed. Greco and Rose, 90. Medieval conduct books often cite both Christian and pagan women as exempla. The *Miror des bonnes femmes,* for example, includes Dido and Lucrece; and Philippe de Mézières, in his *Livre de mariage,* links Griselda to classical virtuous women. And in *The Book of the Knyght of the Towre,* the narrator wishes to "speke of the good wydowes ladyes of Rome / the whiche whan as they held them clenly in theyr wydowhede they were worshipfully crowned in signe and token of chastyte" (148).

[87] Illouz, *Cold Intimacies,* 4.

[88] Jessica Brantley, *Reading in the Wilderness: Private Devotion and Public Performance in Late Medieval England* (Chicago: University of Chicago Press, 2007), 15.

[89] See also Clark, "Constructing the Female Subject in Late Medieval Devotion," 166–67. For the public and private functions of books of hours, see Lawrence R. Poos, "Social History and the Book of Hours," in Wieck, *Time Sanctified,* 33–38.

of honor, piety, and domesticity. She therefore equals or even excels virgins and the female religious, women who traditionally live apart from the lay household. This leveling of the prestige associated with maidens and wives in private devotion may explain why Dorigen includes both categories of women in her litany. In addition to the fifty maidens of Lacedomye (V.1379–85), she also praises Teuta's "wyfly chastitee" (V.1453) and Artemesie's "parfit wyfhood" (V.1451).

As the *Tale* progresses, Dorigen undergoes a rapid change in her role from that of a courtly heroine to a domestic wife. Aurelius initially calls her his "sovereyn lady deere" (V.1070) or "madame" (V.967); after he releases her from her vow, however, he calls her a "wife" for the first time (V.1539). By then, Dorigen's transformation through shame is complete, and "hoom unto hir housbonde is she fare" (V.1546). Not quite a minoritized female suicide, Dorigen instead assumes the universalized role of an obedient wife, an elevated figure within conduct literature: this is her shameful becoming. For Aurelius, she is "the treweste and the beste wyf" (V.1539), a characterization that alludes to her marital pledge (V.758). Therefore, Dorigen does seem to fulfill her part of the matrimonial contract; at least that much appears to be the case for the men involved. Moving from praise to lecture, Aurelius immediately turns her into an exemplum of wifehood: "But every wyf be war of hir biheeste! / On Dorigen remembreth, atte leeste" (V.1541–42). While Aurelius is the alleged speaker, the Franklin, as the narrator, could also be interjecting his own voice here. It is therefore possible to hear, through the layered male voices, the Franklin representing himself as a writer of conduct books that instruct all wives and, implicitly, their husbands.

In foregrounding Dorigen's "verray feere" (V.1347) that triggers her affective engagement with shame, the Franklin alludes to the Aristotelian conception of shame as a species of fear; specifically, shame is the fear of ill repute. The strong affinity between shame and fear demonstrates the capacity of shame for binding with other affects and forming what Silvan Tomkins calls "affect-shame binds." Indeed, all affects can form complexes among and beyond themselves, creating a "great variety of admixtures of affect with cognitive, behavioral, and event references."[90] Because many affects are socialized through techniques of

---

[90] Silvan Tomkins, *Affect, Imagery, Consciousness,* vol. 3 (New York: Springer, 1963), 51.

shaming, a diverse range of situations could activate affects that are then bound to shame and impressed on memory; an individual's experience and behavior are mediated through the hybridized effects of these affect formations. One can thus imagine an assemblage of shame-binds at work in *The Franklin's Tale*—shame-*fere,* shame-*pite,* shame-*trouthe,* shame-*routhe,* shame-*gentillesse*—that incorporates not only other affects but also ideals and conditions of *gentil* conduct. Within Dorigen's litany, the ability of shame to mutate and adhere is manifest in Dorigen's capacity to attach herself, at least performatively and mimetically, to exemplary female suicides, and to create such affective identity-binds, or masks, as Dorigen-Lucretia, Dorigen-Teuta, and Dorigen-Penelope. This is one effect of exemplarity: (re)citation ending in adhesion. But in a moment of sudden illumination, Dorigen ironically gestures at the potential absurdity of her attempts at affective binding. The possibilities for her list of exempla, she realizes, are theoretically ad infinitum: "Mo than a thousand stories, *as I gesse,* / Koude I now telle as touchynge this mateere" (V.1412–13, my emphasis). As Tomkins remarks, "The number of different complex assemblies of affects and perceived causes and consequences is without limit."[91] In the midst of weeping and swooning, Dorigen nevertheless catches herself.

Underlying Dorigen's performative litany is the logic of conditionality that keeps circling back not to the marital vow "I do" but to the performative "Shame on you." It might be more precise to label Dorigen's complaint as a conditional speech act in which, according to Eve Sweetser, "the speaker presents the performance of a speech act as taking place in the conditional mental space established by the protasis [the *if*-clause]."[92] Each exemplary female suicide on Dorigen's list represents a possible model of conduct for her to emulate; each woman's history becomes a mental space that she imagines herself occupying. In drawing up a series of conditionals and analogies between herself and the exempla, Dorigen inadvertently establishes a "remote past" of virtuous wives and a "remote future" of herself as a possible suicide, both of which elide the shameful crisis in the present that she, in suspense, is afraid to confront.

In contrast to Arveragus, who is unable to name his shame, Dorigen

[91] Ibid., 50.

[92] Eve Sweetser, "Mental Spaces and the Grammar of Conditional Constructions," in *Spaces, Worlds, and Grammar,* ed. Gilles Fauconnier and Eve Sweetser (Chicago: University of Chicago Press, 1996), 318–33 (327).

deliberately invokes shame in order to defer its actualization. She desperately drags the past into the present in order to forestall any concrete experience of shame while seeking to identify with "a set of social coordinates that [exceed] her own historical moment" and constructing herself as a "future dead person" who appears destined to join the pantheon of virtuous women.[93] But her litany creates only a suspensive future in which she exists only as a potential female suicide. The spectral effect of shame on Dorigen, which disrupts any linear teleology, can be understood in terms of Pierre Bourdieu's notion of emotion as "a (hallucinatory) 'presenting' of the impending future, which . . . leads a person to live a still suspended future as already present, or even already past, and therefore necessary and inevitable—'I'm a dead man,' 'I'm done for.'"[94] But Dorigen's difficulty lies in the fact that, as long as she continues to lament, she is not yet done for by anything or anyone. Like Arveragus, who dances around shame, Dorigen too cannot bring herself to do or say, "Now, I kill myself." She can offer only scripted reruns of "Years ago, such and such women killed themselves." But in so doing, Dorigen locks herself within a temporal nowhere, tiptoeing around other people's death wishes without an unequivocal course of action or guidance. Her quasi-conduct book, her litany, teeters on the verge of collapse. Not yet dead, Dorigen is imminently dying.

At the *Tale*'s most precarious moments, shame remains iterable but never fully realizable as productive of a stable identity for Dorigen— either a female suicide or a good wife. Toward the end of her litany, Dorigen evokes the pagan wife Bilyea (V.1455), who, according to Jerome, is famed for being tolerant of her husband's bad breath.[95] The apparent incoherence in Dorigen's complaint is more than an unconscious slip on her part from serious moralizing to comic posturing. From its start, the catalogue of exemplary women has presented problematic models of identification for Dorigen, who will never be a Lucretia or a Teuta. In her minoritizing act, Dorigen presumes the existence of a discernible, essential, and emulable identity to which she has access. But as Butler has shown, gender is a performance, a "copy of a copy," and

[93] Elizabeth Freeman, "Packing History, Count(er)ing Generations," *NLH* 31 (2000): 727–44 (728). I borrow the term "future dead person" from Carla Freccero; see Freccero, Carolyn Dinshaw, Lee Edelman, et al., "Theorizing Queer Temporalities: A Roundtable Discussion," *GLQ* 13.2–3 (2007): 177–95 (184).

[94] Pierre Bourdieu, *The Logic of Practice,* trans. Richard Nice (Stanford: Stanford University Press, 1990), 292 n. 2.

[95] *Sources and Analogues of the Canterbury Tales,* ed. Robert M. Correale and Mary Hamel, vol. 1 (Rochester: Brewer, 2002), 62–63.

the faith in a natural origin is only a normalizing myth.[96] Dorigen's collection of clichés therefore enacts a similar clash of exemplary discourses and captivity to the dissonant platitudes that plague the conduct genre. Instead of her imposition of the same interpretation on all exempla, Dorigen's relationship to her litany is marked by a persistent incoherence. Like the disobedient and ill-fated wife in the *Ménagier* who cannot find an exact conduct prescription in her *cedule* that addresses her current predicament, Dorigen cannot be minoritized because there is not a single, simple, or coherent minority identity available to her. By the time she invokes Bilyea, there has been a movement definitively away from female martyrdom to the household and good wifely conduct.

Shame Management

Jennifer C. Manion suggests that it is "the way in which an ashamed person manages her shame that establishes its usefulness in any particular situation."[97] One does not know precisely which *trouthe* Dorigen is upholding when she sets out to meet Aurelius in the garden. Is it the marriage vow that she has made to Arveragus (V.759)? Or her playful promise to Aurelius (V.998)? Or both? Regardless of her motives, Dorigen ends up becoming an exemplary wife who has successfully managed her body and avoided public shame. But what do *treweste* and *beste* mean? Are they the universal answers to the difficulty of *si bene facias?* Or are they just as murky to define?[98]

Aurelius's characterization of Dorigen as the *trewest wyf* resonates with Arveragus's admonishment to her that "*Trouthe* is the hyeste thyng that *man* may kepe" (V.1479, my emphasis), thereby linking directly the

[96] Judith Butler, *Gender Trouble: Feminism and the Subversion of Identity* (New York: Routledge, 1999), 41.

[97] Jennifer C. Manion, "Girls Blush, Sometimes: Gender, Moral Agency, and the Problem of Shame," *Hypatia* 18.3 (2003): 21–41 (35).

[98] The Middle English *trouthe* encompasses a complex range of meanings that do not neatly sort into categories of public and private. See Richard Firth Green, *A Crisis of Truth: Literature and Law in Ricardian England* (Philadelphia: University of Pennsylvania Press, 1999). *Trouthe* can assume four main areas of meaning: legally, as "a promise, a pledge of loyalty"; ethically, as "honor, integrity"; theologically, as "divine righteousness" or "absolute truth"; and intellectually, as "correspondence, exactitude" (9). *Trouthe* thus refers, on the one hand, to the condition of agreements between people, and, on the other hand, to absolute divine truths independent of social relations. Like shame, *trouthe* straddles the nebulous boundaries between public socialization and private individuation.

idea of *trouthe* to male honor.[99] However, the fundamental problem in the *Tale*—one of body and identity—is that Dorigen, in her initial self-representation and conduct, is not a man. What Arveragus demands of her is an impossibility. When she agrees to (or obeys?) Arveragus's request, "half as she were mad" (V.1511), Dorigen is acting neither as a chaste wife/suicide nor as an obedient wife. As the *Tale* torques from the "I do" to the "Shame on you," the only identity option left to her is uncannily a queer one. Dorigen, consciously or not, assumes the identity of a "manly wife," for she manages to keep the highest thing that a *man* may keep.

Some readers have argued that Arveragus and Dorigen's marriage betrays a conflict between courtly love, in which women dominate, and secular marriage, in which men exert control.[100] However, the *Tale's* insistent engagement with shame via technologies of conduct works to destabilize power differentials along dichotomies of men/women or the public/private. The good wife or the good husband's shame is simultaneously *privé* and *apert*. Conduct literature, ostensibly affirming a rigid gender division of spiritual and secular labors, paradoxically works to undo gender and blur social hierarchy. In *The Book of the Knyght of the Towre*, a good lady possesses as much renown as a good knight: "For men ought to doo and bere as moche worship and honour to a good

---

[99] While the Middle English *man* may also denote a person of either sex, there is an inherent gendered asymmetry. See Steven F. Kruger, *The Spectral Jew: Conversion and Embodiment in Medieval Europe* (Minneapolis: University of Minnesota Press, 2006); Carol J. Clover, "Regardless of Sex: Men, Women, and Power in Early Northern Europe," in *Studying Medieval Women: Sex, Gender, Feminism,* ed. Nancy F. Partner (Cambridge, Mass.: Medieval Academy of America, 1993), 61–85 (75); and Thomas Laqueur, *Making Sex: Body and Gender from the Greeks to Freud* (Cambridge, Mass.: Harvard University Press, 1990). The ancient one-sex model, "the idea that male and female are not opposed states of being but rather different points of development on a single continuum of sex" (Kruger, *Spectral Jew,* 74), posits men as the privileged state of being (Clover, "Regardless of Sex," 75) and women as "inverted, and less perfect men" (Laqueur, *Making Sex,* 26). Some medieval writers, such as Petrarch and Christine de Pizan, reimagine the feminine in positive and useful ways by associating it with (quasi-)manliness. Petrarch's Griselda has a "virilis senilisque animus" ("mature, manly spirit") (Correale and Hamel, eds., *Sources and Analogues,* 1:115), and Christine states that a female household manager should have the "courage d'omme" ("heart of a man"); see *Le livre des trois vertus,* ed. Charity Cannon Willard and Eric Hicks (Paris: Honoré Champion, 1989), 150. As Kellie Robertson points out in *The Laborer's Two Bodies: Literary and Legal Productions in Britain, 1350–1500* (New York: Palgrave, 2006), estate management was one avenue for gentry housewives to become "like a man" (129).

[100] See, for instance, Hansen, *Chaucer and the Fictions of Gender,* 267–92; and Mark N. Taylor, "Servant and Lord / Lady and Wife: The *Franklin's Tale* and Traditions of Courtly and Conjugal Love," *ChauR* 32.1 (1997): 64–81.

lady or damoysel as to a good knyght or squyer."[101] The good wife, who successfully manages her shame, is not inferior to the good husband. For Dorigen, what shame makes possible is a queer minority identity, a female masculinity that exposes masculinity as primarily a prosthetic, "technical special effect."[102] And if she is capable of detaching gender roles from biology—teacher, household manager, and husband—and appropriating them in her litany, there is potentially no limit to how far or how dangerously she could continue *in pley*.

The Franklin himself exemplifies the gender and class hybridity of the middling sorts. As historians and Chaucer critics have repeatedly pointed out, in the late Middle Ages, franklins occupied an ambiguous social category without a clearly delineated identity or status. While they were, by definition, freeholders without military or labor obligations, franklins were not strictly a single identifiable professional category.[103] Chaucer's Franklin, nominally a small landholder, is also a lay bureaucrat who has held positions as diverse as a "knyght of the shire" (I.356), a "shirreve" (I.359), and a "contour" (I.359). And though he professes to be "a burel man" (V.716), the Franklin is nevertheless much concerned with the symbolic capital of *gentillesse*. More important, the Franklin presents himself as the nexus linking the aristocracy and the middling group. Serving the interests and tastes of the two strata, he welds the genres of romance and conduct literature together and seeks to please both the nobility, exemplified by the Knight, and the bourgeoisie, represented by the Merchant, among his fellow pilgrims. Chaucer characterizes the Franklin as a great "housholdere" (I.339) who enjoys "pleyn delit" (I.337) and whose home is never without "mete and drynke" (I.345). Household consumption, as traffic in material goods, necessarily blurs the distinction between the public and private. Moreover, avid consumption presupposes diligent management; under emotional capitalism, the manager is a rational, responsible being who regulates labor relations and affections in order to maximize productivity.[104] The Franklin's success in life is a testament to his effective man-

---

[101] *The Book of the Knight of the Towre,* ed. Offord, 152.

[102] Judith Halberstam, *Female Masculinity* (Durham: Duke University Press, 1998), 3.

[103] For a summary of the critical debate over the Franklin's status and ambiguity, see Elizabeth Mauer Sembler, "A Frankeleyn Was in His Compaignye," in *Chaucer's Pilgrims: An Historical Guide to the Pilgrims in the Canterbury Tales,* ed. Laura C. Lambdin and Robert T. Lambdin (Westport, Conn.: Greenwood Press, 1996), 135–44.

[104] Illouz, *Cold Intimacies,* 11–12.

agement of household conduct and affects—except possibly those of his son. Oddly enough, he is a good wife.

As he attempts to finish his tale, the Franklin asks: "Which was the mooste fre, as thynketh yow?" (V.1622). In other words, if the tale's various virtualizations and actualizations of shame serve only to uphold proper conduct, who emerges as the most "gentil"? Glenn Burger suggests that "[a]ccess to the cultural capital of gentility allows subjects to be 'fre' in the old sense of giving of their worth . . . while manifesting freedom in the modern sense of individual autonomy."[105] But realizable freedom also depends on the realizability of shame; both are social attention signals that can be bought, sold, and exchanged within affective economy. Shame, blurring categorical differences of gender, class, and publicity, exerts its force on affective modes of sociality and invades the seemingly private, autonomous, and *fre* selves constructed by the tale. If shame is a potential to be trafficked, so too can *gentillesse* circulate from Arveragus, to Aurelius, to the Clerk of Orleans, and implicitly to the Franklin. By invoking the unfinished doing of shame as social leverage, the Franklin becomes a trafficker in affective potential, a shame manager who surveys and preserves the condition of household order and the fiction of companionate conduct.

---

[105] Burger, *Chaucer's Queer Nation,* 114–15.

Selling Alys: Reading (with) the Wife of Bath

Roger A. Ladd
University of North Carolina at Pembroke

HERE IS NO REAL QUESTION that consensus over Geoffrey Chaucer's Wife of Bath continues to elude critics; even attempts to challenge the ongoing critical conflict directly, such as H. Marshall Leicester Jr.'s assertion that "of course there is no Wife of Bath,"[1] have not really led to any resolution. Because of the *Prologue* and *Tale*'s complex intersection of class, gender, and rhetoric, there also remains substantial critical anxiety over this material: as Lee Patterson puts it, "[T]ell me what you think of the Wife of Bath, runs the implicit formula, and I'll tell you what I think of you."[2] This sense of critical risk deepens when addressing the Wife's economic identity, when one encounters the initial reaction to Mary Carruthers' now-influential article "The Wife of Bath and the Painting of Lions." For her trouble in sorting out a reasonable economic context for a wife in Bath involved in the cloth trade, Robert Jordan in one letter to *PMLA* pats her on the head and suggests that Carruthers does not understand poetics, and James Wimsatt in another suggests that she is "seeking answers to questions that are beside the point."[3] Certainly that was the 1970s, and critical interests (and accept-

---

[1] H. Marshall Leicester Jr., "Of a Fire in the Dark: Public and Private Feminism in the *Wife of Bath's Tale*," *Women's Studies* 11 (1984): 175 (157–78); most influentially quoted by Elaine Tuttle Hansen, *Chaucer and the Fictions of Gender* (Berkeley and Los Angeles: University of California Press, 1992), 35.

[2] Lee Patterson, *Putting the Wife in Her Place: The William Matthews Lectures, 1995* (London: Birkbeck College, 1995), 1.

[3] Mary Carruthers, "The Wife of Bath and the Painting of Lions," *PMLA* 94 (1979): 209–22; reprinted in and cited from *Feminist Readings in Middle English Literature: The Wife of Bath and All Her Sect,* ed. Leslie Johnson and Ruth Evans (New York: Routledge, 1994), 21–51. Jordan's letter appears on pages 950–51, and Wimsatt's on 951–52 of *PMLA* 94; I quote from 951. Carruthers presents a spirited rejoinder on 952–53. Whether or not anyone might now disagree with Carruthers's overall conclusions, this exchange reveals methodological tensions that persist in Chaucer studies. Carruthers

able gender dynamics) have changed, but there remain tensions between multiple and largely incompatible strands of Wife of Bath criticism. We examine her and her textuality from a variety of overlapping perspectives, including her subjectivity as a wife or widow, her feminist and/or antifeminist hermeneutics, her role as either a positive or negative pseudofeminine mouthpiece for a male author, her use or misuse of sources, her "glosing," and so on.

While several studies have focused on socioeconomic issues concerning Alys,[4] including Carruthers's assessment of the cloth trade in Bath and discussions of her dower economics by such luminaries as D. W. Robertson Jr. and Lee Patterson, recent scholarship makes it increasingly worth our while both to gender the Wife's estate status and "estate" her gender status specifically in terms of her textuality. As Jeanie Grant Moore points out in a discussion of the Wife's widowhood, no one ever thinks of Alys as the "Weaver of Bath."[5] We ignore the Wife's gender at our peril (and only rarely do),[6] but if we read Alys in the London context of the poet, her estate status as a clothier, thin as it is, invokes an area of late fourteenth-century textuality that is becoming much better understood: the complex textual and material nexus of the guild classes, London scribes, and London poets, including Chaucer or

---

herself pursues this tension in the afterword to the article's 1994 reprint (37–42). She notes that "this essay struck a raw nerve among Chaucerians" (37), and argues that "the impulse to shut the Wife up comes from readers, whom she variously frightens, repels and attracts, as we variously respond to her power" (42).

[4] Critical practice differs on whether to follow line 320 of *The Wife of Bath's Prologue*, which names her "Alys," or line 804, which names her "Alisoun." I adopt the name used first, which has the advantage of avoiding any confusion with Alys's "gossib," also named "Alisoun" (lines 529–30). Geoffrey Chaucer, *The Wife of Bath*, ed. Peter G. Beidler, Case Studies in Contemporary Criticism (Boston: Bedford/St. Martin's, 1996). Material from *The Wife of Bath's Prologue* and *Tale* will be taken from Beidler's edition, which is more recent than *The Riverside Chaucer;* the latter will be used for all other Chaucer citations: Geoffrey Chaucer, *The Riverside Chaucer,* gen. ed. Larry D. Benson (Boston: Houghton Mifflin, 1987). Beidler's edition does not prefix line numbers with a fragment number except in his presentation of the Wife's *General Prologue* portrait, but his line numbers generally correspond with those of Fragment III or Group D of Benson's edition. All citations of verse will be by line number.

[5] Jeanie Grant Moore, "(Re)Creations of a Single Woman: Discursive Realms of the Wife of Bath," in *The Single Woman in Medieval and Early Modern England: Her Life and Representation,* ed. Lauren Amtower and Dorothea Kehler (Tempe: Arizona Center for Medieval and Renaissance Studies, 2003), 133–46 (133).

[6] For a helpful overview of contrasting feminist approaches to Alys and her *Prologue* and *Tale,* see Jennifer L. Martin, "The *Crossing* of the Wife of Bath," in *The Canterbury Tales Revisited: 21st Century Interpretations,* ed. Kathleen A. Bishop (Newcastle upon Tyne: Cambridge Scholars Publishing, 2008), 60–74.

John Gower. *The Wife of Bath's Prologue* and *Tale* reveal the extent to which Chaucer's blurring of the Wife's economic and textual identities participates in a larger analysis of mercantile identity, and thus engages with the discursive communities of London poets and guilds that shared a common scribal community. More specifically, the complexity of Alys's responses to both her sources and the varying discourses from which she is constituted reflects only in part her fictive gender; beyond her function as a male poet's representation of a "wife," Alys in her highly mixed textuality participates in what I have elsewhere seen as an available form of guild-class resistance to antimercantile satire, one that Chaucer critiques through his mercantile characters' inability (or unwillingness) to comprehend complex discourse.[7] By displacing this "mercantile" textuality in a somewhat altered form onto a figure much more subtly mercantile than the examples I have previously discussed, Chaucer is able to present his reader with a more biting satire of that textuality.

The Wife's Economic Context, or, Getting Alys to London

Before looking at how the Wife's *Prologue* and *Tale* enable Chaucer to develop his ongoing analysis of the nature of satire, however, it is important to address what we do know about Alys's economic identity and estate position and ultimately justify reading her in a London context. While Chaucer generously informs us about the character's personal life, most notably her five marriages and her friendship with her namesake "gossib" (529), he dedicates only a few lines directly to her economic activities. We do know from the *General Prologue* portrait that she lived "beside Bathe" (I.445), and that "of clooth-making she hadde swich an haunt, / She passed hem of Ypres and of Gaunt" (I.447–48). She is clearly depicted with a certain village sort of wealth from the beginning, with her "ten pound" coverchiefs (I.454) and pilgrimages to Jerusalem, Rome, Santiago de Compostela, and Cologne. Her own *Prologue* adds the details that she has acquired her early husbands' "lond and . . . tresoor" (III.204), that she owned at least one sheep, Wilkyn (432), that her fourth husband had reason to travel a hundred miles to London for

---

[7] For the larger context of antimercantile satire, see Roger A. Ladd, *Antimercantilism in Late Medieval English Literature* (New York: Palgrave, 2010); on Chaucer's mercantile characters' lack of comprehension, see Roger A. Ladd, "The Mercantile (Mis)Reader in *The Canterbury Tales*," *SP* 99 (2002): 17–32. The current essay is an extension of this previous work on merchants and Chaucer's satire.

a whole season (550), that her household was large enough to employ Jankyn as a clerk (595), and that later, as her husband, Jankyn could afford the apparently quite large "book of wikked wives" (685).[8] She makes one reference to "spinning" (401), which comes across as more figural than literal, listed along with deceit and weeping as inherent skills of women (401–2).[9] She also describes herself as "faire and *riche* and yong and wel bigon" (606, emphasis added), though given that she describes herself as "yong" at the tender age of forty, all four terms might require a certain skepticism.

Mary Carruthers was the first scholar to address these material details in any depth, and she largely reinforces Alys's connection with Bath.[10] Carruthers argues that "clooth-making" denotes Alys as an entrepreneurial clothier, rather than as an artisanal weaver.[11] Carruthers's interpretation of these lines would make Alys "engaged in the most lucrative trade possible,"[12] from "the richest of provinces";[13] even while married, such a wife might have had independent business interests, and would

[8] On the availability of such manuscripts, see Ralph Hanna III and Traugott Lawler, ed., *Jankyn's Book of Wikked Wyves,* vol. 1: *The Primary Texts* (Athens: University of Georgia Press, 1997), 2–8.

[9] See Heather Hill-Vásquez, "Chaucer's Wife of Bath, Hoccleve's Arguing Women, and Lydgate's Hertford Wives: Lay Interpretation and the Figure of the Spinning Woman in Late Medieval England," *Florilegium* 23.2 (2006): 269–95.

[10] Economic historian E. M. Carus-Wilson does refer to Alys in passing as Chaucer's "west-country clothier, that redoubtable goodwife living near Bath," in her "Trends in the Export of English Woollens in the Fourteenth Century," *Economic History Review* n.s. 3.2 (1950): 177 (162–79). D. W. Robertson Jr. points out this reference in his " 'And For My Land Thus Hastow Mordred Me?': Land Tenure, the Cloth Industry, and the Wife of Bath," *ChauR* 14.4 (1980): 403–20 (418 n. 20).

[11] Carruthers, "The Wife of Bath and the Painting of Lions," 22–23; 43 n. 8. One can see in great detail the sort of arrangement an extraordinarily successful clothier might employ a century and a half later in a passage in Thomas Deloney's late sixteenth-century *Iacke of Newberie,* in which the title character inherits from his wife (a widow) a house with roughly a thousand workers: in his house "there stood two hundred Loomes full strong," with two hundred boys "making quils," a hundred women "carding hard with ioyfull cheere," two hundred maidens who "in that place all day did spin," one hundred and fifty children "in poore array / . . . picking wool," fifty shearmen, eighty rowers, forty dyers, and twenty fullers. The household also employs a butcher, brewer, baker, five cooks, and six "scullian boyes." Deloney describes the economy of a later century than Chaucer, and probably exaggerates for effect, but Newbury (in Berkshire) is only fifty miles or so from Bath (in Somerset), and even if we doubt Deloney's numbers, he shows the variety of related trades upon which a preindustrial clothier might call. Thomas Deloney, *Iacke of Newberie,* in *The Works of Thomas Deloney,* ed. Francis Oscar Mann (Oxford: Clarendon Press, 1912), 1–68 (20–21).

[12] Carruthers, "The Wife of Bath and the Painting of Lions," 22.

[13] Ibid., 23.

certainly have been responsible for her husband's local business interests when he traveled.[14] In contrast, this material occupies only two lines of *The General Prologue*, and Chaucer invested far more energy in the depiction of Alys's marital arrangements than in her other business arrangements. Carruthers makes a good case for Alys's identity as a clothier in the context of Bath, but the Wife is described as such very much in passing.

While the most memorable aspects of Alys's marriages concern sex and violence, her marital history also has an economic component through her apparent inheritance of her early husbands' wealth, and subsequent sharing of that wealth with Jankyn. D. W. Robertson Jr. reinforces Carruthers's focus on Bath and Somerset when he argues on the basis of her land transactions that the Wife must have been "a bondwoman," which he sees as fitting her iconography.[15] As he considers likely village and rural holdings in Bath, and observes the character of the cloth trade in the region, he concludes the Wife's pattern of land inheritance to be rural.[16] This firm connection to a particular provincial location starts to dissolve, however, when Lee Patterson digs deeper, arguing that "the more one knows about medieval property law, the more puzzling do the Wife's allusions become."[17] Questioning Robertson's certainty, Patterson concludes that "this tale of possessive individualism is told with such frugality of circumstantial detail that the historical investigator is thwarted at every turn, especially since in some

[14] Ibid., 23, 26. On the Wife's economic independence, see Patterson, *Putting the Wife in Her Place*, 25, 29. Brian Gastle presents an extended analysis of Alys as a *femme sole* in his "*Femme sole* and Mercantile Writing in Late Medieval England," Ph.D. diss., (University of Delaware, 1998), 116–35.

[15] Robertson argues that according to late feudal land-tenure law, "land could not be devised or willed to someone else," with "exceptions in burgage tenure in some towns . . . and among villeins on some manors" (404). In the case of burgage tenure, he argues, widows in some boroughs could inherit "tenements, shops, and manufacturing facilities," while rural unfree widows "often entered the holdings of their deceased husbands, sometimes even alienating them on their own behalf after they had remarried" (406). "And For My Land," 403–6.

[16] Ibid., 410. Robertson also suggests that her wealth was a more likely attraction for her earlier husbands than her sexuality. He even shares an example of a thoroughly remarkable bondwoman of the fifteenth century, Margery Haynes, whose holdings included several mills and a considerable household ("And For My Land," 411–13).

[17] He points out, for example, that Robertson's unfree husband-to-wife land inheritance pattern was not typical in the fourteenth century. He also asks, "[H]ow . . . could she have had five marriages without her feudal lord taking an interest in any of them?" Patterson, *Putting the Wife in Her Place*, 23–27 (27).

cases what she tells us will not compute with any of the possible arrangements for marital property available at the time."[18] Where Chaucer's presentation of Alys's profession was merely thin, his presentation of her real estate holdings is deeply ambiguous, or even contradictory—while it feels thicker than the other economic material, it never resolves into an unequivocal impression of her economic identity. It is therefore important not to fixate too much on a context around Bath, both because that context "will not compute," and because when she is read in a London context (see below), her economic and contextual details connect more effectively to the larger satire of her characterization.

What does emerge from our attempts to place Alys's social and economic identity into a firm context is a sense of implicit, rather than explicit, identity—we can tease these details into conformity with the social reality of the period, as both Carruthers and Robertson do, but not in a stable sense, because of the ambiguities Patterson recognizes. The similar dynamic at work in another area of Alys's social identity, that of her "array" (338), suggests that this represents a consistent approach on Chaucer's part. Interpreting Alys's clothes, Laura F. Hodges applies a depth of contextual information to nearly every detail in the *General Prologue* portrait, and ultimately sees Alys as using her professional expertise to present herself, a reading that reinforces Alys's social status as a wealthy clothier.[19] These details also start to connect Alys to London, in that it is the London silkwomen whom Hodges can present

[18] Indeed, where Robertson saw indications in the property exchanges that Alys would have been a bondwoman, Patterson sees her as a *femme sole*. Patterson, *Putting the Wife in Her Place*, 25–29.

[19] Dividing the many details of Alys's wardrobe into two costumes, one for church and another for travel, Hodges attests to the overall expense of the former costume. She notes that this outfit with its elaborate headdress both reinforces satiric stereotypes of women's array, and "demonstrates [Alys's] knowledge of fine quality in fabric and familiarity with special weaving techniques" (363). Similarly, the details of her travel costume, with its "foot-mantel" (I.472), wimple, and big hat, "proclaim her cosmopolitan traveling experience and, thus, her economic status, and possibly even her civic and martial responsibilities" (367). Laura F. Hodges, "The Wife of Bath's Costumes: Reading the Subtexts," *ChauR* 27.4 (1993): 359–76 (363–67). See also her *Chaucer and Costume: The Secular Pilgrims in the General Prologue* (Cambridge: D. S. Brewer, 2000), 161–86. Peter G. Beidler adds to our understanding of the travel outfit by determining just what a "foot-mantel" is, and explaining that this "set of loose leggings" would have very sensibly protected the Wife's expensive clothing from the inevitable filth of medieval travel. "Chaucer's Wife of Bath's 'Foot-Mantel' and her 'Hipes Large,'" *ChauR* 34.4 (2000): 388–97 (389). Beidler's demonstration of a foot-mantel while standing on a table remains a memorable Kalamazoo moment, which he recalls in the headnote to the reprint of this article in Peter G. Beidler, *Chaucer's Canterbury Comedies: Origins and Originality* (Seattle: Coffeetown Press, 2010), 91–104.

as a context for Alys's clothes.[20] The costume material is not quite as murky as Alys's real-estate transactions or her cloth business, in the sense that it receives more sustained description in *The General Prologue*, and in that it links directly to the antifeminist material that so dominates *The Wife's Prologue*.[21] However, that antifeminist angle reveals a key similarity here between the portraits of the Wife and the Merchant in *The General Prologue*. I have argued elsewhere that the deliberate ambiguity of the Merchant's portrait allows potential readers to support *both* anti- and pro-mercantile readings of the Merchant,[22] and Chaucer employs the same "both-and" method here. On the one hand, Hodges primarily emphasizes the social identity suggested by the Wife's clothing; on the other hand, Elaine Whitaker demonstrates the possibility for a morally condemnatory reading of the Wife's coverchiefs as "accessories of the devil."[23] While I prefer the more contextual to the more symbolic reading, what matters is the similarity here to how Chaucer handles the Merchant in *The General Prologue*—a reader expecting traditional estates satire of either the Merchant or the Wife will (like Whitaker) find textual support for those readings, but a reader also has the possibility of seeing those details more innocently (like Hodges), as a faithful description of the guild classes' deliberate and careful self-fashioning through appearances.[24]

What makes this ambiguity between descriptive and satiric details more than just a Chaucerian idiosyncrasy is the extent to which, like the ambiguity of the Merchant's portrait, it reflects a set of larger social

[20] Hodges, "The Wife of Bath's Costumes," 369 n. 6.

[21] See also Thomas Jay Garbáty, "Chaucer's Weaving Wife," *Journal of American Folklore* 81.322 (1968): 342–46 (343–44). Garbáty's suggestion that Alisoun's weaving reflects a "traditional connection of the bawd with the cloth trade" (345) is suggestive, but as he himself acknowledges, ultimately unprovable: "[T]he questions tease, but can never be answered" (346).

[22] Ladd, *Antimercantilism*, 79–86.

[23] Elaine E. Whitaker, "Chaucer's Wife of Bath and Her Ten Pound Coverchiefs," *Publications of the Arkansas Philological Society* 15 (1989): 27 (26–36).

[24] Ladd, *Antimercantilism*, 80–81. For a slightly different perspective on the role of critical expectations in the interpretive process, see Stanley E. Fish, "Interpreting the *Variorum*," *Critical Inquiry* 2.3 (1976): 465–85 (467–68). I cannot quite go all the way down the rabbit hole with Fish, but his description of how different readers can find valid textual support for incompatible readings is quite apt to *The General Prologue*, and Chaucer in general. A more recent exploration of this literary principle in terms of "inferencing" is Helen Barr's "Religious Practice in Chaucer's *Prioress's Tale:* Rabbit and/or Duck?" *SAC* 32 (2010): 39–65; Barr argues that "in reading the lines of the verbal text of *The Prioress's Tale*, the duck of orthodoxy or the rabbit of heterodoxy are both present, depending on the interpretive presuppositions of the reader" (39).

concerns over the social type represented by each pilgrim, Merchant or Wife. We will have an easier time connecting such social concerns to the type represented by Alys, however, if we stop looking for them in Bath. Barbara A. Hanawalt demonstrates the complexity of the social type of the London wife in her recent work on wives in the late medieval economy; she points out that "few women became entrepreneurs. Necessary as female labor was, it had less of an economic impact on London's capital formation than the money and property that passed through women in the form of inheritance, dowry, dower, and their role in the consumer economy."[25] Aside from its London context, this description of economically active wives more aptly fits Alys than any of the economic identities above, which creates an apparent paradox: Alys might be a wife *of Bath,* but the ambiguities of her representation reflect social concerns about the guild-class wives *of London.* Our developing understanding of a specifically London context for women's involvement in the economy is essential for our understanding of Alys's economic identity, precisely because she is *not* from London. Her economic activities are apt to be read entirely differently, depending on whether one understands them in a London or Somerset context. In her village "beside Bathe," she represents a purely local economic prominence, one that supports Chaucer's characterization of her as a narrator and sets the terms for her complex economic relationships with her husbands. Read in a London context, however, in a poem by a London native written for an audience more directly familiar with the women of the guild classes,[26] Alys's vague business affairs will inevitably blur with those of women much closer to home. This allows Chaucer his characteristic ambivalence, familiar from his satire of the estate of merchants— since Alys is not from London, she can satirize women like the London silkwomen without doing so inescapably and thus provoking resistance to his satire.[27] This move is similar to the Merchant's namelessness in

---

[25] Barbara A. Hanawalt, *The Wealth of Wives: Women, Law, and Economy in Late Medieval London* (Oxford: Oxford University Press, 2007), 160. She goes on to outline the many forms of unpaid labor that women contributed to their families as economic units (161), and to highlight the activities of those few women who did go into business on their own.

[26] A prime example of such women would be the silkwomen, who typically both married and worked with mercers; see Anne F. Sutton, *The Mercery of London: Trade, Goods, and People, 1130–1578* (Burlington, Vt.: Ashgate, 2005), 116.

[27] This notion of Alys's characterization as integral to a process of deferral is not unique to this analysis; Theresa Tinkle argues that Chaucer uses his characterization of Alys to insulate himself from her challenges to textual authority: "This chameleon-like persona functions as the poet's protective disguise, allowing him to engage the heated

The General Prologue, substituting a geographical misdirection for the anonymity of a character type to combine with thick descriptive detail.[28]

Silkwomen are not the only women in medieval London who would have been brought to mind by Chaucer's depiction of Alys the clothier, but for several reasons they are worth a closer look, not least because we know enough about them to make comparison possible. The silkwomen of London were not clothiers as such, but, like Alys, they were involved in the cloth trade: they made "silk thread and ribbon,"[29] and also small accessories and piece goods that might then be sold in mercers' (often their husbands') shops.[30] They also lacked their own guild,[31] a point they would have in common with a rural clothier like Alys. And as manufacturers of expensive clothing accessories, and as a group with a well-known and intimate connection with the mercers responsible for selling high-end luxury fabrics, they would have been strongly associated with exactly the sort of clothing opulence described in the Wife's portrait in *The General Prologue.* For that matter, the mercers, who sold the silkwomen's piece goods and other textile luxuries, were long associated with those coverchiefs that are so central to Alys's self-presentation.[32] The silkwomen could also be conduits of wealth through marriage, albeit not necessarily in the manner described by *The Wife of Bath's Prologue.* Anne F. Sutton observes that "some [mercer] dynasties ran in the female line," and she names several mercers who left their holdings to their daughters' husbands.[33] Silkwomen would also have been quite familiar to Londoners doing business in the Mercery, because although their silk work might be something done behind closed doors,

---

controversies circulating in his culture while distancing himself from 'Alison's' subversive challenges to traditional authority." "Contested Authority: Jerome and the Wife of Bath on 1 Timothy 2," *ChauR* 44.3 (2010): 284 (268–93).

[28] Ladd, *Antimercantilism,* 85.

[29] Hanawalt, *Wealth of Wives,* 150.

[30] Sutton, *Mercery of London,* 9.

[31] Hanawalt, *Wealth of Wives,* 39.

[32] "Cuevrechiés a dames" are included in the inventory of the speaker of the c. 1300 French poem *Dit du mercier,* and in John Gower's *Mirour de l'omme* mercers also sell "courchiefs." "Le 'Dit du mercier,'" ed. Philippe Ménarde, in *Mélanges de langue et de littérature du Moyen Âge et de la Renaissance offerts à Jean Frappier, professeur à la Sorbonne, par ses collègues, ses élèves et ses amis* (Geneva: Droz, 1970), 2:797–810; line 48; John Gower, *The Complete Works of John Gower,* ed. G. C. Macaulay, 4 vols. (Oxford: Clarendon Press, 1899–1902), 1:1–334; line 25291. On the ubiquity of coverchiefs as mercery, see also Roger A. Ladd, "The London Mercers' Company, London Textual Culture, and John Gower's *Mirour de l'omme,*" *Medieval Clothing and Textiles* 6 (2010): 129, 142–45 (127–50).

[33] Sutton, *Mercery of London,* 193.

a silkwoman married to a mercer would have "managed the shop [when her husband was away], bought raw materials and marketed on her own behalf or on her husband's, made the goods, trained the apprentices and children, and over[seen] employees."[34] The silkwomen could also become more publicly visible, which is a major reason for considering them here: in 1368, they petitioned the mayor to do something about the Lucchese merchant Nicholas Sardouche, who had cornered the market in silk. Although Sardouche was subsequently arrested, he ultimately bought a royal pardon; he was killed by a mercer in a brawl not long afterward.[35] Given that books, like mercery, represented elite merchandise, Chaucer's readers and the mercers' customers would presumably have overlapped to some extent. Taste and other factors would determine whether one bought books, mercery, or both, but only those who could afford either would have such a choice. Chaucer's audience in the well-known *Troilus* frontispiece has clearly been to the Mercery.[36]

Alys's property deals also invoke a London context, one not limited to the silkwomen. Although Robertson and Patterson note that rural land law would not facilitate the land accumulation in the Wife's *Prologue*, Hanawalt notices that under the "borough" law of London, widows held onto their dowers into later marriages,[37] though sometimes they had to go through legal proceedings to recover their dowers upon their husbands' deaths.[38] This made guild-class widows very attractive potential spouses, and there was even an "upswing in remarriage among urban women at the end of the fourteenth century and into the fifteenth

[34] Ibid., 202.
[35] Ibid., 116; Hanawalt, *Wealth of Wives,* 177–78. For a good overview of the London rivalry with Italian merchants, see Craig E. Bertolet, " 'The Slyeste of Alle': The Lombard Problem in John Gower's London," in *John Gower: Manuscripts, Readers, Contexts,* ed. Malte Urban (Turnhout: Brepols, 2009), 197–218 (199–209).
[36] For a reasonable picture of that illustration from Cambridge, Corpus Christi College Library MS 61, see Laura Kendrick, *Chaucerian Play: Comedy and Control in the Canterbury Tales* (Berkeley and Los Angeles: University of California Press, 1988), figs. 22–23; Kendrick clearly sees the clothing in this picture as mercantile, as she interprets the scene as "emblematically" representing "a *puy* as the audience for Chaucer's play," and goes on to discuss the London *puy* as a "mutual-aid" literary society (169–70) for wealthy London merchants. For a discussion of the memory of the defunct London *puy* in Chaucer's time, see my "The London Mercers' Company, London Textual Culture, and John Gower's *Mirour de l'omme,*" 132–33. See also Joyce Coleman, "Where Chaucer Got His Pulpit: Audience and Intervisuality in the *Troilus and Criseyde* Frontispiece," *SAC* 32 (2010): 103–28.
[37] Hanawalt, *Wealth of Wives,* 8.
[38] Ibid., 97–104.

century."[39] In addition to the remarriage of widows moving capital between merchant houses, London women were also directly involved in the real-estate market, largely within the constraints set by the rules for dowers. They did not sell much property, but they were quite involved in leasing and commercially exploiting the property they owned.[40] Imagining an early reader encountering Alys of Bath, it seems entirely likely that she would have fit directly into that reader's understanding of London women of the merchant estate: she dressed well, remarried readily, and accumulated and managed property much like a London guild-class widow. It might not be possible (or necessary) to locate all of the details of her property "beside Bathe," but it does not seem clear that the ambiguity of her economic identity would even have occurred to a London reader more familiar with the interplay between marriage, business, and property in the city. For that matter, one hesitates to expect Chaucer necessarily to know or care about the fine points of land tenure in Somerset, though of course his familiarity with London is generally accepted as a given.[41]

Textual Alys

This sense of Alys's economic identity leads, then, to the whole question of the more discussed side of her identity, her textuality. One of the few areas in *The Wife of Bath's Prologue* where critics generally agree is that something interesting is going on with her discourse, in particular in terms of her use of sources. Indeed, although she seems to take liberties with her sources throughout, Chaucer presents the Wife (and himself) as quite impressively well read.[42] It is hard to be sure whether this aspect of her characterization invokes London guild-class women in the same way that her economic activities do, since we know rather less about their reading habits than we might like; of course, the same could be

[39] Ibid., 108. Hanawalt presents the example of Thomasine Bonaventure, who grew wealthy through serial marriage; Bonaventure started out a servant, married thrice, and was able to pay a trumped-up fine of £1,000 to Henry VII (111).

[40] Ibid., 164–69.

[41] See, for example, Ardis Butterfield, ed., *Chaucer and the City* (Cambridge: D. S. Brewer, 2006).

[42] Theresa Tinkle provides a useful overview of critical attitudes to Alys's textuality in "The Wife of Bath's Marginal Authority," *SAC* 33 (2010): 67–101, though she does persist in considering Alys to belong to "the artisan class" (70); she also refers to "lower, artisan class" terms of representations of Alys by Skelton and Lydgate in "Contested Authority," 291.

said for London guild-class men.[43] Hanawalt makes it clear that "some women certainly read for pleasure and edification and left books in their wills or inherited books."[44] While one doubts that the rabid misogyny of the "book of wikked wives" (685) would suit the taste of the average silkwoman, it does seem reasonable on the basis of Hanawalt's and Sutton's overviews of their business and reading activities to suppose that the sorts of wealthy London widows whom Alys so resembles exercised more than basic literacy, as well as the pretty good oral memory required for serious business. What this means in terms of the *Canterbury Tales* is that we need to look much more closely for points of similarity between the Wife of Bath and the other tale-tellers of the mercantile estate, particularly in terms of how they handle texts.

I have discussed this issue at some length elsewhere, arguing that Chaucer consistently represents male merchant characters as lacking in their ability to mix discourses, and unable or unwilling to read carefully in general, a shortcoming that limits their susceptibility to the correction of satire.[45] Lee Patterson characterizes merchants as "a class in search of a legitimizing ideology,"[46] and we can see this with the Merchant in his narration of his own tale, which in many ways seeks such an ideology through a hodge-podge of clerical and aristocratic discourses. The Merchant also misreads the Clerk's *Envoy* badly, not seeing its implicit contrast between the idealized world of Griselda and the differently stereotyped world of the Wife of Bath. We see a similar difficulty with complex comprehension in the rather nicer but clueless *Shipman's Tale* merchant, who seems not quite to get his wife's clever puns at the end of the tale.[47] Nancy M. Reale suggests that this move can be seen in a wider selection of pilgrims,[48] and while she understates

[43] Since Chaucer himself came from the guild class, it would be a mistake to underestimate the level of education possible (if not typical) in the city.

[44] Hanawalt, *Wealth of Wives,* 37. The classic study of women's books remains Susan Groag Bell's "Medieval Women Book Owners: Arbiters of Lay Piety and Ambassadors of Culture," *Signs: Journal of Women in Culture and Society* 7.4 (1982): 742–68, but it focuses mostly on the books of a much higher social stratum. She does attest to the increasing book ownership of the higher and lower "bourgeoisie," however (747–48).

[45] Ladd, "The Mercantile (Mis)Reader," 17–32.

[46] Lee Patterson, *Chaucer and the Subject of History* (Madison: University of Wisconsin Press, 1991), 330. My discussion of the mixture of aristocratic and clerical discourses in the *Merchant's* and *Shipman's Tales* is much indebted to Patterson's study (333ff.).

[47] Ladd, "The Mercantile (Mis)Reader," 26–30.

[48] She argues that "it is precisely this ability to decode language that is at center stage in the *Canterbury Tales,* as his wide variety of pilgrims allows Chaucer to demonstrate time and again how critical interpretive skill is for the newly emerging business model of society." Nancy M. Reale, "Companies, Mysteries, and Foreign Exchange:

the extent to which characters explicitly connected to the merchant estate can be expected to bear the symbolic weight of commerce in Chaucer's estates satire, her invitation to consider this pattern more broadly leads directly to the Wife of Bath. Given the extent to which Alys's economic identity fits into that of London mercantile women like the silkwomen, Chaucer seems to invite this comparison as well.[49]

He also rewards it. In terms of her discourse, there remains considerable debate over just what we are to make of the Wife's consistent pattern of selective citation. One of the best-known and most obvious examples is her citation of 1 Corinthians 7:3: "Let the husband render the debt to his wife, and the wife also in like manner to the husband."[50] She renders that verse, "I have the power duringe all my lif / Upon his proper body, and noght he. / Right thus th'apostle tolde it unto me" (III.158–60); she omits the reciprocity of the marriage debt. Theresa Tinkle chides modern readers who take this selective citation to require a serious challenge to Alys's hermeneutic by medieval readers, arguing that "lopsided scriptural arguments are apparently the norm [in the late Middle Ages], not the exception,"[51] but Alys's pattern of reading only the part that fits her agenda matches the pattern of the other mercantile readers in the *Canterbury Tales*. Alys also has a much-discussed (and entirely understandable) tendency toward tension with her patristic sources, particularly Jerome's *Adversus Jovinianum*. What to make of this pattern is less clear, of course; Carolyn Dinshaw raises the citation from 1 Corinthians in a discussion of how Alys's use of glossing "indicts [male glossators'] motivations as similarly carnal" to her own.[52] Graham D. Caie, in contrast, notes that many manuscripts include glosses correcting or otherwise adding to this partial citation,[53] and suggests that "the glossator could ensure that the reader was not deceived by the Wife's

---

Chaucer's Currency for the Modern Reader," in *The Canterbury Tales Revisited*, ed. Bishop, 256–80 (274).

[49] Identifying the Wife as "bourgeois" is not new of course. Stewart Justman argues that "in the Wife of Bath, Chaucer pictures the folly of the bourgeoisie—its appetite for goods both social and economic—as the ancestral license of Woman." "Trade as Pudendum: Chaucer's Wife of Bath," *ChauR* 28.4 (1994): 344–52 (345).

[50] *Rheims New Testament*, in *The Catholic Comparative New Testament* (Oxford: Oxford University Press, 2005), 1132.

[51] Tinkle, "The Wife of Bath's Marginal Authority," 81.

[52] Carolyn Dinshaw, *Chaucer's Sexual Poetics* (Madison: University of Wisconsin Press, 1989), 124.

[53] Graham D. Caie, "The Significance of the Early Chaucer Manuscript Glosses (with Special Reference to the *Wife of Bath's Prologue*," *ChauR* 10.4 (1976): 350–60 (355).

false logic and her persuasive misinterpretations of Scripture and Jerome."[54]

My own sense of what Chaucer has the Wife trying to do is probably
closer to Dinshaw's, but Caie's scholarship raises an important point:
while one might look at glosses as an approach to the text (analyzed by
Dinshaw in gendered terms), they also represent a valuable window into
the reading experience.[55] There are several key elements of the manuscript glosses that one needs to consider. One point is that they clearly
were a major component of the *mise en page* of many manuscripts; Caie
characterizes the Ellesmere manuscript glosses as "written in as large
and as careful a hand as the actual text, which is placed off-centre to
make room for the glosses."[56] The glosses in British Library Additional
manuscript 5140 are also very impressive, though it is a much later
manuscript than Ellesmere or Hengwrt.[57] However, sometimes they
were *not* a key component. The Hengwrt manuscript contains exactly
two glosses for the Wife's *Prologue:* "Questio" on the left at line 115,
and a "Nota" at a bracket enclosing lines 633–36.[58] The glosses are

[54] Ibid., 351. Note that Tinkle strongly disagrees with Caie's interpretation of those
glosses' function in "The Wife of Bath's Marginal Authority," though her 1998 article
"The Wife of Bath's Textual/Sexual Lives" sees the glosses more critically: "[T]he steady
marginal pointing of difficulties in her exegetical practice fosters habitual readerly suspicion and urges us continually to pause over her adequacy as a translator, to notice
that her texts barely support her interpretations" (73). The glosses "authorize Alisoun's
classicism, astrology, and misogyny; they call into question her biblical hermeneutics"
(73). "The Wife of Bath's Textual/Sexual Lives," in *The Iconic Page in Manuscript, Print,
and Digital Culture*, ed. George Bornstein and Theresa Tinkle (Ann Arbor: University
of Michigan Press, 1998), 55–88. Susan Schibanoff also disagrees strongly with Caie's
interpretation: "The New Reader and Female Textuality in Two Early Commentaries
on Chaucer," *SAC* 10 (1988): 71–108 (73–76).
[55] This is a principle much developed by Theresa Tinkle in "The Wife of Bath's
Marginal Authority," as she argues that the fifteenth-century glosses of *The Wife of
Bath's Prologue* reflect the tastes and attitudes of the gentry (71, 87) who formed a
market for those manuscripts.
[56] Caie, "Significance," 350.
[57] *The Wife of Bath's Prologue on CD-ROM,* ed. Peter Robinson (Cambridge: Cambridge University Press, 1996). The manuscript description on the CD-ROM suggests
a date of around 1501–3, based on its attribution to Henry Dene, Archbishop of Canterbury.
[58] Ibid. Ellesmere and Additional 5140 (Ad[1]) do represent highly distinct traditions
of the glosses; Stephen Partridge in his note in the electronic edition explains, "In Ad[1]
and En[3] the glosses are longer and more numerous, and as Schibanoff (1988) has shown,
they begin to 'pull away' from the sources of the text, but they are nevertheless concentrated in the opening lines of The Wife of Bath's Prologue, where the Wife points
clearly to her sources, and almost without exception are drawn from the Vulgate. By
contrast, El and the related manuscripts contain glosses at some lines which are glossed

also not consistent across manuscripts; Stephen Partridge identifies "six distinct efforts to provide *The Wife of Bath's Prologue* with an apparatus of Latin citations."[59] Not all of these would be equally learned of course, and there remains marked debate about whether the source glosses ultimately come from Chaucer or represent later recognition of his sources, or both.[60] Disputed authorship notwithstanding, the Latinity of these glosses represents another key feature, because they would not be equally accessible to all readers. Perhaps not unlike the Latin glosses in manuscripts of John Gower's *Confessio Amantis,* these Latin glosses strike Caie as a "sign of prestige," and he also suggests that they would be aimed at the " 'new readers,' the laity who could now read without the

in no other manuscript; the glosses in these manuscripts draw on sources ranging well beyond the Vulgate and the collections of aphorisms which appeared in basic school-texts, and at lines where no specific source is named; and finally, many of these glosses are drawn from Jerome's *Adversus Jovinianum,* which is alluded to near the end of The Wife of Bath's Prologue but is by no means clearly marked in the text in the first 200 lines, where many of the glosses appear. . . . We must therefore consider seriously the possibility that many of the El glosses derive from Chaucer himself; at the least, we cannot imagine that scribal or editorial introduction of El's extensive apparatus was in any way typical or routine for an English manuscript." "The Manuscript Glosses to The Wife of Bath's Prologue," in *The Wife of Bath's Prologue on CD-ROM,* ed. Robinson.

[59] Partridge, "The Manuscript Glosses to The Wife of Bath's Prologue."

[60] Partridge notes that there are really "four kinds of glosses"—"source glosses," "headings," "explanatory glosses," and "deictic" (pointing) glosses—and outlines the complete critical history of the glosses. He also suggests that the Ellesmere glosses, at least, might "derive from Chaucer himself" (ibid.). See also his "Glosses in the Manuscripts of Chaucer's 'Canterbury Tales': An Edition and Commentary," Ph.D. diss. (Harvard University, 1992). Caie suggests a preference for Chaucer as the author; Graham D. Caie, "The Significance of Marginal Glosses in the Earliest Manuscripts of *The Canterbury Tales,*" in *Chaucer and Scriptural Tradition,* ed. David Lyle Jeffery (Ottawa: University of Ottawa Press, 1984), 75–88 (76). Tinkle endorses Partridge's judgment that the Ellesmere glosses are Chaucer's, and provides a useful bibliography on the subject ("The Wife of Bath's Marginal Authority," 74 n. 21). Schibanoff argues that "someone who annotated both the Hengwrt and Ellesmere manuscripts could not, of course, also be Chaucer. But that does not rule out the possibility that this glossator attempts to sound *like* Chaucer in the Ellesmere manuscript. . . . I suggest that another part of the 'hoax' of the Ellesmere manuscript may be the invention of pseudo-Chaucerian glosses, glosses meant to appear as authentic" ("The New Reader," 92). Hanna and Lawler argue that "there is only a minimal probability that these glosses are by Chaucer, and all are probably decisions about textual presentation made by the producers of individual *Canterbury Tales* manuscripts" (85); aside from three that they cannot rule out as authorial, "the remaining thirty citations of 'book of wikked wyves' material cannot be by Chaucer" (86), on the grounds that materials introduced into the textual tradition in the Ellesmere manuscript cannot be authorial. Given a choice between Partridge and Tinkle on one side and Hanna, Lawler, and Schibanoff on the other, the question of the authorship of the Ellesmere glosses must be considered still open.

guidance of the clergy."[61] Of course, it has become apparent that there is considerably more going on with those *Confessio Amantis* glosses than meets the eye,[62] but my real point concerns the variable utility of these glosses to a vernacular reader. Certainly for a well-educated reader who can understand them, the Ellesmere glosses would help to fill in the contexts of all of those borrowings from Jerome. For a purely vernacular reader, however, they would be entirely decorative, signs that a manuscript like Ellesmere is just that fabulous. For a reader of the Hengwrt manuscript or others with a similar lack of glosses for this particular text, they are simply absent.

Reading the Wife

What does this mean for one's reading of *The Wife of Bath's Prologue* and *Tale,* specifically her use of discourses? It might mean quite a bit, in the sense that the source glosses crediting Jerome, particularly the Ellesmere glosses, can have a major effect on how a reader views Chaucer's creation of the Wife's own discourse.[63] For a reader not all that familiar with Jerome, or one accustomed to highly selective citation, she would really be quite impressive in her command of clerical and intellectual discourse. She refers regularly to the Bible, mentions "Protholome" (182, 324), has classical references such as "Argus" (358) and Metellius (460), and when describing Jankyn's book, indicates that its authors include "Valerie and Theofraste, . . . Seint Jerome, . . . Tertulan, Crisippus, Trotula, and Helowis" (671–77), and even Ovid (680). The Pardoner may even see her as "a noble prechour in this cas" (165), though it is not clear whether he is being ironic, or whether being praised by the Pardoner can be a good thing. On a surface level at least, Chaucer shows

---

[61] Graham D. Caie, "'Glosyinge is a glorious thing': Chaucer's Rhetoric, Manuscripts, and Readers," *Hiroshima Studies in English Language and Literature* 46 (2001): 1–12 (5).

[62] Joyce Coleman, "Lay Readers and Hard Latin: How Gower May Have Intended the *Confessio Amantis* to Be Read," *SAC* 24 (2002): 209–35 (219–25). See also such studies as Robert F. Yeager, "English, Latin, and the Text as 'Other,'" *Text* 3 (1987): 251–67; Siân Echard, "Glossing Gower: In Latin, in English, and *in absentia:* The Case of Bodleian Ashmole 35," in *Re-Visioning Gower,* ed. R. F. Yeager (Asheville, N.C.: Pegasus Press, 1998), 237–56, and Richard K. Emmerson, "Reading Gower in a Manuscript Culture: Latin and English in Illustrated Manuscripts of the *Confessio Amantis,*" *SAC* 21 (1999): 143–86.

[63] Schibanoff takes this even further with her characterization of the glosses in British Library MS Egerton 2864, in which "this glossator is determined to have the last word in his verbal duel with Alison—and does" ("The New Reader," 80).

Alys mastering a highly allusive clerical discourse; only when one recognizes her selective quotation, recasting, and outright alteration of her sources does one realize that she is either directly challenging or failing at this discourse. Either way (and I think she is actually doing both), Chaucer gets to show off his own reading at the same time that Alys's approach to clerical discourse resembles that of the Merchant. Unlike the Merchant, who unsuccessfully mixes clerical and aristocratic discourses in the same tale, Alys saves her aristocratic material for her *Tale* and thus avoids some problematic tensions between those discourses.

There is another significant difference, though; the discourse Chaucer has her subvert is one that directly satirizes her in estate terms. That is, where *The Merchant's Tale* is not really about merchants (despite some confused critical readings of January), the Wife's *Prologue* and *Tale* are both ultimately about gender and marriage, the *Prologue* drawing heavily from clerical discourse and the *Tale* taking a more or less aristocratic form. This is important because it makes even a glossless reader much more likely to notice the extent to which she is bending her source materials in the *Prologue,* and it makes her treatments of those texts a response to their content, as well as a performance of classed discourse. While a reader would have to know *Adversus Jovinianum* reasonably well to catch all of the ways in which the glossator highlights her liberties with Jerome's text, some of the biblical citations, such as the significantly partial quote of 1 Corinthians 7.3 mentioned earlier, would be familiar to many readers—the concept of the marriage debt was hardly a secret, and people knew that it went in both directions.[64] Thus, depending on the reader and the availability of source glosses, Alys might come across as well read but self-serving, or she might come across as creatively bending or maybe working within the rules of scholarly disputation, or she might come across as catastrophically and dangerously unable to use biblical, theological, and classical texts in accepted ways. Regardless of the reader's interpretation, his or her attention will and should be held more by the subject matter, marriage and gender, than by what Alys reveals about her limitations as a user of texts: the similarity to the Merchant is there, but Chaucer directs our attention away from that similarity through our engagement with her subject matter.

[64] See, for example, Elizabeth M. Makowski, "The Conjugal Debt and Medieval Canon Law," in *Equally in God's Image: Women in the Middle Ages,* ed. Julia Bolton Holloway, Constance S. Wright, and Joan Bechtold (New York: Peter Lang, 1990), 129–43. Also available online at http://www.umilta.net/equally.html.

A reader of a highly glossed manuscript is more likely to observe the depth of what Caie critiques as "textual harassment,"[65] but even a London silkwoman reading the *Prologue* and *Tale* might be expected primarily to notice Alys's discussion of marriage and gender, rather than her use of sources or her economic identity.

That is not to say, however, that Chaucer is not using his depiction of the Wife of Bath as part of a larger pattern of interrogating mercantile patterns of discourse. It is hardly unusual to read economic or even mercantile elements in her *Prologue*.[66] While the content of Alys's discursive experimentation directs the reader away from her economic identity, the manner of that experimentation is very consistent with what we see in the Merchant (down to their ire over marriage expressed in somewhat socially inappropriate ways)[67] and *The Shipman's Tale*. There are even some faint echoes of *The Shipman's Tale* in Alys's *Prologue:* she invokes, for example, a pun on good and goods very common in mercantile material when she tells one of her old husbands, "thou shalt not both . . . be maister of my body and of my good," a line reminiscent of the merchant's admonition to his wife in *The Shipman's Tale* to "keep bet thy good" (VII.432).[68] Alys's fine clothing also recalls the way that the wife of *The Shipman's Tale* claims to have spent the hundred francs on her "array" (VII.418), though that wife's clothing never receives the detail dedicated to Alys's wardrobe.[69] One might also note that Alys's vigorous defense of serial marriage supports a common social practice of the estate group she so resembles, urban guild-class women. Chaucer is up to something interesting here. I argued before that Chaucer focuses on mercantile discursive problems as a way of interrogating why satire might not work on such a group.[70] With Alys, Chaucer seems to take that approach to satire even further, by imagining how such discursive practices might even counter satire, through energetic reconstruction of

---

[65] Caie, "Glosyinge is a glorious thing," 12.

[66] Peggy A. Knapp, for example, observes Alys to be "situated on a borderline between a discourse based on learning and one based on money." "Alisoun Weaves a Text," *PQ* 65.3 (1986): 387–401 (396).

[67] For an insightful reading of the Merchant and Alys, see Tara Williams, "The Host, His Wife, and Their Communities in the *Canterbury Tales*," *ChauR* 42.4 (2008): 383–408.

[68] Ladd, *Antimercantilism*, 27–30, 43, 93–99.

[69] On the hundred francs' buying power, see Peter G. Beidler, "The Price of Sex in Chaucer's *Shipman's Tale*," *ChauR* 31.1 (1996): 5–17; reprinted in Beidler, *Chaucer's Canterbury Comedies*, 116–32.

[70] Ladd, "Mercantile (Mis)Reader," 30–32, and *Antimercantilism*, 99–100.

clerical/satirical discourse. In Alys's *Prologue,* the object of satire fights back, because unlike the merchants represented in the Merchant's or Shipman's tales, Alys uses her mercantile (mis)reading to come right out and defend herself both against and with the terms of antifeminist satire.

Telling the Tale

There also remains the question of just what Alys's actual *Tale* contributes to this larger satire. Here again the contrast to the Merchant seems relevant, in the sense that Alys's Arthurian romance separates out the aristocratic element of the mix of clerical and aristocratic discourses in *The Merchant's Tale.* It would be a mistake to overstate just how aristocratic this *Tale* might be, particularly given the details of the old woman's speech about the nature of *gentillesse* (III.1106–1216),[71] but on a surface level at least, this tale of knights and ladies represents a primarily aristocratic world (one that can be quite cruel to the commons). This world seems preoccupied with "gender and sovereignty,"[72] though sovereignty itself is a tricky concept to place socially. Although at one level it seems like a primary concern of the aristocracy who wielded political sovereignty, it is not at all clear that the old woman in the *Tale* is really talking about politics as such.[73] The *Tale* is even sometimes seen as ultimately giving way to "mercantile concerns" rather than Arthurian fantasy.[74] My point here is not particularly to pin down the tale as "mercantile" or "aristocratic," but to note that critical challenges to

[71] I follow here Susanne Sara Thomas's suggestion that the term "hag" is highly problematic in scholarship of this tale. "The Problem of Defining *Sovereynetee* in the *Wife of Bath's Tale," ChauR* 41.1 (2006): 87–97 (88).

[72] Susan Crane argues that the main issues of this tale, "gender and sovereignty . . . are of concern to Alison"; she characterizes the *Tale*'s romance genre as one that "celebrates women's emotive power instead of undermining it." "Alison's Incapacity and Poetic Instability in the Wife of Bath's Tale," *PMLA* 102 (1987): 20–28 (20–21). See also Tison Pugh, "Queering Genres, Battering Males: The Wife of Bath's Narrative Violence," *Journal of Narrative Theory* 33.2 (2003): 115–42. Crane further argues that the tale cannot fully resist satire, and its shifts between genres undermine Alys's own sovereignty (26–27).

[73] Indeed, Thomas suggests that the term "sovereignty" refers more to self-determination than to power over others, more personal than political. "The Problem of Defining *Sovereynetee,*" 94–96. See also Manuel Aguirre, "The Riddle of Sovereignty," *MLR* 88.2 (1993): 273–82 (278).

[74] Patricia Clare Ingham, "Pastoral Histories: Utopia, Conquest, and the Wife of Bath's Tale," *TSLL* 44.1 (2002): 34–46 (35).

the effectiveness of Alys's aristocratic discourse demonstrate its distinct limitations. On the one hand, some readers see romance (and Arthurian material) as inherently aristocratic,[75] but on the other hand, this *Tale* seems far more tied to its teller than others of the *Canterbury Tales,* and the bracketing of the tale with Alys's strong characterization in her *Prologue* and the *Tale*'s envoy (1253–64) reinforces that connection. As a result, the issues of gender that so dominate the *Prologue* resurface in the *Tale,* sometimes in tension with its ostensibly aristocratic terms.

Indeed, the *Tale*'s differences from John Gower's *Tale of Florent* in the *Confessio Amantis* show how the material could have been much more overtly aristocratic. As Peter G. Beidler points out, although Chaucer's and Gower's tales are clearly variations on the same basic story, many plot elements differ, and in general Gower's version is more effectively aristocratic. Florent is of a considerably higher social rank than the knight in *The Wife of Bath's Tale,* and his "crime" of killing a man in a fair fight is far less transgressive than the clearly criminal rape in *The Wife of Bath's Tale.* Florent can be trusted throughout to keep his word, and Gower's old woman turns out to be a princess under an enchantment.[76] Even if Chaucer was not using Gower's tale as a direct source, these differences underline the ways in which Alys as a narrator seems connected to her *Tale.* As Beidler puts it, "Parody or not, Chaucer's tale is a story about how a young man learns a measure of nobility by making impulsive mistakes and by coming into contact with two women."[77] The differences, such as the rape, the intercession of Guinevere, the inclusion of the old woman's lecture on "gentilesse," and the much more overtly sexual nature of the knight's final choice, foreground gender issues in Chaucer's version, whereas Gower's version foregrounds nobility. If, like the Merchant, Alys is constructed as trying to capture an aristocratic discourse, her personality from the *Prologue* still comes through; even the clerical discourse with which she wrestles in the *Prologue* makes its appearance as the old woman cites Roman philosophers

---

[75] See, e.g., Pugh, "Queering Genres," 116.

[76] Peter G. Beidler, "Transformations in Gower's *Tale of Florent* and Chaucer's *Wife of Bath's Tale*," in *Chaucer and Gower: Difference, Mutuality, Exchange,* ed. R. F. Yeager (Victoria, B.C.: English Literary Studies, University of Victoria, 1990), 100–114; reprinted in Beidler, *Chaucer's Canterbury Comedies,* 72–90. Beidler notes in this edition that following the recommendation of Lorraine K. Stock (and in agreement with Thomas, note 71 above), he shifts his uses of the term "hag" to "old woman" in the reprint.

[77] Ibid., 87.

and analyzes the nature of poverty.[78] This approach, involving what Jamie C. Fumo characterizes as "strategies of deferral or . . . dilation,"[79] comes across as deliberate, and these fractures and digressions work to memorable effect.

If in the *Tale*, however, Chaucer represents Alys's attempt to master aristocratic discourse in tandem with the clerical discourse in her *Prologue*, her mastery is partial at best. On the one hand, the *Tale* is a success: as Beidler points out, critics tend to prefer it to Gower's version.[80] On the other hand, its success comes largely from the ways in which it breaks down as an example of aristocratic discourse, such as the eruptions of Alys's preoccupation with gender and sexuality, and the return to the tone of the *Prologue* in the envoy—as Pugh suggests, Alys's failure to master an aristocratic form is central to the *Tale*'s overall effect.[81] Given that *The Tale of Florent* is probably earlier,[82] and is much

[78] She cites Valerius (1165), Seneca and Boethius (1168), and Juvenal (1192). Her discourse on poverty (1199–1206) is perhaps more overtly clerical in tone.

[79] Fumo continues by suggesting that the multiplication of digressions ultimately challenges "our preconceived expectations of what narrative *should* be." "Argus' Eyes, Midas' Ears, and the Wife of Bath as Storyteller," in *Metamorphosis: The Changing Face of Ovid in Medieval and Early Modern Europe,* ed. Alison Keith and Stephen Rupp (Toronto: Centre for Reformation and Renaissance Studies, 2007), 129–50 (148–49).

[80] Beidler, "Transformations," 72–73. Success can be measured in terms beyond critical interest, of course, but certainly in terms of other measures, like publication history, copies of the text sold, or number of film/television adaptations, there is no real contest. Closer to Chaucer and Gower's own time, consider the mention of Alys in John Lydgate's "Disguising at Hertford": "And for oure partye the worthy Wyf of Bathe / Cane shewe statutes moo than six or seven, / Howe wyves make hir housbandes wynne heven, / Maugré the feonde and al his vyolence." John Lydgate, *Mummings and Entertainments,* ed. Claire Sponsler, Middle English Texts Series (Kalamazoo: Medieval Institute Publications, 2010), lines 168–71. On the overall likeability of Alys as character and narrator, see Al Walzem, "Peynted by the Lion: The Wife of Bath as Feminist Pedagogue," in *The Canterbury Tales Revisited,* ed. Bishop, 44–59 (50–51).

[81] Pugh discusses the persistence of "a fabliau sensibility" in *The Wife of Bath's Tale* ("Queering Genres," 120).

[82] The initial version of the *Confessio Amantis* is usually dated "between 1386 and 1390." John Gower, *Confessio Amantis,* ed. Russell A. Peck, vol. 1, 2nd ed., Middle English Texts Series (Kalamazoo: Medieval Institute Publications, 2006), 36. Wim Lindeboom pushes the *terminus a quo* back to 1384, in "Rethinking the Recensions of the *Confessio Amantis,*" *Viator* 40.2 (2009): 319–48 (320). Larry D. Benson's chronology of the *Canterbury Tales* in *The Riverside Chaucer* dates the earliest of the tales to 1388, with "most" probably written 1392–95, and finishing touches until Chaucer's death (xxix). Certainly given the references to Alys in *The Clerk's Tale* (IV.1170) and "Lenvoy de Chaucer a Bukton" (line 29), some version of *The Wife of Bath's Prologue* would have to predate those two works; Jane Chance dates "Lenvoy de Chaucer a Bukton" to 1396, in "Chaucerian Irony in the Verse Epistles 'Wordes Unto Adam,' 'Lenvoy a Scogan,' and 'Lenvoy a Bukton,'" *PLL* 21.2 (1985): 115–28 (116 n. 3). If, as I suggest below, Chaucer was still tinkering with the Wife of Bath and her *Tale* late enough for distinct

more straightforwardly aristocratic in its tone and details, this is also a failure that one can reasonably expect a reader to notice. As the *Confessio Amantis* and *Canterbury Tales* circulated in much the same milieux,[83] a significant proportion of Chaucer's readers should have been able to recognize the difference in Alys's approach. This use of a potentially familiar romance story thus allows Chaucer to present Alys's use of discourse somewhat differently from what I have argued is the case for *The Merchant's Tale*. Both the Merchant and Alys attempt unsuccessfully to master both clerical and aristocratic discourse. Unlike the Merchant's fractured and overtold fabliau, however, Alys's *Prologue* and *Tale* find a much more effective thematic coherence around the central issues of gender and marriage, despite the inherent contrast between aristocratic and clerical antifeminist takes on marriage. Because Alys's materials are so much more focused thematically than the Merchant's, the reader's attention to the gender satire of both *Prologue* and *Tale* distracts that reader from seeing the extent to which Alys's discourse follows the pattern that Chaucer establishes for his male merchant-estate characters.[84] The concentration of Alys's speaking persona around the concerns raised by her gender, then, distracts not only from material indicators of her mercantile estate but also from mercantile elements in her approach to discourse.

Fixing Alys's Text

This sense of the centrality of Alys's persona to Chaucer's satire then leads to a major difficulty with *The Wife of Bath's Prologue* and *Tale*—their overall textual instability. Chaucer seems to have been not entirely

---

versions to appear in the Hengwrt and Ellesmere manuscripts, the final version of *The Wife of Bath's Tale* at least most likely postdates *The Tale of Florent*. Lest one get too confident about this sort of chronology, however, Kathryn L. Lynch outlines the parade of assumptions that underlie most Chaucer dating in her "Dating Chaucer," *ChauR* 42.1 (2007): 1–22. A rough simultaneity would suffice for my point that many readers would be familiar with both versions, and the aristocratic romance form that both tales follow was well established—consider, for example, the history of critics trying to establish a direct link between Chaucer and the Auchinleck manuscript, as described (if not ultimately supported) by Christopher Cannon, "Chaucer and the Auchinleck Manuscript Revisited," *ChauR* 46.1–2 (2011): 131–46 (132–33).

[83] Medieval audience is obviously a vexed question, but a number of recent studies have discussed the scribes who produced these works; see below.

[84] Indeed, the pattern distracted me from seeing the parallel in my earlier work on mercantile discourse in the *Canterbury Tales,* and I was actually looking for this sort of similarity.

certain how he wanted to contextualize this particular text within the
Canterbury Tales as a whole, an instability that suggests the complexity
of the intersection between mercantile discourse, Alys's gender, and
Chaucer's other interests in the *Canterbury Tales,* such as the subject of
marriage. Although as a general thing with the *Canterbury Tales* we do
not usually have a sense of Chaucer's creative process, there do seem to
be several stages of composition for *The Wife of Bath's Prologue* and *Tale;*
Chaucer's emphasis shifts subtly from stage to stage. The earliest stage
is conjectural at best, but consider Estelle Stubbs's suggestion of an early
version consisting of *The Man of Law's Tale* endlink with "Wif of Bathe"
where various manuscripts now have "Squire, Summoner or Shipman";
this text would promise the reader that the Wife's "joly body schal a
tale telle" (II.1185), and promise "litel Latyn" (II.1190), perhaps indicating a glossless *Prologue*. Stubbs suggests that such a version would
have "a shorter form of the Wife of Bath's Prologue."[85] However much
shorter this ur-*Prologue* might be, it might then have been followed by
what is now *The Shipman's Tale,* where

> The sely housbonde, algate he moot paye,
> He moot us clothe, and he moot us arraye,
> Al for his owene worshipe richely,
> In which array we daunce jolily.
> And if that he noght may, par aventure,
> Or ellis list no swich dispence endure,
> But thynketh it is wasted and ylost,
> Thanne moot another payen for oure cost,
> Or lene us gold, and that is perilous.
>
> (VII.11–19)

While this passage can be made to work for the Shipman, perhaps by
imagining some sort of satiric impersonation of the Wife of Bath, it
would also work extremely well for Alys herself; after all, "all is for to
selle" (414).[86] Such an early conception would very much accentuate the

[85] Estelle Stubbs, "'Here's One I Prepared Earlier': The Work of Scribe D on Oxford,
Corpus Christi College, Ms. 198," *RES* n.s. 58, no. 234 (2007): 133–53 (150).
[86] The classic articulation of the argument in favor of *The Shipman's Tale*'s composition
for the Wife of Bath as a teller is William W. Lawrence, "Chaucer's Shipman's Tale,"
Speculum 33.1 (1958): 56–68; for a challenge to much of the (il)logic involved in interrogating Chaucer's intentions too closely, specifically in terms of the teller of *The Shipman's
Tale,* see Joseph A. Dane, "The Wife of Bath's Shipman's Tale and the Invention of
Chaucerian Fabliaux," *MLR* 99.2 (2004): 287–300 (294–98). Dane does concede that
"it is not unreasonable to claim that the speaker should be a woman" for the lines I cite

mercantile aspects of the Wife's characterization through the juxtaposition of her *Prologue* behavior and that of the fabliau wife, through the
mercantile setting of the tale, and through its placement right after *The
Man of Law's Tale,* which has its own examples of flawed mercantile
discourse.[87] Certainly such a combination of tale and prologue would
retain a focus on gender in terms of feminine misbehavior, but it would
lack the rhetorical effect of the competing clerical and aristocratic discourses between Alys's *Prologue* and *Tale* in the extant versions. This
early phase of the Wife's *Prologue* and *Tale* can never be more than conjectural, but it would be thematically consistent, and it has some supporting textual hints if not irrefutable evidence.

The later two phases then have the advantage of actually existing in
early manuscripts. If we contrast the Hengwrt and Ellesmere texts of
the Wife's *Prologue* and *Tale,* there are two major differences: the Hengwrt, generally thought to be the earlier of these two very early manuscripts,[88] lacks any significant glosses, and also lacks several passages
that tend to strengthen antifeminist readings of the *Prologue,* including
the dream of the bloody bed (575–84), and the passage including the
lines, "Venus me yaf my lust, my likerousnesse, / And Mars yaf me my
sturdy hardinesse" (611–12).[89] As Theresa Tinkle puts it, "Hengwrt's

---

above (295), though he points out that "no manuscript attempts to correct the presumed lack of agreement between speaker and pronoun and the only edition to my
knowledge that does so is Urry's of 1721. There is no evidence that these pronouns
bothered any scribe or reader before this" (295). Because of these reasonable doubts, I
here present the notion of Alys telling that fabliau as a possibility rather than a probability. Note, however, that Andrew Galloway simply labels *The Shipman's Tale* as "the tale
originally assigned to her, then transferred to the Shipman." "The Account Book and
the Treasure: Gilbert Maghfeld's Textual Economy and the Poetics of Mercantile Accounting in Ricardian Literature," *SAC* 33 (2011): 65–124 (97).

[87] See Ladd, "Mercantile (Mis)Reader," 19–25.

[88] Stubbs, " 'Here's One I Prepared Earlier,' " 143–45. She later explains that "some
layers of Cp [Oxford, Corpus Christi College MS 198] may represent a pre-Hg period,
others suggest changes in-line with Hg [Hengwrt; Aberystwyth, National Library of
Wales, MS Peniarth 392] and access to the Hg thinking. The same is true of Ha4
[London, British Library, Harley MS 7334] and El [Ellesmere; San Marino, Calif., Huntington Library, MS EL 26 C9]. This must surely suggest a close working relationship
between Adam [Pinkhurst], Scribe D, and perhaps even with the author himself" (151).

[89] These passages lead to a major question in Chaucerian editing studies, which is
what we are supposed to do when good early manuscripts disagree. Beverly Kennedy
argues that these passages are not authentically Chaucerian, "given that five of these
passages have a very limited manuscript attestation, that they are all misogynous in
import as well as clumsily inserted into Chaucer's text, and that some of them work to
disambiguate that text concerning the Wife's sexual morality." "The Variant Passages
in the Wife of Bath's Prologue and the Textual Transmission of *The Canterbury Tales:
The 'Great Tradition' Revisited," in *Women, the Book, and the Worldly: Selected Proceedings*

Alisoun does not seem especially destined to martial hostility, is less given to undermining herself, and appears less purposely deceitful."[90] The Ellesmere text, then, has both the source glosses pointing out all of the Wife's discursive shortcomings, and the passages accentuating her "likerousnesse." Given Hengwrt's lack of source glosses, my hypothetical ur-version would presumably also lack the glosses, so what we would have would be:

- Phase A (hypothetical): *The Man of Law's Tale* endlink, with the "joly body"; glossless *Wife of Bath's Prologue* lacking the bloody bed; mercantile fabliau for a tale.
- Phase B (Hengwrt): Not linked to *The Man of Law's Tale;* glossless *Wife of Bath's Prologue* lacking the bloody bed; Arthurian tale about sovereignty in marriage.
- Phase C (Ellesmere): Not linked to *The Man of Law's Tale;* heavy source glosses for *The Wife of Bath's Prologue;* additional antifeminist passages; Arthurian tale about sovereignty in marriage.

If this sequence is even remotely right, and phases B and C do have solid manuscript evidence, what we see is Chaucer toning down the Wife's mercantility, but not removing it altogether.[91] Indeed, as Theresa

---

of the St Hilda's Conference, 1993, ed. Lesley Smith and Jane H. M. Taylor, vol. 2 (Cambridge: D. S. Brewer, 1995), 85–101 (91). Much of Kennedy's argument is essentially aesthetic, however (she is very free with phrases like "the clumsy way" [90] and "crudity of their style" [93]), and her sense of the editorial issues is very dependent on the work of Norman Blake (see her notes 3 and 7), with its close adherence to the Hengwrt manuscript. For an instructive contrast between Blake's approach and a less Hengwrt-centric approach to editing the *Canterbury Tales,* see N. F. Blake, "The Ellesmere Text in the Light of the Hengwrt Manuscript," in *The Ellesmere Chaucer: Essays in Interpretation,* ed. Martin Stevens and Daniel Woodward (San Marino, Calif.: Huntington Library, 1995), 205–24, and Ralph Hanna III, "(The) Editing (of) the Ellesmere Text," in ibid., 225–43. Beidler in his edition brackets the added lines and concludes that "because the matter will not likely be settled for some time—if ever—it seems best to present these lines in their 'proper' place, but to call attention to their problematic authorship" (*The Wife of Bath,* 64n.). For a more recent argument in favor of the lines as authentically Chaucerian, see Orietta Da Rold, "The Significance of Scribal Corrections in Cambridge University Library ms. Dd.4.24 of Chaucer's *Canterbury Tales,*" *ChauR* 40.4 (2007): 393–438 (395, 408). Clearly there is some debate here, but it is not at all clear how a late revision by Chaucer, only available to Adam Pinkhurst after his completion of the Hengwrt manuscript, would be distinguishable from a scribal interpolation. If Pinkhurst could not tell the difference, are we sure we can?

[90] Tinkle, "The Wife of Bath's Textual/Sexual Lives," 61.

[91] Tinkle argues that "we have no evidence that [Chaucer] tried to give his works a fixed authorial form" (ibid., 62); such a view would consider these differences less a progression than parallel versions always expected to coexist: "The work's historical form is multiplicity" (63).

Tinkle suggests, uses of the term "profit" in Ellesmere in locations using "parfit" in Hengwrt "accentuate Alisoun's aggressively mercantile eroticism,"[92] though Tinkle also argues for Ellesmere's reinforcement of Alisoun as a "misogynistic stereotype," and a relatively stronger stress on her gender.[93] If, as Simon Horobin suggests, the scribe Adam Pinkhurst was copying Hengwrt from separate fragments, without a sense of where the *Canterbury Tales* as a whole were going,[94] the differences in *The Wife of Bath's Prologue* between Hengwrt and Ellesmere could reflect either revisions in Chaucer's own text that were ongoing at the time or the existence of multiple versions in circulation. We know that there were two versions, but we cannot know whether Chaucer expected to withdraw the Hengwrt version.[95] If those versions represent a revision process, we can see Chaucer directing the reader much more explicitly toward seeing Alys's discursive transgressions in terms of her gender while at the same time encouraging us to see her in antifeminist (rather than antimercantile) terms. Given that he repurposed *The Shipman's Tale* and its presentation of mercantile discourse, and that he was able to build the Merchant's *Prologue* from the Wife's *Prologue* through the Clerk's *Envoy,* he retains the sense of merchants as a problematic audience and also develops this notion into his exploration of how someone like Alys might attack a different sort of satire from the inside.

Thus we see two related approaches on Chaucer's part: the represen-

---

[92] This is a fairly subtle point in Tinkle's argument, which cannot be done justice here; see ibid., 64.

[93] Ibid., 68.

[94] Simon Horobin, "Adam Pinkhurst, Geoffrey Chaucer, and the Hengwrt Manuscript of the *Canterbury Tales,*" *ChauR* 44.4 (2010): 351–67 (364–65). For the identification of Pinkhurst as Chaucer's scribe, see Linne R. Mooney, "Chaucer's Scribe," *Speculum* 81.1 (2006): 97–138.

[95] Horobin mentions the familiar note informing the Hengwrt reader that there is no more to *The Cook's Tale,* which makes it clear that Chaucer was not alive at the end of the Hengwrt's production ("Adam Pinkhurst," 358), and suggests, "perhaps the reason that Pinkhurst did not have all the text to hand when he began copying was not because it was still being composed, but because it was being copied by other London scribes" (365). This possibility is quite convincing, in the light of his sense of the copying business in London at the time (366), but does not rule out the possibility that the different circulating exemplars for Hengwrt and Ellesmere represent different stages of composition. See also Heather F. Windram, Christopher Howe, and Matthew Spencer, "The Identification of Exemplar Change in the *Wife of Bath's Prologue* Using the Chi-Squared Method," *Literary and Linguistic Computing* 20.2 (2005): 189–204 (194–97), for a statistical analysis of the differences between Hengwrt and Ellesmere. On the copying industry more generally, see Linne R. Mooney, "Locating Scribal Activity in Late Medieval London," in *Design and Distribution of Late Medieval Manuscripts in England,* ed. Margaret Connolly and Linne R. Mooney (York: York Medieval Press, 2008), 183–204.

tation of merchants as particularly unlikely to learn from satire because of their lack of discursive sophistication,[96] and the similar but more focused representation of Alys successfully wrestling with antifeminist satire through her own discursive performances. There are similarities between these two implicit critiques of satire in that both use mixtures of clerical and aristocratic discourse, both rely on merchant-estate characters' perceived lack of expertise at those discourses, and both address issues that would really matter to a reader who belonged to the social groups being satirized. Chaucer's representation of Alys as so overtly focused on gender and marriage, however, displaces that representation's similarity in structure to Chaucer's representations of male merchant-estate characters, with the result that, just as Alys can satirize London wives because she is not one, she can also satirize London merchants through her similarities to them.

Alys's Audience

This then leads back to the manuscripts, this time in terms of Chaucer's audience. One question that comes up whenever one addresses merchants as a social group in Chaucer is whether fine points of satire on merchants are really relevant, since merchants have not been seen as a major audience for Chaucer. The question of the extent to which Chaucer might have been writing for a mercantile audience does not lend itself to clear proof, as Chaucer does not directly mention such an audience, and we lack a large body of Chaucer manuscripts with merchants' ownership marks on them. But the possibility remains worth considering and would fit with what we know of his later audience. Tinkle argues for an extensive gentry audience for the *Canterbury Tales* in the fifteenth century, for example,[97] and older assumptions about Chaucer's courtly audience continue to be complicated.[98] The classic study of Chaucer's audience remains Paul Strohm's chapter of that title in his

[96] Ladd, "Mercantile (Mis)Reader," 31–32.

[97] Tinkle, "The Wife of Bath's Marginal Authority," 71.

[98] See, for example, Coleman, "Where Chaucer Got His Pulpit." See also Kate Harris, "Patrons, Buyers, and Owners: The Evidence for Ownership and the Rôle of Book Owners in Book Production and the Book Trade," in *Book Production and Publishing in Britain, 1375–1475*, ed. Jeremy Griffiths and Derek Pearsall (Cambridge: Cambridge University Press, 1989), 163–99, and Carol M. Meale, "Patrons, Buyers, and Owners: Book Production and Social Status," in ibid., 201–38.

Social Chaucer, which has the benefit of naming names,[99] and it is clear that Chaucer's initial audience did include quite a social range, from the aristocracy on down. The vexed question, then, is how far down. We do know that some merchants did eventually own copies of Chaucer,[100] but in the absence of direct address to a mercantile audience, critics have hitherto assumed that there was not much of one. There are, however, two reasons to be skeptical of this assumption. One reason is internal to the *Canterbury Tales:* as I am trying to suggest here, Chaucer is very attentive to issues relevant to the merchant estate, both in the terms that I have suggested previously and also in terms of Alys's strong resemblance to London merchant-estate women, the similarities between her discourse and that of the Merchant, and the overall sense of her materialism, which has caught the eye of so many scholars.[101]

The other reason to wonder about a mercantile audience for Chaucer is to shift the question from "Whom do we think Chaucer wanted to read the *Canterbury Tales?*" to "Who do we know was actually in the same room as a *Canterbury Tales* manuscript?" The latter of course yields a much shorter list, but it is a tantalizing one: aside from limited manuscript ownership evidence (which, like the manuscripts themselves, is all from after Chaucer's lifetime), the people we know most certainly were in contact with the *Canterbury Tales* were the scribes. Many of them are anonymous, especially for the later manuscripts, but both Hengwrt and Ellesmere were copied by Adam Pinkhurst.[102] Pinkhurst was by the turn of the fifteenth century routinely employed by the Mercers' Company and had written at least one major public document for that guild, its 1387 petition to the king's council,[103] as well as a 1385 petition requesting a "permanent deputy" for Chaucer as controller of the wool custom.[104] Without some reason to imagine that Pinkhurst performed his literary commissions in an entirely separate location from his guild commissions,[105] it seems quite probable that at some point representatives

---

[99] Paul Strohm, *Social Chaucer* (Cambridge, Mass.: Harvard University Press, 1989), 47–83.

[100] Sutton, *Mercery of London,* 168.

[101] Andrew Galloway reinforces the overall mercantility of Alys's discourse, particularly in terms of her use of accounting terminology, in his "The Account Book and the Treasure," 94–97. Galloway's whole discussion of Chaucer (92–103) reinforces my sense of Chaucer's understanding of and attention to mercantile culture.

[102] Mooney, "Chaucer's Scribe," 98.

[103] Ibid., 106–12.

[104] Horobin, "Adam Pinkhurst," 354.

[105] Mooney, "Locating Scribal Activity," 184–86.

of the Mercers' Company (or their paperwork, at least) should have crossed paths with either the Hengwrt or Ellesmere manuscripts, neither of which would have been quick jobs. Although some scribes, like Thomas Hoccleve, might have had to do commissions in a less official location than that of their day jobs,[106] more freelance ones like Pinkhurst would presumably not have had quite so official a workplace as a royal clerk. Mooney suggests that he might have worked in "space allocated to the Mercers' Company within the Hospital of St Thomas of Acon,"[107] which certainly would have put his other copying work in the presence of guild members. It is also clear that these scribes did not specialize in single authors or genres; Mooney outlines Pinkhurst's varied production,[108] and "Scribe D" similarly worked on a variety of texts, including Gower and Chaucer.[109] Pinkhurst was not the only scribe with a guild affiliation, either; as Marion Turner points out, "Chaucer's earliest known scribe (Adam Pynkhurst), the first known owner of a *Canterbury Tales* manuscript (John Brynchele), and the earliest-known reader of *Troilus and Criseyde* (Thomas Usk) were all employed as scribes for major London livery companies"—Pinkhurst with the Mercers, Brynchele with the Tailors, and Usk with the Goldsmiths.[110] As Turner suggests, what these connections indicate is a very real possibility of a guild-class audience for Chaucer,[111] and certainly quite straightforward guild-class

[106] Mooney does suggest that some scribes, such as "clerks of the Privy Seal, Chancery, [and] the Exchequer" might have "taken commissions for copying books in their lodgings after hours" ("Locating Scribal Activity," 194), and describes Thomas Hoccleve doing so for a *Confessio Amantis* manuscript (194–95).

[107] Ibid., 198.

[108] In addition to his professional work for the Mercers and the petition for Chaucer, Mooney attributes to Pinkhurst several works by Chaucer, part of a *Confessio Amantis,* and a *Piers Plowman.* "Chaucer's Scribe," 98–99.

[109] Kathryn Kerby-Fulton and Steven Justice, "Scribe D and the Marketing of Ricardian Literature," in *The Medieval Professional Reader at Work: Evidence from Manuscripts of Chaucer, Langland, Kempe, and Gower,* ed. Kathryn Kerby-Fulton and Maidie Hilmo (Victoria, B.C.: English Literary Studies, University of Victoria, 2001), 217–37. Estelle Stubbs has recently proposed John Marchaunt, Common Clerk of the city of London as Scribe D; she notes Marchaunt's hand both on a number of literary documents and on a variety of city records, including some that concern Ralph Strode. Her work suggests the value of considering traffic in Guildhall in the context of literary production. "Gower's Scribe: The London Implications," paper presented at the Second International Congress of the John Gower Society: "John Gower in Iberia: Six Hundred Years," Valladolid, Spain, July 2011.

[110] Marion Turner, "Usk and the Goldsmiths," *NML* 9 (2007): 139–77 (140).

[111] Turner goes into considerably more detail about the authorial role of known scribes like Pinkhurst or Usk, and the rising guild-class literary audience, in "Conflict," in *Middle English,* ed. Paul Strohm (Oxford: Oxford University Press, 2007), 258–73. She argues that "these guilds [the Goldsmiths and Mercers], so profoundly bound up

access to Chaucer from a very early point, even that point when the text of *The Wife of Bath's Prologue* and *Tale* was changing from the Hengwrt to the Ellesmere version.[112]

It is this manuscript context, then, that makes an analysis of Alys's social position crucial in our understanding of the *Canterbury Tales'* London context. Regardless of how closely Chaucer might have worked with Pinkhurst or any other scribe,[113] he certainly had every reason to be aware of working scribes' social and professional circles, and to be aware of the ways that manuscripts circulated. Presumably he knew where his own books had come from at least, and however we read "Chaucers Wordes Unto Adam, His Owne Scriveyn," it is worth considering how the guild-class audience available to working scribes might be addressed by Chaucer's work.

In the case of *The Wife of Bath's Prologue* and *Tale,* I have tried to suggest above how the final form of the text strongly calls to mind guild-class women while retaining a degree of protective ambiguity to deflect the possibility of such a reader taking offense. Based on that similarity, established through the telling characterization of Alys as a multiply widowed woman in the cloth trade, Chaucer connects the Wife to his larger treatment of the merchant estate, though his focus on gender more than class distracts the reader from that identification at the same time that he shows Alys finding more success with the pattern of merchants' failed discourse than I observed in *The Man of Law's Tale, The Shipman's Tale,* and, most important, *The Merchant's Tale.* The complicated textual history of the Wife of Bath and her *Prologue* and *Tale* then suggests the possibility that just what to do with the Wife was something Chaucer had to think about for a while, with the apparent

---

in civic conflict, were also closely connected to the literary culture of late fourteenth-century London" and notes that both Mercers and Goldsmiths paid Lydgate to write them mummings (266). For those mummings, see Lydgate, *Mummings and Entertainments,* ed. Sponsler.

[112] One might productively question why a scribe like Pinkhurst would *not* show an ongoing copy of a text like the *Canterbury Tales* to one of his clients able to afford such a thing.

[113] This remains a vexed question; Mooney argues for a close working relationship between Pinkhurst and Chaucer ("Chaucer's Scribe," 105), while Horobin argues that despite their past contacts, Chaucer was *not* in contact with Pinkhurst during the copying of the Hengwrt manuscript ("Adam Pinkhurst," 364). Alexandra Gillespie, however, suggests that though there is "circumstantial" evidence linking Chaucer to Pinkhurst, it is not "conclusive," and questions Mooney's reading of "Chaucers Wordes Unto Adam, His Owne Scriveyn." "Reading Chaucer's Words to Adam," *ChauR* 42.3 (2008): 269–83 (270).

revisions possibly abandoning a more directly mercantile characterization of her, and most certainly accentuating both her *Prologue*'s composite discourse and its antifeminist effect through the added passages and source glosses. That overall effect then adds another dimension to a larger issue that Chaucer was working on: how to make satire work. I have previously asked how a bad reader would learn from satire, since Chaucer shows merchant-estate characters misunderstanding discourses around them. One solution to that problem would be to educate those bad readers by showing them the consequences of their inability, but another solution, tried here with the Wife of Bath, would be to displace the critique onto another estate, in this case the estate of women, and then to show a pattern whereby one could make sense despite being caught between discourses. Women and wives were traditionally treated as a category by estates satires,[114] but oddly enough, this Wife is ambiguously criticized both in traditional antifeminist terms and also in the same terms male merchant-estate characters are elsewhere. Perhaps, then, one purpose in Chaucer's portrayal of Alys, and in particular a reason to give her a profession and a social class (even vaguely), is to create a character in which guild-class readers of either gender can recognize their discursive patterns, without necessarily noticing that they were being critiqued in those terms. Chaucer so effectively develops this critique in gendered terms by the end, though, that the Wife's mercantile qualities have remained largely submerged.

[114] See, e.g., Jill Mann, *Chaucer and Medieval Estates Satire* (Cambridge: Cambridge University Press, 1973), 121–27.

Chaucer and the Oxford Renaissance of Anglo-Latin Rhetoric

Martin Camargo
University of Illinois at Urbana-Champaign

W RITING OVER EIGHTY YEARS AGO, John M. Manly posed the questions that have shaped scholarly debate over the nature and extent of Chaucer's debt to medieval rhetoric ever since: "What . . . was medieval rhetoric? Who were its principal authorities in Chaucer's time? And what use did Chaucer make of methods and doctrines unmistakably due to the rhetoricians?"[1] In his answer to the first question, Manly restricted medieval rhetoric to a set of formal precepts that fell into three categories: "(1) arrangement or organization; (2) amplification and abbreviation; (3) style and its ornaments."[2] Especially among the generation immediately following the 1926 publication of Manly's landmark essay, that definition prevailed and shaped many subsequent studies devoted to identifying the various rhetorical figures employed in Chaucer's poetry.

Those who wrote such studies also accepted Manly's answer to his second basic question: the principal sources of rhetorical doctrine for Chaucer and his contemporaries were the Latin textbooks composed in the late twelfth and early thirteenth centuries by Matthew of Vendôme, Geoffrey of Vinsauf, and others, several of which were made available in modern printed editions by Edmond Faral only two years before Manly explored their influence on Chaucer.[3] Often referred to as *artes poetriae,* these are treatises on general composition, a genre that Douglas Kelly has designated more precisely as "arts of poetry and prose."[4] The most

---

[1] J. M. Manly, "Chaucer and the Rhetoricians," *PBA* 12 (1926): 95–113 (98).
[2] Ibid., 99. Under the first category, Manly has in mind chiefly instruction on how to begin and end a composition (see 99–101).
[3] Edmond Faral, *Les arts poétiques du xiie et du xiiie siècle* (Paris: Champion, 1924).
[4] Douglas Kelly, *The Arts of Poetry and Prose,* Typologie des sources du Moyen Âge occidental 59 (Turnhout: Brepols, 1991). This is still the best study of the genre.

Studies in the Age of Chaucer 34 (2012):173–207
© 2012 The New Chaucer Society

popular among the arts of poetry and prose, Geoffrey of Vinsauf's *Poetria nova* (1200–1202, revised up to c. 1215), survives in more than two hundred manuscript copies and is cited twice by Chaucer.[5]

Manly's answer to his third question was that Chaucer made extensive use of the formal techniques he had learned from Geoffrey of Vinsauf and his fellow rhetoricians but distanced himself from this kind of artifice as he matured as a poet: "To any student of his technique, Chaucer's development reveals itself unmistakably, not as progress from crude, untrained native power to a style and method polished by fuller acquaintance with rhetorical precepts and more sophisticated models, but rather as a process of gradual release from the astonishingly artificial and sophisticated art with which he began and the gradual replacement of formal rhetorical devices by methods of comparison based upon close observation of life and the exercise of the creative imagination."[6] Since the 1960s, scholars have taken issue with the "unmistakably" in Manly's formulation in order to document the ways in which Chaucer's artistic success came not despite but *by means of* his "rhetorical" poetics. Leading the way was Robert O. Payne, whose 1963 book *The Key of Remembrance* remains the most comprehensive and nuanced appreciation of Chaucer's creative experimentation with the rhetorical conception of poetry anatomized in the arts of poetry and prose and embodied in previous literary works, both Latin and vernacular, that belong to the tradition they epitomized.[7] More recent scholarship has expanded the scope of inquiry beyond the formalistic elements of structure and style to include, for example, the construction of rhetorical ethos,[8] argument from the attri-

---

[5] On the reception of the *Poetria nova* (*PN*), see especially Marjorie Curry Woods, *Classroom Commentaries: Teaching the "Poetria nova" Across Medieval and Renaissance Europe* (Columbus: Ohio State University Press, 2010). Manly puts special emphasis on Geoffrey of Vinsauf and his masterpiece: "Every educated man [in Chaucer's fourteenth-century audience] remembered Master Gaufred and some perhaps knew by heart his famous lamentation [of King Richard I (*PN* 368–430)], for the *Nova Poetria* was one of the principal text-books on rhetoric and was studied in the schools with a zeal devoted perhaps to few modern school books" ("Chaucer and the Rhetoricians," 96).

[6] Manly, "Chaucer and the Rhetoricians," 97.

[7] Robert O. Payne, *The Key of Remembrance: A Study of Chaucer's Poetics* (New Haven: Yale University Press, 1963). For an excellent survey of the scholarship on Chaucer and rhetoric from 1926 through the mid-1970s, see also Robert O. Payne, "Chaucer and the Art of Rhetoric," in *Companion to Chaucer Studies,* ed. Beryl Rowland, rev. ed. (Oxford: Oxford University Press, 1979), 42–64.

[8] Robert O. Payne, "Chaucer's Realization of Himself as Rhetor," in *Medieval Eloquence: Studies in the Theory and Practice of Medieval Rhetoric,* ed. James J. Murphy (Berkeley and Los Angeles: University of California Press, 1978), 270–87; Martin Camargo, "Rhetorical Ethos and the 'Nun's Priest's Tale,'" *Comparative Literature Studies* 33 (1996): 173–86.

butes of persons,[9] and persuasion through careful attention to audience and occasion (*kairos*) in Chaucer's works.[10] Rita Copeland's studies of Chaucerian rhetoric as both a metadiscourse and a conceptual scheme for textual production have been especially important in this ongoing effort to broaden and deepen our understanding of rhetoric as it shapes and informs Chaucer's work.[11]

Also in the 1960s, James J. Murphy assailed another of Manly's confident claims, namely, that the rhetorical "methods and doctrines" employed by Chaucer were "unmistakably due to the rhetoricians" and, therefore, what Manly had defined as "medieval rhetoric" could have reached Chaucer only through the arts of poetry and prose by Matthew of Vendôme and Geoffrey of Vinsauf. In his 1964 essay "A New Look at Chaucer and the Rhetoricians," Murphy argued that "there is very little evidence of an active rhetorical tradition in fourteenth-century England" and that the evidence cited to support the influence of the arts of poetry and prose on Chaucer's works could just as easily be used to demonstrate influence by any number of other, more readily available works, particularly those used to teach grammar.[12]

The assumption, usually unstated, behind the position Murphy sought to refute is that Chaucer would have encountered the arts of poetry and prose as a schoolboy, while acquiring basic literacy in Latin at a grammar school in the late 1340s and early 1350s.[13] As long as one equates medieval rhetoric with stylistic elaboration and ornamentation,

---

[9] Marjorie Curry Woods, "Chaucer the Rhetorician: Criseyde and Her Family," *ChauR* 20 (1985): 28–39. See also Payne, *Key of Remembrance,* 180–83.

[10] David Wallace, *Chaucerian Polity: Absolutist Lineages and Associational Forms in England and Italy* (Stanford: Stanford University Press, 1997), chap. 8: "Household Rhetoric: Violence and Eloquence in the *Tale of Melibee,*" 212–46, 450–60.

[11] For an excellent overview that synthesizes her own with other recent scholarship, see Rita Copeland, "Chaucer and Rhetoric," in *The Yale Companion to Chaucer,* ed. Seth Lerer (New Haven: Yale University Press, 2006), 122–43.

[12] James J. Murphy, "A New Look at Chaucer and the Rhetoricians," *RES* n.s. 15 (1964): 1–20 (2).

[13] In the most recent scholarly biography, Derek Pearsall says that Chaucer probably was sent to a nearby grammar school to learn Latin but adds that his education in a noble household was more important than his formal education: *The Life of Geoffrey Chaucer: A Critical Biography* (Oxford: Blackwell, 1992), 29–34 ("Chaucer's Education; Chaucer's Latin"). Donald R. Howard, in his own slightly earlier biography, also indicates that Chaucer would have been sent to a grammar school in his neighborhood at around age seven but is more willing to speculate about what he might have learned there: *Chaucer: His Life, His Works, His World* (New York: Dutton, 1987), 19–27 ("Early Education"). Howard includes "rhetoric" among the subjects regularly taught in the grammar schools and singles out the *Poetria nova* as a textbook used for such instruction (26).

in particular with rules for producing the figures of speech and thought, as most earlier scholars had done, it is difficult not to assume that Chaucer learned the basics of "rhetoric" at some point between the ages of seven and fourteen. Proceeding from that assumption, Murphy was right to point out that those stylistic precepts were not the exclusive property of the arts of poetry and prose. The pedagogical materials and methods of those treatises had been in use for centuries, many of the sources dating from antiquity, before Matthew of Vendôme and Geoffrey of Vinsauf synthesized and adapted them into a teachable system tailored to contemporary needs. Even if Chaucer learned to use the "colours of rethorik" chiefly through his formal education in Latin—rather than through imitation of vernacular poetry, for example—he could have found the necessary information in standard grammar textbooks such as the *Doctrinale* by Alexander of Villa Dei and the *Graecismus* by Évrard of Bethune, and even in encyclopedic works such as the *Catholicon* by John Balbus of Genoa.[14] Without explicit attribution or clear verbal echoes, it is impossible to trace Chaucer's use of conventional stylistic ornament to a specific textbook or even a specific type of textbook among the many potential sources that would have been available to his grammar-school teachers.

Chaucer did provide such evidence of his debt to the *Poetria nova,* by translating a brief passage from it in *Troilus and Criseyde* and citing its author by name in *The Nun's Priest's Tale.* Unlike Murphy, I count these explicit references as demonstrating Chaucer's familiarity with Geoffrey of Vinsauf's most famous treatise and as increasing the likelihood that he knew other rhetorical treatises as well. However, the new evidence that I will offer strongly suggests that in quoting and citing the *Poetria nova,* Chaucer was not evoking memories of the elementary exercises that he, along with the members of his audience, had practiced as children in grammar school.[15] More likely, Chaucer was reacting to a body of newly recovered rhetorical texts that included the *Poetria nova,* along

[14] Murphy correctly notes the widespread availability of the grammatical textbooks ("New Look," 3–5, 16–18); but the encyclopedists were cited just as frequently by medieval English grammar teachers.

[15] An example of a recent study that seems to conflate the *Poetria nova,* or at least the part of it that Chaucer cites in *The Nun's Priest's Tale,* with the elementary exercises of the grammar-school classroom is Peter W. Travis, *Disseminal Chaucer: Rereading "The Nun's Priest's Tale"* (Notre Dame: University of Notre Dame Press, 2010), chap. 2: "*The Nun's Priest's Tale* as Grammar School Primer, Menippean Parody, and *Ars Poetica,*" 51–117 (*PN* 368–430 is discussed on 84–92).

with other arts of poetry and prose and probably some of the ancient treatises and the commentaries on them. The rediscovery of such texts was part of a broader "renaissance" of rhetoric, centered on Oxford, that began in the second half of the fourteenth century and lasted through at least the first quarter of the fifteenth century. Chaucer's encounter with this new burst of intellectual and pedagogical activity as an already mature poet, in the 1380s, immediately transformed his awareness of and attitude toward rhetoric as a discipline and continued to have an impact on his poetry for the remainder of his career.

It is no mere coincidence that the *Poetria nova* is the one art of poetry and prose to which Chaucer explicitly refers. Both within and beyond England, Geoffrey of Vinsauf's art of rhetorical composition in 2,121 Latin hexameters was by far the best known, most frequently copied and excerpted, and most influential example of its genre. From England alone, at least thirty-three manuscripts preserve all or part of the treatise.[16] Ten of these English copies were produced during the first half of the thirteenth century, within a generation or so of Geoffrey's composing the work.[17] By the latter half of the thirteenth century, however, the number of copies produced—or at least the number preserved—falls off dramatically. Only three English copies survive from the rest of the thirteenth century,[18] and only a single copy survives from the beginning of the fourteenth century.[19] Not one English copy of the *Poetria nova* survives from the middle of the fourteenth century, the period when Chaucer would have attended grammar school. However, clear signs of a strong and lasting revival of interest appear toward the end of the century. No fewer than fourteen copies of the *Poetria nova* can be dated

[16] For a more detailed account of the material covered in the following pages, see Martin Camargo, "The Late Fourteenth-Century Renaissance of Anglo-Latin Rhetoric," *Philosophy and Rhetoric* 45 (2012): 107–33.

[17] Cambridge, Corpus Christi College, MS 406; Cambridge, Trinity College, MS R.3.29 and MS R.3.51; Glasgow, Hunterian Library, MS Hunterian V.8.14; Oxford, Bodleian Library, MS Add. A.44 (excerpts), MS Bodley 656 (excerpt), MS Digby 104, MS Laud misc. 515, and MS Rawlinson C.552 (excerpts); York, Minster Library, MS XVI.Q.14.

[18] Cambridge, Trinity College, MS R.14.22; London, British Library, MS Egerton 2261 and MS Harley 3775.

[19] Oxford, Bodleian Library, MS Auct. F.1.17. Bruce Harbert uses this manuscript to illustrate the form in which Chaucer typically would have encountered works by classical and pseudoclassical poets: "Chaucer and the Latin Classics," in *Writers and Their Background: Geoffrey Chaucer,* ed. Derek Brewer (Athens: Ohio University Press, 1975), 137–53 (esp. 138–41).

to the period encompassing the last decades of the fourteenth century and the first decades of the fifteenth century.[20]

Chaucer's best chance of reading the *Poetria nova* is thus likely to have come in the last quarter of the fourteenth century, when fresh copies once again became readily available in England after a century or more of severely diminished production. Of course, he could have read a thirteenth-century copy or a more nearly contemporary copy made on the Continent, where production of *Poetria nova* manuscripts continued unabated or even—in parts of central Europe and Italy—increased during the fourteenth century.[21] When all of the relevant evidence is considered, however, it seems far more likely that Chaucer would have encountered the *Poetria nova* in the 1380s, in the context of a more comprehensive, deliberate recovery of older rhetorical materials by English scholars, many of whom drew on those materials to compile new treatises on rhetoric.

The distinctive chronology of the English manuscripts containing the *Poetria nova* holds true for every one of the twelfth- and thirteenth-century arts of poetry and prose that circulated in England. Although the total number of exemplars is much smaller for any given treatise than it is for the *Poetria nova,* the uniformity of the cumulative record appears to indicate a sudden and marked interest in the genre that was well under way by the end of the fourteenth century. The pattern is particularly clear in two prose treatises that survive chiefly or solely in manuscripts written in England. Geoffrey of Vinsauf's textbook in prose, the *Documentum de modo et arte dictandi et versificandi,* which he must have completed shortly before the death of King Richard I in

---

[20] Berlin, Staatsbibliothek, Stiftung preussischer Kulturbesitz, MS Lat. qu. 515; Douai, Bibliothèque municipale, MS 764; Durham Cathedral, Dean and Chapter Library, MS C.IV.23; Durham, University Library, MS Cosin V.v.2; London, British Library, MS Cotton Cleopatra B.vi and MS Cotton Titus A.xx (excerpt); Oxford, Balliol College, MS 263 and MS 276; Oxford, Bodleian Library, MS Bodley 496 (excerpts), MS Digby 64, and MS Selden Supra 65; Oxford, Corpus Christi College, MS 144; Paris, Bibliothèque nationale, MS nouv. acq. lat. 699; Worcester Cathedral, Chapter Library, MS Q.79. The remaining five copies date from the fifteenth century: London, British Library, MS Royal 12.B.xvii (excerpt) and MS Royal 12.E.xi; Oxford, Bodleian Library, MS Bodley 832 (excerpt) and MS Laud misc. 707; Oxford, Corpus Christi College, MS 132.

[21] For a list of the manuscripts known to contain the *Poetria nova,* see Woods, *Classroom Commentaries,* 289–307. Chaucer could have secured a fresh copy while traveling in Italy as an adult, for example, but is unlikely to have encountered one while studying grammar as a child.

1199, is preserved in two thirteenth-century English manuscripts and three English manuscripts that range in date from the early to the mid-fifteenth century.[22] The chronological distribution of the four English manuscripts that contain the *De arte versificatoria et modo dictandi* (1215–16) by Geoffrey of Vinsauf's English contemporary Gervase of Melkley is almost identical: one copy dates from the early thirteenth century, while the remaining three copies are from the late fourteenth or early fifteenth century.[23] Even a work that was written in France, Matthew of Vendôme's *Ars versificatoria* (before c. 1175), exhibits a similar pattern in its English circulation, albeit with an imbalance favoring the earlier rather than the later phase of copying. Of the nine manuscript copies that may be of English provenance, six are from the thirteenth century (most of them from the first half of the century) and three are from the late fourteenth or the early fifteenth century.[24] Finally, there is no evidence that the *Parisiana poetria* (c. 1220; revised 1231–35) by John of Garland, an Englishman who spent his teaching career in France, circulated in England before the last quarter of the fourteenth century. While none of the six surviving manuscript copies on which Traugott Lawler based his critical edition is obviously Eng-

[22] The thirteenth-century copies are in Cambridge, Corpus Christi College, MS 217, and Glasgow, Hunterian Library, MS Hunterian V.8.14. The fifteenth-century copies are in Durham Cathedral, Dean and Chapter Library, MS C.IV.25; London, British Library, MS Royal 12.B.xvii; and Paris, Bibliothèque nationale, MS nouv. acq. lat. 699. N. R. Ker, *Medieval Manuscripts in British Libraries,* 5 vols. (Oxford: Clarendon Press, 1969–2002), vol. 3 (1983), 142–43, records a two-page fragment of the *Documentum* that he thinks might be French, used as binding leaves in an English manuscript whose main contents are J. of Hildesheim, *Historia trium regum* (s. xiv/xv): Lincoln, Muniments of the Dean and Chapter, MS Di/20/3, fols. 41r–42v (s. xiii[1]).

[23] Early thirteenth century: Glasgow, Hunterian Library, MS Hunterian V.8.14; fourteenth/fifteenth century: Douai, Bibliothèque Municipale, MS 764; Oxford, Balliol College, MS 263 and MS 276.

[24] Franco Munari lists nineteen manuscripts containing all or part of the *Ars versificatoria,* in *Mathei Vindocinensis Opera,* vol. 1: *Catologo dei manoscritti* (Rome: Storia e Letteratura, 1977): #30, 37, 43, 47, 50, 51, 60, 61, 70, 77, 79, 83, 87, 92, 101, 105, 110, 124, 126. As many as nine of these are from England, including six that date from the thirteenth century: Durham Cathedral, Dean and Chapter Library, MS B.III.33; Glasgow, Hunterian Library, MS Hunterian V.8.14 (formerly 511); London, British Library, MS Add. 23892; Oxford, Bodleian Library, MS Misc. Latin D 15 (excerpts); Warminster (Wilts.), Library of the Marquess of Bath, MS Longleat 27 (excerpts); and York, Minster Library, MS XVI.Q.14 (excerpts). Three date from the second half of the fourteenth century through the first half of the fifteenth century: London, British Library, MS Cotton Titus A.xx (excerpts), and Oxford, Balliol College, MS 263 and MS 276.

lish, at least one copy of the *Parisiana poetria* was in England by 1389. The work is cited in several English manuscripts from the first half of the fifteenth century, and it is a major source for several chapters of the anonymous English rhetorical treatise known as *Tria sunt,* which probably was compiled near the end of the fourteenth century.[25] In this case, the quest to recover twelfth- and thirteenth-century arts of poetry and prose may well have extended across the Channel.[26]

Arts of poetry and prose were not the only examples of older "rhetorical" texts that were sought out for renewed study in their own right and for reuse as sources for new textbooks in England during the second half of the fourteenth century. The revival also encompassed the literary texts that were cited as models by the authors of the arts of poetry and prose. These included both the classical poetry of antiquity and the classicizing Latin poetry of the twelfth century, as well as prose texts deemed worthy of imitation. Copies of such works often appear together with the arts of poetry and prose or with newly composed rhetoric textbooks in English manuscripts of the late fourteenth and early fifteenth centuries.[27] There is also evidence to suggest that new attention was paid to the ancient rhetorical treatises, in particular Cicero's *De inventione* and the anonymous *Rhetorica ad Herennium,* which in the Middle Ages was attributed to Cicero. For example, early in the fifteenth century, Hugh Legat, a Benedictine monk who had studied at Oxford, brought together twelfth-century copies of the *De inventione* and *Rhetorica ad Herennium* belonging to his house of St. Albans, arranged to have them newly rebound, and proclaimed the

---

[25] Traugott Lawler, ed. and trans., *The "Parisiana poetria" of John of Garland* (New Haven: Yale University Press, 1974), xix–xxi. A copy (now lost) is recorded in John Whytefelde's 1389 catalogue of the books in the library of the Priory of the Blessed Virgin Mary and St. Martin, Dover: *Dover Priory,* ed. William P. Stoneman, Corpus of British Medieval Library Catalogues, 5 (London: The British Library, 1999), 135–36, item H.IIII.327(c). For citations of the *Parisiana poetria* in Oxford, Bodleian Library, MS Douce 52, and London, British Library, MS Harley 670, see Martin Camargo, *Medieval Rhetorics of Prose Composition: Five English "Artes dictandi" and Their Tradition* (Binghamton: Medieval and Renaissance Texts and Studies, 1995), 9 (esp. n. 25), 88. The *Tria sunt* is discussed in greater detail below.

[26] The only thirteenth-century art of poetry and prose that seems to have escaped the fourteenth-century English dragnet entirely is the *Laborintus* (after 1213; before 1280) by Eberhard the German. It survives in more than forty manuscript copies, second only to the *Poetria nova,* but its circulation apparently was limited almost exclusively to the German-speaking regions of central Europe.

[27] For some examples, see Martin Camargo, "Beyond the *Libri Catoniani:* Models of Latin Prose Style at Oxford University ca. 1400," *Mediaeval Studies* 56 (1994): 165–87.

fact of having done so on the flyleaf of the codex (London, British Library, MS Harley 2624). Evidence of a different sort comes from the *Tria sunt,* whose compiler appears to have consulted the *Rhetorica ad Herennium* directly when defining and illustrating the rhetorical figures and an even wider range of ancient and medieval sources, including the *De inventione,* in treating the attributes of persons and actions.[28]

The prominent role that Oxford-trained Benedictine monks played in the fourteenth-century renaissance of rhetoric extended beyond collecting and recopying older, often neglected texts. Hugh Legat of St. Albans also wrote a commentary on John of Hauville's *Architrenius,* and other Benedictines contributed commentaries, *accessus,* and glosses to rhetorical texts and literary texts employed in teaching rhetoric.[29] Benedictines also were among those who created new rhetorical treatises from the older texts that they or their fellow monks had rescued from obscurity. An especially good example is Thomas Merke, a Benedictine monk of Westminster Abbey, who wrote the *Formula moderni et usitati dictaminis* ("A Rule for Modern and Familiar [Prose] Composition") around 1390, probably while resident at Oxford.[30] One of the more popular among the new textbooks, Merke's letter-writing handbook (*ars dictandi*) survives in eleven English manuscripts, most of them from the early fifteenth century.[31] It is divided into three parts, consisting of brief

[28] Martin Camargo, "Latin Composition Textbooks and *Ad Herennium* Glossing: The Missing Link?" in *The Rhetoric of Cicero in Its Medieval and Early Renaissance Commentary Tradition,* ed. Virginia Cox and John O. Ward (Leiden: Brill, 2006), 267–88 (275, 278–79, 286–88). Since publishing this essay, I have discovered additional sources employed in the treatment of the attributes, including the twelfth-century commentary on the *De inventione* by Thierry of Chartres and the commentary on Alan of Lille's *Anticlaudianus* (c. 1212) by Ralph of Longchamp.

[29] For many examples (including Legat) from one of the larger houses, see James G. Clark, *A Monastic Renaissance at St Albans: Thomas Walsingham and His Circle, c. 1350– 1440* (Oxford: Clarendon Press, 2004). On the role of the Benedictines in the late medieval renaissance of rhetoric in England, see also Martin Camargo, "Rhetoricians in Black: Benedictine Monks and Rhetorical Revival in Medieval Oxford," in *New Chapters in the History of Rhetoric,* ed. Laurent Pernot, International Studies in the History of Rhetoric 1 (Leiden: Brill, 2009), 375–84.

[30] Camargo, ed., *Medieval Rhetorics,* 105–47. See also James J. Murphy, "A Fifteenth-Century Treatise on Prose Style," *Newberry Library Bulletin* 6 (1966): 205–10. Murphy (207–8) believes that Merke wrote his treatise during a later stay at Oxford, between 1401 and his death in 1406. For the evidence favoring the earlier date, see Camargo, *Medieval Rhetorics,* 116–17.

[31] Chicago, Newberry Library, MS 55; Dublin, Trinity College, MS 424 and MS 427; Lincoln, Cathedral, Chapter Library, MS 237; London, British Library, MS Additional 24361 and MS Harley 5398; Oxford, Balliol College, MS 263; Oxford, Bodleian Li-

introductory remarks followed by more extended treatments of the "essential" and the "accidental" parts of a letter:

1. Prologue and definitions
2. Essential parts of a letter:
   a. greeting (*salutatio*)
   b. introduction (*exordium*)
   c. statement of facts (*narratio*)
   d. request (*petitio*)
   e. conclusion (*conclusio*)
3. Accidental parts of a letter:
   a. rhythmical clause endings (*cursus*)
   b. rhetorical figures (*colores rhetorici*)
   c. stylistic variation through changes in a key word (*conversio*)
   d. stylistic variation through modifying a key word with other words (*determinatio*)
   e. stylistic faults (*vitia*)

The contents of Merke's *ars dictandi* illustrate several characteristic features of the rhetoric textbooks produced in the course of the Oxford-centered revival.

Most of the other new rhetoric textbooks are anonymous and cannot be dated so precisely, but at least three of them probably were composed during Chaucer's lifetime, since the earliest copies are written in English hands from around the turn of the fifteenth century. Two of these also show signs of Benedictine authorship. *Tria sunt,* a new art of poetry and prose that is among the most comprehensive works in this genre, was almost certainly composed by a Benedictine monk, probably at Oxford, in the late fourteenth century.[32] Preserved in thirteen English manuscripts, it was at least as popular as Merke's contemporary *ars dictandi.*[33]

---

brary, MS Rawlinson D.232 and MS Selden Supra 65; Oxford, St. John's College, MS 172 and MS 184.

[32] Martin Camargo, "*Tria sunt:* The Long and the Short of Geoffrey of Vinsauf's *Documentum de modo et arte dictandi et versificandi,*" *Speculum* 74 (1999): 935–55. An edition with facing English translation, and a separate commentary, are in preparation.

[33] The earliest copies (s. xiv/xv) are in Cambridge, Trinity College, MS R.14.22; Douai, Bibliothèque municipale, MS 764; London, British Library, MS Cotton Cleopatra B.vi; Oxford, Balliol College, MS 263. All of the other copies are from the fifteenth century, mainly its first few decades: Berlin, Staatsbibliothek, Stiftung preussischer Kulturbesitz, MS Lat. qu. 515; Cambridge, Pembroke College, MS 287; Cambridge, Sidney Sussex College, MS 56; Chicago, Newberry Library, MS 55; Oxford, Bodleian Library, MS Douce 147, MS Laud misc. 707, MS Rawlinson D.893 (one leaf from what probably was a complete copy), and MS Selden Supra 65; Worcester Cathedral, Chapter Library,

In all copies it is divided into the same sixteen chapters, usually provided with descriptive headings that vary little from one copy to another:

Primum capitulum est de principio naturali et artificiali et de octo modis principii artificialis.

Secundum de prosecucione materie et quibus terminis precedencia subsequentibus copulentur.

Tercium de octo modis prolongandi materiam et eam inueniendi et de artificio epistolas componendi.

Quartum de septem modis abbreuiandi materiam et de consideracione materie quibus ornatibus vestiatur.

Quintum de decem speciebus transumpcionis quibus ornata difficultas efficitur et scripturarum grauitas aperitur.

Sextum de hiis in quibus omnis ornatus attenditur et in quibus diccionibus melior sit ornatus.

Septimum de ornata facilitate et de determinacione, quod est potissimum elocucionis condimentum, et de coloribus verborum et sentenciarum.

Octauum de officio omnium colorum et quomodo figure coloribus reducuntur.

Nonum de arte inueniendi ornata verba quibus omnis ruditas quibusdam nouitatis flosculis exornetur.

Decimum de execucione materie illibate.

Undecimum de execucione materie communis.

Duodecimum de attributis persone et negocio, quorum artificio proprietates materie comparantur.

Terciumdecimum de stilis poeticis et modernis et eorum proprietatibus.

Quartumdecimum de sex viciis capitalibus in dictamine quolibet euitandis.

Quintumdecimum de generibus sermonum et varietatibus carminum.

Sextumdecimum et vltimum de conclusione et quomodo sit sumenda.[34]

1. On natural and artificial beginnings and the eight methods for artificial beginnings.
2. On the continuation of the subject matter and transitional expressions.
3. On the eight ways of generating and lengthening the subject matter and about the technique for composing letters.

MS Q.79. While this article was in press I discovered two further copies, in Ferrara, Biblioteca comunale Ariostea, MS Classe II.206 (s. xiv), and Bologna, Biblioteca comunale dell'Archiginnasio, MS A.163 (s. xv).

[34] These headings or *capitula* are repeated as part of Chapter 16, at the very end of the *Tria sunt,* here quoted from the base text for my edition (Worcester Cathedral, Chapter Library, MS Q.79, fol. 158r–v).

4. On the seven ways of shortening the subject matter and about how to decide which verbal ornaments to use in adorning a given subject matter.

5. On the ten kinds of "transumption" [metaphorical language], by means of which one produces "ornamented difficulty" and reveals the weightiness of what one has written.

6. On matters that concern all verbal ornamentation and on the words that provide the best ornamentation.

7. On "ornamented facility" [nonmetaphorical figures] and on "determination" [qualifying one word with another], which is the principal seasoning of style, and on the colors of words and thoughts.

8. On the functional categories into which all of the colors can be sorted and how the "figures" correspond to the "colors."

9. On the art of discovering ornamented words that enable one to beautify every uncouth expression with "fresh flowers."

10. On developing an original subject matter.

11. On developing a familiar subject matter.

12. On the attributes of persons and actions, by means of which one provides the characteristic details that are suited to a particular subject matter.

13. On the "poetic" and the "modern" styles and their characteristics.

14. On the six chief faults to be avoided in any kind of composition.

15. On the genres of discourse and the varieties of poetic compositions.

16. On conclusions and how they should be produced.

A third rhetorical treatise is preserved in four English manuscripts from the fourteenth through the early fifteenth centuries, where it is called both *Floridi dictaminis compendium* ("Compendium of Flowery [Prose] Composition") and *Compendium artis dictatorie* ("Compendium of the Art of [Prose] Composition").[35] In a copy that belonged to Benedictine monks who studied at Canterbury College, Oxford, it is said to have been composed by "a certain monk of S."[36] Each of the

[35] Oxford, Bodleian Library, MS Selden Supra 65 (s. xv in.); Oxford, Balliol College, MS 263 (s. xiv/xv); Cambridge, Corpus Christi College, MS 358 (s. xiv); Douai, Bibliothèque municipale, MS 764 (s. xiv/xv).

[36] MS Selden Supra 65, fol. 134r: "Explicit compendium artis dictatorie compositum [MS: composito] a quodam monacho de S. anno domini Millesimo lxiiij° etc." The date in the explicit (1064) cannot be accurate, since the treatise cites several works from the thirteenth century. Perhaps it is a corruption of 1364, which fits the evidence better.

six chapters into which it is divided is provided with a descriptive heading:[37]

1. On the parts of a composition and their order.
2. On the beginnings, divisions, and endings of sentences.
3. On the faults to be avoided.
4. The ornamentation of words.
5. The ornaments of thoughts.
6. The proper method of oral delivery.

While the *Tria sunt* and the *Compendium artis dictatorie* vary little in structure and contents from one copy to another, the same is not true of my final example. In the two fullest copies, it contains five parts, and in one of these the scribe has given it the title *Forma dictandi* ("A Model for Composing [Prose *or* Letters]"); but its constituent parts appear separately or in various combinations in English manuscripts of the thirteenth through the fifteenth centuries, suggesting that it is more purely a compendium than the other three textbooks in the sample group.[38] The sequence of parts in the two "complete" copies is as follows:

1. General prologue; Prose rhythm (*cursus*) A
2. Prose rhythm B
3. Divisions of a sentence (*distinctiones*)
4. The colors of rhetoric in order (*colores rhetorici seriatim*)
5. In praise of Bartholomew (*ad laudem Bartholomei*)

[37] The translated portions of the rubrics, from the copy in MS Selden Supra 65, are: de dictacionis partibus et ordine (fol. 126v); de clausularum principiis, scissuris et terminis (127r); de viciis euitandis (128r); ornatum verborum (129r); sentenciarum ornamenta (131r); modum debitum proferendi (132v).

[38] The complete copies (both s. xiv/xv) are in London, British Library, MS Harley 3224 (with title) and Oxford, Balliol College, MS 263. A third manuscript contemporary with these (Douai, Bibliothèque municipale, MS 764) begins with the final leaf of what may have been a complete copy. Other English manuscripts that contain a majority of the parts, in sequence, are London, British Library, MS Cotton Cleopatra B.vi (s. xiv/xv; parts 1, 3–4); MS Cotton Nero A.iv (s. xiv; parts 2–4 [imperf.]); and MS Harley 3300 (s. xv; parts 1–4 [imperf.]). Parts 4 and 5 occur together in a thirteenth-century English manuscript (Cambridge, Trinity College, MS R.14.40) and widely separated from one another in a fourteenth-century English manuscript (Cambridge, Corpus Christi College, MS 358). Another English manuscript of the fourteenth century (Oxford, Magdalen College, MS Lat. 6) contains an incomplete copy of Part 4. Part 1 occurs alone in Oxford, Bodleian Library, MS Bodley 310 (s. xiv ex.), and Part 3 and a version of Part 2 occur separately and in reverse order in MS Bodley 832 (s. xv²).

The *Formula moderni et usitati dictaminis,* the *Tria sunt,* the *Compendium artis dictatorie,* and the *Forma dictandi* are almost certainly not the only textbooks that were produced as a direct result of the renaissance of rhetoric that began in the second half of the fourteenth century. Some such works inevitably will have been lost, while others may have been written within Chaucer's lifetime but survive only in later copies.[39] As will be evident from the lists of their contents, the treatises for which there is strong evidence of fourteenth-century circulation share certain emphases that shed light on the concerns of those who were responsible for the renewed interest in rhetoric and which may help to explain Chaucer's interest in the results of their labors.

These four treatises have one shared feature that is not obvious from their tables of contents. Each draws principally if not exclusively on sources that are more than a century older. In his *Formula moderni et usitati dictaminis,* Thomas Merke combines material on the theory of letters and the "essential" parts of a letter from the *Summa dictaminis* (c. 1228–29) by Guido Faba and the *Ars dictandi* (1208–1209) by Thomas of Capua with still more extensive borrowings from Geoffrey of Vinsauf's *Documentum de modo et arte dictandi et versificandi* (s. xii ex.) and *Poetria nova* (s. xiii in.), on natural and artificial order, amplification and abbreviation, and all of the "accidental" parts of a letter except prose rhythm.[40] The contemporary *Tria sunt* is equally dependent on sources from the twelfth and early thirteenth centuries for most of its contents. It quotes at length not only from Geoffrey of Vinsauf's *Poetria nova* and *Documentum de modo et arte dictandi et versificandi* (probably a later version [s. xiii in.] that has not survived), but also from the arts of poetry and prose by Matthew of Vendôme (*Ars versificatoria;* s. xii ex.) and Gervase of Melkley (*De arte versificatoria et modo dictandi;* s. xiii in.), as well as from "rhetorical" poets of the same vintage, most notably Alan of Lille (*De planctu Naturae, Anticlaudianus*). When the compiler ventures beyond such sources, it generally is to cite the ancient rhetorical texts,

---

[39] The *Compilacio de arte dictandi* by Master John of Briggis, to cite only one example, could have been composed as early as 1380, when its probable author's name begins to appear in the records of Merton College, Oxford. However, the single extant copy was made during the first half of the fifteenth century (Oxford, Bodleian Library, MS Douce 52). For a discussion and edition of this work, see Camargo, *Medieval Rhetorics,* 88–104.

[40] Merke's treatment of rhythmical clause endings (*cursus*) derives from a text found in several late fourteenth- and fifteenth-century English manuscripts, including copies of the anonymous *Forma dictandi* (it is what I have called "Prose rhythm A" in Part 1). See Camargo, *Medieval Rhetorics,* 146 (note to lines 514–54).

such as the *Rhetorica ad Herennium* and Horace's *Ars poetica,* that were major sources for the arts of poetry and prose, as well as the classical poetry on which the classicizing verse of Alan of Lille and his contemporaries was modeled. Were it not for a few scattered quotations and references to later works, the *Tria sunt* could as easily have been composed in the early thirteenth century as in the late fourteenth century. Although much shorter and more tightly organized than the *Tria sunt,* the *Compendium artis dictatorie* is still more eclectic in the sources it claims, if not those it actually uses. The treatise opens with a list of sources that includes Cicero, Aristotle, Quintilian, Isidore [of Seville], and Marbod [of Rennes] and concludes with a list of twelfth- and thirteenth-century letter collections, by Peter of Vinea, Richard of Pophis, and Peter of Blois, that exemplify the epistolary eloquence that it seeks to inculcate. Like the other three textbooks, the *Forma dictandi* contains a substantial amount of much earlier, newly recovered rhetorical materials, but, unlike them, its adaptation of those materials to contemporary needs is limited to their juxtaposition with more recently composed materials. It is not impossible that the compiler of the *Forma dictandi* was the author of one or more of the initial three parts of the textbook, none of which is attested before the fourteenth century; but the remaining two parts probably were written as companion pieces during the late twelfth or early thirteenth century, since they are preserved together in an English manuscript written early in the thirteenth century, and were not linked to the other three parts until late in the fourteenth century.

Even in his simple act of assembling what were originally at least three and possibly five discrete texts, the compiler of the *Forma dictandi* exemplifies another important tendency of the fourteenth-century English "rhetoricians": when searching out and incorporating source materials, they liked to juxtapose and compare different authorities on topics of particular interest. Thus, the first two parts of the *Forma dictandi* offer contrasting treatments of the *cursus,* and the *Compendium artis dictatorie* compares sources on major topics such as the rhetorical figures (chapters 4 and 5) and the rules governing oral delivery (Chapter 6). Juxtaposition and comparison are most pervasive in the *Tria sunt,* with its multifaceted and comprehensive treatment of the rhetorical figures from a variety of angles based on sources that range from the *Rhetorica ad Herennium,* through five different arts of poetry and prose, to the late antique and early medieval grammarians and encyclopedists (see chapters 5–8 and 10–12). The use of different combinations of sources seems to have helped each of the teachers who composed such textbooks to establish his unique niche within what would have been a crowded field in the schools at Oxford during the late fourteenth century, and the desire to gain a competitive advantage by using sources not available elsewhere must have been a strong incentive for recovering rhetorical texts, such as the arts of poetry and prose, that had languished in libraries for generations. This drive to differentiate is evident even when two authors used the same authority to treat a given topic. Both Thomas Merke and the compiler of the *Tria sunt* made extensive use of Geoffrey of Vinsauf's *Documentum de modo et arte dictandi et versificandi* and *Poetria nova,* for example, but Merke adapted Geoffrey's teaching on artificial and natural order and on amplification and abbreviation to create his own schemes for epistolary *exordia* and *narrationes,* respectively, while the compiler of the *Tria sunt* based his epistolary doctrine on what must have been a rare copy of the revised *Documentum de modo et arte dictandi,* which contained a discussion of letters found nowhere else.

Besides their use of newly rediscovered source materials in novel combinations, the rhetorical textbooks written in the late fourteenth and early fifteenth centuries share several areas of emphasis. Chief among these is letter writing, whether the textbook in question is a dedicated treatise on the subject (i.e., an *ars dictandi*), such as Merke's *Formula moderni et usitati dictaminis,* or is closer in scope and emphasis to the earlier arts of poetry and prose, as are the *Tria sunt* and, on a smaller scale, the *Compendium artis dictatorie,* or is somewhere in between, as is the *Forma dictandi.* In the *Tria sunt,* letters are treated in some detail as a special instance of amplification, in an appendix to the third chapter;[41] they are discussed briefly in the fifteenth chapter, as one of several types of rhetorically constructed texts; and examples of epistolary conclusions are provided in the sixteenth chapter. The first chapter of the *Compendium artis dictatorie* is devoted to the parts of a letter, which the author, in keeping with his classicizing tendencies, equates with the six parts of an oration (*exordium, narratio, divisio, confirmatio, confutatio, conclusio*) rather than the standard five parts of a medieval letter (*salutatio, exor-*

---

[41] On this appendix, see Martin Camargo, "Toward a Comprehensive Art of Written Discourse: Geoffrey of Vinsauf and the *Ars dictaminis,*" *Rhetorica* 6 (1988): 167–94 (edition of the Latin text: 186–92), and Camargo, introduction, translation, and annotation of an excerpt from *Tria sunt,* Chapter 3, in *Medieval Grammar and Rhetoric: Language Arts and Literary Theory, AD 300–1475,* ed. Rita Copeland and Ineke Sluiter (Oxford: Oxford University Press, 2009), 670–81 (English translation of the appendix on letter writing: 674–81).

dium, narratio, petitio, conclusio) recognized by Merke and the compiler of the *Tria sunt*. The second chapter takes up the most distinctive elements of epistolary style, the rhythmical cadences of the *cursus* and the division of sentences into their constituent segments, called *distinctiones* (comma, colon, and period), with cross-references to the discussion of letter parts in Chapter 1. The *cursus* and *distinctiones* are also the subjects of parts 1–3 of the *Forma dictandi,* a textbook that is concerned almost exclusively with matters of style.

The subject of the remaining two parts of the *Forma dictandi*—the figures or "colors" of rhetoric—is a second area of emphasis in all four of the textbooks under consideration. Like the corresponding sections of the *Formula moderni et usitati dictaminis* (Part 3.b), *Tria sunt* (chapters 5 and 7), and *Compendium artis dictatorie* (chapters 4 and 5), Part 4 of the *Forma dictandi* contains definitions and illustrations of the *colores.* In Part 5, the figures of speech are used in the exact order of their treatment in Book 4 of the *Rhetorica ad Herennium* to produce a rhetorical encomium of an archdeacon named Bartholomew. Examples of the same technique—probably the basis of a classroom exercise—also appear in Geoffrey of Vinsauf's *Poetria nova* (figures of speech: lines 1098–1217; figures of thought: lines 1280–1527), which is exactly contemporary with the earliest surviving copy of what became parts 4 and 5 of the *Forma dictandi* (s. xiii in.).[42] Select figures also are prominent among the methods for achieving brevity and amplitude, as discussed in Merke's *Formula moderni et usitati dictaminis* (Part 2.c) and the *Tria sunt* (chapters 3 and 4).

A third shared emphasis, oral performance, overlaps in interesting ways with the other two. This topic is most explicit in the *Compendium artis dictatorie,* which devotes the last of its six chapters to the theory and practice of oral performance. Many of its contents are paraphrased from the *Rhetorica ad Herennium* and concern the need to match one's manner of delivery to the level of style one employs (the subdued, the moderate, or the grand); but the author also includes specific instructions on performing epistolary texts whose style is based on the *cursus* and the *distinctiones.*[43] These remarks are a reminder that both the *cursus*

---

[42] As part of a larger project on the rhetorical figures, I have completed a preliminary edition of the texts in question, titled "Colores rhetorici seriatim" and "Magister Berentinus ad laudem Bartholomei" in the earliest manuscript copy.

[43] *Compendium artis dictatorie,* Chapter 6, has been edited and translated into English by Martin Camargo, "Epistolary Declamation: Performing Model Letters in Medieval English Classrooms," in *Studies in the Cultural History of Letter Writing,* ed. Susan Green

and the *distinctiones* are auditory techniques whose effects are fully realized only in oral performance. Thus, in devoting significant space to these topics, both Merke's *Formula moderni et usitati dictaminis* (Part 3.a) and the anonymous *Forma dictandi* (parts 1–3) implicitly share the emphasis of the *Compendium artis dictatorie* on oral performance. Only the *Tria sunt* fails to emphasize speaking or reading aloud to the same extent. While the two model letters in the appendix to Chapter 3 are composed in accordance with the rules of the *cursus* and *distinctiones,* the treatise lacks any explicit treatment of the *distinctiones* and includes the *cursus* among several types of prose rhythm described and illustrated in the short Chapter 13.[44] Nonetheless, *Tria sunt* does consider in some detail what amount to auditory effects; for example, in its teaching on the figures of speech (Chapter 7), whose special relevance to letters composed in the "Gregorian" style is noted in Chapter 13. Another topic that the *Tria sunt* shares with several other contemporary textbooks, the vices of style, also reveals an underlying presumption of oral performance. Many of the stylistic faults identified in the *Tria sunt* (Chapter 14), the *Formula moderni et usitati dictaminis* (Part 3.e), and the *Compendium artis dictatorie* (Chapter 3) are auditory defects that impede the pleasure and/or comprehension of listeners rather than readers.

The relative neglect of a topic emphasized elsewhere, such as the rarely explicit treatment of oral performance in the *Tria sunt,* could actually have been a deliberate response to the simultaneous circulation of so many new and old rhetorical treatises in late fourteenth-century Oxford. As was shown earlier, one response to the competition was to innovate, by finding new source materials or by creating a novel synthesis from materials already in use; but another could have been to focus on certain topics while de-emphasizing others, secure in the knowledge that those who wished to study them would have no shortage of alternatives. The manuscripts recording the Oxford renaissance of rhetoric offer clear evidence that it was in fact a common practice to copy two or more

---

(San Marino, Calif.: Huntington Library Press, in press), appendix. On the oral performance of medieval letters, see also Martin Camargo, "Special Delivery: Were Medieval Letter Writers Trained in Performance?" in *Rhetoric Beyond Words: Delight and Persuasion in the Arts of the Middle Ages,* ed. Mary Carruthers (Cambridge: Cambridge University Press, 2010), 173–89.

[44] Some readers of the *Tria sunt* took steps to remedy this relative neglect. In two of the manuscripts, a kind of appendix on the rules of the *cursus* has been copied immediately after the *Tria sunt:* Douai, Bibliothèque municipale, MS 764, fol. 108r–v, and London, British Library, MS Cotton Cleopatra B.vi, fol. 89v.

textbooks together, a good indication that those who created and used such codices recognized and valued the complementarity of their contents. The thirteenth-century English manuscripts containing arts of poetry and prose rarely follow the same pattern, though they do include one exceptionally rich anthology of textbooks and school poetry;[45] but during the late fourteenth and early fifteenth centuries, it became normal to copy or bind several rhetoric textbooks together, as evidenced by at least a dozen English examples from this period.[46]

By the last quarter of the fourteenth century a significant revival of rhetoric was under way, as Englishmen dusted off old copies of rhetorical texts, made new copies of some of them, and composed or compiled textbooks combining older with more recent doctrine on the *colores rhetorici,* oral delivery, and especially letter writing, all of which they frequently gathered into larger collections. The provision of multiple perspectives on topics of special interest, which privileges critical analy-

---

[45] Glasgow, Hunterian Library, MS Hunterian V.8.14 (c. 1225). On this well-known collection, see especially Edmond Faral, "Le manuscrit 511 du 'Hunterian Museum' de Glasgow: Notes sur le mouvement poétique et l'histoire des études littéraires en France et en Angleterre entre les années 1150 et 1225," *Studi medievali* n.s. 9 (1936): 18–121; and Bruce Harbert, *A Thirteenth-Century Anthology of Rhetorical Poems* (Toronto: Pontifical Institute of Mediaeval Studies, 1975).

[46] The following sigla designate treatises discussed in this essay and preserved, in whole or in excerpts, in the manuscripts indicated: *AV* (Matthew of Vendôme, *Ars versificatoria*), *CAD* (*Compendium artis dictatorie*), *Doc* (Geoffrey of Vinsauf, *Documentum de modo et arte dictandi et versificandi*), *FD* (*Forma dictandi*), GerM (Gervase of Melkley, *De arte versificatoria et modo dictandi*), Merke (Thomas Merke, *Formula moderni et usitati dictaminis*), *PN* (Geoffrey of Vinsauf, *Poetria nova*), *TS* (*Tria sunt*). Early thirteenth-century English manuscripts containing two or more rhetoric textbooks: Glasgow, Hunterian Library, MS Hunterian V.8.14 (*AV, PN, Doc,* GerM); York, Minster Library, MS XVI.Q.14 (*AV, PN*). Fourteenth- and fifteenth-century manuscripts: Berlin, Staatsbibliothek, Stiftung preussischer Kulturbesitz, MS Lat. qu. 515 (*PN, TS*); Cambridge, Corpus Christi College, MS 358 (*FD, CAD*); Cambridge, Trinity College, MS R.14.22 (*PN, TS*); Chicago, Newberry Library, MS 55 (Merke, *TS*); Douai, Bibliothèque municipale, MS 764 (*PN,* GerM, *FD, CAD, TS*); London, British Library, MS Cotton Cleopatra B.vi (*PN, FD, TS*) and MS Royal 12.B.xvii (*PN, Doc*); Oxford, Balliol College, MS 263 (*AV, PN,* GerM, *FD, CAD, TS*) and MS 276 (*AV, PN,* GerM); Oxford, Bodleian Library, MS Bodley 832 (*PN, FD*), MS Laud misc. 707 (*PN, TS*), and MS Selden Supra 65 (*PN,* Merke, *CAD, TS*); Paris, Bibliothèque nationale, MS nouv. acq. lat. 699 (*PN, Doc*); Worcester Cathedral, Chapter Library, MS Q.79 (*PN, TS*). Two of these manuscripts—MS Bodley 832 and MS Royal 12.B.xvii—are from the third quarter of the fifteenth century and record the spread of the rediscovered materials to provincial schools rather than their initial revival at Oxford. On these two manuscripts, see Martin Camargo, "Grammar School Rhetoric: The Compendia of John Longe and John Miller," *NML* 11, special issue, "Medieval Grammar and the Literary Arts," ed. Chris Cannon, Rita Copeland, and Nicolette Zeeman (2010, for 2009): 91–112.

sis over mechanical imitation, the Oxford provenance of the new textbooks and many of the most important manuscripts, and the marked emphasis on novel approaches to letter writing are features that are more suited to intermediate and advanced students than to elementary students and further suggest that at its height the English renaissance of rhetoric was motivated by intellectual curiosity as well as pedagogical necessity.

What had sparked this revival whose traces are so abundant in the manuscript record? At least part of the answer should be sought among the many Benedictine monks who played such a prominent role as collectors, scribes, compilers, and authors of the rhetorical texts that define it. In particular, it seems significant that the revival of rhetoric coincides precisely with a dramatic increase in the numbers of Benedictines at Oxford during the second half of the fourteenth century. Pope Benedict XII's bull *Summi magistri,* issued in 1336, included the provision that each of the English monasteries should send at least one monk to study at the university. Larger houses were required to send one out of every twenty monks. The effects of these new regulations became evident over time, for example, in the founding of two new Benedictine colleges at Oxford—Canterbury College (1361) and Durham College (1381)—to help relieve the pressure on Gloucester College, which had housed scholar monks since 1283. The goal of the student monks was to progress as quickly as possible to the higher faculties of theology and canon law in order to spend as little time as possible away from the monastic community, but this goal conflicted with the university's requirement that a lengthy arts course be completed first. The monks who tried to circumvent this requirement by devising their own substitute for the university arts course would have ransacked their libraries for relevant materials, in the process very likely rediscovering rhetorical texts that had remained unread and all but forgotten for a century or more. The activities of one such Benedictine, Hugh Legat of St. Albans, have been mentioned already. There is also evidence of student monks carrying manuscripts containing rhetorical texts between their mother houses and the monastic colleges at Oxford, where they had the potential to have an impact on a broader spectrum of scholars.[47]

[47] Cambridge, Sidney Sussex College MS 56, which belonged to monks who studied at Durham College, and Oxford, Bodleian Library, MS Selden Supra 65, which belonged to monks who studied at Canterbury College, are two good examples. In addition to Clark, *A Monastic Renaissance,* and Camargo, "Rhetoricians in Black," on the Benedictines at Oxford, see also R. B. Dobson, "The Religious Orders 1370–1540," in *The*

Even if the monks' wish to bypass normal curricular requirements was instrumental in setting the revival of rhetoric in motion, building and sustaining that revival through at least the first quarter of the fifteenth century depended on creating broader interest in the subject. In fact, the topics that are foregrounded in the fourteenth- and fifteenth-century textbooks reveal some of the ways in which rhetorical treatises would have benefited a wide range of Oxford scholars. The ability to compose official letters was a necessity for anyone taking on significant administrative duties in a monastery, an episcopal chancery, or a secular context. The rhetorical art of letter writing (*ars dictaminis*) had developed to meet a growing need for clerks with this skill, and Oxford had come to be the preeminent center for such instruction in England. By the mid-fourteenth century, practical training in the composition of letters and other quasi-epistolary documents was offered primarily by specialists operating on the margins of the university, as part of what has been called the "business course," which had evolved over several generations. The letter-writing textbooks created by the business teachers were short on rhetorical theory and long on models to imitate, and the grammar masters who worked within the university quickly seized the opportunity to exploit the newly recovered rhetorical materials in competing textbooks that reversed those proportions. They typically situated letters within a more general theory of composition, brought the full range of stylistics to bear on their composition, and incorporated at most only a few model letters.[48] Whether in a true *ars dictandi* such as Thomas Merke's *Formula moderni et usitati dictaminis* or an art of poetry and prose such as the *Tria sunt,* the success of their approach extended well beyond the confines of the Benedictine community and of Oxford itself, helping to spread the effects of the rhetorical renaissance throughout England.

The emphasis on oral performance in connection with letters also was a contributing factor to the broader impact of the Oxford rhetorical

---

History of the University of Oxford, vol. 2: *Late Medieval Oxford,* ed. J. I. Catto and Ralph Evans (Oxford: Clarendon Press, 1992), 539–79.

[48] The Oxford "business course" was first identified and labeled as such by H. G. Richardson, "Business Training in Medieval Oxford," *American Historical Review* 46 (1941): 259–80. On the competing approaches to teaching the *ars dictaminis* at Oxford, see Camargo, *Medieval Rhetorics,* 20–32, and "If You Can't Join Them, Beat Them; or, When Grammar Met Business Writing (in Fifteenth-Century Oxford)," in *Letter-Writing Manuals and Instruction from Antiquity to the Present,* ed. Carol Poster and Linda C. Mitchell (Columbia: University of South Carolina Press, 2007), 67–87.

renaissance. All medieval writers of official letters understood that they were composing for the ear as much as for the eye, but explicit acknowledgment of that fact was especially rare in the more formulaic textbooks that competed with the new varieties produced at Oxford during the last quarter of the fourteenth century. One consequence of a fresh look at sources such as the *Rhetorica ad Herennium* and even the *Poetria nova* was increased attention to oral delivery as a component of rhetoric in general and letters in particular. Awareness of oral performance as a component of epistolary rhetoric is fully explicit in the *Compendium artis dictatorie*. The practical relevance of speaking skills for a practitioner of letter writing is made especially clear in another *ars dictandi* that belongs to the same tradition but took its present form in the first decades of the fifteenth century rather than the last decades of the fourteenth century. The first part of this anonymous treatise, in which the general principles of letter writing are set forth, is a personification allegory in which Queen Rhetoric presides over her court with the assistance of her secretary the Nightingale. Most of this introduction is devoted to the aural dimensions of the *ars dictaminis*—the *cursus* and the *distinctiones*—the components of which are represented as court functionaries who are summoned to present oral reports to the monarch. A different bird performs each cadence of the *cursus,* referred to as a "song," while the more theoretical points are made in formal speeches by the Nightingale and her fellow officers the chancellor Comma, the treasurer Colon, and the almoner Period.[49] Here the rules governing oral performance of letters are personified in roles that mirror those of their intended practitioners.

Oral delivery was an important concern for other, more historically and geographically specific reasons in Oxford during the late fourteenth century. The controversy over John Wyclif's ideas, centered at Oxford, gave rise to a substantial body of polemical literature, especially in the form of sermons but also including letters and other forms of propaganda. Oxford monks were important participants in the campaign against the Wycliffite heresy, a fact that gave practical relevance to their interest in the rhetoric of oral performance.[50] Mishtooni Bose notes that

[49] *Regina sedens Rhetorica,* ed. Camargo, *Medieval Rhetorics,* 169–219 (176–86).
[50] Patrick J. Horner compares fourteenth-century with fifteenth-century Benedictine preaching against Lollardy in "The King Taught Us the Lesson: Benedictine Support for Henry V's Suppression of the Lollards," *Mediaeval Studies* 52 (1990): 190–220. In the context of her broader survey of opposition to Lollardy, Mishtooni Bose discusses or mentions briefly the preaching and other propaganda of the Benedictines Nicholas Rad-

academic writers increasingly recognized real danger in the potential appeal of Wyclif's ideas to a broader public beyond the academy: "[I]t was increasing concern for the way in which Wyclif's arguments might play in the wider world, rather than disagreement simply with his arguments, that fuelled the opposition to him."[51] As public controversialists, in other words, they needed rhetorical skill both in oral performance and in audience assessment to counter the rhetorical effects of their opponents' arguments.

The concern with delivery can be detected even in the emphasis on the "colors" in the rhetorical textbooks of the Oxford renaissance. The figures of speech, the ones whose effects depend more on sound than on sense, are the colors that are described most consistently and illustrated most profusely in the works of the rhetoricians. If knowledge of the figures was essential for the production of "performable" texts, it was equally essential for the interpretation of authoritative and artfully constructed texts. The classical and classicizing poems that were rediscovered along with the rhetorical treatises could not be analyzed properly and understood fully without this knowledge. With their exhaustive catalogues, definitions, and illustrations of the figures, the *Rhetorica ad Herennium* and the medieval rhetorical treatises that drew upon and supplemented it were thus a precious resource for the study of such texts, and their direct influence can be traced in the commentaries and glosses of fourteenth- and fifteenth-century students and teachers. A treatise such as the *Tria sunt* simultaneously functioned as a manual for rhetorical composition and a reference guide for rhetorical exegesis, which it often illustrated through commentary on excerpts from ancient poets and highly rhetorical twelfth-century poets as well as appropriation of extracts from earlier commentaries on classical texts. In the milieu that

---

cliff, Robert Rypon, William Binham, Uthred of Boldon, Adam Easton, John Wells, John Whethamstede, and Thomas Brinton: "The Opponents of John Wyclif," in *A Companion to John Wyclif: Late Medieval Theologian,* ed. Ian Christopher Levy, Brill's Companions to the Christian Tradition 4 (Leiden: Brill, 2006), 407–55. See also Clark, *A Monastic Renaissance,* 1–2 and passim; and Alan J. Fletcher, *Late Medieval Popular Preaching in Britain and Ireland: Texts, Studies, and Interpretations,* Sermo: Studies on Patristic, Medieval, and Reformation Sermons and Preaching 5 (Turnhout: Brepols, 2009), 76–82. Siegfried Wenzel notices a "definite resurgence of interest in preaching among Benedictines . . . near the end of the fourteenth and early fifteenth centuries," including but not limited to the preaching of sermons against Wyclif's heresy: *Monastic Preaching in the Age of Chaucer,* Morton W. Bloomfield Lectures on Medieval English Literature 3 (Kalamazoo: Medieval Institute Publications, 1993), 2 (on monastic preaching against the Lollards, see 15–16).
[51] Bose, "Opponents of Wyclif," 429–36 (432).

produced and sustained interest in the *Tria sunt* and treatises like it, imitation and interpretation, textual production and textual analysis, were complementary activities that drew considerable energy from the Latin rhetorical texts that were recovered, recopied, and repurposed by Chaucer's English contemporaries.

Among those contemporaries, Thomas Merke is the best example of how an ambitious and talented monk could translate this renewed study and teaching of rhetoric into a career that took him far beyond the schools of Oxford and the Benedictine community. In 1397, less than a decade after he had composed his treatise on letter writing at Oxford, Merke was consecrated as bishop of Carlisle. He also belonged to the inner circle of advisers to King Richard II, in whose company he was captured by Henry Bolingbroke, the future King Henry IV, in 1399. While few monks rose to the same level of involvement in secular politics as Merke, many combined a strong interest in the theory and practice of rhetoric with direct engagement in the major political and theological controversies of the day. An excellent example from the generation following Merke's is John Whethamstede, who studied at Oxford in the first decade of the fifteenth century and, as abbot of St. Albans, continued to pursue his "literary" interests even as he dealt with the Wycliffite heresy and the Wars of the Roses.[52] If these and other Benedictines found the newly revived rhetoric so useful both within and beyond the cloister, it seems likely that at least some of their fellow Englishmen, laymen included, would have recognized its value as well.[53]

---

[52] David R. Carlson, "The Civic Poetry of Abbot John Whethamstede of St. Albans (†1465)," *Mediaeval Studies* 61 (1999): 205–42, and "Whethamstede on Lollardy: Latin Styles and the Vernacular Cultures of Early Fifteenth-Century England," *JEGP* 102 (2003): 21–41. John Lydgate of Bury St. Edmunds, another Oxford-trained Benedictine, was one of several monks who wrote highly rhetorical poetry in the service of Lancastrian claims to dynastic legitimacy. Christopher Cannon, "Monastic Productions," in *The Cambridge History of Medieval English Literature,* ed. David Wallace (Cambridge: Cambridge University Press, 1999), 316–48 (340–48), discusses this "emphatic movement of monastic writing in the fifteenth century out into the main line of English literary writing" (348).

[53] Chaucer was by no means alone among Middle English poets of his and succeeding generations in his complex engagement with rhetoric. See, for example, James J. Murphy, "John Gower's *Confessio Amantis* and the First Discussion of Rhetoric in the English Language," *PQ* 41 (1962): 401–11; Rita Copeland, "Lydgate, Hawes, and the Science of Rhetoric in the Late Middle Ages," *MLQ* 53 (1992): 57–82; and J. Allan Mitchell, "John Gower and John Lydgate: Forms and Norms of Rhetorical Culture," in *A Companion to Medieval English Literature and Culture, c. 1350–c. 1500,* ed. Peter Brown (Oxford: Blackwell, 2007), 569–84.

Born around 1342, Chaucer would have completed his early training in Latin grammar long before this Anglo-Latin renaissance could have influenced his teachers directly and probably even before it developed any real momentum. This is not to rule out indirect influence from some of the rhetorical sources that were about to be recovered and repurposed. By Chaucer's day, the contents of the arts of poetry and prose by Matthew of Vendôme and Geoffrey of Vinsauf are likely to have been absorbed into standard teaching materials and practices, even if the treatises themselves no longer were readily available. In this attenuated and probably anonymous form they could well have been used by Chaucer's grammar-school teachers. But it is not until the 1380s that Chaucer shows signs of firsthand acquaintance with Geoffrey of Vinsauf's *Poetria nova,* at a time when that work and other rhetorical treatises contemporary with and much older than it were still being rediscovered and were beginning to generate the new treatises described above. It was this "second wave" of their reception in England and the intellectual energy it generated that shaped Chaucer's explicit response to rhetoric in his own works. His encounter with "rethorike" as a newly reinvigorated discipline whose theory and practice were the subject of lively interest at England's premier center of higher education sparked a noticeable shift toward a deeper and more complex engagement with rhetorical doctrines and techniques.

A sophisticated and cosmopolitan poet and civil servant with close personal connections to the intellectual, political, and social elites of late fourteenth-century England, Chaucer could hardly have missed the broader impact of the renaissance of rhetoric under way at Oxford. Whether he knew Simon Southerey, Thomas Merke, or other monk rhetoricians personally, he certainly had direct access to intellectual developments at Oxford through friends such as Ralph Strode, a one-time fellow of Merton College, to whom he dedicated *Troilus and Criseyde.* The same ideas were current in learned circles with strong Oxford connections, both in Chaucer's native London and in the larger monastic houses located nearby, such as St. Albans.[54] Whether from scholars who studied and taught at Oxford or a still larger group of writers and intellectuals with ties to Oxford, Chaucer would have had ready access to

---

[54] For one such network, which included the Oxford-trained monk of St. Albans Simon Southerey, see V. H. Galbraith, "John Seward and His Circle: Some London Scholars of the Early Fifteenth Century," *Medieval and Renaissance Studies* 1 (1943): 85–104, and Clark, *Monastic Renaissance,* 218–26.

both the newly recovered and the newly composed rhetorical texts, as well as any scholarly debates about the nature and purpose of rhetoric.

Clear signs of Chaucer's enhanced awareness of and intensified interest in rhetoric, complete with direct quotation of Geoffrey of Vinsauf and references to other authorities on the subject, first appear in *Troilus and Criseyde,* a poem that he probably began in the early 1380s and completed by about 1386.[55] Earlier works such as *The Book of the Duchess* and *The Parliament of Fowls* have been described as "rhetorical" largely on the basis of their abundant use of the figures that are defined and illustrated in *Rhetorica ad Herennium,* Book 4, and in most medieval arts of poetry and prose; but as Murphy and Payne correctly observe, Chaucer could have learned how to employ figural language from many sources, ranging from elementary school texts to the vernacular poetry that was his immediate model. As Payne and Copeland, in particular, have demonstrated, Chaucer's poetics were rhetorical in other ways as well, and his propensity for reflecting on his poetic craft already pervades these early poems. While rhetorical theory provides concepts and terminology that are useful for analyzing the early poems, however, Chaucer nowhere avails himself of these resources, not even in his most metapoetic moments.

The only passage from the early poems that comes close to invoking rhetoric does so only to exclude it through comparison to something better. The Black Knight's catalogue of Lady White's many virtues includes her "goodly, softe speche," which he praises by saying, "Of eloquence was never founde / So swete a sownynge facounde."[56] "Eloquence" is not the same thing as "rhetoric," to be sure, and whatever Chaucer meant by the term, his interest is in the natural beauty of the lady's speech that surpasses any sweetness of sound that eloquence may achieve, presumably through learned artifice.

In *The House of Fame,* a work that Chaucer could have written any

---

[55] "Rethorice" is mentioned briefly but positively in Chaucer's translation of Boethius, *De consolatione Philosophiae* (*Boece* II.pr. 1.41–44), a project that coincided with his composition of *Troilus and Criseyde.* On Chaucer's translating the *Boece* as rhetorical activity, see Rita Copeland, "Rhetoric and Vernacular Translation in the Middle Ages," *SAC* 9 (1987): 41–75, and *Rhetoric, Hermeneutics, and Translation in the Middle Ages: Academic Traditions and Vernacular Texts* (Cambridge: Cambridge University Press, 1991), esp. 142–49.

[56] *Book of the Duchess,* 919, 925–26. Chaucer quotations are from *The Riverside Chaucer,* gen. ed. Larry D. Benson (Boston: Houghton Mifflin, 1987). Further quotations are referenced parenthetically in the text.

time between 1374 and 1386, rhetoric is more explicitly elided, but in a more ironic key. The word "rethorike" appears only once in this poem, when the loquacious eagle asks "Geffrey" whether he has been speaking

> Withoute any subtilite
> Of speche, or gret prolixite
> Of termes of philosophie,
> Of figures of poetrie,
> Or colours of rethorike?
>
> (855–59)

Here the "colours of rethorike" are invoked only as one of several kinds of "hard langage" (861) that are not being used. In fact, the eagle's speech has been filled with "figures" and "colours," especially those involving repetition, which he employs even in his rhetorical question. But the allusion to rhetoric is fleeting and superficial, the use of the *colores rhetorici* dismissed as but one among other potential sources of prolix and obscure discourse. If Chaucer wrote *The House of Fame* before the early 1380s, then this passage might count as further evidence of his not yet having felt the effects of the rhetorical revival; but even if he wrote it later, perhaps even shortly after he completed *Troilus and Criseyde*,[57] its satire is one of several characteristic dimensions of Chaucer's complex response to rhetoric.

The relative indifference to rhetoric in the earliest poems stands in sharp contrast to the explicit engagement with rhetoric in *Troilus and Criseyde* and many of the works that followed it. Payne has said that "the kind of criticism practiced in the rhetorical manuals [he has just mentioned Geoffrey of Vinsauf] will yield a more satisfactory analysis of *Troilus and Criseyde* than of any other major Chaucerian piece,"[58] and I would argue that this is due in no small part to the freshness of Chaucer's encounter with a newly available body of rhetorical texts and the richer conception of rhetoric that they offered.

---

[57] Helen Cooper mounts a strong argument for dating the poem to 1384, in "The Four Last Things in Dante and Chaucer: Ugolino in the House of Rumour," *NML* 3 (1999): 39–66. The more traditional, earlier dating is based especially on the poem's use of octosyllabics, like *The Book of the Duchess,* rather than pentameter, as in *The Parliament of Fowls* and *Troilus and Criseyde.*

[58] Payne, *Key of Remembrance,* 173. He goes on to say of Chaucer: "We know that he read and weighed critically the treatises themselves" (175); but he does not say when he thinks Chaucer might have studied them.

Chaucer's heightened awareness of rhetoric is especially evident in his decision to refashion one of Boccaccio's central characters as a skilled, self-conscious rhetorician who approaches the task of seducing his niece Criseyde on behalf of his friend Troilus as a problem of rhetorical invention. Having learned the source of Troilus's sorrow and promised to provide a remedy, Pandarus leaves his friend:

> And went his wey, thenkyng of this matere,
> And how he best myghte hire biseche of grace,
> And fynde a tyme therto, and a place.
> For everi wight that hath an hous to founde
> Ne renneth naught the werk for to bygynne
> With rakel hond, but he wol bide a stounde,
> And sende his hertes line out fro withinne
> Aldirfirst his purpos for to wynne.
> Al this Pandare in his herte thoughte,
> And cast his werk ful wisely or he wroughte.
>
> (I.1062–71)

Here Chaucer not only recognizes that rhetoric encompasses more than attractive artifice but also cites as his authority one of the chief sources that mediated the discipline's renewed prominence in England. The metaphor in which the narrator compares Pandarus's careful forethought to a builder's mental blueprint (lines 1065–69) renders into English the very words that Geoffrey of Vinsauf used to describe the first stage of rhetorical invention early in the *Poetria nova:*

> Si quis habet fundare domum, non currit ad actum
> Impetuosa manus: intrinseca linea cordis
> Praemetitur opus . . .
>
> (*PN,* 43–45)

While others have noted the unacknowledged citation of Geoffrey of Vinsauf and invoked this passage as evidence for Chaucer's interest in rhetoric, less attention has been paid to the pervasive and complex engagement with rhetorical argumentation that it signals. As Pandarus turns careful forethought, the first stage of rhetorical invention, into purposeful action in the unfolding narrative, Chaucer continues to draw on rhetorical precepts that were not previously part of his repertoire and that were to be found in some of the rhetorical manuals he is likely to have encountered at the very moment when he was reconceiving and complicating the character of the willing go-between. We are allowed to glimpse the inventional process in action on several occasions, as when Pandarus tells himself that the indirect approach (*insinuatio*) will be most persuasive even as he tells Criseyde that he will use no "subtyl art" (II.255–73).[59] Pandarus is marked explicitly as a practicing *rhetor* in other ways as well, for example, in his ability and willingness to argue *in utramque partem* on issues such as fortune and fidelity in love (cf. III.1618–38 and IV.380–427). He even takes on the role of rhetoric teacher, most literally when he plays the *dictator* to give Troilus a brief lesson in how to compose an effective love letter (II.1002–8, 1023–43).

Letter writing was one of the characteristic emphases of the revival of rhetoric at Oxford, and Chaucer exploited the conventions of the *ars dictaminis* in *Troilus and Criseyde* to lay the foundations for what developed into an important genre in the Middle English literature of the fifteenth and sixteenth centuries: the verse love epistle.[60] Equally revealing about Chaucer's knowledge of rhetorical studies at Oxford is a passage from the *Canterbury Tales* in which the Host instructs the Clerk of Oxenford on stylistic decorum even as he reminds us why an Oxford scholar would have found it useful to acquire proficiency in letter writing:

> Telle us som murie thyng of aventures.
> Youre termes, youre colours, and youre figures,
> Keepe hem in stoor til so be ye endite
> Heigh style, as whan that men to kynges write.
> Speketh so pleyn at this tyme, we yow preye,
> That we may understonde what ye seye.
>
> (IV.15–20)

The Host's plea for plain speech underscores his own social class and his lack of formal education. Part of Chaucer's point here is that even a

---

[59] Cf. also Diomede's reflections on how best to woo Criseyde away from her Trojan love (V.92–105). In the speech in which she tries to persuade Troilus that she can leave Troy and still return (IV.1264–1414), Criseyde includes references to her rhetorical strategy (e.g., lines 1282–95) and bases a key part of her argument on the attributes of persons (lines 1368–1400), an element of classical rhetoric that received special emphasis in medieval teaching on rhetorical invention.

[60] Martin Camargo, *The Middle English Verse Love Epistle,* Studien zur englischen Philologie n.s. 28 (Tübingen: Niemeyer, 1991).

London innkeeper who is a relative ignoramus in academic matters knows that one goes to Oxford to learn how to compose the elaborately artificial (and to him incomprehensible) documents employed in royal correspondence. It was not for the scholastic study "Of Aristotle and his philosophie" (I.295), but for the recently revived study of rhetoric that Oxford was known to every bleary-eyed man and barber in late fourteenth-century England.

The association between rhetorical training, the use of figure-intensive "high style," and service to kings is reiterated in *The Nun's Priest's Tale*, where Chaucer apostrophizes Geoffrey of Vinsauf by name in order to lament his own inability to match the Latin rhetorician's mastery of the figure apostrophe:

> O Gaufred, deere maister soverayn,
> That whan thy worthy kyng Richard was slayn
> With shot, compleynedest his deeth so soore,
> Why ne hadde I now thy sentence and thy loore,
> The Friday for to chide, as diden ye?
> For on a Friday, soothly, slayn was he.
> Thanne wolde I shewe yow how that I koude pleyne
> For Chauntecleres drede and for his peyne.
>
> (VII.3347–54)

Chaucer refers here to what was Geoffrey of Vinsauf's most famous poem, a lament for King Richard I in a series of apostrophes to Normandy, Friday, the soldier who shot the fatal arrow, Death, Nature, and God, which was included as an example of amplification in the *Poetria nova* (lines 368–430) but also circulated separately. The reference to Geoffrey of Vinsauf as "maister" and the double emphasis on learning ("sentence," "loore"), not to mention the fact that the allusion is a digression (another method of amplification: *PN* 527–53) in the form of an apostrophe within a series of apostrophes that also functions as a digression, indicates that Chaucer invokes the poem not as an independent historical artifact that was copied into certain chronicles but rather in the context of the thirteenth-century art of poetry and prose that had been given new currency through the contemporary revival of rhetoric.[61]

---

[61] On the independent circulation of the lament for Richard, see Karl Young, "Chaucer and Geoffrey of Vinsauf," *MP* 41 (1943): 172–82 (172–76). Murphy, "New Look,"

In passages such as these, we may glimpse behind Chaucer's characteristic irony the practical perspective of a court poet who earned his living as a bureaucrat in the king's service, as he assessed and absorbed the rhetorical lore newly emanating from Oxford. When he actually represents a practicing courtier, in *The Squire's Tale,* Chaucer has his narrator draw explicit attention to the value of training in rhetoric and specifically in oral delivery to the performance of a courtier's duties, in this case duties of an ambassador that Chaucer had performed himself on more than one occasion. The knight who delivers gifts and an accompanying message to the royal court of King Cambyuskan perfectly matches his gestures to his language as the art of rhetoric teaches one to do: "Accordaunt to his wordes was his cheere, / As techeth art of speche hem that it leere" (V.103–4). His language ("speech") and gestures ("contenaunce"), which could not be bettered even by the epitome of courtly eloquence, "Gawayn" (89–97), far exceed the capacities of the Squire, who admits that he "kan nat sowne his stile" (105) and must content himself with conveying "that . . . he mente" (108). Although apparently not trained in rhetoric himself, the Squire does not make the distinction between natural and artificial eloquence that the Black Knight seemed to make, at least in the case of his lady love. In applying the inexpressibility topos to descriptions of noble persons and customs, for example, he invokes the trained rhetorician and the hypersophisticated nobleman as seemingly interchangeable standards for supreme eloquence. To describe the beauty of Canacee would require a "rethor excellent" who "koude his colours longynge for that art" (38–39), while the elegant feast celebrating Cambyuskan's birthday could be described properly only by the ultimate courtly connoisseur, "Launcelot" (287). Perhaps it is no coincidence that the only two examples of amplification through description offered in the *Poetria nova* (554–667) are on the same topics singled out by the Squire as beyond his capabilities: an extended description of a beautiful woman and one of a royal feast. Chaucer might not have needed these precise epideictic skills in his ser-

---

12–14, believes that Chaucer would have been more likely to encounter the lament as an independent poem than as part of the *Poetria nova.* If this were so, however, Chaucer would have had no particular reason to associate this example of apostrophe with digression, as he clearly does in the passage from *The Nun's Priest's Tale.* According to the *Poetria nova* (lines 219–689), amplification is achieved by eight methods: repeating the same meaning in different words, circumlocution, comparison, apostrophe, personification, digression, description, and opposition.

vice to the court, but he surely would have valued the ability to read aloud and elaborate on an official letter,[62] perhaps one whose elegant language he had a hand in drafting, in the presence of a powerful lord and his entourage.

While Chaucer recognized that skill in writing letters, employing figural language, and speaking in public could help advance the career of a royal servant, he also realized that knowledge of rhetoric could be abused. He was not an academic, and we should not expect him to juxtapose different authorities on rhetoric as the Oxford masters did. However, he does provide multiple perspectives on exactly the aspects of rhetoric that were emphasized in the contemporary revival. For example, he can use highly figured language with little apparent irony when the genre demands it, as he does in the chivalric epic that is *The Knight's Tale;* but he also can draw attention to the way such language often masks dubious intent with a pleasing appearance, as when he has Criseyde refer to her uncle Pandarus's artful *insinuatio* as a "paynted proces" (II.424) calculated to undermine her virtue. In between these extremes, Chaucer can use the Franklin's professed ignorance of the rhetorical figures, or "colours of rethoryk" (V.726), to help characterize an upwardly aspiring country gentleman's struggle to position himself with respect to the aristocracy:

> But, sires, by cause I am a burel man,
> At my bigynnyng first I yow biseche,
> Have me excused of my rude speche.
> I lerned nevere rethorik, certeyn;
> Thyng that I speke, it moot be bare and pleyn.
> I sleep nevere on the Mount of Pernaso,
> Ne lerned Marcus Tullius Scithero.
> Colours ne knowe I none, withouten drede,
> But swiche colours as growen in the mede,
> Or elles swiche as men dye or peynte.
> Colours of rethoryk been to me queynte;
> My spirit feeleth noght of swich mateere.
>
> (V.716–27)

[62] The Squire also observes that the courtly ambassador "with a manly voys seide his message, / . . . Withouten vice of silable or of lettre" (V.99, 101), certainly indicating that his language was grammatically correct and free of barbarism but perhaps also suggesting that he spoke from a prepared text written in the romance equivalent of the *cursus*.

The Franklin's preemptive apology recalls his effusive, if qualified, flattery of the Squire's "gentilesse," especially his age-appropriate "eloquence" (V.673–81), and perhaps is meant to elevate that flattery to its sincerest form through imitation. If so, the Franklin is imitating far too literally the Squire's polite (if all-too-accurate) disclaimers of rhetorical knowledge and ability. He belabors what should be passed over lightly, even to the point of showing off his awareness that the supreme authority on the "colours of rethoryk," about which he supposedly knows nothing, is Cicero (as the reputed author of the *Rhetorica ad Herennium*). Also like the Squire, his apologies do not stop him from using the colors frequently, ostentatiously, and less than expertly. Perhaps his mangling of Cicero's name as "Scithero" is meant to signal that while he may have dipped into some of the recently recovered rhetoric textbooks, his mastery of their contents is limited.[63] The desire to flatter by imitating and the eagerness to display one's superficial book learning also can be seen in the Franklin's response to one of the Squire's least successful rhetorical displays, the aborted circumlocution couched in cosmological allegory that is all we have of the third part of his incomplete tale (V.671–72). The Franklin recognizes the rhetorical device well enough to imitate it but apparently has not understood the rules sufficiently well to realize that the figure does not include the pedagogical gloss that would have accompanied it in a schoolbook:

> Til that the brighte sonne loste his hewe;
> For th'orisonte hath refte the sonne his lyght—
> This is as muche to seye as it was nyght—
>   (V.1016–18)[64]

Frequent reuse of examples to illustrate the figures makes it difficult to prove direct influence from a particular textbook, but the Franklin had in mind something like the following example of circumlocution, from Chapter 9 of the anonymous *Tria sunt:*

---

[63] The Franklin's use of the full name "Marcus Tullius Scithero" (V.722), rather than the medieval schoolmen's more typical "Tully," is a further sign that he is trying to impress even as he feigns humility.

[64] Cf. *Troilus and Criseyde* II.904–5 (the sun), which Payne interprets as sending up the excesses of the rhetoricians' "stylistic prescriptions" ("Chaucer and the Art of Rhetoric," 49–50). Chaucer used similar stylistic techniques repeatedly in *TC,* Book V—e.g., lines 274–80 (dawn), 1016–20 (sunset), 1107–10 (sunrise)—but minus the gloss and with no apparent parodic intent or effect.

Veritatem splendide producit [circumlocutio], ut in Virgilio:
Et iam prima novo spargebat lumine terras
Titanis croceum linquens Aurora cubile. (*Aen.* 4.584–85: Tithoni)
ut sit sensus: "Iam diescebat"

When the Franklin apologized for his "rude speche," he inadvertently but appropriately aligned himself with the unformed grammar-school boys (*rudibus*) who were the least knowledgeable among the intended users of the textbooks that treated the colors of rhetoric.

While he often mocks the misuse of figural language with playful irony, Chaucer is more troubled by the misuse of oral delivery, another characteristic concern of the Oxford rhetoricians. The ability to move listeners to action by means of voice and gesture is both a powerful and a morally ambivalent rhetorical tool, and Chaucer acknowledges its dangerous appeal with darker and deeper irony. The most self-conscious and, by his own account, the most accomplished performer among the pilgrims is also the most immoral, and this deceiving Pardoner delights in describing his enthusiastic manipulation of voice and gesture to enthrall his audience of rustic dupes:[65]

> "Lordynges," quod he, "in chirches whan I preche,
> I peyne me to han an hauteyn speche,
> And rynge it out as round as gooth a belle,
> For I kan al by rote that I telle.
>
> . . .
>
> "Thanne peyne I me to strecche forth the nekke,
> And est and west upon the peple I bekke,
> As dooth a dowve sittynge on a berne.
> Myne handes and my tonge goon so yerne
> That it is joye to se my bisynesse."
>
> (VI.329–32, 395–99)

A different sort of irony may be at work in Chaucer's representation of the Pardoner's opposite, a speaker whose subject matter is so uniform and whose oral delivery is so monotonous that the Host orders him to

[65] For recent assessments of the Pardoner's oratory, see Claire M. Waters, *Angels and Earthly Creatures: Preaching, Performance, and Gender in the Later Middle Ages* (Philadelphia: University of Pennsylvania Press, 2004), esp. 31–56, 187–97; and Martin Camargo, "How (Not) to Preach: Thomas Waleys and Chaucer's Pardoner," in *Sacred and Profane in Chaucer and Late Medieval Literature: Essays in Honour of John V. Fleming,* ed. Robert Epstein and William Robins (Toronto: University of Toronto Press, 2010), 146–78.

liven up his performance so that his listeners will not lose consciousness
and risk falling from their horses into the mud:

> "Ye," quod oure Hooste, "by Seint Poules belle!
> Ye seye right sooth; this Monk he clappeth lowde.
> . . .
> "Sire Monk, namoore of this, so God yow blesse!
> Youre tale anoyeth al this compaignye.
> Swich talkyng is nat worth a boterflye,
> For therinne is ther no desport ne game.
> Wherfore, sire Monk, daun Piers by youre name,
> I pray yow hertely telle us somwhat elles;
> For sikerly, nere clynkyng of youre belles
> That on youre bridel hange on every syde,
> By hevene kyng that for us alle dyde,
> I sholde er this han fallen doun for sleep,
> Althogh the slough had never been so deep;
> Thanne hadde your tale al be toold in veyn.
> For certeinly, as that thise clerkes seyn,
> Whereas a man may have noon audience,
> Noght helpeth it to tellen his sentence."
>   (VII.2780–81, 2788–2802)

As the Host concludes, if no one is listening, your wisdom has no effect.
For those members of Chaucer's audience who were aware of the rhetorical revival under way in Oxford, the ignorant Host's rhetoric lesson
concealed a sly joke. The speaker whose rhetorical shortcomings the
Host chides is none other than a worldly monk who prides himself on
his classical learning (VII.1971–82). Chaucer not only engages all the
key topics of the contemporary renaissance of rhetoric in his poetry but
also, in this particular passage, indicates the group most responsible for
the revived interest in the theory and practice of rhetoric, even as he
ironically suggests that not every member of the monastic community
will have paid proper attention to his rhetoric lessons.[66]

[66] This article has benefited from the responses of those who heard versions presented
at Siena, Bologna, Oxford, and Bristol. I wish to thank the members of those audiences
for their questions and comments, especially James Clark and Laura Ashe, from whom
I have happily borrowed insights about the English Benedictines and the Franklin's
literalism, respectively. My greatest debt is to Rita Copeland, who read the article before
and after it was submitted for publication, each time suggesting new ways to clarify
and strengthen its argument.

John Lydgate Reads *The Clerk's Tale*

Jonathan Stavsky
The Hebrew University of Jerusalem

Ille referre aliter saepe solebat idem

Ovid, *Ars amatoria* 2.128

F IFTEENTH-CENTURY ENGLAND DID NOT LEAVE US its own version of the story of patient Griselda. Between the death of Chaucer and
the Griselda revival of early modern England,[1] all that remains of this
heroine are precisely her remains: scattered references to, and verbal
reminiscences of, *The Clerk's Tale*.[2] Yet these remains, too, have a story
to narrate. As Richard Firth Green has recently demonstrated, paying
close attention to the contexts in which Griselda's tale was read and
retold can yield valuable insights about the meaning—or meanings—of
her troubled marriage to Walter.[3]

Particularly fascinated by Griselda, John Lydgate conjures her up in
many of his writings, from such minor lyrics as "A Ballade on ane Ale-

I wish to thank Lawrence Besserman, David Wallace, and two anonymous readers
for *SAC* for their sincere and thorough engagement with my argument.

[1] For an extensive list of analogues from the last novella of Boccaccio's *Decameron* to
twentieth-century adaptations, see Raffaele Morabito, "La diffusione della storia di
Griselda dal XIV al XX secolo," *Studi sul Boccaccio* 17 (1988): 237–85. The diverse uses
to which the Griselda story was put in England during the sixteenth and seventeenth
centuries are treated in Lee Bliss, "The Renaissance Griselda: A Woman for All Seasons," *Viator* 23 (1992): 301–43. See also Judith Bronfman, *Chaucer's Clerk's Tale: The
Griselda Story Received, Rewritten, Illustrated* (New York: Garland, 1994), esp. 53–61.

[2] Another source for studying the reception of *The Clerk's Tale* is the manuscripts in
which it is transmitted. This is explored in Daniel S. Silvia, "Some Fifteenth-Century
Manuscripts of the *Canterbury Tales*," in *Chaucer and Middle English Studies in Honour of
Rossell Hope Robbins*, ed. Beryl Rowland (London: George Allen & Unwin, 1974),
153–63; Seth Lerer, "Rewriting Chaucer: Two Fifteenth-Century Readings of *The Canterbury Tales*," *Viator* 19 (1988): 311–26; and James Weldon, "The Naples Manuscript
and the Case for a Female Readership," *Neophil* 93 (2009): 703–22. All three studies
demonstrate Lydgate's influence on the reception of the *Tale*.

[3] Richard Firth Green, "Griselda in Siena," *SAC* 33 (2011): 3–38.

Seller"[4] to more ambitious productions such as the *Troy Book*[5] and the *Fall of Princes*.[6] In so doing, he provides a record both of the *Tale*'s reception and of the central role it played in his appropriation of Chaucerian poetics. A number of Lydgate's allusions have been examined in the past,[7] whereas others have gone unnoticed, especially in passages where Griselda is not mentioned by name, though also in some where she is. Previous work on Griselda has dealt almost exclusively with authors who rewrote her story rather than with authors who made other uses of it. Studies of Lydgate have considered his attitude to Griselda in a more general context; hence, they have confined their analysis to a few selected passages. As a result, the full scope of Lydgate's engagement with *The Clerk's Tale* remains undocumented and often misunderstood. The present study is the first to focus specifically and extensively on this important feature of Griselda's fortunes and Lydgate's poetry.

Two examples from the field of Lydgate scholarship ought to clarify

---

[4] "A Ballade on ane Ale-Seller," in *The Minor Poems of John Lydgate,* ed. Henry Noble MacCracken and Merriam Sherwood, 2 vols., EETS e.s. 107 and o.s. 192 (London: Kegan Paul, Trench, Trübner & Co., and Oxford University Press, 1911, 1934), 2:429–32.

[5] *Troy Book,* ed. Henry Bergen, 4 vols., EETS e.s. 97, 103, 106, and 126 (London: Kegan Paul, Trench, Trübner & Co., and Oxford University Press, 1906–35).

[6] *Fall of Princes,* ed. Henry Bergen, 4 vols. (Washington, D.C.: Carnegie Institution, 1923–27).

[7] Some of Lydgate's references (and one by the fifteenth-century poet John Metham) are listed in *Five Hundred Years of Chaucer Criticism and Allusion (1357–1900),* ed. Caroline F. Spurgeon, 6 vols. (London: Kegan Paul, Trench, Trübner & Co. and Oxford University Press, 1914–25), 1:17, 18, 39, 47. See also studies by Dona Faraci, "Griselda in Inghilterra: Fortuna di un personaggio ed etimologia di un nome," in *La circolazione dei temi e degli intrecci narrativi: Il caso Griselda,* ed. Raffaele Morabito (L'Aquila: Japadre, 1988), 39–56, esp. 40–41; Seth Lerer, "Writing Like the Clerk: Laureate Poets and the Aureate World," in his *Chaucer and His Readers: Imagining the Author in Late-Medieval England* (Princeton: Princeton University Press, 1993), 22–56; Bronfman, *Chaucer's Clerk's Tale,* 51; David R. Carlson, "The Chronology of Lydgate's Chaucer References," *ChauR* 38 (2004): 246–54; Maura Nolan, "Lydgate's Literary History: Chaucer, Gower, and Canacee," *SAC* 27 (2005): 59–92; Maura Nolan, "Tragedy and Comedy: Lydgate's Disguisings and Public Poetry," in her *John Lydgate and the Making of Public Culture* (Cambridge: Cambridge University Press, 2005), 120–83; Larry Scanlon, "Lydgate's Poetics: Laureation and Domesticity in the *Temple of Glass,*" in *John Lydgate: Poetry, Culture, and Lancastrian England,* ed. Scanlon and James Simpson (Notre Dame, Ind.: University of Notre Dame Press, 2006), 61–97; Christine F. Cooper Rompato, "Stuck in Chichevache's Maw: Digesting the Example of (Im)Patient Griselda in John Lydgate's 'A Mumming at Hertford' and 'Bycorne and Chychevache,'" in *At the Table: Metaphorical and Material Cultures of Good in Medieval and Early Modern Europe,* ed. Timothy J. Tomasik and Juliann M. Vitullo (Turnhout: Brepols, 2007), 73–93; and Andrea Denny-Brown, "Lydgate's Golden Cows: Appetite and Avarice in *Bycorne and Chychevache,*" in *Lydgate Matters: Poetry and Material Culture in the Fifteenth Century,* ed. Lisa H. Cooper and Andrea Denny-Brown (New York: Palgrave Macmillan, 2008), 35–56.

why a detailed approach to his use of *The Clerk's Tale* is called for. Despite their contrasting evaluations of Lydgate, Seth Lerer and Larry Scanlon agree that his reading of the *Tale* is crucial to his self-definition as a poet. According to Lerer,

As one of the most popular of Chaucer's fictions in the fifteenth century, [*The Clerk's Tale*] provided more than story line or character for later imitators. It presented, too, a paradigm for a writer's relationship to a deceased author and a living patron. Its Prologue bequeathed to an English readership a way of understanding poetic authority as forms of political sanction (laureate) and rhetorical finesse (aureate), while its Envoy dramatized the strategies for controlling . . . audience response. . . . [Lydgate] seems to live out the condition of the Clerk. He has mined the Clerk's performance for its vocabulary of poetic praise, its subservient narrative stance, and its overall dramatic structure. . . . Like the Clerk, Lydgate presents vernacular translations of exemplary texts drawn from a humanist past. Like the Clerk, too, he must translate both over languages and over time. . . . While much of Lydgate's career concerns itself with acting out these strategies, it is the *Fall of Princes* that develops fully and explicitly the stance of what I will call "writing like the Clerk."[8]

Lerer then proceeds to argue that however closely Lydgate models his persona on Chaucer, the Lancastrian poet fails to grasp the complexity of his master's literary and historical vision. Published in the early days of the movement to reappraise Lydgate, Lerer's account soon found itself on the wrong side of the critical fence.[9] Contesting this and similar accounts, Scanlon bases his analysis of Lydgate's poetics on another poem that is rife with Chaucerian—and Clerkly—resonances: *The Temple of Glass.*[10] "[I]mportant to Lydgate both as a bearer of vernacular authority

[8] Lerer, *Chaucer and His Readers*, 24–25.

[9] Although sympathetic readings of Lydgate began to be published in the middle of the twentieth century, the view of Lydgate as epigone dominated his reception from the Renaissance until the 1990s. A good survey and critique of this position is found in Chapter 2 of James Simpson's *Reform and Cultural Revolution*, Oxford English Literary History, vol. 2, 1350–1547 (Oxford: Oxford University Press, 2002), esp. 34–50. See also the editors' introduction to *John Lydgate: Poetry, Culture, and Lancastrian England*, ed. Scanlon and Simpson, 1–11. The current Lydgate revival began with David Lawton, "Dullness and the Fifteenth Century," *ELH* 54 (1987): 761–99. A number of important monographs and essay collections have since appeared. In addition to those mentioned in the footnotes above, see *Nation, Court, and Culture: New Essays on Fifteenth-Century English Poetry*, ed. Helen Cooney (Dublin: Four Courts, 2001).

[10] *The Temple of Glas*, ed. Josef Schick, EETS e.s. 40 (London: Kegan Paul, Trench, Trübner & Co., 1891).

and as an example of female virtue," Griselda, he argues, "effect[s] a conflation between female agency and poetic authority." Rather than a narrow concern with fame, Scanlon identifies several discourses at work in this dream vision, all of which converge in the mediating figure of Griselda. "In this way the poem offers a particularly literal confirmation of [Isobel] Armstrong's notion of the aesthetic as transformative, 'working over' the Chaucerian materials out of which it is constructed." This process "uses Griselda's constancy to rewrite the erotic, which, thus rewritten, makes poetry's incomplete and unending transformation of loss at once more accessible and more ethical."[11]

Scholarly trends aside, both Lerer and Scanlon offer cogent readings of the works they have chosen as representative of Lydgate's oeuvre. Yet neither scholar's interpretive framework can quite be made to fit the text chosen by the other. Whereas *The Temple of Glass* is no mere allegory of poetic authority (*pace* Lerer), one would be hard-pressed to find any profound expressions of moral authority in the eulogies to poets scattered throughout the *Fall of Princes* (*pace* Scanlon). Herein lies the rub: without comprehensive knowledge of Lydgate's use of *The Clerk's Tale*, we can neither decide between Lerer's and Scanlon's paradigms nor develop an alternative paradigm that would accommodate the disparate sources upon which each of them draws. In order to work out such a paradigm, there is no choice but to undertake a close and comparative reading of as wide a corpus as can be processed without turning out a catalogue of allusions.

The figure of Lydgate that emerges from the present study reconciles the partial descriptions offered by Lerer and Scanlon, while bringing to the fore some unexpected facets of his poetry. Despite the ideal of Petrarchan laureateship to which he was devoted, and despite the aureate diction that he supposed would raise him to Parnassian heights, I argue that Lydgate's poetics is mutable, conversational, and feminized (in accordance with his own shifting conception of womanhood). With Lerer, I hold that Lydgate, more than Chaucer or any other Middle English writer, is obsessed with securing his fame: this is the end of his literary efforts. With Scanlon, I insist that his desire for recognition admits of its own high seriousness (as well as tantalizing humor, which Scanlon does not sufficiently emphasize): these are the means by which he strives

---

[11] Scanlon, "Lydgate's Poetics," 80, 69, and 91. I return to Scanlon's reading of *The Temple* in my discussion of this poem.

to attain popularity. However, whereas both scholars focus on particular works, this study demonstrates that Lydgate's unique blend of *sentence, solas,* and self-promotion unfolds along a horizontal axis. Although some of his writings are surprisingly complex, the breadth of his vision can be appreciated only by ranging across his immense literary output. By continually reorienting his perspective, Lydgate regales his followers with diverse food for thought, delectation, and subsequent dissemination. What keeps this banquet interesting is not so much the wholesomeness of individual courses as it is the heated conversation that he expects to take place during and between them. Literature, for Lydgate, is essentially a process of talking and being talked about.

The Clerk's Tale both provided Lydgate with a theme to rework in his poetry and taught him how to use his kaleidoscopic art in order to spark debate. Of course, not every text examined in the following pages relies heavily on the *Tale;* yet the effects of these writings are inevitably colored by Lydgate's attempt to emulate the air of controversy with which Chaucer imbues the story of Griselda. Ever since Elizabeth Salter's groundbreaking reading of *The Clerk's Tale,*[12] scholars have come to appreciate its combination of an (ostensibly) absolute moral, inherited from Petrarch's Latin version, and the plurality of voices reintroduced by Chaucer. According to Michaela Paasche Grudin, Chaucer's "treatment of the Griselda story enhances, rather than softens, its paradoxical elements."[13] As Carolyn Dinshaw suggests, the "attractiveness" of the story "lie[s] in its hermeneutic difficulty," so that "each translation— each literary treatment—provides an interpretation" of its problems: thanks to his "Griselda-like position," the Clerk is able to appreciate this very quality.[14] At once chronicling and shaping what Lesley Johnson

---

[12] Elizabeth Salter, *Chaucer: The Knight's Tale and the Clerk's Tale* (Great Neck, N.Y.: Barron's Educational Series, 1962), 37–65.

[13] Michaela Paasche Grudin, "Chaucer's *Clerk's Tale* as Political Paradox," *SAC* 11 (1989): 63–92 (79).

[14] Carolyn Dinshaw, *Chaucer's Sexual Poetics* (Madison: University of Wisconsin Press, 1989), 132–33 and 136. Other studies that emphasize the polysemous and paradoxical nature of *The Clerk's Tale,* as well as its author's departure from Petrarch, include Bernard S. Levy, "The Meanings of *The Clerk's Tale,*" in *Chaucer and the Craft of Fiction,* ed. Leigh A. Arrathoon (Rochester, Mich.: Solaris Press, 1986), 385–409; John M. Ganim, "Carnival Voices and the Envoy to the *Clerk's Tale,*" *ChauR* 22 (1987): 112–27; Lars Engle, "Chaucer, Bakhtin, and Griselda," *Exemplaria* 1 (1989): 429–59; William McClellan, "Bakhtin's Theory of Dialogic Discourse, Medieval Rhetorical Theory, and the Multi-Voiced Structure of the Clerk's Tale," *Exemplaria* 1 (1989): 461–88; David Wallace, " 'Whan She Translated Was': Humanism, Tyranny, and the Petrarchan Academy," in his *Chaucerian Polity: Absolutist Lineages and Associational Forms in England and Italy* (Stanford: Stanford University Press, 1997), 261–98; and Robert R. Edwards,

calls the "talking point" of "Griselda's story,"[15] Lydgate seeks to exploit the "buzz" surrounding the mysterious figure of Griselda, but does so in a way that differs starkly from his model. Instead of inventing his own densely polysemous and paradox-ridden character, Lydgate revisits her story over and over again throughout his long career, each time contriving a Chaucerian moment that encapsulates a new reaction to the fourteenth-century source. Even if the positions he adopts on certain occasions fall short of Chaucer's open-ended liberalism and deserve to be criticized as such, a wider perspective reveals that Lydgate is capable of manipulating different worldviews—if still within the orthodox purview—rather than underwriting a single dominant ideology.

The structure of this study mirrors the way in which I believe that Lydgate's oeuvre is designed to be read. My analysis follows a thematic instead of a strictly chronological order: I am more concerned with producing an anatomy of Lydgate's engagement with *The Clerk's Tale* than with reconstructing the development of his reading over time, if such may at all be established. In order to flesh out the gendered logic that underlies his appropriation of the Griselda story, and consequently his poetics in general, I shall chart the diverse attitudes to women that emerge from his Chaucerian allusions.[16] I begin with references to Griselda that appear to praise women, continue to others that disparage them, and then dwell on some ironic attempts to do both in his minor as well as in his more substantial writings. From antifeminist satire I proceed to works that undertake, with varying degrees of seriousness, to "rehabilitate" female nature and the relations between men and women by reinterpreting *The Clerk's Tale.* Finally, I shall look at the more skeptical approach to worldly affairs (including the story of Griselda) taken by some of Lydgate's religious poetry, but shall then cast doubt on his

---

" 'The sclaundre of Walter': The Clerk's Tale and the Problem of Hermeneutics," in his *Chaucer and Boccaccio: Antiquity and Modernity* (Houndmills: Palgrave, 2002), 128–52. A survey of (mostly) twentieth-century scholarship is provided by Charlotte C. Morse, "Critical Approaches to the *Clerk's Tale,*" in *Chaucer's Religious Tales,* ed. C. David Benson and Elizabeth Robertson (Cambridge: Brewer, 1990), 71–83.

[15] Lesley Johnson, "Reincarnations of Griselda: Contexts for the *Clerk's Tale?*" in *Feminist Readings in Middle English Literature: The Wife of Bath and All Her Sect,* ed. Ruth Evans and Lesley Johnson (London: Routledge, 1994), 195–220 (195).

[16] Lydgate's changing representations of women are noted by Alain Renoir, "Attitudes Toward Women in Lydgate's Poetry," *ES* 42 (1961): 1–14; and A .S. G. Edwards, "Lydgate's Attitudes to Women," *ES* 51 (1971): 436–37. Other than a Ph.D. dissertation by Karol Lynn Walchak, *The Four Faces of Lydgate's Women: The Minor Poems* (University of Nevada, 1995), which I have not been able to consult, I know of no study of Lydgate and women that spans a large part of his oeuvre.

attempt to solve the ambiguities of literature. In each of these configurations, the form of his writing assumes the qualities that Lydgate identifies as female or associates with Griselda or one of her substitutes.

In Praise of Women and Poets

Lydgate's references to Griselda are usually traceable to the narrative frame encasing her story: a eulogy to Petrarch appears before the narrative proper, which, in turn, is followed by the Clerk's concluding words—partly translated from Petrarch's own conclusion—and an *Envoy* ascribed in the rubric of most manuscripts to Chaucer (rather than the fictional narrator).[17] Lerer disapproves of this focus: by "subordinat-[ing]" the "narrative . . . to the social facts of its telling," Lydgate makes "the Prologue and Envoy swell out of proportion; they become read as the most salient features of the *Tale,* offering stories of authorial and patronly subjection and the strategies for praising the source and placating the public."[18] Admittedly, Lydgate pays more attention to Griselda's *Nachleben* than he does to the account of her life (though he does from time to time allude to passages from the *Tale* proper). Yet his concern with poetic fame does not blot out the other issues raised by the *Prologue,* the tale's conclusion, and *Envoy.* On the contrary, he celebrates the diverse reactions to *The Clerk's Tale,* which accompany its "original" telling within the *Canterbury Tales* frame story and begin to shape its future reception.

In addition to being portrayed in the *Prologue* as a model of literary excellence, Griselda figures in the tale's conclusion and *Envoy* as an impossible ideal of female conduct; as an allegory of humanity's relation to God and the troubles of this world; and as a person or kind of person who once existed but is now eclipsed by real-life women—who, in turn, are more akin to the Wife of Bath. Overdetermined by its context, the *Tale* confronts us with a threefold interpretive dilemma: Is Griselda's behavior plausible or even desirable? Does her story redound to the favor or discredit of women? And is Alisoun of Bath a better alternative? As Charlotte Morse suggests, "If Chaucer had not added endings be-

---

[17] Thomas J. Farrell argues that the *Envoy* would have been read as Chaucer's own composition rather than as the Clerk's ironic conclusion to his tale, which most critics (for example, John Ganim in his essay referred to in note 14 above) take it to be. See "The 'Envoy de Chaucer' and the *Clerk's Tale,*" *ChauR* 24 (1990): 329–36. Lydgate, at any rate, shows no sign of distinguishing between the conclusion and the *Envoy.*

[18] Lerer, *Chaucer and His Readers,* 39.

yond the moral conclusion . . . interpretation of the *Clerk's Tale* would be more stable, readers less perplexed."[19] Yet perplexity turns out to be a poetic goldmine for Lydgate: by repeatedly harking back to *The Clerk's Tale,* he uses this complex and paradoxical narrative to carve out an identity for himself as a writer—not by reducing its multiple voices to an overriding concern with literary tradition, as Lerer maintains, but, conversely, by playing these voices off against one another.

Lydgate typically refers to Griselda in conjunction with other examples of female virtue and beauty. His penchant for combining simile, name-dropping, and potentially endless amplification, though monotonous by modern standards, is not without its subtlety.[20] Close attention to his poetry reveals that Lydgate is capable of using commonplaces in sophisticated and self-reflexive ways, which attest to his deep familiarity with Chaucer's works and close attentiveness to the contexts in which they are likely to become conversation pieces. Praising his beloved, the speaker of "The Floure of Curtesye" claims she is

> As Hester meke, lyke Judith of prudence
> Kynde as Alcest or Marcia Catoun,
> And to Grisylde lyke in pacience,
> And Ariadne of discrecioun,
> And to Lucrece, that was of Rome toun,

[19] Morse, "Critical Approaches to the *Clerk's Tale,*" 71.

[20] This combination of tropes appears in other late medieval poems and lyrics, such as Lydgate's "On Gloucester's Approaching Marriage" (*Minor Poems,* ed. MacCracken and Sherwood, 2:601–8). Composed around the time of Lydgate's death, John Metham's *Amoryus and Cleopes* writes of its dedicatee, Lady Katherine Stapleton: "And yff I the trwthe schuld here wryght, / As gret a style I schuld make in euery degre, / As Chauncerys [i.e., Chaucer] off qwene Eleyne, or Cresseyd, doht endyght; / Or off Polyxchene, Grysyld, or Penelope; / As beuteus, as womanly, as pacyent, as thei were wunt to be, / Thys lady was, qwan I endytyd this story" (*The Works of John Metham,* ed. Hardin Craig, EETS o.s. 132 [London: Kegan Paul, Trench, Trübner & Co., 1916], 1–81, lines 2170–75). Of special interest are several of the poems ascribed to "Ch" in the University of Pennsylvania MS French 15 (*Chaucer and Poems of "Ch,"* ed. James I. Wimsatt [Cambridge: Brewer, 1982], esp. fols. 77d and 81b–d). In another poem from the same collection (fols. 76a–b), a fourteenth-century "Wife's Lament," the female speaker identifies with the plights of Dido, Medea, and Helen, thereby anticipating Lydgate's positive portrayal of these heroines. As Derek Pearsall points out, Lydgate's accumulative style also characterizes the writings of such fourteenth-century classicizing friars as Robert Holcot. See *John Lydgate* (Charlottesville: University Press of Virginia, 1970), 38–40. The heuristic value of amplification in Lydgate's poetry is discussed in Lois B. Ebin, *Illuminator, Makar, Vates: Visions of Poetry in the Fifteenth Century* (Lincoln: University of Nebraska Press, 1988), 36–37.

> She may be lykened, as for honeste,
> And for her faythe, vnto Penelope.[21]

Such figures as Odysseus's wife Penelope, Cato's Marcia, Lucrece, and the biblical Esther and Judith are traditionally regarded as paragons of merit. However, Lydgate's strings of references also include more dubious examples:

> For good she is, lyke to Polycene,
> And in fayrnesse to the quene Helayne
>
> . . .
>
> And wyfely trouthe, if I shal nat fayne,
> In constaunce eke and faythe, she may attayne
> To Cleopatre[.]
>
> (190–91, 193–95)

And from another poem:

> Wyfly trouthe with Penolope,
> And with Gresylde parfyt pacyence,
>
> . . .
>
> . . . and al þe diligence
> of fayre Dydo, pryncesse of Cartage:
> Al þis haþe nature sett in youre ymage.[22]

Does Lydgate imply that despite their bitter ends, Dido, Cleopatra, and Helen of Troy deserve to be remembered for their finer moments? By emphasizing the "diligence / of fayre Dydo," for example, he calls attention to her grandeur as portrayed in Book I of the *Aeneid*.[23] Or do these fallen women serve as foils to the superior worth of the speaker's lady, as "The Floure of Curtesye" suggests?

> For though that Dydo with wytte sage
> Was in her tyme stedfast to Enee,

[21] "The Floure of Curtesye," lines 197–203, in *Minor Poems,* ed. MacCracken and Sherwood, 2:410–18.

[22] "A Ballade, of Her That Hath All Virtues," lines 8–9, 12–14, in *Minor Poems,* ed. MacCracken and Sherwood, 2:379–81.

[23] I shall return to Lydgate's ambivalent representation of Dido in my discussion of the two envoys to her story in the *Fall of Princes.*

> Of hastynesse yet she dyd outrage,
> And so for Iason dyd also Medee;
> But my lady is so auysee
> That, bountie and beautie bothe in her demeyne,
> She maketh bountie always souerayne.
>
> (211–17)

Perhaps, as Lydgate was to imply at a later stage of his career, his questionable similes are due to the paucity of truly virtuous heroines:

> This poete [Chaucer] wrot, at request off the queen,
> A legende off parfit hoolynesse,
> Off Goode Women to fynde out nynteen
> That dede excelle in bounte and fairnesse;
> But for his labour and [his] bisynesse
> Was inportable his wittis to encoumbre,
> In al this world to fynde so gret a noumbre.[24]

The spiteful remark that caps this passage becomes even more provocative when one considers the Chaucerian resonance of the word "inportable": "This storie is seyd nat for that wyves sholde / Folwen Grisilde as in humylitee / For it were inportable, though they wolde."[25] As we shall see, Lydgate often uses the implausibility of Griselda's story to disparage the whole of womankind; even so, the more respectful attitude noted above is not canceled by the irony of the last passage. Rather, it remains an interpretive possibility that Lydgate evokes alongside his more familiar misogynistic stance.

One way or another, Lydgate's smorgasbord of virtuous and quasi-virtuous female characters draws attention to his rhetorical prowess, manifested in his copious invention and gift for manipulating the facts to suit his present needs. Thus displaying his skill, Lydgate hopes to imitate the poetic luminaries of the fourteenth century, whom he credits not only with supreme eloquence but specifically with having written the lives of women like Griselda:

> And thus be writyng he [Petrarch] gat hymsilff a name
> Perpetuelli to been in remembraunce,

---

[24] *Fall of Princes*, ed. Bergen, I.330–36.
[25] *Clerk's Tale*, IV.1142–44. Chaucer's works are quoted from *The Riverside Chaucer*, gen. ed. Larry D. Benson (Boston: Houghton Mifflin, 1987).

> Set and registred in the Hous of Fame,
> And made Epistles of ful hih substaunce
> Callid Sine Titulo; & mor hymsilff tauaunce,
> Of famous women he wrot thexcellence,
> Gresilde preferryng for hir gret pacience.
>
> (*Fall of Princes* IV.120–26)

The Chaucerian diction in which this encomium is couched suggests that Lydgate's Petrarchism is actually inspired by the Clerk's recasting of Petrarch, whose image he again recasts along the lines of his reworking of the *Tale.* If Petrarch composed Griselda's story "hymsilff tauaunce"—and Chaucer, as noted in Book I of the same poem, "[e]nditid" the "Cantirburi Talis," including the *Clerk's,* "ful weel in our language" (I.337–48)—so will Lydgate at least refer to this heroine and other emblems of laureateship. However, such gestures to literary tradition are no mere acts of adulation. Much as he worships Petrarch (and Chaucer for having achieved Petrarchan fame), Lydgate, like any Silver Age writer, makes up in variety what he supposedly lacks in authority by constantly repositioning his objects of reference. Although he does not always give special prominence to Griselda, whose name often appears side by side with many others, she is representative of Lydgate's poetics in a way that Penelope and Lucrece are not. Whereas these heroines are drawn from classical antiquity, their renown long since established, Griselda haunts Lydgate's imagination owing to the paradox of her being a contemporary classic. Not surprisingly, his self-portrait in the prologue to the *Siege of Thebes* is partly modeled on the Clerk.[26]

Returning to his love lyrics, we find that Lydgate's subtle interplay of reverence and irreverence with regard to legendary good women forms part of a broader campaign to aspire for poetic mastery over the fictional beloved, as well as other figures of authority. By employing a frustrated lover persona, Lydgate at once exaggerates his praise and calls the real worth of its object into question. "A Ballade, of Her That Hath All Virtues" is addressed to a lady who, graced with Griselda's patience (see quotation above) and every good quality under the sun, nevertheless lacks pity for her desolate lover. The "myrrour and verray exemplayre" of "wommanhede" (29–30) turns out to be tainted by "daunger" (36), the courtly term for haughtiness. It seems that if the addressee does not

---

[26] For this borrowing, see Robert R. Edwards's marginal notes to the *Siege of Thebes* (Kalamazoo: Medieval Institute Publications, 2001), lines 73–74, 90, and 167.

wish to join the ranks of famous heroines who have fallen from grace, she had better show favor to the speaker.

"The Floure of Curtesye" (with its reference to Griselda, cited above) devises a more complex situation: though his beloved is commended for "hauyng aye pyte / Of hem that ben in trybulacion" (150–51), the speaker's plight remains the same. He is "so ferre . . . hyndred from [the lady's] grace / That saue Daunger" he has "none other mede" (80–81; cf. 254). Repeatedly asserting his failure "[o]f her goodnesse to make discrypcion" (186), he links together poetic and sexual potency in a remarkable passage that deserves to be quoted at length:

> And though that I, for very ignoraunce,
> Ne may discryue her vertues by and by,
> Yet on this day, for a remembraunce,
> Onely supported vnder her mercy,
> With quakyng honde, I shal ful humbly
> To her hynesse, my rudenesse for to quyte,
> A lytel balade here byneth endyte.
>
> Euer as I can supprise in my herte,
> Alway with feare, betwyxt drede and shame,
> Leste out of lose any worde asterte
> In this metre to make it seme lame;
> Chaucer is deed, that had suche a name
> Of fayre makyng, that, withouten wene,
> Fayrest in our tonge, as the laurer grene.
>
> We may assay for to countrefete
> His gaye style, but it wyl not be;
> The welle is drie, with the lycoure swete,
> Bothe of Clye and of Caliope[.]
>
> (225–42)

The effects of this predicament are both debilitating and humorous: like Chaucer in the proem to Book IV of *Troilus and Criseyde* (13–14), the speaker's hands tremble as he barely manages to keep his words from limping out of meter. Were he not to enjoy the lady's mercy, he might fail altogether. However, in refusing his courtship, she must settle for a less than perfect panegyric that redounds unfavorably upon herself as its recipient: "to you thus I me excuse / That I aqueynted am not with no muse," the speaker protests (181–82). Ultimately, the poem dwindles into a "lytel balade," which both imitates the ending of *The Parliament of Fowls* and falls short of its happy resolution (246–66). Chaucer, we are told, would have done a better job, perhaps enjoying better luck with his amorous pursuits as well. His green laurel stands in contrast with the speaker's lack of "lycoure,"[27] the same fluid with which April impregnates the earth in *The General Prologue* (I.1–4). However, now that he is dead like Petrarch and Griselda before him (IV.36–38 and 1177), now that his authorial stipulation at the end of his "litel tragedye" that "non myswrite" or "mysmetre" it "for defaute of tonge" (*TC* V.1786 and 1795–96) cannot be fulfilled owing to the unsurpassable greatness of his own "tonge," those writing in his shadow must find other ways to join the Muses' company. This Lydgate does by concealing his subtle ironies and allusions—for example, to Chaucer's statements about literature in the prologue and conclusion to *The Clerk's Tale*—under a screen of poetic inadequacy, which the addressee may or may not be able to pierce.

"A Lover's New Year's Gift" faces a similar challenge. When the speaker professes "[i]ff I shal reherce also Gresyldes pacyence, / My lady haþe, I dare wel sey, more passing eloquence / To reherse by and by hir vertus alle efeere," the credit for this original compliment goes to Lydgate, who sets the terms of a contest that he is sure to win by dint of his intimate acquaintance with *The Clerk's Tale*.[28] The reference to Griselda revises three passages from the *Tale* where her virtues are "rehearsed," two of which occur before and one shortly after her marriage. In the first, the narrator begins his description with a phrase that draws as much attention to its speaker as it does to its subject: "But for to speke of vertuous beautee, / Thanne was she oon the faireste under sonne" (*CT* IV.211–12). Next, the perspective shifts to Walter, who is at this stage confident in his ability to judge for himself the young woman's worth,

> Commendynge in his herte hir wommanhede,
> And eek hir vertu, passynge any wight
> Of so yong age, as wel in chiere as dede.
> For thogh the peple have no greet insight

[27] For the importance of this term in Lydgate's critical vocabulary, see Ebin, *Illuminator, Makar, Vates,* 12 and 26–27.

[28] "A Lover's New Year's Gift," lines 42–44, in *Minor Poems,* ed. MacCracken and Sherwood, 2:424–27.

> In vertu, he considered ful right
> Hire bountee, and disposed that he wolde
> Wedde hire oonly, if evere he wedde sholde.
>
> (IV.239–45)

In the third passage, the Clerk observes:

> For though that evere vertuous was she,
> She was encressed in swich excellence
> Of thewes goode, yset in heigh bountee,
> And so discreet and fair of eloquence,
> So benigne and so digne of reverence,
> And koude so the peples herte embrace,
> That ech hire lovede that looked on hir face.
>
> (IV.407–13)

These passages codify and to some extent define the stock vocabulary that Lydgate uses to extol women: "vertu," "beautee," "wommanhede,"[29] "excellence," "bountee," and so forth. Tellingly, "eloquence" is not a quality that Lydgate typically attributes to them. Its appearance in this passage and in "A Lover's New Year's Gift" sharpens the paradoxical nature of their clerkly encomia: while Griselda and the beloved are praised for being eloquent, this art is actually being practiced by the discerning male observer.[30]

Although it is certainly possible to read his love lyrics for their attitude to women, Lydgate may well have had an additional object in mind. Some critics detect a blend of self-deprecation, flattery, and covert irony similar to that examined above in Lydgate's addresses to his patrons.[31] By penning his seemingly undistinguished poems of courtly

---

[29] According to Tara Williams, the word "wommanhede" is a Chaucerian coinage that is especially relevant to *The Clerk's Tale*. See "'T'assaye in thee thy wommanheede': Griselda Chosen, Translated, and Tried," *SAC* 27 (2005): 93–127.

[30] William Rossiter pushes this point even further by arguing that "[w]hen one reads the opening stanza of Lydgate's description of the perfect lady [in "A Ballade, of Her That Hath All Virtues"], one cannot help but notice that almost every adjective may be read as reflecting back upon the descriptive strategy that the poet employs in order to convey 'Her.'" See "'Disgraces the name and patronage of his master Chaucer': Echoes and Reflections in Lydgate's Courtly Poetry," in *Standing in the Shadow of the Master? Chaucerian Influences and Interpretations*, ed. Kathleen A. Bishop (Newcastle upon Tyne: Cambridge Scholars, 2010), 2–27 (7).

[31] See Lawton, "Dullness and the Fifteenth Century"; Scott-Morgan Straker, "Propaganda, Intentionality, and the Lancastrian Lydgate," in *John Lydgate: Poetry, Culture, and Lancastrian England*, ed. Scanlon and Simpson, 98–128; and Robert J. Meyer-Lee, *Poets and Power from Chaucer to Wyatt* (Cambridge: Cambridge University Press, 2007).

love, the Monk of Bury could have been using a well-established formula to deplore his service not to Cupid's court but to the English
court.[32] After all, tongue-in-cheek homage to a fictional lady would not
have raised many eyebrows among those familiar with the genre, as
opposed to more direct confrontation with real, mostly male authorities.
Thanks to her association with Chaucer and Petrarch, Griselda becomes
a figure of the prestige the poet claims for himself over and against the
patrons whose favor he courts and whose praise he sings—while failing
to receive due recompense for his effort. However, this subversive potential is achieved at a cost. Not only does Griselda become an instrument
in Lydgate's rhetorical arsenal, subjected to him as she had been to Walter; but in serving his poetic and political ends, she loses the dignity
that has made her worthy of being recorded in the literary hall of fame.

Both overdetermined and overworked by Lydgate, the figure of
Griselda points to a tension that cuts across his poetry. For Lydgate,
Griselda is the quintessential topic of, not a participant in, conversation.
Together with his "lady," she represents the fame to which he aspires
through his poetry rather than the actual creative process. This split,
which Lydgate tries to cover up by transposing his eloquence to the
fictional beloved, has some troubling consequences. On the one hand,
he is among the first writers to conceive of authorship—or laureateship—as celebrity: rearranging the excerpt from the *Fall of Princes* IV
quoted above, one might say that an author's "name" precedes and
authenticates the "substaunce" of his "writyng." On the other hand,
Lydgate invests an inordinate amount of effort in the hope of achieving
laureate status. As the following sections of this study will argue, the
frustration that comes from this double bind is often vented in misogynistic terms, which confuse the vehicle ("wommanhede") with the tenor
(fame) of Lydgate's self-referential discourse. At once reviling and revel-
ing in female "duplicity," Lydgate exacerbates the contradictions inher-

---

[32] While the love lyrics are notoriously difficult to date, I accept Pearsall's suggestion
that they belong to Lydgate's "period of comparatively close contact with the court" in
the 1420s. John Shirley's rubrics to "A Ballade, of Her That Hath All Virtues," as well
as to *The Temple of Glass,* record the commission of "a squyer þat serued in loves court"
or "[un] amoreux," respectively, but Pearsall argues that such information is not specific
enough to be credible. Elsewhere Shirley attributes the speaker's views to Lydgate himself. See *John Lydgate (1371–1449): A Bio-bibliography* (Victoria, B.C.: English Literary
Studies, University of Victoria, 1997), 31. Whether commissioned or not, these poems
are clearly exercises in style that either lack a female referent or are not primarily concerned with this person.

ent in his quest for laureateship so as to attract notoriety—which, after all, is a form of fame. Nevertheless, his acute awareness that he will never become a second Petrarch also leaves open the possibility of working through his sense of inadequacy by revalorizing women.

Antifeminism and Antiphrasis

The last piece included under the heading of "Courtly Love" in Mac-Cracken's *Minor Poems* is a farewell to Cupid that builds on the disappointment expressed in the previous lyrics and marks another turn in their attitude to Griselda. "For cruwel Daunger was my guyde / Withoute mercy oþer grace," complains the speaker of "The Servant of Cupyde Forsaken."[33] The poem's envoy, an epitome of male chauvinism, alludes once more to Chaucer:

> To alle wymmen þis compleynt
> With cursed hert I nowe direct,
> Whos corage is euer emeynt
> With doubulnesse, such is þe sect,
> Which soþely no man may correct,
> Youre nature haþe so double a face,
> Whos galle ay newe doþe infect
> Þe sugre of men in euery place.
>
> (65–72)

Lydgate's idiosyncratic use of "sect" instead of "sex" goes back to the concluding words of *The Clerk's Tale*. Swearing by the "Wyves love of Bathe[,] / Whos lyf and al hire secte God mayntene / In heigh maistrie" (IV.1170–72), the narrator proceeds to sing a ballad in praise of domineering wives. Chaucer's ending may be read as sarcastic or affirmative of reality. "The Servant of Cupyde Forsaken" clearly supports the former view: if no woman may "folwen Grisilde as in humylitee," women shall instead suffer the speaker's abuse.

This poem lays the groundwork for understanding Lydgate's misogynistic references to *The Clerk's Tale*, whose authority he frequently invokes when attacking the alleged duplicity of women. "A Ballade on an Ale-Seller," addressed to a conniving barmaid of scanty apparel (cf. 9),

---

[33] "The Servant of Cupyde Forsaken," lines 5–6, in *Minor Poems,* ed. MacCracken and Sherwood, 2:427–29.

remarks by way of understatement that she will not be "compare[d]" to "trewe Grisilde . . . To Lucrece nor vnto Penelope" (35–36; cf. *CT* IV.1185–87). Disillusioned by her "doubilnesse" (63), the speaker now wishes the tapster to have a taste of her own medicine. In the *Fall of Princes,* the wife of Candaules, king of Lydia, is "[c]allid for beute cosyn to Nature, / And worthi eek, yiff I shal nat feyne, / To be comparid to Griselde or Eleyne" (II.3379–81)—only to be accused by the narrator of causing her husband's ruin when a knight who desires her murders the king.[34] Although one might argue that pairing Griselda and Helen together is meant to contrast faithful with untrue wives, the antifeminist gibe with which the episode concludes acknowledges only the latter kind: "Alas, a queen, or any gret pryncesse / Assente sholde hir fame for to trouble, / But yiff Nature excuse hem to be double" (II.3421–23). Lydgate's wholesale condemnation of women, as well as his blurred distinction between the Griseldas and Helens of this world, comes dangerously close to justifying Walter's suspicion of his wife.

More allusively phrased though no less sweepingly misogynistic is the false panegyric to female virtue in *Reson and Sensuallyte,*[35] the bulk of which Lydgate added to his translation of the French original.[36] When the narrator claims "[t]her sect ys no thing lunatyke" (6177), a marginal note in Bodleian Library MS Fairfax 16 is careful to note that he is speaking *per antiphrasim,* in the opposite sense to that intended. Echoing Griselda's humble submission to Walter's "assayes" (cf. *CT* IV.537–39, 545–46, 597–609, 677–79, 918–31), as well as the Clerk's conclusion and the *Envoy,* he lauds the quiet forbearance of women:

> For oonly of humilyte
> They suffren al that men wil seyn,
> And kan nat speke a worde ageyn;
> Meknes hath so her tonge nayled,
> Thogh they with anger be assayled,
> They be as Muet as a ston.
> A mouthe they han, her tonge ys gon,
> For of kyndly providence

---

[34] Laurent de Premierfait's French translation of Boccaccio's *De casibus virorum illustrium,* which Lydgate used as his crib, does not mention Griselda. See Faraci, "Griselda in Inghilterra," 41.

[35] *Reson and Sensuallyte,* ed. Ernst Sieper, 2 vols., EETS e.s. 84 and 89 (London: Kegan Paul, Trench, Trübner & Co., 1901–3), lines 6155–586.

[36] Pearsall, *John Lydgate,* 118.

> They be professed to silence.
> Ther ys no man that wyl sey nay
> That hath hem preved at assay.
>
> (6262–72)

This passage is so riddled with equivocation that it assumes the very quality that the narrator ironically pretends to admire in women: they are praised not for accepting their husband's will but for repressing their objection, angered though they may be.

Likewise couched in antiphrasis, and labeled so by the London book producer John Shirley,[37] the poem "Beware of Doubleness" adds another twist to the topos of false advice to women. It starts by arguing that contrary to all things sublunary, women alone are free of "variaunce" (1). The point is pressed to absurdity when Delilah's shearing of Samson is ascribed to her "innocence" (83).[38] None too surprisingly, the poem's envoy subverts its pseudofeminist moral:

> O ye women whiche ben enclyned,
> By influence of youre nature,
> To ben as pure as golde y-fyned,
> In your trouthe for to endure,
> Arme your-selfe in stronge armure,
> Leste men assayle youre sikernesse;
> Sette on your brest, your-self tassure,
> A myghty shelde of doublenesse.[39]

Whereas the Clerk believes that "the gold" of modern-day Griseldas "hath now so badde alayes / With bras, that thogh the coyne be fair at ye, / It wolde rather breste a-two than plye" (IV.1167–69), the above passage suggests that women are naturally and unadulteratedly good but must protect themselves from men by means of duplicity.[40] Accord-

---

[37] Ibid., 217.

[38] Both in his "Examples against Women" (*Minor Poems,* ed. MacCracken and Sherwood, 2:442–45, line 69) and in the *Fall of Princes* (I.6418), Lydgate calls Samson's lover "Dalida the double." As Nigel Mortimer argues, the *Fall of Princes* version of Samson and Delilah differs from its sources in highlighting the female protagonist's duplicity. See *John Lydgate's "Fall of Princes": Narrative Tragedy in Its Literary and Political Contexts* (Oxford: Clarendon Press, 2005), 200–202.

[39] "Beware of Doubleness," lines 97–104, in *Minor Poems,* ed. MacCracken and Sherwood, 2:438–42.

[40] The blatantly antifeminist "A Balade: Warning Men to Beware of Deceitful Women" (*Chaucerian and Other Pieces,* vol. 7 of *The Complete Works of Geoffrey Chaucer,* ed. Walter W. Skeat [London: Oxford University Press, 1897], 295–96) also echoes these

ing to this logic, even Griselda's obedience to Walter appears like an act of deception—an interpretive possibility that the Clerk himself raises but then discards (IV.691–93).[41] The notion, however, evidently appealed to some readers. In the fifteenth-century miscellany held in Naples, Biblioteca Nazionale, MS XIII.B.29, which contains a version of *The Clerk's Tale,* the *Envoy* is immediately followed by Lydgate's conclusion to "Beware of Doubleness."[42]

Returning to the *Fall of Princes,* we find two more passages that are modeled on the Clerk's antiphrastic conclusion to his tale. Once favored by Fortune, Theseus has erred in believing his second wife Phaedra's false accusation of his son Hippolytus, whom she "[l]oued ageyn kynde . . . [b]ut he to hire was contrarious" (I.4449–50). As a result, the son is "slayn / Withynne a char" (I.4457–58) and the wife commits suicide "ageyn al womanheed" (I.4460). The moral of the story, according to "Bochas," is that "[w]ithoute preeff" husbands should "nat leeue to soone her wyues" and other tellers of "talis" (I.4493–95). The narrator proceeds to expatiate on the evils of hasty judgment for several dozen stanzas, but suddenly changes his course by reporting that

> Bochas heer, I not what he doth meene,
> Maketh in his book an exclamacioun
> Ageynes women, that pite is to seene—
> Seith how ther lyne, ther generacioun
> Been off nature double off condicioun,
> And callith hem eek dyuers and onstable,
> Beestis rassemblyng that been insaciable.
>
> (I.4719–25)

This generalization runs against the point that Lydgate has so far been stressing: because "[s]um men sey trouthe, and summe be variable," the

---

lines from *The Clerk's Envoy* by pointing out first that "Men deme hit is right as they see at y" (6) and then that "Al is nat gold that shyneth! Men, take hede; / Hir galle is hid under a sugred wede" (25–26). The attribution of this poem to Lydgate was called in question by MacCracken in *Minor Poems,* ed. MacCracken and Sherwood, 1:xlix. For an argument in favor of Lydgate's authorship, see A. G. Rigg, "Some Notes on Trinity College, Cambridge, MS O.9.38," *N&Q* n.s. 13 (1966): 324–30 (327–28).

[41] Another late medieval exercise in antiphrasis, the anonymous poem "Abuse of Women" refers explicitly to Griselda: "ffor by women was neuer man begiled, / ffor they be of þe condicion of curtes gryzell" (18–19). The burden of this lyric uses clerkly Latin to signal its true intent: "Cuius contrarium verum est." See *Secular Lyrics of the XIVth and XVth Centuries,* ed. Rossell Hope Robbins (Oxford: Clarendon Press, 1955), 35–36.

[42] Weldon, "The Naples Manuscript," 706.

"prynce . . . [s]holde weel examyne afforn or that he deeme" (I.4618–
20). Women, it would appear, are guilty *a priori* and therefore need not
even be examined.

Despite his initial embarrassment, the narrator soon finds a way to
capitalize on the weakness of these misogynistic claims: "[Bochas] men-
eth off women that be born in Cret, / Nothyng off hem that duelle in
this contre: / For women heer, al doubilnesse thei lete" (I.4726–28).
Then again, calling all women in England faithful is still open to the
charge of judgment without proof. Seeking to substantiate his argument, Lydgate alludes to Griselda-like wives who are tried by their husbands:

> Blessid be God, that hath hem maad so meek,
> So humble and feithful off ther condiciouns;
> For thouh men wolde cause and mater seek
> Ageyn ther pacience to fynde occasiouns,
> Thei han refusid al contradicciouns,
> And hem submittid thoruh ther gouernaunce,
> Onli to meeknesse and womanli suffraunce.
>
> I speke off alle, I speke nat off on,
> That be professid onto lowlynesse;
> Thei may haue mouthes, but language haue thei non:
> Alle trewe husbondis can bern heroff witnesse;
> For weddid men, I dar riht weel expresse,
> That haue assaied and had experience,
> Best can recorde off wifli pacience.
>
> (I.4733–46)

As in *Reson and Sensuallyte,* the narrator adduces the "assayes" that husbands such as Walter have inflicted on their wives in order to prove
their "meeknesse," "suffraunce," and "pacience." Yet whereas the Clerk
insists that Griselda is an exceptional woman and cautions men not to
follow Walter's suit, here Walter and Griselda become a model for Lydgate's description of the quintessential English couple. This humorous
train of thought easily admits logical contradictions: in the next stanza,
the narrator draws on the Clerk's distinction between God's "preev[ing]
folk" but not "tempt[ing]" them (IV.1153, 1155) to claim that "[m]en
sholde attempte no maner creature, / And namli women, ther meeknesse for to preue" (I.4751–52). While this statement is more in line with

the Clerk's warning to husbands, it completely subverts his theological argument—as well as the original moral of Theseus's tragedy, which Lydgate struggles to recover as he returns to his translation of "Bochas."

The story of Dido from the *Fall of Princes* contains another interpolation that recalls the Clerk's antiphrastic conclusion to his tale. What Chaucer has done to Petrarch's endorsement of "vertuous suffraunce" (IV.1162), Lydgate will now do to Boccaccio's ethical posture. Although his additions may have been intended as comic relief, their darker implications are liable to leave readers more troubled than amused. Initially following "Bochas" in "wr[i]t[ing] hir chaste liff" (II.2152), the narrator denies Dido's involvement with Aeneas (II.2157–60) and portrays her as a martyr who would rather commit suicide than surrender her chastity to a local king (II.2059–65, 2129–42).[43] Whereas Boccaccio's and Laurent de Premierfait's versions end with an encomium of Dido, who, in Lydgate's words, "ded[e] fyne, / With liht off trouthe alle widwes tenlumyne" (II.2176–77), the English poet appends his own envoy to this conclusion, thereby refashioning Dido into a counter-example for women. "Noble matrones, which han al suffisaunce / Off womanhed" (II.2199–200) are urged to "countirfet[en] in speche and daliaunce / Alle thynge that sowneth unto stedfastnesse" (II.2215–16) while acquiring many "freendis" (II.2221) so as to "best encresen in richesse" (II.2223), not unlike the Wife of Bath. To wit, they should "do[n] their auauntage,—/ Contraire to Dido, that was queen off Cartage" (II.2232–33). The *Envoy* to *The Clerk's Tale* may leave the reader wondering whether a lifetime of marital strife is truly better for women than Griselda's extreme though ultimately rewarded meekness, but in this passage from the *Fall of Princes*, the dilemma becomes a choice between adultery and suicide, both of which are mortal sins. Even Dido, who allegedly opted for the more honorable alternative, stands "accusid off Ouide" (II.2151), her good name ever in doubt.[44] More disturbingly, by suggesting that Griselda-like constancy is a mere cover for marital

[43] For the long history of this representation of Dido, see Mary Louise Lord, "Dido as an Example of Chastity: The Influence of Example Literature," *Harvard University Bulletin* 17 (1969): 22–44. Lord believes that Lydgate's rewriting of Boccaccio "comes as a fresh note of practicality in a long series of pious admonitions to sterner virtue by other writers" (226).

[44] For Lydgate's ironic allusions to *The Man of Law's Tale*, and possibly *The Clerk's Tale* as well, in the story of Canacee from the *Fall of Princes*, see Nolan, "Lydgate's Literary History."

infidelity, the narrator unwittingly plays the part of the villain in the popular story of the righteous woman calumniated with adultery.[45]

Some of Lydgate's most startling uses of antiphrasis occur at an earlier stage of his career. Book III of the *Troy Book,* a translation of Guido delle Colonne's *Historia destructionis Troiae,*[46] contains a long misogynistic rant, supposedly meant to cure Troilus of his doomed love for Criseyde. While the narrator is careful to ascribe this passage to Guido (4264, 4270, 4303, 4322, 4329), no reader of Lydgate will fail to recognize the emphasis on women's duplicity, as well as a quotation lifted from *The Wife of Bath's Prologue:* "al is for to selle" (4329; cf. *CT* III.414).[47] His amplified diatribe, which effectively accuses all women of prostitution, goes beyond anything we find in Guido. Having apparently had his fill, the narrator suddenly exclaims "Þus techeþ Guydo, God wot, & not I!" (4343) and launches a counterattack on the Latin author: "So generally her secte to discryve," he explains, "made nat, þoruȝ indiscrecioun, / Of good nor badde noon excepcioun" (4356–58).[48] The word "secte" from the conclusion of *The Clerk's Tale* is again alluded to, only this time ostensibly *in bono.* However, the pendulum soon swings in the opposite direction to Guido's harangue as the narrator begins to extol the whole of womankind: "I dar wel affermen by þe rode, / Ageyn oon badde ben an hundrid gode" (4361–62; cf. 4393–

---

[45] The popularity of unjustly accused heroines in late medieval England is attested by such works as *The Pistel of Swete Susan, Octavian,* and *Le Bone Florence of Rome.* For these stories as the "immediate narrative context for Chaucer's tale of Griselda," see Karl Reichl, "Griselda and the Patient Wife: The Popular Tradition in Middle English Narrative," in *La storia di Griselda in Europa,* ed. Raffaele Morabito (L'Aquila: Japadre, 1990), 119–36 (120).

[46] Guido de Columnis, *Historia destructionis Troiae,* ed. Nathaniel Edward Griffin (Cambridge, Mass.: Mediaeval Academy of America, 1936).

[47] In the Latin *Historia,* Guido directs his invective at women's lack of "constancia," which gives rise to "mutabilitas" and "varietas" (XVIIII, fol. 84r). For Lydgate, by contrast, the root of all evil is duplicity.

[48] These distinct allusions to *The Wife of Bath's Prologue* and *The Clerk's Tale* in a work composed between 1412 and 1420 should qualify David R. Carlson's assertion that "John Lydgate gives no direct evidence of having known or known of Geoffrey Chaucer's *Canterbury Tales* until about 1421–22, when Lydgate wrote the prologue to his *Siege of Thebes*" ("The Chronology of Lydgate's Chaucer References," 246). If the *Life of Our Lady,* whose quotations from *The Clerk's Prologue* are discussed below, was indeed commissioned by Henry V and composed between 1409 and 1411 (for a summary of contrary arguments, see Pearsall, *John Lydgate,* 285–86, and *Bio-bibliography,* 19–20), then Carlson's theory is further called into question. At any rate, I cannot agree with Carlson that Lydgate's *Life* "mentions only unspecified 'dyteȝ withoutyn eny pere' (2.1641) that Chaucer had written. It does not show (and so need not be taken to manifest) particular direct knowledge" (249).

97). This assertion effects a complete reversal of Ecclesiastes' dictum: "One man among a thousand I have found: a woman among them all I have not found."[49] To support his statistical claim, the narrator cites the legend of Saint Ursula and the Eleven Thousand Virgins martyred in Cologne (4370–83). Unfortunately, in his seeming eagerness to defend women, he concludes with a specious argument that makes him lose the case: since one cannot "holden or restreyne" the "cours" of nature (4403)—like an unruly wife, "she wil nat be guyed be no reyne" (4404)—male readers must (like Griselda?) "þanke God and take paciently: / For ʒif wommen be double naturelly, / Why shulde men leyn on hem þe blame?" (4407–9).

Lydgate was evidently pleased with himself for having penned this tour de force of pro- and antifeminist discourse, or at least anxious that his readers should not overlook it, for he repeats the same move several times throughout the *Troy Book:* with reference to Medea (I.2072–135) and Helen (II.3536–68).[50] These passages from Lydgate's first epic may well have provided the model for the kind of criticism his contemporaries would later voice at his disparaging attitude toward women. The best-known specimens of such criticism are Shirley's marginal notes to "The Servant of Cupyde Forsaken" and to the *Fall of Princes* excerpts in British Library MS Harley 2251,[51] as well as the poem in reproof of Lydgate contained, alongside several of his works, in Bodleian Library MS Fairfax 16.[52] Appended to the story of Samson and Delilah, the Harley passage likewise proceeds from insulting women in Boccaccio's name to making amends in Lydgate's (I.6511–734). "[B]e my trowth

[49] Ecclesiastes 7:29. All biblical quotations and references are from the Douay-Rheims Bible Online, http://www.drbo.org/. In the Authorized Version, as well as the Masoretic text, the verse number is 28. "Beware of Doubleness" also stands Ecclesiastes's dictum on its head, though in a more elusive and ambiguous fashion: "Salamon was not so sage / To fynde in hem noo doublenesse" (63–64). The double negative could be read both as emphasizing a profeminist statement and as denying it.

[50] For these and other passages, see Pearsall, *John Lydgate,* 134–35. An excellent study of the topos in general is Jill Mann, *Apologies to Women: Inaugural Lecture Delivered 20th November 1990* (Cambridge: Cambridge University Press, 1991), esp. 17–20.

[51] See Aage Brusendorff, "Lydgate and Shirley," in *The Chaucer Tradition* (Oxford: Clarendon Press, 1967 [1925]), 453–71; A. S. G. Edwards, "John Lydgate, Medieval Antifeminism, and Harley 2251," *Annuale Mediaevale* 13 (1972): 32–44; and Pearsall, *John Lydgate,* 75.

[52] The poem, dated between 1438 and Lydgate's death in 1449, has been edited by Eleanor Prescott Hammond, "A Reproof to Lydgate," *MLN* 26.3 (1911): 74–76. For a recent discussion of its possible author, his relations with Lydgate, and previous scholarship on this issue, see Meyer-Lee, *Poets and Power,* 136–39.

ye wilbe shent" and "Be pees or I wil rende this leef out of your booke," writes Shirley apropos of this text, in reminiscence of the Wife of Bath.[53] Although it is tempting to take his grievances at face value as being genuine expressions of indignation, one must not ignore Shirley's conclusion, which is humorous rather than indignant: "There is no goode wommane that wilbe wroth ne take no quarell agenst this booke as I suppose." Elsewhere, when "Lydgate speaks of women's truth and fidelity, Shirley asks laconically, 'A daun Iohan, est yvray?' "[54]

The London bookmaker likewise uses the verb *shenden* in a positive sense (a Middle English equivalent of "damn you!") when commenting on the third version of Lydgate's "Four Things That Make a Man a Fool":

> Wurship, women, wyne, vnweldy age
> Maken men to fonne for lakke of ther resoun;
> Elde causeth dulnesse and dotage;
> Worship causeth chaunge of condicioun;
> Excesse of wyne blyndeth discrecioun;
> And bookes alle, that poetes wroot and radde,
> Seyn women moste maken men to madde.[55]

To which Shirley adds: "Ye wilbe shent, Dane Iohan Lidegate for your triew seyeng."[56] It seems that Lydgate, his detractors, and, to a certain extent, Chaucer's Clerk partake of the same devices and use them to similar ends. As Jill Mann observes, "[T]heir ritual yea-and-nay saying about women . . . is an easy way to create a controversy that will attract interest, an easy way to win the reader's involvement."[57] This air of controversy depends for its effectiveness on continual tension among Guido the author, Lydgate the translator, and the various personas touted by the latter, which become more and more difficult to tell apart from one another. The more one reads, the less one knows to whom one should attribute the misogyny of the text. Lydgate heightens this tension by writing in a highly intimate, confessional tone:

---

[53] For this reminiscence, I am indebted to Mann, *Apologies to Women,* 20.

[54] Quoted in Pearsall, *John Lydgate,* 75. Brusendorff translates the French as follows: "Oh, Dan John must have been in his cups when he wrote that!" ("Lydgate and Shirley," 466).

[55] "Four Things That Make a Man a Fool, and Other Sayings of Don Iohan," lines 15–21, in *Minor Poems,* ed. MacCracken and Sherwood, 2:708–10.

[56] See also Brusendorff, "Lydgate and Shirley," 465.

[57] Mann, *Apologies to Women,* 20.

in good feith, I am riȝt wroþe with al,
Þat he [i.e., Guido] with hem [women] list so to debate;
For Ire of whiche, þe latyn to translate,
Inwardly myn herte I felte blede,
Of hiȝe dispit, his clausis for to rede[.]
(*Troy Book* III.4348–52)

In an earlier passage, the narrator goes so far as to hope that Guido "schulde reseyue duely his penaunce; / For ȝif he died with-oute repentaunce, / I am dispeired of his sauacioun" (I.2123–25). Such brazen statements bring the reader to a state of aporia: we must assume either that Lydgate underwent a true yet extraordinarily short-lived conversion experience in his attitude toward women or that he was so convinced that misogyny was part of the natural order of Creation that, having at first pretended to oppose it, he was willing to stake his own salvation by relapsing into antifeminist discourse at the end of this episode. Neither assumption seems tenable.

Through his use of antithesis, Lydgate attempts to deprecate women, defend them, travesty this defense, and exculpate himself in the process, all to his reader's delight—or indignation. This literary ploy takes the carnivalesque mode of the conclusion to *The Clerk's Tale* and its *Envoy* to the extreme. By radicalizing the poetics of the Clerk's conclusion, Lydgate exposes some of the troubling consequences lurking beneath its jovial surface. Whether or not he intended to criticize medieval antifeminism, he certainly offers a brilliant exploration of its contorted rhetoric, thereby making his poetry a *locus classicus* for contemporary debates on, and jokes at the expense of, female virtue. Although he does not seem to have been genuinely offended by misogyny, it was probably not an end in itself for Lydgate, but a means to provoke reaction from his readers by dramatizing his own encounter with such texts as *The Clerk's Tale* that appear to praise women or others, like the *Historia destructionis Troiae,* that denigrate them. Judging by Shirley's marginalia and the "Reproof to Lydgate," he certainly achieved this purpose.

In Search of a New Griselda

Other works by Lydgate imply a different reading of *The Clerk's Tale* that is perhaps less adverse to female dignity: Griselda's model womanhood is not impossible but temporarily unavailable. In this new config-

uration, the poet's role is to revive female virtue (or fame) rather than
merely to grieve over its loss. According to the *Envoy,* now that "Grisilde
is deed, and eek hire pacience" (IV.1177), modern women should not
attempt to imitate her "[l]est Chichevache," the legendary beast that
feeds on patient wives, "swelwe [them] in hire entraille" (1188). Lydgate's "Bycorne and Chychevache" follows Chaucer's lead up to a point
but rejects the finality of his conclusion; after all, one may still hope for
the revival of defunct ideals. Originally accompanied by (or woven on)
a series of tapestries,[58] the poem devises a situation that appears to be
as static as the cloth that depicts it: all patient wives are devoured by
Chichevache; all husbands of impatient wives are devoured by the
beast's mate Bycorne; and marriage is therefore impossible. Lydgate
concludes by lamenting the "double cheyne" in which husbands, caught
between their rebellious wives and the rapacious Bycorne, are supposedly "[l]ynkeld."[59] However, this deadlock is one that he cannot or will
not consistently maintain without allowing for some kind of outlet.

Borrowing liberally from the *Envoy* to *The Clerk's Tale* (as well as from
The Monk's Tale), the poem describes the complaint of a woman about
to be consumed by Chichevache:

> O noble wyves, beoþe wel ware,
> Takeþe ensaumple nowe by me,
> Or ellys, afferme weel I dare,
> Yee shal beo ded, yee shal not flee;
> Beoþe crabbed, voydeþe humylitee,
> Or Chychevache ne wol not fayle
> You for to swalowe in hir entrayle.
>
> (71–77)

The beast's victim embodies both Griselda and the Clerk: once a submissive wife, she now follows the Clerk's lead in cautioning her sisters
against becoming Griseldas. By repenting of her patience at the final
hour, she may be hoping to escape perdition—or rather, ingestion. Chichevache's own grievance (which ignores her feast in the previous scene)

---

[58] The difficulty of knowing exactly how "Bycorne and Chychevache" was displayed,
performed, or read is discussed by Claire Sponsler, "Text and Textile: Lydgate's Tapestry
Poems," in *Medieval Fabrications: Dress, Textile, Clothwork, and Other Cultural Imaginings,*
ed. E. Jane Burns (New York: Palgrave Macmillan, 2004), 19–34 (26–29).

[59] "Bycorne and Chychevache," line 133, in *Minor Poems,* ed. MacCracken and Sherwood, 2:433–38.

refers twice to Griselda. The beast specifies that her "feding . . . [i]s of wymmen þat beon meeke, / And lyche Gresylde in pacyence, / Or more, þeyre bountee for to eeke" (85–88). This combination of simile and hyperbole is reminiscent of Lydgate's love lyrics, which are populated by Griselda-like women. Chichevache, however, claims she is unable to come upon any:

> I trowe þer beo a dere yeere
> Of pacyent wymmen nowe þeos dayes;
> Who greueþe hem with worde or chere,
> Let him be-ware of suche assayes;
> For it is more þane thritty Mayes
> Þat I haue sought frome lande to londe,
> But yit oone Gresylde neuer I fonde.
>
> I fonde but oone, in al my lyve,
> And she was deed sith go ful yore;
> For more pasture I wil not stryve
> Nor seeche for my foode no more,
> Ne for vitayle me to enstore;
> Wymmen beon wexen so prudent
> Þey wol no more beo pacyent.
>
> (92–105)

Chichevache models her moan on Ecclesiastes 7:29. However, unlike the biblical author, she concedes to having once found a patient wife— possibly Griselda, who, as the Clerk informs us, is "deed, and eek hire pacience," leaving us with a "world [that] is nat so strong . . . [a]s it hath been in olde tymes yoore" (IV.1177, 1139–40). According to the logic of the new dispensation, wifely virtue becomes a contradiction in terms: prudence no longer complements patience but actually negates it. Even so, this is already a far cry from the rabidly misogynistic statements quoted in the previous section: in "Bycorne and Chychevache," women are the victims of insatiable beasts, or at worst their collaborators, but they are not such beasts themselves. The same air of pessimism inspires the final lament of the poem, spoken by an old husband who has (*mirabile dictu*) just lost his spouse to the "hungry, megre, sklendre, and lene" beast (79), a physical description one may at this stage come to doubt. Partly taking his cue from the Clerk and partly reversing his moral, the widower insists that "for it is an inpossyble, / To fynde euer suche a wyff, / I wil lyve sool during my lyff" (110–12). "The irony," observes Christine Rompato, "is that this Walter-like husband is not innocent, for it is his fault that his wife is being eaten. He does not seem to have learned patience from this experience; therefore, despite his warnings, we have no fear that he will ever be eaten by Bycorne. The warning of the double chain is noticeably empty, since as a husband he has suffered neither of these claims."[60] None of these complainers is therefore quite what he or she would like to appear. All three have read *The Clerk's Tale* and try, albeit unconvincingly, to use it to their advantage. Their studied behavior belies the vicious circle of "Bycorne and Chychevache," which seems at first to unfold regardless of the characters' volition. The static vision of the poem is further undermined by its confused handling of time: how many wives has Chichevache devoured? Is the same act of devouring portrayed several times?[61] Have women become insubordinate "nowe of nuwe" (113) or long ago? Moving back and forth in the "halle . . . parlour or . . . chaumbre" where Shirley tells us the tapestries were displayed, some spectators might have looked for a different way to make sense of what lay in front of them.

Lydgate provides us with a clue by modeling "Bycorne and Chychevache" on another well-known biblical intertext. The phrase "dere yeere" quoted above, as well as the coupling of "twoo beestis oon fatte a noþer leene" (Shirley's heading to the second stanza), recall the seven years of dearth prophesied by Joseph in Genesis 41, which lead to a surprising reunion with his family and a promise to feed and support them (45:18 and 50:21). While the only logical escape from the double bind in which the beasts place men and women is to renounce the conflictual view of marriage, Lydgate could simply have had in mind an unexpected reversal of Fortune's wheel in the husbands' favor, as it certainly had smiled on the "werþy citeseyn of London," who, according to Shirley, commissioned the poem.[62]

---

[60] Rompato, "Stuck in Chichevache's Maw," 88.

[61] Chichevache is shown devouring a patient wife twice—before and after her complaint—to which may be added her own reference to the "oone" she "fonde . . . in al [her] lyve." Christine Rompato argues that Griselda is to be understood on all three occasions (7–8). Far from solving the poem's contradictions, this suggestion makes even more confusing its shift between the distant past, the near past, and the present.

[62] In "Lydgate's Golden Cows," Andrea Denny-Brown reads "Bycorne and Chychevache" as a critique of avarice that is undermined by its own lavish presentation. Another study by the same author links this poem to Lydgate's topical satire "Horns Away" (*Minor Poems,* ed. MacCracken and Sherwood, 2:662–65), which condemns the fashionable sporting of forked headdresses by women. While "Horns Away" does not refer explicitly to Griselda, it does echo (37) the reference to "archewyves" in the *Envoy*

An open ending of this kind is likewise suggested by the play *A Mumming at Hertford,*[63] a pageant of antifeminist stereotypes whose chief interest (other than its plentiful allusions to Chaucer) lies in showing the detrimental effect of these stereotypes on the relations between men and women. Originally performed to a noble audience that included Henry VI when still a child, the *Mumming* presents a group of rustic, henpecked husbands who come before the young ruler supplicating protection from their wives. In the words of Rompato, "These abused husbands become like Griselda in their overly patient natures. The narrator of the mumming refers to the men as 'holy martirs, preued ful pacyent' (135), which invokes Griselda's full patience. The poem also asserts that the men suffer a "tourment verray *importable*" ([13]; emphasis added), the very word Chaucer uses for Griselda's ordeal in the *Clerk's Tale.*"[64] The wives, who have obviously taken *ensaumple* from Chichevache's victim, are given an opportunity to argue their side. So sure are they of winning the case that, if need be, they "wol darrein it in chaumpcloos by bataylle" (166). Be that as it may, judicial battle is soon rejected in favor of forensic debate. To prove that "parfyte pacyence / Parteneþe not to wyves nowe-adayes" (172–73), they cite "Gresyldes story," which "recordeþe pleinly soo" (176). The "worthy Wyff of Bathe," similarly a legal precedent (168–69), proves that abusive wives guarantee salvation to their spouses in reward for marital purgatory (170–71): an argument that the husbands themselves have previously sought to enlist on their behalf (85–90). Like the characters in "Bycorne and Chychevache," both parties have learned their respective lessons from the Clerk's conclusion and *Envoy* and try to bolster their case by referring to this canonical text. Sadly, the Chaucerian ideal of companionate marriage is excluded from the start: "Þer was no meen bytweene hem for to goone" (67).

Unable to pass a verdict, a spokesman on behalf of the king reaffirms the status quo until such time as "man may fynde some processe oute by lawe, / Þat þey shoulde by nature in þeyre lyves / Haue souerayntee

---

to *The Clerk's Tale* (*CT* IV.1195), an allusion that Pearsall also notes in *John Lydgate,* 218. Tellingly, the female role models whom Lydgate contrasts with the archwives share a number of Griselda-like attributes, such as "pacence" ("Horns Away," 63). Thus both poems, each with its own relation to fabric and its own Chaucerian moments, are rooted in contemporary social reality. See *"Povre* Griselda and the All-Consuming *Archewyves," SAC* 28 (2006): 77–115 (112–14).

[63] *A Mumming at Hertford,* in *Minor Poems,* ed. MacCracken and Sherwood, 2:675–82.

[64] Rompato, "Stuck in Chichevache's Maw," 83.

on þeyre prudent wyves, / A thing vnkouþe, which was neuer founde" (242–45). Part adjournment, part messianic prophecy, this open ending is reminiscent of the unnamed "man of gret auctorite," whom the dreamer glimpses at the end of *The House of Fame* (2158). The play concludes with some traditional if not very practical advice to men, who should "be-ware . . . or þey beo bounde" in matrimony (246). While the rustics can hardly be expected to produce a novel argument that would liberate them from their "seruage" (250),[65] nor is the tender-aged Henry capable of restoring order to a world allegedly turned upside down, there is nothing to prevent the sophisticated Lydgate from attempting to do so, at least within the confines of his verse. In addition to the sense of "legal action," the Middle English word *processe* quoted above could also mean "story."[66] Accordingly, whoever is able to devise another interpretation of *The Clerk's Tale* adduced by the wives to justify their behavior, or another text to whose authority husbands may appeal, will presumably win the king's favor and succeed in changing the prevailing view of marriage. This cultural transformation, which rulers, judges, and lawgivers have failed to bring about, necessitates the power of persuasion that only a poet can muster.[67]

Lydgate rises to the occasion by endeavoring to "correct" or redefine female nature in accordance with the values "properly" exemplified by Griselda and other virtuous heroines, thereby claiming a key public role for his poetry. The story of Olympias, mother of Alexander the Great, from the *Fall of Princes* initially capitalizes on this queen's tempestuous life to revile all women, alluding once again to Ecclesiastes (IV.2451–54), but gradually shifting its perspective to depict her as the antithesis

[65] This word echoes Walter's initial objection to matrimony: "Ther I was free, I moot been in servage" (*CT* IV.147). Yet his subjects' plea for marriage proves to be more compelling. It seems that had he read the *Mumming,* Walter might never have espoused Griselda.

[66] *Middle English Dictionary,* s.v. "proces," senses 4 and 3, respectively.

[67] Maura Nolan criticizes *A Mumming at Hertford* for "strip[ping] away" the *Canterbury Tales'* "multiplicity of voices and the multivalence of narrative, setting in their place a series of oppositions—husbands and wives, Griselda and the Wife of Bath—that demand not narrative but legal resolution." *John Lydgate and the Making of Public Culture,* 162. The ambivalent meaning of "processe" should qualify at least the latter part of this assessment. For other perspectives on the intersection of gender, law, politics, and hermeneutics in the *Mumming,* see Heather Hill-Vásquez, "Chaucer's Wife of Bath, Hoccleve's Arguing Women, and Lydgate's Hertford Wives: Lay Interpretation and the Figure of the Spinning Woman in Late Medieval England," *Florilegium* 23 (2006): 169–95; and Nicole Nolan Sidhu, "Henpecked Husbands, Unruly Wives, and Royal Authority in Lydgate's *Mumming at Hertford,*" *ChauR* 42 (2008): 431–60.

of "manerys that be femynyne" (2562). Lydgate concludes with an envoy to "Noble Princessis, set hih in dignite" (2598), entreating them to embrace "pacience" (2612) and "suffraunce" (2617), qualities deemed suitable to their "sect" (2631) both "of old auctorite" and "bi disposicioun" (2619–20). Apart from revising the Clerk's conclusion and *Envoy*, as well as a passage in the *Mumming at Hertford* where the impatient wives appeal to "þe statuyt of olde antiquytee" (213), this injunction also takes issue with the Wife of Bath's privileging of "experience" *(CT* III.1). It now appears that experience does not contradict but rather supports patriarchal authority.

A notably different approach is taken by the "Epistle to Sibille," dedicated to Lydgate's patron Lady Sibylle Boys of Norfolk.[68] Although one versed in his writings may hear an echo of Ecclesiastes and the Clerk's conclusion in the lines "Who is þat cane nowe fynde suche tweyne, / Or of þeire secte one verraily in dede, / Whiche þat list in labour do suche peyne, / Thorugh diligence longinge to womanhede?" (8–11), the poem turns out to be a paraphrase of the Ode to the Valiant Woman from the Book of Proverbs (31:10–31), rare in the Lydgate canon for unambiguously praising a female subject. By refusing to produce a misogynistic turn of the screw, the speaker restores the original meaning of Proverbs 31:10 ("Who shall find a valiant woman?"), which the Clerk has reversed in the lines "It were ful hard to fynde now-a-dayes / In al a toun Grisildis thre or two" (IV.1164–65).[69] The "verba factoris" that precede the envoy of this poem similarly revise the *Envoy* to *The Clerk's Tale* (IV.1183–87), as well as the ending of *Troilus and Criseyde* (V.1835–38):

> O yee wyves and wydowes moste entiere,
> And godely maydens yonge and fresshe of face,
> What ever be sayd as in þis matere,
> Ful humbully I putt me in youre grace,
> And remembreþe every houres space

---

[68] "An Epistle to Sibille," *Minor Poems,* ed. MacCracken and Sherwood, 1:14–18. "Sibille"/"Cybille" is mentioned in Shirley's heading to the poem and by the speaker in the envoy (135). MacCracken's identification of the dedicatee with Sibylly Boys is accepted by most scholars. For her life, social activity, and relevance to understanding the "Epistle" (as well as Lydgate's "A Tretise for Lauandres"), see Anthony Bale, "A Norfolk Gentlewoman and Lydgatian Patronage: Lady Sibylle Boys and Her Cultural Environment," *MÆ* 78 (2009): 261–80.

[69] This allusion is noted by Alfred I. Kellogg, "The Evolution of the 'Clerk's Tale,'" in *Chaucer, Langland, Arthur: Essays in Middle English Literature* (New Brunswick, N.J.: Rutgers University Press, 1972), 276–329 (314).

> Þat moder of vyces is wilful ydelnesse,
> And grounde of grace is vertuous besynesse.
>
> (127–33)

Instead of a perpetual battle of the sexes or the doomed love affairs of pagan tragedies, the "Epistle" recommends a life of biblically sanctioned "besynesse." Griselda may be dead, but her spirit continues to inspire other women, not so much to patience as to active devotion. Just as "[s]he knew wel labour but noon ydel ese" (*CT* IV.217), so is Sibylle called to "gif ensaumple" (13) and to "[l]et hir labour, avoydyng ydelnesse / Vsinge hir handes in vertuous besynesse" (139).[70]

Lydgate's *Temple of Glass* undertakes a more thorough engagement with the questions raised by *The Clerk's Tale*. This dream vision brings together a lovelorn lady and knight, each of whom feels spurned by the other. Tellingly, the knight's complaint is reminiscent of Lydgate's own lyric verse (e.g., 743–49). A benevolent Venus consoles the lovers one after the other, makes each swear a vow of permanent fidelity, and weds the couple. The poem refers twice to Griselda: first in the phantasmagoria of afflicted lovers that the dreamer witnesses upon his entrance to the temple (75–76) and next in Venus's reply to the lady, who has "[w]ithoute chaunge or mutabilite" in her "peynes ben so pacient, / To take louli [her] aduersite" (385–87). "Grisilde," says the goddess, "was assaied atte ful, / That turned aftir to hir encrese of Ioye" (405–6). The same lesson is then imparted to the knight, whom Venus urges to be as "constant as a walle" (1153), a phrase Chaucer had used of Griselda (*CT* IV.1047).[71] Having begun on a rather confused note, the poem gradually coheres into a vision of harmonious love. Instead of Chaucer's "man of gret auctorite," in *The Temple of Glass* a woman (or rather a goddess) takes charge.

Although this dream vision is often read in conjunction with Lydgate's love lyrics, which it admittedly resembles in other ways, it has little in common with their use of *The Clerk's Tale* to depict male-female relationships. In the words of Larry Scanlon,

---

[70] As Frances Manetti Biscoglio argues in her study of *The Wives of the Canterbury Tales and the Tradition of the Valiant Woman of Proverbs 31:10–31* (San Francisco: Mellen Research University Press, 1993), the biblical ode also underlies Chaucer's portrayal of his female characters. Of special relevance to Lydgate's poem is the "concentrated repetition of the word 'bisy' and 'bisynesse,' found more frequently in [*The Clerk's Tale*] than in [its] Latin or French sources" (120). Cf. also Kellogg, "The Evolution of the 'Clerk's Tale,'" 302.

[71] I owe this observation to Scanlon, "Lydgate's Poetics," 90.

When Lydgate's Venus enjoins [Griselda-like] constancy to the male beloved, she takes literally the Clerk's Petrarchan moral—that Griselda's example applies to "every wight, in his degree" ([IV].1145). She takes it literally in another way as well. It is no . . . longer a simple exhortation for spiritual forbearance in the abstract. Venus has returned it to the domestic sphere from which Griselda's example originates and made it the basis for an entirely mutual erotic contract, as binding on men as on women. Moreover, the figure also resonates with the poem's central conceit. The poem dramatizes the constancy, the durability, of poetry by transforming it into the temple's transparent walls.[72]

Scanlon's otherwise superb analysis overlooks the fact that *The Temple* reworks not only Chaucer but also the poetics of Lydgate's other writings.[73] As such, this transformation is at once more radical and more ephemeral than may appear at first. Notoriously difficult to date,[74] *The Temple* can neither be made into, nor advertises itself as, the high point of its author's career, the culmination and resolution of his engagement with the perennial problems of love and literature. Rather, its walls— together with the authority that Lydgate bestows on Venus, Griselda, and other valiant women—turn out to be as brittle as "ise Ifrore" (20).[75] Unable to offer permanent refuge, they instead provide Lydgate with a much-needed yet fleeting fantasy of escape from the contradictions that both afflict and enable his creative process.

From Griselda to the Virgin Mary and Back Again

Far from being essentially misogynistic, Lydgate's writings resemble Chaucer's in their commitment to explore different, often clashing view-

---

[72] Ibid., 91.

[73] More accurately, *The Temple of Glass* and the "Epistle to Sibille" revise the particular readings of *The Clerk's Tale* that underlie the poems to which I have so far referred. According to Green, the Griselda story "throw[s] into stark contrast two competing models of marriage—the patriarchal and the cooperative, or, to borrow David Wallace's terminology (since the personal is always political), the absolutist and the associational" ("Griselda in Siena," 22). Whereas Green argues that the cooperative model was more prevalent among late medieval readers in England and northwestern Europe, the foregoing discussion suggests that Lydgate and those who chose to read his works side by side with Chaucer's were also disposed to a conflictual view of marriage, at least as a literary trope.

[74] According to the latest edition, the possible date of composition for this poem "rang[es] from 1400 all the way to 1438." See John Lydgate, *The Temple of Glas,* ed. J. Allan Mitchell (Kalamazoo: Medieval Institute Publications, 2007), 4.

[75] For Scanlon's interpretation of this simile, see "Lydgate's Poetics," 72.

points while exposing their merits, weaknesses, and consequences. It is in religion that Lydgate, Chaucer, and other medieval authors found confirmation of the uncertain nature of reality, as well as refuge from worldly transience and unaccommodating circumstances—a haven that secular literature can provide only temporarily and imperfectly. Appropriately, some of Lydgate's pious and contemplative poems give a new meaning to the Griselda story. Like Chaucer's *Parson's Tale* and *Retraction,* and to a certain extent the Clerk's own conclusion to his tale, they disavow the laureate tradition of which this heroine is emblematic. The unexpected recasting of Chaucer in these poems adds a meta-literary dimension to their piety while simultaneously rising above the paradoxes of this world embodied by Griselda.

"That Now Is Hay Some-Tyme Was Grase" interprets her death as one more instance of "transmutacion"; the ballad closes with a vision of another world where "[t]her is no heye but all fresh grase."[76] "A Valentine to Her That Excelleth All" acknowledges that "Gresylde whylome hade gret pacyence." However, the speaker claims to have found a worthier love, whose identity is soon revealed: "Þis goodely fresshe called is Marye."[77] By substituting the Virgin Mary for Griselda as his ideal of womanhood, Lydgate undertakes a radical revision of the gendered logic that, I have been arguing, informs his poetics. In his *Life of Our Lady,* a dense cluster of Chaucerian resonances that we have encountered in his secular writings is translated to the domain of divine history. About to drink bitter waters in order for the "bisshopes" to determine whether her pregnancy with Jesus is the product of illicit intercourse,[78] the Virgin Mary

> all way constant, as a wall
> In thought ne chere, abaschede neuer a dele
> Ne in hir hert, dredyth not at all
> But vpon god, trustyth all waye wele
> That he of trouthe, shall trye oute the stele[.][79]

[76] "That Now Is Hay Some-Tyme Was Grase," lines 2, 136; for Griselda's death, see 59–62. *Minor Poems,* ed. MacCracken and Sherwood, 2:809–13.

[77] "A Valentine to Her That Excelleth All," lines 64, 73, in *Minor Poems,* ed. MacCracken and Sherwood, 1:304–10.

[78] This episode ultimately derives, via a late medieval version of the Nativity Gospel of Pseudo-Matthew, from the second-century Protevangelium of James. See the introduction to the *Life of Our Lady,* 81–84, in *A Critical Edition of John Lydgate's Life of Our Lady,* ed. Joseph A. Lauritis, Ralph A. Klinefelter, and Vernon F. Gallagher (Pittsburgh: Duquesne University Press, 1961).

[79] Ibid., lines II.1509–13.

Faced with this "hard assay" (II.1508), Mary follows the Clerk's Petrarchan advice to "be constant in adversitee" *(CT* IV.1146) while disregarding its attendant ambiguities. Placed between the Annunciation and the Incarnation, the apocryphal story of Mary's trial is followed by Lydgate's often-quoted commendation of Petrarch's and Cicero's "Retorykes swete" (II.1623), now "dede alas and passed into faate" (II.1627). Praised for having "enlumyne[d]" England's "[r]ude speche" (II.1636) with "golde dewe dropes, of speche and eloquence" (II.1633),[80] Chaucer is likewise "ygrave" (II.1628). This encomium is often taken at face value as indicative of Lydgate's taste for aureate versification. Not enough attention has been paid to his refashioning of *The Clerk's Prologue* to suit the purpose of a devotional text.[81] Just as Chaucer's Clerk laments that Petrarch "is now deed and nayled in his cheste; / I prey to God so yeve his soule reste" *(CT* IV.29–30), so does Lydgate "[p]ray for [Chaucer], that liethe nowe in his cheste / To god above, to yeve his saule goode reste" (II.1654–55).

Drawing on the epilogue of *Troilus and Criseyde,* the proems to Books II and IV, and very possibly *The Second Nun's Prologue,* Lydgate continues:

> And as I can, forth I woll procede
> Sythen of his helpe, ther may no socour be
> And though my penne, be quakyng ay for drede
> Neythir to Cleo, ne to Caliope
> Me luste not calle, forto helpe me
> Ne to no muse, my poyntell forto gye
> But leve all this, and saye vnto Marye
>
> O clene castell, and the chaaste toure
> Of the holy goste, mothir and virgyne
> Be thou my helpe, counsel and socour
> And late thy stremes, of thy mercy shyne
> Into my breste, this thryde boke to fyne

---

[80] Compare Lydgate's reference in the *Troy Book* to the "gold dewe-dropis" of Chaucer's "rethorik" (II.4699). For the precise meanings attached by Lydgate to such concepts as illumination and rhetoric, see Ebin, *Illuminator, Makar, Vates,* 19–48.

[81] Some notable exceptions are Nancy Bradley Warren, *Spiritual Economies: Female Monasticism in Later Medieval England* (Philadelphia: University of Pennsylvania Press, 2001), 145–47; and Robert Meyer-Lee, "The Emergence of the Literary in John Lydgate's *Life of Our Lady," JEGP* 109 (2010): 322–48.

> That thorugh thy supporte, and benyng grace
> It to performe, I maye haue tyme and space.
>
> (II.1656–69)

Characteristically, Lydgate vies with Chaucer by adopting his rhetorical strategies. So intense is this engagement that he replays Chaucer's own contention with the origin of vernacular authority, Dante, only to create (perhaps unknowingly) a Dantean moment with a particularly Lydgatean twist. If Dante must bid farewell to the pagan genius of Virgil in order to reach paradise under Beatrice's guidance, so does Lydgate pay his final respects to the Christian authors Chaucer and Petrarch, whom he brazenly places on a par with Cicero. Instead of these dead writers, he substitutes Mary's inspiring presence, which he has already called upon in the prologue to her *Life* (I.50–63). Moreover, in addressing the Virgin as "the chaaste toure / Of the holy goste," he specifically invokes her at the time of her pregnancy. The subject of his work and its source of illumination are therefore represented as identical.[82] Such perfect unity is denied from the author of Griselda's story, which, as the Clerk insists, takes place in a world very different from his own.[83] Nor can the imperfect relationship portrayed in "The Floure of Curtesye" stop the speaker's pen from quaking. In writing the *Life of Our Lady* and other devout poems, the Monk of Bury has found a genre in which he can outdo Chaucer and Petrarch.[84]

Conclusion: Lydgate's Many Griseldas

Modern readers—whether believers or nonbelievers—may choose not to accept the religious solution outlined above. Nevertheless, Lydgate's

[82] According to Meyer-Lee, this unity characterizes Lydgate's secular encomia as well (*Poets and Power,* 56–61). While his transcendental praise of temporal authorities is certainly influenced by religious forms of expression, Lydgate nevertheless tries to maintain a distinction between the two.

[83] As Wallace argues in *Chaucerian Polity,* when translating Petrarch's version of the Griselda story, Chaucer works against the idealizing tendency of the Latin author, thereby recovering the historical awareness displayed by the last tale of Boccaccio's *Decameron.*

[84] Lydgate's *Legend of St. Petronilla* (*Minor Poems,* 1:154–59) and *Legend of St. Margaret* (*Minor Poems,* 1:173–92) are likewise colored with the distinctive vocabulary of *The Clerk's Tale*—or, more accurately, Lydgate's other poems that allude to it: "parfyte pacience" (*Petronilla,* 16) "inportable"/"importable" (*Petronilla,* 18 and *Margaret,* 236), "with-oute doublenesse" (*Margaret,* 159), and so forth. The prologue to the latter legend is especially rife with Chaucerian echoes, many of which are found in the *Life of Our Lady.* The influence of the Griselda story on Lydgate's legends of virgin martyrs is briefly suggested by Mary-Ann Stouck, "Chaucer and Capgrave's *Life of St. Katharine,*"

work is rich enough to suggest an alternative ending to this study. The last poem to which I shall refer, a ballad in critique of slander, admits that even if all women had "Gresildis humble pacience . . . ʒit dar I seyne, & triste right wel this, / Somme wicked tonge wole sey of hem a-mys."[85] Certainly, Walter is capable of inventing such popular "murmur" as a pretext for putting away Griselda (*CT* II.624–44), thereby "saying amiss" of his wife. Like the marquis's tongue, poetry is a tool that is liable to be abused: while its shifting perspectives, learned allusions, and savvy *doubles entendres* may teach and delight the reader, they can also be hurtfully dishonest. What sense is there for a poet to accuse womankind of duplicity or "lunacy" when his own work revels in contradiction? Having pledged in "A Lover's New Year's Gift" to be his lady's "truwe man, withoute doublenesse" (7), having sworn by the cross in the *Troy Book* that he believes most women are virtuous, and having renounced these statements, is Lydgate in any position to pass judgment on other people's fickleness, real or imagined? By obliging us to come to terms with the historical author's dubious morality, such questions destabilize the self-referential aureate world that he seeks to create through his secular verse, as well as the alternative poetics of his religious writings, grounded in timeless Christian truth. But they also encourage us to look for texts in which Lydgate does not "say amiss."

Elaine Tuttle Hansen has accused the Clerk (and those modern critics who follow his lead) of using multiple morals, subtle ironies, and comic relief to diffuse Griselda's enigmatic female virtue, a threat to men like Walter and Chaucer.[86] Similar charges could be brought against Lydgate, whose numerous references to *The Clerk's Tale,* each differing in tone from the others and manipulating different levels of signification, risk turning its heroine into a cipher. However, one must not forget that for all her mysterious qualities—indeed because of them—Griselda is also powerfully attractive to her husband, as well as to subsequent writers and readers. The proliferation of trials, possible meanings, literary versions, references, and scholarly interpretations that

---

American Benedictine Review 33 (1982): 276–91 (277); and Karen A. Winstead, *Virgin Martyrs: Legends of Sainthood in Late Medieval England* (Ithaca, N.Y.: Cornell University Press, 1997), 132 n. 52.

[85] "A Wicked Tunge Wille Sey Amys," lines 108, 112–12, in *Minor Poems,* ed. MacCracken and Sherwood, 2:839–44.

[86] Elaine Tuttle Hansen, "The Powers of Silence: The Case of the Clerk's Griselda," in *Chaucer and the Fictions of Gender* (Berkeley and Los Angeles: University of California Press, 1992), 188–207.

characterize her story may thus be seen as repeated attempts not to drain it of its meaning but rather to celebrate and multiply its polysemy.

When Lydgate read *The Clerk's Tale,* he discovered both a rich quarry of Chaucerian resonances and a model for his own conception of poetry. One aspect of this model, expounded in *The Clerk's Prologue* and explored by Lerer and others, is the ideal of the laureate/aureate poet capable of telling the story of Griselda, a *monumentum aere perennius* that will outlive its author, "subgit . . . to alle poesye" (*TC* V.1790). Yet a no less important lesson that Lydgate learned from the *Tale* and its narrative frame is that poetry is a constantly shifting process, a *carmen perpetuum,* with which the poet must work very hard to keep up. And Lydgate does keep up by giving us not one but many Griseldas: Griselda the muse, Griselda the haughty beloved, Griselda the antithesis of contemporary women, Griselda the exemplary spouse, Griselda who falls short of being the Virgin Mary, and Griselda the victim of misrepresentation. All attest to the great vitality of the literary tradition inspired by this heroine. Lydgate's unique contribution to this tradition can now be more fully appreciated.

Desire Out of Order and *Undo Your Door*

Nicola McDonald
University of York

THIS IS AN ESSAY about romance and desire, but not the kind of desire we usually associate with romance. Its focus is a young woman's physical intimacy with a disfigured corpse in *Undo Your Door,* a Middle English verse romance (better known as *The Squire of Low Degree*) that is preoccupied with the genre's capacity not only to articulate desire but to contain the disorder that it inevitably produces. It argues that readers' discomfort with her errant conduct has produced persistent misreadings, both purposeful and inadvertent, since at least the second half of the sixteenth century. Moreover, it suggests, those misreadings are inseparable from an impulse to circumscribe Middle English romance, to render its desires benign and readily intelligible. Romance is an enormously powerful cultural discourse; it both scripts our desires, as it does for the protagonists of *Undo Your Door,* and seeks to organize them into legible and socially acceptable forms. At the same time, our desire for romance, particularly our desire as modern readers for historical or archaic forms, affects the kinds of meaning that we attribute, indeed that we *want* to attribute, to the Middle English romances. First published c. 1520, and extant in a complete version only from the 1550s, *Undo Your Door* is commonly regarded as a relic of an outmoded genre. Ostensibly backward looking in its choice of form and subject matter, its achievement can only be understood as a critique of romance's limitations, as a cultural ideology and an aesthetic form. Too medieval to warrant the attention of early modernists and too late to secure a spot in the canon of Middle English romance, *Undo Your Door* awkwardly straddles the "great divide" that continues not only to structure our desire for the past but to condition the kinds of desire we allow that past to narrate.

Studies in the Age of Chaucer 34 (2012):247–75
© 2012 The New Chaucer Society

"otherwise called the squyer of lowe degree"

Undo Your Door is an early Tudor verse romance first printed by Wynkyn de Worde, c. 1520, and then again by William Copland, c. 1555–60. A radically abbreviated version also survives in the seventeenth-century Percy Folio.[1] Over the past few decades, it has attracted a body of criticism, often nuanced and sympathetic, that has nonetheless failed to consider seriously its most dramatic episode: the princess of Hungary's seven-year-long intimacy with the mutilated corpse that she mistakes for her lover.[2] Scholarship's palpable discomfort with the princess's misplaced desire (it is routinely ignored or diminished) is, however, nothing new. Sixteenth-century readers were likewise disquieted by the errant narrative and they were the first to try to impose some kind of familiar order on it.

[1] Both *Undo Your Door* and *The Squier,* as the Percy version is entitled, have been newly edited, for the first time in over one hundred years, by Erik Kooper in *Sentimental and Humorous Romances* (Kalamazoo: Medieval Institute Publications, 2005). All citations are from this edition.

[2] Sustained modern interest in the romance is datable to Kevin Kiernan, "*Undo Your Door* and the Order of Chivalry," *SP* 70 (1973): 345–66. Although his contention that the poem is a "humorous" "anti-romance" (345–46) has been contested, he effectively put its self-conscious disruption of generic convention at the center of the critical agenda. Questions of metanarrativity and storytelling preoccupy, respectively, Carol Fewster, *Traditionality and Genre in Middle English Romance* (Cambridge: D. S. Brewer, 1987), Chap. 5, and A. C. Spearing, *The Medieval Poet as Voyeur: Looking and Listening in Medieval Love-Narratives* (Cambridge: Cambridge University Press, 1993), Chap. 9, both of whom offer highly nuanced readings of the romance's distinctive poetics. Most recently, Myra J. Seaman, "The Waning of Middle English Chivalric Romance in 'The Squyr of Lowe Degre,'" *Fifteenth-Century Studies* 29 (2003): 174–99, has proposed that the text's acute self-awareness works to critique the genre's value system and to demonstrate its incompatibility with life in Tudor England. Seaman's historicizing impulse is indebted to Spearing, who was the first to give particular significance to the date of first publication, and subsequently Seth Lerer, *Courtly Letters in the Age of Henry VIII: Literary Culture and the Arts of Deceit* (Cambridge: Cambridge University Press, 1997), esp. 65–70, who tries to map its "topical allusiveness" (67). More narrowly concerned with the question of parody proposed by Kiernan are: Bryan Rivers, "The Focus of Satire in *The Squire of Low Degree*," *ESC* 7 (1981): 379–87, who shares his sense of parodic *intent* but emphasizes "the sexual timidity of the princess" (386); and Glenn Wright, "'Other wyse then must we do': Parody and Popular Narrative in *The Squyr of Lowe Degre,*" *Comitatus* 27 (1996): 14–41, who argues instead for its "multi-layered *reception*" (38), encompassing both "straight" and parodic readings. In a rather different vein, and one that so far has had little echo in mainstream scholarship, Margaret J. Allen, "The Harlot and the Mourning Bride," in *The Practical Vision: Essays in English Literature in Honour of Flora Roy,* ed. Jane Campbell and James Doyle (Waterloo, Ont.: Wilfred Laurier University Press, 1978), 13–28, and Huston Diehl, "'For no theves shall come thereto': Symbolic Detail in *The Squyr of Lowe Degre,*" *American Benedictine Review* 32 (1981): 140–55, not only highlight the remarkable proliferation of religious detail in the romance but propose sources and putative devotional meanings.

The original title of the romance, attested on the title page of the earliest print and in the day book of John Dorne, a bookseller in Oxford in 1520 (who sold two copies, priced at three-and-a-half pence each), is *Undo Your Door*.[3] This essay argues that *Undo Your Door* not only has the advantage of primacy, but that it puts the princess and her door at the center of the romance and prevents us from skipping over what happens when she undoes it. In the middle of the night, stark naked, the princess opens her door. She finds a disfigured corpse, assumes it is her lover, the squire, and takes it into her chamber. She eviscerates and embalms it, then locks it in a coffin that she puts inside a tomb at the head of her bed. Every day for seven years, the princess takes the corpse out of its monumental casing, embraces and kisses it. Ultimately, it disintegrates. At this point, the real squire returns from seven years of adventuring (summed up in a short seventeen lines) and the couple is reunited. They marry and—convention would suggest—live happily ever after.

Although medieval titles are more fluid than their modern counterparts (and much medieval poetry is untitled), the nomenclature of Middle English romance, in both manuscript and print, is remarkably predictable. The majority of extant romances bear the name of the knight whose adventures the narrative charts. John Dorne, for instance, also records sales of *Syr Eglemour* and *Syr Isambras*. All of the romances in the Auchinleck manuscript (Edinburgh, National Library of Scotland, MS Advocates 19.2.1), for which titles survive, are likewise assimilated to the men (or occasionally women) whose stories they narrate.[4] Even in more miscellaneous collections like Manchester, Chetham's Library, MS 8009, the romances are uniformly identified with their male protagonist: *Torrente of Portyngale, Bevys of Hampton,* and *Ipomadon.* In Oxford, Bodleian Library, MS Douce 261, where generic attributions are insistently flexible, the hero is still, necessarily, eponymous: *The Hystorye of the Valyaunte Knyght Syr Isenbras, The Treatyse of Syr Degore,* and so on.[5] For all of their descriptive simplicity, titles like these are ideologically

---

[3] "Day-book of John Dorne, Bookseller in Oxford, A.D. 1520," ed. F. Madan, Oxford Historical Society, *Collectanea* 1, ed. C. R. L. Fletcher (Oxford, 1885), 71–177 (100, 116).

[4] In Auchinleck, titles survive for the following romances: *Þe King of Tars, Reinbrun Gij sone of Warwike, Sir Beues of Hamtoun, Of Arthour & of Merlin, Lay le Freine, Otuel a Kniȝt, Horn Childe & Maiden Rimnild,* and *King Richard.*

[5] Maldwyn Mills, "Generic Titles in Bodleian Library MS Douce 261 and British Library MS Egerton 3132A," in *The Matter of Identity in Medieval Romance*, ed. P. Hardman (Cambridge: D. S. Brewer, 2002), 125–38.

charged. They work hard to privilege the trajectory of the knight—the pursuit and satisfaction of *his* desires—while simultaneously diminishing the claims of competing story lines, other desires. Wynkyn de Worde, the foremost printer of Middle English romance, printed nineteen editions of twelve verse romances.[6] Among these, *Undo Your Door* uniquely breaks with generic convention. Right from the start, from the illustrated title page (a feature of print marketing that de Worde himself introduced into England),[7] the narrative is explicitly at odds with standard romance practice. In a context in which knights lend their names to narratives almost by default, *Undo Your Door* is deliberately not *The Squire of Low Degree*. In other words, instead of reinforcing the cultural and structural paradigms that the *Squire* necessarily implies, *Undo Your Door* proposes alternative strategies of interpretation, alternative desires.

The impulse to efface difference, to refuse its consequences is, however, powerful. The hardening conservatism of printers and their marked preference for standardized products (in terms of format, layout, and decoration as well as subject matter) in an uncertain print economy is well documented. But the transformation of *Undo Your Door* into something more conventional, forty or so years after it was first printed, cannot be dismissed as merely pragmatic. *The Squyr of Lowe Degre* first appears on Copland's title page; yet it is not original to him. As the colophon indicates, popular perception of the narrative was shifting. "Thus endeth undo your doore," he writes, "otherwise called the squyer of lowe degre."[8] Here Copland provides us with a rare glimpse into the dynamics of textual reception at a time when the romance canon was conspicuously narrowing.[9] Contemporary readers were, it seems, divided between the familiar and the extraordinary, between the illusion of order

---

[6] Carol Meale, "Caxton, de Worde, and the Publication of Romance in Late Medieval England," *The Library,* 6th series, 14 (1992): 283–98. From surviving evidence, de Worde printed the following romances, in addition to *Undo Your Door* (*STC* 23111.5), and where his titles survive, I have included them: *Arthur and Merlin* (*STC* 17840.7, 17841 ["A lytel treatyse of þe byrth & prophecye of Marlyn"], 17841.3); *Bevis of Hampton* (*STC* 1987, 1987.5, 1988.6); *Degaré* (*STC* 6470 ["Syr Degore"]); *Eglamour of Artois* (*STC* 7541); *Generides* (*STC* 11721.5, 11721.7); *Guy of Warwick* (*STC* 12541); *Ipomydon* (*STC* 5732.5, 5733); *Octavian* (*STC* 18779 ["Octauyan the Emperoure of Rome"]); *Richard Coeur de Lion* (*STC* 21007; 21008 [both entitled "Kynge Rycharde cuer du lyon"]); *Torrent of Portyngale* (*STC* 24133.5); *Tryamour* (*STC* 24302).

[7] Martha Driver, *The Image in Print: Book Illustration in Late Medieval England and Its Sources* (London: British Library, 2004), 82.

[8] *The Squyr of Lowe Degre* (London: William Copland, c. 1555–60), sig. E.iv–verso.

[9] A. S. G. Edwards, "William Copland and the Identity of Printed Middle English Romance," in *The Matter of Identity,* ed. P. Hardman, 139–47.

(predicated on a readily identifiable, culturally sanctioned center of meaning) and the disorder that any kind of undoing, inevitably, threatens. And the contest was, nominally at least, soon over. In 1560, John Kynge was licensed to print "the squyre of low degre" (although he seems not to have done so); in 1575, Captain Cox was said to include a "squyre of lo degree" in his repertoire; and by 1589, the Protestant Nashe dismissed "the Squire of low degree" as yet another of the absurdities penned by "exiled Abbie-lubbers."[10] Before the century was out, *Undo Your Door* disappeared and, with it, the challenge to normative desire occasioned by the princess and her undoing.[11]

And modern scholarship has done little to reverse the trend. In its newest edition, the first since 1904, the *Squire* is represented as entirely benign, a "sentimental" story of "social mobility" and the "difference between reputation and wealth."[12] Middle English verse romance is, today, a degraded genre, its aesthetics impoverished and its ideologies circumscribed. *The Squire of Low Degree* matches our assumptions about romance narrative, and what it can achieve, much more neatly than the enigmatic *Undo Your Door*. At the same time, the inadequacies—in plot, motivation, and resolution—that are thrown up by reading *Undo Your Door* as the *Squire* (Mead, the first modern editor, for instance, remarks: "[The] squire is the central figure—or is intended to be. Yet . . . he has little or nothing to do")[13] work to confirm the genre's limitations. As A. S. G. Edwards puts it: what remains of the *Squire* are "late, corrupt,

---

[10] *A Transcript of the Registers of the Company of Stationers of London 1554–1640,* ed. Edward Arber; 5 vols. (London: privately printed, 1875–94), 1:fol. 48b (128); *Robert Langham: A Letter,* ed. R. J. P. Kuin (Leiden: Brill, 1983), 53; Thomas Nashe, *The Anatomie of Absurditie* in *The Works of Thomas Nashe,* ed. R. B. McKerrow, rev. F. P. Wilson, 5 vols. (Oxford: Blackwell, 1958), 1:11.

[11] For all that *Squire of Low Degree* shifts attention away from the princess, sixteenth-century readers, unlike modern ones, seem not to have regarded the newly eponymous squire as a typical romance hero. In late sixteenth-century sources (see the detailed list of allusions to a "squire of low degree" in Shakespeare, Nashe, Beaumont, and Fletcher compiled in *The Squyr of Lowe Degre,* ed. William E. Mead (Boston: Ginn, 1904), xiii, he is a distinctly base character. The *Squier*'s popularity through the end of the sixteenth century, and indeed beyond, as attested by its inclusion in the Percy Folio (where the squire is a villain from the outset), merits closer scrutiny. A London bookseller, for instance, shipped fifty unbound copies of "Squire of low degre" (by far the largest number of copies of a single title in the whole shipment) to Scotland in 1586. Donald Robertson, "A Packet of Books for Scotland," *Bibliothek* 6 (1971–73): 52–53. I am grateful to Jordi Sánchez Martí for this reference.

[12] This description comes from the publisher's website, but it matches the tenor of Kooper's introduction (which studiously avoids any discussion of the princess's necrophilia) and readily reflects critical consensus.

[13] *The Squyr of Lowe Degre,* ed. Mead, lxxx.

reflections of a design that was initially imperfect."[14] My point is not to suggest that there has been no interesting work on the poem; on the contrary, it has attracted more sustained analysis than almost any other of the Middle English verse romances. But, rather, that as long we continue to elide the narrative with the squire, we can never fully appreciate its remarkable audacity. What happens when the princess undoes her door is not a "bit of grotesquerie" designed to "spice up the story"; nor is it "immediately forgotten" once the squire returns.[15] It is the focal point of a narrative wholly preoccupied with desires that are out of order.

Ordering Desire

Romance is, of course, always preoccupied with desire, whether erotic, material, political, or, more rarely, spiritual. A romance tells the story of someone (usually a knight) who wants something (usually sex, money, and/or power) and who, after a few adventures (to get rid of the competition), ends up getting it.[16] What exactly the knight wants and the detail of how he goes about getting it change from narrative to narrative. Likewise, the desires with which he has to compete are heterogeneous and often multiple. But, despite the variance of incident and preoccupation, the basic principle remains the same. As my crude plot summary implies, desire is at once the subject matter of romance and the energy (or, to borrow Peter Brooks's formulation, the "motor force")

[14] A. S. G. Edwards, "Middle English Romance: The Limits of Editing, the Limits of Criticism," in *Medieval Literature: Texts and Interpretations,* ed. Tim W. Machan (Binghamton, N.Y.: Medieval and Renaissance Texts and Studies, 1991), 91–104 (103).

[15] Lee C. Ramsey, *Chivalric Romances: Popular Literature in Medieval England* (Bloomington: Indiana University Press, 1983), 197.

[16] Middle English verse romance is notoriously difficult to treat as a single, coherent genre; indeed, "defining romance" is characterized by Helen Cooper as "one of the more time-wasting exercises." But "equally clearly," Cooper remarks, medieval authors, and their readers, did work with a "set of generic expectations." Helen Cooper, "Thomas of Erceldoune: Romance as Prophecy," in *Cultural Encounters in the Romance of Medieval England,* ed. C. Saunders (Cambridge: D. S. Brewer, 2005), 171–87 (177). My discussion of romance and desire focuses primarily on that "loose confederation" of Middle English verse narratives, readily identifiable, I would argue, to both the author of *Undo Your Door* and his readers, that one might call love and adventure or, to borrow Cohen's term, "identity" romances, which follow a young man's successful pursuit of (the usually twinned fantasies of) social advancement and heterosexual union. Jeffrey Jerome Cohen, *Of Giants: Sex, Monsters, and the Middle Ages* (Minneapolis: University of Minnesota Press, 1999), xviii. I suggest, however, that it is applicable to Middle English verse romance more widely, in spite of its variety of structure and subject matter.

through which its story is produced.[17] What distinguishes romance as a genre is the way in which its form so regularly coincides with its content; the inception, pursuit, and satisfaction of desire (usually the eponymous hero's) give romance its distinctive shape and at the same time are what romance is all about.

And what distinguishes desire, in romance as in life, is that it is inherently disruptive. Desire makes us dissatisfied and stimulates us into action; only when we have what we want, when our desire is extinguished, can we return to the state of rest, or sated quiescence, from which we started. In narrative terms, in particular in the case of traditional narrative forms (like romance and most novels), desire precipitates a disorder that it is the purpose of the story to reorder. At the beginning of a romance a desire is aroused: a knight falls in love with a lady. The plot is set in motion when the knight sets out to win her and, in doing so, upsets the status quo. Inevitably, he comes into conflict with one or more incompatible desires (of a rival, a parent or guardian, even the lady herself) that are needed to generate the narrative. "A knight falls in love with a lady; she loves him in return; they marry" is not a romance; not because romances are not about love and marriage, but because as long as the knight's desire is uncontested there is, literally, no story. Indeed, the romance can survive only as long as the disorder that desire occasions. When the knight's desire is satisfied (he wins the lady), a new order is inaugurated (they marry) and the romance ends abruptly.

The paradox of desire is that it exists only prior to satisfaction, yet it is always compelled to seek satisfaction, the fulfillment that is, necessarily, its own end. It is this tension between dilation and closure that gives romance its distinctive dynamic. So, while the genre is famous for its dilatory aesthetic—the knight moves from one adventure to the next in a seemingly endless postponement of satisfaction—it is also insistently mindful of the end that its reader, if not its hero, knows it will achieve. Romance's reputation for conservatism is predicated not simply on its typical resolutions—which usually affirm prevailing social and sexual hierarchies—but on the way in which it works hard to make these resolutions seem like the most desirable *solutions* to the problems that the narrative has raised. The pared-down, action-driven plots of Middle English romance lay bare the process by which traditional narrative forms

---

[17] Peter Brooks, *Reading for the Plot: Design and Intention in Narrative* (Cambridge, Mass.: Harvard University Press, 1992; first published 1984), 48.

strive to achieve the artificial coherence that discontented modernists have so vehemently rejected. *Sir Eglamour* (a romance that, like *Undo Your Door,* is recorded among John Dorne's sales) illustrates the kind of romance dynamic I am talking about.[18]

When Eglamour falls in love with Christabelle, daughter of the earl of Artois (who loves him in return), he specifically articulates his desire as a function of closure and underscores the coincidence of desire and narrative: "she myȝt be myn at myn endyng" (105). Her father, Sir Prynsamour, assents to their union on condition that Eglamour complete three increasingly difficult tasks: to kill a hart, a boar (both the property of giants), and finally a dragon. Like the characters who mark out the teleological process of adventure as a succession of "poynts" ("'What,' seyd þe erl, 'and þis poynt be done? / Thow getys anoþur iurnay sone'" (346–47); "He sayde, 'I haue don poyntes two / . . . / þer is a poynt vndon'" (706–12), the narrator counts off the knight's successes, identifying them with formal narrative divisions: "þys ys þe fyrst fytte" (344), "this ys þe secund fytte" (624). But the anticipated "third fytte" is missing. Although Eglamour successfully completes his third task, when he returns to Artois he finds that the earl has exiled Christabelle, along with the lovers' infant son Degrebelle, and both are assumed dead. The expected "endyng" is deferred; Eglamour, knight and narrative, is still "vndon." Although he doesn't know it (the structuring of the second half of the romance, unlike the first, is apparent only to the audience), there are three new tasks for Eglamour to complete: he needs to find Christabelle and Degrebelle (who is now separated from his mother, having been abducted by a griffin) and to get rid of the earl, who, as in many romances, proves to be the real obstacle to the young knight's satisfaction, which comes fifteen years later. After winning her in a tournament, Degrebelle marries his mother only to have Christabelle discover, when she sees the griffin on his coat of arms, their real kinship. Degrebelle demands a second tournament, which Eglamour ("homwarde bowne" [1195] after fifteen years in the Holy Land) wins, defeating his son with a smack of his sword. It is now Eglamour's turn

---

[18] *Sir Eglamour of Artois,* ed. Frances E. Richardson, EETS o.s. 256 (London: Oxford University Press, 1965). *Eglamour* survives in three manuscripts: Cambridge, Cambridge University Library, MS Ff.2.38; Lincoln, Lincoln Cathedral Library, MS 91; and London, British Library, MS Cotton Caligula Aii. Although all three versions share the same dynamic, the (virtually identical) copies in Cotton Caligula Aii and CUL Ff 2.38 are the most explicit in structuring it as a textual dynamic; all citations are from the Cotton Caligula Aii version.

to be recognized, from the token on *his* coat of arms (a mother and child drowning at sea). Reunited, the family returns to Artois, where the earl, Prynsamour, falls from the tower to which he had escaped when Eglamour first discovered his treachery (fifteen years earlier when the "third fytte" was left undone) and breaks his neck. Eglamour marries Christabelle and Degrebelle marries Organate, an heiress won by Eglamour on his second adventure. All extant versions of the romance finish on the word "ende."

What *Eglamour* demonstrates so emphatically, with a bit of corporal punishment and a fortuitously spare heiress, is that romance is as much about the ordering of desire into culturally sanctioned ends as it is about desire itself. Although resolution always coincides with satisfaction, precisely which desires are, or rather *can be,* satisfied is determined by forces that are both external to the romance and sustained by it. For all that disorderly desires are necessary to—are actively courted by—the narrative, closure demands that they are systematically eradicated and replaced with the kind of orderly satisfaction that the exogamous heterosexual union so neatly represents. And *amour* (the defining principle of both father and suitor) is never simply erotic. The desires that preoccupy *Eglamour* are also social, political, and even, briefly, religious; and satisfaction requires that all of them are properly policed. Eglamour's fifteen-year interlude in the Holy Land, where he lives among "heden men" (1017), is a suggestive case in point. Condensed into a mere six lines, his adventures are reduced to the claim that "full dowȝtyly he hym bar" "agayn þem þat lyued wrong" (1018, 1020). The episode, if we can call it that, has no function other than an ideological one. The Christian order on which the resolution is ultimately predicated—"Ihesu bryng vs to hys blys / that neuyr schall haue ende!" (1376–77)—refuses to accommodate *any* challenge to its hegemony, even though Islam has, ostensibly, nothing to do with the plot. Romance satisfaction is all about righting wrongs; but it is also all about delimiting a particular notion of what *is* right.

"The Squire of Low Degree"

So far, I have been treating romance as if it were reducible to a single, straightforward plot, one that accords more readily with modern stereotypes (Knight in Shining Armor seeks Damsel in Distress, as countless personal ads put it) than with the genre's characteristic exuberance. Yet, for all that the corpus resists easy generalization, it is precisely this model, what critics of Victorian fiction often call the marriage plot, that *Undo Your Door* proposes as its framework: "It was a squyer of lowe degré / That loved the kings doughter of Hungré" (1–2); 1125 lines later, "that yong man" (now a king) "and the quene his wyfe, / With joy and blysse they led theyr lyfe" (1127–28). I want to call this framework narrative "The Squire of Low Degree," using roman font to distinguish it from the (italicized) title that was later attributed to *Undo Your Door*. It is not confined to first and last lines and can be summarized as follows. A lowborn squire, in service at the Hungarian court, falls in love with the king's daughter. While he is lamenting the futility of his love in an enclosed garden, the princess overhears him. She opens her window, returns his love, and agrees to marry him on condition that he first prove himself as a knight. A jealous steward tries to intervene, the two rivals fight, and the steward is killed. The squire goes off for seven years, adventuring in Italy, Spain and Portugal, the Mediterranean and the Holy Land, and wins his spurs. He returns to the court and to the princess. The king consents to the couple's marriage, the festivities last forty days, and, shortly afterward, the squire is crowned king. At this point, it might be hard to understand my objection to standard titling practice.

Undo Your Door is a remarkably self-conscious narrative. The poet is at least as familiar as modern scholars with the power of the genre's conventions, as well as their inadequacies. And this is nowhere more evident than in the way in which the squire and the princess, both voracious consumers of popular narrative, knowingly exploit romance stereotypes to formulate their own desires. *Guy of Warwick* and *Libeaus Desconus,* in particular, are explicitly cited by both lovers as models for *their* romance, and the princess is unique in surviving Middle English texts as a *character* who retells episodes from another romance (*Libeaus Desconus*) to advance her own story. But their debt to the genre is still more absolute; without romance's familiar narrative and attendant tropes, which together function as the impetus for desire and the structure around which it is organized, there would, quite literally, be no romance. The story of the squire and the princess offers an arresting testimony to the genre's capacity to order desire before it is even imagined.[19]

---

[19] The romancer thus anticipates Žižek: "The fundamental point of psychoanalysis is that desire is not something given in advance, but something that has to be constructed—and it is precisely the role of fantasy to give the coordinates of the subject's desire, to specify its object, to locate the position the subject assumes in it. It is only

Yet, as critics have long recognized, *Undo Your Door* is also distinguished for the way that it manipulates generic convention to destabilize our expectations of just about everything: plot, agency, and resolution, in particular.[20] It invokes conventional romance-structuring devices only to pervert their expected trajectories, and description always supersedes action; the progress of the narrative, which is already marked by brusque, unexplained transitions, is repeatedly arrested by rhetorically ornamented stasis. In addition, there is an extraordinary amount of direct discourse, almost all of which promotes articulation over execution. Aside from a fatal skirmish in a corridor and the princess's preparation and entombment of the resulting corpse, very little actually happens. *Undo Your Door* is completely invested in the practices of romance, yet it refuses to conform to them. The plot summarized above, while faithful to the rudiments of the text, completely misrepresents the narrative dynamic, gives the squire a prominence that is wholly undeserved, and excludes several fundamental episodes. Innocuous though it sounds, it mutilates *Undo Your Door* almost beyond recognition.

In short, *Undo Your Door* takes "The Squire of Low Degree" and forcefully resists the kind of ordering that it represents. It violently decenters the squire as both lover and adventurer (his seven years of exploits merit only seventeen lines, roughly comparable with the attention given to the king's dinner and the decoration of the princess's bed) and ensures that his eventual union with the princess (who spends those same seven years kissing a corpse) is never more than utterly contrived. In doing so, it undoes our confidence in romance's ability to contain the impulse to disorder that is inherent in desire.

Coming Undone

As we might expect, desire is construed right from the start of *Undo Your Door* as a threat to the established order. The squire's desire for a princess undermines the logic of social hierarchy, while the steward's desire for that same princess is both structurally and sexually excessive (one desire, one man too many). Both of these threats converge to start

---

through fantasy that the subject is constituted as desiring: *through fantasy, we learn how to desire.*" Slavoj Žižek, *Looking Awry: An Introduction to Jacques Lacan Through Popular Culture* (Cambridge, Mass.: MIT Press, 1991), 6.

[20] The way in which *Undo Your Door* has what Wright calls an "inside/outside relationship with romance" ("'Other wyse then must we do,'" 16) is well recognized; see Fewster, *Traditionality and Genre,* Chap. 5.

the plot moving forward: the squire goes adventuring to compensate for his "low degree," while the steward's jealousy precipitates the men's fatal rivalry. As in most romances, the threats that these desires represent do not exceed the narrative's resolution. The steward is killed off; the squire is made a king; and the final coupling reestablishes both social and sexual order. What is striking about *Undo Your Door,* however, is the way in which both of the initiatory threats are quickly and summarily dismissed. The king immediately expresses his complete indifference to the squire's social inferiority and the squire kills the steward before he sets off on his adventures. Unlike what we find in most romances, the removal of neither threat generates much narrative interest. The focus, rather, is elsewhere, on desires that cannot be assimilated into, or explained away by, the final resolution.

The king of Hungary's violent infatuation with his daughter's lover, the squire who serves in his hall, is the first overt articulation of a formally aberrant desire. Just when the usual romance coordinates have fallen into place (the squire and the princess have declared their love; the squire is about to depart on adventure; the steward prepares to betray them), the king sees the squire as if for the first time. "Full sodenly" (331) he is arrested by his manly beauty, fixes him with his gaze and is unable to eat; he can think of nothing else:

> The kynge behelde the squyer wele,
> And all his rayment every dele.
> He thought he was the semylyest man
> That ever in the worlde he sawe or than.
> Thus sate the kyng and eate ryght nought,
> But on his squyer was all his thought.
>
> (333–38)

The king's desire, of course, functions queerly, not only because it is directed toward a man, but because of the way in which it explicitly reconfigures an easily recognizable motif for heterosexual love at first sight.[21] The disorder that it effects results from poetic displacement as much as sexual errancy. The king's desire is arresting because it ruptures

---

[21] The closest analogy is *Ipomadon,* ed. Rhiannon Purdie, EETS o.s. 316 (Oxford: Oxford University Press, 2001), lines 184–95. See also *Emare,* lines 397–404, in *The Middle English Breton Lays,* ed. A. Laskaya and E. Salisbury (Kalamazoo: Medieval Institute Publications, 1995) and *Floris and Blancheflour,* lines 398–400, in Kooper, *Sentimental and Humorous Romances.*

the kinds of normative correlations (between gender and desire, between men of divergent social status, between fathers and daughters, and between language and meaning) that the narrative, up to this point, has been working hard to establish. And then it is over; eight lines of libidinal intensity that, explicitly at least, are not worked into the rest of the story. The king, as dumbfounded as the audience, tries to make sense of it all and comes up with nothing: "he wyst not wherfore nor why" (332). Hermeneutic indeterminacy is formally acknowledged (as it will be again, later in the romance), but the disruption produced by the king's desire for his future son-in-law is not forgotten. By positing a desire that is extraneous to the amorous economy of romance and explicitly recognizing its unmanageability, *Undo Your Door* makes possible other desires that likewise refuse to be managed. From this point on, nothing is quite what romance has taught us to expect.

The Naked and the Dead

When the squire cuts the throat of the king's treacherous steward, he ostensibly succeeds, as I have already remarked, in eliminating one of the primary obstacles to (his and his narrative's) satisfaction. Yet in doing so, he catapults his rival not out of the story but into the princess's chamber, thereby precipitating a startling reconfiguration of her desire. Paradoxically, the squire's one act of martial prowess, what is conventionally the meat and potatoes of romance, works to reward his enemy, the now-dead steward, with the physical intimacy that both men want, and from which the squire is wholly excluded. At the same time, it decisively shifts the focus away from the squire to the princess and to the playing out of her desire. I now want to turn to the undoing of the princess's door, the episode to which the romance's original title so insistently points and the only satisfaction that its narrative actually demands. The fact that this satisfaction comes in the middle of the story, rather than at the end, is typical of its challenge to normative models of meaning.

Throughout the romance, the princess's door is coded as a site of erotic desire with the threat of its rupture (what, in effect, we are waiting for) tantamount to that of sexual intercourse. The king is the first to identify his daughter's intact body with her enclosed chamber, a common medieval equivalence traceable to both the *porta clausa* of Ezekiel (44:2) and the *hortus conclusus* of the Song of Songs (4:12), when he authorizes the steward to guard over her but to act only if the squire attempts to "come" "within" or "breke" "her chamber" (431, 437). And it is an analogy to which the princess herself readily subcribes. Interpreting the squire's repeated demand for entry (his volley of "undo your doors") as a threat to her chastity, she rebuffs him—"I wyll not my dore undo" (551)—and elaborates: "kepe I shall my maydenhede ryght, / tyll ye be proved a venturous knyght" (575–76). But the princess does, of course, undo her door; and when she does she is tellingly "naked as she was borne" (673). This is a detail that modern readers have tended to overlook, but it is deliberate (aroused from her bed by the squire's knocking, she pulls on a "mantell of golde" [548]; by the time she opens the door, she has lost it) and far-reaching. While most romance heroines do eventually get around to opening their doors, what stands out here is that it is not only a dead man that the princess takes "in her armes" and then "into" her "chamber" (683–84), but the *wrong* dead man.

We never learn why the king's men strip the squire, dress the dead steward in his clothes, and leave the defaced corpse outside the princess's door (before bundling the squire off to the king, who sends him back on his adventures). It is the haunting question that the princess herself asks, twice: "Alas! Father, why dyd ye so?" (987, 1043), and it remains unanswered. The king's motivations are baffling—sometimes, as we saw above, even to himself—and his interventions in the narrative, a finger in every plot, are invariably unsettling. The *effect* of the gruesome hoax is, however, easier to grasp. In addition to sparking the princess's necrophilia, it formalizes the process of structural and thematic doubling through which romance meaning is so often made and unmade. Distracted by the squire's putative eponymity, few scholars have, in fact, noticed the easy coincidence between the princess's two lovers; and indeed the impulse to preserve the squire's, apparently necessary, distance from the treacherous steward Sir Maradose, who is the only character to merit a personal name, has repeatedly led scholars to misread even basic plot details. There is, I want to argue, little to distinguish the two men, neither of whom makes for a conventionally satisfactory romance hero. This is nowhere more evident than in the preamble to their fight, which both men win and lose. The episode has caused some confusion.

Having secured the king's support for his proposed adventuring, the squire departs. Less than one mile out, however, he tells his companions that he has forgotten "to take leve" (499) of the princess (*we,* on the other hand, know that he "toke his leve" of her more than two hundred lines earlier [282]); and so he returns to the castle, alone and at night. He sneaks in by the rear entrance, his sword drawn, and pounds at the sleeping princess's chamber. The much-anticipated demand for entry, with its repeated invocation of the poem's title, neatly exposes the strategies—courtly come-ons, manipulative lies, and displaced threats of violence—that the squire exploits as he attempts to satisfy his desire, prematurely and unsuccessfully. It is a moment of proleptic irony:

> Anone he sayde: "Your dore undo!
> Undo," he sayde, "nowe, fayre lady!
> I am beset with many a spy.
> Lady as whyte as whales bone,
> There are thyrty agaynst me one.
> Undo thy dore, my worthy wyfe,
> I am besette with many a knyfe.
> Undo your dore, my lady swete,
> I am beset with enemyes great;
> And, lady, but ye wyll aryse,
> I shall be dead with myne enemyes.
> Undo thy dore, my frely flour!
> For ye are myne and I am your."
> (534–46)

The squire, of course, does not yet know that the steward and his men have surrounded the chamber and are waiting for the "treason" that "walketh wonder wyde" (520)—waiting, in other words, to catch the squire redhanded, which they do.[22] The only oddity is that the steward and his men do not take the squire as he tries to force his entry but instead wait, allowing the lovers time to talk romance through the still-closed door. The squire's attempt to cajole the princess into her own violation—an act that was codified as treason in late medieval Eng-

---

[22] That the squire initially *pretends* to be ambushed, in order to trick the princess into opening her door, has gone unnoticed by scholars sympathetic to the squire, who instead charge the poet with a strange failure, that of omitting to tell us that the steward begins his attack on the squire at the very moment, if not before, the squire starts his knocking (Spearing, *The Medieval Poet as Voyeur,* 185; Kiernan, "*Undo Your Door,*" 361). Seaman, "The Waning of Middle English Chivalric Romance," likewise, believes the squire's claim to have "overlooked bidding his lady adieu" (176), whereas, I argue, the narrator's careful phrasing—"*he sayd he had forgete /* to take leve of that lady fre" (498–99)—alerts us to the squire's duplicity from the start of the episode.

land[23]—effectively recalls his first disclosure of desire. Right at the outset, he fantasizes about being either a chivalric hero (like Libeaus
Desconus, Gawain, or Guy) *or* a brute like Colbrand, the loathsome
giant of *Guy of Warwick*. The squire wants the princess—"no man
[should] have her but I" (85)—and makes it clear that if he can't live
up to the example of the romance hero, then the villain will do just as
well.[24]

Once this underlying affinity between squire and steward is recognized, the integrity of the lover's pairing is compromised. The assumption, fundamental to romance ideology, that the lovers are uniquely and
ineluctably "right" for each other is exposed for what it is: a fiction;
which is, after all, what propels their coupling in the first place. The
squire and the princess are both inveterate romance readers and both
turn to romance paradigms to articulate their desire. Yet, while the
squire can only lament what he isn't—"ryche," "gentyll," "bolde," or
"doughty" (69, 73, 77, 81)—the princess takes matters into her own
hands and models a knight in shining armor out of her unpromising
suitor: she dresses the squire up in a set of fantastic knightly duds, details the direction and duration of his quest, and offers him the material
support necessary to accomplish it. As Kiernan and others have noticed,
the outfit that the princess provides for the squire is not only "outlandish" (with its multihued, ostrich-feather headpiece and flower-bedecked
blue shield), it is the stuff of fiction.[25] And not simply because it draws
on fiction for its authority (no one but a romance knight would ever
wear this kind of getup). But rather, because it is realized only in the
princess's imagination, the squire—unlike his romance kin—never actually gets to wear it. The point here is that for the princess the lover,
appropriately labeled AMOR, is the *product* of her own desire (which
she, of course, has learned from reading romance). The squire—as he
sits in the garden, underneath the princess's window, desiring her—is

---

[23] The Treason Act of 1352 made the violation of the king's eldest daughter, unmar-
ried, an act of treason. *Statutes of the Realm*, 11 vols. (London: Record Commission,
1810–28), 1:319–20 (320). In the Percy Folio, the squire, forced to flee England for
Hungary after having "wrought a forffett against the crowne" (2), is guilty of treason
from the outset.

[24] Fewster's contention (*Traditionality and Genre*, 132), that by citing Guy *and* Colbrand as models the squire does not discriminate between their different roles, underes-
timates his cunning and determination. Medieval readers (the squire included) would
have had no difficulty in recognizing Colbrand as the quintessential romance villain.

[25] Kiernan, "*Undo Your Door*," 352.

simply the (most convenient) object, or screen, onto which the princess can project that desire.

And this is what she does again when, aroused and naked, she opens her door and finds the dead steward. The only difference is that this time the princess manufactures her lover quite literally. It is a scene that is at once tender and shockingly carnal, played out on the evisceration, embalming, and entombment of a corpse and in which traditional gender roles are exploded. For the only time in the romance, a woman takes a man in her arms. She carries the corpse into her chamber, where she opens it up, intimately searches out its bowels (commonly understood as the locus of feeling or emotion) before saturating it in preserving fluid. Although Middle English "seren" ("she sered that body with specery, / with vyrgin waxe and commendry" [687–88]) does not have the explicit sexual connotation of its modern English gloss ("impregnated with wax" is how the *Middle English Dictionary* puts it),[26] it is hard to escape the contextual significance of the "virgin" wax that the naked princess (yes, she is still naked) uses to prevent the body's corruption. It is a consummation, but only of sorts. And it by no means signals the satisfaction of the princess's desire, which is instead focused on the ornamented marble tomb at the head of her bed. Here, in a thrice-locked maple coffin, the princess puts the embalmed corpse; and daily for seven years she undoes it, embracing and kissing a lover who is, paradoxically, much more real, more material than the squire ever was, until it crumbles, from overuse, into "powder small" (931).

A Peculiar Passion

The princess's intimacy with a corpse is unorthodox, but what is just as surprising is that it takes its inspiration from popular devotion to Christ's passion, the flamboyantly macabre brand of piety that flourished, especially in the vernacular and among devout women, in later medieval England. A number of readers have noticed the poem's debt to religious culture; *Undo Your Door* makes unusually insistent, albeit fractious, use of religious language and popular religious motifs.[27] But the importance of

[26] *MED,* cīren (v); "seren" is an alternative spelling.

[27] Both Allen, "The Harlot and the Mourning Bride," and Diehl, "'For no theves shall come thereto,'" demonstrate something of the extent to which *Undo Your Door* is steeped in late medieval devotional culture, although Diehl's insistence on reducing an elusive text to a coherent spiritual meaning is unconvincing. The way in which, at every turn, *Undo Your Door* exploits religious language, motifs, and structural paradigms—the

the cult of the Passion merits further scrutiny. From the moment the squire enters the "gardyn that was full gaye" (26), that conventional locus of romance desire, Christ's death haunts the poem's erotics:

> And in the arber was a tre,
> A fayrer in the world might none be:
> The tre it was of cypresse,
> The fyrst tre that Jesu chose.
>
> (29–32)

The cypress was identified by medieval writers as one of the four trees used to make the cross of the Crucifixion (alongside the cedar, palm, and olive) and the notion that Jesus chose it first had common currency in later medieval England.[28] But the decision to privilege it in a romance garden is not haphazard. It signals an obsession with the Passion that informs the romance's poetics as well as its structure. A couple of key examples will illustrate what I mean.

When the squire declares his love for the princess ("lady, I thee praye," "let me not in daunger dwell" [145, 147]), he frames his supplication with pious oaths, those romance formulae that, common though they are, nuance the narrative. Both of the squire's oaths invoke events associated with the Passion—"For hym that dyed on Good Frydaye" (146) and "For his love that harowed hell" (148)—and while the latter is well attested, the reference to Good Friday is unique to *Undo Your Door*.[29] The princess responds ("I shall thee love agayne" [154]) with a Passion-oath of her own, "By him that dyed on a tre" (151), at once mimicking the squire and reinforcing the collocation of secular and sacred passion (there are no other pious tags in the romance). More important, Christ's dead body stands, quite literally, between the squire and the satisfaction of his desire. Devotion to it is determined, by the princess, to be the necessary condition of the lovers' union. Delineating the squire's quest, she directs him to "fyght thre Good Frydayes" (200) at Rhodes (the Crusader kingdom held by the Hospitallers until 1523), in

---

Marian imagery that characterizes the squire's annunciation of desire, for instance, or the provocative identification of the princess as "the kings doughter of Hungré" (2), a designation more commonly attributed to Elizabeth of Hungary, whose revelations were printed twice by Wynkyn de Worde—is, like its use of romance convention, determinedly off-kilter.

[28] See *MED* cīpres (see [n]).

[29] Roger Dalrymple, *Language and Piety in Middle English Romance* (Cambridge: D. S. Brewer, 2000), 229–30, 222.

order to secure a knighthood, and then to make offerings at "the sepulchre" (240) to prove himself the "venturous knyght" (250) worthy of
her maidenhead. It is another of the romance's disruptive doublings:
while the princess, a tomb in her chamber, is rapt in devotion to the
dead steward, the squire is preoccupied with the Holy Sepulchre and
the sexual reward that it offers.

The Passion likewise inflects both the original title and the action
that it anticipates. Unlike standard romance titles, *Undo Your Door* invites decoding, and although it refuses to be reduced to a single, mono-
lithic meaning, what scholarship has thrown up is its wide devotional
resonance.[30] The motif of Christ as a wounded, bloodied lover knocking
in vain at the door of his beloved's chamber is sufficiently well documented in preaching manuals, sermon exempla, and lyric poetry, in
both Latin and the vernacular, to suggest that it was (to borrow Siegfried Wenzel's formulation) "common property."[31] "Vndo þi dore, my
spuse dere," an English lyric preserved under the rubric "Passio Christi"
in the vast alphabetized collection of the Franciscan John Grimeston (d.
1372), is the most well known example of its use and I reproduce it
here:

> Vndo þi dore, my spuse dere,
> Allas! wy stond i loken out here?
>   Fre am i þi make.
> Loke mi lokkes & ek myn heued
> & al my bodi with blod be-weued
>   For þi sake.
>
> Allas! allas! heuel haue I sped,
> For senne iesu is fro me fled,
>   Mi trewe fere.
> With-outen my gate he stant alone,
> Sorfuliche he maket his mone
>   On his manere.[32]

[30] See Allen, "The Harlot and the Mourning Bride," 21–23, and Lerer, *Courtly Letters in the Age of Henry VIII,* 68–69.

[31] Peter Dronke, *Medieval Latin and the Rise of the European Love Lyric,* 2nd ed., 2 vols. (Oxford: Clarendon Press, 1968), 1:269–71; Rosemary Woolf, *The English Religious Lyric in the Middle Ages* (Oxford: Clarendon Press, 1968), 50–51. Siegfried Wenzel, *Verses in Sermons: "Fasciculus morum" and Its Middle English Poems* (Cambridge, Mass.: Medieval Academy of America, 1978), 119.

[32] Carleton Brown, *Religious Lyrics of the XIVth Century,* 2nd ed., rev. G. V. Smithers (Oxford: Clarendon Press, 1952), 86.

Moreover, as the scriptural citation that prefaces Grimeston's copy of the lyric makes clear, the motif derives its authority from Chapter 5 of the Song of Songs, a chapter whose detail and dynamic correspond suggestively with the morbid drama of *Undo Your Door*'s central episode: the lover's demand for entry, the beloved's delay, and its consequences, including his sudden disappearance and her resultant love-longing.[33]

For the later Middle Ages, there was of course nothing inherently disruptive about the fusion of Christ's Passion with romance. The suffering of the incarnate Christ up to the point of death was conceived of, in learned and popular piety, as *the* supreme act of love; and the only proper response to it was to love the contorted, leaking body back. From its beginnings in the twelfth century (in the prayers of Anselm, the sermons of Bernard of Clairvaux, and in the writings of their contemporaries), the piety that was to fuel medieval Europe's most extraordinary devotional practices looked to the nuptial imagery of the Song of Songs, as well as its highly sensual lyricism, to articulate the love between Christ (as *sponsus* or bridegroom) and the soul (as *sponsa* or bride).[34] The devotee's desire for Christ as a lover-knight was a devotional commonplace;[35] and its longed-for satisfaction found expression in a fantasy of

---

[33] Song of Songs 5:2–8, from the Douay-Rheims translation of the Vulgate, runs as follows: "I sleep, and my heart watcheth; the voice of my beloved knocking: 'Open to me, my sister, my love, my dove, my undefiled: for my head is full of dew, and my locks of the drops of the nights.' I have put off my garment, how shall I put it on? I have washed my feet, how shall I defile them? My beloved put his hand through the key hole, and my bowels were moved at his touch. I arose up to open to my beloved: my hands dropped with myrrh, and my fingers were full of the choicest myrrh. I opened the bolt of my door to my beloved: but he had turned aside, and was gone. My soul melted when he spoke: I sought him, and found him not: I called, and he did not answer me. The keepers that go about the city found me: they struck me: and wounded me: the keepers of the walls took away my veil from me. I adjure you, O daughters of Jerusalem, if you find my beloved, that you tell him that I languish with love" (www .drbo.org). Grimeston prefaces his copy of the lyric with citations of Song of Songs 5:2 and Revelation 3:20 ("Behold, I stand at the gate, and knock"), a verse commonly glossed as an allusion to this episode in the Song of Songs.

[34] Rachel Fulton, *From Judgement to Passion: Devotion to Christ and the Virgin Mary, 800–1200* (New York: Columbia University Press, 2002), and Sarah McNamer, *Affective Meditation and the Invention of Medieval Compassion* (Philadelphia: University of Pennsylvania Press, 2009) both offer impressively thorough, although divergent, accounts of the origins and early development of passional piety. The early work of Ann Astell, *The Song of Songs in the Middle Ages* (Ithaca: Cornell University Press, 1990), and E. Ann Matter, *The Voice of My Beloved: The Song of Songs in Western Christianity* (Philadelphia: University of Pennsylvania Press, 1990), is, however, still useful for the period after 1200.

[35] Rosemary Woolf, "The Theme of Christ the Lover-Knight in Medieval English Literature," *RES* 13 (1962): 1–16.

total, self-annihilating union with the man-God. The *literal* meaning of the "book of loue" (as Middle English writers sometimes called the Song) was, however, always a sticking point for medieval theologians, as was the reputation of its putative author, the historical King Solomon: "lecher or prophet," as Ann Astell puts it.[36] The vast exegetical tradition that grew up around the Song (it was the book of the medieval Bible that was most commented on) was, in effect, an attempt to control the poem's carnal impulse, and its likely effect on a carnally inclined audience, through the imposition of a "correct" *spiritual* meaning. Yet what it produced, particularly in the outpouring of devotional literature in the vernacular, was the most searching, the most comprehensive, and the most unfettered amorous discourse to emerge from medieval Europe. The kind of uninhibited exploration of desire and intimacy that is found everywhere in the devotional literature of late medieval England—its insights readily rivaling those of modern theorists—is not only unmatched but is unimaginable in the secular literature of the same period.

One of the most distinctive features of devotional writing is the enthusiasm with which it calls forth a whole panoply of transgressive desires, often but not exclusively sexual: not (in the manner of the penitentials) to exhaust them, but to press them into the service of its own amorous project. In fact, much of the power of this kind of writing comes from its purposeful flouting of normative models of discourse, as well as desire, which can neither comprehend nor contain the vastness of Christ's love and the gory excess of self-sacrifice that is its most articulate expression. Although the term would have to wait until the nineteenth century to be invented, the desire that lies, inescapably, at the heart of popular Passion devotion is necrophilia; and while it may have been sanctified, it was never sanitized.[37] Christ crucified—his body all

---

[36] Astell, *The Song of Songs in the Middle Ages*, 27.

[37] The term was coined by Richard von Krafft-Ebing in his *Psychopathia sexualis* (Stuttgart: Enke, 1886), translated into English in 1892, but the practice was certainly familiar to medieval writers. A widespread religious exemplum (Frederic C. Tubach, *Index Exemplorum: A Handbook of Medieval Religious Tales* [Helsinki: Academia Scientiarum Fennica, 1981], 1268), found in, for instance, *An Alphabet of Tales: An English Fifteenth-Century Translation of the "Alphabetum Narrationem" of Etienne de Besançon*, ed. Mary M. Banks, EETS o.s. 126 (London: Kegan Paul, Trench, Trübner, 1904), 1:93, and *Jacob's Well*, ed. Arthur Brandeis, EETS o.s. 115 (London: Kegan Paul, Trench, Trübner, 1900), 219, records the story of a monk who, on the death of his lover, takes her body to his cell and, as it corrupts, learns to despise fleshly desire. John Mandeville also tells of a knight whose "paramour" had recently died: unable to control his lust, he "wente in the nyght vnto hire tombe & opened it & went in & lay be hire," begetting on

bloody, his limbs mangled, his face hideous—enflamed desire. Some sought satisfaction by putting fingers or whole hands in his wounds, others crawled into the gaping gash in his side.[38] Catherine of Siena, whose "holy desyre" was to "bygrope" Christ "more gredily," covered herself in a garment soaked in his blood and drank deep from his open side, coming up from another "rauysshyng" "yet thursty."[39] The speaker of *A Talkyng of þe Love of God,* his mouth suddenly filled with a wondrous strange taste ("a tast wonder ferli") of love, was stirred into frenzied action by the sight of his mutilated lover:

> I lepe on him raply as grehound on herte, al out of my self, wiþ loueliche leete, and cluppe in myn armes þe cros bi þe sterte. Þe blood I souke of his feet; þat sok is ful swete. I cusse and I cluppe and stunte oþerwhile as mon þat is loue mad and seek of loue sore. . . . I cluppe and I cusse as I wood wore. I walewe and I souke I not whuche while. And whon I haue al don ȝit me luste more.

> [I leap at him swiftly as a greyhound at a hart, quite beside myself, in loving manner, and fold in my arms the cross at the lower end. I suck the blood from his feet; that sucking is extremely sweet. I kiss and embrace and occasionally stop, as one who is love-mad and sick with love-pain. . . . I embrace and I kiss, as if I was mad. I roll and I suck I do not know how long. And when I am sated, I want yet more.][40]

And in return, Christ on the cross stretched out his arms to embrace, and inclined his head to kiss, countless devotees.[41] A rampant desire for

---

her a hideous serpent and causing the city of Cathaillye to sink into the Mediterranean. *Mandeville's Travels,* ed. Paul Hamelius, EETS o.s. 153 (London: Oxford University Press, 1919), 1:16–17.

[38] See, for instance, the injunction in the MS Bodley 423 version of the Middle English *De institutione inclusarum:* "Crepe in-to that blessed syde where that blood and water cam forthe, and hyde the ther as a culuer in the stoon, wel likynge the dropes of his blood, til that thy lippes be maad like to a reed scarlet hood." *Aelred of Rievaulx's "De institutione inclusarum": Two English Versions,* ed. John Ayto and Alexandra Barratt, EETS o.s. 287 (London: Oxford University Press, 1984), Chap. 14, lines 863–66.

[39] *The Lyf of Saint Katherin of Senis,* ed. Carl Horstmann, *Archiv* 76 (1886): 33–112, 265–314, 353–91 (87, 88, 93, 105).

[40] *A Talkyng of þe Loue of God,* ed. and trans. Mary Salvina Westra (The Hague: Martinus Nijhoff, 1950), 60–61 (punctuation mine).

[41] The image of the crucified Christ "inclin[ing]" "hys hed to kysse" and "spredyng" "hys armys to clyppe" his "blessed and happy spowse" is remarkably commonplace. For instance: *The Tretyse of Loue,* ed. John H. Fisher, EETS o.s. 225 (London: Oxford University Press, 1951), 15; *A Talkyng of þe Loue of God,* 6; *Aelred of Rievaulx's "De Institutione Inclusarum";* Chap. 15, lines 603–4 (MS Bodley 423), and Chap. 11, lines 380–81 (Vernon MS). It lies, no doubt, behind Margery Kempe's desire that "the crucifix schuld losyn hys handys fro the crosse and halsyn hir in tokyn of lofe," *The Book of Margery*

a dead (or dying) lover was, in sum, proper to passion devotion; and by the fifteenth century, what Jennifer Bryan calls the "English hunger" for this kind of devotional material—native and Continental, translated, adapted, excerpted, and amplified—was virtually insatiable.[42]

In manuscript and early print, romance circulates in close proximity to its devotional counterpart; and lay readers, women prominent among them, had demonstrably catholic tastes. Wynkyn de Worde ran a healthy trade in romance, but he made more money peddling piety, much of which was the kind of "private devotional erotica" discussed above.[43] For the laity, indeed, the practice of reading was inseparable from that of Passion devotion. The alphabet, prefixed by a cross and concluded with an amen, was itself a prayer whose purpose was to facilitate the "prickynge" of "feruent disire," by a focusing of the reader's attention on the "very ymage of loue."[44] "Closed well" (94) within her chamber, the princess of Hungary's view of the world is literally filtered through "ymagery" (95), the stories illustrated in the "royall glas" (94) of her oriel window: she is the consummate (female) reader. While scholarship has concentrated on her rich diet of romance, her outlandish

---

Kempe, ed. Lynn Staley (Kalamazoo: Medieval Institute Publications, 1996), I.4, lines 306–7.

[42] Jennifer Bryan, *Looking Inward: Devotional Reading and the Private Self in Late Medieval England* (Philadelphia: University of Pennsylvania Press, 2008), 111.

[43] Ibid., 12. Wynkyn de Worde published, among other devotional volumes, two editions of *The Lyf of Saint Katherin of Senis* (1492? and 1500?), to both of which are appended *The Reuelacions of Saynt Elysabeth the Kynges Doughter of Hungary;* two editions of *The Tretyse of Loue* (c. 1493 and 1532); five editions of Walter Hilton's *Scale of Perfection* (between 1494 and 1533); four editions of Nicholas Love's translation of the *Meditationes vitae Christi* (between 1500 and 1530); an abbreviated version of *The Book of Margery Kempe* entitled *A Short Treatyse of Contemplacyon* (1501); *The Contemplacyons of the Drede and Loue of God* (1506), wrongly attributed to Richard Rolle; the *IIII Leues of a Truelove* (1510), which shares its title page woodcut (Hodnett, no. 1009) with *Undo Your Door* (see Seth Lerer, "The Wiles of a Woodcut: Wynkyn de Worde and the Early Tudor Reader," *HLQ* 59 [1996]: 381–403); the *Orcharde of Syon* (1519); *The Complaynte of the Louer of Cryst Saynt Mary Magdaleyn* (1520); and John Ryckes's *The Ymage of Loue* (1525). On de Worde as a publisher of devotional material, see George R. Keiser, "The Mystics and the Early English Printers: The Economics of Devotionalism," in *The Medieval Mystical Tradition in England: Exeter Symposium IV,* ed. Marion Glasscoe (Cambridge: D. S. Brewer, 1987), 9–26, and A. S. G. Edwards and Carol Meale, "The Marketing of Printed Books in Late Medieval England," *The Library,* 6th series, 15 (1993): 95–124.

[44] For the alphabet as a prayer, see Nicola McDonald, "A York Primer and Its Alphabet: Reading Women in a Lay Household," in *The Oxford Handbook of Medieval Literature,* ed. Elaine Treharne and Greg Walker (Oxford: Oxford University Press, 2010), 181–99 (186–87). *The Prickynge of Love,* ed. Harold Kane, Salzburg Studies in English Literature (Salzburg: Institut für Anglistik und Amerikanistik, 1983), 210, 14; John Ryckes, *The Ymage of Loue* (London: Wynkyn de Worde, 1525), sig. E.vi.

adventures with a corpse are, I want to suggest, more readily attribut-
able to her "studye" in "bokes of contemplacion."[45] When she is presented with the disfigured body of the man whom she believes to be her
lover, the ever resourceful princess effectively turns over the leaf and lets
the most popular literature of the day script her response.

Reinventing herself as a recluse (always the *ideal* of the contemplative,
whom even lay readers were instructed to imitate in their own devotions), the princess appropriates the desires proper to that most extreme
religious profession and relentlessly pursues their satisfaction. She reconfigures her conventional romance enclosure as a form of entombment,
readily submits to the rigor of ascetic discipline, finds her pleasure (as
Spearing has already noted apropos the extravagant catalogue of courtly
riches offered her by her father)[46] in renunciation, and busies herself
with a vigorous daily routine of passional exercise: until, dead to the
world, she is all but dead to herself. In this alternative narrative of desire, satisfaction is, fleetingly, hers. In a grammatical slippage that has
troubled modern editors, the princess realizes the fantasy of mimetic
identification that is *imitatio Christi:* "one flesshe," "one loue," "one
deth," in the words of the fifteenth-century *Tretyse of Loue.*[47] "Thus ye
have kept your enemy here, / pallyng more than seven yere" (1029–30),
charges the king as he reveals to his daughter (who immediately falls
down in a "dead sownyng" [1048]) the awful truth about her misdi-
rected desire. As long as the subject of "pallyng" (fading away) remains
equivocal—is it "ye" (the princess), "enemy" (the steward), or both?—
the princess is formally indistinguishable from her dead lover.[48] But
what makes the spectacle of her morbid devotion so disorderly is not (as
she and her father think) that she practices it on the wrong man (the
steward, not the squire), but that she substitutes a carnal lover for Christ

---

[45] Whether or not the princess's devotional "studye" is "overmoche," as her near-
contemporary Caxton would have it, it is one of the interpretative cruxes of the romance. *Caxton's Blanchardyn and Eglantine,* ed. Leon Kellner, EETS e.s. 58 (London:
Trübner, 1890), 1. The relationship between the date of both first and second publication (c. 1520 and c. 1555–60, respectively) and the romance's devotional politics merits
further attention, but is outside the scope of this essay.

[46] Spearing, *The Medieval Poet as Voyeur,* 188.

[47] *The Tretyse of Loue,* 60.

[48] Kooper, like Donald Sands before him (*Middle English Verse Romances* ([New York:
Holt, Rinehart, and Winston, 1966], 276), seeks to resolve the grammatical equivocation, providing alternative glosses ("languishing" or "decaying") depending on who is
properly the subject of "pallyng" (see the note to line 1030, *The Squire of Low Degree,*
ed. Kooper, 169).

and puts flesh on a practice that is properly spiritual. When Christ gets into bed with Margery Kempe, he invites her to "take" him "boldly" not in her arms, but in the "armys of [her] *sowle*"; likewise the energetic foot sucker cited above apprehends "swete Ihesu," his "lemmon" in his "soule," "wiþ al hol muynde."[49] Taking up "the mantell and the rynge" (955), the traditional signs of religious profession, the princess consecrates herself, again using familiar language ("I am a mayden for thee" [957]), *to the squire:* "To Chryst I shall my prayers make, / Squyer, onely for thy sake" (959–60). In doing so, she explicitly ruptures—she undoes—the logic of the discursive system that licenses or, to use Georges Bataille's term again, "sanctifies" her necrophilia, that makes it thinkable, and plunges us instead into the *un*thinkable, into the heart of transgressive desire itself.[50]

Love in a Box

The heavily ornamented marble tomb at the head of the princess's bed, in which the dead steward's remains are "closed" (689), is a monument to the princess's desire. Just as she, "closed" (94) in her chamber, by the sealed door and the ivory pins that spear her windows shut, is the familiar monument to the romance hero's desire. One is embedded in the other. In the paradigmatic romance (like "The Squire of Low Degree"), in which adventuring is the knight's prerogative, narrative desire coincides, as I have already suggested, with his desire: the beautiful, fabulously wealthy, titled woman in her magnificently decorated chamber, waiting to be won, epitomizes everything he wants. Women's lives, by contrast, are conventionally plotless.[51] What the woman wants, as she waits in her chamber, does not typically interest the Middle English romances, except insofar as it coincides with what the hero wants. Helen Cooper has argued that romance texts often evidence the "desirability of active female desire," a woman who sets her sights on a man and goes after him.[52] But what this usually boils down to is that the wealthy

[49] *The Book of Margery Kempe,* I.36, lines 2106–7; *A Talkyng of the Loue of God,* 58, 60.

[50] Georges Bataille, *Eroticism: Death and Sensuality,* trans. Mary Dalwood (London: Calder, 1962), 90.

[51] Felicity Riddy, "Middle English Romance: Family, Marriage, Intimacy," in *The Cambridge Companion to Medieval Romance,* ed. Roberta L. Krueger (Cambridge: Cambridge University Press, 2000), 235–52 (240).

[52] Helen Cooper, *The English Romance in Time: Transforming Motifs from Geoffrey of Monmouth to the Death of Shakespeare* (Oxford: Oxford University Press, 2004), 220.

heiress, like Lavine in the twelfth-century *Roman d'Eneas,* to whom Cooper traces the model, knows before the eponymous hero does that her wealth, lands, and reproductive capacity are what he (and the narrative) wants and so manages her desire accordingly. The *Eneas* cannot, however, make sense of Dido's unruly passion: Eneas has to move on; Dido has to die.

Undo Your Door, as we have seen, eschews knightly adventuring. Instead, it telescopes us into the woman's chamber and tries to imagine what she does in there, waiting. Her closeted desire is the hermeneutic puzzle at the core of the romance. Waiting is what women like Felice and the lady of Synadowne (the heroines of *Guy of Warwick* and *Libeaus Desconus,* respectively) do, and the comparison with *Libeaus,* in particular, is instructive.[53] Imprisoned by two magicians who have transformed her into a winged, woman-faced "worme" (2067), the lady of Synadowne waits the full duration of the romance to be rescued by Gawain or one of his kin. When Libeaus finally defeats her captors, the "worme" goes directly up to him and brazenly kisses him on the mouth. The spell is broken; the monstrous cladding falls to the ground; and a beautiful woman stands naked before Gawain's son. His reaction is curious: "The[r]for was Lybeous *woo*" (2093). Face to face with unfettered female desire, the knight is wretched and distressed. It is not until the woman offers him castles and herself in marriage and agrees to be ruled by "Arthures will" (2114)—until she is able both to articulate and to submit herself to male desire—that Libeaus can be "glad and blythe" (2115), secure in the knowledge that the satisfaction that the romance provides will, after all, be his. The king of Hungary, who watches his daughter through her window, also tries, belatedly, to accommodate her aberrant desire within the classic romance model: "a trewer lover than ye are one / was never yet of fleshe ne bone" (1085–86), he tells the princess as preparations are made for her marriage to the squire. But his words only serve to flag up their own inadequacy. Seven years of intimacy with a slowly disintegrating corpse is so in excess of even the exaggerated demands of "true love," the fantasy that many romances still claim to offer, that we cannot but be reminded of the disorder occasioned by the princess's desire.

Lee Ramsey's claim that, with the squire's return, the princess's "gro-

---

[53] *Lybeaus Desconus,* ed. Maldwyn Mills, EETS o.s. 261 (London: Oxford University Press, 1969); all citations are from this edition (London, Lambeth Palace, MS 306).

tesquerie" is "immediately forgotten" characterizes more accurately critical responses to the so-called *Squire of Low Degree* than the dynamic of the romance itself. Indeed, for all of their sensitivity to the romance's extraordinary peculiarity ("strange and whimsical," "haunting," even "zany" are common assessments),[54] the kind of willing amnesia to which Ramsey and others testify is only conceivable once the narrative acquires its new title. (It is hard to imagine how readers of *Undo Your Door* could repress all trace of what happens when the princess undoes her door.) At the same time, Ramsey (and others like him) betrays a confidence in the power of the "happy ending" that is not borne out by the text, which works instead to highlight the failure of that ending to contain the multiple and divergent desires of the king and his daughter, the squire and the steward. The standard romance resolution—abrupt and perfunctory—is always self-consciously artificial. Its very tidiness, neatly wrapping up a carefully patterned plot, makes the familiar romance order not natural, as it would have us believe, but utterly contrived. The illusion of coherence is fundamentally an ideological tactic; and its capacity to close down the errancy common to both language and desire is never assured.[55] But what distinguishes the final movement of *Undo Your Door,* from which the princess is, in fact, almost totally excluded (after she swoons in the squire's arms, she is never heard from again), is the way in which the king forges his own union with the squire, at once recalling his desire for the young knight *and* his investment in his daughter's romantic adventures.[56] In a move that is unmatched in ex-

---

[54] Joseph Ritson, *Ancient Engleish Metrical Romanceës,* 3 vols. (London: G. and W. Nichol, 1802), 3:344; Spearing, *The Medieval Poet as Voyeur,* 177; Kiernan, "*Undo Your Door,*" 346.

[55] The totalizing impulse of even apparently "closed" texts, like *Eglamour,* is inevitably imperfect. For instance, following his third adventure, Eglamour lingers for a full year in the bedchamber of a Roman princess, thus delaying his return to his pregnant lover and precipitating her (and his son's) exile.

[56] Note the way in which verbal repetition, characteristic of romance, works not only to identify the squire's greeting of his insentient lover with that of her father, but structurally brackets the squire's amorous attentions within those of the king (printed in boldface):

> And downe she fell in dead sownyng.
> **The kyng anone gan go,**
> **And hente her in his armes two.**
> . . .
> She fell in sownyng by and by.
> The squyer her hente in armes two,
> And kyssed her an hundreth tymes and mo.
> There was myrth and melody

tant Middle English romances, where succession conventionally demands the death of the incumbent, the king of Hungary, after forty days of wedding celebrations, crowns the squire king: two men, one office. In formally reproducing himself, the king not only escapes the death sentence commonly meted out to fathers in the family romance (a radical but common prelude to romance closure), but he transforms his daughter into "the quene his wyfe" (1127), a substitute for her shadowy mother, and completes the confusion of identities that has haunted the narrative. As in so many romances, desire *is* at last domesticated; but in *Undo Your Door,* this offers no promise of order.

In the study of medieval English literature, romance occupies a funny place. Readily identified as *the* medieval genre (synonymous with the period itself even, and not just in the popular imagination), it is with few exceptions completely peripheral to the debates that most excite medieval scholars. With a reputation for ideological and aesthetic conservatism, Middle English verse romance in particular is simply not a form that we imagine being used to wrestle with pressing cultural issues, about, for instance, women's devotional practice or the function of fiction.[57] Long-standing critical assumptions about romance continue, often in very basic ways, to restrict the achievement of *Undo Your Door.* I have already discussed modern editorial (and with it scholarly) resistance to the original title. Likewise, most scholars have been reluctant to credit the romance's date of first publication (c. 1520) with serious interpretative significance. Despite evidence to the contrary, many still date *Undo Your Door* to the fifteenth century, when the idea of writing a new romance seems less outlandish; and, just as oddly, the few who do take c. 1520 seriously nonetheless privilege the later title, unnecessarily (and sometimes unproductively) skewing their understanding of its his-

---

. . .
The kyng in herte he was full blithe,
He kissed his doughter many a sithe
With melody and muche chere.
(1049–91)

[57] For a recent discussion of late romance "look[ing] back . . . [to] older and safer traditions," as a "stabilizing model to hold as an ideal," see Helen Cooper, "Romance After 1400," in *The Cambridge History of Medieval English Literature,* ed. David Wallace (Cambridge: Cambridge University Press, 1999), 690–719 (694, 695); my essay has sought to demonstrate the contrary: that, like Cooper's Chaucer, romance has the capacity to "challenge" "safe thinking" (693).

torical particularity.[58] This essay has sought to chart some of the ways in which *Undo Your Door* purposefully resists the impulse to order desire; much work still needs to be done. The romance's popularity all throughout the sixteenth century (and beyond) is not, as Donald Sands would have us believe, "peculiar."[59] The transformation of *Undo Your Door* into *The Squire of Low Degree,* and later the Percy Folio's abbreviated *Squier,* is rather a testament to its extraordinary vitality.

[58] Mead was the first to demonstrate (*contra* Percy, Warton, and later Skeat, who supposed it a source for *Sir Thopas*) that the romance must postdate Chaucer; he fixed on a date of "about 1450, or possibly a decade earlier" (*Squyr of Lowe Degre,* lxxvi). More recently, Derek Pearsall, "The English Romance in the Fifteenth Century," *Essays and Studies* n.s. 29 (1976): 56–83, has argued that it should be dated "not much earlier" than its earliest print (66). Although its distinctive lexis, already identified by Mead as "suspiciously late" (lxxvi), readily confirms a date in the first decades of the sixteenth century, scholars have nonetheless been reluctant to leave the Middle Ages, as conventionally defined, wholly behind; for instance, see Kooper, *The Squire of Low Degree:* "a date in the late fifteenth century will now meet with little opposition" (127); and Seaman, "The Waning of Middle English Chivalric Romance": "originally produced c.1450–1520" (175). Both Spearing, *The Medieval Poet as Voyeur,* and Lerer, *Courtly Letters in the Age of Henry VIII,* by contrast, map the romance's preoccupations onto the erotic and political machinations of the early Henrician court but continue to treat the squire as if he were eponymous.

[59] Sands, *Middle English Verse Romances,* 249.

Penitential Discourse in Hoccleve's *Series*

Robyn Malo
Purdue University

> Had I be for an homicide iknowe
> Or an extorcioner or a robbour,
> Or for a coin clipper as wide yblowe
> As was my seeknesse, or a werriour
> Aȝein þe feith, or a false maintenour
> Of causes, þouȝ I had amendid me,
> Hem to han mynged had ben nicete.
>
> . . .
>
> But this is al another caas, sothly.
> This was the strook of God; he ȝaf me þis. . . .
> In feith, frende, make I thenke an open shrifte,
> And hide not what I had of his ȝifte.[1]

I N THIS PASSAGE from Thomas Hoccleve's *Series,* the narrator makes several important claims: he has not committed a serious crime or sin; God was the root cause of his illness; he should not, therefore, hesitate to advertise—to confess—his recovery as widely as possible. In explaining his situation, Hoccleve refuses to identify himself as a sinner in absolute terms.[2] Instead, he redefines confession: the rhymes "shrifte"

Many thanks to Shannon Gayk, Michael Johnston, Ethan Knapp, Sarah Tolmie, and David Watt, all of whom read and generously commented on drafts of this article. Earlier versions of this essay were presented at a colloquium at Indiana University–Bloomington in November 2010 and at the Sewanee Medieval Colloquium in April 2011. I am grateful to participants at both for their feedback. *SAC*'s anonymous readers all provided invaluable comments that strengthened this essay. Any infelicities that remain are, needless to say, my own.

[1] Thomas Hoccleve, *"My Compleinte" and Other Poems,* ed. Roger Ellis (Exeter: University of Exeter Press, 2001), D 64–70, 78–79, 83–84. All quotations are from this edition and will be cited parenthetically by section and line number. Abbreviations will be as follows: *C* (*Complaint*); *D* (*Dialogue*); *JW* (*Tale of Jereslaus' Wife*); *LD* (*Learn to Die*); *JF* (*Jonathas and Fellicula*).

[2] Throughout this essay, I refer to both the narrator and author of the *Series* as Hoccleve. But for some of the attendant problems in conflating narrator and author in Hoccleve's work, see David Watt, "'I this book shal make': Thomas Hoccleve's Self-Publication and Book Production," *LSE* 34 (2003): 133–60 (149).

and "ʒifte" suggest the possibility that confession—shrift—might comprise an explanation of what God sends, rather than a laundry list of transgressions. The entirety of the *Series,* in fact, supplies us with a complex response to and engagement with late medieval confessional discourse, which Hoccleve neither embraces nor rejects. He rejects, instead, the idea that confession enables the expression of the self *only* in terms of sin. In the *Complaint* and *Dialogue,* the narrator's primary concern is not with examining or justifying his behavior, but rather with *what he is:* "Uppon a look is harde men hem to grounde / What a man *is.* Therby the sothe is hid" (*C* 211–12; my emphasis). That shrift facilitates the expression of God's grace and individual identity inverts the widely accepted idea that the medieval "sinner recognizes himself not by what he is but by what he has done."[3] Hoccleve's narrator, rather than rejecting confessional discourse outright, wishes to recognize himself for and confess what he is.

It will be the argument of this essay that in the *Series,* Thomas Hoccleve appropriates penitential discourse to argue for the narrator's sanity and sinlessness—and that this confessional project dovetails with the narrator's desire to protest his innocence.[4] A group of five poems composed between 1419 and 1422,[5] the *Series* consists of the *Complaint,* in which the narrator laments that in spite of his recovery from mental illness, his friends reject him; the *Dialogue,* which dramatizes a conversation between the narrator and a friend, centering on whether to circulate

[3] Lee Patterson, *Chaucer and the Subject of History* (Madison: University of Wisconsin Press, 1991), 393.

[4] By contrast, Stephan Kohl juxtaposes the articulation of the self with medieval discourses of sin, suggesting that "Hoccleve indeed tried to write an account of his life in terms of individual development *rather than* a typically medieval *exemplum* of the reformed sinner" ("More than Virtues and Vices: Self-Analysis in Hoccleve's 'Autobiographies,'" *Fifteenth-Century Studies* 14 [1988]: 115–27 [115]; my emphasis). Kohl's point is an important one, but his unspoken assumption is that medieval religious discourse and autobiography are mutually exclusive. As I seek to demonstrate here, the modes of confession and autobiography are not so easy to separate and, in the context of the *Series,* should be thought of as interdependent. J. A. Burrow has similarly argued that the use of convention does not foreclose the possibility of self-exploration and autobiography, though he does not take up confessional discourse per se. See "Autobiographical Poetry in the Middle Ages: The Case of Thomas Hoccleve," *PBA* 68 (1982): 389–412, esp. 389–400.

[5] On the dating of the holograph copy of the *Series,* Durham University Library MS Cosin V.III.9, see Ellis, "Introduction," *"My Compleinte" and Other Poems,* 10. For a detailed discussion of the dating, manuscript history, and compilation of the *Series,* see David Watt's work-in-progress, *Exemplars and Exemplarity: The Making of Thomas Hoccleve's "Series."* I am grateful to David for sharing his monograph with me.

the *Complaint;* the *Tale of Jereslaus' Wife,* a translation of a narrative and moralization from the *Gesta Romanorum; Learn to Die,* a translation of Henry Suso's *Ars moriendi* in the *Horologium sapientiae* (c. 1334);[6] and the translation of another tale and moralization from the *Gesta,* entitled *Jonathas and Fellicula.*[7] This poem has been regarded both as a "loose anthology"[8] and as a more unified whole;[9] but there has yet to be a sustained discussion of how elements of the confessional form pervade and link the *Series.* Hoccleve's use of penitential language demonstrates both the unity of this poetic work and its dogged commitment to self-expression.[10] Confessional motifs not only unite the poems of the *Series*—they also reveal the work to be organized around the narrator's

[6] See Benjamin P. Kurtz, "The Source of Occleve's *Lerne to Dye,*" *MLN* 38 (1923): 337–40. On Hoccleve's treatment of his source text, see Steven Rozenski Jr., " 'Your Ensaumple and Your Mirour': Hoccleve's Amplification of the Imagery and Intimacy of Henry Suso's *Ars Moriendi,*" *Parergon* 25 (2008): 1–16.

[7] Although I cite from Ellis, for the sake of convenience I have adopted the titles from *Hoccleve's Works: The Minor Poems,* ed. F. J. Furnivall, EETS e.s. 61 (New York: C. Scribner, 1892), with the exception of *Jonathas and Fellicula,* which Furnivall calls the *Tale of Jonathas.*

[8] Ethan Knapp, for instance, comments that "the multiplicity of tales following the 'Dialogue' carries an implication that the *Series* is organized only as a loose anthology with no real conclusion" (*The Bureaucratic Muse: Thomas Hoccleve and the Literature of Late Medieval England* [University Park, Pa.: Pennsylvania State University Press, 2001], 161). For similar assessments, see Matthew Boyd Goldie, "Hoccleve's Psychosomatic Illness and Identity," *Exemplaria* 11 (1999): 23–52 (51–52); and Lee Patterson, " 'What Is Me?': Self and Society in the Poetry of Thomas Hoccleve," *SAC* 23 (2001): 437–70 (443–44, 450).

[9] See Penelope Doob's often-contested argument that the *Series* as a whole has as its "central theme the usefulness of physical disorder for recalling men to spiritual sanity" (*Nebuchadnezzar's Children: Conventions of Madness in Middle English Literature* [New Haven: Yale University Press, 1974], 220). Others who note thematic unity in the *Series* include Robert J. Meyer-Lee, "Hoccleve and the Apprehension of Money," *Exemplaria* 13 (2001): 173–214 (211–12); and Stephen Langdell, who outlines common threads in the *Series,* including Hoccleve's narratorial interjections and emphasis on "the element of haste" (" 'What World Is This? How Vndirstand Am I?' A Reappraisal of Poetic Authority in Thomas Hoccleve's *Series,*" *MÆ* 78.2 [2009]: 281–99 [290]). See also Christina von Nolcken's influential reading of *Learn to Die* as the thematic anchor of the *Series,* which as a whole takes up "its author's own preparation for death" (" 'O why ne had I lerned for to die?': *Lerne for to Dye* and the Author's Death in Thomas Hoccleve's *Series,*" *Essays in Medieval Studies* 10 [1993]: 27–51 [43]); and, more recently, Watt's argument that we should consider the *Series* in its entirety as a metaphor for memory (*Exemplars and Exemplarity,* 13).

[10] On confession as producing the means for self-definition, though in different terms from those I use here, see Katherine C. Little, *Confession and Resistance: Defining the Self in Late Medieval England* (Notre Dame: University of Notre Dame Press, 2006), 5–15, 20–25. Masha Raskolnikov surveys medieval confessional literature, reframing medieval psychology in terms of the self as constituted by sin and suggesting that confessional language organizes "a coherent narrative of sin" ("Confessional Literature, Vernacular Psychology, and the History of the Self in Middle English," *LitComp* 2 [2005]: 1–20 [3,

impulse to communicate his inner self to a wide audience. It is simply not the case that Hoccleve "bows to the demands of his accuser,"[11] abandoning his original intention to circulate a written defense of his sanity. Instead, in deploying elements of the confessional form throughout the poem, Hoccleve yokes together the tales from the *Gesta* with the *Complaint, Dialogue,* and *Learn to Die,* revealing the poem as a whole to explore not only the problem of identity—a topic many have taken up with respect to the *Complaint* and *Dialogue,* but seldom the rest of the *Series*[12]—but also to suggest the difficulties with some conventions of mainstream penitential discourse. Forms of confession were hugely popular in late medieval Europe, particularly in fifteenth-century England, where they "flourished"—indeed, we may even consider the genre "especially an English one."[13] As Michael Cornett explains, the form of

---

12]). See also Raskolnikov, *Body Against Soul: Gender and Sowlehele in Middle English Allegory* (Columbus: The Ohio State University Press, 2009), 11–20.

[11] Langdell, " 'What World Is This?' " 286.

[12] For investigations of inner identity, madness, and fragmentation in the *Complaint* and *Dialogue,* see the following studies: J. A. Burrow, "Autobiographical Poetry in the Middle Ages"; Burrow, "Hoccleve's *Series:* Experience and Books," in *Fifteenth-Century Studies,* ed. Robert F. Yeager (Hamden, Conn.: Archon Books, 1984), 259–73 (260, 268). While Burrow notes the narrative arc of the *Series,* he nonetheless concludes that "the two *Gesta* stories . . . have no direct bearing on Hoccleve's personal circumstances" ("Experience and Books," 269). See also Goldie, "Hoccleve's Psychosomatic Illness and Identity"; Knapp, *The Bureaucratic Muse,* 163–74; Kohl, "More than Virtues and Vices"; Richard Lawes, "Psychological Disorder and the Autobiographical Impulse in Julian of Norwich, Margery Kempe and Thomas Hoccleve," in *Writing Religious Women: Female Spiritual and Textual Practices in Late Medieval England,* ed. Denis Renevey and Christiania Whitehead (Toronto: University of Toronto Press, 2000), 217–43 (218–34); Stephen Medcalf, "Inner and Outer," in *The Later Middle Ages,* ed. Medcalf (London: Methuen, 1981), 108–71; David Mills, "The Voices of Thomas Hoccleve," in *Essays on Thomas Hoccleve,* ed. Catherine Batt (Turnhout: Brepols, 1996), 85–107; and James Simpson, "Madness and Texts: Hoccleve's *Series,*" in *Chaucer and Fifteenth-Century Poetry,* ed. Julia Boffey and Janet Cowen (King's College London: Centre for Late Antique and Medieval Studies, 1991), 15–29.

[13] Michael Cornett identifies more than 440 copies of 198 Latin, French, and English forms of confession that survive from c. 1200 to c. 1500 ("The Form of Confession: A Later Medieval Genre for Examining Conscience," Ph.D. diss. [University of North Carolina at Chapel Hill, 2011], 29). More than half of these surviving copies of confessional forms are from fifteenth-century England. Discussions of confession typically locate the beginnings of later trends in the canon *Omnis utriusque sexus* from the Fourth Lateran Council of 1215, a canon that resulted in the translation and wide dissemination of vernacular confessional manuals in England and on the Continent. For what is still the most comprehensive overview of medieval confessional practice, see Thomas N. Tentler, *Sin and Confession on the Eve of the Reformation* (Princeton: Princeton University Press, 1977); and Tentler's earlier essay, "The Summa for Confessors as an Instrument of Social Control," in *The Pursuit of Holiness in Late Medieval and Renaissance Religion,* ed. Charles Trinkaus and Heiko A. Oberman (Leiden: Brill, 1974), 103–25, especially 109–17. Leonard E. Boyle's response, "The Summa for Confessors as a Genre, and Its Reli-

confession "presents the grammar of sin, the matrix of possibilities in a discourse for practice from which penitents must recognize what is relevant to their own cases."[14] The penitential discourse of such confessional forms—along with that of treatises such as the fifteenth-century *Jacob's Well* and of manuals for confessors—clearly informed Hoccleve's own writing. In crafting tales from the *Gesta Romanorum* and in translating Suso's *Ars moriendi*, Hoccleve amplifies elements of these texts that center on self-expression and public confession. Throughout the *Series,* he explores the intersections of a public self-defense and confessional language.

While *Jereslaus' Wife* and *Jonathas and Fellicula* seem at first glance unrelated to the narrator's mental health and social difficulties, then, their focus on confession enables Hoccleve to continue his meditation on the perils of self-expression—just as this meditation enables his commentary on the limitations of mainstream confession. In the *Tale of Jereslaus' Wife,* for instance, the empress reclaims her identity through the auricular and public confessions of those who sinned against her. By contrast, in *Jonathas and Fellicula,* Fellicula's confession results in her spectacular death, illustrating that understanding the self in terms of sin might have dire consequences. Such a move is recursive, reminding the reader that in the *Complaint* and *Dialogue,* the narrator struggles against the limitations of categories of sin and madness. So, too, the focus of the *Gesta* tales and *Learn to Die* on confession and inner identity demonstrates that we ought to consider these portions of the *Series,* every bit as much as the *Complaint* and *Dialogue,* in examining the relationship between the inner self and public narration.

Hoccleve's appropriation of penitential discourse is hence critically important to the *Series:* it allows him to keep on talking about himself even after he has promised not to. Penelope Doob and a few others have characterized Hoccleve's oeuvre as generally penitential but have stopped short of examining how Hoccleve engages with fifteenth-

---

gious Intent," is in the same volume, 126–30. But see also the collection *Handling Sin: Confession in the Middle Ages,* ed. Peter Biller and Alastair Minnis (York: York Medieval Press, 1998), particularly Biller's helpful introduction, "Confession in the Middle Ages," 1–34; and, more recently, Richard Newhauser, "Introduction: Cultural Construction and the Vices," in *The Seven Deadly Sins: From Communities to Individuals,* ed. Richard Newhauser (Leiden: Brill, 2007), 1–17, and Abigail Firey, ed., *A New History of Penance* (Leiden: Brill, 2008).

[14] Cornett, "The Form of Confession," 26.

century penitential forms.[15] Explorations of Hoccleve's struggle with the boundaries between inner and outer sometimes refer to his "confessional style" but do not unpack in detail precisely what this style entails or what it tells us about the narrator or about the *Series*.[16] It is clearly inaccurate to say, as Doob does, that Hoccleve's illness metaphorically signals "the crippling state of sin which is the subject of the poem."[17] Hoccleve insists on the opposite reading: that his suffering is neither the result of nor represents sin. I think we need to take the narrator's claims about sin and confession seriously. If the illness the narrator suffers is not the result of sin but is rather God's gift, what effect does this interpretation have on how we understand the *Series?* And what might this tell us about Hoccleve's engagement with fifteenth-century religious discourse? Based on her assessment that in Hoccleve's *Regiment of Princes,* confession and heresy are "inextricably linked," Katherine C. Little has argued that Hoccleve retreats from confession, first envisioning it as a "site of solely personal, private concerns" but ultimately "emptying [the confessional genre] of its power to define the self and its power to console."[18] This may be true of *The Regiment of Princes.* But Little does not

[15] See Doob, *Nebuchadnezzar's Children,* 208–31; and Medcalf, "Inner and Outer," 132–33. On the importance of the penitential lyric to Hoccleve's work (the *Male regle* in particular), see Eva Thornley's influential essay, "The Middle English Penitential Lyric and Hoccleve's Autobiographical Poetry," *NM* 68 (1967): 295–321. Few since have discussed the importance of devotional literature to Hoccleve's configuration of self-identity (though many cite Doob and Thornley). While Jennifer Bryan, *Looking Inward: Devotional Reading and the Private Self in Late Medieval England* (Philadelphia: University of Pennsylvania Press, 2008), revives this important discussion, she focuses almost exclusively on Hoccleve's Marian lyrics, referring only sporadically to what she calls Hoccleve's "confessional protestations" (181) or "confessional paradigm" (202).

[16] Medcalf, "Inner and Outer," 133. Medcalf refers both to Thornley's article and to Hoccleve's indebtedness to Augustine's *Confessions,* particularly Augustine's descriptions of his misspent youth. Also citing Thornley, Lee Patterson registers the "penitential context" of the *Male regle* ("'What Is Me?': Self and Society in the Poetry of Thomas Hoccleve," 438). Although Burrow, who discusses both Thornley's and Doob's approaches to the *Male regle,* acknowledges the "confessional sentiments" in the *Male regle* ("Autobiographical Poetry in the Middle Ages," 410) and rightly criticizes Penelope Doob's dismissal of this poem's autobiographical elements, his essay—which focuses on what Burrow calls the "conventional fallacy" (389–400) and on Hoccleve's three autobiographical roles: ideal citizen, friend and colleague, and petitioner (402–12)—does not take up confessional discourse explicitly. And in his overview of Hoccleve's life and works, Ethan Knapp remarks only in passing that *Learn to Die* "anchors much of the *Series* thematically around the importance of penitence and confession" ("Thomas Hoccleve," in *The Cambridge Companion to Medieval English Literature, 1100–1500,* ed. Larry Scanlon [Cambridge: Cambridge University Press, 2009], 191–203 [200]).

[17] Doob, *Nebuchadnezzar's Children,* 228.

[18] Little, *Confession and Resistance,* 113, 117, 128.

discuss the *Series,* and Hoccleve's complex engagement with confession in that text differs from what Little describes. There the narrator dissociates confession from the recognition and expression of sin—not to *empty* confession of its consolatory power, but rather to reimagine this consolatory power.[19] Ultimately, I will make three suggestions related to this claim: first, that Hoccleve subverts a central metaphor of the penitential form—the self as mirroring a particular sin—implying, instead, that it is possible to create self-identity rather than merely to reflect it from available discourses;[20] second, that Hoccleve's preoccupation with confession unites both the *Series* as a whole, and the *Series* with Hoccleve's earlier confessional poem, the *Male regle* (c. 1405–6); and third, that the confessional narratives of the *Series* also have much to tell us about fifteenth-century religious discourse. In borrowing and revising elements of the vernacular confessional forms that were widespread by the fifteenth century, the *Series* illustrates how a concept can supersede its component parts. Masha Raskolnikov has recently observed that confessional texts, including guides to sin and the self, could help "[e]veryday people . . . think narratively about their own selves."[21] I think that to some degree, confessional discourse serves this purpose in the *Series.* Hoccleve's text, however, engages with taxonomies of sin partly to suggest that these categories are inadequate for constructing a narrative of the self. And yet the *concept* of confession is still useful: Hoccleve dismisses or troubles some of its most recognizable attributes but nonetheless seems unwilling to do away with "shrifte."

Narrating the Sinful Self

While the *Series* frequently equates the purging of sin with *reflecting* available discourses and identities—as in the personification of the Seven

[19] In his assessment of Hoccleve's "The Address to Sir John Oldcastle," Andrew Cole similarly notes Hoccleve's conflicted attitude to confession. Cole suggests that Hoccleve is "so keen to formulate a merciful orthodoxy in this poem . . . that he even accepts a Wycliffite position on confession," exhibiting a "flexible orthodoxy" and coming very close to the Wycliffite view that only God was the appropriate audience for confession. See Cole, *Literature and Heresy in the Age of Chaucer* (Cambridge: Cambridge University Press, 2008), 105, 113–14.

[20] On the mirror and forms of confession, see Cornett, "The Form of Confession," 41–56, 63–70. According to Cornett, "The fifteenth century saw a huge increase in the use of mirror-titles paralleling the diffusion of forms of confession, and many manuscripts containing a form of confession also include *speculum* literature, particularly the pseudo-Augustinian *Speculum peccatorum*" (41–42).

[21] Raskolnikov, *Body Against Soul,* 12.

Deadly Sins[22]—Hoccleve presents confession as a concept that enables the expression, even creation, of "what a man is." By contrast, the moments in the *Series* that privilege sacramental confession—such as the exhortations of the image of death in *Learn to Die*—fall under the rubric of reporting, of merely repeating or inhabiting (rather than revising or reimagining) the various commonplaces of confessional discourse.[23] Throughout the *Series,* Hoccleve draws on the confessional commonplace that in verbalizing sin the penitent projects his inner, sinful self outward. The author of the *Boke of Penance,* a "versified form of confession" appended to one copy of the fourteenth-century northern poem the *Cursor Mundi,*[24] equates confession with precisely this kind of exposure:

> Þe toþer point is shrift of mouþ
> to make to prest our synnis couþ
> opinli ham to knaw.
> Wiþ-out glosing truli to shaw . . .
> Shrift is opin shewing of brest . . .
> of synnis þat man myn of mai.[25]

In contrast to Hoccleve's configuration of the relationship between the self and sin, these lines implicitly associate the "brest" with "synnis"— for in revealing the inside, the sinner will, specifically, "make to prest [his] synnis couþ." This kind of manual envisions a very particular kind of interior: one defined primarily by categories of sin. Such a model precludes the existence of a self outside of sin.[26] Mary Braswell goes so far as to suggest that a sinner retains his or her individuality only before confession; from this perspective, "personality is composed of those *par-*

<hr/>

[22] On representations of the Seven Deadly Sins in late medieval literature, see Morton W. Bloomfield, *The Seven Deadly Sins: An Introduction to the History of a Religious Concept, with Special Reference to Medieval English Literature* (East Lansing: Michigan State College Press, 1952), 160–243. More recently, see Richard Newhauser, ed., *The Seven Deadly Sins: From Communities to Individuals* (Leiden: Brill, 2007).

[23] On some of these commonplaces, see Little, *Confession and Resistance,* 50–63.

[24] Cornett, "The Form of Confession," 27.

[25] *Boke of Penance,* in *Cursor Mundi: A Northumbrian Poem of the Fourteenth Century,* ed. Richard K. Morris, EETS o.s. 68 (London: Kegan Paul, Trench, Trübner & Co., 1874–93), lines 26092–95, 26110, 26112.

[26] In her discussion of the *Pricke of Conscience,* Jennifer Bryan examines the configuration of the self in terms of "slime, worms, lice, stinking carrion, and excrement," showing that many models of self-knowledge associate interiority with dirt, "loathsome blood and slime of the womb" (*Looking Inward,* 63).

ticular sins which he has committed in his own inimitable way."[27] By extension, absolution strips away identity.[28] If we envision medieval self-hood as deriving in some way from categories of sin, Braswell's claim resonates. According to this model, making an "open shrifte" entails exposing sin, specifically in order to be treated. As the author of *Jacob's Well*, a mid-fifteenth-century vernacular penitential treatise, explains,

þowȝ deed flesch be kut out of a wounde . . . þi wounde, þowȝ, nedyth to be pourgyd, wyth a drawyng salue; ellys it wolde rotyn & festryn aȝen. Ryȝt so, þowȝ þi dedly synne be kut out, wyth sorwe of herte, fro þe pyt of þi conscyens, ȝit þi conscyens nedyth to be pourgyd, wyth a drawyng salue of clene schryfte.[29]

This passage turns on a commonplace in confessional literature: the priest as physician, who facilitates the healing of the diseased penitent.[30]

Images of bodily corruption reinforce the association in confessional manuals between inner identity and sin. By presenting sin as vomit, stench, or inner rottenness, these manuals imply that without the sacramental grace of mainstream religious practices, the body is merely a container for sin. The leitmotif in *Jacob's Well* correlates the discharging of fetid water from a well with confession: "Here-beforn I told ȝow of a welle, & of a pytt of lust, þat is, ȝour body, & how full it is of corrupte watyr. . . . Þerfore ȝou nedyth, in gostly labour, to scopyn out þis corrupte watyr of curs, wyth the scoope of penauns."[31] This passage depends upon the reader's acceptance that without the help of sacramental confession, she or he is merely a vessel for corruption: "Þis wose [ooze] in ȝoure pyt is euery dedly synne. Ffor ȝoure body gaderyth euere more wose of synne . . . þer-fore, ȝoure body is a foul wosy pytt"; the interior

---

[27] Mary Flowers Braswell, *The Medieval Sinner: Characterization and Confession in the Literature of the English Middle Ages* (Rutherford, N.J.: Fairleigh Dickinson University Press, 1983), 13 (emphasis in original). For a similar approach, see Jerry Root, who argues that the vernacular confessional manuals of the thirteenth and fourteenth centuries aimed to create a "'space to speke' for the lay population," thereby creating "a new cultural construction of the self." See *Space to Speke: The Confessional Subject in Medieval Literature* (New York: Peter Lang, 1997), 1.

[28] Braswell, *The Medieval Sinner*, 22.

[29] *Jacob's Well: An English Treatise on the Cleansing of Man's Conscience,* ed. Arthur Brandeis, EETS o.s. 115 (London: Kegan Paul, Trench, Trübner & Co., 1900), 178–79.

[30] On the trope of priest as physician, see Karma Lochrie, *Covert Operations: The Medieval Uses of Secrecy* (Philadelphia: University of Pennsylvania Press, 1999), 26; and Thornley, "The Middle English Penitential Lyric," 298–99.

[31] *Jacob's Well,* 64–65.

of such a body "stynketh."[32] For the *Jacob* author, to describe the interior is to describe corruption. So, too, in the *Speculum sacerdotale,* a fifteenth-century collection of sermons, a repentant friar characterizes his misbehavior as "stynkynge synnes,"[33] an image suggestive of entrails, rotten food, and decay. The author of the *Speculum sacerdotale* confirms that sin is like food—like what we consume, and therefore inside of us[34]—in his exhortation to fast from sin as we would from food: "Let vs faste also fro lecherie, fro glotonye, fro hatreden and stryfe and alle wyckidnes. Let vs absteyne vs fro metes but more fro vicis."[35] Similarly, a sermon from a fourteenth-century vernacular collection compares the vomit of a drunk man to confession: "It is tauȝth in fisike þat a vomyte is a profitabull medecyn to suche dronkon men. And þis vomyte to oure porpose is þe sacrament of confession."[36] The metaphor likens the act of confession—and, by extension, the interior—to vomit, to inimical matter that must be expunged from the body.

The description of pride in *Jacob's Well* confirms that, in the context of confessional language, interior identity stems largely from sin. There the author argues that taking credit for one's virtues or fortune is to be "prowd in herte": "Þe grace of fortune, of goodnes, of prosperyte, of vertewys, þat þou hast of god, þou thynkyst þat þou hast hem of god for þi gode werkys, & þat þou hast wel deseruyd hem. Or ellys þe loue, worschype, rycches, whiche þou hast of god, þou thynkyst þat þou hast hem of þi good gouernaunce, wytist it þi-self, & noȝt god."[37]

Throughout this section, the author presents as fundamentally disordered the belief that the self ("þi-self")—including one's works ("þi

---

[32] Ibid., 68.

[33] *Speculum sacerdotale,* ed. Edward H. Weatherly, EETS o.s. 200 (London: Oxford University Press, 1936), 60.

[34] For Raskolnikov, confessional language "stressed the self's vulnerability to sin, conceived as something that both attacks the self from without and is generated from within." "Confessional Literature," 1.

[35] *Speculum sacerdotale,* ed. Weatherly, 56.

[36] *Middle English Sermons,* ed. Woodburn O. Ross, EETS o.s. 209 (London: Oxford University Press, 1960), 240. *Piers Plowman* includes a particularly colorful version of this image: "Ac Gloton was a gret cherl and a grym in the liftyng, / And koughed up a cawdel in Clementes lappe. / Is noon so hungry hound in Hertfordshire / Dorste lape of that levynge, so unlovely it smaughte!" William Langland, *The Vision of Piers Plowman: A Critical Edition of the B-Text,* ed. A. V. C. Schmidt (London: Everyman, 1995), V.354–57. On this passage as representing "an integral part of the process of contrition" and drawing on the penitential motif of a dog eating vomit, see M. Jane Toswell, "Of Dogs, *Cawdels,* and Contrition: A Penitential Motif in *Piers Plowman*," *YLS* 7 (1993): 115–21 (117). My thanks to Sarah Tolmie for drawing this analogue to my attention.

[37] *Jacob's Well,* 69.

gode werkys") or prudent behavior ("þi good gouernaunce")—is the root cause of doing well. One should recognize instead that "þou hast [these things] of god." By contrast, the penitent is to understand his or her sin as an inner cancer, sprung from within. As the *Jacob* author explains, sin makes the sinner "foulere þan þe deuyl"[38]—and as is commonplace in penitential manuals, the penitent alone must take responsibility:

> Þy shryfte shal be al of þy selue,
> Of þyn owne propre dede,
> And bewreye noun ouþre, y þe forbede.
> Þyn owne folye þou shalt seye
> And noun ouþer body bewreye.[39]

In this passage from *Handlyng Synne,* an early fourteenth-century translation of the Anglo-Norman *Manuel des péchés,* Robert Mannyng of Brunne clearly identifies sin as arising from the deeds of the self ("þy selue"; "þyn owne propre dede").[40] Unlike "gode werkys," which the *Jacob* author insists be attributed to God, "folye" is "þyn owne." While it is prideful to be satisfied with good works, then, it is necessary to own and be sorrowful for "þi synne."[41] It follows from such a configuration—which dismisses the possibility that the self can do good—that an accurate narrative of self must be a narrative of sin.

In the *Complaint* and *Dialogue,* however, the narrator establishes that although his own interior is not marred by sin, he still wishes to make a confession: "In feith, frende, make I thenke an open shrifte, / And hide not what I had of his [God's] ȝifte" (D 83–4).[42] As I suggested above, the end-rhymes "shrifte" and "ȝifte" substantially revise a basic premise of late medieval confession: that "shrifte" exposes a sinful and

---

[38] Ibid., 170.

[39] Robert Mannyng, *Handlyng Synne,* ed. Idelle Sullens (Binghamton, N.Y.: Medieval and Renaissance Texts and Studies, 1983), lines 11620–24.

[40] On Mannyng's translation of the *Manuel* and commitment to vernacular theology, see Jennifer Garrison, "Mediated Piety: Eucharistic Theology and Lay Devotion in Robert Mannyng's *Handlyng Synne,*" *Speculum* 85 (2010): 894–922 (895–99). This passage from *Handlyng Synne* stems from a commonplace of confessional literature: that it is sinful to blame others for your own actions. But at the same time, in emphasizing the possessive adjective "þy" Mannyng—like the author of *Jacob's Well*—identifies sin as *belonging* to a particular individual in a way that virtue cannot.

[41] *Jacob's Well,* 168, 170 (emphasis added).

[42] Mannyng similarly exhorts readers to be open in their confessions: "Þat þou ne lette for no shame / To telle opunly þy blame" (*Handlyng Synne,* 10851–52).

diseased self, in need of healing. The narrator of the *Series* proposes, instead, a narrative of the healed self. In so doing, he implicitly redefines confession as the exposition of both suffering and recovery—not of sin. His suggestion that he make an "open shrifte" indirectly challenges the mainstream idea that, as Mannyng explains,

> Yn tokenyng to holde vs lowe
> And oure wykkednes for to knowe,
> Hyt ys ordeyned þurgh goddes ȝyfte
> To man for to knowe oure shryfte.[43]

In Mannyng's configuration, God's gift is confession itself, which enables both the knowledge and expression of "oure wykkednes." In this case, the end-rhymes "ȝyfte" and "shryfte" affirm the divine ordination of sacramental confession and, by extension, the authority of the mainstream church. I am not suggesting that Hoccleve derives his rhyme from Mannyng's—the constraints of form are far more likely to have informed Hoccleve's choice. More important for this essay is the difference in Mannyng's and Hoccleve's conceptions of "shryfte": for Mannyng, "shryfte" denotes the expression of our wickedness for the purpose of absolution and healing; for Hoccleve, "shryfte" suggests, instead, the expression of "what a man is," comprising the interior life more broadly construed than sacramental definitions of confession allow. What is more, the narrator of the *Series* desires a public confession. His desire to express, publicly, who he is transforms confession from the description of particular sins—controlled by a priest, as Karma Lochrie has argued[44]—to the communication of the self.

Hoccleve in fact begins the *Dialogue* by expressing this desire:

> "But this is al another caas, sothly.
> This was the strook of God; he ȝaf me þis.
> And sithen he hath withdrawe it curteisly,
> *Am I not holden it out?* O ȝis."
> (*D* 78–81; emphasis added)

In this passage, which immediately follows the narrator's assertion that he is no sinner (not "for an homicide iknowe" [64], for instance), Hoc-

---

[43] Ibid., 11339–43.
[44] Lochrie, *Covert Operations*, 26.

cleve identifies God as the root cause of his infirmity and recovery and affirms that in order to demonstrate his sanity he must confess his story. The express purpose of such a confession is that it be circulated among the very people who doubt his recovery and, as Hoccleve corrects the friend, still "of me speke in myn audience / Ful heuily" (44–45). In this instance, the narrator presents confession as an advertisement of his recovered self. For while his "brainseke[ness]" manifested itself clearly enough—he mirrors, in his physical bearing, the symptoms of one who is unstable (C 127–33)[45]—the narrator's inner stability is apparently not so easy for others to interpret. In response to this difficulty, Hoccleve seeks to create his own reflection: in the responses of those around him, and indeed, in an actual mirror.

Confession and Reporting in the *Series*

One of the best-known and most frequently cited passages in Thomas Hoccleve's oeuvre, the narrator's "many a saute" in front of his mirror anticipates the *Series*' extended meditation on the perils of perception and misperception. At this point in the *Complaint,* the narrator, realizing that he has either failed to convey his sanity or that his friends have failed to comprehend it, jumps in front of the mirror, "Thinking, 'If that I looke in þis manere / Amonge folke as I nowe do, noon errour / Of suspecte look may in my face appere'" (C 163–65). Regardless of whether we understand this moment as proof positive of Hoccleve's malady, one thing is clear: the narrator attempts to construct his own identity, using the mirror to discern his "looke" and to arrange his own face accordingly. Although he focuses initially on what men "seiden" about him—the series of physical behaviors that, taken together, constitute mental instability, including throwing his "looke aboute" (C 121) and walking in the stilted manner of a deer (128)—he quickly moves to the idea that, rather than mirroring others' descriptions of him, he can reclaim the construction of his self. As he puts it, "My spirites labouriden euere ful bisily / To peinte countenaunce, chere and look" (148–49). In this moment, Hoccleve identifies himself as the rhetor, the "peinte[r]," the one who will assign particular images and metaphors to himself, rather than simply repeat the descriptions that others assign. Moreover, the mirror passage

[45] For Hoccleve's description of his malady as corresponding to late medieval medical conventions of madness, see Goldie, "Hoccleve's Psychosomatic Illness and Identity," 25–33.

directly follows this decision to "peinte [his own] countenaunce." In this context, the narrator is not merely attempting to ensure that he appears sane, but also, more importantly, presenting the mirror as an image for self-definition.

From the beginning of the *Complaint,* then, Hoccleve establishes his desire to be an "auctor" rather than a "reportour." My use of these terms is not accidental. The narrator introduces them explicitly at the end of the *Dialogue,* in defending himself against accusations of misogyny: "Therof was I noon auctour. / I nas in þat cas but a reportour / Of folkes tales. As they seide, I wroot" (*D* 760–62). To some degree, such an assertion is conventional, recalling Chaucer's apology in *The General Prologue* of the *Canterbury Tales.* But in this moment, Hoccleve nevertheless distinguishes between what he copies and what he creates. Such a distinction is important for the *Complaint* and *Dialogue* where, as I have already suggested, the narrator rejects the modes of self-definition based on madness and sin and articulates the difficulty in doing so. As he laments, "'Wiche is the beste way / My troublid spirit for to bringe in rest?'" (*C* 173–74). And while Hoccleve concludes that action will assuage his anxiety—"preue may the dede" (224), as he comments—he closely associates deeds with words, as the following selection of passages demonstrates. Here, having realized that he cannot necessarily control his appearance, he acknowledges that

> Man by hise dedis and not by hise lookes
> Shal knowen be. As it is written in bookes,
> Bi taaste of fruit men may wel wite and knowe
> What that it is. Othir preef is ther noon. . . .
> Uppon a look is harde men hem to grounde
> What a man is. Therby the sothe is hid. . . .
> By commvnynge is the beste assay.
>   (*C* 202–5, 211–12, 217)

Rejecting the idea that others will understand him through his physical appearance, the narrator concludes that his actions ("hise dedis") express who he is. Yet as he introduces this idea, he immediately resorts to the authority of the written word ("as it is written in bookes"). From the beginning of this section, then, deeds are imbricated with words. Indeed, the assertion that "othir preef is ther noon" refers most directly not to deeds, but rather to what is "written in bookes"—to, in other words, *auctoritas*. Throughout these stanzas, in fact, Hoccleve presents words and deeds as equivalent. To wit, he derives the claim that "preue may the dede" (*C* 224) from his assurance that "commvnynge is the beste assay" (217) and thereby aligns communication and language with action—and with confession.

"Commvnynge" is, I would suggest, in direct contrast to reporting. To be a reporter is to gossip, as so many of the narrator's sometime friends do: to repeat or "clappe" (*D* 489) what men "sein" (*C* 181). While we might understand mainstream confession as a kind of "reporting," expressing the self through categories of sin, the narrator of the *Complaint* and *Dialogue* presents confession as a kind of "commvnynge" instead: constructing identity and rejecting clear-cut definitions, rather than reflecting categories that are already available. In reassigning the image of the physician to God, for instance, Hoccleve reimagines how sacramental confession enables self-definition:

> God me deuoided of the greuous venim
> That had enfectid and wildid my brain.
> See howe the curteise leche moost souerain
> Vnto the seke ȝeueth medicine
> In nede, and hym releueth of his greuous pine.
>
> (*C* 234–38)[46]

In confessional manuals such as *Jacob's Well*, the metaphors of physician and disease represent the priest and interior sin; that God "deuoided" the narrator of his sin is reminiscent of the image of confession as vomiting. But here, God is the "curteise leche moost souerain" who "me deuoided" of inner poison. In this configuration, the narrator has direct access to God's healing "medicine." More radically still, although he uses an image from confessional literature—the image of the body as a container for sin, which a physician must scoop out—Hoccleve does not identify "greuous venim" as sin. Instead, he explains that this poison "enfectid and wildid my brain," and that God heals him from this disease. In other words, while Hoccleve employs the metaphor of poison, he does so to describe an actual malady, rather than to describe sin. In "unmetaphoring the metaphor" of illness and reassigning the role of

---

[46] See also *D* 85–94: "If that a leeche curid had me so— / . . . / A name he shulde han had for eueremo"; "The benefice of God not hid be sholde. / Sithen of myn heele he ȝaf me þe triacle, / It to confesse and þanke hym, am I holde."

physician to God, the narrator lays the foundation for the idea that confession can enable self-expression beyond paradigms of sin.[47]

In general terms, then, it would seem that reporting has little effect on perception and belief; witness the narrator's frustration that, no matter how many times his friends at the Privy Seal affirm that he has recovered, his detractors "helden her wordis not but lees" (*C* 300). In this case, his friends repeat, rather than construct, what they know about him. Moreover, as he makes clear in the *Dialogue,* it is as easy to repeat hearsay as truth: "I woote what men han seide and seien of me" (*D* 37). Indeed, the remainder of the *Dialogue* centers on whether or not to allow the *Complaint* "forth to goo / Amonge þe peple" (*D* 23–24). The narrator ultimately concedes that he should keep his suffering to himself and translate works that will appeal to his patrons. However, Hoccleve is remarkably consistent about when to keep silent and when to speak out. As he explains to his friend, "And to reherse his gilte wich him accusiþ, / Honour seith nay there he scilence excusiþ" (*D* 76–77). In other words, he argues that only guilt justifies silence, when in traditional paradigms, guilt is the only thing that emanates from the self and necessitates sacramental confession. But Hoccleve presents innocence, not sin, as the prerequisite to confession: "The benefice of God not hid be sholde. / Sithen of myn heele he ȝaf me þe triacle, / It to confesse and þanke hym, am I holde" (*D* 92–94). This passage yet again renders God as the confessional doctor—and yet again revises confession as the expression of healing rather than of disease. Although he asks the friend for "assistence / And help. What I shal make, I yow byseeche" (*D* 656–57); and although he agrees to keep "cloos" about his mental illness, subsequent narratives affirm this position: in the absence of wrongdoing, public expression of the self is not only acceptable but ideal, even necessary.

The parallels between the *Complaint, Dialogue,* and *Tale of Jereslaus' Wife* make it clear that in translating the *Tale of Jereslaus' Wife,* Hoccleve highlights the perils of keeping quiet and the role of confession in reconstructing the empress's identity. The story proceeds as follows: an empress, who presides over the empire in her husband's absence, refuses the advances of her brother-in-law; he retaliates by leaving her to die, stripped and suspended "by hir heer / Vpon an ook" (*JW* 234–35). A

---

[47] In private correspondence, Sarah Tolmie used the phrase "unmetaphoring the metaphor"; I am grateful for her permission to use it here.

benevolent earl rescues her, but a member of his household, enthralled with the empress, murders the earl's daughter when he cannot sate his desire (*JW* 342–50). The earl—unaware of her identity, as she does not tell him who she is—then banishes the empress. Her credulous nature unshaken by her misfortune, she rescues a thief about to be executed and appoints him her servant (*JW* 448). The thief succumbs to greed and conspires with a shipman to lure the empress to the shipman's boat, where she resists the shipman's overtures by praying for deliverance and causing a storm. The beleaguered empress then enters a nunnery and develops the ability to cure disease. In the meantime, the sinners endure horrible illnesses: leprosy, blindness and deafness, gout, and dementia (*JW* 698–715), and not knowing who she is, they seek her out in order to be healed.

Hoccleve renders this virtuous "and specially pitous and merciable" (*JW* 11) protagonist as, like Hoccleve himself, more sinned against than sinning. The similarity between the narrator of the *Complaint* and *Dialogue* and the empress does not end there, however. For the narrator employs the same vocabulary of expression and silence in *Jereslaus' Wife* as he does in the *Complaint* and *Dialogue*. This lexicon is not present in the *Gesta Romanorum*, Hoccleve's source for these stories.[48] When the earl rescues the empress from the oak tree, for instance, "Shee wolde by no way / Deskeuere what shee was, ne what fallace / Was doon to hir. *Cloos shee kepte hir ay*" (*JW* 282–84; emphasis added). So, too, when the knight falsely accuses her of murder,

> This innocent lady no word ageyn
> Spak, for shee spoken had ynow beforn,
> Excusynge hir, but al was in veyn, . . .
> And, sikirly, wheras þat no credence
> May been had, wysdam conseilith silence.
> (*JW* 421–23, 426–27)[49]

[48] For the Latin versions of these narratives, see the *Gesta Romanorum*, ed. Hermann Oesterley (Hildesheim: Georg Olms Verlagsbuchhandlung, 1872; rpt. 1963), 466–70 ("De mulierum subtili decepcione"), and 648–54 (beginning "Octavianus regnavit"). Unless Hoccleve was working from a radically different text from the *Gesta* as we now have it, he is responsible for the details about the inner, hidden thoughts of Fellicula and the empress, as well as the expansive use of confessional discourse in both translations. It would seem that Hoccleve amplified these stories in such a way that both emphasizes what he has in common with the empress in particular, and foregrounds interiority and confession in general.

[49] In this instance, the narrator of the *Gesta* comments merely that the empress departs immediately, "dolens et tristis" ("sorrowing and disconsolate") (650).

Here the narrator editorializes the empress's decision not to explain herself further, imputing to her the same logic by which Hoccleve initially determined to keep his thoughts to himself: when no one will believe you, it is better not to speak. As the narrator acknowledges, there is always a chance that others will regard the truth as "not but lees" (*C* 300). This moment recalls the narrator's earlier decision to keep "scilence, / Lest þat men of me deme wolde, and sein, / 'Se howe this man is fallen in aȝein'" (*C* 180–82). So, too, before he determines that "commvnyng" is the best approach, he explains that, like the empress, "kepte I me cloos" (*C* 145), lest others disbelieve him:

> And this I demed wel and knewe wel eke,
> Whatso þat euere I shulde answere or seie,
> They wolden not han holde it worth a leke.
> Forwhy, as I had lost my tunges keie,
> Kepte I me cloos.
>
> (*C* 141–45)[50]

The passage anticipates the empress's own dilemma and decision not to speak "whereas þat no credence / May been had." Given Hoccleve's own conclusion that in fact "commvnynge is the beste assay," in describing the empress in the same terms he uses to describe himself, he implies that her decision to keep silent might not be the right one. She has, after all, done nothing wrong.

According to Hoccleve's reworking of the confessional paradigm in the *Complaint* and *Dialogue,* then, the empress is in an ideal position to "braste oute" (*C* 35) with her story and reclaim her royal position. However, she never has to do so. Instead, when those who "had hir doon so greet aduersitee" (*JW* 770) seek healing, she mandates that they confess: "Noon þat is heer Y cure can. / . . . / But if þat they an open shrifte make / Of hir offenses dirke and synnes blake" (*JW* 773, 776–77). These lines echo both Hoccleve's resolution—"In feith, frende, make I thenke an open shrifte" (*D* 83)—and, by extension, the convention that "Shrift is opin shewing of brest."[51] The identity of the sinners is restricted to their sins, so much so that Hoccleve describes the emperor's brother as the "mirour of malice and iniquitee" (*JW* 697), and the empress herself

---

[50] See also *C* 32 and *D* 28.
[51] *Boke of Penance,* 26110.

refers to their diseases as a "miroure" of their sins (*JW* 727). These characters reflect the sins they have committed.

Their confessions, however, ultimately affirm the empress's story, and their narratives have more to do with her innocence than with their sins. The homicidal knight, for instance, having listened to the brother-in-law's narrative about how he abused the empress, muses that he does not know that lady,

> But as my lord the erl rood on huntynge
> In a foreste ones, wel woot Y this,
> A fair lady he fond hangynge, iwis,
> On a tree by hir heer . . .
>
> (*JW* 857–60)

The knight disproportionately focuses on what happened to this woman (the empress): of the thirty lines of his confession, all but one illuminates the empress's suffering. Having murdered a child, he spends a solitary clause admitting his guilt: "I kilde the chyld" (*JW* 878). While he also sinned in falsely accusing the empress, murder is surely a more serious act. But in keeping with the focus in the *Complaint* and *Dialogue* on "commvnynge" and truth, the concern here is not so much with the knight's actions as with vindicating the empress. So, too, before he confesses, the rescued thief labels the empress a "lady beninge and good" (*JW* 890), extolling her virtues for eleven of the seventeen lines of his "shrifte." The shipman follows suit. At the opening of this scene, the empress herself forces the brother-in-law to tell the entirety of her story. Addressing the emperor, she convicts her brother-in-law of failing to make "hool shrifte ne pleyn" (*JW* 795). To be sure, the character omits both his sin of lust and of his leaving the empress for dead, hanging from a tree by her hair. But more crucially, in doing so, he fails publicly to narrate the empress's own suffering. In this context, then, to make an open and complete confession is to give an account of the empress herself. That Hoccleve emphasizes this account is borne out by his expansion of the story's end: in the *Gesta,* the empress is reunited with her husband immediately following the confessions. But Hoccleve's version highlights that she was, up to that point, hiding herself: "This emperice list no lenger hyde / What þat shee was, but spak . . . / And hem hir face shewid anoonright" (*JW* 921–22, 929).

Taxonomies of Sin in the *Male regle,*
Jonathas and Fellicula, and *Learn to Die*

These confessions are thus not merely descriptive, cataloguing sins (such as murder) and examining the conscience in order to determine the motivation for a particular sin. (The knight, for instance, never goes into detail about his lust for the empress.) Instead, these confessions enable the empress to reveal who she is and, in addition, vindicate her in front of those who abused her. We might understand such a narrative as compensatory in some way for Hoccleve's own public suffering, affirming that when confession is not limited to the cataloguing of sins, it can enable self-definition—even self-reclamation. By contrast, Hoccleve's engagement with both mainstream categories of sin and images of confession in the earlier poem, the *Male regle* (c. 1405–6), *Learn to Die,* and the tale of *Jonathas and Fellicula* demonstrates that to some extent, these modes limit narratives of the interior to descriptions of sin and decaying innards. As with the *Tale of Jereslaus' Wife,* Hoccleve modifies the *Jonathas and Fellicula* of the *Gesta,* adding material that foregrounds his own apparent concern with how confession works. Taken together with the rest of the *Series,* these works problematize engaging with confessional discourse on its own terms.

Hoccleve's *Male regle* describes the narrator's misspent youth and imminent death—"so rype vnto my pit / þat scarsely I may it nat asterte" (95–96), as the narrator explains. This penitential autobiography envisions the narrator's life in terms of "riot and excesse": "It sit nat vnto me / þat mirour am of riot and excesse / To knowen of a goddes pryuetee" (329–31). This image of a mirror does not conjure Hoccleve's strained "many a saute" to his mirror in the *Complaint,* at which point the narrator attempts both to regulate and to construct his outward appearance. Instead, the mirror of the *Male regle* is entirely mimetic: the narrator takes on and then displays—mirrors—the attributes of these sins. While the concern in the *Complaint* is that none will comprehend the narrator's interior life, the narrator of the *Male regle* reflects widely known commonplaces. According to available discourses, particularly those of the tavern sins, Seven Deadly Sins, and penitential lyric, as scholars have noted, he does not create or articulate an identity so much as inhabit one.[52]

---

[52] But see Knapp's cautionary note that in the *Male regle,* "Hoccleve artfully moves the reader back and forth between the expectation of some steamy confession and the realization that there is not really anything much to confess. . . . Insofar as his poem is

Because others have treated Hoccleve's employment of these commonplaces in the *Male regle,* I will dwell on them only briefly here. Hoccleve begins the poem in a traditional penitential mode, decrying his sickness and age, and condemning his behavior in youth: "Myn vnwar yowthe kneew nat what it wroghte, / This woot I wel" (41–42):

> For seelde is seen þat yowthe takith heede
> Of perils þat been likly for to fall,
> For, haue he take a purpos, þat moot neede
> Been execut. No conseil wole he call.
>
> (73–76)

Eva Thornley has shown the degree to which the section on youth draws from the penitential commonplace of wasted youth and impending age.[53] Moreover, the sins of Hoccleve's youth correspond to the conventions of confessional manuals. Among these sins is gluttony; though "Reson me bad" to eat and drink in moderation,

> wilful youthe nat obeie leste
> Vnto þat reed, ne sette nat therby.
> I take haue of hem bothe [food and drink] outrageously
> And out of tyme. Nat two yeer or three,
> But xxti wyntir past continuelly,
> Excesse at borde hath leyd his knyf with me.
>
> (107–12)

In such instances, Hoccleve describes his youthful self in terms of the attributes of specific sins (gluttony, for instance), such that he personifies his youth as the very thing that refuses Reason and embraces "excesse."

---

autobiographic, it is a confession of failures" (Ethan Knapp, "Bureaucratic Identity and the Construction of the Self in Hoccleve's *Formulary* and *La Male Regle,*" *Speculum* 74 [1999]: 357–76 [373–74]). On the Seven Deadly Sins in the *Male regle,* see Thornley, "The Middle English Penitential Lyric," 311–19. In "The Professional: Thomas Hoccleve," *SAC* 29 (2007): 341–73, Sarah Tolmie reads the *Male regle* as "trying to sort out the proprietary discourse of the vernacular poet whose authority is neither aristocratic-courtly nor religious-clerical" (347). Tolmie's interest is not in penitential modes per se, but rather in how Hoccleve appropriates *exempla* concerning tavern sins in order to examine the tavern as a "place of business" as well as the "labor performed by urban service professionals" (356–57).

[53] Thornley argues that the *Male regle* "stems from the lyrical tradition of regret for a misspent youth which has been followed by infirmity and the fear of death" ("The Middle English Penitential Lyric," 303). For Thornley's discussion of this commonplace, see 300–303, 306–8. See also Patterson, *Chaucer and the Subject of History,* 389.

Yet while Hoccleve spends the better part of this poem describing himself in terms of sin, he ends the poem with a frequently cited question:

> Ey, what is me, þat to myself thus longe
> Clappid haue I? I trowe þat I raue.
> A, nay, my poore purs and peynes stronge
> Han artid me speke as I spoken haue.
>
> (393–96)

As Robert J. Meyer-Lee sums it up, "Hoccleve concludes, in effect, 'I'm not mad, I'm just out of cash.'"[54] But there is something more at play in these lines. Ostensibly, the narrator has spent the entire poem explaining "what [was and] is me": one who was profligate in youth and now, approaching death, regrets his misspent past—or regrets that because of his misspent past, he suffers physically and financially. And yet, given the detail with which Hoccleve articulates his condition, the question "what is me" resonates strangely. At 448 lines, only 392 of which Hoccleve devotes to his sinful state, the poem is hardly "longe." That he justifies this "rav[ing]" by reminding the reader of his poverty certainly demonstrates Hoccleve's more general concern with money. However, when Hoccleve surmises, "I trowe þat I raue," he refers back to the previous 392 lines of poetry, suggesting that what he has written up to that point has little meaning. According to Hoccleve, the poem itself neither answers the question "what is me" nor employs language that would enable it to do so. Hoccleve thereby registers not only a need for money but also, obliquely, an attitude of skepticism toward the very discourse the poem employs—that of confession. The corollary is that available confessional identities (the gluttonous taverngoer, the prodigal spender, the wasted youth) do not define the self so much as personify various mainstream attributes of sin.

So, too, the tale of *Jonathas and Fellicula* problematizes a commonplace of confessional discourse: that the exposition of the insides results in healing. In this case, Hoccleve literalizes the image of confession as vomit (or some kind of bodily discharge) and presents this effluvium as what precipitates, rather than alleviates, suffering and death. Hoccleve translates this particular tale from the *Gesta Romanorum* at the behest of

---

[54] Meyer-Lee, "Hoccleve and the Apprehension of Money," 174.

his friend, but, as with the *Tale of Jereslaus' Wife*, Hoccleve nevertheless remains committed to his exploration of confession and inner identity. Jonathas, an emperor's son, inherits three extraordinary gifts: a ring that ensures his popularity; a brooch that yields whatever he desires; and a magic carpet that carries him wherever he wishes (*JF* 99–115). Upon arriving at school, Jonathas takes up with an immoral woman, Fellicula, who pries from him the secrets of his three treasures and then steals them all for her own benefit. That Fellicula represents the ill-fated sinner is made clear by her behavior at the outset of this narrative, when, after she pilfers the ring, she fakes its theft by someone else: "She wepte, and shewid outward cheer of wo, / But in hir herte was it nothyng so" (*JF* 244–45). Clearly the disparity between Fellicula's countenance and "herte" is proof positive of her duplicity. But these lines are also suggestive of the *confessio ficti*—the confession of an imposter and, in this case, manufactured contrition as well, for tears constituted one of the most acceptable signs of contrition.[55] Although Hoccleve is hardly groundbreaking here, the moment suggests that it is possible to fake the attributes of virtue—that these attributes do not accurately define the self, which in Fellicula's case, festers. Moreover, Hoccleve adds this detail to the narrative of the *Gesta,* which includes nothing about Fellicula's inner state.

But it is only after Fellicula steals the magic carpet (having left Jonathas at the ends of the earth), and after Jonathas makes his way back home, where he gains fame as a "maistreful . . . leche" (*JF* 595), that she repents her evil ways. Fellicula's death illustrates the literal consequences of a confessional metaphor—that shrift is like vomit. This metaphor often works in tandem with the confessional commonplace of the physician doctor, whose treatment of disease represents the priest's treatment of sin. With Fellicula's fate, the narrative complicates the notion that narrating sin leads to healing. In this case, Fellicula, having prospered by her ill-gotten treasures (*JF* 592), falls "into greet seeknesse" (*JF* 593). Again, in the context of penitential discourse, this sickness is tantamount to Fellicula's many indiscretions. Fellicula's search for a physician thus represents her search for a confessor—in this case, Jonathas, who, as Meyer-Lee observes, "becomes a priest-figure."[56]

---

[55] For the *confessio ficti* as it appears in literature, see Patterson, *Chaucer and the Subject of History,* 385, 400–402. Tentler discusses the *confessio ficti* in *summae confessorum;* see *Sin and Confession,* 274–75, 279.

[56] Meyer-Lee, "Hoccleve and the Apprehension of Money," 212.

While Hoccleve damns Fellicula as "the welle of deceyuable double-nesse" (JF 590), there is no clear sense that she seeks a physician for any other reason than to be healed. In other words, as a metaphor for the penitent Christian, Fellicula fits the bill: she understands that she is sick and needs a doctor. Her own plea to Jonathas underscores her apparent sincerity as a contrite sinner:

> "A, sir," seide shee, "for Goddes sake,
> þat way me shewe and Y shal folwen it,
> Whateuere it be, for this seeknesse sit
> So ny myn herte þat Y woot nat how
> Me to demene."
>
> (JF 612–16)[57]

One might argue that Fellicula's remorse stems from her disease and that her contrition is therefore imperfect, even unacceptable; but insofar as disease represents sin, one might also suggest that Hoccleve renders Fellicula as seeking respite precisely from her transgressions. Jonathas's answer is commensurate with such a reading: "Lady, yee muste openly yow confesse, / . . . / . . . elles nat in the might / Of man is it to yeue a medecyne" (JF 617, 621–22). Of course, Jonathas's tone is not surprising. He could hardly be expected to embrace the woman who robbed him of his friends, fortune, and position. And yet Hoccleve frames his response in terms of confessional discourse: in order to expose his or her insides, the penitent must confess "openly." Thus far, it is reasonable to expect absolution: Fellicula is diseased; she seeks a doctor; she plans the open exposition of her sins. Indeed, even the narrator's identifying Fellicula as the "mirour of shame" suggests as much (JF 637)—in this case, as in the Male regle, the character merely reflects the attributes of a specific sin.

But in spite of what appears to be a conventional narrative employing easily recognizable metaphors of sin, Fellicula's confession is hardly successful. Indeed, Jonathas does not accept her confession, resolving in-

---

[57] In the Gesta, while Jonathas informs the woman that, without confession, his medicine will not help her ("Medicina sua non valeret ei, nisi prius confiteretur omnia peccata sua" [468]), the narrator does not describe the deceptive woman as expressing penitence or as suffering (468–69): "Illa vero alta voce confitebatur, quomodo Jonatham decepisset de annulo, monili et panno et quomodo eum in loco deserto reliquisset bestiis ad devorandum." ("She confessed, in a low voice, that she had cheated him of his ring, necklace, and cloth, and left him in a desert place to be devoured by beasts.")

stead "to doon his cure, / Cure mortel, way to hir sepulture" (*JF* 650–51). Such a response inverts the expectations the reader may have of the confessional physician—the priest—whose job is to offer the spiritual cure (absolution) that ensures the penitent's hope for attaining heaven. Jonathas takes the opposite approach, poisoning Fellicula with the very fruit and water that sickened him on his journey home:

> He thoughte reewe shee sholde . . .
> And of þat watir hir he yaf to drynke
> Which þat his flessh from his bones before
> Had twynned . . .
> Of the fruyt of the tree he yaf hir ete
> Which þat him made into the leepre sterte,
> And as blyue in hir wombe gan they frete
> And gnawe so þat change gan hir herte.
> Now herkneth how it hir made smerte.
> *Hir wombe opned and out fil eche entraille*
> *That in hir was* . . .
> (*JF* 652, 654–56, 659–65; my emphasis)

Jonathas locates after confession—"reewe shee sholde"—what should come before. He thereby behaves as an ill-trained physician: Fellicula does, after all, request that he "þat way me shewe and Y shal folwen it, / Whateuere it be." To state the obvious, the priest is then to examine the penitent's sorrow for his or her sins—not after the confession and as punishment. Indeed, Jonathas capitalizes on a secondary meaning of "reewe" as payment, rather than sorrow or contrition, in order to set up what amounts to revenge. This inverted absolution results in what we might regard as Fellicula's second (and literalized) confession, in which she spills her insides for all to see—in stark contrast to the *Gesta,* which states merely that Fellicula died and includes none of Fellicula's explicitly confessional speech.[58] Hoccleve's image draws from the confessional metaphor of scooping out the insides, as I discussed above: "Herebeforn I told ȝow of a welle, & of a pytt of lust, þat is, ȝour body, & how full it is of corrupte watyr. . . . Þerfore ȝou nedyth, in gostly labour,

---

[58] The Latin text emphasizes her suffering: she dies ("spiritum emisit") in torment ("dolores interiores senciens lacrimabiliter"), but she neither speaks about penitence nor *vomits forth* her insides. See the *Gesta Romanorum,* 469. For a discussion of excessive interiority as connected to femininity, see Ruth Nissé, " 'Oure Fadres Olde and Modres': Gender, Heresy, and Hoccleve's Literary Politics," *SAC* 21 (1999): 275–99.

to scopyn out þis corrupte watyr of curs, wyth the scoope of pen-auns"[59]—and once again, Hoccleve unmetaphors illness, this time graphically. In this context, Fellicula's literal disembowelment reads as the direct consequence, rather than as the metaphorical expression, of her confession.

Insofar as Hoccleve modifies both tales as they appear in the *Gesta,* he emphasizes the importance of "commvnynge" and the self-destructive nature of mainstream confession. One is tempted to suggest that the empress in the *Tale of Jereslaus' Wife* absolves the sinners because in tell-ing her story they enact a kind of "commvnynge." Fellicula's confession, by contrast, is neither so involved nor compendious in its description of Jonathas. Instead, she articulates a conventional desire to do whatever the physician commands—perhaps connoting, on some level, the peni-tent sinner who conforms precisely to orthodox categories of sin. Hoc-cleve does not report the contents of her sin, summarizing merely that she recites "how falsly" she had behaved to Jonathas, "as yee han herd aboue" (*JF* 631, 633).[60] In its lack of individual detail, her confession differs markedly from those in the *Tale of Jereslaus' Wife.* That Jonathas determines that her "cure" will be death cues the reader to the coming inversion of confessional discourse, when, rather than experiencing heal-ing, Fellicula evacuates her insides.

Hoccleve's modification of these tales might seem commensurate with what Little identifies as Hoccleve's retreat from confession, which, in her reading of *The Regiment of Princes,* Hoccleve ultimately abandons "in favor of exemplary narrative as the site of self-definition."[61] Yet, as this essay has shown, throughout the *Series,* Hoccleve engages with rather than rejects or retreats from confession, to the point of exploring its utility as well as its drawbacks. Unlike the rest of the *Series, Learn to*

---

[59] *Jacob's Well,* 64–65. See also Ross, *Middle English Sermons,* 240. Hoccleve employs the metaphor of vomit in *The Regiment of Princes* as well, where the old man explains that confession is the necessary corollary to "besy thoght": "But if a vomyt after folwe blyve, / At the port of despeir he may arryve" (F. J. Furnivall, ed., *Hoccleve's Works: The Regiment of Princes,* EETS e.s. 72 [London: Kegan Paul, Trench, Trübner & Co., rpt 1996], 272–73). Bryan discusses this section of the *Regiment* as exemplifying the danger of "excesses of . . . introspection" (*Looking Inward,* 196). A turn to Patterson's discussion of contrition and despair is instructive, however: if the penitent experiences contrition but does not expose his sins to the priest, he is in danger of festering inwardly. See Patterson, *Chaucer and the Subject of History,* 374–97.

[60] Hoccleve here *omits* information that the *Gesta* includes. Cf. the *Gesta Romanorum,* 466–70.

[61] Little, *Confession and Resistance,* 117.

Die presents penance and mainstream confession as the remedy for being forgotten and ostracized. The poem, a translation of Suso's *Ars moriendi,* comprises an interior dialogue between a "disciple" (*LD* 87) and the image of a dying man who will convince the disciple "to lerne for to die" (*LD* 50). The concerns of this dying youth, an image of lost "good precious tyme" (*LD* 234), dovetail with those of the narrator of the *Male regle* and stem from confessional discourse.[62] Christina von Nolcken has argued that *Learn to Die* distills the central concern of the *Series,* which for von Nolcken comprises an extended meditation on the narrator's anxiety over his impending death.[63] As James Simpson puts it, "as both person and author . . . Hoccleve is dying."[64] But I think we might also consider that, taken together with the rest of the *Series,* the image of death in *Learn to Die* also expresses Hoccleve's own conflicted attitude to mainstream confession, sin, and death. As the image exhorts Hoccleve, "Let me be your ensaumple and your mirour, / Lest yee slippe into my plyt miserable. / [. . .] / In holy wirkes your tyme occupie" (*LD* 295–96, 300). The image of the mirror, yet again, reflects the narrator's own shortcomings, so that he might turn away from vice and spend his time wisely. But unlike the physical mirror of the *Complaint,* before which Hoccleve attempts to construct and perform his public identity, the "mirour" of the dying man presents mainstream and conventional actions of charity and mercy as evidence of inner identity, sanity, and goodness. The image of death does not suggest, as Hoccleve does elsewhere in the *Series,* that confession might be a narrative of health, that God heals disease regardless of institutional paradigms— quite the opposite, in fact.

Learn to Die foregrounds, instead, "penance" (*LD* 322) and suggests that God's mercy is contingent on acknowledging how one "haast offendid" (*LD* 333). Such a moment differs markedly from the narrator's insistence, in the *Complaint* and *Dialogue,* that he has done nothing wrong—that his confession will describe not his sin but God's "ʒifte." The confessional moments in *Learn to Die,* by contrast, adhere closely to mainstream guidelines: "plener confessioun / Make of thy gilt, and

---

[62] On the inclusion of *Learn to Die* in the Huntington holograph, see Watt, "'I this book shal make,'" 137–48. On *Ars moriendi* as an increasingly popular genre in late medieval England, see von Nolcken, "'O why ne had I lerned for to die?'" 29–30, 40; and Watt, *Exemplars and Exemplarity,* 189–90.

[63] See von Nolcken, "'O why ne had I lerned for to die?'"

[64] James Simpson, *Reform and Cultural Revolution* (Oxford: Oxford University Press, 2002), 430.

satisfaccioun / And asseeth [amends] do" (*LD* 480–82). This plain or open confession does not, as in the *Complaint* and *Dialogue,* describe "what a man is," but rather catalogues guilt and offers sacramental ritual as the solution. What is more, the image of death bears marked similarities to the narrator of the *Complaint* and *Dialogue;* it "acts exactly like Hoccleve himself had done earlier in the *Complaint,*" in Simpson's phrase.[65] The image, like Hoccleve, expresses bitterness at the fickleness of the world: "Y haue espyd the frendshipe is ful streit / Of this world. It is mirour of deceit" (*LD* 454–55). This assertion reflects both the changeable attitude the narrator discovered in his former friends, and his observation, in the *Complaint,* that "stablenesse in this worlde is ther noon" (*C* 9). So, too, just as the narrator bewails the rejection "of hem þat weren wonte me for to calle / To companie" (*C* 75–76), the image of death characterizes the soul as complaining that "the worldes fauour cleene is fro me went. / Forsake Y am. Frendshippe Y can noon fynde. / . . . / Slipt out of mynde / I am" (*LD* 505–6, 508–9). These parallels suggest that Hoccleve is not without sin, whatever his claims to the contrary. Moreover, the similarities between the image and Hoccleve suggest a certain amount of self-doubt and anxiety, both about the function of confession and self-expression, and about whether the narrator actually deserves to be accepted back into the community. Has he really done nothing wrong? Does his mirror image reflect his inner self? Although the poem resolves some of these anxieties in the graphic conclusion of *Jonathas and Fellicula,* seemingly underscoring the inutility and even danger of sacramental confession, *Learn to Die* raises a question central to the poem: What sorts of self-expression will be well received? Is it better in the end to conform to convention, embrace taxonomies of sin, madness, social stereotypes? These are complications the poem raises but does not—perhaps cannot—resolve, except to rest in the paradoxical hope that one might find a receptive audience. It is suggestive, as Steven Rozenski Jr. points out, that Hoccleve's additions to Suso's text focus precisely on issues of isolation, loneliness, and the desire to be reintegrated into the community.[66]

This hope for rehabilitation, which stems in part from Hoccleve's

---

[65] Ibid.

[66] Rozenski Jr., " 'Your Ensaumple and Your Mirour,' " 14. On *Learn to Die* as expressing both the poet's isolation and desire for a return to the community, see Burrow, "Hoccleve's *Series:* Experience and Books," 269; and Simpson, *Reform and Cultural Revolution,* 430–32.

appropriation of confessional discourse, suggests the possibility of a new kind of fifteenth-century confession, one that envisions a public and secular audience. In the *Series,* Hoccleve is clearly preoccupied with what kind of behavior will, in Simpson's phrase, earn "social reincorporation" and/or redemption: for the empress, for Fellicula, for the image of the dying man, and, perhaps most centrally of all, for himself. But insofar as he presents only those without sin as unequivocally deserving of mercy, Hoccleve removes forgiveness from its sacramental context, reframing it as the acknowledgment of public sin against a guiltless individual. The *Series* is not univocal in advancing this idea, of course, and as the discussion above indicates, *Learn to Die* is in conversation with the mainstream devotional paradigms that present all people as sinners in need of repentance. And yet Hoccleve does not end the *Series* with this relatively comforting idea. Instead, he closes his meditation with the translation of the tale of *Jonathas and Fellicula,* reminding the reader of his consistent revision of confessional paradigms throughout the work. In so doing, the *Series* engages with one of the most fundamental questions raised by vernacular penitential manuals: If our identity is *only* in sin, what is left? As Lee Patterson has suggested, the answer seems to be despair[67]—and ultimately, in his depiction of Fellicula's suffering, Hoccleve highlights and problematizes this despair. This revision of confessional paradigms troubles the received wisdom about the relationship between confession and interiority in the early fifteenth century, suggesting that we might look beyond images of sin, decay, and death for evidence of medieval selfhood—suggesting, indeed, that the individual may fashion his or her own identity, even in front of a mirror.

[67] On how late medieval definitions of contrition focus on the connection between selfhood and sin, and hence closely resemble definitions of despair, see Patterson, *Chaucer and the Subject of History,* 374–97; and Little, *Confession and Resistance,* 113–15.

COLLOQUIUM: *ANIMALIA*

Introduction

Gillian Rudd
University of Liverpool

T HERE IS A PROBLEM when it comes to talking about animals that is hinted at in the title of this paper colloquium. *Animalia* now signals the group, animals, as distinct from vegetables and minerals. Those within this group are distinguished from vegetables by their inability to convert inorganic matter into organic matter (which means they have to consume organic matter in order to live) and from minerals by being organic rather than inorganic. In the Middle Ages, animals were distinguished by being things that had breath (*anima*) and the term could include all such creatures, so that it lumped humans and nonhumans together. While these were the technical divisions, there was and is also the familiar and persistent division, human/animal, which has given rise to so much discussion over what we humans mean when we use the term "animal" and what we ought to mean. Animal studies is now again troubling the waters of human identity and moral (in)action. The meeting of animal studies with ethics and literary study has resulted in a surge of discussion marked by the sudden rash of journals devoting space to the topic. Among these, two are of particular relevance to medievalists: *PMLA* dedicated a special number to animal studies in 2009, and in 2011 *postmedieval* brought out its special number "The Animal Turn." These two confirm current interest in the area, but it is a *renewed* interest, not a new one. The work of Beryl Rowland alone testifies that animals have long furnished topics for debate in medieval circles, with Jill Mann's book on beast fable carrying on and developing that tradition of scholarship, while Joyce Salisbury's *The Beast Within* offers a more animal-studies viewpoint.[1] The arrival of broader ecocriti-

---

[1] Jill Mann, *From Aesop to Reynard: Beast Literature in Medieval Britain* (Oxford: Oxford University Press, 2009); Joyce Salisbury, *The Beast Within: Animals in the Middle Ages* (London: Routledge, 1994).

Studies in the Age of Chaucer 34 (2012):309–10
© 2012 The New Chaucer Society

cism in medieval studies was affirmed by Barbara Hanawalt and Lisa Kiser's collection *Engaging with Nature*.[2]

It is thus into a well-established field of debate that the following colloquium enters. The group of contributors gathered here comes from a variety of backgrounds and interests, but all have agreed to focus for a short space on the animal in some form or another; to offer a short initial piece and then to respond in brief to what the others in the group have written. These responses are by no means final words on the topics or even on the papers here offered. Rather, they are ways into discussion yet to be held, indications of routes that may be followed at leisure and in more depth elsewhere.

We begin with Lisa J. Kiser's consideration of instances of animals in the *Canterbury Tales* that do not fit the prevailing types of the fourteenth century. From there we move to Susan Crane's discussion of the crucial and perhaps unexpected roles of the three domestic animals (housecat, pig, and capon) in *The Summoner's Tale* and then on to Gillian Rudd's discussion of the figurative use of animals in the Host's comments that top and tail *The Nun's Priest's Tale*. This is followed by David Scott-Macnab's observations about Chaucer's use of hunting, followed by David Salter, who draws our attention to the oddity of the comedy of Palamon and Arcite fighting like dogs over a bone. Dogs take us to Karl Steel's dead pets and the *canis* legend, and our dog finally becomes a werewolf in the piece by Jeffrey J. Cohen that concludes the formal paper part of our virtual colloquium.

<hr />

[2] Barbara Hanawalt and Lisa J. Kiser, eds., *Engaging with Nature: Essays on the Natural World in Medieval and Early Modern Europe* (Notre Dame: University of Notre Dame Press, 2008).

The Animals That Therefore They Were: Some Chaucerian Animal/Human Relationships

Lisa J. Kiser
Ohio State University

I N HER STILL-USEFUL BOOK about Chaucerian animals, Beryl Rowland argues that the poet consistently tends to "rely on tradition and iconography" in his animal allusions, a point that many of us, in our day-to-day practical criticism, might easily concede.[1] But in this essay, I want to confront a handful of animal references that have bothered me over the years because "tradition and iconography" haven't entirely fulfilled Rowland's promise. These references, which seem irrational given their contexts and intractable even in the face of the valuable current scholarship they have sponsored, continue to haunt me.

I

In *The Pardoner's Tale,* when the youngest rioter visits the apothecary to purchase the poison designed to do away with his two companions, he comes up with a plausible fiction to justify his grisly purchase, presumably to distract the druggist from his actual intentions. He mentions rodents, of course, certainly common enough pests in medieval households, but then he spins out a more detailed and entirely unnecessary animal-centered scenario: "and eek ther was a polcat in his hawe, / That, as he seyde, his capouns hadde yslawe, / And fayn he wolde wreke hym, if he myghte, / On vermin that destroyed hym by nyghte" (855–58). This scene, wherein formerly male animals, now with weak and nonnormative bodies that lack the testicular edge that might allow them to

---

[1] Beryl Rowland, *Blind Beasts: Chaucer's Animal World* (Kent: Kent State University Press, 1971), 16. See also 44 and 166.

Studies in the Age of Chaucer 34 (2012):311–17
© 2012 The New Chaucer Society

effectively resist an attack, are viciously slain by a predator, seems uncannily to reflect something close to the Pardoner's own identity. What exactly that might be is hard to capture without closing down the interpretive richness of Chaucer's character. Yet we are asked, I think, to meditate on these dead capons, to see in them a vulnerability that carries over to the Pardoner himself. Are they offering up for view and consideration an image of the Pardoner that he himself has carefully crafted as a vehicle for coyly "outing himself" before his audience? Or, to follow a different line of inquiry, do they reflect a buried, perhaps even a totally repressed, desire for the kind of spectacular death that the capons themselves are victims of? However one decides to link this animal scene to *The Pardoner's Prologue* and *Tale* (and there are many different ways in which one might do so), the image of the dead and dying capons seems important—doubly so given Chaucer's typical care as a writer. Although these animals are deeply sublimated, a fact signaled, perhaps, by the way in which Chaucer tucks them deep inside a fiction-within-a-fiction, and although their damaged bodies are incompatible with the confident self-presentation of the speaker with whom they seem to be aligned, they stand out as abject tokens of something that is being signaled, even if it is impossible to try to pin down.

Other things might be said about the oddness of this animal moment in *The Pardoner's Tale.* Neither the capons nor the doomed polecat that attacks them have any extensive medieval social or literary history that would overdetermine their possible significance in this tale. There are no polecat/capon fables and myths, for example, or heraldic devices, or proverbs, or well-known saints' lives that feature either of these animals. Dragging little or no cultural baggage along with them, they remain resolutely literal, unlike the elaborate animal metaphorizing of the Pardoner's sexual identity that goes on in the *General Prologue,* where he's compared to a mare, a gelding, a goat, and a hare, all common animals that serve as symbols of lechery or male sexual deficiency drawn from common medieval systems of signification. In other words, the polecat and the capons, though acting a bit like personal psychic totems for the Pardoner, "represent while escaping representation."[2]

II

The Wife of Bath's Prologue teems with animal life, mostly the sort that one commonly associates with domesticity. There are spaniels, geese,

[2] The phrase is Donna Haraway's, in *Simians, Cyborgs, and Women: The Reinvention of Nature* (New York: Routledge, 1991), 188.

oxen, horses, asses, cats, sheep, pigs, and sows—some of these animals appearing in the Wife's own richly metaphorical discourse and some appearing in the reported discourse of either her husbands or the misogamist literature they channel. The one animal, however, that seems to recur is the lion, an "extreme" animal deployed most frequently in the Wife's descriptions of her angry spouses, two of whom are compared to a "wood leoun" during arguments (III.429, 794). To match them in their power and rage, the Wife describes herself as a "leonesse" (637) during these shouting matches, and her rhetorical purpose here is to present herself as equal to these predatory and domineering adversaries. Lions, too, form the centerpiece of the Wife's "Who peyntede the leon" argument; in the fable she refers to, the lion is an interesting animal in part because its strength makes it a viable displacer of the human in any imagined chain of being based on sheer power—and the Wife clearly admires this beast's attempt to overturn the usual animal/human hierarchy. Lions (along with their "extreme" partners, dragons) are also used against the Wife in the misogynistic tradition; she quotes *The Book of Wicked Wives* as inveighing, "Bet is . . . thyn habitacioun / Be with a leon or a foul dragoun / Than with a woman usynge for to chyde" (775–77). On the face of it, then, one is tempted to see the Wife's leonine self-fashioning—and her awareness of the lion as an image imposed upon her by others—as central to her identity.

But buried in her Prologue is another zoomorphism, one that competes with the Wife's identity as lion. She is a mouse: "Yet was I nevere withouten purveiance / Of mariage, n'of othere thynges eek. / I holde a mouses herte nat worth a leek / That hath but oon hole for to sterte to, / And if that faille, thanne is al ydo" (570–74). The mouse is of course the quintessential prey animal for humans with traps as well as for a large number of beasts from the biggest carnivores (avian and animal both) down to the household cat, and although its vulnerability might not always be appreciated by those involved in attempts at eradication of this invader of human foodstores, the mouse that lives in the Wife's analogy—and looms so large in her self-conception—is a desperate beast on the run. To be sure, the Wife may be admiring the animal's fabled resourcefulness here, but her attention is also drawn to the spectacle of doom that the animal frequently provides to onlookers, the moment when all "is ydo." Chaucer himself has visualized such a moment in the Prioress's portrait, where a mouse's entrapped and bleeding body stands exposed to view. The mouse, living in a habitat positively electrified by generalized threat, seems to creep out of some psychic recess in the Wife's unconscious and disturb the overt rhetoric of her construction of herself as a powerful agent of her own survival.

III

In *The Knight's Tale* and *The Clerk's Tale,* the principal female characters turn to irrational animal fantasies to give structure to their anxieties. Emelye wants to avoid, at all costs, becoming like Acteon, the hunter whose own domestic hounds attack him and eat him after Diana transforms him into a stag—"keepe me fro thy vengeaunce and thyn ire, / That Attheon aboughte cruelly" (I.2302–3)—a fate that seems strangely inappropriate to her own circumstances.[3] In a tale that contains a number of frightening scenarios involving animals turning on humans (the boars killing Atalanta and Meleager, the sow eating the child, the wolf eating the man, the lion and the tigress attacking the hunters, etc.), the anxiety-ridden Emelye has chosen perhaps the worst of them to concentrate on, partly because the role of the human actor is suddenly and inexplicably reversed; a guiltless human is now forced to endure what his prey habitually undergoes, and the prime movers of his torture are the very companion animals he once trusted. In *The Clerk's Tale,* Griselda (again quite irrationally, given the aristocratic status of her offspring) worries about the bodies of her "dead" children; three times she creates a vivid verbal portrait of their corpses being eaten by beasts, especially dogs and birds, being treated, that is, just as the bodies of dead animals are—as abandoned carrion (IV.570–72; 680–83; 1093–95). The image of their bodily desecration persists even after she has been reunited with them, documenting its tenacious hold on her consciousness. In this fantasy, again one of predation gone haywire, animal bodies are replaced with innocent human ones, and Griselda is portrayed as someone who holds fast to the belief (*pace* Christian doctrine) that the self is entirely dependent on bodily form, that it is "almost impossible to envision personal survival without material continuity."[4]

---

[3] In "Medieval Romance and Feminine Difference in *The Knight's Tale,*" *SAC* 12 (1990): 47–63, Susan Crane also notes the seeming inappropriateness of Emelye's specific fear here; she resolves the problem by reading the passage as a version of the love-hunt convention (57).

[4] Caroline Walker Bynum, *The Resurrection of the Body in Western Christianity, 200–1336* (New York: Columbia University Press, 1995), 247. In "Chaucer and Everyday Death: *The Clerk's Tale,* Burial, and the Subject of Poverty," *SAC* 23 (2001): 255–87, Kathy Lavezzo analyzes these moments as expressing Griselda's anxiety about social

Her persistent fantasy also suggests that her children's imagined bodily dismemberment after death somehow brings them pain along with dishonor.

IV

It is hard to deal with these four troubling Chaucerian moments; each seems odd and incompletely analyzed by the context that encloses them, and each seems, socioculturally or historically, "nonfigurative." Each suggests that some aspect of the human self, in some circumstances, can be powerfully evoked by the animal—but these are not "cyborgian" moments, or examples of "distributed cognition" or even of the "prosthetic self."[5] All four seem to be shaped with the predator/prey model as their deep structure, and though each offers a slightly different permutation of that model, each casts the speaker (or, as with Griselda, her loved ones) in the role of vulnerable prey. Because all four moments are imaginary (i.e., the scenarios do not involve *actual* interactions with animals by any of the characters who relate them but are, rather, creations of their imaginations), and because all four seem to be telegraphing anxiety of some kind, it is tempting to adopt a psychoanalytical framework—and I have followed that impulse by crudely deploying some of that framework's vocabulary. But finally, it seems just as convincing to argue that there is a reflexive, perhaps even corporal, dimension to these images as well; that is, the sponsoring site of these fictions seems to be a sort of "psycho-somatic" nexus, with which Chaucer is experimenting. The animal actors in these fictions offer images of animal bodies in trouble (as in the examples drawn from the Pardoner's and the Wife's discourse) or human bodies that first become animal and then experience trouble (as with Emelye and Griselda). In all four cases, the zoomorphizing definitely suggests that when pain and the prospect of death are in view, the animal simply "comes to mind."

In both the ethical and ontological branches of the Enlightenment

---

status; she does not address the animal-centeredness of the passages, nor does she fully confront the fact that Griselda's fear should be (but is not) resolved by Christian teaching (per Bynum).

[5] These concepts surrounding the definition of posthuman selfhood are drawn from Haraway, *Simians, Cyborgs, and Women;* Katherine Hayles, *How We Became Posthuman: Virtual Bodies in Cybernetics, Literature, and Informatics* (Chicago: University of Chicago Press, 1999); and David Wills, *Prosthesis* (Stanford: Stanford University Press, 1995).

and post-Enlightenment European philosophical tradition, of course, there is a long, though intermittently articulated, thread of thought about the role of "embodiedness" in the human/animal relationship, stretching from Jeremy Bentham's observation that "they suffer" through Derrida's haunting and often-cited words, "Mortality resides there, as the most radical means of thinking the finitude that we share with animals, . . . the possibility of sharing the possibility of this nonpower, the anguish of this vulnerability and the vulnerability of this anguish."[6] Philosophers have indeed faced, if not explained, what Chaucer is reaching for here, and those working within the field of critical animal studies are well aware of its existence in the philosophical tradition. But as Cora Diamond has argued, perhaps philosophy's tools can't adequately build a framework in which to contain it. Literature, such as Chaucer's, may be equipped to capture it better.[7]

If suffering animals sometimes come to mind when Chaucer's characters are themselves in situations of "nonpower," to use Derrida's phrase (the Pardoner and the Wife are widely identified as marginalized, and Emelye and Griselda are female victims of male plots of varying levels of threat), do homologies between animals and humans occur when Chaucer is attempting to represent other psychosomatic states, especially those that do not involve an element of vulnerability? Is the animal/human boundary sometimes reified rather than eroded in the poet's deployment of animal reference? Consider the Squire, a character brimming with the confidence and self-satisfaction that comes with youth, the security of high social status, and the promise of an untroubled future. One of the Squire's fascinations is with the "steed of bras," an entirely mechanical beast that weirdly prefigures the later Cartesian "animal machines" that theorized and then repressed animal suffering into invisibility. Clearly, the privileged and not-yet-disenchanted youth

---

[6] Jacques Derrida, "The Animal That Therefore I Am (More to Follow)," trans. David Wills, *Critical Inquiry* 28 (2002): 369–418 (396). Surveys of (and commentary on) post-Enlightenment philosophical positions involving sentience and "embodiedness" in cross-species relationships can be found in Kelly Oliver, *Animal Lessons: How They Teach Us to Be Human* (New York: Columbia University Press, 2009); Ralph R. Acampora, *Corporal Compassion: Animal Ethics and Philosophy of Body* (Pittsburgh: Pittsburgh University Press, 2006); and Matthew Calarco, *Zoographies: The Question of the Animal from Heidegger to Derrida* (New York: Columbia University Press, 2008), esp. Chap. 4.

[7] Cora Diamond, "The Difficulty of Reality and the Difficulty of Philosophy," *Partial Answers* 1.2 (2003): 1–16. See also Stephen Mulhall, *The Wounded Animal: J. M. Coetzee and the Difficulty of Reality in Literature and Philosophy* (Princeton: Princeton University Press, 2009).

resides in a psychic world where easily acquired tech support seems to be all one needs to ensure immortality, either for the steed or, analogously, for oneself. The animal-that-can't-die is thus a provocative companion for one who realizes none of the "finitude we share with animals."

Cat, Capon, and Pig in
The Summoner's Tale

Susan Crane
Columbia University

FOR LITERARY ANIMALS, the star turns, we might say, have long been figurative—the lion as king, the faithful turtledove—rather than literal—the cat as mouser, the pig as pork. Our analytical sensibilities thrill to the animal tropes, to distinguishing the metalepsis of the sacrificial lamb from the symbolic presence of the devil in the fox.[1] Scholarship can too easily come to see literary animals *only* as figures for human concerns. Chaucer's poetry often deploys animals to figurative ends, but occasionally his works also evoke an animal's physical presence on the narrative scene. In *The Summoner's Tale,* two moments of concrete representation assign narrative significance to cohabitation with animals and even ponder an ethical dimension of cross-species relationship.

In the first of these moments, Friar John shoos a housecat off the bench of his bedridden host in order to make room for his own posterior and his several accessories. The briefly evoked housecat differs from the more characteristic deployment of animals in *The Summoner's Tale.* In this more familiar strategy, animals figure the gross embodiment of humankind and the dichotomous relation of human body to eternal soul—the body always pulling away from virtue and threatening the soul's health. Following this familiar teaching, the intercessory prayers of friars have a special effectiveness because "We lyve in poverte and in abstinence, / And burell folk in richesse and despence / Of mete and drynke, and in hir foul delit."[2] In a diegesis Bakhtin would have appreciated, the precise opposite of abstinent prayer is a sick man's fart, a supremely animal

---

[1] Susan Crane, *Animal Encounters: Contacts and Concepts in Medieval Britain* (Philadelphia: University of Pennsylvania Press, 2012 forthcoming), Chap. 3.

[2] Geoffrey Chaucer, *The Canterbury Tales,* in *The Riverside Chaucer,* gen. ed. Larry D. Benson, 3rd ed. (Boston: Houghton Mifflin, 1987), *The Summoner's Tale,* III.1873–75. Hereafter cited in parentheses in my text by fragment and line number.

act: "Ther nys no capul, drawynge in a cart, / That myghte have lete a fart of swich a soun" (III.2150–51). Just as bestial as this physical excess is imperfect faith: the friar imagines laymen and Jerome's adversary Jovinian waddling and belching as they pray, "Fat as a whale, and walkynge as a swan . . . Lo, 'buf!' they seye, '*cor meum eructavit!*'" (III.1930, 1934). And the squire who works out the partition of the sick man's fart calls it a fair exchange for the friar's dissembling sermon that morning. According to the Summoner, Friar John's and all friars' base pleasures corrupt their spirituality so completely that they are to spend eternity lodged under the devil's huge tail. The carthorse, whale, swan, and devil are repulsive in their oversized physicality; they figure an opposition between embodiment and virtue that the sick man Thomas illustrates as fully as the friar. In his illness, says his wife, he is as angry as a biting ant and he groans "lyk oure boor, lyth in oure sty" (III.1825, 1829).

On this ugly scene of humankind's subjection to physicality, the cat driven from the bench has a contrasting referential status: it works on conception by remaining a literal creature rather than a figure for human embodiment. Two more such creatures, capon and pig, are invoked as the friar orders his dinner. Cat, capon, and pig are all caught in the tale's net of references to the incompatibility of bodily and spiritual well-being, but all three also remain important as cohabitants in domestic space. When the friar arrives at Thomas's house,

> "*Deus hic!*" quod he, "O Thomas, freend, good day!"
> Seyde this frere, curteisly and softe.
> "Thomas," quod he, "God yelde you! Ful ofte
> Have I upon this bench faren ful weel;
> Heere have I eten many a myrie meel."
> And fro the bench he droof awey the cat,
> And leyde adoun his potente and his hat,
> And eek his scrippe, and sette hym softe adoun.
>
> (III.1770–77)

The thanks of this frequent guest veer toward presumptuousness as he invokes merry meals of the past and settles down comfortably (in three clauses no less) next to his suffering bedridden host. Several small disturbances to Thomas's domestic space—the fleeing cat, the setting down of hat, staff, and scrip, the settling in, the expectation of a meal—are preliminary to the friar's speeches of "false dissymulacioun" (III.2123).

But the fleeing cat is different from the scene's other moving parts; the cat exceeds bench, scrip, hat, staff, and meal in having a capacity for displeasure. The full satiric effect of the friar's entrance is available only when the cat represents a sentient living cat. When the tale's cat evokes the unequivocal displeasure of living domestic cats as they are displaced from a favored seat, his displeasure seconds Thomas's displeasure, redoubling the effect of disturbance to domestic space. The awareness of this double disturbance arises not from the reader's sensitivity to figuration but instead from the reader's knowledge of ordinary housecats. As a creature rather than as a sign, the displaced cat intensifies the comedy of oblivious selfishness: for Friar John, upsetting a household is irrelevant in comparison to the "myrie meal" he is anticipating.

The friar's menu choices offer the other point in *The Summoner's Tale* when animals contribute to meaning as animals, alongside their figuration of the problematic of human embodiment. Thomas's wife inquires "What wol ye dyne?" (III.1837) and the friar provides one of his glorious *glosing* answers:

> "Now, dame," quod he, "now *je vous dy sanz doute,*
> Have I nat of a capon but the lyvere,
> And of youre softe breed nat but a shyvre,
> And after that a rosted pigges heed—
> But that I nolde no beest for me were deed—
> Thanne hadde I with yow hoomly suffisaunce.
> I am a man of litel sustenaunce;
> My spirit hath his fostryng in the Bible.
> The body is ay so redy and penyble
> To wake, that my stomak is destroyed."
> (III.1838–47)

The friar's mask of politesse and abnegation slips up and down as he struggles to conceal his bodily appetites behind his faked commitment to the spirit. He manages to begin by asking for little, but not by asking for plain; his attempt at the French elegance of a gourmet (just a little chopped liver) yields in a breath to the gross pleasures of a gourmand (and a whole pig's head). Presumably the head is that of "oure boor, lyth in oure sty," a substantial part of the household's wealth that Thomas's wife has unfortunately mentioned as she described her husband's groans. The friar now deploys three tactics to control his failure of control: declaring the indulgent meal to be no more than "hoomly suffisaunce"; rolling out one of his fictions that the spirit controls the body in his religious practice; and demurring that he would not want any beast to die on his account—"I nolde no beest for me were deed."[3] This is a very odd assertion. The friar's other self-presentations tend toward cliché, masking his deceptions with innocuous commonplaces: "I walke and fisshe Cristen mennes soules," "My spirit hath his fostryng in the Bible," "We han this worldes lust al in despit" (III.1820, 1845, 1876). No such commonplace is in circulation that animals should not die to provide dinner.

To be sure, *The Summoner's Tale* is structured around the commonplace that spiritual and bodily engagements are mutually exclusive. In Christian practice, this conviction gave rise to asceticisms in diet, dress, and devotions. The point of such abnegation in Christian teachings is spiritual advancement, not the protection of nonhuman animals from death. In declaring that "I nolde no beeste for me were deed," Friar John is shifting away from the conventional ideological structure for abstinence—that spirituality is superior to earthly engagements—to a new ideological ground—that a superior spirituality would not will the death of a beast.

This idea is most likely to have come into Friar John's stock of pious dissimulations from the teachings of Saint Francis, although I have found no trace of it in Franciscan texts. Scholars have noted a few clues that the Summoner's friar may be a Franciscan.[4] Like other fraternal and monastic orders, Franciscans were abstemious in their diets rather than animal-protectionist. But the *First Life of St. Francis* by Thomas of Celano offers a pattern of animal protection in Francis's life. The saint is said to have cherished rabbits rescued from snares, admonishing one of them, "Why did you allow yourself to be deceived like this?" He "was moved by the same tender affection toward fish, too, which, when they had been caught, and he had the chance, he threw back into the water, commanding them to be careful lest they be caught again." He rescued lambs from slaughter and had them raised by one of his supporters,

---

[3] The shift in mood from indicative "have I" at III.1839 to conditional "I nolde" at III.1842 hedges or hesitates about the protestation even as it is put on the table. He does not intend that Thomas's wife should put down the cleaver, only that she should recognize his wonderful holiness.

[4] *The Summoner's Tale* in *Riverside Chaucer*, explanatory notes to lines III.1755, 1770, 2186–87.

"and he commanded him not to sell them at any time, nor to do them any harm, but to keep them, feed them, and take care of them conscientiously."[5]

The *First Life* however does not formulate these anecdotes into a teaching on whether or not to eat animals, nor do any of these anecdotes survive into Thomas's *Second Life*. Moreover, Thomas adds in the *Second Life* a bizarre anecdote in which Francis endorses universal meat eating: one year when Christmas fell on a Friday and Brother Morico suggested that the brothers should abstain from eating meat that day, Francis objected, " 'You sin, Brother, calling the day on which the Child was born to us a day of fast. It is my wish,' he said, 'that even the walls should eat meat on such a day, and if they cannot, they should be smeared with meat on the outside.' "[6] In sum, Friar John's principle "I nolde no beest for me were deed" is consonant with the behavior of Francis in the *First Life,* but the *First Life* does not overtly cast this unorthodoxy as a principle of conduct, and the *Second Life* seems at pains to suppress even the latent principle in its revised account of Francis's life and works.

Friar John, I propose, is echoing a Franciscan teaching that survived orally from the founder's lifetime into the fourteenth century but did not survive in the order's authorized texts—a teaching that killing animals is contrary to spiritual love. Oral circulation could explain how this unorthodox principle has joined the friar's repertoire of dissimulations: he is not inventing a whole new standard of pious behavior but borrowing it, along with his more commonplace pieties, from his Franciscan milieu. Like his familiar "My spirit hath his fostryng in the Bible," his unorthodox "I nolde for me no beest were deed" is well suited to camouflaging his self-indulgence, but the latter invokes a spirituality so radical that it has left no official trace. By this principle, eating animals is not consonant with spirituality because it involves taking animal lives. Friar John invokes life and death as the only relevant difference between his hostess's "softe breed" and the capon and pig. His hesitation about killing, reminiscent of Francis's earliest biography and perhaps taken from

[5] Thomas of Celano, *First Life of St. Francis,* trans. Placid Hermann, in *St. Francis of Assisi: Writings and Early Biographies: English Omnibus of the Sources for the Writings of St. Francis,* ed. Marion A. Habig, 4th rev. ed. (Chicago: Franciscan Herald Press, 1983), 279, 280, 295 (paragraphs 60, 61, 79).

[6] Thomas of Celano, *Second Life of St. Francis,* trans. Placid Hermann, in *St. Francis of Assisi: Writings and Early Biographies,* 521–22 (paragraph 199).

Franciscan oral tradition, propels the reader into a little vortex of ethical questions: Should animals die for dinner? Would it be better for our spiritual health if they did not? How should animal life be valued? Capon and pig are swept up in illustrating the friar's gluttony, but they also enjoy this startling moment of significance as, precisely, a capon and a pig whose life and death are a subject for reflection. Friar John opens this ethical chasm beneath his feet, then steps quickly back to safer ground by professing moderation: his envisioned meal is just "hoomly suffisaunce" and "litel sustenaunce."

The capon and pig, like the cat leaping from the bench, diagnose the friar's spiritual weakness specifically through their embodied vulnerability. But Chaucer evokes these creatures' presence before and after Friar John's intrusion as well, as members of a household that encompasses domestic animals. "Oure boor, lyth in oure sty" is out there grunting and the cat is enjoying a favorite spot on the bench when Friar John shows up. The friar's visit interrupts the progress of several lives. Just as Thomas is not merely a diagnostic for the friar's heedless selfishness but also a man in pain, so too his creatures have that doubled status of revelatory figures and sentient beings. Attending to both statuses intensifies the satire and deepens the seriousness of the friar's depiction.

"rather be used / than be eaten"?
Harry Bailly's Animals and
The Nun's Priest's Tale

Gillian Rudd
University of Liverpool

I N 1975, UMBERTO ECO TRAVELED IN HYPERREALITY, visiting in passing the San Diego zoo. This zoo was, according to him, "unquestionably the one where the animal is most respected. But it is unclear whether this respect is meant to convince the animal or the human."[1] Respect and conviction continue to trouble animal studies as we are repeatedly encouraged to examine what respect entails, how it is best expressed, or, in Jacques Derrida's case, to examine the anxiety attendant upon suspecting that the cat who shares his bathroom may not respect him at all.[2] Likewise, to posit that animals might need convincing is to admit that they are capable not just of complex thought processes but also of skepticism. But of what is it that we and the animals are to be convinced? Our similarity? Our difference? Or that in persisting in thinking in terms of similarity and difference we persist in an error of understanding both of what it means to be human and to be animal? Marianne Dekoven's record of her "visceral" experience at the San Diego zoo, which made her aware of the possibility of a "two-way interaction with the animals," refracts her reading of Eco and Derrida, but also indicates that there are many for whom such an experience is still revelatory, or even yet to come.[3] Over and again, as the work of

---

[1] Umberto Eco, *Travels in Hyperreality,* trans. William Weaver (London: Picador, 1986), 49.

[2] Jacques Derrida, "The Animal That Therefore I Am (More to Follow)," trans. David Wills, in *Critical Inquiry* 28 (2002): 369–418. Although highly influential, the unremittingly anthropocentric (if not Derrida-centric) stance of this piece renders it problematic to animal studies.

[3] Marianne Dekoven, "Why Animals Now?" Guest column in *PMLA* 124.2 (March 2009): 361–69 (366).

Studies in the Age of Chaucer 34 (2012):325–30
© 2012 The New Chaucer Society

Erica Fudge has shown, humans are exercised by where we may draw the line between us and the rest of the animal world and, having drawn it, how, why, when, and where we may then cross or blur that line.[4] Various tropes have been used to portray this process, from binary opposition to dividing abyss, from human-animal continuum to a sliding scale of anthropomorphism. Each of these is open to refinement: following Julia Kristeva, binary opposition admits expansion into a third term, the abject, where the animal may be found alongside those humans or human attributes deemed beyond taboo; thanks to Susan Crane, we are no longer restricted to sliding up and down a continuum, but may rather oscillate between terms that themselves are not necessarily fixed points on such scales.[5] Yet whatever the terms of the debate, those core elements of respect and conviction are to be found, lurking or explicit, but still unresolved.

Eco also visited the Middle Ages on his travels, describing them as "the root of all our currently 'hot' problems," which is why "it is not surprising that we go back to that period every time we ask ourselves about our origin" (65). No surprise, either, that animal studies and medieval studies should meet. In many cases, such as Derrida's, the exploration of the animal is indeed inspired by questions about human origin or identity. If that is always so, we are stuck indeed, endlessly contemplating our own worth while ostensibly seeking to understand the worth of others. The best we can hope for is that occasional moments of imagination will liberate us from such relentless egocentrism and admit at least the possibility of conceiving of something outside the human that is not dependent upon it, something that may be appreciated without necessarily being valued in terms of its use to humans. However, if such moments do exist, I am not sure we find them in Chaucer. What we do find are some illustrations of the complex animal/human relations that inform our language and habits of thought.

---

[4] See Erica Fudge, *Perceiving Animals* (Basingstoke: Macmillan, 2000), and E. Fudge, R. Gilbert, and S. Wiseman, eds., *At the Borders of the Human* (Basingstoke: Macmillan, 1999).

[5] Derrida refers to and refines his notion of abyss in "The Animal That Therefore I Am," 398–400. Malcolm Pittock explores the animal-human scale in "Animals as People—People as Animals: The Beast Story with Special Reference to Henryson's *The Two Mice* and *The Preaching of the Swallow*," in *Language and the Subject*, ed. K. Simms (Amsterdam: Rodopi, 1997), 163–72. Kristeva presents her concept of the abject in *The Powers of Horror*, trans. Leon S. Roudiez (New York: Columbia University Press, 1982). Susan Crane offers the term "oscillation" in "Chivalry and the Pre/Postmodern," *postmedieval* 2.1 (2011): 69–87 (70).

The Host's heavy-handed humor that bookends *The Nun's Priest's Tale* offers two examples of the way animals routinely figure in our human habits of thought and language. In the first instance, Harry Bailly makes mocking reference to the "jade" (VII.2812) on which the Priest rides. In the immediate context of the exchange between Host, Knight, Monk, and Nun's Priest, the rather overhearty exhortation not to be cast down because he rides a poor horse creates a silent contrast between the Priest's comparative poverty and lack of worldly status and the affluent Knight, whose "horse was good" (I.74). Susan Crane has recently drawn our attention to the way horses in particular are regarded almost as prosthetics for a knight.[6] That reading could be extended to the Priest here, leading us to consider the ways in which this rather less than impressive horse is just as much of an additional limb for the Priest as the charger is for the Knight. Indeed Harry Bailly's jocular consolation hinges on the fact that the nag may look unimpressive, but as long as she can fulfill her function, that's all that matters. The point may be decoded further, leading to comments on the Priest's unworldly nature—as he is not troubled by the look of his mount, or his poverty, since he cannot afford a better—and to his mild nature as he does not rise to the Host's gibe. All such readings are valid enough, but they appropriate the horse into the human social world so fully that the actual beast all but disappears from view. Importantly, though, this is an actual beast: the horse is present, and while its age and condition may be read as reflecting on its rider in a variety of ways, it remains a real horse even if it is also offered up as a metaphor.

The second example forms the core of the Host's response to this tale and is both more obvious and less literal, at least on the surface. Harry Bailly's laddish term "trede-foul" (VII.3451) apparently compliments the Priest for being a fine specimen of virile manhood, while highlighting the fact that his post forbids him exercising his libido, however strong it may be. Given that opening remark about the broken-down horse, though, there is also the possibility of another, more snide, interpretation: that the Nun's Priest is in fact incapable of any "fowltreading." In contrast to those opening barbed remarks on the jade, the simile that shapes his concluding words does not have an actual, physically present referent (there is no real bird on the road). Not that that is necessary for the simile to work, far from it. The point of the "trede-

---

[6] Ibid., 76.

foul" reference is that it invokes the "what everyone knows" of received knowledge that makes up "cockerel," without being troubled by too much direct knowledge of the species in question, let alone an individual bird. It is worth noting that the choice of the generic "fowl" for this simile reflects the world of the tale just heard, subtly contributing to the blurring of boundaries between the clearly fictional frame of the beast fable about Chaunticleer and the familiar references to animals that make up our daily linguistic "real" world. Harry's speech illustrates how much our ways of talking about being human rely upon animals as referents, metaphorical or not. But it also reinforces the divide human/ animal that designates animal behavior as both enviable and not quite respectable when performed by a human.

Harry's two animal allusions seem very different at first sight. In the first, the animal referred to is physically present and it is that particular horse's appearance that enables his comments about its rider. In the second, the bird is not present, not even figuratively as Chaunticleer, although that link exists. This difference in the presence or absence suggests a level of contrast that is not in fact as marked as it may appear. At bottom, both these uses of the animal are metaphorical and both deny the animal in question any agency or self-identity—this despite the fact that in each case it is what the animal *does* that provides the point of comparison and thus its linguistic value. The jade's looks are an important element, but the crucial thing is whether or not she "goes," while it is "going" of a rather different kind that is key to the "trede-foul" quip. So while it is tempting to think in terms of a sliding scale with these two examples acting as opposite end points (real and physically present horse—generic and absent fowl), we must also acknowledge that they share the common ground of being useful to the Host only for how they are made to reflect human characteristics and identity. These two instances are thus prime examples of the human habit of appropriating the animal world across the board, from language to physical life.

The Host takes human precedence for granted in his thoroughgoing anthropocentric world, which is surely the world Chaucer inhabited, and *The Nun's Priest's Tale* is likewise thoroughly human-centered. In this familiar fable, all the animals are part of the human domestic sphere, including the fox, who may not be domesticated, but who is very much part of a chicken-keeper's world since the need to guard against foxes is a recognized element of keeping hens. The fox is interpolated into the human world twice over: metaphorically by being part of a beast fable with the whole Reynard tradition behind him, and literally by entering the chicken run. Within the fable, as we would expect, the animal bodies shift seamlessly between being physically accurate for their species and being in effect human bodies with animal additions. This leads to some contradictory details, as when, human-fashion, the fox carries the cock on his back (VII.3334, 3405) while also holding him, foxlike, in his mouth, made apparent when Chaunticleer "brak from his mouth" (VII.3416). Such fluctuation between human and animal partly dissolves the divide between humans and others, but the very familiarity of such fluctuation allows us to maintain a double-think that means we can attribute the "human" aspects of the animals concerned to their role in a fable, rather than admitting that responses we call "human" are not exclusive to our species. However, there are other animals in this tale whose reactions to events take for granted a common human/animal response. In this group also are humans whose presence is every bit as generic as that of the animals—we do well to remember that not every human who appears in a tale is an individual.

As the reactions of Eco, Derrida, and Dekoven show, how we speak of animals reflects not just how we see them but also how we think they see us, where "see" is both visual and cognitive. In fact, it is less a matter of how we speak/write *of* animals as of how we speak/write *with* them. The scene of chaos toward the end of *The Nun's Priest's Tale* is a case in point. Animals not previously mentioned in the fable are drawn into a confusion in which some are reacting to the fox and others simply to the uproar. The final rhetorical flourish is to liken this melee of animals and humans to Jack Straw, the 1381 rebels, and the Flemings they wished to kill; a simile in which humans are not being compared to animals, but animals to humans. The analogy allows comparisons to flow in both directions while the comic intent masks a rather disturbing attitude. It is superficially funny to align panicking Flemish and Jack Straw rebels to flapping, squawking birds and stampeding beasts; on the next level, it betrays a callous lack of concern for the people involved, who are dismissed as merely distressed livestock; finally, there is a yet more serious bottom note in that all these animals owe their existence to being livestock; their role is to provide food or goods in the form of milk, eggs, wool, and finally their own carcasses, as they are the livelihood of the widow, her daughters, and, presumably, the other villagers. The hullabaloo of lines VII.3375–401 gives us both literal

329

animals fleeing an unidentified fear in a heightened moment of stock comedic uproar and terrified humans caught up in a riot. The moment is fleeting; the beasts begin as literal animals in a moment of slapstick chaos, but are immediately slewed sideways into an analogy that makes the actual animals disappear behind the terrified Flemish and Jack Straw rebels. These people are in turn swiftly set aside as mere comic matter in a fast-paced conclusion to a lively fable, but we may now be left to ponder that all of those mentioned in this depiction of chaos are there to be consumed, literally or metaphorically; actually and/or economically.

Meanwhile, cock and fox end the tale in a cameo in which their animal physical forms are visually present, but their competing moral interpretations of events leave them at one remove from these animal selves. It is in this thoroughly metaphorical mode that Chaucer's Priest leaves us, knowing that to read his tale simply as "a folye, / As of a fox, or of a cok and hen" (VII.3438–39) is impossible. Perhaps, in this day, we could take as the lesson not Chauntecleer's assertion nor Russell's warning, but Gillian Hanscombe's parenthetical comment in her poem "Sometimes seeing is l/ike": [7]

> (If they could
> choose, they'd rather be used
> than be eaten, rather be metaphors).

---

[7] Gillian Hanscombe, "Sometimes seeing is l/ike daffodils or lilac," in Suniti Namjoshi, *The Blue Donkey Fables* (London: Women's Press, 1988), iii.

The Animals of the Hunt and the Limits of Chaucer's Sympathies

David Scott-Macnab
University of Johannesburg

WHEN DRYDEN DESCRIBES the multifarious collection of characters that Chaucer assembled for the pilgrimage to Canterbury, he declares himself overwhelmed by the sheer diversity of the group and the strongly drawn presence of each individual; so much so that he gives up trying to summarize their specific qualities. "But enough of this," he says, "There is such a Variety of Game springing up before me, that I am distracted by my Choice, and I know not which to follow. 'Tis sufficient to say according to the Proverb, that here is God's Plenty."[1] Dryden's admiring observation that "here is God's Plenty" continues to be quoted regularly, especially in popular appreciations of Chaucer,[2] and it may therefore provide a useful starting point for this essay, in which I shall argue that, in contrast with Chaucer's thoughtful and strongly imagined depictions of human characters, his writings show a marked lack of sympathy for animals as quarries of the hunt. Such creatures, I shall argue, fail to engage Chaucer's empathetic imagination, and consequently (and ironically) fail to contribute to the totality of one's sense of "God's Plenty" in his work. From an ecocritical perspective, this constitutes what may be termed a "significant silence" in Chaucer's overall achievement, and one that can be thrown into sharp relief by other works in which such silence is broken.

I shall begin by observing that, for a writer who displays so much curiosity and knowledge about so many aspects of the world, Chaucer appears to be only passingly interested in the sport of hunting and even

---

[1] John Dryden, *Fables Ancient and Modern; Translated into Verse from Homer, Ovid, Boccace, & Chaucer* (London: Jacob Tonson, 1700), Preface (n.p.).

[2] For example, Joan Acocella, "All England: 'The Canterbury Tales' Retold," *New Yorker* (December 21 and 28, 2009), 140–45 (140).

Studies in the Age of Chaucer 34 (2012):331–37
© 2012 The New Chaucer Society

less concerned with hunting as a means of subsistence. One looks to Chaucer in vain for anything like the extended accounts of deer, boar, and fox hunts found in *Sir Gawain and the Green Knight,* the meticulous stalking of the stag described in the *Parlement of the Thre Ages,* or Arthur's strenuous pursuit of a boar in *The Avowynge of Arthure.* This is not to say that Chaucer is ignorant of contemporary hunting practices; on the contrary, as I have argued elsewhere, Chaucer's hunting lexicon shows that he was as well acquainted with the technicalities of the aristocratic sport as he was with other specialized subjects, from astronomy to law to rhetoric.[3] Such knowledge is apparent in numerous passing references to hunting that are scattered throughout Chaucer's work, such as his statement concerning the Monk that, "Of prikyng and of huntyng for the hare / Was al his lust" (I.191–92); the simile in *The Merchant's Tale* revealing that the sly Damian "gooth as lowe / As evere dide a dogge for the bowe" (IV.2013–14); and Pandarus's advice to Troilus to "hold the at thi triste clos, and I / Shal wel the deer unto thi bowe dryve" (II.1534–35).[4] Powerfully evocative as such allusions are, they do not constitute accounts of hunts, and in this regard it is noteworthy that the only hunts that Chaucer does describe in any detail are hart hunts; furthermore, there are only three of them, all remarkably brief. These are to be found, in chronological order, in *The Book of the Duchess* (c. 1369: 372–86), *The Legend of Good Women* (c. 1386: 212–17), and *The Franklin's Tale* (c. 1395: V.1189–94). Together, these descriptions of hunts add up to a mere twenty-seven lines in Chaucer's entire oeuvre, which is considerably less than the eighty-one lines devoted to the first day's hunting in *Sir Gawain and the Green Knight* (1150–77, 1319–71).

Of course, Chaucer's tally could be increased by including Theseus's hunt in *The Knight's Tale* (I.1673–95), but the problem with that passage is that most of it is devoted to the preparations and anticipation of the event, and it is unclear whether the hunt itself ever gets properly under way. I have also excluded from my tally those lines in *The Book of the Duchess* and *The Legend of Good Women* leading up to the hunts proper,

---

[3] See, for example, my " Re-examination of Octovyen's Hunt in *The Book of the Duchess,*" *MÆ* 56 (1987): 183–99; " 'Of prickyng and of huntyng for the hare': General Prologue to *The Canterbury Tales* I 191," *JEGP* 104 (2005): 373–84; "Polysemy in Middle English *embosen* and the Hart of *The Book of the Duchess,*" *LSE* 36 (2005): 175–94.

[4] All references to Chaucer are to *The Riverside Chaucer,* gen. ed. Larry D. Benson, 3rd ed. (Boston: Houghton Mifflin, 1987). The dates given for Chaucer's works below are those postulated by this edition.

since I am concerned here with Chaucer's depictions of hunting itself, and his treatment of the quarries in each of those hunts.[5] For what is striking in this regard is that Chaucer shows no sympathy for the animals that are to be run down or shot down and no imaginative engagement with their plight.

My point can be demonstrated more effectively by directly comparing Chaucer's words in the relevant passages:

The Book of the Duchess (372–86):

Whan we came to the forest syde,
Every man dide ryght anoon
As to huntynge fil to doon.
The mayster-hunte anoon, fot-hot,
With a gret horn blew thre mot
At the uncouplynge of hys houndes.
Withynne a while the hert yfounde ys,
Yhalowed, and rechased faste
Long tyme; and so at the last
This hert rused and staal away
Fro alle the houndes a privy way.
The houndes had overshote hym alle
And were on a defaute yfalle.
Therwyth the hunte wonder faste
Blew a forloyn at the laste.

The Legend of Good Women (1212–17):

The herde of hertes founden is anon,
With "Hay! Go bet! Pryke thow! Lat gon, lat gon!
Why nyl the leoun comen, or the bere,
That I myghte ones mete hym with this spere?"
Thus seyn these yonge folk, and up they kylle
These bestes wilde, and han hem at here wille.

The Franklin's Tale (1189–94):

He shewed hym, er he wente to sopeer,
Forestes, parkes ful of wilde deer;

---

[5] I have accordingly also excluded the brief account of Cenobia's exploits in the wild in *The Monk's Tale* (VII.3445–52), as this does not refer explicitly to hunting. Likewise, the short comparison in *The Romaunce of the Rose* in which the narrator is said to be

> Ther saugh he hertes with hir hornes hye,
> The grettest that evere were seyn with ye.
> He saugh of hem an hondred slayn with houndes,
> And somme with arwes blede of bittre woundes.

It may immediately be seen that these episodes fall into two distinct categories: one comprising hunts that are directed at herds of harts (*The Legend of Good Women* and *The Franklin's Tale*) and the other (*The Book of the Duchess*) the pursuit of a single hart with hounds. The latter is the hunt *par force,* or "with strength," the most prestigious form of the medieval hunt, and one that was practiced as an elaborate ceremony.[6] I shall deal with *The Book of the Duchess* first, for in such an individualized hunt we may reasonably expect some sense of the battle of wits and energies that made hunting the hart *par force* such a popular sport; or some sense of the concomitant desperation and exhaustion of the harried quarry. Yet it is plain to see that Chaucer's imaginative gaze fails to take account of the experiences of the hart as quarry. While plenty of attention is devoted to the preparations of the excited hunting party (344–71), the hart is described in the most perfunctory, impersonal manner as having been found and pursued with shouts and horn calls for a long time before stealing away "Fro alle the houndes a privy way," and so forcing an abrupt halt to proceedings. In short, in *The Book of the Duchess,* Chaucer simply does not engage with the ordeal of being hunted from the perspective of the quarry itself.

The same is true of Chaucer's two massed hunts, which is probably to be expected on account of their being shorter and so less likely to accommodate narrative complexity. Indeed, in both episodes, the hunted harts, by their anonymous multiplicity, and by the brevity of Chaucer's descriptions, are figured in the most rudimentary way. In Dido's hunt in *The Legend of Good Women,* Chaucer's narrative focus takes in the herd of harts only glancingly. After capturing the energetic hue and cry of the event in a single line devoted to hunting calls (1213), Chaucer shifts his attention to the frustrations of the vigorous youths taking part in the hunt, revealing that, for them, a herd of harts is a

---

hunted by the God of Love as if he were a deer (1449–54), and the fleeting reference to Troilus's hunting in *Troilus and Criseyde,* III.1780: neither passage provides an actual description of hunting.

   [6] See also Marcelle Thiébaux, *The Stag of Love: The Chase in Medieval Literature* (Ithaca: Cornell University Press, 1974), 21–40; John Cummins, *The Hound and the Hawk* (London: Weidenfeld and Nicolson, 1988), 32–46.

poor substitute for the lions or bears that they would prefer to encounter heroically with their spears. There is thus no space here for contemplating the potential miseries of the "bestes wilde" that these youths kill and "han . . . at here wille" (1217). Turning to Chaucer's account of the illusion of a hunt presented to Aurelius in *The Franklin's Tale,* we find that this, too, presents its harts distantly and anonymously, revealing only that they have "hornes hye, / The grettest that evere were seyn with ye," and that "somme with arwes blede of bittre woundes." The animals in both these hunts are little more than emblematic figures occupying elaborate tableaux, much as they do in Paolo Uccello's *The Hunt in the Forest,* or the Cranachs' paintings of the stag hunts of the electors of Saxony, and they are treated with comparable emotional detachment.[7]

Although sympathy with the plight of hunted animals is not widespread in medieval English literature, it can be shown to be strongly imagined when it does occur. A particularly poignant example is the short, anonymous poem known as "The Mourning of the Hunted Hare," which purports to recount the long lament of a hare over the hardships of its life. The hare declares its life to be one long torment, leading it to plead:

> Dere-worth god, how schal I leve
> And leyd my lyve in lond?
> Frov dale to doune I am i-drevfe;
> I not where I may syte or stond![8]

The hare proceeds to describe how it is tormented by hunters, including on Sundays and in winter snow, and how it is driven away from vegetable gardens by cursing housewives bearing staves. In short,

---

[7] Uccello's *The Hunt in the Forest* (c. 1460) in the Ashmolean Museum, Oxford. *The Stag Hunt of the Elector Frederick the Wise* (1529) by Lucas Cranach the Elder and *The Stag Hunt of the Elector John Frederick of Saxony* (1544) by Lucas Cranach the Younger are in the Kunsthistorisches Museum, Vienna.

[8] Rossell Hope Robbins, ed., *Secular Lyrics of the XIVth and XVth Centuries* (Oxford: Clarendon Press, 1952), no. 119 (107–10), lines 5–8. I use the title in the *New Index of Middle English Verse,* ed. Julia Boffey and A. S. G. Edwards (London: British Library, 2005), no. 559. I quote from the long version of the poem (found in National Library of Wales, MS Brogyntyn II.1 [*olim* Porkington 10], fols. 81v–83v], Robbins, *Secular Lyrics,* 107–10. I have made small editorial adjustments, such as using capital *F* in place of the editor's *ff,* by removing unnecessary hyphens in words such as *A-non, a-waye, vp-on,* and by silently correcting *world* in line 57.

> There is no best in þe world, I wene,
>> Hert, hynd, buke ne dowe,
> That suffuris so myche tene
>> As doth þe sylly wat—go where he go.
>>> (57–60)

Paradoxically, the hare is grateful for the pride and sporting instincts of gentlemen, who will never beat it to death with a vulgar club. Consequently, "Of all þe men þat beth alyue / I am most behold to genttylmen!" (67–68). Even so, the hare remains well aware of the ignominious end that awaits it:

> As sone as I can ren to þe laye,
>> Anon þe greyhondys wyl me have;
> My bowels beth i-þrowe awaye,
>> And I ame bore home on a stavfe.
> Als son as I am come home,
>> I ame i-honge hye vpon a pyne,
> With leke-wortes I am eette anone,
>> And whelpes play with my skyne!
>>> (69–76)

Returning to Chaucer, it will be seen that the closest that he comes to expressing comparable awareness of a harried quarry's plight is in *The Shipman's Tale*, when the concupiscent monk, Daun John, in his first moves to seduce his hostess, jokes about old husbands, comparing them to weary hares that have been pursued by hounds all night:

> "Nece," quod he, "it oghte ynough suffise
> Fyve houres for to slepe upon a nyght,
> But it were for an old appalled wight,
> As been thise wedded men, that lye and dare
> As in a fourme sit a wery hare,
> Were al forstraught with houndes grete and smale."
>> (VII.100–105)

The adjectives "wery" and "forstraught" amply suggest the anguish of the frightened, exhausted animal, but the simile to which these words contribute is lewdly humorous in a way that precludes sympathy for the hare as much as for the fraught husband cowering from his amorously demanding wife.

Turning to the Prologue to *The Legend of Good Women,* it is possible to detect a distant note of pathos when the narrator hears the joyful song of "The smale foules . . . / That from the panter and the net ben scaped," and who now join together to sing in scorn of the fowler who had "hem made awhaped / In wynter, and distroyed hadde hire brood" (F 130–33). But the pathos is faint, for the sorrows of winter are said to be a distant memory, and the fowler with his nets is a rustic figure engaged in a churlish occupation, very remote from the aristocratic hunts that Chaucer describes in the passages examined above.

In conclusion, my observations are not intended as criticism of Chaucer, or an attempt to diminish his achievement. My aim is simply to draw attention to one aspect of his portrayal of the hunt—that locus of violent engagement between human and animal worlds—to point out that even Chaucer's urbane and expansive vision had its limits: that his portrayal of "God's Plenty" goes only so far in certain respects. By confronting this aspect of Chaucer's work, we are forced to consider possible reasons for it, and here I would suggest that Chaucer is probably deferring to the tastes and values of the courtly world for which he so often wrote. While his hart hunts evoke the sense of excitement that made the sport so popular with high-status medieval hunters, they depict nothing of the exhaustion or despair of the quarry itself. It should be apparent that for Chaucer to confront the wretchedness of such animals imaginatively would be to question the priority of his patrons' experiences and, by implication, an entire ideological framework concerning human-animal relations. It is for this reason that ecocritics will look to Chaucer in vain for anything like the sympathetic depiction of the experiences of the hare in the anonymous lyric I examine above.

"We stryve as dide the houndes for the boon": Animals and Chaucer's Romance Vision

David Salter
University of Edinburgh

I N THIS ESSAY, I will examine two brief episodes from *The Knight's Tale* to explore how Chaucer makes use of the comic potential of animals in order to reflect upon the complex and multifarious nature of romantic love. My interest here is not with Chaucer's attitudes toward animals per se; in both of the episodes I will discuss, he draws on highly conventional and proverbial ideas about the animals concerned, which he accepts without question. Rather, focusing on just a couple of passages, I will examine how Chaucer deploys received opinions about animals as a way of opening up new and complicating perspectives on what is perhaps the central concern not just of *The Knight's Tale* itself but of all romance: the resolutely human predicament of being in love. In this way, my focus will be on the way in which the distinctive use of animals in *The Knight's Tale* can shed some light on Chaucer's characteristic attitude toward the genre of romance.

The first of these incidents occurs immediately after the tale's two protagonists, Palamon and Arcite, have fallen in love at first sight with Emelye, whom they both observe from their shared prison cell, as she is gathering flowers in her garden one May morning. During the bitter argument that ensues, as the two knights hotly dispute their competing claims for Emelye, Arcite momentarily appears to adopt a more measured and realistic appraisal of their chances of winning her love:

> And eek it is nat likly al thy lyf
> To stonden in hir grace; namoore shal I;
> For wel thou woost thyselven, verraily,
> That thou and I be dampned to prisoun

Studies in the Age of Chaucer 34 (2012):339–44
© 2012 The New Chaucer Society

> Perpetuelly; us gayneth no raunsoun.
> We stryve as dide the houndes for the boon;
> They foughte al day, and yet hir part was noon.
> Ther cam a kyte, whil that they were so wrothe,
> And baar awey the boon bitwixe hem bothe.
> And therfore, at the kynges court, my brother,
> Ech man for hymself, ther is noon oother.
> Love, if thee list, for I love and ay shal;
> And soothly, leeve brother, this is al.
> Heere in this prisoun moote we endure,
> And everich of us take his aventure.
>
> (I.1172–86)

Here Arcite takes a step back from the intensity of his quarrel with Palamon to offer—through the medium of the briefest of beast fables—a moral commentary on his and his cousin's unhappy predicament. This opens up a radical new perspective on the sudden eruption of conflict between the two knights, who unexpectedly find themselves rivals for Emelye's love. Having both fallen in love with Emelye, the knights level ferocious accusations and recriminations against each other, briefly yielding to a moment of clarity and insight as Arcite becomes aware of just how absurd it is for two prisoners, sentenced to perpetual captivity, to argue over a woman who lives beyond their prison walls, and who is ignorant of their very existence. It is the absurdity of this situation that then suggests to Arcite the exemplary fable of the two dogs arguing over a bone.

The analogy of course is far from flattering for the two knights, for at one and the same time it would seem to reduce them to the level of beasts, and to demean and belittle their romantic attachment—the ennobling love that romance conventionally celebrates—to the level of mere animal appetite. However, it is worth noting that the beast fable that Arcite briefly recounts is one whose moral he does not, or perhaps cannot, follow. Rather than accepting the moral logic of the narrative and dismissing his longing for Emelye as either futile or worthless or both, Arcite chooses to draw a different conclusion, reading into the fable the inevitability of human conflict in the pursuit of individual self-interest. So instead of seeking to reform himself, or at least amend his behavior by reflecting on the exemplary animal tale, Arcite implicitly acknowledges his own animal nature. And then having accepted, as it were, the beast within himself, he concludes his comments in the manner of a typical romance protagonist, by submitting to the spirit of chance or *aventure*, presumably in the hope that, like the archetypal heroes of romance, he will experience a reversal of fortunes and achieve his desired goals.

On one level, this analogy between knightly protagonists and canine scavengers accords with the deeply pessimistic interpretation of the human condition to which *The Knight's Tale* gives such sustained expression. Palamon and Arcite are repeatedly overwhelmed by seething, animalistic passions that they are powerless to control. Particularly when they are engaging in physical combat, the bestial is forever bursting through the veneer of their human civility, paralyzing or at least sabotaging their ability to act rationally. For instance, when fighting in the wooded grove outside Athens toward the end of the second part of the tale, Palamon is compared to a "wood leon" (1656), Arcite to a "crueel tigre" (1657), and the two collectively to "wilde bores" (1658), and these images, and variations on them, recur throughout the narrative. Within the tale, it is the figure of Theseus who seeks to resist these irrational, entropic forces that are constantly threatening to plunge the action into chaos. Theseus attempts to contain and control the knights' brutality and irrationality by insisting that they conduct and mediate their conflict through the civilizing institution of chivalry. One of the ways in which the tale has traditionally been read is in terms of this tension between order and chaos: between the civilizing, socially ameliorating efforts of Theseus and the knights' animalistic passions, which are forever breaking out of the civilizing straitjacket that Theseus seeks to impose on them.

But rather than exploring the ways in which Chaucer uses animals to reflect upon the human condition, what I would like to do in this brief essay is examine what animals can tell us about his understanding of, and his attitudes toward, the genre of romance. If we return, once again, to Arcite's miniature beast fable, what is perhaps worth noting is how, for Arcite—and presumably for Chaucer as well—the comical and the absurd can exist alongside the serious and the morally earnest. The image of two dogs fighting over a bone that ultimately eludes them both, captures on one level the ridiculousness of the knights' predicament, but the comical perspective that it opens up complicates but does not negate the intensity and the seriousness of their feelings for Emelye. And this mixture of emotions and registers, the combination of the intense, the serious, and the comical, is highly characteristic of Chaucer's romance vision. It is evident in that same scene in the wooded grove, where Palamon and Arcite are metaphorically transformed into wild beasts while fighting. Their deadly combat is interrupted by the arrival of Theseus, who having been persuaded to grant the two clemency after initially condemning them to death, then reflects in an extended speech, which he milks for all of its comic potential, upon the universal folly of lovers. And while the speech is too long to quote in its entirety, it is worth considering a short passage from it:

> But this is yet the beste game of alle,
> That she for whom they han this jolitee
> Kan hem therfore as muche thank as me.
> She woot namoore of al this hoote fare,
> By God, than woot a cokkow or an hare!
> But all moot ben assayed, hoot and coold;
> A man moot ben a fool, or yong or oold—
> I woot it by myself ful yore agon,
> For in my tyme a servant [of the God of Love] was I oon.
> And therfore, syn I knowe of loves peyne
> And woot hou soore it kan a man distreyne,
> As he that hath ben caught ofte in his laas,
> I yow foryeve al hoolly this trespaas . . .
>
> (I.1806–18)

It is striking just how swiftly the trajectory of the narrative moves from the single-minded intensity of Palamon and Arcite's mortal combat, through the swift dispatch of Theseus's sentence of execution, to his comic reflection on the lovers' folly, which he recognizes as a universal human phenomenon and that becomes the basis for his show of mercy. The shift in tone from the potentially tragic (with the threat of death hanging over the knights) to the comic is reflected in the narrative's abrupt change in register. What is at first presented as a bitter battle to the death, with the protagonists fighting up to their ankles in blood, comes to be characterized by Theseus in humorous and much more colloquial language as a "jolitee" and "hoote fare." Significantly, to accentuate the absurdity of the scene, Theseus employs a couple of comically deflating and seemingly unromantic images drawn from the animal kingdom: according to Theseus, Emelye is as ignorant as a cuckoo or a hare of the knights' existential struggle to win her love.[1] Just as the two hounds fighting over the bone appeared to be at odds with the serious tone one might expect of courtly romance, so a cuckoo and a hare, proverbial for their foolishness and madness, would seem to be singularly inapposite animals to compare to a courtly lady such as Emelye, who elsewhere in the tale is treated with the utmost reverence and seriousness. When writing about this passage, Beryl Rowland notes that "the lapse from high style to homely colloquialism" that is reflected in the comparison "contributes a flippancy to [Theseus's] speech, which is consistent with his down-to-earth character."[2] But one could argue that it is not just flippancy that Theseus exhibits here. Rather, it can be seen as a mature ability to recognize the absurdity in extreme passion, even as it responds to the knights' very serious investment in their passionate desire. Unlike tragedy, which relies—at least in its more extreme forms—on a uniform high seriousness of tone, it is a defining feature of romance that it is capable of incorporating multiple, and here diametrically opposed perspectives, on the same character or action, without either negating the other.

In the two vignettes I have briefly examined, the comparisons that Chaucer draws between the human and animal worlds would seem deliberately to be made to the detriment of his human characters. In the socially conservative, highly class-conscious milieu of medieval romance, where the animal kingdom was thought to reflect the hierarchies of human society, beasts such as kites, cuckoos, and hares were regarded as plebeian in nature, and so hardly fitting creatures to be compared to the aristocratic protagonists of the genre. Even the two hounds, although traditionally considered fit companions for romance's knightly protagonists, are used as part of the poem's broader strategy of reduction and deflation. Chaucer's use of animals in these two instances enables him to introduce and consolidate the theme of folly into his explorations of erotic desire. Throughout the tale, just as we find in Chaucer's romances more generally, folly—along with the comic situations that arise from it—is treated not only as a defining feature of the

---

[1] The editors of *The Riverside Chaucer*, gen. ed. Larry D. Benson (Boston: Houghton Mifflin, 1987), note that some manuscripts have a variant reading of this line, substituting the phrase "than woot a cukkow *of* an hare" for "than woot a cukkow *or* an hare." Whichever reading we choose, the effect of the line remains the same, puncturing the high seriousness of the situation with the intrusion of the low and the comical.

[2] Beryl Rowland, *Blind Beasts: Chaucer's Animal World* (Kent: Kent State University Press, 1971), 95.

male hero but also as a universal and unavoidable attribute of the human condition. In a way that could be said to anticipate Shakespeare's comedies two centuries later, Chaucer's romances have a breadth and complexity of vision that are able to encompass and integrate startlingly different perspectives, moods, and emotions concerning what it feels like and what it means to be in love. And reflecting the practice of so many late medieval writers, Chaucer can be seen to articulate human truths about the nature of love through animal comparisons.

Ridiculous Mourning: Dead Pets and Lost Humans

Karl Steel
Brooklyn College, City University of New York

O NE MAY DAY, a knight goes out to join a nearby tournament. His wife follows, while their two nurses climb a tower to see the hubbub below, leaving behind both the knight's greyhound and his infant son. Then from a crack in an ancient wall, woken by the noise, an adder emerges and heads for the baby. The adder and dog struggle: the cradle's overturned, the adder wounds and poisons the dog, but the dog finally prevails. When the nurses come home, they find a room covered with blood, the baby nowhere to be seen, and amid all this, the dog, howling with pain. They run away, the knight's wife intercepts them, and they tell her the dog has gone mad and killed the baby. She in turn tells her husband, who rushes home to be met by his dog, who stands and proudly puts its forepaws on the knight's chest. The knight cuts his dog in two and then orders the cradle removed. Seeing the baby underneath, unharmed and happy, "thay fanden alle / How the cas was byfalle, / How the naddir was yslawe / That the grewhound hadde to-drawe" (874–77).[1]

This is the *canis* legend, perhaps best known to medievalists from Stephen of Bourbon's account of the dog-saint Guinefort.[2] The story finds its widest distribution in the many versions of *The Seven Sages of Rome*, where it numbers among several told to caution a father against believing his wife's lies and rashly executing his son.[3] Even in itself, *canis*

---

[1] Jill Whitelock, ed., *The Seven Sages of Rome: Midland Version,* EETS 324 (Oxford: Oxford University Press, 2005).

[2] Jean-Claude Schmitt, *The Holy Greyhound: Guinefort, Healer of Children Since the Thirteenth Century,* trans. Martin Thom (Cambridge: Cambridge University Press, 1983).

[3] For a useful survey of the tradition, see Hans R. Runte, "Canis: The Dog File," *Society of the Seven Sages,* February 21, 2011, http://myweb.dal.ca/hrunte/sss_2.html#Dog.

Studies in the Age of Chaucer 34 (2012):345–49
© 2012 The New Chaucer Society

reaffirms a set of medieval proverbs that distinguish the steady love of dogs from the mutable affections of women.[4]

The knight thus errs by betraying an aristocratic—and interspecies— company of men.[5] But he betrays much more than this: uniquely, in this, the Midlands version of *The Seven Sages,* he goes out into his orchard, finds a fish pond, and "for dule of hys hounde . . . lepe in and sanke to gronde" (884–85). The suicidal knight commits something far worse than self-murder. He absurdly betrays the human community as a whole by treating as a grievable life or even as a friend what should be understood only as a divinely provided tool, like all animals. Irrational animals, Aquinas explains, cannot be the subjects of direct charity: since they lack the free will that would allow them to choose good, humans can wish no good for them; for the same reason, humans can have no authentic friendship with animals; animals' inescapable mortality also bars them from charity, since humans wish other humans charity "based on the fellowship of everlasting happiness."[6]

Had the dog actually killed the baby, the knight would therefore have done right in killing it for the simple reason that in the human system animals are worth less than any human. Their lives do not merit the same respect and certainly not the same mourning. In the terminology of Judith Butler's recent work, frames of representability, like the one Aquinas establishes between humans and animals, divide grievable lives from nonlives, whose loss does no injury or no lasting injury to a community.[7] Like any community, the human community sustains itself as much by the deaths it does not acknowledge as by the deaths it does.

---

[4] Yasmina Foehr-Janssens, "Le chien, la femme et le petit enfant: Apologie de la fable dans *Le roman des sept sages de Rome,*" *Vox romanica* 52 (1993): 147–63, points to the *Roman des deduis,* which observes that "amour de chien n'est pas muable" (a dog's love is not changeable), *Aeneid* IV.569, "mutabile semper femina" (women are always changeable), and the *Folie Tristan* of Oxford, which directly contrasts the nobility of dogs to the trickery of women (155).

[5] For a recent treatment of interspecies chivalric masculinity, see Susan Crane, "Chivalry and the Pre/Postmodern," *postmedieval* 2.1 (2011): 69–87.

[6] Thomas Aquinas, *Summa theologica,* trans. Fathers of the English Dominican Province, 3 vols. (New York: Benziger Bros., 1947), 2a2ae q25, a. 3. For Christian friendship, see James McEvoy, "The Theory of Friendship in the Latin Middle Ages: Hermeneutics, Contextualization, and the Transmission and Reception of Ancient Texts and Ideas, from c. AD 350 to c. 1500," in *Friendship in Medieval Europe,* ed. Julian Haseldine (Stroud: Sutton, 1999), 3–44.

[7] See Judith Butler, *Precarious Life: The Powers of Mourning and Violence* (New York: Verso, 2004), and Butler, *Frames of War: When Is Life Grievable?* (New York: Verso, 2009).

For humans to know themselves as human, what they call animal must be outside the frame.

However, while the knight loves his child dearly, he considers his greyhound "anoþer iuel" (736), his other love. He proves this love by killing himself. The wise horse Bonus Amicus in the *Otia imperialia* kills itself when its master dies.[8] The knight has become like this horse. He grieves like an animal lover, like someone who loves animals, like an animal that loves. In grieving an improper object, the knight splits himself altogether from the human community. His frame has slipped. What he does can make no sense, for outside of this and a handful of other medieval texts—*Bevis of Hampton,* for example—there is no medieval allowance for according any animal the status of "friend" or "sworn brother," categories of classical and medieval chosen kinship that might justify the knight's valuation of his dog above his own family and, especially, above his wife.[9] For the knight to remain himself, which is to say, for him to remain socially legible, he must frame others appropriately. Being in a community, as Sara Ahmed tells us in *The Promise of Happiness,* means following the right happiness scripts: "We can think of gendered scripts as "happiness scripts" providing a set of instructions for what women and men must do in order to be happy, whereby happiness is what follows being natural or good. Going along with happiness scripts is how we get along: to get along is to be willing and able to express happiness in proximity to the right things."[10] So too with humans and animals, humans and pets. Following the script correctly means investing in the right happiness objects and, also, in the right *un*happiness objects, which for the human community requires that animals must die like animals, some regretted and missed, but most unmourned, discarded, and unthought.

In his essay "Pet Grief," Lawrence Rickels describes it sharply: "We keep the individual animal close to us until death opens wide a mass grave. Everyone likes your adorable pet and spends quality time giving the animal an interspecial context for life. But when the loved one goes: shut up and get a replacement." The dead pet is, as Rickels writes, the

[8] Gervase of Tilbury, *Otia Imperialia: Recreation for an Emperor,* ed. and trans. S. E. Banks and J. W. Binns (Oxford: Clarendon Press, 2002), 740–43.

[9] For example, see Robert Stretter, "Rewriting Perfect Friendship in Chaucer's *Knight's Tale* and Lydgate's *Fabula Duorum Mercatorum,*" *ChauR* 37 (2003): 234–52.

[10] Sara Ahmed, *The Promise of Happiness* (Durham: Duke University Press, 2010), 59.

"lost loss,"[11] a death the human community refuses to take seriously. Note, then, the misspelled title of Stephen King's novel *Pet Sematary,* which itself thematizes the peculiarities and presumptive childishness of grieving for pets, as does an online guide to a Pet Cemetery in the Presidio, which calls it "fairly redolent with lugubrious kitsch . . . sweet, disheveled, slightly loonie [*sic*]."[12]

The knight has refused to give up his loss. He lets himself go more than slightly loony. The loss has astonished the knight by compelling him to recognize his shared vulnerability with what the human community can recognize as only a dog. He is shocked to find himself wounded by what he did: to discover himself to be a murderer, and to have murdered what the human system believes only to be killable, if even that. So astonished, he surrenders his legible social existence. He disorients himself from the socially mandated happiness objects. He refuses to be or finds himself unable to remain recognizable as a family man, at least as a member of the exclusively human family. He becomes dead to what had been his world. Even in other versions of the *Seven Sages,* where he exiles himself, he still slips outside the human community's frame of representability to join his dog in nonlife.

Pet love may not be sufficient to challenge human supremacy. If some of our best friends are dogs, pet love may do nothing to impede the violence through which the human sustains itself as human.[13] After all, medieval chivalric self-perception necessarily had room for the love of dogs, horses, and hawks—to a certain point. And pet love can be no certain guide for action. In *The Gift of Death,* Derrida asks "how would you ever justify the fact that you sacrifice all the cats in the world to the cat that you feed at home every morning for years, whereas other cats die of hunger at every instant? Not to mention other people?"[14] The unjustifiable arbitrariness of love might indeed be a perfect form of re-

[11] Laurence A. Rickels, "Pet Grief," in *Diana Thater: Gorillagorillagorilla,* ed. Adam Budak and Peter Pakesch (Cologne: König, 2009), 72.

[12] Dr. Weirde, "Presidio Pet Cemetery Survives Toxic Scare," *Found SF,* October 30, 2011, http://foundsf.org/index.php?title = Presidio_Pet_Cemetery_Survives_Toxic_Scare.

[13] See the critique of the "logic of the pet" by Jonathan Elmer and Cary Wolfe in Cary Wolfe, *Animal Rites: American Culture, the Discourse of Species, and Posthumanist Theory* (Chicago: University of Chicago Press, 2003), 104.

[14] Jacques Derrida, *The Gift of Death,* trans. David Wills (Chicago: University of Chicago Press, 1995), 71. On the injustice of love, see also "Neighbors and Other Monsters: A Plea for Ethical Violence," in Slavoj Žižek, Eric L. Santner, and Kenneth Reinhard, *The Neighbor: Three Inquiries in Political Theology* (Chicago: University of Chicago Press, 2006), 182.

sponsibility, which to be worthy of being called responsibility can follow no pattern and must risk all, without knowing beforehand what it will settle on and without knowing in advance where it can stop.

Judith Butler, like others, speaks of the "transformative effect of loss," whose transformations cannot be known "in advance" or "charted or planned."[15] But within proper frames, there is only so far the transformation can go. When grief has a proper object, there will be rituals and community recognition; here grief finds a home, and the griever will find a home in it. Proper grief—for a fellow human, for a family member, a compatriot, an already known and publicly recognized neighbor—may be a private catastrophe but will do nothing to change the frame. This is a grief with a justifiable object; it makes sense. By contrast, the knight's astonishing grief for a dog that had done everything right might knock askew our human frames. The knight's stupid excess may illustrate the self-abandonment that follows from giving up the presumption of human superiority.

Literature may offer us few sharper examples of the dangers of this responsibility than the pet lover who, like Christ's perfect disciple, hates what had been his family (Luke 14:26). This is a charity that, against Aquinas's teaching, disdains the human. To be sure, given the knight's love for misogynist homosociality, especially given his suicide, what he does cannot simply be imitated or admired. We nonetheless may still find here tools to unthink the human; we may find a way of mourning and unhappiness that, in refusing to be well adjusted, in refusing to go along with the right kinds of happiness and unhappiness, opens "up other possibilities for living,"[16] which must require other possibilities for dying. It requires something other than just asking our companions to go along with us; it requires losing oneself, leaving off human certainty, come what may.

[15] Butler, *Precarious Life*, 21.
[16] Ahmed, *Promise of Happiness*, 79.

The Werewolf's Indifference

Jeffrey J. Cohen
George Washington University

A WEREWOLF IS THE PROBLEM of animal difference expressed in monster's flesh. This compound creature asks how intermixed with the bestial (*-wolf*) the human (*were-*) might already be. All that is civilized, ennobling, and sacred is lost in fleshly tumult with lupine appetites, impulses, and violence. The werewolf would seem the ideal monster to query the suppression of "the animal part within us all."[1] Yet a warning that this monstrous admixture is not so easy to make a universalizing metaphor inheres in the fact that Latin possesses no common noun for the creature. Lycaon might be transformed by an angry god into a wolf, and might (in Ovid's narration) inhabit briefly an interstitial space where he possesses human and bestial qualities, but at transformation's end one term replaces another, *vir* to *lupus.* When Gervase of Tilbury in the *Otia imperialia* is describing men who metamorphose under lunar influence, he observes: "In England we have often seen men change into wolves [*homines in lupos mutari*] according to the phases of the moon. The Gauls call men of this kind *gerulfi,* while the English name for them is *werewolves, were* being the English equivalent of *uir.*"[2] Gervase must employ French and English words to gloss his Latinate circumlocution.[3]

As its etymologically admixed nature suggests, the werewolf is a hy-

---

[1] Joyce E. Salisbury, "Human Beasts and Bestial Humans in the Middle Ages," in *Animal Acts: Configuring the Human in Western History,* ed. Jennifer Ham and Matthew Senior (New York: Routledge, 1997), 9–22. Salisbury is arguing for more sympathy toward the animal within. See also her book *The Beast Within: Animals in the Middle Ages* (New York: Routledge, 1994).

[2] Gervase of Tilbury, *Otia Imperialia: Recreation for an Emperor,* 87–89, I.15.

[3] Although Gervase is dubious about many animal transformations, the werewolves seem to be a true change of body. See the thorough discussion in Leslie A. Sconduto, *Metamorphoses of the Werewolf: A Literary Study from Antiquity Through the Renaissance* (Jefferson, N.C.: McFarland, 2008), 35–38.

brid monster. Caroline Walker Bynum has argued that hybridity is a dialogue in which "contraries are simultaneous and in conversation with each other."[4] The werewolf is therefore not an identity-robbing degradation of the human, nor the yielding to a submerged and interior animality, but the staging of a conversation in which the human always triumphs. Hybridity is therefore a simultaneity of unequal differences. As Karl Steel has demonstrated, this overpowering of animal possibility by human exceptionality is a ceaseless, fraught, and violence-driven process. Humans are made at animal expense. Steel points out that a werewolf's raising the problem of "the animal part that is within us all" is possible only "if humans are understood to have discrete 'animal' and 'human' parts."[5] As idealized differences, these categories need to be produced and stabilized repeatedly: the only way to maintain such separations is through more violence.

As admonitory figures, werewolves would seem to warn us why species difference must remain firm. So keen is the desired division between animal and human that many medieval werewolves are not true composites but humans encased in lupine skin, awaiting liberation. Gerald of Wales describes natives of Ossory cursed by Saint Natalis to don wolf fur and live as beasts. Under these animal garments, their bodies remain unaltered.[6] Two of these transformed Irish villagers announce their appearance to a group of startled travelers with the resonant words "Do not be afraid." Wolf skin is peeled back to reveal an ordinary woman inside. The werewolves deliver a human message, an anthropocentric horror story about being entrapped in an alien encasement. What human would not seek an immediate release from enclosure within such degrading and disjunctive corporeality? If this hybrid form stages a dialogue, the conversation is one-sided. Who speaks the animal's narrative? Who could wish for such a monster's impossibly amalgamated body? Who could desire such a life?

Cursed and pedagogical creatures, werewolves cannot be a happy lot. The citizens of Ossory bewail their compulsion. Yet medieval literature also describes werewolves cheerful in their composite bodies: the clever

---

[4] Caroline Walker Bynum, *Metamorphosis and Identity* (New York: Zone Books, 2001), 160.

[5] Karl Steel, *How to Make a Human: Animals and Violence in the Middle Ages* (Columbus: Ohio State University Press, 2011), 12.

[6] Gerald of Wales, *The History and Topography of Ireland*, trans. John O'Meara (London: Penguin Books, 1982). For an influential treatment of the episode stressing its stabilities of forms, see Bynum, *Metamorphosis and Identity,* 15–18, 106–11.

Alphonse, who teaches the young lovers to disguise themselves in animal skins in *Guillaume de Palerne;* the forest-loving protagonist of *Melion,* who discovers in wolf fur a success never realized while an ordinary husband and vassal; Bisclavret, who when trapped in animal form attains a satisfaction denied as a quotidian knight. Animality is supposed to be a despised state, the abject condition against which humanity asserts itself. The werewolf knows better. This monster inhabits a space of undifferentiated concurrency, in the doubled sense of a *running together* and a *mutual assent.* The werewolf offers neither a conversation (which too easily becomes a conversion) nor a dialogue (weighted in advance toward human domination), but a pause, a hesitation, a concurrence during which what is supposed to be contrastive remains coexistent, in difference, indifferent. Werewolves do not reject the stony enclosure of castles for arboreal wilds. They are not proto-romanticists or early avatars of Bear Grylls. What is most intriguing about the state of unsettled animality that they incarnate is its irreducible hybridity, its ethical complexity, and its dispersive instability, pro-animal yet posthuman.

Perhaps that sounds too affirmative for so fierce a creature. In *Bisclavret,* Marie de France glosses "werewolf" in harsh but familiar terms:

> Garualf, c[eo] est beste salvage:
> Tant cum il est en cele rage,
> Hummes devure, grant mal fait,
> Es granz forez converse et vait.
>
> [A werewolf is a savage beast:
> while his fury is on him,
> he eats men, does much harm,
> goes deep in the forest to live.][7]

Marie vividly describes the bestiality incarnated by this monster, its sylvan existence of uncontrolled violence, even anthropophagy. Who would embrace such animal life? Bisclavret. A well-respected knight four days of the week and a forest-dwelling wolf the other three, Bisclavret is not unhappy. His mistake is to confide the secret of his dual

---

[7] *Bisclavret,* 9–12, in Marie de France, *Lais,* ed. Alfred Ewert, intro. Glyn S. Burgess (Bristol: Bristol Classical Press, 1995); translation from Robert Hanning and Joan Ferrante, *The Lais of Marie de France* (Durham, N.C.: Labyrinth Press, 1978). Further references by line numbers.

nature to his wife. Unlike the werewolves described by Gerald of Wales who don lupine skins, Marie's knight simply removes his clothing and stashes the garments in the hollow of a woodland rock. Once "stark naked" (*tut nu*), he tells his fearful spouse, the following adventure (*aventure*) inevitably arrives:

> Dame, jeo devienc bisclavret:
> En cele grant forest me met,
> Al plus espés de la gaudine,
> S'i vif de preie e de ravine.
>
> (63–66)

> [My dear, I become a werewolf:
> I go into the great forest,
> in the thickest part of the woods,
> and I live on prey I hunt down.]

This account of roaming the forest is significantly less violent than the vision of lycanthropy with which the *lai* opens. The wolf's sustenance in the forest depths is described as *preie,* which could be deer, rabbits, and foxes. Or not. What matters is that unlike the opening gloss, no invitation is extended to consider brutality against specific bodies. Bynum therefore sees a vast difference between the *garvalf,* the Norman word for the savage werewolf of tradition, and Marie's own *bisclavret,* the term of unknown origin that is supposed to be its Breton equivalent.[8] I wonder, though, if these two nouns can be so easily separated and suspect that Marie is up to something more complicated and inventive.

Bisclavret hesitates to reveal his covert life. He fears he will lose his "very self" ("me meïsmes en perdrai") if this secret becomes known. Yet although he admits his second nature to his wife with apprehension, he speaks it without shame. He arrives home from his three wolfen days *joius e liez,* happy and delighted (30). Time in the forest vivifies. His wife is terrified by this knowledge and certain she will never desire to share a bed with him again (102). Feigning passion for a neighbor, she arranges to have Bisclavret's clothing stolen, trapping him in animal form. Bisclavret's anger at his wife is immense, his revenge brutal: when she comes to the court where he has become the king's favorite pet, he bites

[8] Bynum, *Metamorphosis and Identity,* 170–71.

the nose from her face. Torture compels the disfigured woman to reveal her crime, and she admits the stealing of his transfigurative clothes.

Strangely, however, when the vestments are returned to a lupine Bisclavret, he looks upon them with indifference: "he didn't even seem to notice them"(280). A councillor suggests that the former knight is too modest to dress in public. Critics generally find this intratextual interpretation persuasive. Bisclavret's shame signals his readiness to abandon his animality and return to civility. Yet the councillor's words are nonsensical. Why would Bisclavret feel shame? Certainly not at his nakedness: he is covered in fur, and he is refusing to dress, not to strip. The clothing is a potent materialization of his humanity. Why would shame inhere in a return to that superior state? Marie de France's *lais* are usually crafted around densely symbolic objects that might be described as *parabolic,* an adjective for parables (stories) as well as parabolae (curved orbits). To enter into relation with a parabolic object is to be swept into an unexpected narrative that alters the trajectory of one's life, spinning it around a novel center of accelerating gravity. Everything changes at such encounters. These objects are *aventure* in material form: the ship in *Guigemar,* the hawk and sword in *Yonec,* the swan in *Milun.* Why would Bisclavret demonstrate such apathy toward the thing that can restore human being?

Werewolves' bodies are convenient animal vehicles for meditating upon human identity in the Middle Ages. They are theologically rich and pose difficult questions about identity and continuity, as Bynum has shown. They often prove to be less hybrid than they at first appear: unzip the wolf skin and out pops the human who had always been dwelling inside. Werewolves easily become allegories, reaffirming the superiority of the human, their natural dominance and difference. So why would a werewolf, through a dogged lack of interest, suggest he is at home in a shaggy form? Could it be that Bisclavret is simply indifferent to a return to quotidian humanity, and thus offers no reaction at all to these powerfully symbolic accoutrements?

As a knight, Bisclavret is noble and loved. His three days spent prowling the forests in a wolf's body detracted nothing, and he returns home refreshed. The forest is a place of privacy. He resists telling his wife about his lupine sojourns because he fears the loss of that space, her love, his selfhood. He places his clothing in the hollow of a rock by an ancient chapel to gain something that he knows imperils his life as husband and neighbor: a space inhuman (lived among vegetation and beasts, filled with violence but also shared with trees, other animals, stones) and innovative (he creates and sustains a precarious existence). This hybrid space is also too easily annexed back into the orbit of ordinary human lives. Bisclavret in his wolf body earns the king's affection through an act of submission, kissing the monarch's stirrup and making his readiness to serve visually evident. Well fed and watered, full of proper submission but also ready to unleash proper violence, he is at once like a favorite hunting dog and like a good household knight. He learns the equivalence between two forms that seemed mutually exclusive, learns their indifference.

Immediately upon his restoration, Bisclavret is beheld asleep upon the royal bed. His wife—the one who did not want him in her bed any more—is banished. Her female children inherit her noselessness, an infinitely repeating historical sign of the misogyny that has limned this tale, with its closing vision of a thoroughly homosocial world. And perhaps with that trading of one dreary bed for another we realize the reason for Bisclavret's unresponsiveness to the offered clothing. He returns from his wolf's form to a startlingly familiar scene, one that he thought he had trotted away from long ago. How sad his departure from lycanthropy must be, as an ephemeral but invigoratingly uncertain world yields to soft beds and predictable human vistas "a tutdis," *forever.*

Responses

In what Susan Crane described as "scholarly haiku," the colloquium participants offered initial responses to the collected papers in around one hundred words. Those responses are given here without further comment. Full discussion must take place elsewhere, but taken together these responses go some way to indicate the directions open for animal studies in Chaucer and medieval studies generally.

DS-M: Given the symbolic weight that animals are so often made to bear in medieval literature, I think Susan Crane makes an important point in emphasizing that animals are sometimes simply that, rather than figures for something else. Karl Steel's discussion of the knight's response to his murder of his greyhound prompted me to return to medieval hunting manuals to remind myself of the special significance afforded hunting dogs in aristocratic circles—some sense of which may be found in Edward of York's regretful statement (in *The Master of Game*) that "The moost defaute of houndes is þat þei lyuen not longe inowe."

SC: Karl Steel's greyhound offers an ethical as well as an affective challenge. To kill the greyhound may be to sin against love, but it also does an enormous injustice to the hound. The master's awakening to the hound's virtue in contrast to his own injustice contributes to his complete "self-abandonment." Analogously, the "undifferentiated concurrency" of Jeffrey Cohen's werewolf offers a cross-species distribution of justice. Who within *Bisclavret* is punishing the wife—anthropophagous wolf, loyal hound of the king, or wronged husband? For Aquinas, no ethical question can refer to animals, yet these two tales place greyhound and werewolf inside the ethical circle.

DS: Susan Crane's discussion of the cat in *The Summoner's Tale* brings to mind the detail from *The Miller's Tale* of the hole at the foot of Nicholas's bedroom door through which "the cat was wont in for to crepe" (I.3440). Both hint at human lives led in conditions of extremely close proximity, even intimacy, with cats, although the narrators are silent about whether these are simply instances of utilitarian cohabitation based on mutual self-interest, or if the cats' access to the most private of human spaces might imply that there is something more involved: possibly that there is an emotional component to the relationship.

LK: Given the frequency with which our essays address the framing of human identity and the animal/human divide, it is interesting to note how often Chaucer self-identifies with nonhumans (the hound seeking a hare in the *Prioress-Thopas Link,* the puppy in *The Book of the Duchess,* the mouselike prey in the claws of *The House of Fame's* eagle, the caged bird in *The Manciple's Tale,* etc.). He even becomes a kind of plant in his imitation of the daisy's pattern of tracking the sun in *The Legend of Good Women.* Finally, as a "popet," he is only a sign of a human, having no independent life whatsoever. How might we analyze Chaucer's attempts at emptying himself of humanity?

KS: Several essays here seek out those Chaucerian animals irreducible to symbolic appropriation: his cats and polecats, his cervids, and so on. *The Reeve's Tale* offers others: the clerks' horse, disappearing with a "wehee" (I.4066) after wild mares, and the clerks themselves, returning from their chase "wery and weet, as beest is in the reyn" (I.4107). Often lassoed into signifying the tale's wild sexual energy, the horse might instead be seen as nearly escaping the story by following its own desires. As for the clerks, they return as animals: not irrational, but rather vulnerable bodied subjects caught by the weather, whether they like it or not.

JJC: I wonder about what we have all taken for granted . . . or for granite. Jill Rudd observes in her opening remarks that animal comes from *anima,* and marks a creature possessing breath. Dividing animals from humans is therefore an unceasing labor. Separating both from mere minerals is easy. One group is organic and lively, the other inert. Yet as Dorigen suspected when she looked at the coast of Brittany and saw rocks intending harm, medieval people knew that stones are filled with agency. Read any lapidary, and you'll find the inorganic version of a bestiary. If medieval thinkers could find such vivacity in the lithic, why can't we?

GR: David Scott-Macnab's suggestion that Chaucer's hunting elements reflect a court audience made me wonder if they also betrayed Chaucer's more urban than court sympathies. Perhaps, then, the wry comedy Salter observes in the dogs outwitted by the hawk may contain irony at the expense of the courtly class. I was struck by Chaucer's lack of empathy when writing animals, further highlighted by the contrasts offered by Steel and Cohen. Chaucer seems to access the animal only from within a securely human viewpoint; when his attention is elsewhere, the animal itself finds more space, as Crane's and Kiser's examples suggest.

REVIEWS

DAVID AERS. *Salvation and Sin: Augustine, Langland, and Fourteenth-Century Theology.* Notre Dame: University of Notre Dame Press, 2009. Pp. xv, 284. $38.00.

David Aers's latest journey toward ecclesiological understanding makes for an intriguing read. In five densely argued and heavily documented chapters, he provides close and passionately engaged readings of Augustine of Hippo on conversion; William of Ockham on grace, predestination, divine power, and the sacraments; Thomas Bradwardine on these same topics in his attacks on the Pelagianism of late fourteenth-century "modern" theology; Julian of Norwich's response to her question "What is synne?" in the context of her theology of agency, redemption, and reconciliation; and, in the longest chapter (and in important ways as an *a priori* concern), William Langland's theology of sin, grace, and agency. The fact that some of these works are in the vernacular is not of primary importance to their analysis here as theological texts. It is, indeed, one of the valuable contributions of Aers's work to demonstrate that all of these texts deserve to be interrogated seriously for their theology (xiii–xiv).

"Theology" is, then, the first of the terms used in the title of the study that requires some clarification: Aers's work in this book is in the field of systematic theology. He is most concerned with the choices authors have made in their arguments touching on the question of agency in the Christian conception of redemption, that is to say, the interplay between divine grace and human action in performing good works in the process of salvation of the human soul. What takes center stage in the analysis are the consequences of these authors' choices and what they say about the authors' standing in Aers's interpretation of the tradition of Christian dogmatics, mainly through Augustine and Aquinas. One will also find Karl Barth quoted here as a primary source defining this tradition alongside medieval authors. It follows, second, that for Aers the word "sin" in the title designates a general state of sinfulness. This conception is not limited to original sin; it includes as well the continuing possibility of the human will to refuse to be drawn to redemption, to act against "the good that is common to all whose source and end is God" (138). But only rarely (see, e.g., 104–5) does the book take into account the exacting and concrete analysis and classification of acts of sinfulness that loom so large in fourteenth-century pastoral thinking. What precisely constitutes a sin, at what precise point an action becomes delegitimized as evil, and what precisely a sinner must do about this to continue in the process of the soul's salvation as a member of the community of the church—these are ever-present and urgent questions in the moral theology of the later Middle Ages, but they are not part of the tight focus of this study.

The procedure Aers follows is to contrast his own views with recent trends in the scholarship of the authors he is investigating that incorrectly problematize the authors' place in the contexts of the Christian tradition emphasized here or that have insufficiently focused on the difficulties of placing the authors within this tradition. Charles Taylor's view of Augustinian radical reflexivity, or semi-Pelagian readings of *Piers Plowman,* belong to the former category; in the latter are Rega Wood on Ockhamite theology, readings of Bradwardine that uncritically apply the term "Augustinian" to his works, and Denise Baker on Julian's "correction" of the medieval Church's "ideology of sin."

The reader will find many searching and important observations here. The consequences of Julian's conception of humanity's two-part soul, a higher portion that remains forever in contact with God, encompassing an unfallen will, and a lower portion that wills to sin, are, as Aers notes, "congruent with the Manichean belief that Augustine recalls" (164). When Julian then equates sinfulness with suffering that cannot transcend itself, rather than with an act of the will turning away from God, the result is a moral vision that shows distinctive differences from common Christian teaching on these topics (157). As Aers further argues, under the pressure of combatting the Pelagian emphasis on human agency in redemption, Bradwardine insisted to such a degree on God's freedom in offering grace that in his theology human action, including that of the priesthood, disappears. The sacrament of penance becomes a sign of prior justification, not the instrument employed by divine power to achieve it (75). This makes grace something extrinsic to human action, and Aers argues that it also sidelines Christology, but these do not seem to be enough as defining elements to warrant claiming that Bradwardine ironically reproduces "key features" of the "modern" theology that characterizes Ockham (79). The dividing line between these two theologians' ideas of redemption is defined more decisively by the wholesale investment in human agency (Ockham) or in divine power (Bradwardine).

What amounts in effect to the path between these extremes is, for Aers, occupied by Augustine and Langland. Recounting Augustine's view of the human will as both acting and being acted on in the process of redemption, Aers notes that the bishop of Hippo's view "pervades my own reflections on salvation, sin, and agency in *Piers Plowman*" (95). In fact, his interpretations of both authors' works suffuse each other in this study. The emphasis on the social implications of sin in Augustine's thought is designed to counter Charles Taylor's identification of an essential "inwardness" there (3–4), and sin as a disruptive force in the community has also been commented on emphatically by Aers in Langland's allegory, a poem that is described here as "profoundly social" (111). Certainly, though, the gaps between Augustine and Langland are just as telling. Aers rejects "semi-Pelagian" readings of the salvation of Trajan in *Piers Plowman,* finding in this episode only a stage of development that points "beyond itself to the later Christological and Trinitarian narratives" (126) more in line with Augustinian conceptions, but surely this episode opens up, rather than forecloses, the possibility of the salvation of the just pagan (cf. esp. C XII.98–99) in ways that go beyond Augustinian thought. In the specifics of their reflections on sin, Augustine and Langland also understandably demonstrate quite divergent interests. The bishop, to take only one example, found ways to reassure the aristocratic Proba that she need not reject her immense possessions and fabulous wealth as a sign of avarice (see *Epistle* 130), while the rich have a much more problematic existence in the community in *Piers Plowman.* Such matters grow out of and have important consequences for the social reach of sin in the communal life of the Church. Although they and other issues concerning sin and salvation in the context of fourteenth-century moral and pastoral theology are largely left in the background, as an engaged analysis of systematic theology *Salvation and Sin* is a valuable and provocative investigation of the authors it focuses on.

RICHARD NEWHAUSER
Arizona State University, Tempe

ANTHONY BALE. *Feeling Persecuted: Christians, Jews and Images of Violence in the Middle Ages.* London: Reaktion Books, 2010. Pp. 254. £29.00; $45.00.

At the beginning of *Feeling Persecuted: Christians, Jews and Images of Violence in the Middle Ages,* Anthony Bale briefly invokes the Grimm brothers' story, "The Boy Who Had to Learn Fear," to suggest that fear is, in part, a performance and "pain rethought as its aesthetic assumption" (9). His book proceeds to examine, with extraordinary scholarly dexterity, all manner of material culture from the eleventh through the fifteenth centuries—including manuscript illuminations, sculptures, building structures, paintings, literary texts—to consider how objects displaying violence by Jews against Christians succeeded in occasioning performances of horror and fear. In fact, Bale's brilliance resides in his ability to look across multiple kinds of medieval media from England, France, Germany, Italy, Spain, and the Low Countries to investigate how these apparatuses were able to engender particular kinds of affective responses, enabling empowered Christians to feel themselves the victims of persecution by Jews, a largely disempowered—often displaced—minority.

Regarding "the book" as a recreational object that could "touch, impress, hurt or wound the reader or viewer" (19), Bale focuses, in his opening chapter, on an illustration from the fourteenth-century Luttrell Psalter, one of the most beautifully illuminated manuscripts of its time. Beneath the directive, "ne timueris," "do not be afraid," the Luttrell manuscript reveals a picture of Jesus, nearly naked and bound to a column, beaten by two Jews. Bale acknowledges that although medieval Jews were typically marginalized, with such depictions medieval Christians imagined themselves spiritually strong but physically weak, easy victims of this predatory, brutal minority culture. He writes, "[T]here is a clear difference between 'actual' power (which medieval Christians almost universally had over Jews) and that which is imagined (in which Christians valorized weakness and martyrdom and represented themselves as under attack from Jews and others)" (24). But what interests him about this picture, and what continues to interest him throughout the remainder of his study of violence, is not so much its political or even social implications. Rather, it is the aesthetic reception that Bale finds of consequence, how medieval Christians would have appreciated "[a] fixed point of purity in a moving sea of cruelty, the superlative beauty and innocence of Christ . . . contrasted with the Jews' foulness" (14). He is interested in the interrelationship between texts and audience, in the various ways reading texts of all varieties allows audience members to nurture miseries they have never endured, even—as with Chaucer's *Prioress's Tale*—to believe themselves imitatively suffering torments of victims that may never have been victimized.

As he pursues this argument, Bale considers the affective influence of images of the Virgin Mary enduring the agony of her son's Crucifixion, morbid medieval lullabies, blood libel narratives, and injunctions against swearing oaths like a Jew—all teaching the medieval Christian to relish and nurture pain, fear, and suffering. He offers up a brief "history of ugliness," commenting on how representations of the Jewish profile function as a kind of shorthand in medieval art and literature to suggest "the tainted or heretic Jewish soul" (65). Such images are particularly damning in medieval depictions of the Passion, where tormentors, among them the sponge-bearer at the Crucifixion who offers Jesus false relief in the form of a vinegar-soaked sponge, are readily identifiable as Jews, marked by their excessive corporeality, their rounded foreheads, slanting noses, and, in the case of Judas Iscariot, red—possibly blood-soaked—hair. Bale considers the many versions—across a number of different media—of the story of Jephonius, a Jew who, at the Funeral of the Virgin, dares to touch Mary's bier and is rewarded for his impudence with either a withered hand, a severed hand, or having his hand(s) become stuck to the conveyance. This story, part of a long tradition fantasizing Jewish hostility to the Virgin Mary, is repeated in art and literature—including the N-Town mystery cycle's "Funeral of the Virgin" play. It calls upon its audience to see themselves as part of a Christianity continuously threatened by Jewish persecution, even as that audience believes the Virgin is gloriously assumed into heaven while those who torment her deservedly suffer here on earth.

In perhaps his most intriguing chapter, Bale engages imaginings of Jerusalem, a city that for medieval Europeans was simultaneously filled with the memory of violences performed by disfigured, treacherous, murderous Jews against their Savior and, somehow, devoid of Jews altogether. Visits to Jerusalem are made by pilgrims seeking to reenact the sufferings of Jesus at the hands of the Jews. But pilgrimages are so arranged that these pilgrims never encounter a Jew, or even visit Old Testament sites. *Imitatio Christi,* which requires that the Christian understand himself the object of Jewish antagonism, is performed in the absence of antagonists. The Jerusalem of medieval pilgrimage becomes a simulacrum, a copy of a city that never really existed. But because even the most managed pilgrimages were still both extremely dangerous and very expensive, throughout the Middle Ages copies of Jerusalem attractions begin to spring up during Europe. Medieval pilgrims could ultimately, in the safety of their homelands, reenact the sufferings of their Lord in copies of copies of the Holy City, imagining violence performed on them by Jews in places that had long been Jew-free.

For all that Bale's *Feeling Persecuted* is a scholarly tour de force, it still left this reader deeply troubled. Bale is aware of the sometimes horrific offenses committed by the Christian majority against Jews during the Middle Ages—he occasionally references these crimes. But he is unwilling to draw one-to-one correlations between the way medieval media depicted Jews and the atrocities that individuals and states performed against this minority. Bale rejects the idea of a long and continuous anti-Semitism, infecting Europe from the Middle Ages through the Third Reich. He insists that "texts, images and polemics of hatred can, but do not always, translate into physical violence or political disempowerment and physical and political attacks do not always reflect hatred" (184). For Bale, "[e]quating medieval violence—symbolic or real—with modern persecution is lazy history which reifies 'anti-Semitism' as a constant in which Jews are simply victims of a larger transhistorical 'phenomenon' (the 'anti-Semitic') over which one could have no control because of its inevitability and its foundational role in European, Christian culture" (185). Bale goes so far as to argue that Jews from the Middle Ages to the present day are every bit as guilty of drawing religious and cultural valorization by participating in devotions animated by the idea of victimhood. As he brings his book to its conclusion, Bale asks, "Is it possible that some medieval Christians and medieval Jews could have a readerly, imaginative world, structured around horror, emotion, affectivity, empathy and aesthetic violence, which is neither seamlessly connected to the terrible violence which punctuates the Jewish historical experience in medieval Europe nor able to be explained away by psychoanalysis?" (188). Unfortunately, I think the answer may be no. Bale contends that "medieval Christians did not know what catastrophes would eventually befall the Jews of Europe" (185). Perhaps not, but it is hard to imagine that medieval Christians would have been deeply troubled by those catastrophes.

MARTIN B. SHICHTMAN
Eastern Michigan University

BETTINA BILDHAUER. *Filming the Middle Ages.* London: Reaktion Books, 2011. Pp. 264. £25.00; $40.00.

It was once a commonly held view that the persistent and lively tradition of popular medievalism in the twentieth and twenty-first centuries—the re-creation, invocation, and rehabilitation of the Middle Ages by postmedieval culture—could only ever be an amusing, decorative afterthought to the medieval "real." Far less serious than eighteenth- and nineteenth-century revivalism in architecture, poetry, social ideology, and the arts and crafts movement, modern medievalism in fiction and film could be assessed and graded, much like student work, as more or less historically accurate; and it could be patronized, much like popular culture in general, as the product of amateurs and enthusiasts. Naturally, filmmakers, novelists, and fans would be drawn to the self-evidently intriguing Middle Ages, but their knowledge of its precise intricacies would be limited. Nevertheless, medievalism might still have a useful function if it directed undergraduates toward the study of medieval history and literature.

Some medieval scholars may still think along these lines, but they ignore at their peril a new generation of scholarly work that interrogates the medievalist project from a perspective of active engagement with what it can tell us about our relationship with the past and, indeed, why medieval culture itself should still matter to us.

Bettina Bildhauer's provocative study, *Filming the Middle Ages,* marches close to the vanguard of such work. It is perhaps less of a game-changer than Carolyn Dinshaw's *Getting Medieval,* but along with Nickolas Haydock's wonderful *Movie Medievalism* (2008), Bildhauer's book is an authoritative study of medievalist film that will shape future criticism of both medievalism and historically oriented cinema.

Bildhauer steps deftly through previous traditions of criticism and scholarship. She acknowledges the tempting critical tendency to judge medievalist cinema according to standards of historical accuracy, but she proposes a more productive approach, one that focuses on "the subversive and critical *potential* of medieval film—partly as a corrective to the dominant understanding of almost all films set in the Middle Ages as conservative" (21).

Filming the Middle Ages offers a fresh voice of analysis and commentary. Its texts include a number of the usual suspects, and it will be an indispensable book for teaching, but its orientation is firmly toward European and, indeed, German film. In effect, it proposes a new canon and a new genre of films, along with a new term. Sidestepping the interminable difficulties of terminology around "medievalism" and its cognates, Bildhauer proposes to describe as *medieval film* all films that are set in the Middle Ages, or that are treated *as* "medieval" in the premodernity attributed to them by the film industry and in their reception. There are clear advantages here: unlike poetry or fictions that have clearer antecedents in the Middle Ages, cinema has no substantial medieval analogues to confuse us. For Bildhauer, medieval film names a distinctive genre, a corpus that is held together by features that can be described on two levels. First, medieval film shares a relatively stable set of visual codes and thematic patterns. Second, these films often share a number of less well recognized preoccupations: with time (a concept that also features in Haydock's book); with a semiotic and ideological hierarchy that privileges the visual over the textual (despite the familiar opening trope of the medieval manuscript or book); and with a form of subjectivity that can be described as "post-human."

This threefold thesis is played out neatly over three sections, each with three chapters that move with ease between familiar and less familiar films, often candidly focusing on German cinema and its implications for national history. There are substantial discussions of *The Seventh Seal, Joan of Arc* (1928), *The Hunchback of Notre Dame, The Da Vinci Code, A Canterbury Tale, The Name of the Rose,* and *Beowulf,* all familiar fare in studies of medieval film. But there are other treasures to be explored in this rich and engaging study. Bildhauer's summaries of less familiar films are concise and engaging, and supplemented by many small black-and-white stills. These are not always of high quality—content is privileged over form throughout, especially in the cover image (a still from Murnau's *Faust,* from 1926)—but they certainly help to tell the story of medieval film's preoccupation with the haunting otherness of the past and its insistence on its own capacity to mediate that past for us. Indeed, cinema itself, and not just medieval film, is a medium that has often been described as "medieval," akin to the cathedrals of the Middle Ages, for example, in its "visuality, collectivity and non-chronology" (221). The book's conclusion brilliantly interrogates these three assumptions, insisting on the mutual and historical imbrication of medieval film, film studies, and medieval studies.

As Bildhauer points out in her introduction, a number of commentators (Lindley, Haydock, Finke and Shichtman) draw attention to the way medieval films construct the Middle Ages as a fantasy of modernity, rather than as a historical past that might be connected through chronological continuity with the present. *Filming the Middle Ages* works from this same premise, but it attempts to move the discussion one step further by wanting to make this a generic feature of medieval films. To emphasize this point, the book is almost completely uninterested in the historical Middle Ages, though it is often engaged by the historical context of medieval film production, especially, for example, in Weimar Expressionism. Certainly Bildhauer eschews the tendency to "correct" the representation of the past in medieval film, though she is obliged to point out several times that she does not share the assumptions of these films about the medieval past.

Bildhauer's quarrel with medieval film is exemplified most passionately in the first chapter of the third section, in her account and critique of Luis Trenker's *Condottieri* (1937), "a highly reactionary, politically despicable example of how in the Middle Ages the individual was allegedly subsumed into a collective body" (152). This film was a German-Italian co-production celebrating the life of Giovanni de' Medici (1498–1526). Bildhauer shows how in Italian cinema the film is read as "a straightforward allegory of Benito Mussolini's leadership" (153), while the German context privileged an affinity between Giovanni and Adolf Hitler (SS members were employed as extras, playing the mercenaries who gathered under Giovanni's leadership). The film's narrative is patchy in its political details, permitting easy appeals to national unity and heroic leadership for both Italian and German audiences. Most disturbingly for Bildhauer, though, *Condottieri* naturalizes the ideological fantasies of collective identity and an idea of homeland that is defined only by one's birth: these values are clearly shared with those of National Socialism (170). Bildhauer closes this chapter by linking the film's "objectionable ends" to "the currently fashionable introduction of affect into one's relationship to history," and she concludes with a ringing call to a more critical scholarly mode: *"Condottieri* . . . holds onto the illusion that everything was better in pre-modernity. Scholarship instead should aim to analyse and thereby shatter such illusions" (171).

This last sentence is a rare *aporia* in the text, something of a relapse into the historical (and political) imperative to correct medieval film's misrepresentations of the Middle Ages. It suggests there is still more work to be done in balancing the competing desires and intellectual programs of medievalism and historicism. *Filming the Middle Ages* is an important step along the way.

STEPHANIE TRIGG
University of Melbourne

PETER BROWN. *Geoffrey Chaucer.* Oxford: Oxford University Press, 2011. Pp. xvi, 254. £8.99; $13.95 paper.

As a spin-off from the World's Classics series, Oxford's "Authors in Context" will command a wide readership, so it is good to report that Peter Brown's thoughtful volume on Chaucer is packed with accurate information, intelligent negotiation between texts and contexts, and interpretations that command respect.

In Chaucer's case, the chief problem confronting anyone who would anchor the writer to pertinent "social, cultural, and political contexts," as is the general aim of this series, is where to ground the discussion and how to structure it. Brown means to eschew the temptations of fictionalizing and of "short-circuiting" (so as to fill tantalizing gaps), which in his view bedevil attempts to work either from life-records or from historical superstructure to the poetry. His preferred approach is looser: "to take a topic with roots in life records, Chaucer's poetry and historical writing alike, and present a conspectus" (18–19). As a result, the book is not governed by historical chronology but is topic-based; nor is it (to any significant extent) thesis-driven; nor does it develop through supposed evolutions in Chaucer's poetry and interests, except insofar as it begins with the topic "Finding a Voice," as exemplified in *The Book of the Duchess.* That subsection crowns the initial chapter, which summarizes Chaucer's life and discusses his self-representation, the early reception of his work, and some impediments to contextualizing that work.

An idea of the management of the numerous topics scattered in the book will be apparent from the contents of two of the seven chapters. Chapter 2, "The Social Body," covers "social structures," "religion and piety," "the Black Death," "the wars of Edward III," "revolt," and "the reign of Richard II." Chaucerians will often feel on familiar ground here. Thus Chaucer is considered "elliptical" (27) in response to social tensions, and this is seen as a tendency reinforced by his own allegedly "liminal" social status. A little less routine is the connection suggested between contemporary lay piety's emphasis on individual moral responsibility and the poetry's habit of apportioning judgment to the reader. Then there is Brown's bracingly direct argument that Chaucer fundamentally wrote as a Christian, all the more able to interweave religious and secular motifs in *The Miller's Tale* for fun because he was an author working in a culture "profoundly and securely Christian" (37). Brown encapsulates the late fourteenth-century social body well in parts of this chapter: but it is perhaps symptomatic of the hold-all tendencies of the book's method that an account of "the wars of Edward III" is made to slot in here on the pretext that waging war "was a dominant activity of the society Chaucer knew" (45).

Brown's "conspectus" approach restricts his own interpretative endeavors in Chapter 2 and some others, but not in Chapter 4, "Society and Politics." ("Politics" here seems to be meant in the frustratingly diffuse sense that the term has recently attracted in the world of literary criticism.) The chapter's topics are "personal identity," "authority," "status," "women and gender," "chivalry," and "peace." Here there *is* a thesis, that Chaucer understands the individual to be generally "an unstable amalgam of a number of possible identities" and accordingly explores "identities in flux" (104, 106)—as demonstrated by slippages in the pilgrim Merchant's attitudes and by slippages disclosed by figures in his tale. Griselda is then analyzed as a contrasting figure, whose identity does not fragment within *The Clerk's Tale*'s topical probing of the ideology of authority. The chapter's further subsections accommodate analyses of *The Franklin's Tale* (status anxiety), *The Wife of Bath's Prologue* and *Tale* (women, gender, then chivalry), and *Melibee* (peace).

Brown's concise writing sustains interest in these readings from the *Tales* and keeps up a pressure of response. He alerts readers to inherited falsifications: in the "thematically connected narratives, sometimes referred to as 'the marriage group,'" marriage is "not so much the topic as the means of representing other issues" (122). On second thoughts, does this not leave the fundamentally flawed notion of a marriage "group" in place? Four pages later, *The Franklin's Tale* is unwarily identified as "the tale that concludes 'the marriage group.'" The present reviewer also became uneasy about one or two of the book's other mild inconsistencies. Donald Howard is ticked off for fantasizing that Chaucer "saw" the rebels enter London beneath his flat in Aldgate. But Brown himself maintains a fantasy: the fantasy of the "performance" of Chaucer's texts. That *The Book of the Duchess* was commissioned and that its "performance" was a public event, moves in the course of the book from being plausible hypothesis to having the status of fact. For sure it is possible, even likely; and most scholars will agree that Chaucer writes with an expert sense of an audience. But to harp on Chaucer as a "performance poet" risks the very charge of fictionalizing that Brown is keen to escape.

Other small caveats of different kinds will occur to every Chaucerian who reads this book. To the present reader, one signal omission in an otherwise impressive chapter, "Science and Technology," is that Chaucer's concept of mental *impressioun,* so effectively investigated by David Burnley, is negligibly treated, by contrast with optical theories (the subject of another book by Brown) that are somewhat more remote from the texture of the poet's language. It seems even more odd that so little is said about confession, a topic that once would have been absolutely *de rigueur* in a general book on Chaucer. Here it appears only in some incidental sentences about *The Wife of Bath's Prologue.* Finally, a silence that will be nothing less than cacophonous to many in the Chaucer community in the second decade of the twenty-first century is the refusal to engage with the vexed question of the charge of *raptus* laid against Chaucer. Brown mentions the charge once or twice in passing but without acknowledging its critical notoriety: he offers no comment. That will surely pique the very same readers who will otherwise much enjoy the tautness of the book's writing, the numerous touches of idiomatic modernity, and the alert thoughtfulness of engagement on many fronts. (Actually the market for the book is a little hard to discern. Given the careful orientation supplied by passages of narrative paraphrase for readers who may have little acquaintance with Chaucer as yet, and for whom the meaning of the term "elegy" needs to be explained, it is slightly perplexing that words such as *domicella* and *coulisse* remain unglossed.)

These are nevertheless minor reservations in relation to the achievement of this project. Brown's coverage is both immense and quietly commanding. He is quite the impresario in his contextual handling of *Troilus and Criseyde*. His book introduces us to phenomena such as Lollardy and scholastic debate about fate (Chapter 5, "Intellectual Ideas") with the same spirit of enlightening inquiry as it lastly brings in Chapter 7 to "New Contexts"—a cracking fine survey of the use of Chaucer in modern texts and film. Niggling at details of this Author-in-Context volume is inevitable but curmudgeonly. What Brown achieves is deeply informed, professional, and attractively written: a book that can be recommended with substantial confidence to undergraduates everywhere, and that Chaucer scholars can beneficially use as a whetstone to sharpen up their own views.

ALCUIN BLAMIRES
Goldsmiths, University of London (Emeritus)

JOHN A. BURROW and HOYT N. DUGGAN, eds. *Medieval Alliterative Poetry: Essays in Honour of Thorlac Turville-Petre.* Dublin: Four Courts Press, 2010. Pp. 229. €55.00; $70.00.

This *festschrift* offers a good snapshot of the state of thinking on the works conventionally classified as belonging to the Middle English alliterative corpus, the subject of Turville-Petre's major study, *The Alliterative Revival* (1977). No one here reconsiders that book's larger arguments, and indeed some might come away from this collection wondering whether the concept of an alliterative corpus, not to mention revival, is still a going concern. The editors, rather than foreground this or any other characteristic of the collection, offer only a 150-word preface and present the essays in alphabetical order by author's last name. Still, a reading of the volume produces some interesting threads of interest across the contributions while also signaling some of the limitations of "alliterative poetry" as a governing principle.

John Scattergood's "On the Road: Langland and Some Medieval Outlaw Stories" is the only poor fit, *Piers Plowman* here just exemplifying the standard literary approach to outlaws. The most interesting source of pressure on the concept of an alliterative corpus comes in the form of the contribution that most fully engages with Turville-Petre's approach, Michael Calabrese's enjoyable "Alliterative Wombs." Calabrese adds "images of the womb and analogous spaces of nurturing, safety, and re-birth" to the topics the honorand identified as those at which alliterative poets excelled (54). Calabrese marshals ample evidence from *Cleanness, The Wars of Alexander, Piers Plowman,* and *The Siege of Jerusalem,* but I kept hearing a voice as I read: "Leeve mooder, leet me in!" If the phenomenon is best exemplified in *The Pardoner's Tale,* how helpful is the descriptor "alliterative" at all?

This question of how individual alliterative poems relate to external sources or milieux keeps coming up as one works through the volume. Robert Adams catalogues the similarities between Langland and the Dutch religious figure Geert Grote, including, he says, their eschatological outlook and devotion to *"traditional Catholic dogma"* (35; emphasis his). The essay seems intended to shore up support for his beliefs about Langland, which have proved contentious, but it is unclear how Grote's embodiment of them helps the cause. Richard F. Green argues that the English translator of *Guillaume de Palerne* responded to particular interests (physiology, pacifism, the poor) of his patron, Humphrey de Bohun, but any long narrative poem might provide such evidence. Ralph Hanna says five features of Langland's Tree of Charity "are certainly derived from" the *Glossa ordinaria* on the Song of Songs, which features some similar employments of the gardening metaphor (128). He does not think "that there can be a great deal of doubt" about his claims (133). More exposition and less hectoring would have benefited this effort, which makes few concessions to the virtues of clarity and logic.

Other approaches are more successful in negotiating such difficulties. Ad Putter sensibly argues that in assessing *Cleanness*'s homiletic passages we need to look to biblical versifications such as the *Cursor mundi,* which "are valuable repositories of the apocryphal lore, the received wisdom and textual variants, that made the medieval Bible so different from our own" (184). And Andrew Galloway's new identification of John of Tynemouth's mid-fourteenth-century universal history as a major source for *The Siege of Jerusalem* is wholly convincing, relying on often exact verbal parallels, and reducing the minimally necessary number of sources for the *Siege* from the five postulated by Hanna and David Lawton to three.

Two other contributions that approach such magisterial levels are A. V. C. Schmidt's and John Burrow's, both on Langland, whose "profoundly original exploration of the sacramental significance of blood," inspired by the Easter liturgy and its religious iconography, is the former's topic (217). The editors might profitably have brought Schmidt's analysis of the pervasive imagery of blood and the piercing of the body into conversation with Calabrese's study of womb imagery, or his description of Langland's religious vision as "in a wide sense sacramental" (217) with Adams's assertion that the poet held "a subjective view of the sacrament [of the altar]'s efficacy" (33).

Ilyke (ME "similarly, likewise"), Burrow's essay on the lives of Piers the Plowman through A, B, and C might have been fruitfully juxtaposed with Derek Pearsall's on the character of C. My use of a Middle English term offers one reason, for both of these distinguished critics discuss the enormous implications of a single-letter emendation by Russell and Kane, whereby Langland no longer says that Patience is *ilyk* (like) Piers, but that he prayed for food, and *ilyk{e}* so did Piers, now a ghostly presence at the feast (46, 157). Burrow points out that "the Piers of C does not have x-ray eyes" as does his B equivalent, who can see people's thoughts (48), and that taken as a whole Piers exemplifies "in succession the lives of Dowel, Dobet and Dobest" (52). Pearsall's essay is not as captivating as Schmidt's and Burrow's because fair chunks of it have appeared in the introduction to his 2008 edition and in his contribution to the *Yearbook of Langland Studies*'s cluster in memory of George Kane, *ilyke* published in 2010.

All of the remaining contributions are well worth reading. A. S. G. Edwards and Nicola Royan extend the scope of alliterative poetry in time and place, respectively, the former focusing on works of the sixteenth-century Blage manuscript, the latter on Old Scots verse. Hoyt N. Duggan offers an ornery response to Putter, Stokes, and Jefferson's arguments regarding the prosody of the alliterative long line: they are wrong, in effect, because they cannot be right. Finally, Judith Jefferson's analysis of the table of contents of a sixteenth-century copy of *Piers Plowman* (CUL Gg.4.31) was one of my favorites, even if she indicates neither how well her topic accords with Turville-Petre's study of another sixteenth-century *Piers* manuscript, nor that she provides one of the most detailed accounts of early responses to alliterative poetry, indeed medieval narrative poetry at large, that we have.

In a review of a volume of *YLS*, Turville-Petre observed an "unease

STUDIES IN THE AGE OF CHAUCER

about the state of the edited text" of *Piers Plowman,* though "only one of the essays directly addresses issues of editorial practice" (*RES* n.s. 46 [1995]: 65). Things have not changed much: Adams and Calabrese do not say what editions they cite; Hanna, Burrow, and Pearsall say they use Athlone, though the latter two present the identical passage in different ways; Scattergood uses Pearsall's 1978 edition of C; and Schmidt cites himself. Only Pearsall addresses questions of editing Langland at any length. This and other features, such as the lack of any engagement with David Lawton's "Unity of Middle English Alliterative Poetry" (*Speculum* 58 [1983]: 72–94) or Christine Chism's *Alliterative Revivals,* either indicate a larger unease about the status of alliterative poetry as a coherent object of study, or manifest a refreshing sense that we can stop going over and over an earlier generation's obsessions with the concepts of "revival" and the editing of *Piers Plowman* and turn to the particulars. After all, as Nicola Royan and Judith Jesch's portrait of the scholar and a quick survey of his publications reveal, this is precisely what Thorlac Turville-Petre has been doing so wonderfully in the thirty-five years since the appearance of *The Alliterative Revival.*

LAWRENCE WARNER
University of Sydney

KIRSTY CAMPBELL. *The Call to Read: Reginald Pecock's Books and Textual Communities.* Notre Dame: University of Notre Dame Press, 2010. Pp. xi, 310. $38.00.

The first large-scale study of Reginald Pecock and his works since the 1980s demands the attention of all scholars interested in fifteenth-century religious culture, literature, theology, and the interactions between orthodoxy and heterodoxy. Campbell's book does not disappoint, as she invites the reader on a journey through the construction of Pecock's textual communities, his ideas on lay religiosity, his reliance on reason and the authority of the Bible.

The introduction offers a brief survey of modern scholarship concerned with that increasingly contested term, "vernacular theology," and the blurring of distinctions between orthodoxy and heresy, which has been a particularly welcome feature of recent scholarly enquiry.

Campbell aligns herself firmly with the progressive camp, which is skeptical about the ontological status of these categories, and she seeks to locate Pecock's writings within a religious and intellectual milieu that is more fluid and contingent than has often been acknowledged. Pecock is introduced as someone who "thinks big" (8) about the reform of preaching and teaching, his ideas being on a similar scale to those of Arundel in drafting his Constitutions—although with very different intentions and results. The scholarly debate stimulated by Nicholas Watson's groundbreaking *Speculum* article of 1995 has, I think, resolved itself into a more nuanced perception of the effects of Arundel's legislation than Campbell allows; she, like many other medievalists, appears to regard its intention as at best the prescriptive regulation of theological speculation, at worst its prohibition. I suspect there is still some work to be done here to produce a more fine-grained view, but that is clearly not a major concern of this book, which is described as focusing on "the contents of Pecock's writings" (5). That does not quite encapsulate Campbell's project; she is much more interested in locating Pecock within textual and religious communities than with the minutiae of his texts. Thus anyone seeking a detailed exploration of the contents of his works must look elsewhere.

The opening chapter, "Pecock's Audience," might more accurately be entitled "Pecock's Audiences," as Campbell seeks to sketch out the intended, historical, and implied audiences for her subject's works. This is no easy task; while Pecock's writings are littered with references to the kinds of reading practices he demands from his readers, and the prologues paint a colorful but impressionistic picture of actual reading events, there is very little real evidence upon which she can base her audience sketches. As a result, the dividing lines between the different categories become increasingly blurred, and at times the "historical" audience and the "ideal" audience seem to be presented as one and the same. Part of the difficulty may lie in the assumption that Pecock was clear about his audience's expectations, and that he viewed his audience as broadly, though not completely, homogeneous. My own reading of his works suggests that at least some of the time he struggled unsuccessfully to address "an" audience that he recognized to be radically fragmented. Nevertheless, there is some fascinating detail here about Pecock's metropolitan milieu; Campbell argues a good case for his familiarity with members of the Mercers' Guild and their concerns, and indeed perhaps those of other craft guilds, though these receive less attention.

Chapters 2 and 3 focus on Pecock's radical ideas for the reform of theological education for the laity, including his construction of an educational program that, he claims, would render all other such initiatives superfluous. The novelty of his project is demonstrated convincingly, in particular his emphasis on the provision of books, which could usefully be further contextualized in relation to Pecock's infamous views on preaching bishops. It would be interesting to see Campbell speculate further about the practicability of putting Pecock's program into practice. Most of the examples she mentions of lay individuals practicing structured routines of reading and devotion are, of course, from the wealthiest classes, and it is not always easy to see how readily these practices would translate to the lower orders. However, the emphasis that she places upon the development of the mixed life gestures toward some fascinating possibilities. The fourth chapter is, in some respects, a little less satisfying, primarily because its discussion of reading practices is largely dependent upon works by Pecock to which he refers in other writings, but which are no longer extant. Campbell does the best she can with the hints that remain, and her thoughtful discussion of meditation, contemplation, and mystical union with God is for me one of the highlights of the book.

The "book of reason" and the Bible are the respective concerns of Chapters 5 and 6. The importance—indeed, the supremacy—that Pecock affords to reason in many fields of inquiry is surely one of the most distinctive features of his writing, and thus it richly deserves the attention it receives here. Campbell is particularly interested in the impact that this reliance on reason has upon the notion of the textual community, creating "a common ground within the textual community by getting everyone thinking along the same lines" (152). She discusses Pecock's use of syllogism and analogy and notes his indebtedness to a philosophical tradition embracing both Aristotle and Aquinas; yet in so doing, she seems to me to underplay the radical nature of this approach in the context of fifteenth-century vernacular theological writing. Her exploration of the place of the Bible within Pecock's intellectual framework is nuanced and skillful, delicately balancing his objections to the Lollard emphasis on *sola scriptura* with the need to acknowledge the crucial importance of the Bible to the understanding of the Christian faith. Campbell locates Pecock's solution in his insistence that biblical exegesis remains the preserve of the clergy, an assertion given added weight by his own refusal to provide illustrative examples that might be seen to encourage excessive lay curiosity. This discussion leads elegantly into the final chapter, which explores lay/clerical relations in Pecock's imagined textual community, in which Pecock's ambivalence about the relationship between the clergy and laity is well argued. On the one hand, he envisages a world of friendly, loving relations, in which both parties are united in mutual exploration of the Christian faith; on the other, the traditional hierarchical structure remains to underpin such relations. Campbell provides an interesting discussion of changing ideas about "natural" social relations, drawing on the work of Andrew Galloway and Anne Middleton to suggest a nonhierarchical model for interaction based on "mutuality, commonality, affinity, and reciprocity" (233). This is intriguing, but I am not entirely convinced that the reciprocal, affinity-based relationships she posits are necessarily at odds with an estates-based hierarchy; there is scope for the two models to coexist, and this is surely what Pecock is envisaging in his work. This may simply be me wanting to have my cake and eat it too, but I believe the same might be said for Pecock and his imaginary model of lay/clerical relations.

Campbell's book provides a fascinating study of one of the most prominent, yet least understood, writers of the mid-fifteenth century. Her unwavering focus on Pecock's textual communities, however difficult they may be to define, ensures that her work will be of great service not only to scholars of Pecock, but to all with an interest in fifteenth-century literary and religious studies.

SARAH JAMES
University of Kent, Canterbury

DAVID R. CARLSON, ed. *John Gower: Poems on Contemporary Events: The Visio Anglie (1381) and Cronica tripertita,* with a verse translation by A. G. Rigg. Toronto: Pontifical Institute, 2011. Pp. 419. $150.00.

ELISABETH DUTTON, JOHN HINES, and R. F. YEAGER, eds. *John Gower, Trilingual Poet: Language, Translation, and Tradition.* Cambridge: D. S. Brewer, 2010. Pp. 358. £60.00; $99.00.

Both of the books under review make a notable contribution to the study of Gower, who emerges here as an erudite and wide-ranging poet in Latin, French, and English. In *Poems on Contemporary Events,* David Carlson and A. G. Rigg make accessible Gower's *Visio Anglie* and his *Cronica tripertita.* Both are important "eye-witness" accounts of the political upheavals that afflicted England in the last quarter of the fourteenth century. The *Cronica tripertita* follows the reign of King Richard II, beginning with the rebellion of the Lords Appellant, through to the Wonderful and Merciless Parliaments, and culminating in the deposition of Richard by Henry IV. The chronicle is written in leonine hexameters (translated by Rigg into rhyming couplets), and its approach to historiography is both highly poetic and highly biased. The influence of prophetic literature is felt in its allegorical veiling. For instance, Thomas of Woodstock, leader of the rebellion against Richard, is code-named the Swan; Thomas de Beauchamp, Earl of Warwick, is the Bear, and so on. To ensure that readers were able to follow the argument, the verse was accompanied by Latin prose glosses (presumably composed by Gower himself) that decode the allegory. Gower's Lancastrian sympathies are ever-present. The tripartite structure of the chronicle gives an early indication of his allegiance: the first part, dealing with the Lords Appellant, is the *opus humanum;* the second book, concerning Richard's revenge, is the *opus inferni;* and the third part, on Henry's usurpation, is the *opus in Cristo.*

The *Visio Anglie,* in unrhymed elegiac couplets (here rendered in unrhymed pentameters) offers a fascinating apocalyptic vision of the peasants' revolt and its immediate aftermath. In an allegorical move familiar from Gower's *Vox clamantis,* the peasants are grotesquely portrayed as repugnant animals (dogs, boars, foxes, and the like). However, the visionary poet does not remain a detached observer of this troubled world: Passus 16 suddenly sees him fleeing from his own home and then wandering in paranoid terror in the woods—only to be rescued by a ship that carries him and other noblemen through the storm. The moral to be drawn from all this, Gower thinks, is that greater repression is essential, for "peasants always plot toward our death, / If they can subjugate the noble class" (2099–100).

As Carlson and Rigg explain in their introduction, one of the reasons these two works should matter to students of Gower is that Gower himself envisaged them as an integral part of his *magnum opus.* This *magnum opus* as he conceived it was also tripartite in structure, consisting of the English *Confessio Amantis,* the French *Mirour de l'omme,* and the Latin *Vox clamantis,* to which Gower subsequently added the *Visio Anglie* and *Cronica tripertita* as, respectively, Book 1 and the final conclusion. Carlson's edition is based on careful consideration of the surviving manuscript, and Rigg's translation is eminently readable, though on a few occasions it bears only a very loose resemblance to the original. Line 1265, "Milicies cessit paciensque locum dedit ire," does not really mean "In sufferance, knights yielded place to wrath," but rather "knighthood yielded to, and with forbearance surrendered ground to, wrath." And while Rigg translates lines 1163–64, "Quicque magis celebres fuerant hoc tempore ciues, / Sicut oues mortis procubuere manu," as "All citizens were at that time close packed: like sheep they fell before the hand of death," line 1163 presumably means (literally): "Whichever citizens were at time more renowned."

The collection *John Gower, Trilingual Poet* also focuses attention on Gower's non-English output, though the *Confessio Amantis* is by no means neglected. Because there are twenty-five essays in total, I restrict myself to a select few. George Shuffleton examines the relationship between Gower's *Confessio* and the Middle English verse romances; these no doubt influenced him, but (like Chaucer) Gower was not keen to acknowledge his debts to the tradition of popular romance. Tamara F. O'Collaghan examines Gower's discussion of alchemy in Book VII of the *Confessio,* and sheds light both on Gower's reading and on his later reputation as an alchemical authority (based on the inclusion of relevant excerpts from Gower in fifteenth- and sixteenth-century alchemical treatises). Peter Nicholson contrasts Chaucer's fondness for irony, "his awareness that the same words and actions can be understood in more than one way, and our . . . constant process of discovery of that which is unexpressed" (207), with Gower's directness: "[t]hings are what they seem in the *Confessio Amantis*" (216). In his readings of individual tales, Nicholson is persuasive, but it has to be said that the *Confessio*'s frame narrative is ironic in a way that Chaucer's *Canterbury Tales* is not. The confessor, as John Burrow points out in his essay, is "a Christian priest retained in the household of a great lady . . . subject to her commands, but . . . also a father who performs the high offices of the priesthood" (218). In other words, Genius is at once a priest and a servant of Love, and to declare (without a hint of irony) that "all of the ethical instruction that Genius provides to Amans fails to turn him into a perfect human being" (Nicholson, 216) is to miss the point that Genius, *qua* Venus's priest, is mainly interested in turning Amans into a perfect *lover*. And, of course, his failure in that regard is predicated on yet another irony, which is that "Amans" is revealed to be only slightly more credible as a lover than is old January in *The Merchant's Tale*. The person whom we fancied to be "Amans," and who fancied himself as lover, too, is the old-age pensioner John Gower. If that does not count as a "discovery of that which is unexpressed," then I don't know what does.

As the title of the collection indicates, Gower's French and Latin writings receive plenty of attention. Cathy Hume raises the question "Why did Gower write the *Traitié?*" The usual answer is that Gower wanted to offer his advice about how to maintain matrimonial harmony, but as Hume rightly points out, Gower's real purpose seems to be to show that adulterers come to sticky ends. It need not necessarily follow that Gower aimed the *Traitié* at some of the high-profile adulterers whom Hume mentions (Edward III, John of Gaunt), but the status of the *Traitié* as a straightforward marriage treatise will now need to be reconsidered. Nigel Saul in "John Gower: Prophet or Turncoat?" shows that Gower's reactionary response to the peasants' revolt was representative of his class. Finally, Andrew Galloway develops the implications of Gower's own immersion in the dream world of the *Visio Anglie*. Galloway argues that the theme of the *Visio* is reason led astray by appetite, and this theme is exemplified not only in the revolting peasants but also, and more memorably, in the person of the terrified dreamer who wanders through an apocalyptic landscape (like Lysander in *A Midsummer Night's Dream*) "amazedly, half sleep, half waking." A number of essays in *John Gower, Trilingual Poet* are good companion pieces to Gower's *Visio Anglie*, which I am sure will gain a wider audience now that it can be read in the edition and translation by Carlson and Rigg.

AD PUTTER
University of Bristol

KATHY CAWSEY. *Twentieth-Century Chaucer Criticism: Reading Audiences.* Farnham: Ashgate, 2011. Pp. xi, 185. £55.00; $99.95.

In this volume, Kathy Cawsey identifies and analyzes major trends over a hundred years of Chaucer criticism through the work of six critics and their conceptions of Chaucer's audience. As she takes us through a survey that begins with George Lyman Kittredge's dramatic principle and concludes with Lee Patterson's new historicism, her insightful judgments and comparative perspective bring into sharp relief the arguments, discussions, and assumptions under which the world of Chaucer criticism has progressed over the last century. The retrospective she provides for her envisioned audience of graduate students offers an overview of the subject, a useful map of the terrain whose peaks and valleys they may not yet have encountered. For those she terms the "more mature scholars" who might read the book, she reveals unexpected similarities between seemingly distinct critical approaches. Over its course, her analysis also raises a series of implicit questions that go to the heart of the practice of literary criticism in general and to Chaucer criticism in particular.

The rationale for the book is to define and analyze what Cawsey terms the "audience function" in the work of the various critics she discusses. She builds her analyses on the plausible theory that in the literary criticism of medieval literature defining an audience means defining a text, in essence drawing parameters for what and how it means. The book focuses on six critics familiar to all Chaucerians—George Lyman Kittredge, C. S. Lewis, E. Talbot Donaldson, D. W. Robertson, Carolyn Dinshaw, and Lee Patterson. In each case, Cawsey's intelligent analysis reveals that the "audience function" for these critics is essentially a projection of his or her own learning and cultural perspective. For different critics in different cultural circumstances, Chaucer is various things. In one view, he is a universal author accessible to all, a position Kittredge and Donaldson share, although they come to it in very different ways. For Lewis, Robertson, and Patterson, Chaucer is a medieval author whose audience lived within a culture that must now be substantially recovered. For Carolyn Dinshaw, Chaucer and his audience are best understood by reading from the margins and appreciating the multiplicity of perspectives that gender and cultural difference— medieval and modern—bring to a text.

The various chapters of the book provide detailed exposition of each critic's assumptions about audience, literature, and the past. Kittredge "at once universalizes his own response and assumes a universality of readers" (26) in a medieval world not radically different from ours because, while human culture changes, human nature remains constant. C. S. Lewis "uses the refined and educated nature of his vision of Chaucer's audience as a defence for his own reading . . . that will allow gentle humour in Chaucer, but nothing that might portray him as mocking or ironizing the courtly ethos in which Lewis situates Chaucer's writings" (47). E. Talbot Donaldson, in contrast, imagined Chaucer's audience as "capable of humour, alive to dramatic and structural irony, undisturbed by irreverence" (57). For Donaldson, the "careful" modern reader could prise meaning from a text's formal and structural elements that would be "more-or-less the same response to the same text" (67) as a medieval reader might have. Donaldson did allow for the semantic instability of language over time, but beyond that concession to cultural change, he regarded historical context as substantially inaccessible. His critical method, famously rooted in his elevation of irony, means that the skeptical "distance" inherent in that mode becomes central to how Chaucer's audience engaged his texts.

Donaldson's position was opposed by D. W. Robertson's contention that truths and aesthetic values deemed universal are "historically contingent and transitory." Robertson argued that while the re-creation of the past is inherently impossible, some effort to recover culture is necessary to understand how Chaucer's audience understood his work. The result was Robertsonian criticism, a focusing lens of Christianity, especially the Augustinian doctrine of charity, and an assumption that Chaucer's medieval audience was used to "reading" both the created world and texts as representative of religious truth. Cawsey points out that for Robertson, Chaucer's texts were about something more than their surface level, and that his imagined medieval audience would have seen in the duality between letter and spirit a sense of distance between assertion and meaning akin to the distance Donaldson's readers perceived at work in irony.

In Cawsey's analysis, Carolyn Dinshaw seems to be the most radical of the six in her conception of the diversity of Chaucer's medieval audience—the educated male reader implicit in earlier criticism is displaced by a sense of the multiplicity of backgrounds and circumstances members of Chaucer's medieval audience brought to his work. This audience as well as characters within Chaucer's texts are all "readers" of the world, but not in the way that Robertson imagined, not through a single lens of religion but through a kaleidoscopic splintering of different visions. Concluding with Lee Patterson, Cawsey identifies new historicism with Patterson's research that finds Chaucer's medieval audience in the documents of the past, blending historical evidence, modern theory, and close reading to recover not the general or the typical, but the unique and subjective, and its relationship to structures of power and discourse.

In the course of the book, Cawsey highlights implicit assumptions that have shaped Chaucer studies for nearly a century—the assumed bookishness of Chaucer's audience, its maleness, its putative interest in reading a text by "unraveling words and gestures so as to see to the heart of things" (Saul N. Brody, "Making a Play for Criseyde: The Staging of Pandarus's House in Chaucer's *Troilus and Criseyde, Speculum* 73 [1998]: 115–40 [140]). The volume does such a good job with the critics it selects that it invites further exposition. Without directly engaging the subject, Cawsey's work calls attention to the continual, serial projection of modern academic, scholarly, and cultural assumptions onto Chaucer's texts through definitions of his medieval audience. In her conclusion, she contrasts the cost of the universalizing principles of the early twentieth century to the particular subjectivity of recent criticism, and suggests that a combination of the two might prove a more useful way of understanding both Chaucer and his audience. But that suggestion begs a larger question: that of why these six critics achieved the influence each has undeniably exerted over the scholarship and attitudes of Chaucerians. It is hard to quarrel with the importance of the figures Cawsey has selected, but they do not represent all the modes of scholarly criticism or all the important critical influences of the last century. Other critics exerted tremendous influence and earned tremendous admiration for their scholarly and critical work, without founding or representing a distinct line of critical inquiry. What is different about the figures she has selected? The answer may lie in the intersection of Chaucer criticism and contemporary culture. Part of the value of this volume is its implicit invitation to think about how the idea of "Chaucer's audience" functions as a mirror of widely accepted contemporary interests and assumptions. The interplay among critic, culture, and text is a fascinating subject worth addressing directly. Cawsey's book leaves the reader wishing there had been one more chapter in which to consider it. Given the clarity of her exposition, we can hope that she may address the implications of this volume in the future.

CAROLYN P. COLLETTE
Mount Holyoke College

K. P. CLARKE. *Chaucer and Italian Textuality*. Oxford: Oxford University Press, 2011. Pp. viii, 234. £60.00; $110.00.

This study reconstructs what Chaucer's Italian "library" may have looked like, in order to suggest the reverberations of Italian textuality in his writings and to redirect source study to texts as they were actually available, with marginal spaces filled with glosses, illustrations, and catchwords. Focusing on Boccaccio, his readers, and *The Wife of Bath's Prologue* and *Clerk's Tale* in the Hengwrt and Ellesmere manuscripts, Clarke stresses Chaucer as a reader of Italian textuality and an author of the "whole page." Methodologically, the study seeks to use variable manuscript witnesses not only to infer instances of reception but also to reclaim the aim of Lachmannian textual studies: reconstructing the author.

Two chapters concern forms of Italian textuality that may have shaped Chaucer's reading of classical works. Chapter 1 suggests an Italian Ovidian tradition behind *The Legend of Good Women;* the Florentine notary Filippo Ceffi's translation of the *Heroides* exemplifies the different kind of Ovid available in Italy. Chapter 2 treats Boccaccio not as an author of texts but as a producer of books. He copied and annotated not only his own works, like the *Teseida,* but also works by others, especially Dante, and the textuality of his autographs provides models for the negotiation of text and margin that Chaucer may have experienced in his reception of Statius as well.

Chapter 3 initiates the study's main focus, how the textuality of the *Decameron* shaped the experience of its early readers, including Chaucer. Boccaccio exercised considerable control over the textual and material construction of his books. Four early copies of Boccaccio's *Decameron* produced by and for Florentine mercantile readers serve as models of Chaucer's encounter with this work. It sometimes circulated in fragmentary forms, as exemplifed by the oldest witness, which Clarke (following Marco Cursi) associates with the Buondelmonti banking family and thus the political-financial networks associating Florence and Naples. In addition, he argues, two other manuscripts promote reading practices that arise from their physical structure. Thus the illustrated catchwords of the autograph Hamilton 90 (Berlin, Staatsbibliothek preussischer Kulturbesitz) work to prompt an active, forward-and-backward thematic reading; they bridge "a physical gap by proleptically recalling" words the reader has not yet read. Attributed to Boccaccio himself, the catchwords are so imbricated that they "are incarnations of the text rather than parallel figures who interact with it" (101, 102). The Capponi codex illustrations visually inscribe both Boccaccio as author and a female audience vulnerable to the erotic potential of the book, whose cognomen (drawn from *Inferno* V's allusion to Lancelot and Guinevere) is "prencipe galeotto" (104). Sadly, no reproductions from either manuscript are included, making the argument more difficult to follow.

From the beginning, the story of Griselda has prompted accounts of readerly reception; Petrarch, for example, supplemented his Latin translation with an account of two readers, one moved to tears, the other disbelieving. The high point of Chapter 3 is a detailed examination of *Decameron* X.10 in the Mannelli codex, whose sometimes idiosyncratic glosses (reproduced in Appendix 1) record the responses of an early "copista per passione"—an amateur reader of a mercantile family. Clarke does not claim the Mannelli codex as a source for Chaucer's *Clerk's Tale,* but rather adduces it as a contemporaneous context for reading the *Decameron* in 1384 (113). Mannelli's glosses show remarkable emotional engagement (Gualtieri is "pazzo," crazy). Most striking is Griselda's imagined marginal response when her silent submission becomes too much to bear: " 'Pisciarti in mano Gualtieri! Chi mi ristora di dodici anni? Le forche?' (f. 170rb), 'Go piss on your hand Gualtieri! Who'll give me back twelve years? The gallows?' " (122). The Mannelli codex exemplifes the "varied textuality" (128) of Chaucer's contact with Italian vernacular and Latin sources. In a recurrent gesture linking Boccaccio's own bookmaking to that of his early readers, Clarke suggests that these texts exposed Chaucer to "a complex mode of authorial self-presentation" (128). Clarke's conception of Boccaccio's practice of authorship is so expansive that even resistant readers like Mannelli, owing to similar treatment of margins, layout, and paratext, are drawn into the matrix of authorial book production.

The logic of Clarke's use of readerly practices to get at authorship becomes apparent in Chapter 4, which treats contrasting negotiations of textual authority of the Wife of Bath and the Clerk in the Hengwrt and Ellesmere manuscripts. Ellesmere's careful layout and glosses (Appendix 2 provides glosses from both manuscripts) not only put hermeneutic pressure on readers but also suggest authorial activity. Although evidence for Chaucer's responsibility for the Ellesmere glosses remains elusive, Clarke extends Chaucer's authorial activity—like that of Boccaccio—to marginal spaces. Our rapidly changing knowledge about early Chaucer manuscripts allows Clarke to absorb the common scribe, Adam Pinkhurst, into the matrix of authorship, thus suggesting Chaucer's responsibility for the Ellesmere glosses. (Thus he circumvents the absence of glosses for *The Wife of Bath's Prologue* in Hengwrt, possibly produced during Chaucer's lifetime, in favor of those in Ellesmere, which was posthumously produced.) Situated alongside a text about reading and the negotiation of authority, the glosses become part of the authorial conception of the Wife, who models a form of textuality differing from Jankyn's book. The glossed Ellesmere recapitulates Jankyn's fictional encounter reading his antifeminist compilation and "glossing" the Wife's body, with the difference that the Wife subverts the texts that purport to define her. Drawing the manuscript glosses into the fiction, she models a more challenging form of reading, completed only in the margins of the manuscript.

Clarke's treatment of *The Clerk's Tale* as a macaronic "whole page"—a different negotiation of authority—demonstrates that the glosses come from Petrarch's Latin translation of *Decameron* X.10 rather than from the French intermediary. Supplying Latinity to the tale, they quote Petrarch on Griselda's virtue, wisdom, and political acumen, as well as Walter's discernment of her virtues. The margins provide space for different voices, giving the characters "room to breathe" (155) and nudging readers toward the Petrarchan source. The multiplication of voices is echoed in the "Envoi de Chaucer," which Clarke reads as a declaration of Chaucerian authorship and a humorous recognition that the world cannot handle too many Walters or Griseldas. Despite the glosses' reinforcement of the characters, then, the *envoi* puts a limit on the tale's exemplary value—and thus departs from Petrarch's reading of Boccaccio.

This stimulating study offers absorbing readings of the interplay of text and margin, author and readers, in the construction of the whole page. It brings the best recent Italian textual scholarship to bear on Chaucer's connections. Clarke uses an approach that usually derives readerly practice, rather than authorial activity, from the evidence of glossed manuscripts; indeed the chief gap is the scanty awareness of work on Chaucer manuscripts as evidence of reception (the Chaucer Project's hypertext *Wife of Bath's Prologue* makes this especially accessible). It seems slightly perverse to retake the margins as authorial space, and I am skeptical about the utility of merging Chaucer's first scribe into a composite author function. I miss the independent agency of historical, potentially resistant readers. The necessarily speculative nature of Chaucer's reconstructed reading experience is reflected in this review's initial "may haves"; nevertheless, Clarke's conceptual provocation to take textuality into account in source study is welcome.

KARLA TAYLOR
University of Michigan

LISA H. COOPER. *Artisans and Narrative Craft in Late Medieval England.* Cambridge: Cambridge University Press, 2011. Pp xiii, 278. £55.00; $90.00.

This wide-ranging book about artisans in medieval culture is engaging and insightful. Rather than pursuing one overarching argument about the social function of artisans in the Middle Ages, *Artisans and Narrative Craft in Late Medieval England* pursues what Lisa Cooper calls a "multi-faceted historiography" of artisans through their representation in literary and nonliterary texts (11). What I most admire about this study is Cooper's ability to discover artisans and artisanal concerns in texts where we might not expect to find them: instructional vocabularies, fabliaux, spiritual allegories, and mirrors for princes. In presenting an innovative survey of medieval genres, the book fulfills its promise to offer "a useful account of the varied roles that artisans and artisanal imagery play in late medieval didactic and imaginative writing" (4).

The book's chapters are organized by genre, and Cooper examines texts about, for, and (in some cases) by artisans; the disparate narrative contexts range from Anglo-Saxon texts for monks to fifteenth-century bilingual manuals for merchants. By traversing diverse social spaces, Cooper demonstrates that artisans occupy "*multiple* roles in medieval English literature" (15, her italics). Shape-shifting, multitasking artisans serve many narrative conventions and discursive aims—pedagogical, vocational, spiritual, or political—and comprise crucial tools for thought for medieval writers. (The implicit pun on "tools" is my own; Cooper adapts Lévi-Strauss, asserting artisans are "good to think with" [7].)

The introduction to *Artisans and Narrative Craft in Late Medieval England* establishes the study's aims, with an excursus on Chaucer. Cooper notes that the poet aligns poetry making with artisanal craft, but that he also takes pains to distinguish between literary composition and the creation of physical artifacts (11–14). Chapter 1 examines understandings of craft production in pedagogical vocabularies, from Ælfric's tenth-century *Colloquy* to Caxton's *Dialogues in French and English* (c. 1480–83). Cooper reveals how these texts provide insight into perceptions of artisans and their social positioning, and she draws upon Bourdieu to argue that the texts also confer cultural capital upon their readers, pursuing symbolic profit and material gain (22).

Chapter 2 explores artisanal community and domesticity in the masons' *Constitutions,* Chaucer's *Miller's Tale,* and anonymous texts about artisans (*The Debate of the Carpenter's Tools, The Wright's Chaste Wife,* and *The Smyth and His Dame*). The fifteenth-century *Constitutions,* which interweave legends and didactic materials, "provide a substitute, if metaphorical, home" for medieval masons who were largely itinerant (58). In making this argument, Cooper astutely observes that masons lacked an established guildhall and formed contingent communities that were reconstituted at one construction site after another. Transitioning to fabliaux as examples of "medieval domestic fiction" (83), Cooper explores how poems about artisanal households manage concerns about domestic order and social harmony.

Chapter 3 traces how Deguileville's *Pèlerinage de la vie humaine* exploits imagery of artisanal craft and labor and how such phenomena are transformed in Lydgate's English translation. Cooper demonstrates that "both metaphorical craft language and actual (if nonetheless still allegorical) scenes of craft practice are the means by which the pilgrim-narrator is informed" on theological matters, and she persuasively argues that artisanal production often comprises the poem's epistemology (107). The reading of Occupation, a net-maker by trade, is compelling: Cooper shows that Lydgate adapts this figure to mitigate the radical threat it poses to conservative notions of social hierarchy (136–40).

Chapter 4 turns to political education, revealing how texts in the mirror for princes tradition employ the figure of the artisan to theorize social hierarchy and proper relations between rulers and subjects. Opening with Alfred's Old English translation of Boethius's *Consolation of Philosophy,* Cooper invokes kingly *cræft* (an interpolation absent in the original Latin) to establish the conceit of "the ruler as master *artifex* of the realm" (146). This ruler-as-artisan construct is traced through reiterations over time. In Lydgate's *Fall of Princes* (c. 1431–38), artisanal craft is expressly linked to modes of linguistic translation and poetic composition. In Caxton's *The Game and Playe of the Chesse* (1474 and 1483), the interdependence of the estates constitutes a key concern. I found the close reading of Caxton most compelling when Cooper attends to the graphic layout of the printed text (181–84). Cooper notes the interplay between the text and its illustrations, observing that the placement of occupational woodcuts across the printed pages of the book "reinforces the horizontal quality of its social vision" (182).

The epilogue to *Artisans and Narrative Craft in Late Medieval England* provocatively explores the notion that a pervasive "craft nostalgia" underlies both medieval texts and contemporary forms of online gaming (such as *Second Life*) that incorporate role-playing and virtual labor (192). Cooper nicely observes that such cultural phenomena "enact both linguistic and cultural translation . . . transfer[ring] images of craft practice from one language, time and place, to another" (193).

Each chapter is compelling in its own way, and Cooper's "multifaceted" approach invites readers to entertain fruitful connections across texts. This being said, I wondered if Cooper's frequent invocation of the "image" or "figure" of artisanry undersells the complexity of these chapters. Invoking "the artisan" as a narrative device in medieval texts is a strategic choice on Cooper's part; such a formulation allows her to pivot gracefully from discussions of artisanal identity to artisanal labor or artisanal social relationships, all of which are slightly different things. On the whole, artisanry is much *more* than a trope. I would say Cooper hits the nail on the head (as it were) in asserting that medieval culture sees the artisan not just as a "figure" but also as a "social person" (conceptual category) that is "good to think with" (6–7). Ultimately, this book surpasses its mission of tracing how artisans are depicted or "imagined" in medieval texts; it actively encourages us to adopt an artisanal orientation toward knowledge itself.

As wide-ranging as this study is, certain aspects of *Artisans and Narrative Craft in Late Medieval England* felt underdeveloped. Throughout the book, I wondered if Cooper was invested not so much in "narrative" craft as in theorizing figuration more broadly. Many close readings often do not discuss narrative per se but something I might call "discursive craft" (if not the art of rhetoric). Cooper maintains that *texts* are the focus of this study and not the physical products created by medieval artisans themselves, but a more sustained engagement with created texts as artifacts (with their own material histories) could have enriched the book's titular focus on narrative as craft. Insofar as this book traverses Latin, French, Old English, and Middle English texts, I felt that the practice of translation was given inadequate treatment. The epilogue and the discussion of Lydgate in Chapter 4 align features of poetic translation with artisanal craft, but Cooper's inclination to think in terms of narrative tends to obscure linguistic difference precisely when texts render it most visible (for instance, in Caxton's *Dialogues,* or the French-English peregrinations of Deguileville).

Quibbles aside, I find this study engaging, informative, and thought-provoking. Given its subtle and nuanced readings of craft discourses in texts across medieval genres and media, *Artisans and Narrative Craft in Late Medieval England* has the potential to lay the groundwork for many productive discussions.

Jonathan Hsy
George Washington University

Rita Copeland and Peter T. Struck, eds. *The Cambridge Companion to Allegory.* Cambridge: Cambridge University Press, 2010. Pp. xxiii, 295. £55.00; $95.00 cloth, £18.99; $29.99 paper.

Coming up with a comprehensive and yet pithy definition of allegory is notoriously difficult—and, strikingly, in this *Companion,* Rita Copeland and Peter Struck do not even try. Instead, they offer a history of the ways in which *allegory* and associated terms such as *enigma, symbol,* and *hyponoia* ("under-meaning") have been used and understood in the West, from the earliest Greek texts to the early twenty-first century. In the process, Copeland and Struck rebut a long-standing devaluation of allegory that condemns it for erasing individual or historical particularity in favor of totalizing and reductively applied doctrine. By drawing productively on philosophy, theology, rhetoric, literature, and the arts, the *Companion*'s detailed histories reveal that our understanding of allegory, rather than allegory itself, has heretofore been reductive and over-general.

Indeed, one of the distinctive features of Copeland and Struck's approach is that it defines nearly everybody as in need of the kinds of basic orientation that the Cambridge *Companion*s have traditionally provided to students and beginning teachers. Outside the confines of this volume, few are simultaneously conversant with Stoic allegoresis, eleventh-century Islamic philosophical allegories, Bernard Silvestris, Dante's *Convivio,* fourteenth-century poetry, allegorical drama, Protestant exegesis, the differences between late antique and Romantic Neoplatonism, Walter Benjamin and Paul de Man, and late twentieth-century allegorical performance art. For Copeland and Struck, however, these historically disparate test cases are the empirical shoals on which theoretical statements about allegory have repeatedly foundered. Here, instead, they are converted into sites for defining allegory as a series of historically specific "practices" and "habits of thought" to which the volume invites us to awaken (2).

For readers of *Studies in the Age of Chaucer,* the most valuable chapters are likely to be those that address medieval allegory and its late classical antecedents, as well as—perhaps surprisingly—the essays on the twentieth-century recuperation of allegory at the end of the book. One disadvantage of presenting the volume as a rhetorical history is that the editors forgo the opportunity to define its theoretical affiliations. When the *Companion* is read backward, however, it becomes clear that Benjamin and de Man, discussed in a pair of lucid essays by Howard Caygill and Steven Mailloux, cast long shadows over the rest of the book. Individual contributions to the *Companion* follow in de Man's footsteps by returning to texts long considered to be axiomatically anti-allegorical, discovering in them more interpretive complexity than had previously been allowed, while Denys Turner refreshingly performs this operation in reverse, exposing the anxiety about, and frustration with, prevailing forms of allegorical reading in seemingly standardized thirteenth- and fourteenth-century accounts of the four levels of biblical exegesis. A number of essays likewise follow de Man by defining *all* nonliteral language or *all* acts of interpretation as allegory. Others restrict allegory to a mode that foregrounds problems of figuration and interpretation that would otherwise be obfuscated; here we hear echoes of Benjamin's positive valuation of allegory as the redemption of a historical ruin, as well as de Man's claim that elevating symbol over allegory constitutes "self-mystification." In important respects, then, these two chapters define the conditions of possibility for the book as a whole.

This is not to say that the medieval has nothing to teach the modern. One of this book's major strengths is that it debunks the idea (prevalent among nonmedievalists and even some medievalists) that medieval allegory contains and minimizes disturbing textual possibilities while modern allegory thematizes, and sometimes celebrates, distance, difference, and fracture. Turner acknowledges the existence of stereotypically bad medieval allegory, citing Denis the Carthusian's "wooden and po-faced" commentary on the Song of Songs, and even recognizes that such foundational thinkers as Origen, Cassian, and Augustine might at first glance seem to use allegory "as a device of Christian tendentiousness, permitting, if not demanding, the evacuation of all literal meaning from the biblical text, especially the evacuation of the literal 'Jewishness' of the Old Testament" (81, 77). Such a view, however, mistakes Origen and Augustine, as well as the later theologians Hugh of Saint Victor, Saint Thomas Aquinas, and Nicholas of Lyra. All of these thinkers demand a scholarly attention to the literal text, an investigation "into text and context, into cultures of writing, rhetorical and literary, different from the reader's own" before the reader proceeds to allegorical interpretation (78). Like anything else, allegory can be done well or badly— but a good medieval allegorist, defined in the period's own terms, reads through the literal text rather than past it.

Jon Whitman's chapter on twelfth-century allegory and Nicolette Zeeman's essay on thirteenth- and fourteenth-century French and English religious allegory confront a similar set of assumptions, albeit from different angles. For Whitman, Bernard Silvestris's *Cosmographia* emphasizes "not the impulse to escape the world but the effort to 'explicate' it" (110). Whitman considers both Bernard's and Alan of Lille's personifications of Nature to be ancestors of the questioning first-person narrator of later medieval dream visions and, indeed, to be tools for investigating human personhood. These complex personifications resist any schema that contrasts mechanistic or emblematic personification allegory with richly detailed mimetic or realistic literary characters. Zeeman attributes the critical tendency to think of medieval allegory as strongly intellectualist or didactic to the tradition of reading allegory through its explicatory discourses. In practice, however, later medieval vernacular religious allegory "talks back" to this language of interpretation, in part by exploiting the incongruity of its terms for ironic, critical, or iconoclastic purposes. Far from being intrinsically more reductive than secular allegory, for Zeeman "religious allegory seems especially often to foreground the unlikeness and the possible discrepancies between the terms it brings together" (149).

The *Companion* also highlights general continuities in allegorical writing and interpretation where a narrowly periodizing reader might see a *sui generis* phenomenon. Glenn Most argues that the Stoics used allegory to reposition texts and practices originally "anchored in the highly specific micro-cultural contexts" of Greek city-states within the broader and turbulent Mediterranean world (28). In so doing, the Stoics established allegory's value for addressing new, cross-cultural audiences, whether a Christian audience for classical epic, a vernacular audience for Latin theology, or even, as discussed in Lynette Hunter's essay on allegory after 1960, a mixed Euro-American and postcolonial audience for the novels of Salman Rushdie and Ben Okri. Struck, in turn, explains the prevalence of dream visions in the emergent vernacular literature of the late Middle Ages through the classical Neoplatonic tradition, transmitted via Macrobius, of commingling allegorical, divinatory, and dream interpretation. For the Neoplatonists, each links an enigmatic scintilla of truth in the lower world to its origin in the One, making the dream a potential site for literary invention.

Although all medieval dream visions are not allegories (except perhaps as defined by de Man), Struck's genealogy does suggest that dream visions belong to a historically defined allegorical tradition. The same can be said of Gower's *Confessio Amantis,* which Copeland and Stephanie Gibbs Kamath describe as the end product of allegorical reading, shorn of its sources' actual allegorizing. What, then, *is* allegory, and how does it relate to its historical tradition, as well as to the category of the literary, both in and beyond the Middle Ages? *The Cambridge Companion to Allegory* equips its readers to formulate increasingly well-informed and productive versions of these questions.

KATHARINE BREEN
Northwestern University

KATE CRASSONS. *The Claims of Poverty: Literature, Culture, and Ideology in Late Medieval England.* Notre Dame: University of Notre Dame Press, 2010. Pp. 389. $40.00.

In *The Claims of Poverty,* Kate Crassons addresses the competing intellectual responses to poverty in later medieval England. In the texts Crassons analyzes—*Piers Plowman, Pierce the Ploughman's Crede,* three Wycliffite sermons, *The Book of Margery Kempe,* and the pageants of the

York cycle—poverty is figurative; it is a theological construct or a legal category, as much as a lived personal or social experience.

The moral status of poverty was central to writings in both the Franciscan and antifraternal traditions in the later Middle Ages; moreover, both labor law and estates satire depend on their audience's understanding of the right relationships between work and wealth. Scholars have certainly recognized the echoes of these contemporary debates in the literature of late medieval England. Crassons's accomplishment in *The Claims of Poverty* is to bring together a range of discourses around poverty and show both their interrelationships and their pervasiveness in the literary culture. Crassons demonstrates that writers from Langland to Kempe to the anonymous authors of the cycle drama were deeply influenced by ongoing theological and political debates about how to understand poverty.

In her first chapter, which deals with *Piers Plowman,* Crassons extends the previous scholarship on Langland's complex and shifting representations of poverty by focusing on the hermeneutic challenges inherent in discourses on poverty. The need to differentiate the truly needy from idlers, and the poem's concern with its characters' labor status, intersects with the poem's organizing question of what it means to do well. In this chapter, the book's longest, Crassons is particularly concerned with the semiotics of poverty. Must need be visible? Can the poor represent themselves, or must their identity be seen (and thus constructed) by others? What does the presence of the needy mean for a community? How can one recognize those worthy of charity? These questions are, Crassons argues, of a piece with *Piers Plowman*'s shifts in voice, genre, and narrative structure, all of which complicate interpretation of the poem. In the different perspectives characters in *Piers Plowman* bring to the questions of how to differentiate the truly needy from idlers, or legitimate from illegitimate means of living, Crassons sees "a certain reluctance on Langland's part to make hard and fast distinctions among the poor" (76).

In Chapter 2, "Poverty Exposed: The Evangelical and Epistemological Ideal of *Pierce the Ploughman's Crede,*" Crassons argues that the author of the *Crede* intentionally elides all of the epistemological questions that Langland associates with poverty and need, replacing them instead with a certainty that one can transparently differentiate true poverty (like that of the plowman) from feigned need (that of the fraternal orders). Crassons argues that the *Crede*'s Wycliffite semiotics and its "willfully impoverished poetics" deny artifice and ambiguity (92), even if the poem's "goal of [perfect] transparency is, of course, ultimately impossible to attain" (132). This argument is persuasive, although it could have been expressed in fewer than forty-eight pages, given that *Pierce the Ploughman's Crede* itself is only 850 lines long. Chapter 2 is, however, a useful bridge between Crassons's first chapter on Langland's ambivalences about poverty and her third chapter on the surprising economic theories evident in some Wycliffite sermons.

Anticlerical Wycliffite writings are a predictable subject for a book about medieval conceptions of poverty, but in her third chapter, "'Clamerous' Beggars and 'Nedi' Knights: Poverty and Wycliffite Reform," Crassons goes beyond the obvious rejection of clerical wealth to show exactly whose economic interests the Wycliffite sermons serve: those of the lay elites. The sermons Crassons cites challenge the notion of apostolic poverty, arguing that Christ valorized work over idleness and that Christ himself was incapable of poverty, since he had natural dominion and literally could not beg. Moreover, the sermons argue that fraternal mendicancy and the church's accumulation of goods both invert the proper distribution of wealth and power, which are rightfully held by lay lords.

Chapter 4 both continues and contrasts with the third, as Crassons demonstrates the paradoxical claims about poverty and dominion that Margery Kempe makes in her *Book*. Kempe claims to renounce her privilege as a member of Lynn's wealthy elite for a life of voluntary poverty and a socially marginal status; Crassons demonstrates, however, that Kempe's is a poverty without need. Throughout her narrative, Kempe retains social superiority to the involuntary poor around her; meanwhile, all of her needs are fulfilled through divine favor. *The Book of Margery Kempe* thus endorses voluntary poverty on its surface while simultaneously demonstrating Kempe's own disdain for the poor and refusal to inhabit her voluntary poverty fully.

The fifth chapter focuses on the York *Entry into Jerusalem, Crucifixion,* and *Last Judgment.* Here Crassons demonstrates that the York Plays stage many of the competing ideologies of poverty that she has itemized in the previous four chapters, as different characters represent diverse social stations and (explicitly or implicitly) espouse different theories of dominion, poverty, and labor. This chapter and Chapter 2 (on *Pierce the Ploughman's Crede*) are the chapters most dependent on the reader's familiarity with the arguments of the rest of the book. The first, third, and fourth chapters (those on *Piers Plowman,* the Wycliffite sermons, and *The Book of Margery Kempe*) seem the most likely to be read in isolation by scholars researching those particular texts.

Appropriately for a final chapter, but also appropriately for plays that stage competing ideologies, the fifth chapter has the most cross-references to the claims of the others, making it an epilogue before the book's actual epilogue, a discussion of Barbara Ehrenreich's 2001 work of undercover anthropology about living as a minimum-wage laborer: *Nickel and Dimed: On (Not) Getting By in America.* Crassons stops short of claiming the direct influence of earlier debates on poverty or of allowing the contemporary analogue to answer to the "so what?" question elicited by the study of distant cultural phenomena. The epilogue notes that reviewers often focus on the question of whether Ehrenreich's outsider analysis was illegitimate rather than on the larger political issue of the challenges facing the working poor. To that extent, debates about *Nickel and Dimed* recapitulate some of the late medieval discourses about poverty that the previous chapters have itemized.

The Claims of Poverty is deeply researched and attentive to the details of its primary texts. Its arguments are informed by semiotics, speech-act theory, cultural materialism, and deconstruction but are made without resorting to the proprietary terminology of those methodologies, making Crassons's book highly readable, even for an upper-level undergraduate. While another study of *Piers Plowman* and labor law or a new demonstration of Margery Kempe's mercantile ideology may appear superfluous, Crassons brings together some familiar concepts in new ways, and her meticulous close readings pay off with new insights about some of the most widely studied texts in the medieval canon.

SARAH A. KELEN
Nebraska Wesleyan University

HOYT N. DUGGAN, Project Director. *The Piers Plowman Electronic Archive.* The Society for Early English & Norse Electronic Texts (SEENET). Seven compact disks. Vol. 1: Robert Adams, Hoyt N. Duggan, Eric Eliason, Ralph Hanna III, John Price-Wilkin, and Thorlac Turville-Petre, eds. *Corpus Christi College, Oxford MS 201 (F).* $77.50. Vol. 2: Thorlac Turville-Petre and Hoyt N. Duggan, eds. *Cambridge, Trinity College, MS B.15.17 (W)*. $80.00. Ann Arbor: University of Michigan Press, 2000. For the Medieval Academy of America and SEENET. Vol. 3: Katherine Heinrichs, ed. *Oxford, Oriel College, MS 79 (O)*. 2004. $50.00; £30.00. Vol. 4: Hoyt. N. Duggan and Ralph Hanna, eds. *Oxford, Bodleian Library, Laud Misc. 581 (L)*. 2004. $50.00; £30. Vol. 5: Eric Eliason, Thorlac Turville-Petre, and Hoyt. N. Duggan, eds. *London, British Library MS Additional 35287 (M)* 2005. $50.00; £30.00. Vol. 6: Michael Calabrese, Hoyt N. Duggan, and Thorlac Turville-Petre, eds. *San Marino, Huntington Library Hm 128 (Hm, Hm²)*. 2008. $50.00/£30.00. Vol. 7: Robert Adams, ed. *London, British Library, MS Lansdowne 398 & Oxford, Bodleian Library, MS Rawlinson Poetry 38 (R)* 2011. $50.00; £30.00. Rochester, N.Y.: Boydell & Brewer.

This magnificent resource takes pride of place in sophistication if not size among the many other massive digitizing projects in literary studies, among them the Dante and Rossetti materials, the Chaucer Project, the huge Middle English database of the University of Michigan Corpus of Middle English Prose and Verse (which includes older editions of *Piers Plowman* by Skeat and Schmidt), the enormous TEAMS Middle English Texts Series—along with the ever-expanding corpora of high-quality medieval manuscript facsimiles on line, especially in England (the whole Parker Library! select Oxford manuscripts, including *Piers* MS F of B!), France, Germany, and Italy. When put together with JSTOR's trove of scholarly articles and Google's (warmly to be thanked) search engine and free scholarly book services, we are simply in a different research world from even ten years ago. This *Archive* and its peers have scarcely begun to be exploited.

Each of the *Archive*'s disks contains complete color facsimiles of the manuscripts treated, presented in two levels of photographic quality (I found no need for the sharper of the two), along with searchable and manipulable transcriptions of the texts and long introductions. The transcriptions, with elaborate but user-friendly hyperlinks, are able to show manuscript features well beyond what used to be called "diplomatic" texts—such things as the color of ink, the "touching" of letters with red, parasigns, cartouches, superscripts, marginalia, catchwords, croppings and various other types of damage to the writing, abbreviation expansions, corrections, and additions. A manuscript like M (vol. 5), with its 5,000 erasures and 3,500 additions by various hands, is surely more manageable for study in this form than in the flesh. Not tagged, for good reason, are grammatical and metrical features of the text. As the editors point out, it is easy for an individual user to construct a concordance of each manuscript's text using various inexpensive or free programs.

A 1994 online prospectus written by Hoyt Duggan, the leader of this project, sketches its origins in his and Robert Adams's dissatisfaction with some features of the great Athlone edition of *Piers* directed by George Kane, specifically in that edition's failure to exploit Duggan's and Thomas Cable's findings about the meter of alliterative *b*-verses, and in its narrow focus on individual lections and single lines as opposed to larger textual units. By 1994, Duggan and Adams were joined by Eric Eliason, Ralph Hanna III, and Thorlac Turville-Petre, and the five, later joined by at least seven other editors, have persisted with the good health and the financial backing—especially that of the Institute for Advanced Technology in the Humanities at the University of Virginia—required for such a project. They have also been supported by the publishers who issued the CDs, and the fragile nature of such support is indicated by the shift of publishers after the first two volumes. Medievalists owe much to Boydell and Brewer. The editors generously credit the large teams of graduate assistants (who have gotten fine training), associate editors, and computer gurus who have made the project feasible. *Noblesse oblige:* the editors rank among the best Middle English scholars in the world.

The goal is to publish in electronic form facsimiles and transcripts of all the manuscripts of *Piers,* together with an edition of the reconstructed archetype of the B version (Bx), and a critical edition of B with explanatory annotation. The team reports that all the B manuscripts have been transcribed, and that the edition of the Bx, done by John Burrow and Thorlac Turville-Petre, is almost ready to be issued. We learn from an article by Robert Adams ("Evidence for the Stemma of the *Piers Plowman* B Manuscripts," *Studies in Bibliography* 53 [2000]: 173–94), and from his introduction to Volume 7, that at least the first draft of the edition of the Bx will be based on machine collation of nine manuscripts and one early print (CCr[1]FGHmLMORW). More narrowly, the team seems to have concluded that, as Adams says (175), "[W]hen both L and M agree with R . . . it is virtually certain that their shared readings represent those of [Bx]." Along with stemmatic considerations, this view is supported by codicological evidence, which the *Archive* persuasively educes, that manuscripts LMRWY were produced by a "loosely organized group working in London during the 1390s and early 1400s."

Volumes 1 and 7, treating the *alpha* group of B manuscripts, are the meatiest of the seven in their analyses of the version's textual tradition in general, but all offer untold riches. All present the text in at least four forms that they call "styles," including a style lightly edited to represent their judgment of what the scribes meant to write, and a style showing all the "tags" (in SGML, later XML) that underlie the detailed representation of the text, warts and all. There are four types of color-coded annotation—paleographical, codicological, textual, and lexical/linguistic—that quickly appear in windows adjacent to the text. (A problem here: the notes are *only* available by passing through links in the text, making it impossible to scan batches of notes). All volumes present exceptionally full introductions—the luxury of other-than-paper production—which describe the manuscripts and treat the script, the dialect, and the language (that is, the phonology).

In his 1994 prospectus, Duggan observed, "Scholars will want complex electronic texts not so much for reading as for what can be done with them." This is true, and obviously printed books and searchable, mechanically manipulable digitized disks have their separate uses and virtues. (One might add that the *Archive* is not for beginners in textual criticism or *Piers* studies.) The most booklike feature of these volumes is their introductions. The manuscript descriptions are models of thoroughness, as are the letter-by-letter descriptions of the various scribal hands, both strikingly enhanced by hyperlinked images of the codicological and paleographical features being discussed. These are an invaluable basis for any argument about the physical situation of the texts, and I should think would be ideal material for teaching manuscript analysis. The massive detail of the sections on dialect and phonology are grounded not in samplings but in precise counts of every feature (e.g., how many times and in what distribution "she" is represented by *heo*) made possible by the machinery and otherwise beyond human ability. This work need not be done again.

The earlier two of these seven volumes had a few weak features since resolved: in the later disks, the special fonts are automatically downloaded, the footnoting mechanics are smoother, and the font size can easily be adjusted for us presbyopics. Both modern text and facsimiles can be printed at home, with varying degrees of difficulty. Some of the

CDs open more readily than others. Regrettably, the toolbar that allows a reader to manipulate the facsimile images, especially to zoom in and out, disappears after the second volume, perhaps by oversight. On the whole, the main procedural problem is that of all electronic material, on disk or online: it can be a bit slow, a bit erratic, and a bit clumsy of navigation. Inevitably information (like dialect determinations) is dispersed that might better be viewed in a conspectus. Later volumes supply a helpful list of the markup tags employed. Yet a mere hour fiddling with these disks enables confident and pleasant use, appropriate to the medium.

The editors seem broadly to share George Kane's skepticism about any "sentimental" interest in "the scribes as critics" and the like. And indeed, that late twentieth-century vogue went too far. But, as Ralph Hanna has repeatedly warned us, the Athlone or Manly-Rickert or other editions of medieval texts have gone too far in the other direction, abstracting scribal readings from their *Sitz im Leben,* from their very physical condition, thus flattening a rich cultural and intellectual history. A fine example of a balancing of these points of view, using the wonderful materials provided by the *Archive,* is Andrew Galloway's essay-review of the first two volumes, "Reading *Piers Plowman* in the Fifteenth and the Twenty-First Centuries: Notes on Manuscripts F and W in the *Piers Plowman Electronic Archive," JEGP* 103 (2004): 232–52.

I leave aside the persuasive argument (Volume 1) that an "F-Redactor" ancestral to the scribe of F was mainly responsible for the wholesale innovations of that text; the intricate analysis (Volume 2) of the relation of the scribe of W to the Hengwrt/Ellesmere scribe; the untangling of some John Bale matters based on the provenance of L (Volume 4); the hitherto unnoticed links between M and the A Version text (Volume 5); the errant analysis of Hm by the Athlone editors (Volume 6; including publication of a difference of opinion among the *Archive* editors); more argument about the status of the *alpha* tradition of the B Version, and tantalizing suggestions about the Rokele (= Langland) and Butt families (Volume 7). Riches upon riches.

To come to what the editors must believe to be their most important quality, their accuracy. Talbot Donaldson once advised me, in his waggish way, never to print a photograph of a manuscript page along with an edition: some reviewer was bound to find transcriptional errors. I collated ten pages of transcription of manuscript F (Volume 1) and four pages of R (Volume 7) against the facsimiles. For comparison, in this stretch of F (B XII.122–XIII.205), I noted two substantive and two trivial errors in the Athlone edition's collation of F. In the *Archive,* in spite of the large amount of information beyond mere letters that the transcriptions include, I found no errors.

STEPHEN A. BARNEY
University of California, Irvine (Emeritus)

GEORGE EDMONDSON. *The Neighboring Text: Chaucer, Boccaccio, Henryson.* Notre Dame: University of Notre Dame Press, 2011. Pp. ix–xii, 280. $40.00 paper.

The word "neighbor" comes with a trail of sweetness. Neighbor bespeaks cordiality and proximity. My neighbor's house is the one I can see from my window. "Neighbor" carries obligation. My neighbor is she or he to whom I am bound by the mere fact of neighboring. It has nostalgic baggage. If you're from the old neighborhood, I will find myself tied to you for reasons of family and shared history. But there are dark sides to neighboring. If good fences make good neighbors, their moderating work also bespeaks the fractiousness of neighbor relations. Love thy neighbor as thyself, a Levitican injunction foundational to Judeo-Christian ethics, is scripted as law to organize community in the face of the hostility endemic to neighbor relations. It is this set of crossovers between fraught impulses of identification and misrecognition, love and violence, that has made the neighbor a rich topic for psychoanalytic theories of identity. The neighbor, according to Freud, is the *Nebenmensch,* the "next man" whose otherness and likeness provoke both identification and aggression. In his writings as well as in writings of Slavoj Žižek, Kenneth Reinhard, and Jacques Lacan, the psychodynamics of neighbor relations are foundational to the emergence of identity and selfhood as well as to political and social ethics.

   The psychodynamics of neighboring, heretofore little studied in relation to medieval writings, also drive textual relationships among Chaucer, Boccaccio, and Henryson in their rewritings of the Troilus story, according to George Edmondson in *The Neighboring Text.* In retelling the story of Troilus, all three writers take up questions of identity and mirroring that are played out among characters within the narrative and that underwrite the uses of the Troy legend as a political fable in pre-modern Europe, with the neighborhood comprising Europe between Florence, London, and Scotland. The Troilus story, that is, is a neighborly text on multiple levels: as a story about a community under siege; as a story about homosocial relationships and the polarizations of courtly love; as a story, exchanged among writers with different political and devotional aims, about community formation itself. Most provocatively, the idea of the neighbor provides Edmondson with a vehicle for rethinking lineal models of medieval literary history. That neighborly relations were more important for the Middle Ages than kinship or genealogy has been productively argued by David Wallace, Paul Strohm, and Aranye Fradenburg, among others. Edmondson breaks important new ground by extending those principles to writers and readers of medieval texts. Lineal genealogies of literary transmission are associated with a concept of nation that does not really apply to premodern Europe, Edmondson argues. Association, guild, fraternity, family: rules for engagement that underwrite premodern social and political communities can apply as well to literary transmission.

The readings of Henryson, Boccaccio, and Chaucer offered here, buttressed throughout by readings of Lacan, Žižek, and Reinhard, are exceptionally rich and fine. If they make a single argument, it is that the neighbor relationships articulated in one text (a neighboring text) get a second play in their narrative reprisals—that Henryson responds to Chaucer and that Chaucer responds to Boccaccio as literary neighbors and also as creators of narratives about neighboring—and of the neighbor's life or death. Following a lucid introduction outlining the central concerns of the book—the idea of the neighbor in psychoanalytic theory, the meaning of Troy in London's political and civic imaginary, and the book's key psychoanalytic concepts (*Nebenmensch, jouissance,* the Thing, the space between two deaths)—the study opens with a reading of Henryson's Scottish response to Chaucer's London *Troilus*. The *Testament,* Edmondson argues, is organized and contoured by English/Scottish neighbor relations, dramatized through the fates of its characters as well as through Henryson's invocations of Chaucer and of Scottish geography. By reanimating Troilus and denying him a real and symbolic death, by inflicting leprosy on Cresseid, and by presenting Chaucer as a neighbor rather than a literary father, hence denying the community of sons that a symbolic father produces, Henryson undoes claims that would tie

England to the glories of Troy and Chaucer to an emerging English literary genealogy.

Chapter 2, "Chaucer's Encounter with the *Filostrato*," takes as its point of departure the question why Chaucer changed Boccaccio's text. If Chaucer can be said to "medievalize" Boccaccio, as C. S. Lewis has famously argued, he does so as a corrective to the impossible identification Boccaccio allows between his narrator and Troilo—impossible because Boccaccio transgresses fundamental laws of identification in linking his narrator with a figure from the pagan past. Henryson diminishes Troilus's legendary status by keeping him alive; Boccaccio does it by giving him an unremarkable death, in striking contrast to the glorious symbolic death accorded Troilo in Boccaccio's sources. As Edmondson puts it, "By undeadening Troilo, [the *Filostrato*] denies medieval Europe its tomb"—denies, that is, the heroic and symbolic death necessary for Troilus and Troy to serve as symbolic props to Europe's glory. Chaucer, in contrast, provides the tomb and corrects misaligned identification, Edmondson argues in Chapter 3, "*Troilus and Criseyde* between Two Deaths." Unlike the *Testament* or *Filostrato*, Chaucer's *Troilus* commemorates the dead, providing Troilus with a symbolic death that serves political and religious ends. Edmondson gives the best explanation I have seen anywhere of Troilus's deathlike passivity—perhaps awaiting his symbolic interment at the poem's end—and for Pandarus's role as courtier, repeatedly staging actions that defer time and catastrophe. Yet if the poem ultimately serves the Law of Christianity, it does so ironically and self-consciously, critiquing the brutalities of courtly love and commenting on the ironies of London's obsession with Troy even as it gives medieval London its requisite fantasy and, in the Christian entombment of Troilus, its symbolic tragedy.

This brief summary hardly begins to do justice to the riches of *The Neighboring Text*—and those riches include as well the energy and elegance of Edmondson's prose and his lively dialogue with other critics. Lucid as it is, the book is not an easy read, particularly for those unfamiliar with psychoanalytic theories of identity. Yet while it might be possible to skip over passages on Lacan and Žižek, that would be to miss the backstory psychoanalysis provides for emotion, genre, ethics, and literary transmission: why Troilus, Criseyde, and Pandarus are driven to act as they do, why these medieval writers cared so much about them and their fates, and why we as readers still care as well. What are the passions—desire, longing, despair, grief—that drive the Troilus story and that drive Chaucer, Boccaccio, and Henryson to retell the story and to tell it as they do? And how are emotions the basis of ethics? The book could perhaps have been titled *The Other Text*, but that would be to shy away from the ethical and affective demands encompassed in the "neighbor." In this dazzling study, Edmondson has found a compelling critical vocabulary for the psychic and communitarian work of these stories of Troy and, long after Troy has lost its political mystique, the reader's continued investments in them.

SARAH STANBURY
College of the Holy Cross

ROBERT EPSTEIN and WILLIAM ROBINS, eds. *Sacred and Profane in Chaucer and Late Medieval Literature: Essays in Honour of John V. Fleming.* Toronto: University of Toronto Press, 2010. Pp. vii, 238. $60.00.

The distinguished Chaucerian, Princetonian, and blogger John V. Fleming retired in 2006. He continues to add to a learned and wide-ranging oeuvre (his most recent book is a study of the literary representation of the USSR in the Cold War West) that includes the editing (with Thomas J. Heffernan) of the second *Studies in the Age of Chaucer* (1986). This is the second of two *festschrift*s to have appeared. A collection of essays, edited by Michael F. Cusato and Guy Geltner, honoring his work on Franciscan texts and history, came out in 2009 as *Defenders and Critics of Franciscan Life*. The present volume grew out of a symposium arranged in Fleming's honor at Princeton in 2006. The ten essays, all by Fleming's former students, make a lively collection.

In their substantial and thought-provoking introduction, William Robins and Robert Epstein have more to say about the profane than the sacred, seeking to disturb the straightforward binary of sacred and profane by complicating the latter term, which can include senses both of transgressive irreligiosity and of the simply secular. For them, and for contributors to this volume, the profane is "the point at which the sacred and the secular converge" (23).

The first two essays make a nicely complementary pair: both are concerned with biblical women who are the victims of a lustful male gaze, and both extend their inquiry beyond the Middle Ages into the sixteenth and seventeenth centuries. David Lyle Jeffrey writes on Bathsheba, especially in the postmedieval period (culminating with Rembrandt), while Lynn Staley (more substantially) examines Susanna, with particular reference to the self-understandings of victims of religious persecution and legal process, from the Lollards Walter Brut and William Thorpe onward.

The core of the book is provided by five essays on Chaucer's poetry, several of them in close dialogue with John Fleming's own work. Jamie C. Fumo situates Troilus and Criseyde's attitudes to, and belief in, love in relation to fourteenth-century discourses about love for and belief in God, associating Criseyde with what Fleming had identified as "philosophical atheism." William Robins delves rewardingly into Trojan sanitation to find, in Troilus's supposed route to Pandarus's house on the night when he will consummate his love for Criseyde ("thorough a goter, by a pryve wente"), a "strangely fraught nexus of sewage, idolatry, and love" (104). Julia Marvin offers a close reading of the F Prologue to *The Legend of Good Women,* and of the tale of Dido, with the question of old books to the fore. Robert Epstein shows how the generally accepted reading of *The Summoner's Tale* as turning on the opposition of the material and the spiritual is complicated by the fact (increasingly recognized in the late Middle Ages) that money is not material, but "a sophisticated philosophical abstraction" (134) susceptible of learned academic analysis—which Epstein provides by way of Bourdieu and fourteenth-century Oxford. And Martin Camargo finds some telling parallels between the list of *don'ts* given in his advice on preaching style by the fourteenth-century Dominican Thomas Waleys and the performance of the Pardoner. It seems that, in his cocksure estimation of his rhetorical prowess (which we have tended to accept at face value), the Pardoner may have been deluding himself after all. Camargo usefully provides a translation of the relevant chapter of Waleys as an appendix.

Fiona Tolhurst's essay on Margery Kempe is somewhat out on a limb. Her argument, that "Kempe might have had a more basic and more orthodox purpose for writing than critics often suggest" (197), is avowedly a corrective to recent work (especially the books by Karma Lochrie and Lynn Staley) that would see her as radical and (in several senses) heterodox. Such readings do not perhaps have quite the hegemony that Tolhurst assumes, but nonetheless her essay usefully gathers together evidence from the *Book* for Kempe's orthodoxy and conservatism. It does not particularly push back the boundaries of Kempe studies, but it will no doubt be valuable in a teaching context—not something to be sniffed at, in a book dedicated to the man who has made Chaucer's Clerk's "gladly lerne, gladly teche" his own.

The volume concludes with a bibliography of John Fleming's published writings up to 2009, but before that there is Steven Justice's "Preface to Fleming." He describes it as "part essay, part memoir, part encomium" (204), and indeed it is hard to classify. By no means the bland panegyric that a *festschrift* will often contain, it is a serious and in the end compelling reflection on a scholar and teacher that Justice, at least, has found by turns inspiring, frustrating, and fascinating.

This is a fairly short book, but a stimulating one. Some of the essays still have the feel of symposium papers about them: a little short and insubstantial in some cases; opening up a line of inquiry but not really pressing it to its conclusion in a few others. But there is strong and substantial work here, too, perhaps especially in the essays by Staley and by the two editors themselves. They can be congratulated also for pulling together an enjoyable and (for the most part) pleasingly coherent collection.

E. A. JONES
University of Exeter

JAMIE C. FUMO. *The Legacy of Apollo: Antiquity, Authority, and Chaucerian Poetics.* Toronto: University of Toronto Press, 2010. Pp. xvi, 352. $70.00.

This book aims to define the importance for Chaucer, and for the poets who defined the Chaucer tradition in the century following his death, of the figure of Apollo, conceived as "locus of the self-authorizing aspirations of the late-medieval love-poet as well as of the classical convention of the truth-telling *vates*" (11). The author, as imaginatively constructed by Chaucer, was "an Apolline crucible of literary tradition" (15), seriously interested in questions of authority and inspiration.

The introduction locates three main sources for Chaucer's conception of the god. He is largely the Apollo of Ovid, and reflects Ovid's use of the god as a mirror of his own complex, deeply ironic and self-aware conception of the artist. Chaucer's Apollo also reflects the tendency of medieval mythography to make the god "an iconic focus of . . . anxieties surrounding literary paganism" (21): he can be a type of Christ; an image of wisdom; the pagan idol par excellence; or an index to "an ambiguous stage of transition." The silencing of poetry and the breaking of Apollo's instruments in the Manciple's version of an Ovidian tale is Chaucer's "essentially Christian renunciation of a poetic journey inspired by Apollo" (18), and joins him to a well-established tradition. Finally, the Apollo of the *Aeneid* is of great importance for Chaucer, above all in *Troilus and Criseyde*. Fumo interprets the *Troilus* as a retrospective "prequel" to Virgil's poem, reading its portrayal of Apollo "through an Augustinian lens" that emphasizes the role of the god as a destabilizing force, exposing unresolved tensions in Virgil's "epideictic of the founding of Rome" (21).

Fumo devotes a long chapter to Ovid's treatment of Apollo as a "human" god, showing how rarely he appears in a positive light, how often his powers (as healer, teacher, or lover) prove ineffectual and his authoritative posturings absurd. When he appears in the middle of the *Ars amatoria* to deliver the Delphic injunction "know thyself," what he goes on to propose are effective means of self-display—narcissism rather than self-knowledge (51–52). As physician, he has a prominent role in the *Remedia amoris,* but his remedies turn out to be incitements to renewed passion (68–69). Yet Ovid plainly identifies himself with Apollo, who becomes patron, alter ego, and role model for Ovid's own "narcissistic and often self-defeating activity" as poet (48).

The Apollo of the mythographers occupies another long, rather rambling chapter, which shows how the Christianizing mythographers of the fourteenth and fifteenth centuries are anticipated in the favorable treatment of Apollo by Hyginus and Fulgentius, and deals at some length with a range of early Christian materials: the possible appropriation of the myth of Apollo and Python in the Book of Revelation (82); forged oracles attributed to Delphic Apollo acknowledging the arrival of the new, Christian world order (82–86); possible association of Apollo with the priest Apollos of the Book of Acts and Apollyon in Revelation 9:11 (90–94); euhemerist polemic (95–98). Medieval condemnations of Apollo as pagan idol are reviewed with reference to manuscript illustrations and a range of late medieval texts.

Together these two chapters run to a hundred pages, or nearly half the book, and while they are interesting in themselves, it must be said that their length is out of all proportion to their importance for the discussions of Chaucer that follow. Although the author emphasizes the "seminal" importance of Ovid for Chaucer's conception of poetic authority, the chapter on Ovid makes only occasional mention of Chaucer, usually to note his having inherited from Ovid a particular motif, or the canonical version of a mythological story, and we hear almost nothing of Ovid in the chapters devoted to the *Troilus* and the tales of the Squire and Franklin. He of course plays an important role in the concluding chapter on *The Manciple's Tale,* but the Ovidian information necessary to the author's reading of this tale could have been provided much more briefly and efficiently.

The mythography chapter is still more of a loose end. It ranges far and wide, and almost none of the information it gathers together bears significantly on the later chapters. Again, the chapter on *The Manciple's Tale* is a partial exception, but even here the material deployed is random and occasionally confusing, and again it could have been provided more briefly.

That said, there are very good things in the chapters on Chaucer. Much of the *Troilus* chapter could be a commentary on *Troilus and Criseyde* I.70, "Daun Phebus or Appollo Delphicus": the radiant, golden-haired lover, patron of the false joys of Troy, versus the cryptic oracle exploited by calculating priests. Chaucer's treatment of Apollo is part of a critique of the *Aeneid,* balancing the god's traditionally benign attitude toward Troy with suggestions of his failure to protect the city, casting Aeneas as possible traitor and offering no hint of his destined journey to Italy, for which he will claim Apollo's guidance. Noteworthy, too, are a dozen excellent pages on the *Ylias* of Joseph of Exeter, which here receives perhaps its first careful reading by a Chaucerian, and is shown to anticipate many of the complexities of the world of the *Troilus.*

The chapter on the tales of Squire and Franklin does a fine job of demonstrating the coherence of Fragment V, and it argues persuasively that the figure of Apollo is a significant link between the two tales: the high-flying Apollo at the end of *The Squire's Tale* is the measure of an ambition that the Franklin will both gently critique and appropriate to himself. His Aurelius is his version of the Squire, and Aurelius's ineffectual prayer to Apollo sets off the artistic control of the Clerk of Orleans, who saves the day within the *Tale,* and who of course stands for the Franklin himself. Together, the author suggests, the fragmentary glimpse of Apollo at the end of *The Squire's Tale* and Aurelius's abortive prayer anticipate the emphasis on narrative discontinuity in the later portions of the *Canterbury Tales,* and prepare us for the coup de grâce of *The Manciple's Tale,* with Apollo at its center.

At times, the concluding chapter on *The Manciple's Tale* risks following the path of the chapters on Ovid and mythography, in that it introduces a great deal of ancient material that bears at best an oblique relation to the *Tale,* but it succeeds very well in demonstrating how Phoebus is victimized by being placed on the receiving end of an oracular riddle. The role of the crow (and that of the Manciple himself) is usefully compared to that of Cassandra, interpreting Troilus's dream of the boar (*Troilus and Criseyde* V.1450–533). *The Manciple's Tale* does indeed "appropriate the legacy of Apollo to contemplate the death of the author" (227), and the chapter shows how effectively this iconoclastic move prepares for the Christian ending of the Canterbury pilgrimage.

WINTHROP WETHERBEE
Cornell University (Emeritus)

SHANNON GAYK. *Image, Text, and Religious Reform in Fifteenth-Century England.* Cambridge: Cambridge University Press, 2010. Pp. vii, 258. £55.00; $95.00.

Image, Text, and Religious Reform in Fifteenth-Century England explores a set of English discourses on the relation of image and text in the fifteenth century. Intentionally devoid of actual images, Gayk's study focuses instead on vernacular writing in the wake of the Lollard critique and rejection of images at a time when image use was controversial, changing, and closely tied to the church's efforts to regulate lay piety. Building upon the research of such scholars as Margaret Aston, who have surveyed this territory before, Gayk fills in some important gaps by showing that the concern with images was explored by literary writers and theologians such as Thomas Hoccleve, John Lydgate, John Capgrave, and Reginald Pecock. She demonstrates the ways in which these writers "model reformist responses to the changing religious environment of late medieval England" (14), and in so doing forces us to rethink some long-held beliefs about orthodox and heterodox attitudes toward image and text.

In Chapter 1, Gayk looks at a series of "moderate" Lollard texts that advocate their own reformation of the image. While many Lollard writings are known for condemning religious imagery and other forms of imaginative and visual piety, these texts are "surprisingly incarnational" and employ what she calls a "Lollard iconography" (17): pictorial imagery and rhetorical devices that aim to regulate visual literacy. She argues that these writers embrace visual language in order to lead readers into an ethical understanding of images, highlighting the often-overlooked reality that not all Lollards renounced images altogether. Some were keen to provide the devout with their own form of aesthetic education, as she demonstrates. In Chapter 2, Gayk examines the theme of sight and vision in Hoccleve's writings, detailing the ways in which religious images in his poems thematize links between sight and knowledge, optics, and epistemology. In particular, she focuses on the use of the metaphor of eyeglasses to convey the need for regulating vision in order to avoid heresy and error: "Hoccleve suggests a model of 'speculative poetics' in which books are treated as textual spectacles through which images might be better seen and visual experience more effectively mediated" (83). Hoccleve's interest in visionary discourse is revealed to be both orthodox *and* reformist, as well as indebted to contemporary optical theory and theories of the imagination that emphasized the power of images to transform viewers. Hence Gayk reveals Hoccleve's aesthetic ideas to be denser and more variegated than critics have often acknowledged.

Like Hoccleve, Lydgate also seeks to instruct readers in how to view religious images, and Chapter 3 scrutinizes the role of image and text in his writings. Gayk reveals Lydgate to be both conservative and innovative in his attitudes toward images. In his orthodox efforts to regulate lay piety, Lydgate translates clerical, Latinate, and pre-Bernardine modes of affective piety and monastic *lectio* into vernacular poetry—an inherently reformist gesture. This act of translation finds a parallel in his treatment of images, which are also shown to elide boundaries, as Lydgate's writings make concrete some compelling transitions from image to text: moments when material, artistic images such as the *pietà* and Man of Sorrows become textualized. Gayk rightly notes the "permeable boundaries" (110) between image and text in these works and the often mobile, enigmatic transformations between media they exemplify. Indeed, some of Lydgate's poetry was subject to multiform identity and translated from manuscript page to church walls, and his translation of the *Danse macabre*—itself inspired by the painted poem in the cemetery of the Church of the Holy Innocents in Paris—migrated from text to image and back again, eventually making its way into print. This fluid dynamic of transmission can be connected to what Gayk intriguingly calls "the chameleon quality of the image" (3), its capacity for shifting, ever-changing (and often textual) permutation. This is a research area ripe for further exploration, especially in the study of fifteenth-century manuscript art, and Gayk's arguments here will provide an important touchstone.

The subject of Chapter 4 is John Capgrave's treatment of idols and images in his *vita* of Katherine of Alexandria, a text that discredits pagan idol worship in ways often thought of as staging contemporaneous image debates. The difference, Gayk argues, is that Capgrave's treatment of images is invested in preserving and appropriating cultural memory. Like the other authors she has discussed, Capgrave is viewed as providing his readers with an aesthetic education by prompting them to think historically about images across the past and present of Christian history.

In the final chapter, Gayk offers another significant critical intervention illuminating our understanding of Lollardy. Through a consideration of the academic writings of Bishop Reginald Pecock, the clerical reformer who became a tragic victim of ecclesiastical censure, she makes it evident that fifteenth-century discourses about images and iconoclasm are inseparable from ideas about the vernacular during the period. In doing so, she contextualizes anew some of the major fifteenth-century ideological debates that responded to Lollard anti-image polemic. Like several other authors discussed in the book, Pecock is shown to embody radical contradictions. On the one hand, he is radically reformist, not only seeking to empower lay readers by writing in the vernacular and stressing the rational nature of his audience of devout readers, but also involved in urban book circulation. On the other hand, most of his writings about images are essentially conservative. Moreover, for Pecock, images have a public function and social utility; in his view, they are more memorable than texts alone and therefore engage the emotions more effectively. Gayk's discussion illuminates the uniquely interesting position Pecock occupies in the debates about these intersecting discourses.

Gayk's book is filled with some fine close readings and she pays commendable attention to form, suggesting new ways of looking at vernacular religious writing during the period. She explores fascinating links between materiality and textuality in the writings of Hoccleve and Lydgate, and overall presents a compelling synthetic analysis of the fifteenth century's reformist, regulatory poetics. My only criticism of this book is minor: Gayk echoes many recent discussions of Nicholas Love's *Mirror* in her discussion of its proscriptive attempts to regulate lay piety. While it is true that Love advocates a corporeal spirituality rooted in emotional affect and sense perception, a modality that eschews the higher intellect and rationality, these meditative techniques, deeply rooted in monastic practice, were considered to be an appropriate pathway to the divine not only for laypeople but also for clerics and other religious. Overemphasizing this aspect of Love's text unintentionally creates a false dichotomy between a clerical and lay culture of reading, categories that were always more mixed and heterogeneous, even despite the church's attempts at social control.

Gayk has raised some intriguing questions concerning discourses about images within the broader contours of fifteenth-century piety, making new connections between aesthetics, ideology, and vernacular literary practice. Her study reconsiders the textualized spirituality characteristic of the period from a range of fresh, new angles that should be influential in the coming years. This well-informed book will serve as an instructive companion for anyone interested in later medieval English literary history, and Lollardy in particular, as well as art historians and others interested in theorizing the visual culture and incarnational aesthetic of the late Middle Ages.

MARLENE VILLALOBOS HENNESSY
Hunter College, City University of New York

ROBERT HANNING. *Serious Play: Desire and Authority in the Poetry of Ovid, Chaucer, and Ariosto.* New York: Columbia, 2010. Pp. 286. $45.00.

Robert Hanning's engaging, playful, and, despite protestations to the contrary, serious monograph on the seriocomic mode of Ovidian, Chaucerian, and Ariostan narrative begins with a rhetorical gesture that, given the book's impish muse, should not be taken at face value. Because it lacks the rigor of exhaustive engagement with critical scholarship, Hanning reasons, "This is not a scholarly work" (xii).

True, the book is a *vade mecum* that originated as the Schoff Lectures at Columbia University in the fall of 2005. With an argument that is neither linear nor doggedly polemical, it reads with the serendipity of an oral venue. Hanning moves from passage to passage, historical moment to historical moment, delivering insights as provocations to further thought in general preference to deductive conclusions. Its English translations of Ovid's Latin affect a colloquial New Yorkese ("Me miserum" = "Oy vey" [16]) that might seem whimsical for an academic tome were it not for a tonal trueness to the urbane antiestablishmentarianism of the Augustan original. Rather than in sustained argument, coherence resides in that wit and political temper with a hint of fang peculiar to Ovid's humor.

The very fact that this book is being reviewed in a scholarly journal, however, suggests that its publishers at least see it as occupying a niche between the academic and trade markets, albeit without the pomp and bluster of Greenblatt or Bloom. They are correct. Its audience, like that of the *Ars amatoria,* is the rare amateur of great books, someone acquainted with the complete corpus of Chaucer and undaunted by the 39,000 lines of the *Orlando furioso.* That could mean simply a literate reader, or more likely a student—undergraduate or graduate—of classical influence and the rhetorical tradition looking for a path through the Middle Ages to the early modern. In this light, Hanning's opening disavowal should be construed as a *recusatio,* that throroughly Ovidian topos of introduction by which an author dismisses the stuffy authority of his enterprise in order to forge a more casual camaraderie with his reader.

At one hundred pages, Chapter 1, entitled "Ovid's Amatory Poetry," is the longest of the three. It serves as the book's backbone and index of intertextuality. Here Hanning sets for himself the task of defining Ovid's protean personae as they evolve from the supine postures of the *Amores* into the pseudoscientific didacticism of the *Ars amatoria*'s *magister amoris.* In so doing, he traces a hermeneutic fiducial along which to align Chaucer's and Ariosto's later Ovidianism. The center of Ovid's irony, according to Hanning, is "the behavior and the fantasies of certain elite segments of Augustan Roman society" (23), the comic hypocrisy of hot pants in high places that reveals "inevitable contradictions between political and personal agendas" (91). Augustus Caesar is the prime target of this hypocrisy and Hanning diligently, and rightly, builds a poetico-political argument for Ovidian erotic irony on Augustus's Julian Laws of 18–17 BCE that regulated marriage and criminalized adultery among the patricians, and threatened the love poetry that satirized (promulgated?) such sexual license. Hanning notes the irony of Augustus's own sexual license reported by Suetonius, although he might have mentioned, as Macrobius does, the fact that both Augustus's daughter and granddaughter were prosecuted under these same laws. More important, he highlights the politically subversive edge to Ovid's irony that may well have gotten him banished, but certainly provided a model for medieval and early modern textual subversions. Along the way, Hanning explores a series of crucial cultural dichotomies such as *otium* versus *negotium*. The urban *cultus* that Hanning had defined earlier in his career in an influential article reappears in relation to the idea of *decorum* or suitability in a series of finely turned close readings. Now and again, he pauses to gloss pivotal poetic terms such as *membra* and *magister*. Taken alone, this chapter should feature on any university syllabus, undergraduate or graduate, that deals with Ovidian influence on medieval and early modern literature.

Written in the spirit of social disobedience and libertinism that Hanning located earlier in Ovid's anti-Augustanism, "Chaucer: Dealing with the Authorities" celebrates the impieties of author worship. The spotlight here is mainly on the minor poems, although *Troilus* and the *Canterbury Tales* also feature. Seriocomedy, for Hanning, resides in the sly ways Chaucer manages to satirize the classical authors he venerates, throwing stones, as it were, in the "temple ymaad of glas." The rich and insightful treatments of *The Book of the Duchess, The House of Fame, The Parliament of Fowls*, and especially *The Legend of Good Women* reveal an animating paradox in Chaucer that to "follow" an author temporally or textually is to *pretend* to follow in an equivocal game of intertext.

The subtitle to Chapter 3 on Ariosto's *Orlando furioso* makes enough sidelong gestures at other great poems and literary critical works to allow one to expect, somewhat erroneously, an essay on the narrative structure of romance. "Confusion Multiply Confounded, or Astray in the Forest of Desire" echoes, on the first count, Milton's *Paradise Lost*, whose famous Ariostan boast to "soar higher" seems to want to challenge the idea that epic can evolve from heroic romance. On the second count, we cannot help but scent the spoor of Patricia Parker's classic

414

treatment of "error" as a defining structure of romance. Hanning's discussion of *Orlando furioso*'s fusion of "chivalric romance and the feudal epic, also called the chanson de geste" (186) shades into a study of character and the parallel "crisis of desire" that afflicts both Orlando and the narrator. Hanning coins the term "narratorial polyphony" (curiously in contradistinction to Ovid's *Amores* rather than in imitation of the *Metamorphoses*) to describe the authorial persona's shifting postures, the most suggestive of which is the political sycophancy of the courtier, here in deference to the Cardinal Ippolito d'Este. Character analyses follow the errancy of "spatial, mental/moral states" (197) throughout the rest of the essay, culminating in a series of tableaux of "irresistible desire subverting political authority" (247). Recent classicizing work on *Orlando furioso* does little to inform Hanning's pioneering consideration of the poem, making his a unique and uniquely profitable voice in the woods of Ariostan criticism.

If I must admit a weakness to this pleasurable and often challenging tour of the great authors and their works, it would be the book's lack of a clear through-line, or *roter Faden* as the Germans call it. Ovid and his politically inflected discourse run throughout of course, but his spectral presence does not have the same unifying gravity of an argument. What I miss most is the definition of the seriocomic as a genre that might have evolved in quality over the course of the book. How is the seriocomic in Chaucer and Ariosto different, say, from sociopolitical satire in Ovid? Chapter 3 in particular could have done with a discussion of Giraldi Cinzio's and Tasso's theories of romance that would have buttressed the Ovidian influence on Ariosto's notion of narrative structure.

Hanning seems to have sensed this absence and answers, or rather deflects it in an epilogue. Rather than providing a shaping principle to comedy or seriocomedy, he proffers an outline of "some of the aspects of the production, consumption, and evaluation of comedy in twenty-first century America that distinguish it from the circumstances in which Ovid, Chaucer and Ariosto composed and, we assume, performed their comic poetry" (270). The relevance of this modern coda to a premodern study was originally justified most likely by Hanning's own performance before a nonspecialist audience whose experience may have been distant from that of his authors. It distracts more than it adds.

The strengths of this book, however, cannot be evaluated by strictly academic and specialist standards. Despite its form, its mode of performance is resolutely oral. *Serious Play* takes the reader into the classroom of one of the great medievalists of the past half century. I have had the privilege of being in that classroom. Now other serious students of premodern literature will have the opportunity, perhaps their last, to experience Hanning's playful and endlessly stimulating provocations. This is a book to read and reread alone or in the classroom with increments of profit as I have done and will do.

GREGORY HEYWORTH
University of Mississippi

MIRIAMNE ARA KRUMMEL. *Crafting Jewishness in Medieval England: Legally Absent, Virtually Present.* New York: Palgrave Macmillan, 2011. Pp. xix, 243. $85.00.

Long in gestation, this study has more strengths than weaknesses. The principal strength of *Crafting Jewishness in Medieval England* is that it surveys an impressive variety of texts and images from the twelfth century through the fifteenth and illuminates the theme of Jewish otherness in medieval England and the theme of the "Other" in medieval Christian Europe in general. Using postcolonial insights (via the work of Foucault, Homi Bhabha, and others), Miriamne Krummel starts out by linking the mimicry and displacement of Judaism in a contemporary anti-Judaic cartoon with the same ambivalent movement of mimicry and displacement in medieval anti-Judaic supersessionism. Setting the stage, Krummel writes: "Reading Jewishness through the intersection of imaginative and archival works enables me to see that English Jews were not at all absent from medieval English society as was commonly believed—a belief that is ever losing currency among contemporary medievalists" (8). This is promising, but in fact Krummel's "spectral" Jews receive most of the attention. To be sure, the Rolls are helpfully scanned for the "presence" of absent Jews in place-names that refer to "superseded" Jewish ownership. But for Krummel (following Biddick, Fradenburg, Kruger, and others), Jews are either "absent" or "erased," or present mainly in archival memory.

Fortunately, Krummel also sees past the specters and adduces evidence of actual Jews present after the 1290 expulsion, citing records in the Patent Rolls that prove that "the English land [*sic*] and its Court

416

probably welcomed Jews so long as the King desired their presence" (12). Acknowledging that England was not entirely *Judenrein* or "Jew-clean" after 1290, Krummel's thesis is that "neither the 1290 Expulsion nor scriptural typology completely prevented living Jewishness from appearing on the medieval English landscape" (14). How could that happen? Their lands had been expropriated, their presence outlawed—Where was "living Jewishness" to be found? Krummel suggests answers to these questions that will enliven the scholarly conversation.

In Chapter 1, Krummel explicates Edward I's *Statute of Jewry* (1275) and the "racialist impulses in eight thirteenth-century English pictorials [i.e., manuscript illustrations] and one fourteenth-century doodle" (23). As previous scholars have noted, these and similar images and statutes all coincide in defining Jews as bestial, the quintessential, less-than-human "Other." Krummel's contribution is to introduce a postmodern perspective on these familiar anti-Semitic stereotypes by way of theories of agency, the body, the gaze, the panopticon, hybridity, and essentialism.

Chapter 2 treats the liturgical poetry (Heb. *piyyutim*) of Meir, son of Elijah of Norwich (fl. c. 1290), focusing especially on Meir's "Put a Curse on My Enemy." This text reflects Meir's "attempt to reclaim agency and to become a witness to his own experiences" (63). Catastrophes call up memories of earlier catastrophes. As Krummel says, "[r]eseeing and re-membering the 1290 English Expulsion of the Jews through the enormity of the twentieth-century Holocaust are not so much myopic as they are inevitable" (65). Juxtaposing these two Jewish traumatic events may indeed "complicate our understanding of both periods," but the awkwardly expressed claim that it does so "by giving us a glimpse of a medieval Jews' [*sic*] internalization of invisibility and trauma in Meir's *piyyut*" (66) falls flat. In this chapter, page after page repeats large portions of Krummel's 2009 article on Meir of Norwich, partially revised but often cited word for word, and not listed in the bibliography (see Miriamne Ara Krummel, "Meir b. Elijah of Norwich and the Margins of Memory," *Shofar: An Interdisciplinary Journal of Jewish Studies* 27.4 [2009]: 1–23).

In Chapter 3, on *Mandeville's Travels* and the "postcolonial moment" (Tomasch), Krummel provides a sensitive reading of a uniquely intriguing text, "in which Jewishness appears only as deeply buried within the Caspian Mountains" (69). Throughout his travelogue, Mandeville expresses, as Krummel shrewdly says, "a simultaneous fascination with and a repulsion to difference" (69). If this chapter errs on the side of stressing Mandeville's fear over his fascination with Jews and their speaking Hebrew, it makes a plausible case for seeing Mandeville's primary objective to be a counterintuitive quest for cultural "unity, homogeneity, and monoethnicity" (88).

Krummel concedes at the outset of Chapter 4 that "the 'Prioress's Tale' undoubtedly repeats the more standard Christian anti-Judaic sentiment" (91). But in the end, she agrees with Kathleen Hobbs's view that "Chaucer deliberately but strategically deploys anti-Semitic themes and tropes in order to expose and satirize the naïve assumptions and hypocrisies of the Church of his day" (94, 188 n. 32). In her interpretation of *The Prioress's Tale*, Krummel lends credence to her view of Chaucer's cosmopolitan and largely benevolent attitude toward Jews and the idea of Jewishness by effectively applying the postcolonial notion of hybridity, and by adducing other places in Chaucer where we encounter Jews who are anything but hateful or demonic "Others" (especially in *The Monk's Tale, The House of Fame,* and *The Treatise on the Astrolabe;* less convincingly in several other places in the *Canterbury Tales*).

The final two chapters treat Hoccleve's *Complaint of the Virgin* and "The [Croxton] Play of the Conversion." What these texts have in common is that both depart (in their different ways) "from the customary impulse to view Jews antisemitically" (117). Hoccleve's poem, remarkably, "omits a passage of overt anti-Judaism" in a Crucifixion scene that was present in Deguileville's *Le pèlerinage de l'âme,* the source Hoccleve was otherwise copying faithfully. The omission created something rare: "a Crucifixion scene without antisemitism" (118). Krummel astutely observes that Hoccleve's omission of Deguileville's anti-Judaic sentiments should be "read in conversation with the expressions of social marginalization" in Hoccleve's *Complaint* and *Dialogue with a Friend.* Hoccleve's elision of traditional anti-Judaic and anti-Semitic motifs thus provides further evidence of "the depth of Hoccleve's identification with social pariahs" (118).

Chapter 6 provides a close reading of "The [Croxton] Play of the Conversion," a work whose "plot still holds fast to the cultic anti-Judaism that frames the discourse of Latin Christendom" (137). As scholars active since the 1960s have shown, Krummel's claim about the role played by anti-Judaism in "framing" the discourse of Christianity in the West is hard to exaggerate. But in addition to anti-Semitism, in subtle and not-so-subtle ways, the Croxton play raises broader questions of identity (English, Converted Jewish, and lapsed Christian) and "instantiates . . . unsettling anxiety over the secularization of sacred matters" (139). An epilogue, weaving together personal reminiscences and informed medieval historical reflection, brings the book to a satisfying close.

The following omissions or errors of fact in the book should be noted. First, the absence of discussion or even mention of Lollards or Wyclif, heresy or infidels, Langland or *Piers Plowman,* was disappointing. These are contexts in which Jews crop up in interesting ways, and their total neglect creates a significant conceptual gap in the theorizing of medieval English ideas about Jews (virtual or actual). There is no evidence cited to support the assertion that Jewish boys at the age of three (!) began to wear *tallitot* (prayer shawls) (29). This is inconceivable; the widely attested custom among Ashkenazi Jews (Jews primarily of western Europe) was for Jewish males to be awarded a *tallit* at age thirteen and to wear one regularly in prayer only after they married. The discussion of the semiotically significant colors of a black-and-white illustration (Figure 7, on 38–40) is frustrating, to say the least. Proofreading of the book was fairly thorough. But in note 13, 168–69, the transliterated Hebrew terms *Kethuv'im* and *Nevi'im* are switched: *Kethuv'im* are "Writings" and *Nevi'im* are "Prophets," not vice versa. A final bibliographic note: on the subject of the "Jewish nose" (mentioned 33–34 and passim), see Alfred David, "An Iconography of Noses: Directions in the History of a Physical Stereotype," in *Mapping the Cosmos,* ed. Jane Chance and R. O. Wells Jr. (1985), 76–97; and Jay Geller, "(G)nos(e)ology: The Cultural Construction of the Other," in *People of the Body: Jews and Judaism from an Embodied Perspective,* ed. Howard Eilberg-Schwartz (1992), 243–82.

LAWRENCE BESSERMAN
The Hebrew University of Jerusalem

COLETTE MOORE. *Quoting Speech in Early English.* Cambridge: Cambridge University Press, 2011. Pp. xiii, 216. £60.00; $99.00.

Colette Moore's contribution to Cambridge University Press's Studies in English Language series confronts the tension between the pragmatics of a manuscript text and the editorial imposition of different pragmatic systems on its edited version, and so in many ways is about much more than quoting speech. Moore shows that the use of quotation marks in an edited text may conceal earlier strategies for marking speech or may result in distinctly defined speeches where an otherwise meaningful, or artful, underdetermined separation of voices exists in the manuscript version. The result of such editing of texts is, as Moore states, "a pragmatic palimpsest," a figurative use of the term that conveys her notion that the inscription of our modern punctuation systems over preexisting strategies for marking speech is effectively to layer "modern interpretive apparatus onto pre-modern lexical content" (182), a process that ultimately alters the relationship between the text and its reader.

Moore's study is indeed firmly grounded in historical pragmatics and its dimensions are triangular, touching as it does on paleographical, linguistic, and literary aspects of texts. Through case studies, she assesses the textual apparatus on the manuscript page, provides linguistic analysis of corpus data, and brings textual analysis to a broad spectrum of genres (legal, religious, historical, and literary) in order to interpret the ways direct speech is flagged in different textual contexts. Limitations of space preclude a depth that would have given greater satisfaction, but Moore's presentation of short case studies allows for a disciplined and perceptive overview of reported discourse in the late medieval period. She demonstrates some schemes for marking speeches, illustrates the interpretative potential of taking these strategies into account, and therefore promotes careful reading of speeches in premodern texts, by reference to textual and material contexts.

Moore's methodology is clearly laid out in the introduction, in which she discusses the editing of reported speech, with the premise that, whereas the modern convention of quotation marks is "a necessary interpretational layer," their use alters "the pragmatic functions of a [premodern] text, creating a layer of mediation" (10). In the first of her central chapters, Moore describes and analyses some strategies of marking speech, beginning with the material page. Her case studies are based on samples from several manuscripts of *Piers Plowman* and Nicholas Love's *The Mirror of the Blessed Life of Jesus Christ,* chosen for their numerous passages and different levels of reported discourse. While Moore is careful to analyze and explain scribal practice for marking reported discourse, she does not provide a key for her transcriptions, a lack that was compounded by the scarcity of images of manuscript samples against which to compare her transcriptions or descriptions: just two images from manuscripts of *Piers Plowman* are reproduced in an appendix. While Moore identifies a number of ways that scribes could mark direct discourse to guide the reader, she notes that the apparatus is principally employed not so much to flag direct discourse per se as to draw attention to voices of authority.

When she turns to the exploration of lexical marking, Moore's study is on more secure ground. While she takes into account a variety of pragmatic markers (interjections, vocatives, deictic pronouns, tense switching, *explicit* quotatives), she gives special attention to repeated *inquit* phrases. She recasts the idea that such phrases are formulaic by arguing that the most common verbs of speaking demonstrate grammaticalization. This she illustrates through the example of *seien,* "to say." Grammaticalization is defined by syntactical fixing that shifts the lexical component away from having ideational or semantic force. The search of the *Corpus of Middle English Prose and Verse* that Moore undertook for this section had, she admits, its limitations, dependent as it was on editorial quotation marks as indicators of direct speech. While a necessary strategy, this potentially has the drawback of excluding ambiguous discourse that may have been rendered indirect by an editor. Moore also uses corpus data from a sample of legal texts in her illuminating case study of the word *videlicet,* used as a quotative *incipit* to provide textual cohesion. She then turns to the innovations of early printers and compositors for marking speech. She takes as a case study their editing of the "marriage encomium" from *The Merchant's Tale.* This passage, notable for its ambiguously shifting voices, also features in Moore's later discussion of stylistic implications of reported speech.

This preliminary investigation of strategies for marking speech prepares us for textual analysis across different genres: defamation depositions, sermons, and chronicles. The unifying theme of the second chapter is expectations of faithfulness to the spoken word—*de dicto* versus *de re.* Today, a distinction that separates direct from indirect modes of reported speech is the assumption that, in direct discourse, words are quoted verbatim. In the late medieval period, even legal defamation depositions do not require faithfulness to the spoken word in direct discourse. On the contrary, phrases are used that overtly warn that the wording of the utterance is not reported verbatim, though the direct mode is clearly employed. It follows that there can be an ambiguity in levels of discourse as, without adherence to verbatim reproduction, the separation between direct and indirect speech does not meet our modern expectations. Notions of faithfulness to the word are further complicated in vernacular sermons when we confront the question of translation and the quotation of biblical or patristic discourse. Regarding chronicles, Moore goes on to argue that reported speech is "subject to conflicting pragmatic pressures" (124): the incentive for inserting voices is stylistic and rhetorical, providing what is called for in the narrative rather than giving an accurate depiction of past events. Moore takes the position that, without clear definitions of direct and indirect speech, standards of faithfulness are more flexible.

Finally, Moore examines the stylistic implications of reported speech in literary texts. Extracts from the works of Chaucer, *Piers Plowman,* and the works of the *Gawain*-poet provide material for her case studies. Her discussion revisits many of the topics and cruxes with which readers of these works will be familiar. Focusing on interpretational problems caused by indeterminate marking of speeches, she demonstrates how poets may take advantage of a less determined system of quotation, merging or blurring voices to advance artful ambiguity. She notes that a modern editor's more determined marking of speeches through quotation marks is in danger of foreclosing the interpretative potential where indirect speech, direct speech, and straight narrative have greater plasticity.

The period 1350–1600 witnesses both the growth in literacy and private reading and the shift from manuscript to print. Texts reflect the change in reading practices stylistically and rhetorically. This is therefore a particularly important period to observe strategies for quoting speech. The genres from which Moore selects material for her case studies are variously positioned within the oral-written spectrum, incorporating the reporting of "actual" spoken words, imagined utterances in historical speech situations, and fictional narratives. Her investigation into scribal strategies for marking different voices on the material page proves the least sustainable aspect of her three-pronged approach. The strength of her study clearly lies in her identification of pragmatic strategies within the selected texts and her exploration of related interpretative possibilities: a welcome contribution to medieval language and literary studies.

LUCY PERRY
University of Geneva

SUSAN POWELL, ed. *John Mirk's "Festial": Edited from British Library MS Cotton Claudius A.II.* 2 vols. Early English Text Society o.s. 334, 335. Oxford: Oxford University Press, 2009, 2011. Pp. cxlv, 690. £70.00, £75.00; $130.00, $135.00.

John Mirk, an Arrouaisian canon of Lilleshall Abbey, compiled his *Festial,* sixty-four sermons for use by parish priests, "probably in the late 1380s" (1:ix). A lively and undemanding compendium of legend, folktale, and popular history, based mainly on the *Legenda aurea,* it was the most widely used English sermon collection of the pre-Reformation period, and it survives as a whole or in part in more than forty manuscripts. The earliest version (A) followed the order of the Church year; an early revision (B) reordered the sermons into nineteen *Temporale* and forty-five *Sanctorale,* and was itself revised in a post-1434 version (Rev.), which rewrote and augmented it to produce "a more scholarly collection aimed at a more sophisticated audience" (1:ix). In 1483, Caxton published a text of the B version, and the collection remained in print until the Reformation. After that, however, it did not reappear in print until 1905, in the first volume of an EETS edition (e.s. 96) by Theodor Erbe. Erbe's death in World War I meant that his planned second volume, with introduction and notes, was never published. The new EETS edition satisfyingly remedies this loss. A substantial introduction discusses Mirk's life and works, the nature, order, and function of the *Festial*'s sermons, its textual transmission, the "scribal production" of the base manuscript, and the reasons for its choice. The edited text (running across both volumes), which includes additional sermon material from the base manuscript, is meticulously produced and made more accessible by skillful modern punctuation. The second volume also includes comprehensive "Explanatory Notes," a judiciously chosen "Select Glossary," a glossary of proper names, and a list of scriptural references and allusions. The appendices give a tabulation of the contents of each manuscript, descriptions of the individual manuscripts, full collations of the introductory Prayer, the Prologue, and Sermons 2, 14, 24, 34, 39, and 56, a description and discussion of the scribal dialects found in α (London, British Library, MS Cotton Claudius A.II), and a transcription of its list of *festa ferianda.*

The number of the manuscripts of the *Festial* and the complexity of their interrelationships present a daunting challenge to the editor. Erbe chose as his base text Oxford, Bodleian Library, Gough Ecclesiastical

Topography 4 (D), a mid-fifteenth-century manuscript of the A version; Powell prefers an earlier manuscript, Cotton Claudius A.II α, also belonging to the A group but sharing some features with the B version. She concedes that it is "an uneven text, compromised by a piecemeal assemblage of the text, perhaps from different periods, certainly by different scribes using different exemplars which themselves may well have been copied from other different exemplars" (1:lxxxiii). A good case can be pieced together from her introduction for this editorially unorthodox choice, but the theoretical framework underlying it needs to be more explicitly articulated. What kind of edition is she producing? At one point in the introduction (1:cxxii), it is described as a "critical edition," and indeed Volume 1 is advertised on Amazon.com as *A Critical Edition of Mirk's "Festial,"* although this description does not appear on the published title page. But although Powell uses some of the tools of the critical editor to repair textual defects in α, her edition has little in common with the traditional "critical edition." The textual relationships of the manuscripts resist stemmatic analysis (1:cxi), and she makes no attempt to reconstruct an authorial original: "Given the different Hands and exemplars, any attempt to return α to an *Ur*-text closest to Mirk's original would be fundamentally misguided, as well as involving constant and major intervention" (1:cxxii). Her editorial approach is closer, in its conservatism, to that of a "best-text" editor: "The policy is . . . to restrict intervention in the base-text to those cases where omission or error is evident and confirmed by the other manuscripts. . . . Where α is alone in a unique reading (good or bad), that reading is retained, unless so defective or erroneous as to impede sense" (1:cxxi–cxxii). Indeed, one section on α is headed "The Best Text?"; but the question mark is significant. The complex history and uneven nature of the α text (which, like the curate's egg, is only "excellent in parts") make it problematic as a "best text," and Powell's main reason for choosing it is its representative quality: not only is it "a collected edition, assembled from various sources in order to preserve as much of Mirk's vernacular writings as possible" (1:cxxi), but, as a manuscript "pivotal" to the transition between the A and B traditions, it reflects the later development of the work. This editorial strategy is (in my view) a practical and defensible response to the kind of textual tradition where a "living" work continues to evolve after its initial production, but its implications could have been more fully explored.

The difficulty with a base text of this kind is determining what status to give to its divergences from the original. Powell emends lacunae and mechanical errors (1:cxxi–cxxii), but she can be overtolerant of other types of error; since this will undoubtedly become the standard reading text of the *Festial*, its readers have the right to expect an edited text that, wherever possible, makes sense. In the story from the *Gesta Romanorum* about the slave employed to warn victorious generals *Gnothi seauton* ("Know thyself"), the garbled reading in α, *Anothe delytes* (Sermon 25.102) is retained in the edited text, although explained in the notes; similarly the unique α rubric, *De festo Sancti Georgij sermo dicendus ad parochianos vbi sanctus Georgius est patronus ecclesie, quia alibi festum istud celebratur* (Sermon 30.1–2) is baffling as it stands (the notes explain that *non* after *istud* has been lost through a subsequent erasure, presumably after 1416, when the feast began to be celebrated elsewhere). There is a more complex instance in the sermon on the Holy Innocents, where the introductory rhyming division says that they "lyueden here clanly wythout schame, þey dyden wythout blame, and were yfollewed [i.e., baptized] in hure blod at hame" (Sermon 9.8–9). "At hame," found only in the "B" group manuscripts and α, makes unsatisfactory sense; the original rhyme-word must have been "same" (cf. 9.59–60, "Þey weren also folwed in hure same, þat is, in hure owne blod"). There is certainly a problem here, and Powell, who assumes that Mirk's original reading was "in hure same," as in D, is rightly suspicious of *MED*'s suggested translation (s.v. sam(e) *pron.* 2[b]) "in their death." The different manuscript readings, however, could be better explained by an original "in hure blod same," where "same" might be either an adverb ("together"), or an adjective ("very") postposed for the rhyme (cf. Sermon 8.6–7); 9.59–60 (which could be read as "Þey weren also folwed in hure same [þat is, in hure owne] blod") suggests that it was understood as the latter but found difficult.

A few modifications could be suggested to the explanatory notes. The ultimate source of the passage on the Last Judgment in Sermon 1.97–109 is Anselm's *Meditatio* 1; the etymology of "Thomas" as "all man" in Sermon 10.21–22 is not unique to Mirk and is derived from *totus mas* (see Siegfried Wenzel, *Preaching in the Age of Chaucer* [Washington, D.C.: Catholic University of America Press, 2008], 304 n. 12); and the material on the unicorn in Sermon 13.85–96 goes back not to Augustine (in spite of the attribution in the text) but to Gregory's *Moralia in Iob*, 31.15.

These, however, are minor reservations about an edition that successfully fills a large and long-standing gap in late medieval sermon studies.
The product of many years' research, it is scholarly, accurate, immensely
informative, and a pleasure to use. All those interested in the later
medieval English sermon owe a major debt of gratitude to its editor.

BELLA MILLETT
University of Southampton

MARGARET ROGERSON, ed. *The York Mystery Plays: Performance in the
City.* Woodbridge: York Medieval Press, 2011. Pp. xiv, 248.
£50.00; $90.00.

Margaret Rogerson, the editor of this valuable collection of academic,
critical, and practice-based studies, has been a leader in the field of
medieval drama for many years now. With Alexandra F. Johnston, she
edited the inaugural *Records of Early English Drama* on York (1979), and
she returns to the York plays here in a volume revealing the still-vibrant
life of a topic that has held the attention of different academic and nonacademic communities alike over many years. In an expertly managed
set of papers, Rogerson makes a virtue of the eclecticism that now more
than ever characterizes the field, taking the reader from manuscripts to
the material exigencies of wagons; from the unavoidable cognitive blending of reality and fiction in the spectator's mind to the dutiful piety of
late medieval believers imagining the events of Christ's Passion; from
the complex communities that originally produced the plays to the varied goals of those who now perform them half a millennium later. The
voices that join company in this collection come from many different
directions—from the academy, theater, heritage, festival culture,
church, engineering, guildry—and from Australia, Canada, the UK, the
United States, and Israel.

The interpretative matrix of the volume is correspondingly wide, so
that cognitive theory rubs shoulders with medievalism in one essay (Jill
Stevenson), and, in Rogerson's own academic contribution (in addition
to an excellent introduction), Stanislavski's demands on actors prove less
alien to the world of medieval drama than previously thought, if linked

to those of affective piety. Mike Tyler's essay joins traditional literary criticism with Edgar Schein's theory of cultural organizations to explain the effect of familial forces in the Noah play. Pamela M. King, taking a line that archeologists will recognize, valuably nuances the festivity of medieval confraternity by turning to a cognate contemporary event, the Siena *Palio*. There are also tightly analyzed accounts of document, context, and institution included here. For example, in a chapter that will be required reading for anyone interested in the documentary bases for interpreting the public scene, Richard Beadle expertly locates the construction of the York Register in a Ricardian political setting, while Sheila K. Christie takes on definitions of genre, and guild and civic jurisdiction, impressively mapping the history of the Masons' changing involvement in York plays onto their aspirations and ability to work out of religious rather than civic liberties. Rogerson is one of those thoughtful editors who does not balk at providing an index for an essay collection, and so one can find there Artaud and Augustine; the *Middle English Metrical Paraphrase of the Old Testament* and Merleau-Ponty, and many other intriguing entries to demonstrate the uniquely varied hold of medieval drama on the modern imagination.

Literally and symbolically at the center of the volume is a set of papers (some in the form of edited testimonies) from thirteen practitioners addressing the theoretical, physical, and dramatic challenges of putting such plays before a public that might or might not share the faith of those who originally wrote and watched them. These varied and thought-provoking accounts introduce the reader to the practical problems of dealing with physical performance: space, timetabling, nesting owls, alien language, commerce, health and safety, and licensing; but they also engage with wider cultural issues such as how the "live energies" (Gweno Williams) or the "tension and contrast" (Alan Heaven) necessary to drama can be achieved for the modern audience, and what theories of drama or verse-speaking, and what kinds of music, might promote that theatrical success. Drawing both on theory and a particular production in Tel Aviv, Sharon Aronson-Lehavi bridges the worlds of interpretation through textual analysis and performance in a study of how the York *Crucifixion* text makes explicit the practical necessities of production, bearing witness to the aesthetic *and* diachronic priority of staged activity over the written account, and to "gestural, pretextual theatricality as a characteristic of the York plays" (169).

Decades before it became politically expedient to call on the institutions of higher education to prove the social benefit of their research, students and players of medieval drama were engaging with each other and with the local and national communities around them, exploring past identities, but also helping to create contemporary ones, especially for the cities in which this form of theater arose (the case of the York plays is a very good, but not the only, example of this). The present volume, which so acutely shows creative collaboration between different communities in an enterprise from which they all believe they can benefit, would not have been produced if that engagement had not been long-lived. The collection honorably references that earlier work in the field as well as permitting an internationally comparative reflection on past performances (Alexandra F. Johnston). But it does something even more valuable: it prompts the reader to consider why it is that so many people for so long have been engaged in what is, in effect, the public exploration of a cultural simile, probing the gap between the communal, performance culture of faith in the Middle Ages and the desires of our modern, problematically faithful, multicultural, globalized, and shifting identities. On the evidence of this collection of papers, even those who set out conscious that this gap cannot, or should not, be narrowed, do sometimes evince a desire to find analogy with the goals or the techniques or the camaraderie of the first performers. Weaving its way between footnote and text here, one can spot the temptation that a theatrical good and evil that joins us to the past can be known to a degree; that human nature is more enduring than cultural change, and hence that its products can, in a sense, be shared by people across the centuries. And this reviewer is not going to say that that is a false belief, not least because, in the last analysis, how could one *know* that it was false? More compelling, however, is the evidence of the human activity itself in the commitment of the actors and the engagement of the spectators—the implied conversation with those in the past who tried to offer powerful images, to display their own ingenuity, to speak clearly to their fellows, to educate, contemplate the sublime, compete or collaborate, and do the many other things that a play demanded then, and demands now. Rogerson writes, "The object of the collection is to extend debate on medieval performance of the York Plays as a cultural, devotional, and theatrical phenomenon, and to demonstrate the values of modern production as a way of opening up the subject to wider discussion" (1). This collection is well conceived, well edited, and generously illustrated. It is kind to its reader in having footnotes on the page, a good bibliography, index, and a glossary of Middle English words. It contains excellent academic papers and thoughtful, instructive reports from practititoners. It does all it set out to do and more.

JOHN J. McGAVIN
University of Southampton

JESSICA ROSENFELD. *Ethics and Enjoyment in Late Medieval Poetry: Love After Aristotle.* Cambridge: Cambridge University Press, 2011. Pp. vi, 145. £55.00; $90.00.

Medieval scholarship has always recognized as important the question of whether medieval secular philosophy shaped vernacular literature in ways not in tune with Church teaching, and if so, how. In this smart and fast-paced book, Jessica Rosenfeld discovers in medieval texts an important constellation of ideas that seem to stem from Aristotle's *Nicomachean Ethics*. The European transmission in Latin of the entire text of the *Ethics* dates from the thirteenth century, when Aristotle's intellectual standing as a natural philosopher was at its height. Previously, only the first four books had been available; they promoted ethical reflection on the catalogue of virtues and the value of the mean (or "moderation"). The addition of the later books, however, identified the goal of humanity as happiness, endorsing as man's supreme good and final cause a variety of forms of it that include physical and worldly pleasure as well as intellectual happiness and friendship. Such ethical claims could not fail to have a radical impact on medieval thinking since they ran directly counter to an orthodoxy concerned to promote sacrifice in this world and an etherealized version of happiness in the next. How did vernacular authors negotiate this tension?

Rosenfeld explores the ramifications of their responses following a chronological arc from the troubadours to Chaucer. Her argument is multistranded, advancing on several fronts. One of her themes is the question of the relationship between happiness and activity. She also engages with Aristotle's ethical rationalism, assessing the effects of its conflict with the ethics of will or desire that the Middle Ages inherited from Augustine. The most important theme that she works with, however, is that of love, as indicated by her subtitle. The complete text of

Aristotle's *Ethics* valorizes pleasure and enjoyment in mundane relation-ships in a way that challenges the sacrificial and mystical strains in medieval concepts of love, including "courtly love," and that in general opposes any celebration of deferred enjoyment. Her analysis lingers on the *Roman de la rose,* speeds through the *dits amoureux* of Machaut and Froissart together with *The Book of the Duchess,* takes in Deguileville's *Pèlerinage de la vie humaine* and Langland's *Piers Plowman,* and nods rather cursorily at Dante before landing safely on Chaucer, whose most fully discussed text is *Troilus and Criseyde.*

According to Rosenfeld, *Ethics and Enjoyment in Late Medieval Poetry* is addressed to "medieval English literature" (1), a strange claim in view of the fact that (as this overview makes plain) 80 percent-plus of it is about texts in languages other than English. Rosenfeld sometimes gives the unfortunate impression of returning to the bad old days of "sources and analogues" in which non-English works are merely pre-texts for the understanding of real, that is, English, literature. *Ethics and Enjoyment* is indeed most of all about *enjoying Chaucer,* who occupies a place of privi-lege among the *dits* and again at the volume's end; but the irritation that this tired trope of Eng. Lit. arouses in scholars from other disci-plines is to some extent mitigated by Rosenfeld's claim that Chaucer's modernity can best be illuminated by the thinking of Jacques Lacan. For me, it was a pleasure to see the thought of this formidable French ana-lyst, whose seminar on ethics starts out from a direct engagement with Aristotle, weave in and out of the intellectual fabric of Rosenfeld's book, and assume a star role in its coda (160ff.), where similarities between Lacan's "ethics of the real" and the medieval interpretation of Aristote-lian love and contingency are demonstrated (162).

Probably the book's best chapter is the one on the *Rose.* Here Rosen-feld introduces into her overall argument a preoccupation with labor as an ethical category, a category that has more to do with Aristotle's in-sistence on ethics as act than on the familiar duality of active and con-templative ways of life. This irruption of the theme of labor is quite unexpected and appears to be triggered by an accident of translation. Dahlberg renders into English "tot l'afeire vos conterai" (literally "I will recount the whole dealing to you") as "I shall recount . . . how I went to work" (48); but from this unlikely and fragile lead, Rosenfeld develops a fascinating, original, and in the main convincing analysis of an opposi-tion between productive and unproductive activity in the two parts of the *Rose.* Guillaume de Lorris deals, according to Rosenfeld, with "the difficulty of disentangling productive from unproductive labor and the association of labor with both objectless desire and desire for a loved object" (53), whereas the chapter brilliantly concludes, "[Jean]'s version of ethical reading does not seek a moral or even a practical example of living well, but rather a reflection upon oneself and one's desires, bringing with it the pleasure that comes with the labor of rational contemplation" (72). Even though the discussion of some of the texts in subsequent chapters is so rushed as to be hard to take in, the quality of observation is always high, as, for example, when Rosenfeld says of Froissart's *dits* that, unlike Machaut's, they are not "concerned with the impossible pleasure of absolute possession, but with mutual consideration of desire in the face of contingency" (96).

Inevitably, Rosenfeld often gives rather short shrift to writings by thinkers other than Aristotle: the not-lightweight Boethius, for instance, who similarly had much to say about happiness and its relationship with the things of the world. His absence presses on the early chapters until we are shown, persuasively if not unpredictably, how the reception of Aristotle's ethics inflected the medieval reception of the *De consolatione* (Chapter 5). Taking Aristotle as the book's focus also results in nonintellectualist concerns seeming pale beside muscularly philosophical ones; in these pages, there is more discourse on desire than susceptibility to it. While the reader sometimes thirsts for more, what is most impressive about *Ethics and Enjoyment in Late Medieval Poetry* is the crisp, clear command of a huge intellectual field and its exploration across a formidable range of texts. In this I include the treatment of Lacan, an imposing author in his own right, whose uneasy dialogue with Aristotle emerges compellingly in the readings of the medieval literary texts that range between them.

Sarah Kay
New York University

James Simpson. *Under the Hammer: Iconoclasm in the Anglo-American Tradition.* Oxford: Oxford University Press, 2010. Pp. xiii, 222. $45.00; £25.00.

The introduction and four brief chapters of this book (delivered as Oxford University's Clarendon Lectures of 2009) form a companion piece to Simpson's *Burning to Read: English Fundamentalism and Its Reformation Opponents* (2007), and both in turn extend some of his arguments regarding the relation between periodization and political force in *Reform and Cultural Revolution* (2002). The connection to *Burning to Read* is made explicit: England's century of "legislated iconoclasm" (1538–1643) was "partner" to the Reformation's biblical literalism as a "weapon of a radical yet non-progressive modernity" (5). Like that book, too, *Under the Hammer* is unabashed polemic, aiming to prove that violent fundamentalist iconoclasm is not regressive or "medieval," but is rather at the core of western modernity, especially the Anglo-American tradition. In order to press this claim, Simpson moves well beyond his usual focus on late medieval and early modern events, extending his analysis to twentieth-century abstract painting, seventeenth-century English poetry, and especially the Enlightenment, which, he suggests, is "correlative" to the Reformation: "both activate iconoclasm" (10).

Opening with the Taliban's destruction of two monumental Buddha statues (dating from the second century CE) in Bamiyan, Afghanistan, in 2001, Simpson contends that this act, far from being "a regression into medieval barbarism" (3), actually accords precisely with the program of early modern iconoclasm, with parallel movements by revolutionary clerical elites "prepared to wield the hammer, in the name of liberty" (4). Indeed, Simpson finds that it is consistently in the name of liberty—of people and nations—that image-breaking occurs, and it is this freedom from enthrallment that links to the Enlightenment's repudiation of idols and ideologies, a "philosophical iconoclasm" that turns the past into a "museum of error" (11). Iconoclasm is, then, quintessentially modern, an argument that Simpson grounds theoretically upon the politics of representation. Any reconfiguration of jurisdiction, such as the centralization of power in the sixteenth and seventeenth centuries, requires a shift in who is allowed to "re-present" us, which in turn determines "how we allow the past to be made present again" (6). Simpson does not at all engage the long theoretical history of the politics of representation, which to a degree limits the potential of his aspiration that this be "a small book capable of activating a large theme" (17). Nonetheless, his insistence that we pay attention to the connections between iconoclasm and the politics of representation from the Reformation to the present day invigorates our understanding of the processes of periodization, one of his central concerns. Simpson contends that "iconoclasts wish to separate one historical period from another absolutely" by breaking with the previous semiotic system and instituting their own (12–13); he finds, however, that iconoclasm is by nature an unfinishable, recursive process. Periodization, therefore, can never fully succeed.

Chapter 1 focuses on twentieth-century American abstract art, which Simpson reads as antirhetorical, vertical, and exclusive, despite its claim to ahistorical universalism. He first traces abstract art to the Enlightenment, which "must produce an iconoclastic art, purified of all but the rational order." Conversely, it redefines "all cultural and historical particularities as enemies of the rational order and liberty" (26). This interpretation runs contrary to the reception of abstract art as a response to the Holocaust, and Simpson resolves these competing interpretations by suggesting a much deeper source for abstract art (and thus for important aspects of the Enlightenment and modernity): Puritan iconoclasm. Not democratic, but rather the "sign of equality before the absolute," flat abstract art is "painting of non-representation, in all three senses: no re-presenting the past, no intercession, no images" (34). So, too, for post-Reformation Protestant architecture, Simpson claims, particularly the flat, symmetrical, colorless interiors of New England churches. Thus Simpson suggests that not only do images move from church to museum with the "age of Art" and the Enlightenment, but the modern museum (especially MoMA), with "vast white walls and transparent windows," ultimately becomes the "new puritan temple" (48). Paradoxically, this argument depends upon a reductive and single-stranded, tightly periodized sense of "the Enlightenment." Even though he tries to demonstrate the impossibility of historical closure, Simpson never addresses his own reliance upon very traditional periodizations as he works to expose the paradox that absolutist iconoclasm is foundational to the narrative of democracy and its statues of Liberty. He had warned, however, that the book delivers polemic, and such clean argumentative lines enable the book's stark insistence that modernity, essentially iconoclastic, has a fundamentalist core that originates in the Reformation. As Simpson no doubt recognizes, these clean lines, like the "Abstract Art" he critiques, have their own tinge of absolutism.

Chapter 2 pushes the story back to early fifteenth-century England, juxtaposing Lydgate's condemnation of pagan idols with contemporary Lollard iconoclasm, and pairing both with sixteenth-century iconoclastic legislation in order to demonstrate the links between images, imagination, and historical memory. Because images are "lightning rods of historical consciousness" as well as "symptoms of culture," fifteenth-century images prophetically "point to their own demise" (60). The incompleteness of this demise is taken up in Chapter 3. Idolatry "is always a repeatable and a repeated error" (85); thus nothing can arrest iconoclasm in the name of liberty except "statues of Liberty" that "disguise their own status as mesmerizing idol" (86). A study of Milton in the context of the seventeenth-century destruction of images, this chapter reads *Paradise Lost* as "a vigorous but knowingly doomed campaign of idol breaking" (108) and as aggressive toward history and tradition. Through this reading, Simpson shows that breaking "the idol of monarchy" absolutely requires an "iconoclastic creature of emergency" capable of acting without the law (109). Here again one wishes that Simpson had integrated contemporary theories of sovereignty into his discussion (Hobbes, for instance, appears only in a note) as well as the strands of political theory that have long addressed these issues. Nonetheless, his analysis does delineate the function (Simpson would say necessary and paradoxical function) of iconoclasm for absolutism, revolution, and narratives of liberty, and thus intimates its importance for current political and cultural debates.

In his final chapter, Simpson turns squarely to "the Enlightenment," expanding upon his argument in the introduction that iconoclasm such as that of the Taliban accords with Enlightenment attitudes, even though the latter are not *literally* iconoclastic. Instead, the Enlightenment: (1) "exercised a philosophical iconoclasm by describing ideology as false consciousness"; (2) "neutralized the image by placing it in the museum and by calling it Art"; and (3) "commodified the image under the market's hammer" (117). Contrasting Milton's approval of regicide with Edmund Burke's preference for aesthetic decorum, Simpson describes the Enlightenment's "language of taste" as "at every point inflected by recurrent fear of idolatry" (120). This understanding of taste, Simpson argues, was "deeply indebted to Protestant accounts of the Catholic image as capable of working on us and enthralling us." Thus "taste" is the product of a theologically fractured Europe, and "the category of the aesthetic is itself, in sum, a historical product of iconoclasm" (133). It facilitated the passage of the image "from the church to the private, through the semi-public space of the gallery," which "drained the image of much of its life" (130). Simpson clearly mourns this loss of life, and with this refusal of detachment, as with his insistence that "iconoclasm is not somewhere else" (154), he stays true to his critique of "the Enlightenment."

Read as a self-conscious polemic that abjures complication in order to strike a very specific target, *Under the Hammer* provides a bracing argument regarding the relationship between political jurisdiction and periodization, as well as between periodization and the limits placed on history, memory, and imagination.

KATHLEEN DAVIS
University of Rhode Island

KAREN ELAINE SMYTH. *Imaginings of Time in Lydgate and Hoccleve's Verse.* Farnham: Ashgate, 2011. Pp. x, 187. £55.00; $99.95.

Late medieval writers drew upon a rich and varied set of temporal referents, locating events in time by means, *inter alia,* of kings' reigns, the changing months and seasons, the ecclesiastical calendar, astronomical phenomena, and, within each day, by bells, cock-crows, liturgical *horae,* mechanical clocks, and by measurements of the position of the sun. At the same time, authors were engaged with larger timescales of dynasties and empires, as well as the macrocosm of salvation history itself. Karen Smyth's book explores this complex understanding of the temporal, focusing in particular on English literary sources from the first half of the fifteenth century. She investigates the role played by small-scale time-markings in shaping poetic narratives and explores larger-scale time structures within texts (for example, authorial and readerly awareness of the interrelationship of past, present, and future). A lengthy survey chapter is followed by five chapters that consider both narrative time-referents and larger temporal organization in works by John Lydgate (*Troy Book, Siege of Thebes,* and *Fall of Princes*) and Thomas Hoccleve (*Regiment of Princes, Series*), as well as in minor works by these two authors.

Smyth's initial overview of "cultural narratives of time" (15) in late medieval English sources is divided into eight sections (some as short as two paragraphs). It is a wide-ranging discussion, providing much of interest in passing. Yet the treatment of any one aspect is piecemeal and at times superficial. Although Smyth stresses the need for any study of time-consciousness to be context-dependent, her own analysis disregards on occasion differences of genre, date, or purpose, or extrapolates unpersuasively from limited evidence. At times the scholarship appears to be on shaky ground. For example, Smyth cites comments purportedly from John Trevisa's translation (completed in 1387, but here labeled "mid-fourteenth century") of Higden's *Polychronicon* as evidence of self-conscious justification of the use of time-markers as organizational structures in historical narrative (25). Yet the Trevisa quotation comes in fact from his translation of Bartholomaeus Anglicus's *De proprietatibus rerum,* the comment in question being attributed, by Trevisa and by Bartholomaeus, to Isidore of Seville (see *Etymologiae* III.iv.4). Seventh-century comments on the essential role that calculation and computation play in understanding and knowledge cannot serve as fourteenth-century testimony to the role of time-markings in historiography. Elsewhere, Smyth compares a three-line time-marker from *Troy Book* (I.1517–19) with the much more elaborate time calculation that begins the introduction to Chaucer's *Man of Law's Tale* (II.1–14), finding in Lydgate's concision evidence that astronomical reckonings were, by the time of *Troy Book,* a normalized, expected, and hence less elaborate feature of what she somewhat bafflingly calls "vernacular English" (38). Yet the former is a moment of brief scene setting, describing the activities of royal servants as they prepare a midday meal, while the latter is a playfully self-conscious, much-amplified *chronographia* that precedes a warning from the Host about the dangers of wasting time. It may well be, as Smyth asserts but does not demonstrate, that what for Chaucer is novel and diverting has become commonplace and functional for Lydgate (at least in main narrative rather than in his prologues), but the shorthand presentation of evidence makes one doubt some of the sweeping conclusions drawn in this first chapter.

The subsequent chapters exploring literary texts in depth are more profitable. There are suggestive and useful summaries of how time-markers in Lydgate's *Troy Book* unify action or create comparisons between events and of how references to characters' ages operate thematically in both *Troy Book* and the *Fall of Princes.* The chapter on Hoccleve's *Series* explores issues of memory, identity, and reading, demonstrating in respect of temporality Lee Patterson's observation (quoted on 137) that the framing strategies of the *Series* are experimental and evolving rather than fully planned and coherent. Smyth is well read in recent research on Hoccleve and Lydgate and also in recent work on fifteenth-century writing more widely. Her approach is therefore to advance, by means of close examination of time-references, hypotheses that concur with and draw much of their consequence from, for example, work by Paul Strohm, Patterson, and James Simpson, extending readings by increments rather than opening up new fronts. While much of this is enlightening, concentrating the mind on the sheer density of time-references in these poems, occasionally Smyth's intensive attention to temporality causes her to lose sight of basic good judgment in the evaluation of literary evidence. Her argument (74) regarding Lydgate's conscious manipulations of the order of time in phrases such as "nyȝt and day" (*TB* I.1357) and "day and nyȝt" (*TB* V.1966), for example, does not fully persuade because the order in both cases must in large part be due to the demands of rhyme.

Disappointingly, the standard of copyediting and scholarly accuracy on show leaves something to be desired. On a single page, for example, Lydgate's *Disguising at Hertford* becomes first the *Disguising of Hertford* and then, in a footnote referring to a recent article, appears under its alternative title ((but now misspelled and having lost its italicization), as "the Mumming at Herford [*sic*]" (54). There are inconsistencies in the format of entries in the bibliography, sporadic manglings of names and titles (Christopher Baswell becomes "Christopher Canon" [66], Christina von Nolcken "Cristina von Nocklen" [156]), and mistypings of page, book, and line numbers, revealed when one attempts to follow up a reference (see, for example, the latter two entries for Lynn Thorndike in the bibliography). More diligent editorial intervention might also have made the book more pleasing to read. At times the prose is cumbersome, requiring intermittent rereading to negotiate awkward topicalizations and cleft constructions, to decide between two possible meanings, or to extract agency or causation from sentences in the passive voice.

Nevertheless, Smyth's book, *in toto,* reminds us productively of how, particularly in translations of pseudohistorical narratives, there is a constant interplay between past, present, and future, an overarching prudential mode of relations. Likewise, it gives an intricate sense of how these authors locate individual, biographical, or specific moments in time and how these texts negotiate and interrelate the different temporal states of memory, composition, copying, and future reading. Moreover, such close focus on temporality throws into clear relief differences in genre, form, and purpose both within an author's oeuvre and when

437

comparing Hoccleve and Lydgate. Even if it is not as comprehensive, robust, or nuanced as one would wish, *Imaginings of Time* alerts us to the interpretative potential of time-markers and structures, both small and large, within these texts and elsewhere.

JENNI NUTTALL
Wolfson College and St. Edmund Hall, Oxford

THERESA TINKLE. *Gender and Power in Medieval Exegesis.* New York: Palgrave Macmillan, 2010. Pp. xvi, 196. $80.00.

Theresa Tinkle's study of the politics of biblical interpretation is wide reaching in its historical trajectory (the age of Augustine through the late Middle Ages) but organized around a series of case studies linked to "three crucial moments" in the history of exegesis: the establishment of the discourse during the so-called patristic period, its development of (illusory) univocal authority in the twelfth century, and its fragmentation during the ecclesiastical turmoil of the late fourteenth and fifteenth centuries (12). The book's premise is that medieval biblical interpretation was never a disinterested use of scripture, that the operations of exegesis are inevitably shaped by the author's conscious or unconscious agenda and by the political, ecclesiastical, and social circumstances of its production. In Tinkle's words, "exegesis, like politics, is always local" (127).

The range of texts analyzed (Jerome's *Against Jovinian,* two of Chrysostom's sermons, Augustine's *Confessions,* the *Glossa ordinaria,* the Fleury *Slaughter of Innocents,* and *The Wife of Bath's Prologue*) reveals one purpose of this study, which Tinkle directly articulates in a call for an opening of the exegetical canon. Acknowledging the debt that exegetical study owes to the work of Beryl Smalley and scholars following in her wake, Tinkle contends that we can significantly expand upon their work (which focused almost exclusively on academic exegesis) by considering the impact of poets and playwrights on the medieval understanding of scripture. Literary exegesis should not be considered subordinate to academic exegesis; rather, these two modes of writing should be studied intertextually, for they perform similar cultural work in shaping a community's understanding of biblical meaning (Chapter 4, on the Fleury *Slaughter,* illustrates this point especially well).

The narrower focus of this study is the exegetical use of gendered hierarchical inversions, which Tinkle suggests is motivated by the challenges implicit in the call to *imitatio Christi.* The image of a crucified deity necessarily raises questions about the nature of true authority and power, which may not find its basis in traditional masculinity. Tinkle argues that some exegetes respond to this call by inverting hierarchical social models and speaking through feminine or childlike personae. This use of the "woman on top" trope establishes spiritual authority via its difference from traditional social order, but the trope can also be used for the purpose of disparaging assertive, authoritative, and vocal women by exegetes who want to exclude these characteristics from their own self-fashioning. The book's first chapter, "Women on Top in Medieval Exegesis," introduces this topic and establishes Tinkle's methodology as historically informed feminist literary study.

Chapter 2, "Subversive Feminine Voices: The Reception of 1 Timothy 2 from Jerome to Chaucer," is, in a sense, the book in miniature, for it presents the study's historical trajectory and models its overarching argument through a diachronic analysis of interpretations of a single biblical passage ("But I suffer not a woman to teach, nor to use authority over man: but to be in silence"). As Tinkle points out, this passage invites readers either "to side with the apostle, to stand with him in the aura of religious power" or "to dwell imaginatively on those provocative women and to conceive of their unutterable words" (18). The chapter examines the rhetorical strategies that Jerome, Chrysostom, the producers of the *Glossa ordinaria,* and Chaucer's Wife of Bath use to rescript the biblical text's anxiety about feminine speech and subversion. These texts reveal, though in tellingly different ways, a power struggle between ecclesiastical men and lay women. Each constructs a social and gender hierarchy but also exposes the fact that it is contested.

The next three chapters offer sustained engagements with single works from each of the book's three historical periods, in which the trope of the woman on top is instrumental to exegetical authorization. Chapter 3, "Gender Trouble in Augustine's *Confessions,*" demonstrates how Augustine's contradictory performance of gender is part of his authorizing strategy in *Confessions.* When fashioning his episcopal identity, Augustine rhetorically deploys the trope of the woman on top by taking Monica as his role model and finding in her service to God the kind of

STUDIES IN THE AGE OF CHAUCER

imitatio Christi that requires identifying with powerlessness. However, in other cases, such as his arguments against the Manicheans, he relies on conventional hierarchical models that allow him to situate his own position in relation to a masculine learned consensus. Chapter 4, "Affective Exegesis in the Fleury *Slaughter of Innocents,*" argues that this allegory about gentile child martyrs dying for Christ relies on the trope of inversion to align Christian spiritual authority with children and the woman who weeps for them (Rachel, the allegorical *mater dolorosa*). Tinkle compellingly argues that, in the context of the myth of ritual murder of Christian children by Jews, texts like the Fleury *Slaughter* worked with academic exegesis to support the culture of persecution that swept Europe in the twelfth and thirteenth centuries. Chapter 5, "The Wife of Bath's Marginal Authority," offers a study of scribal reception of *The Wife of Bath's Prologue,* an important fictional instance of the woman on top. Tinkle's review of manuscript evidence reveals that, in contrast to modern critics who have assessed the Wife's exegetical failing, scribes who glossed fifteenth-century manuscript copies of the *Tale* highlighted and commented upon Alisoun's scriptural references in a way that presents her as a competent—indeed, uncontested—exegete. As a laywoman who has access to vernacular scripture and defies both it and the men who interpret it, Alisoun poses what should seem a threat to the ecclesiastical establishment; however, this threat dissolves into misogynistic domestic comedy because it is voiced by an unruly and disobedient wife. This choice of voicing is nevertheless significant in that it estranges the masculine point of view, if only momentarily.

One of this study's strengths is Tinkle's nuanced awareness of the complexity of her object of analysis. She notes the unpredictability of the trope of the woman on top and suggests, quite rightly, that "the discursive value of the trope is its flexibility" (125). Medieval social and gender hierarchies were not as ossified as they may be in the popular imagination and were thus interestingly manipulated by exegetes struggling to articulate spiritual authority in nontraditional ways. *Gender and Power in Medieval Exegesis* is a work of many merits, notably Tinkle's lucid analysis of rhetorical strategies and exegetical hermeneutics, as well as her thorough research in what are often distinct areas of specialization. Perhaps most noteworthy, however, is the book's explicit political engagement, which renders it valuable to other intellectual arenas than medieval studies. As Tinkle points out, "biblical hermeneutics change history," and for that reason "scriptural interpretations really matter" (126). Her book may be about the Middle Ages, but its attention to how exegesis is culturally situated has contemporary social relevance. The disinterested scholarship that Tinkle models draws attention to scriptural polysemy, demonstrating that if we expose the ideologies of power that underwrite exegesis, we can demystify exegetical authority and enable disenfranchised voices to become audible. For this reason, I believe the book will, as Tinkle hopes, stand alongside historically informed counter-exegeses that speak out against the rise of fundamentalisms.

JENNIFER L. SISK
University of Vermont

DAVID WALLACE. *Strong Women: Life, Text, and Territory, 1347–1645.* Oxford: Oxford University Press, 2011. Pp. xxxi, 288. £30.00; $55.00.

"Literature is the truest history," begins David Wallace in his introduction to *Strong Women,* because historians produce their own accounts of history based on compiled data, while literary scholars "must give way to voices from the past" (xv). Although I can imagine historians clamoring in protest at this provocative claim for literary scholarship, I would also expect a measure of unease among feminist and queer scholars of the past, who would consider "giving way to voices of the past" a negotiated process. This debatable position of the literary scholar, however, serves for Wallace as the schematic complement to the "premodern speaker [who] awaits her turn on the page." Given the fact that women have had less access to the written page than men historically, Wallace asserts that "it takes a *strong woman* . . . to secure bookish remembrance in future times; to see her life becoming a *life*" (xv–xvi). Wallace cites the *mulier fortis* of Proverbs 31, a medieval stereotype of female virtue, but one that was regulatory and punitive as well (or humorous, as in Chaucer's perversion of the idea in the Wife of Bath). How odd, then, that Wallace chooses this stereotype as the title of his book and the centerpiece of his theme that only strong women "secure" their lives in written forms, tell their own stories. Even lacking the proverbial and medieval contexts of the *mulier fortis,* the "strong woman" argument seems willfully disengaged from feminist scholarship of the past twenty-five years, which has documented and theorized the multiple ways in which an individual woman's strength might not be the whole story. But again, Wallace insists: "Each of these women is a *mulier fortis,* a strong woman: had she been otherwise, her *life* would never have been written" (xix). Take that, Judith Shakespeare and Virginia Woolf!

The strengths of *Strong Women,* however, are many. First, the book straddles two premodern periods, the fifteenth and seventeenth centuries, in a diptych structure: the first part consists of Dorothea of Montau (1347–94) and Margery Kempe (c. 1373–c. 1440); the second takes up two English women, Mary Ward (1585–1645) and Elizabeth Cary (c. 1585–1639). All four women chose the religious life in some form, whether that involved mystical revelations (Dorothea and Kempe), founding their own movement (Mary Ward), or converting to Catholicism and writing plays (Elizabeth Cary). All four are also compatible across their historical and geographical distances for their power to "shock and surprise" (xix). Other connections that Wallace draws among them are that they all struggled with masculine authorities ("for a strong woman to emerge, and get her story written, a man must die," 228); and they all bore up in distinct ways under the pressures of female enclosure and social expectations, particularly with respect to marriage. In addition, however, Wallace is especially interested in inserting these women's lives in historical (and geographical) contexts, implicating them in contemporary events in new ways. Even more important is his attention to the afterlives of the work of all four women as their *lives* become reshaped by twentieth-century political pressures in the process of their recuperation. In both respects, his book makes significant and fascinating contributions to the study of premodern women's religious writing and their twentieth-century afterlives. The "time" of each of these women and their lives is, in Wallace's analysis, *now,* insofar as they came to serve twentieth-century religious and nationalist agendas.

Wallace begins his study with Dorothea of Montau, the Prussian mystic who was a contemporary of Margery Kempe. Dorothea's "life," that is, her biographical trajectory, includes her early self-inflicted asceticism, her arranged marriage, and finally, her enclosure to become Prussia's first anchoress. Wallace seems uncomfortable with Dorothea's mystical practices, such as her severe self-mortification, which causes him to wonder "What is Dorothea's *jouissance?*" (34) in an uncanny echo of Freud's "What do women want?" Considering the wealth of feminist analyses of such practices, it is rather odd that Wallace never engages with them in his pursuit of Dorothea's *jouissance* or the meaning of her bodily asceticism. Wallace is at his best, however, when he considers how Dorothea's *life* comes to signify in her own times (after her death) the triumph of Teutonic Christianity against paganism, or in the twentieth century the compensation of German Catholics for the loss of border territories, the icon of second-wave feminism for Günter Grass, or again, as a figure of "Christian Brotherhood" in a book by Cardinal Josef Ratzinger (Pope Benedict XVI). Not to mention George Eliot's own possible enchantment with Dorothea, a romance that Wallace speculates inspired her own character, Dorothea Brooke of *Middlemarch*.

Wallace turns to Margery Kempe in his second chapter, or rather, he turns to the often ignored second book of her *Book* (because of the German travels recounted in it, which bring her into Dorothea of Montau's orbit). Wallace reviews the complicated story of the rediscovery of Margery Kempe's *Book* in 1934 and Hope Emily Allen's famous identification of the manuscript and subsequent marginalization as an editor in favor of Sanford B. Meech. Beginning with Hope Emily Allen, Wallace examines *TLS* reviews and other writings, in which Margery Kempe assumes the position of exemplar of Englishness as well as "Joan of Arc's English equivalent" (76), protector of the English nation during World War II. Most of the chapter is devoted to Kempe's travel to Gdansk, where Wallace considers the parallels between Kempe's life and Dorothea's. Wallace's titular epithet for Kempe, "anchoritic damsel," however, seems at odds with the "strong women" theme of his book. His explanation for it, that it "bids only to acknowledge, and not to resolve, the mysterious forcefields of her text" (132), only further puzzles.

The final two chapters on Mary Ward and Elizabeth Cary take up many of the parallels with Kempe and Dorothea, including their struggles with male authorities and their travels, particularly in the case of Mary Ward. In addition, Pope Benedict XVI appears again as one of the primary voices of the reemergence of Ward, whom he designated a woman of "heroic virtue" when she was given the title of "Venerable." Elizabeth Cary is the one figure in Wallace's book who does not seem to have a modern afterlife in the sense that she becomes invested with modern nationalistic or religious ideals. After her *Life* was first edited in the Victorian period by Catholic converts, the recent edition by Heather Wolfe instead becomes a scholarly exercise in the difficulty of manuscript reconciliation.

Wallace's book meshes the interests of his previous books on "pre-modern spaces" and premodern women to produce a searching study of the ways in which religious lives and biographies become entangled within their own histories and geographies, as well as the desires of future readers. His contemporary photographs of the premodern places of these women's lives and *lives*—from the bleak, windswept terrain of Dorothea of Montau's native Marienburg to the Gdansk of Margery Kempe's travels, and finally to the alleyways of Elizabeth Cary's Drury Lane—landscape his discussion of their histories and afterlives. To his discussion of these remarkable women and their biographies, Wallace contributes a new and bracing understanding of the multiple ways in which places structured the lives and even bodily practices of religious devotion.

KARMA LOCHRIE
Indiana University

LAWRENCE WARNER. *The Lost History of "Piers Plowman."* Philadelphia: University of Pennsylvania Press, 2011. Pp. xviii, 117. $49.95.

The ABCs of Langland studies keep getting challenged. In the 1980s, we had the Z-text; in the 1990s the idea that the A-text came last; and then in 2002 Lawrence Warner's argument, on the basis of manuscript evidence, that B did not circulate before C, and that the last two passus might have come into B from C ("The Ur-B *Piers Plowman* and the Earliest Production of C and B," *YLS* 16 [2002]: 3–39). Warner's star witness was N^2 (National Library of Wales, MS 733B), an A manuscript with a C continuation, and manuscripts R and F, in the B family but forming a separate group against the fifteen others (W~M). He argued that N^2 is witness to an earlier stage of C transmission than all other C manuscripts, and that its putative ancestor Nx is the source of a number of readings in the B tradition, readings not in the RF line. That is, from the many places where N^2 agrees with W~M and RF is absent or substitutes clearly spurious lines, places that seem to show that N^2 had access to a B manuscript in the W~M family, Warner insisted that the solution is instead that that family had access to an ancestor of N^2, that is, an early C manuscript. His major exhibit was the forty-line "poison of possession" passage in B.XV; he argued that it was composed for C on a loose sheet that went to "the guardian of the ur-B exemplar," who copied it into B, but that it had been returned for the final C-revision before the ancestor of R and F ("RF") was produced—a rather detailed scenario, I must say. And, more detailed yet, the RF scribe likewise adopted many ur-C readings as corrections to his manuscript (some of which were apparently rejected by R, some by F, for the original B reading). That is, though Langland probably wrote ur-B in 1378 or so, it had little circulation; and Bx (the putative latest common ancestor of the B manuscripts) shows C influence, perhaps even owing to C its entire last two passus. Those passus are of course nearly identical in both versions, and Langlandians have supposed that Langland died before revising them, or else that he was satisfied and left them alone. Warner thinks that both originated in C and were then copied into ur-B. He introduced it in 2002 as a "startling new possibility" ("Ur-B," 24) and argued it fully in a further article, "The Ending, and End, of *Piers Plowman* B: The C-Version Origins of the Final Two Passus" (*MÆ* 76 [2007]: 225–50).

Small parts of the argument also appear in "Becket and the Hopping Bishops" (*YLS* 17 [2003]: 107–34) and in *"Piers Plowman* B XV 417–428a: An Intrusion from Langland's C-Papers?" (*N&Q* 51 [2004]: 119–22). The present book gathers together all the strands—and there is some new material as well. In Chapter 1, Warner presents the evidence for his belief that the A version circulated early—he argues that the affiliations imply a total of nineteen now-lost copies, and eventually treats them (with imperfect logic, since they need not all have been pre-1400) as "plenty of evidence for *Piers Plowman* A's substantial fourteenth-century readership" (4) in addition to the three pre-1400 manuscripts we actually have—while ur-B "remain[ed] dormant until readers and scribes had embraced the final, C version" (1). He dismisses the "evidence" that B was available by 1381, particularly John Ball's "Peres Plouȝman" and "do wel and bettre," since they need not be allusions to the poem but, if they are, can be to the A version (though I think he slights Steven Justice's appealing argument that the line "Proditor est prelatus cum Juda qui patrimonium Christi minus distribuit," in B only, lies behind Ball's calling Archbishop Sudbury a traitor). Chapters 2 and 3 do not appear to offer any facts or analyses not already presented in the 2002 article, though there is much reorganization and new argumentation about Kane and Donaldson's blind spots. Chapter

4 is nearly the same as the 2007 *Medium Aevum* article. There is also a thoughtfully designed and thorough index. I found it dizzying to keep the whole complicated array of manuscript evidence clear in my head, and my dizziness was relieved again and again by the index.

In the final chapter, mostly new, Warner moves away from analysis of variants to consider substance. He argues that the changes are all related: that "over the course of the 1380s Langland put together a program that associates friars, illicit sexuality, and the question of *fyndynge* . . . in a series of passages first inscribed on loose sheets that could be read or copied independently and then incorporated into the C and W∼M shapes of the poem" (62), and thus that "the bulk of the passages" that (in his view) went from C into the W∼M family of B are "united thematically." He regards this thematic unity as constituting "final, and as it were external, support for [his] argument that they went from Nx to Bx" (63). I was not convinced by this chapter. Warner cites me to support him, since in my essay "Harlots' Holiness" (*YLS* 20 [2006]: 141–90) I had pointed out that the new lines in C.IX excoriating bishops for laxity in the confessional use the same imagery of salve that appears at the very end of the poem, where the theme is again laxity in the confessional. But I had in fact placed both passages in the much broader context of "harlots' holiness" or false absolution for theft, which I argued is a major theme everywhere in the poem in both B and C, if a little stronger in C. And when Warner argues that B.XV.417–28 (in both RF and W∼M) are "not integral to B" but rather "draft material" for C, because they mention the theme of a proper finding for religious and because he thinks they interrupt Anima's line of thought, he is on dubious ground. He also argued this in his 2004 *Notes and Queries* article. I didn't assent then, and I still don't. The lines do not interrupt the line of thought, but develop the mention of clerks' *coveitise* in line 415, and draw on the *Legenda sanctorum* as Anima has been doing in his entire speech. Also, the lollers in the C.IX passage are not friars but imitation friars, and thus the connection Warner tries to draw between them and Sir Penetrans Domos (64) is factitious. I also dissent from the statement that the C material shared by Ht (Huntington Library 114) and N², which Kane and Russell thought most likely had a common source, "shares . . . many thematic concerns, suggest[ing] the probability that all of this matter originated together and entered circulation in similar form" (63). In fact, that material covers an array of subjects far broader than the attack on friars that ends the last passus; indeed at times it replaces lines about friars with broader lines about religious or about the clergy in general. In short, this last chapter offers very skimpy support for its assertion that the bulk of the passages Warner has been discussing, that is, "about eighty lines from passus 3, 8, 9, 12, 15, and 16"; the final two passus; and "those hundred or so RF/C readings that conflict with W–M/N^2" (62)—all the matter that is in Bx but not in ur-B, and Warner thinks came from C—are united thematically. None of the lines he treats from B VIII, IX, XII, and XVI, for instance, are on the theme. He clearly overreaches here, which I was sorry to see since the rest of the book, though I am not convinced by it, is at least argued with meticulous care.

In the years since the 2002 article, Warner's arguments have been met largely with silence, perhaps because of the dizzying effect I have mentioned. A. V. C. Schmidt in 2008 pointed out that N^2 shows consultation of both main families of C manuscripts (and is therefore necessarily late), and of a B manuscript in the W~M family as well (*Piers Plowman: A Parallel-Text Edition,* vol. 2, Part 1, 8; 208 n. 15), and dismissed Warner's "startling possibility" about the ending as "too startling" (285). Ralph Hanna in 2010 offered a reply in the course of a tribute to George Kane, who had died late in 2009 ("George Kane and the Invention of Textual Thought: Retrospect and Prospect," *YLS* 24 [2010]: 1–20). Briefly, he argues that the affiliations of N^2 make it clear that it belongs late rather than early in the C tradition, that the "editor" (Kane's word) behind it had consulted, beside various C manuscripts, "a very good B manuscript" (rather than an early version of C) (11), and that the scribe of F, finding his exemplar missing a quire between B.VIII.411 and B.XX.26 (lines missing in R), drew on a C copy. Hanna does not, however, confront an important element in Warner's argument: Warner shows that the places in RF where it seems to be contaminated by C correspond overwhelmingly with those where Nx diverged from Cx; he insists that this cannot be coincidental, and it is perhaps his major evidence for his theory that loose sheets were first available to the guardian of ur-B, then unavailable to the RF scribe (46). Both Andrew Galloway (*Choice* 49 [2011], 508) and A. S. G. Edwards (*TLS,* October 7, 2011, 27) praise the boldness and close argumentation of *The Lost History of "Piers Plowman,"* but they raise questions. I find myself in the same boat: the careful argumentation is impressive, but I am not quite ready to see it as the only interpretation of the evidence.

I certainly lean toward Hanna's (and the traditional) view that the last two passus were always in the B version. If the rubrics are authorial, Warner has no case, and I agree with Hanna that they are. And a host of internal considerations also give me pause. There is a certain inevitability in the portrayal in the final passus of how the redemption has played out in the history of the church; ending the poem with the simple piety of Will taking his family to "reverence goddes resurexion" at Easter Sunday mass would be, in a poet of Langland's power, a feeble abandonment of his vision. In particular, I feel a need for a climax to the treatment of the friars' abuse of confession, a full dramatization of the "mooste mischief on Molde," occasioned by their rage for profits, that we have known since the prologue is mounting up fast. And when Conscience leaves Clergye at the end of the banquet in B.XIII, and Clergye says, "Thou shalt se the tyme / Whan thow art wery forwalked; wille me to conseille" (203–4), Langland is almost certainly setting up Conscience's two calls to Clergye in the last passus (B.XX.228, 375). Externally, it is hard to swallow Warner's insistence, crucial to his argument since the ending is in all B manuscripts, that B did not circulate at all until after C was made; what poet, having written B.XI–XVIII (or, in my view, XI–XX), could have kept them in his desk drawer? Another problem is that there are, after all, a number of small regular differences between the B transmission and the C transmission of these passus, at least some of them looking very like corrections in C of metrically faulty B lines. Kane and Donaldson treated them all as scribal errors, but I'm not sure. A third objection is the number of B revisions to A that many perceptive critics have argued must have been made after B.X–XX was written. Although finally I find it hard to offer a definitive adjudication in this review, I have to say that Hanna's elegant arguments support my instinctive skepticism. I hope at least that the publication of Warner's book will occasion still more discussion of these hard matters.

TRAUGOTT LAWLER
Yale University

Books Received

Allen, Mark, and John H. Fisher, eds. *The Wife of Bath's Prologue and Tale.* A Variorum Edition of the Works of Geoffrey Chaucer: *The Canterbury Tales,* Vol. 2, parts 5A and 5B. 2 vols. Norman: University of Oklahoma Press, 2012. Pp. 776. $90.00.

Ashton, Gail. *Brief Lives: Geoffrey Chaucer.* London: Hesperus Press, 2011. Pp. 117. £7.99; $12.95.

Beidler, Peter G. *A Student Guide to Chaucer's Middle English.* Seattle: Coffeetown Press, 2011. Pp. x, 55. $9.95 paper.

Besserman, Lawrence. *Biblical Paradigms in Medieval English Literature: From Cædmon to Malory.* New York: Routledge, 2012. Pp. xvi, 219. $125.00; £80.00.

Binski, Paul, and Patrick Zutshi. *Western Illuminated Manuscripts: A Catalogue of the Collection in Cambridge University Library.* Cambridge: Cambridge University Press, 2011. Pp. xxvi, 506. £175.00; $275.00.

Bolens, Guillemette, and Lukas Erne, eds. *Medieval and Early Modern Authorship.* Tübingen: Narr, 2011. Pp. 323. €49.00; $65.00.

Bose, Mishtooni, and J. Patrick Hornbeck II, eds. *Wycliffite Controversies.* Turnhout: Brepols, 2011. Pp. xiv, 359. €90.00; $120.00.

Donavin, Georgiana. *Scribit Mater: Mary and the Language Arts in the Literature of Medieval England.* Washington, D.C.: Catholic University of America Press, 2011. Pp. xiv, 315. $69.95.

Gillespie, Alexandra, and Daniel Wakelin, eds. *The Production of Books in England, 1350–1500.* Cambridge: Cambridge University Press, 2011. Pp. 396. £60.00; $95.00.

Glaser, Joseph, trans. *Sir Gawain and the Green Knight.* Indianapolis: Hackett, 2011. Pp. liv, 83. $10.95 paper.

Goodman, Lenn E., and Richard McGregor, trans. *The Case of the Animals versus Man Before the King of the Jinn: A Translation from the Epistles of the Brethren of Purity.* Oxford: Oxford University Press, 2012. Pp. xvi, 389. £16.99; $29.95 paper.

Higgins, Iain Macleod, ed. and trans. *The Book of John Mandeville with Related Texts.* Indianapolis: Hackett, 2011. Pp. xxviii, 292. $12.95 paper.

Hoofnagle, Wendy Marie, and Wolfram R. Keller, eds. *Other Nations: The Hybridization of Medieval Insular Mythology and Identity.* Heidelberg: Winter, 2011. Pp. x, 248. €46.00; $69.00.

Jaeger, C. Stephen, ed. *Magnificence and the Sublime in Medieval Aesthetics: Art, Architecture, Literature, Music.* New York: Palgrave Macmillan, 2010. Pp. xii, 274. $84.00.

Karnes, Michelle. *Imagination, Meditation, and Cognition in the Middle Ages.* Chicago: University of Chicago Press, 2011. Pp. xiv, 268. $45.00.

McAvoy, Liz Herbert, and Diane Watt, eds. *The History of British Women's Writing, 700–1500.* New York: Palgrave Macmillan, 2012. Pp. xxvi, 268. $85.00; £55.00.

Newhauser, Richard, trans. Peter of Limoges, *The Moral Treatise on the Eye.* Toronto: Pontifical Institute of Mediaeval Studies, 2012. Pp. xxxiv, 271. $35.00 paper.

Niebrzydowski, Sue, ed. *Middle-Aged Women in the Middle Ages.* Cambridge: Brewer, 2011. Pp. xii, 153. £50.00; $90.00.

Richmond, E. B., trans. Geoffrey Chaucer, *The Merchant's Tale.* London: Hesperus Press, 2011. Pp. xiv, 84. £6.99; $12.50.

Rikhardsdottir, Sif. *Medieval Translations and Cultural Discourse: The Movement of Texts in England, France, and Scandinavia.* Cambridge, Brewer, 2012. Pp. xii, 199. £50.00; $90.00.

Rollo, David. *Kiss My Relics: Hermaphroditic Fictions of the Middle Ages.* Chicago: University of Chicago Press, 2011. Pp. viii, 250. $35.00.

Rooney, Kenneth. *Mortality and Imagination: The Life of the Dead in Medieval English Literature.* Turnhout: Brepols, 2011. Pp. xiv, 304. €100.00; $135.00.

Singer, Julie. *Blindness and Therapy in Late Medieval French and Italian Poetry.* Cambridge: Brewer, 2011. Pp. x, 238. £60.00; $99.00.

Stockton, Will. *Playing Dirty: Sexuality and Waste in Early Modern Comedy.* Minneapolis: University of Minnesota Press, 2011. Pp. xxvi, 175. $22.50 paper.

Swanton, Michael, ed. and trans. *The Lives of Two Offas: Vitae Offarum Duorum.* Crediton: The Medieval Press, 2010. Pp. cii, 210. £65.00; $105.00 cloth, £22.99; $40.00 paper.

Waller, Gary. *Walsingham and the English Imagination.* Farnham: Ashgate, 2011. Pp. xii, 237. £55.00; $85.00.

Winstead, Karen A., trans. John Capgrave, *The Life of Saint Katherine of Alexandria.* Notre Dame: University of Notre Dame Press, 2011. Pp. 203. $25.00 paper.

An Annotated Chaucer Bibliography, 2010

Compiled and edited by Mark Allen and Bege K. Bowers

Regular contributors:

Anne Thornton, *Abbot Public Library* (Marblehead, Massachusetts)
Stephen Jones, *Ball State University* (Indiana)
George Nicholas, *Benedictine College* (Kansas)
Debra Best, *California State University at Dominguez Hills*
Gregory M. Sadlek, *Cleveland State University* (Ohio)
David Sprunger, *Concordia College* (Minnesota)
Winthrop Wetherbee, *Cornell University* (New York)
Elaine Whitaker, *Georgia College & State University*
Michelle Allen, *Grand Valley State University* (Michigan)
Elizabeth Dobbs, *Grinnell College* (Iowa)
Andrew James Johnston, *Freie Universität* (Germany)
Wim Lindeboom, *Independent Scholar* (Netherlands)
Teresa P. Reed, *Jacksonville State University* (Alabama)
William Snell, *Keio University* (Japan)
Denise Stodola, *Kettering University* (Michigan)
Brian A. Shaw, *London, Ontario*
William Schipper, *Memorial University* (Newfoundland, Canada)
Martha Rust, *New York University*
Warren S. Moore III, *Newberry College* (South Carolina)
Cindy L. Vitto, *Rowan College of New Jersey*
Brother Anthony (Sonjae An), *Sogang University* (South Korea)
Stephanie Amsel, *Southern Methodist University* (Texas)
Ana Saez Hidalgo, *Universidad de Valladolid* (Spain)
Stefania D'Agata D'Ottavi, *Università per Stranieri di Siena* (Italy)
Martine Yvernault, *Université de Limoges*
Hillary K. Miller, *University of Alabama at Birmingham*
Cynthia Ho, *University of North Carolina, Asheville*
Margaret Connolly, *University of St. Andrews* (Scotland)

Studies in the Age of Chaucer 34 (2012):453–454
© 2012 The New Chaucer Society

Rebecca Beal, *University of Scranton* (Pennsylvania)
Mark Allen, *University of Texas at San Antonio*
John M. Crafton, *West Georgia College*
Bege K. Bowers, *Youngstown State University* (Ohio)

Ad hoc contributions were made by several contributors, including Michael Murphy of New York, New York. The bibliographers acknowledge with gratitude the MLA typesimulation provided by the Center for Bibliographical Services of the Modern Language Association; postage from the University of Texas at San Antonio Department of English; and assistance from the library staff, especially Susan McCray, at the University of Texas at San Antonio.

This bibliography continues the bibliographies published since 1975 in previous volumes of *Studies in the Age of Chaucer*. Bibliographic information up to 1975 can be found in Eleanor P. Hammond, *Chaucer: A Bibliographic Manual* (1908; reprint, New York: Peter Smith, 1933); D. D. Griffith, *Bibliography of Chaucer, 1908–1953* (Seattle: University of Washington Press, 1955); William R. Crawford, *Bibliography of Chaucer, 1954–1963* (Seattle: University of Washington Press, 1967); and Lorrayne Y. Baird, *Bibliography of Chaucer, 1964–1973* (Boston: G. K. Hall, 1977). See also Lorrayne Y. Baird-Lange and Hildegard Schnuttgen, *Bibliography of Chaucer, 1974–1985* (Hamden, Conn.: Shoe String Press, 1988); and Bege K. Bowers and Mark Allen, eds., *Annotated Chaucer Bibliography, 1986–1996* (Notre Dame: University of Notre Dame Press, 2002).

Additions and corrections to this bibliography should be sent to Mark Allen, Bibliographic Division, The New Chaucer Society, Department of English, University of Texas at San Antonio 78249-0643 (Fax: 210-458-5366; e-mail: mark.allen@utsa.edu). An electronic version of this bibliography (1975–2009) is available via The New Chaucer Society Web page at http://artsci.wustl.edu/~chaucer/ or directly at http://uchaucer.utsa.edu. Authors are urged to send annotations for articles, reviews, and books that have been or might be overlooked.

Classifications

Abbreviations of Chaucer's Works

ABC	*An ABC*
Adam	*Adam Scriveyn*
Anel	*Anelida and Arcite*
Astr	*A Treatise on the Astrolabe*
Bal Compl	*A Balade of Complaint*
BD	*The Book of the Duchess*
Bo	*Boece*
Buk	*The Envoy to Bukton*
CkT, CkP, Rv–CkL	*The Cook's Tale, The Cook's Prologue, Reeve–Cook Link*
ClT, ClP, Cl–MerL	*The Clerk's Tale, The Clerk's Prologue, Clerk–Merchant Link*
Compl d'Am	*Complaynt d'Amours*
CT	*The Canterbury Tales*
CYT, CYP	*The Canon's Yeoman's Tale, The Canon's Yeoman's Prologue*
Equat	*The Equatorie of the Planetis*
For	*Fortune*
Form Age	*The Former Age*
FranT, FranP	*The Franklin's Tale, The Franklin's Prologue*
FrT, FrP, Fr–SumL	*The Friar's Tale, The Friar's Prologue, Friar–Summoner Link*
Gent	*Gentilesse*
GP	*The General Prologue*
HF	*The House of Fame*
KnT, Kn–MilL	*The Knight's Tale, Knight–Miller Link*
Lady	*A Complaint to His Lady*
LGW, LGWP	*The Legend of Good Women, The Legend of Good Women Prologue*
ManT, ManP	*The Manciple's Tale, The Manciple's Prologue*
Mars	*The Complaint of Mars*
Mel, Mel–MkL	*The Tale of Melibee, Melibee–Monk Link*
MercB	*Merciles Beaute*

MerT, MerE–SqH	The Merchant's Tale, Merchant Endlink–Squire Headlink
MilT, MilP, Mil–RvL	The Miller's Tale, The Miller's Prologue, Miller–Reeve Link
MkT, MkP, Mk–NPL	The Monk's Tale, The Monk's Prologue, Monk–Nun's Priest Link
MLT, MLH, MLP, MLE	The Man of Law's Tale, Man of Law Headlink, The Man of Law's Prologue, Man of Law Endlink
NPT, NPP, NPE	The Nun's Priest's Tale, The Nun's Priest's Prologue, Nun's Priest Endlink
PardT, PardP	The Pardoner's Tale, The Pardoner's Prologue
ParsT, ParsP	The Parson's Tale, The Parson's Prologue
PF	The Parliament of Fowls
PhyT, Phy–PardL	The Physician's Tale, Physician–Pardoner Link
Pity	The Complaint unto Pity
Prov	Proverbs
PrT, PrP, Pr–ThL	The Prioress's Tale, The Prioress's Prologue, Prioress–Thopas Link
Purse	The Complaint of Chaucer to His Purse
Ret	Chaucer's Retraction {Retractation}
Rom	The Romaunt of the Rose
Ros	To Rosemounde
RvT, RvP	The Reeve's Tale, The Reeve's Prologue
Scog	The Envoy to Scogan
ShT, Sh–PrL	The Shipman's Tale, Shipman–Prioress Link
SNT, SNP, SN–CYL	The Second Nun's Tale, The Second Nun's Prologue, Second Nun–Canon's Yeoman Link
SqT, SqH, Sq–FranL	The Squire's Tale, Squire Headlink, Squire–Franklin Link
Sted	Lak of Stedfastnesse
SumT, SumP	The Summoner's Tale, The Summoner's Prologue
TC	Troilus and Criseyde
Th, Th–MelL	The Tale of Sir Thopas, Thopas–Melibee Link

Truth	*Truth*
Ven	*The Complaint of Venus*
WBT, WBP, WB–FrL	*The Wife of Bath's Tale, The Wife of Bath's Prologue, Wife of Bath–Friar Link*
Wom Nob	*Womanly Noblesse*
Wom Unc	*Against Women Unconstant*

Periodical Abbreviations

AdI	*Annali d'Italianistica*
Anglia	*Anglia: Zeitschrift für Englische Philologie*
Anglistik	*Anglistik: Mitteilungen des Verbandes deutscher Anglisten*
AnLM	*Anuario de Letras Modernas*
ANQ	*ANQ: A Quarterly Journal of Short Articles, Notes, and Reviews*
Archiv	*Archiv für das Studium der neueren Sprachen und Literaturen*
Arthuriana	*Arthuriana*
Atlantis	*Atlantis: Revista de la Asociacion Española de Estudios Anglo-Norteamericanos*
AUMLA	*AUMLA: Journal of the Australasian Universities Language and Literature Association*
BAM	*Bulletin des Anglicistes Médiévistes*
BJRL	*Bulletin of the John Rylands University Library of Manchester*
C&L	*Christianity and Literature*
CarmP	*Carmina Philosophiae: Journal of the International Boethius Society*
CE	*College English*
ChauR	*Chaucer Review*
CL	*Comparative Literature* (Eugene, Ore.)
Clio	*CLIO: A Journal of Literature, History, and the Philosophy of History*
CLS	*Comparative Literature Studies*
CML	*Classical and Modern Literature: A Quarterly* (Columbia, Mo.)
CollL	*College Literature*
Comitatus	*Comitatus: A Journal of Medieval and Renaissance Studies*
CRCL	*Canadian Review of Comparative Literature/Revue Canadienne de Littérature Comparée*

DAI	*Dissertation Abstracts International*
DR	*Dalhousie Review*
ÉA	*Études Anglaises: Grand-Bretagne, États-Unis*
EHR	*English Historical Review*
EIC	*Essays in Criticism: A Quarterly Journal of Literary Criticism*
EJ	*English Journal*
ELH	*ELH: English Literary History*
ELN	*English Language Notes*
ELR	*English Literary Renaissance*
EMS	*English Manuscript Studies, 1100–1700*
EMSt	*Essays in Medieval Studies*
Encomia	*Encomia: Bibliographical Bulletin of the International Courtly Literature Society*
English	*English: The Journal of the English Association*
Envoi	*Envoi: A Review Journal of Medieval Literature*
ES	*English Studies*
ESC	*English Studies in Canada*
Exemplaria	*Exemplaria: A Journal of Theory in Medieval and Renaissance Studies*
Expl	*Explicator*
FCS	*Fifteenth-Century Studies*
Florilegium	*Florilegium: Carleton University Papers on Late Antiquity and the Middle Ages*
FMLS	*Forum for Modern Language Studies*
Genre	*Genre: Forms of Discourse and Culture*
H-Albion	*H-Albion: The H-Net Discussion Network for British and Irish History, H-Net Reviews in the Humanities and Social Sciences* http://www.h-net.org/reviews/home.php
H-German	*H-German: The Discussion Group for Historians of German around the World, H-Net Reviews in the Humanities and Social Sciences* http://www.h-net.org/~german/
H-HRE	*H-HRE: The Discussion Group for the History and Culture of the Holy Roman Empire, H-Net Reviews in the Humanities and Social Sciences* http://www.h-net.org/~hre/
HLQ	*Huntington Library Quarterly: Studies in English and*

	American History and Literature (San Marino, Calif.)
Hortulus	*Hortulus: The Online Graduate Journal of Medieval Studies* http://www.hortulus.net/
IJES	*International Journal of English Studies*
JAIS	*Journal of Anglo-Italian Studies*
JBSt	*Journal of British Studies*
JEBS	*Journal of the Early Book Society*
JEGP	*Journal of English and Germanic Philology*
JEH	*Journal of Ecclesiastical History*
JELL	*Journal of English Language and Literature* (Korea)
JEngL	*Journal of English Linguistics*
JGN	*John Gower Newsletter*
JHiP	*Journal of Historical Pragmatics*
JMEMSt	*Journal of Medieval and Early Modern Studies*
JML	*Journal of Modern Literature*
JNT	*Journal of Narrative Theory*
JRMMRA	*Quidditas: Journal of the Rocky Mountain Medieval and Renaissance Association*
L&LC	*Literary and Linguistic Computing: Journal of the Association for Literary and Linguistic Computing*
L&P	*Literature and Psychology*
L&T	*Literature and Theology: An International Journal of Religion, Theory, and Culture*
Lang&Lit	*Language and Literature: Journal of the Poetics and Linguistics Association*
Lang&S	*Language and Style: An International Journal*
LATCH	*LATCH: A Journal for the Study of the Literary Artifact in Theory, Culture, or History*
LeedsSE	*Leeds Studies in English*
Library	*The Library: The Transactions of the Bibliographical Society*
LitComp	*Literature Compass* http://www.literaturecompass.com/
MA	*Le Moyen Age: Revue d'Histoire et de Philologie* (Brussels, Belgium)
MÆ	*Medium Ævum*
M&H	*Medievalia et Humanistica: Studies in Medieval and Renaissance Culture*

Manuscripta	*Manuscripta* (St. Louis, Mo.)
Marginalia	*Marginalia: The Journal of the Medieval Reading Group at the University of Cambridge* http://www. marginalia.co.uk/journal/
Mediaevalia	*Mediaevalia: An Interdisciplinary Journal of Medieval Studies Worldwide*
MedievalF	*Medieval Forum* http://www.sfsu.edu/~medieval /index.html
MedPers	*Medieval Perspectives*
MES	*Medieval and Early Modern English Studies*
MFF	*Medieval Feminist Forum*
MichA	*Michigan Academician* (Ann Arbor, Mich.)
MLQ	*Modern Language Quarterly: A Journal of Literary History*
MLR	*The Modern Language Review*
MP	*Modern Philology: A Journal Devoted to Research in Medieval and Modern Literature*
N&Q	*Notes and Queries*
Neophil	*Neophilologus* (Dordrecht, Netherlands)
NLH	*New Literary History: A Journal of Theory and Interpretation*
NM	*Neuphilologische Mitteilungen: Bulletin of the Modern Language Society*
NML	*New Medieval Literatures*
NMS	*Nottingham Medieval Studies*
NOWELE	*NOWELE: North-Western European Language Evolution*
Parergon	*Parergon: Bulletin of the Australian and New Zealand Association for Medieval and Early Modern Studies*
PBA	*Proceedings of the British Academy*
PBSA	*Papers of the Bibliographical Society of America*
PLL	*Papers on Language and Literature: A Journal for Scholars and Critics of Language and Literature*
PMAM	*Publications of the Medieval Association of the Midwest*
PMLA	*Publications of the Modern Language Association of America*
PoeticaT	*Poetica: An International Journal of Linguistic Literary Studies*
PQ	*Philological Quarterly*

RCEI	*Revista Canaria de Estudios Ingleses*
RenQ	*Renaissance Quarterly*
RES	*Review of English Studies*
RMRev	*Reading Medieval Reviews* http://www.rdg.ac.uk /AcaDepts/ln/Medieval/rmr.htm
RMSt	*Reading Medieval Studies*
SAC	*Studies in the Age of Chaucer*
SAP	*Studia Anglica Posnaniensia: An International Review of English*
SAQ	*South Atlantic Quarterly*
SB	*Studies in Bibliography: Papers of the Bibliographical Society of the University of Virginia*
SCJ	*The Sixteenth-Century Journal: Journal of Early Modern Studies* (Kirksville, Mo.)
SEL	*SEL: Studies in English Literature, 1500–1900*
SELIM	*SELIM: Journal of the Spanish Society for Medieval English Language and Literature*
ShakS	*Shakespeare Studies*
SIcon	*Studies in Iconography*
SiM	*Studies in Medievalism*
SIMELL	*Studies in Medieval English Language and Literature*
SMART	*Studies in Medieval and Renaissance Teaching*
SN	*Studia Neophilologica: A Journal of Germanic and Romance Languages and Literatures*
SoAR	*South Atlantic Review*
SP	*Studies in Philology*
Speculum	*Speculum: A Journal of Medieval Studies*
SSF	*Studies in Short Fiction*
SSt	*Spenser Studies: A Renaissance Poetry Annual*
TCBS	*Transactions of the Cambridge Bibliographical Society*
Text	*Text: Transactions of the Society for Textual Scholarship*
TLS	*Times Literary Supplement* (London, England)
TMR	*The Medieval Review* http://www.hti.umich.edu/t /tmr/
Tr&Lit	*Translation and Literature*
TSLL	*Texas Studies in Literature and Language*
UTQ	*University of Toronto Quarterly: A Canadian Journal of the Humanities* (Toronto, Canada)
Viator	*Viator: Medieval and Renaissance Studies*

WS	*Women's Studies: An Interdisciplinary Journal*
YES	*Yearbook of English Studies*
YLS	*The Yearbook of Langland Studies*
YWES	*Year's Work in English Studies*

Bibliographical Citations and Annotations

Bibliographies, Reports, and Reference

1. Allen, Mark, and Bege K. Bowers. "An Annotated Chaucer Bibliography, 2008." *SAC* 32 (2010): 477–578. Continuation of *SAC* annual annotated bibliography (since 1975); based on contributions from an international bibliographic team, independent research, and *MLA Bibliography* listings. 337 items, plus listing of reviews for 92 books. Includes an author index.

2. Chewning, Susannah Mary, Orietta Da Rold, and Katharine Jager. "Later Medieval: Chaucer." *YWES* 89 (2010): 284–308. A discursive bibliography of Chaucer studies for 2008, divided into four subcategories: general, *CT*, *TC*, and other works.

3. Galloway, Andrew. "Geoffrey Chaucer." *Oxford Bibliographies Online.* http://oxfordbibliographies.com, 2010. January 22, 2011. Updatable, annotated bibliography of Chaucer studies, available by subscription only. Arranges individual studies alphabetically under twenty-three categories (plus subsections), providing hypertext links to the original material when possible. Each section/subsection is preceded by a brief, synthesizing introduction, with internal links to cited studies. The bibliography provides various options for saving and exporting citations.

See also no. 38.

Recordings and Films

4. Finke, Laurie A., and Martin B. Shichtman. *Cinematic Illuminations: The Middle Ages on Film.* Baltimore: Johns Hopkins University Press, 2010. xi, 445 pp. 20 b&w illus. The authors survey a range of popular and artistic films, analyzing uses and presentations of the Middle Ages and assessing the interactions of the modern medium and the ancient material. The book includes commentary on Brian Helgeland's *A Knight's Tale*, its depiction of Chaucer, and the role of theatricality in the film and in Chaucer's society.

5. Gielgud, John, presenter, with Anthony Thwaite, comp. *Six Centuries of Verse: Poetry's Greatest Hits Brought to Life.* [U.S.]: Athena; Silver

Spring, Md.: Acorn Media, 2010. 3 DVDs; approx. 410 min. 1 booklet; 17 pp. Dramatized readings of poetry from *Beowulf* to 1984. Disc one (episode 3; track 7; 24 min.) includes the previously published "Chaucer, 1340–1400" (*SAC* 22 [2000], no. 12), an introduction to Chaucer and his works with recitation/dramatization of *PardT*.

6. Murphy, Michael, trans. *"Canterbury Tales": A Reader-Friendly Edition of Geoffrey Chaucer's "Canterbury Tales" Put into Modern Spelling*. http://www.thomondgate.net, [2010]. This updated version of Murphy's computer-based project includes "audioglossed" versions of *GP*, *MilT*, *PardT*, and *NPT* in which readers hear the text in modern pronunciation. In addition, unfamiliar words are glossed to the ear rather than visually.

7. Robinson, Carol L., and Pamela Clements. "Living with Neomedievalism." *SiM* 18 (2009): 55–75. Notes (pp. 65–67) a BBC One production of six tales in *CT* that aims to present the Wife of Bath as "a wonderful, feisty, bawdy, independent woman who is very much alive and living in the 21st century"; a Canadian (Baba Brinkman) who has "retrofitted" *CT* to rap music; and a Wife of Bath restaurant in Wye, Kent.

8. Spearing, Anthony, reader, with the assistance of Hiroshi Miura. *The Canterbury Tales: The Knight's Tale*. Tokyo: Center for Research on Language and Culture, Institute for the Development of Social Intelligence, Senshu University, 2009. 2 CD-ROMs; approx. 145 min. 2-page liner notes. Middle English reading of *GP*, lines 1–78, and the complete *KnT*, divided into 63 tracks.

See also nos. 152, 197, 215.

Chaucer's Life

9. Ashton, Gail. *Brief Lives: Geoffrey Chaucer*. London: Hesperus, 2010. 117 pp. Surveys the array of Chaucer biographies derived sequentially from early accounts and editions, portraits, life records, literature, and popular culture, including recent blogging. Describes Chaucer's early entry into court life, his court duties, spurious works, depictions in manuscripts and editions, implications of the paucity of information about his marriage and death, the changed political climate under Henry IV, Chaucer's literary legacy, and his biological heirs.

10. Carlson, David R. "The Robberies of Chaucer." *ESC* 35.2–3

(2009): 29–54. Legal proceedings following the 1390 roadside theft from Chaucer while he was on the king's business demonstrate the folly of any medieval challenge to hierarchical prerogative by a gang representing antihierarchical attitudes. Theoretically supported by hierarchical authority, pilgrimages are often denounced as profane secularization. Chaucer treats them as examples of the assertion of prerogative and as instances of the conflict between inclusion and exclusion.

11. Kelen, Sarah A. *Langland's Early Modern Identities*. The New Middle Ages. New York: Palgrave Macmillan, 2007. [xi], 225 pp. Kelen studies the reception of William Langland and *Piers Plowman* from the early modern period to the early twentieth century. She focuses on editions of the work and the works it inspired, efforts to identify Langland and construct his biography, and early appreciative criticism. The study includes frequent comparisons with Chaucer's status in literary history and in anthologies of English literature, references to Chaucerian apocrypha (especially *The Plowman's Tale*), and descriptions of biographies and fictional reconstructions of the poets' lives, especially efforts to explore their possible meetings and the lines of influence. See also no. 361.

See also nos. 34, 48, 49, 248.

Facsimiles, Editions, and Translations

12. Crépin, André, et al., trans., with collaboration by Ann Wéry. *Geoffrey Chaucer: "Les contes de Canterbury" et autres œuvres*. Paris: Laffont, 2010. xlvi, 1650 pp. Bilingual edition of the works of Chaucer, based on *The Riverside Chaucer*. Includes *CT, Rom, BD, HF, Anel, PF, Bo, TC, LGW*, short poems, *Astr, Equat*, and French poems attributed to Chaucer. Translators include André Crépin, Jean-Jacques Blanchot, Florence Bourgne, Guy Bourquin, Derek S. Brewer, Hélène Dauby, Juliette Dor, Emmanuel Poulle, and James I. Wimsatt. Provides commentary and indexes. See also no. 340.

13. Cruz Cabanillas, Isabel de, and Nila Vázquez González. "New Approaches in Textual Editing: A Selection of Electronic Editions Under Analysis." *IJES* 5.2 (2005): 193–208. Reviews several online editions of Old and Middle English texts, including some editions and websites that pertain to *CT*.

14. Da Rold, Orietta. "Should We Reedit the *Canterbury Tales*?" *SAC* 32 (2010): 375–82. Comments on questions of "prior circulation and

authorial revision" that were disclosed by the Manly-Rickert edition of *CT* and suggests that recent advances in codicology and the history of the book may offer future editors new perspectives from which to address such questions.

15. Davis, Annie S. "The Kelmscott Chaucer: William Morris's Quest for the Medieval Reader." *DAI* 70.08 (2010): n.p. Davis examines ramifications of the interplay between graphic design and text in William Morris's Kelmscott edition of Chaucer, arguing that the consequent mediation is a precursor to Walter Benjamin's theorized divorce of mechanically reproduced art from "aura" or "authentic presence."

16. Edwards, A. S. G. "Manly and Rickert and the Failure of Method." *SAC* 32 (2010): 337–44. Critiques the Manly-Rickert text of *CT* for inconsistency in treatment of orthographic accidentals and failure to maintain a consistent, identifiable copy-text. Recommends, nevertheless, judicious use of the Manly-Rickert table of variants.

17. Hoekstra, Klaas, trans. *De Canterbury ferhalen*. Leeuwarden: Elikser, 2010. 567 pp. First-time translation of *CT* into Frisian, following Chaucer's verse forms and omitting *Mel* and *ParsT*. Designed for a popular audience rather than a scholarly one. The source text is Albert Baugh's *Chaucer's Major Poetry* (1963), with translation aid from A. Barnouw's Dutch translation, *De vertellingen van de peligrims naar Kantelberg* (1968).

18. Kelly, Henry Ansgar. "Vance Ramsey on Manly-Rickert." *SAC* 32 (2010): 327–35. Summarizes Roy Vance Ramsey's (1994, 2010) defense of the Manly-Rickert text of *CT*, including Ramsey's recognition of the "piecemeal" production of the eight-volume work and his assessment of the dates and scribes of the Hg, El, and Dd manuscripts.

19. Machan, Tim William. "Opportunity's Knock and Chaucerian Textual Criticism." *SAC* 32 (2010): 357–63. The "textual-critical ferment" of the 1980s prompted two "editorial ideas" that have largely (and sadly) been ignored by Chaucer editors and teachers: Derek Pearsall's suggestion that an edition of *CT* should allow the fragments to be arranged variously and Michael Murphy's modern-spelling edition of selections from *CT*.

20. Mann, Jill. "'Learning, Taste, and Judgment' in the Editorial Process." *SAC* 32 (2010): 345–55. Critiques Roy Vance Ramsey's defense of the Manly-Rickert text of *CT* and castigates Ramsey's own methods and practices. The Manly-Rickert edition is valuable for its demonstration that "recension" cannot be used to construct a reliable

text of *CT*, and it provides much useful information—but Ramsey's defense is misguided.

21. Pakkala-Weckström, Mari. "Translating Chaucer's Power Play into Modern English and Finnish." In Alaric Hall, Olga Timofeeva, Ágnes Kiricsi, and Bethany Fox, eds. *Interfaces Between Language and Culture in Medieval England: A Festschrift for Matti Kilpiö*. The Northern World, no. 48. Leiden and Boston: Brill, 2010, pp. 307–27. Pakkala-Weckström compares translations (three modern English and one modern Finnish) of passages from three fabliaux (*MilT*, *MerT*, and *ShT*), examining how well they preserve the politeness features of Chaucer's originals.

22. Phillips, Noelle. "'Texts with Trowsers': Editing and the Elite Chaucer." *RES* 61 (2010): 331–59. Paradoxically, readers of Chaucer are assumed to respond "intuitively" and yet also to need the aid of specialized academic assistance. The Early English Text Society (EETS) and the Chaucer Society played crucial roles in creating this paradox and, despite their egalitarian goals, led readers to rely on professional assistance when approaching the poet's work.

23. Reale, Nancy M. "Chaucer Kowthe in Sondry Londes: *The Canterbury Tales* in Popular Web Culture." In Kathleen A. Bishop, ed. *Standing in the Shadow of the Master? Chaucerian Influences and Interpretations* (*SAC* 34 [2012], no. 114), pp. 257–86. Reale summarizes the versions of Chaucer's tales that abound on the Internet, suggesting that each has its own agenda for re-presenting Chaucer.

24. Sakaida, Susumu, trans. *The Romaunt of the Rose {Bara monogatari}, by Geoffrey Chaucer*. Tokyo: Ogawa Tosho, 1997. 226 pp. Japanese translation of *Rom*.

25. Wakelin, Daniel. "'Maked na moore': Editing and Narrative." *SAC* 32 (2010): 365–73. Explores how the Manly-Rickert edition of *CT* "undoes its own arguments about textual history by noting its own textual history of doubt and contingency," suggesting that Manly and Rickert "tell stories" about the composition of *CT* and that the death of Rickert before completion of the work parallels Chaucer's own death before completion of *CT*.

26. Wilcockson, Colin. "Some Problems in Translating Chaucer's Poetry." *Anglistik* 21.1 (2010): 49–58. Exemplifies several difficulties in translating Chaucer's verse into modern verse or modern prose, commenting on concerns with "tonal register," *rime riche*, semantic change,

taboo words, pronouns of address, the historical present, rhyming tags, and "ingressive" versus intensifying uses of *gan*.

See also nos. 6, 27, 40, 41, 57, 65, 86, 110, 146, 179, 197, 295, 319.

Manuscripts and Textual Studies

27. Boffey, Julia. "Manuscript and Print: Books, Readers, and Writers." In Corinne Saunders, ed. *A Companion to Medieval Poetry* (*SAC* 34 [2012], no. 157), pp. 538–54. Boffey describes the nature and circulation of Middle English poetic manuscripts and early printed editions, with recurrent comments on manuscript production and traces of readers' responses. Draws examples from a wide variety of manuscripts and editions, including those of Chaucer's works.

28. Da Rold, Orietta. "Manuscript Production Before Chaucer: Some Preliminary Observations." *Essays and Studies* 63 (2010): 43–58. Suggests that analysis of the physical makeup of manuscripts is a way to understand the production and use of Middle English texts. Focuses on the multilingualism in texts, the different functions of texts in a single book, and scribal output. Concludes that electronic resources are useful in reevaluating the manuscript production of the eleventh through the fourteenth centuries.

29. ———. "Textual Copying and Transmission." In Elaine Treharne and Greg Walker, with the assistance of William Green, eds. *The Oxford Handbook of Medieval Literature in English* (*SAC* 34 [2012], no. 165), pp. 33–56. Surveys textual practices in Old and Middle English literary culture, focusing on authorial anxieties about scribes, and comparing what is known and surmised about the texts of Ælfric's *Catholic Homilies* and Chaucer's *CT*.

30. Edwards, A. S. G. "The Ellesmere Manuscript: Controversy, Culture, and *The Canterbury Tales*." *Essays and Studies* 63 (2010): 59–73. Studies the reception of the Ellesmere manuscript of *CT* and its use by scholars, concluding that the manuscript is remarkable not only for the poem it records but also for the part it plays in development of modern ideas about the author.

31. Fletcher, Alan J. "What Did Adam Pynkhurst (Not) Write? A Reply to Dr. Horobin." *RES* 61 (2010): 690–710. Argues that the context and argument of Horobin's refutation of Fletcher's earlier essay are

deficient (see *SAC* 31 [2007], no. 30, and *SAC* 33 [2009], no. 16). The question of the role of paleography and historical linguistics in determining scribal attribution remains moot.

32. Hanna, Ralph. "Middle English Manuscripts and Readers." In Corinne Saunders, ed. *A Companion to Medieval Poetry* (*SAC* 34 [2012], no. 157), pp. 196–215. Hanna discusses late medieval English "textual culture," commenting on the production and disposition of manuscripts, habits of collecting and anthologizing individual works, the vagaries of manuscript survival, reading practices, etc. Cites examples from Chaucer's work often, including comments on a facsimile leaf of *TC* (Cambridge, St. John's College, MS L.1, fol. 6v).

33. Horobin, Simon. "Adam Pinkhurst and the Copying of British Library, MS Additional 35287 of the B Version of *Piers Plowman*." *YLS* 23 (2009): 61–83. Paleographical differences between the hands of the Hengwrt and Ellesmere manuscripts of *CT* and of Additional 35287 are more compelling than are the similarities. Horobin suggests that Pinkhurst "was not Chaucer's personal copyist" and focuses on the probability that there was "more cooperation between independent scriveners than we have traditionally allowed."

34. ———. "Adam Pinkhurst, Geoffrey Chaucer, and the Hengwrt Manuscript of the *Canterbury Tales*." *ChauR* 44 (2010): 351–67. A petition in the hand of Pinkhurst requesting that a permanent deputy be appointed to relieve Chaucer of his duties as controller of the wool custom establishes their connection in 1385. However, codicological evidence suggests that the poet "was no longer available for consultation" on the production of Hengwrt even as it provides further proof of collaborative scribal practice in late medieval London.

35. ———. "Manuscripts and Scribes." In Susanna Fein and David Raybin, eds. *Chaucer: Contemporary Approaches* (*SAC* 34 [2012], no. 125), pp. 67–82. Horobin describes recent advances in understanding "late medieval textual culture"—reading habits, book ownership, institutional affiliations, etc.—focusing on the oeuvres of several Chaucerian scribes, discussions of locale and provenance, relationships between Chaucerian and non-Chaucerian contents, and the utility of electronic databases.

36. ———. "The Professionalization of Writing." In Elaine Treharne and Greg Walker, with the assistance of William Green, eds. *The Oxford Handbook of Medieval Literature in English* (*SAC* 34 [2012], no. 165), pp. 57–67. Horobin surveys "complex and contradictory" evi-

dence for the professionalization of writing in England in the late four-teenth and fifteenth centuries, with comments on Chaucer's scribes (including Adam Pinkhurst), Thomas Hoccleve, and others.

37. Iyeiri, Yoko. "Negation in Different Versions of Chaucer's *Boece*: Syntactic Variants and Editing the Text." *ES* 91 (2010): 826–37. Iyeiri investigates negative constructions in five versions of *Bo*, discussing the relative chronology of the witnesses to the text and, more generally, the editing of Middle English texts.

38. Mosser, Daniel W. *A Digital Catalogue of the Pre-1500 Manuscripts and Incunables of the "Canterbury Tales."* Canterbury Tales Project. Birmingham, [Eng.]: Scholarly Digital Editions, 2010. 1 CD-ROM. Comprehensive description of the eighty-four manuscript witnesses to *CT* and four pre-1500 editions, each including contents, tale order, progress of copying, materials, page size, collation, format, hands, illumination, binding, date, language, provenance, and bibliography. Descriptions include links, internal and external, to supporting data. The volume contains an essay on each of the following scribes: B, D, Hammond, Petworth, *Beryn*, and Hooked-*g* (i.e., scribe of the Devonshire group).

39. ———. "The Paper Stocks of the Beryn Scribe." *JEBS* 13 (2010): 63–93. 25 b&w figs. Mosser assesses the watermarks and paper stock of the ten manuscripts attributed to the "Beryn Scribe," to establish their dates and relative chronology.

40. Nakao, Yoshiyuki, Akiyuki Jimura, and Masatsugu Matsuo. "A Project for a Comprehensive Collation of the Two Manuscripts (Hengwrt and Ellesmere) and the Two Editions (Blake [1980] and Benson [1987]) of the *Canterbury Tales*." *Hiroshima Studies in English Language and Literature* 53 (2009): 1–22. A comprehensive comparison of two Chaucer manuscripts and of two editions of *CT*.

41. Ramsey, Roy Vance, with a foreword by Henry Ansgar Kelly. *A Revised Edition of "The Manly-Rickert Text of the 'Canterbury Tales.'"* Lewiston, N.Y.: Edwin Mellen Press, 2010. xxviii, 691 pp. A corrected reprint of Ramsey's 1994 publication (see *SAC* 18 [1996], no. 31), with Kelly's summary of the importance of the volume and its arguments concerning the relationships of the manuscripts (especially Hg, El, and Dd) and the editing of Chaucer's works.

42. Thaisen, Jacob. "Orthography, Codicology, and Textual Studies: The Cambridge University Library Gg.4.27 *Canterbury Tales*." *Boletín Millares Carlo* 24–25 (2005–6): 379–94. Analysis of MS Gg.4.27 of *CT*, combining a codicological approach with analysis of linguistic aspects

such as the graphemic and graphetic variants. This multifocal approach helps identify the process of copying as well as the scribal profile.

43. ———, and Orietta Da Rold. "The Linguistic Stratification in the Cambridge Dd Copy of Chaucer's *Canterbury Tales*." *NM* 110 (2009): 283–97. The authors review previous scholarship concerning Cambridge MS Dd.4.24 and evaluate the linguistic stratification indicated by orthographic variants. They argue that the manuscript appears to date from the late fourteenth century, it originated in London-Westminster, and it should be labeled a type III text of *CT*.

44. Veck, Sonya. "Quat Is This Fairy Burial Mound? The *Gawain*-Poet's Green Moment in *Sir Gawain and the Green Knight*." In Kathleen A. Bishop, ed. *Standing in the Shadow of the Master? Chaucerian Influences and Interpretations* (*SAC* 34 [2012], no. 114), pp. 113–22. Because of the lack of manuscript history, the works of the *Gawain*-poet must be studied in contexts different from those of Chaucer and his London contemporaries. The seriousness of poetic temperament is pronounced throughout the narrative of the poem.

See also nos. 14, 16, 18, 20, 67, 224, 256, 295, 309.

Sources, Analogues, and Literary Relations

45. Bakalian, Ellen S. "Using Reason to Change Their Worlds: The Tale of Rosiphelee and the Tale of Alceone in John Gower's *Confessio Amantis*." In Kathleen A. Bishop, ed. *Standing in the Shadow of the Master? Chaucerian Influences and Interpretations* (*SAC* 34 [2012], no. 114), pp. 82–112. By discussing the tales of Rosiphelee and Alceone from *Confessio Amantis*, Bakalian exemplifies how Gower (in contrast to Chaucer) urges readers to improve their behavior through right reason and rejection of irresponsible passion.

46. Bowers, John M. "Colonialism, Latinity, and Resistance." In Susanna Fein and David Raybin, eds. *Chaucer: Contemporary Approaches* (*SAC* 34 [2012], no. 125), pp. 116–31. Bowers describes Chaucer's treatment of Latin texts throughout his "literary insurgency against [a] foreign incursion"—a kind of postcolonial resistance that is also consistent with Lollard vernacularization. Reads *MLT* as a "rejection" of Bede's authoritative account of the Christianization of England, part of an overall rewriting of history to assert an "English homeland," free of foreign, Latin domination.

47. Butterfield, Ardis. "France." In Susanna Fein and David Raybin, eds. *Chaucer: Contemporary Approaches* (*SAC* 34 [2012], no. 125), pp. 25–46. Butterfield reviews traditional, generally dismissive attitudes toward "Frenchness" in Chaucer criticism and advocates a new awareness of the linguistic complexity that underlies Chaucer's uses of French models and French diction, particularly the interpenetration of international dialects of French in England and on the Continent. Comments in detail on Chaucer's use of Froissart in the opening of *BD* and explores the multilingual—and multicultural—dimensions of puns in *ShT*.

48. Edwards, Robert R. "Italy." In Susanna Fein and David Raybin, eds. *Chaucer: Contemporary Approaches* (*SAC* 34 [2012], no. 125), pp. 3–24. Reconsiders Chaucer's use of Italian sources and his references to Italy and Italian regions (including Rome), focusing on ways that Italy was a geographical and cultural place of strangeness. Authors such as Chaucer and Gower negotiated tensions between strangeness and familiarity. Edwards comments on Chaucer's journeys to Italy (including surmises about an early trip in 1368) and considers how the "multiform contexts of literary influences" complement traditional "comparative and intertextual studies" and encourage consideration of how Italian influences were "transmitted in more than one language."

49. Grosskopf, John Dennis. "Geoffrey Chaucer (c. 1340–1400)." In Laura Cooner Lambdin and Robert Thomas Lambdin, eds. *Arthurian Writers: A Biographical Encyclopedia*. Westport, Conn.: Greenwood Press, 2008, pp. 120–27. Grosskopf summarizes Chaucer's life and assesses allusions to King Arthur and Arthurian motifs and characters in *CT*, commenting on *SqT*, *Th*, *NPT*, *WBT*, and the lack of Arthurian material in *KnT*. Surveys related critical commentary and suggests that Chaucer satirizes Arthurian tradition because of his disillusionment with chivalric ideals.

50. Gutiérrez Arranz, José María. " 'Ovidio medieval': Los mitos Ovidianos en las obras de Geoffrey Chaucer y John Gower." In Pedro P. Conde Parrado and Isabel Velázquez, eds. *La filología latina: Mil años más*. Actas del IV Congreso de la Sociedad de Estudios Latinos, Medina del Campo, May 22–24, 2003. Madrid: Sociedad de Estudios Latinos, 2009, pp. 1579–1601. Surveys Ovid's influence on medieval literature and assesses Chaucer's use of Ovidian myths.

51. Johnson, Eleanor Bayne. "Sensible Prose and the Sense of Meter: Boethian Prosimetrics in Fourteenth-Century England." *DAI* A70.10 (2010): n.p. Considers the alternation between the pedagogy of argu-

ment (prose sections) and pleasure (metrical sections) in *prosimetrum*, arguing that the form of Boethius's *Consolation* was as essential as its content for writers such as Chaucer, Usk, Hoccleve, and Julian of Norwich.

52. Kamath, Stephanie Gibbs, and Rita Copeland. "Medieval Secular Allegory: French and English." In Rita Copeland and Peter T. Struck, eds. *The Cambridge Companion to Allegory*. Cambridge and New York: Cambridge University Press, 2010, pp. 136–47. Kamath and Copeland survey the legacy of philosophical allegory and secular allegory—largely inspired by the *Roman de la Rose*—in late medieval France and, by extension, England. They focus on Machaut, Froissart, and Deschamps and their relative impact on Chaucer, Gower, and Christine de Pizan. In *BD*, *HF*, and *LGW*, Chaucer consistently uses strategies that embed "new and always productive ambiguities about the capacities and limitations of allegory as a literary form."

53. Lavezzo, Kathy. "England." In Susanna Fein and David Raybin, eds. *Chaucer: Contemporary Approaches* (*SAC* 34 [2012], no. 125), pp. 47–64. Traces recent critical engagement with the "problem" of late medieval English national identity in Chaucer, especially as it reflects anxieties about political upheaval, linguistic variety, cultural "hybridity," and English geographical isolation. Lavezzo draws together comments on the Auchinleck Book, *Sir Orfeo*, Higden's *Polychronicon*, and several of the tales in *CT*, especially *Th*, which, she argues, obliquely engages concerns of nation presented directly in *Guy of Warwick*.

54. Rossiter, William T. *Chaucer and Petrarch*. Chaucer Studies, no. 41. Cambridge: D. S. Brewer, 2010. 235 pp. Assesses Chaucer's relationship with Petrarch, focusing on translation theory, humanism, and Chaucer's uses of the Italian writer as source for *ClT* and the "Canticus Troili" of *TC*. Also assesses Chaucer's references to Petrarch in *ClT* and in *MkT*, as well as his interactions with Italians and Italian culture (including the works of Dante and Boccaccio) in London and on his Italian journeys. Comments on Chaucer's notions of translation and literary production, derived from various classical and medieval sources, particularly in comparison with Petrarch's.

55. Yeager, R. F. "The Poetry of John Gower." In Corinne Saunders, ed. *A Companion to Medieval Poetry* (*SAC* 34 [2012], no. 157), pp. 476–95. Considering the possibility that Gower "was the foremost poet of his age," Yeager contrasts the poetic powers of Gower and Chaucer and

compares Gower's poetic techniques in "In Praise of Peace" and *Confessio Amantis* with Chaucer's techniques in *CT*.

56. Yoo, Inchol. "Language, Knowledge, and Power: The Politics of Chaucer's Translation." *DAI* A71.02 (2010): n.p. Argues that Chaucer's texts engage translation as a political tool. *Rom* indicates a balance of resistance to France and outreach to its cultural products; *Bo* can be read as suspicious of royal power during the late Ricardian period; and *ClT* demonstrates how translation (as in the propagandistic translation of Griselda) can be a means of "consolidating" power.

See also nos. 11, 64, 70, 90, 93, 94, 128, 160, 177, 191, 208, 209, 216, 217, 228, 230, 233, 244, 259, 277, 283, 285, 286, 291, 298, 304, 314.

Chaucer's Influence and Later Allusion

57. Barrington, Candace. " 'Forget what you have learned': The Mistick Krewe's 1914 Mardi Gras Chaucer." *American Literary History* 22 (2010): 806–30. Assessing the conservative ideological underpinnings of the pageantry and commenting on its "inability to control the polysemy of Chaucer's texts," Barrington summarizes the history of Mistick Krewe and describes its 1914 parade and party dedicated to "Tales from Chaucer." She examines details of images of the parade floats and associated materials, some perhaps responsive to the 1912 modernization of Chaucer by John Tatlock and Percy Mackaye. See no. 82.

58. Cooper, Helen. "Poetic Fame." In Brian Cummings and James Simpson, eds. *Cultural Reformations: Medieval and Renaissance in Literary History* (*SAC* 34 [2012], no. 121), pp. 361–78. Cooper argues that, despite his own skepticism about fame, Chaucer was the "model of fame" in fifteenth- and sixteenth-century England. Comments on Chaucer's appeal to humanists, to Protestants, and to Catholics and on Chaucer's role as "father" of English poetry.

59. Driver, Martha. "Conjuring Gower in *Pericles*." In Elisabeth Dutton, with John Hines and R. F. Yeager, eds. *John Gower, Trilingual Poet: Language, Translation, and Tradition* (*SAC* 34 [2012], no. 122), pp. 315–25. Driver contrasts Shakespeare's limited attention to Chaucer with his lionization of Gower in *Pericles*, commenting on representations of Gower in modern stage productions of the play.

60. Edwards, A. S. G. "Lydgate in Scotland." *NMS* 54 (2010): 185–

94. Examines the influence of Lydgate in Scotland in the fifteenth and sixteenth centuries, commenting on the manuscript circulation of his poems. Scottish writers' stylistic indebtedness to Lydgate is complicated by the influence of Chaucer's writings on both Lydgate and the Scots poets. Lydgate's verse has only a small place in the literary culture of medieval Scotland.

61. ———. "Poetic Language in the Fifteenth Century." In Corinne Saunders, ed. *A Companion to Medieval Poetry* (*SAC* 34 [2012], no. 157), pp. 520–37. Edwards cites the "pivotal" nature of the 1532 publication of John Gower's *Confessio Amantis* and Chaucer's *Werkes* and explores "Chaucerian modes and language" in fifteenth-century poetry by Hoccleve, Lydgate, Dunbar, and Henryson—a "subject that has yet to receive exhaustive study." Also comments on alliterative tradition, lyric legacies, and "verse translations from the classics."

62. Gelineau, David. "Following the Leaf Through Part of Dryden's *Fables.*" *SEL* 50 (2010): 557–81. Arguing that the sequence of tales in Dryden's *Fables* is significant and meaningful, Gelineau examines a sequence of tales in which Dryden "uses the Chaucerian tales, with their Catholic love of order, to frame his critique of military brutality and to epitomize everything that [King] William has come to reject." The sequence opens with the pseudo-Chaucerian "Flower and the Leaf" and closes with Dryden's version of *WBT*.

63. Gross, John, ed. *The Oxford Book of Parodies*. New York: Oxford University Press, 2010. xix, 339 pp. Surveys parodies in English, including two brief examples from Alexander Pope that parody Chaucer, plus Stanley J. Sharpless's "The Tale of Miss Hunter Dunn [*Geoffrey Chaucer Rewrites Sir John Betjeman*]" (pp. 6–7).

64. Havely, Nick. "From 'Goodly Maker' to Witness Against the Pope: Conscripting Dante in Henrician England." *Textual Cultures: Texts, Contexts, Interpretations* 5.1 (2010): 76–98. Havely documents Dante's reception in sixteenth-century England, focusing on the perception of Dante in relation to England as "empire" and treatments of Dante as a "proto-Protestant" writer. Observes recurrently how Dante and Chaucer were yoked in Henrician literary tradition.

65. Haydock, Nickolas A. *Situational Poetics in Robert Henryson's "Testament of Cresseid."* Amherst, N.Y.: Cambria Press, 2010. xii, 376 pp. 6 b&w figs. Haydock examines poetic authority in Henryson's *Testament* as it simultaneously affirms and seeks to replace *TC*, in effect treating Chaucer's poem in Chaucerian fashion. One of Henryson's three major

works, *Testament* is part of his effort to emulate Virgil and a Scottish response to English literary and political hegemony. Informed by Boethian thought, its depiction of Cresseid was influenced by Saint Jerome's association of tragedy and prostitution, and the work anticipates R. I. Moore's exploration of persecution, René Girard's theory of victimization, and formulations of female subjectivity by Freud, Lacan, and Žižek. *Testament* deeply influenced Shakespeare's *Troilus and Cressida* and, more generally, the Renaissance reception of Chaucer. Haydock's book includes comments on editions of Chaucer and Henryson, Kinaston's Latin translation of *Testament* and *TC,* and the modern reconstruction of Abbot House at Dumfermline Abbey.

66. Higl, Andrew. "Henryson's Textual and Narrative Prosthesis onto Chaucer's Corpus: Cresseid's Leprosy and Her *Schort Conclusioun.*" In Joshua R. Eyler, ed. *Disability in the Middle Ages: Reconsiderations and Reverberations* (*SAC* 34 [2012], no. 124), pp. 167–81. Treating a book or a "corpus" of literature as a body encourages a prosthetic approach to texts and to narratives. Henryson's addition to Chaucer's *TC* in his *Testament of Cresseid* works as a "double prosthesis" in which Henryson seeks to rehabilitate an incomplete narrative (Criseyde's outcome in *TC* is missing) by adding a disability (Cresseid's leprosy) to it.

67. ———— G. "Joining the 'Canterbury Tales': The Story Telling Game and the Interactive Work." *DAI* A70.07 (2010): n.p. Examining how post-Chaucerian writers and critics even to the present day have added and responded to *CT,* Higl argues that their works are analogous to the pilgrims' fictive contest. The dissertation assesses the evidence of reception in select *CT* manuscripts (particularly reception of the Wife of Bath), reactions to *CkT* up through the twenty-first century, Lydgate's uses of *CT,* and *Beryn* and the *Plowman.*

68. Honeyman, Chelsea. *"The Palice of Honour:* Gavin Douglas' Renovation of Chaucer's *House of Fame."* In Kathleen A. Bishop, ed. *Standing in the Shadow of the Master? Chaucerian Influences and Interpretations* (*SAC* 34 [2012], no. 114), pp. 65–81. Honeyman situates *Palice of Honour* within the development of an autonomous tradition of Scottish poetry, addressing the work as a self-aware response to *HF.*

69. Hordis, Sandra M. "Metatextual Resistance in Henryson's *Testament of Cresseid.*" In Kathleen A. Bishop, ed. *Standing in the Shadow of the Master? Chaucerian Influences and Interpretations* (*SAC* 34 [2012], no. 114), pp. 46–64. Hordis argues that Henryson's poem aggressively explores Chaucer's authorial authority. The text was produced in a time of

emergent efforts by the Scots to construct a national identity, and it questions English literary influence.

70. Kamath, Stephanie A. Viereck Gibbs. "John Lydgate and the Curse of Genius." *ChauR* 45 (2010): 32–58. In both *Reson and Sensuallyte* and *Troy Book*, Lydgate establishes the literary authority of English poetry by placing it in the "allegorical landscape" of the *Roman de la Rose*. He frequently follows Chaucer's "method of *Rose* citation," while Genius's anathema in *Troy Book* follows both Gower's and Chaucer's precedent of inserting "internal critiques" into their works.

71. Kern-Stähler, Annette. "Sweet Poison and Its Antidote: *Troilus and Criseyde* and the *Disce mori*." *Anglistik* 21.2 (2010): 171–79. Assesses the location and implications of one stanza from *TC* (1.400–406) as quoted in the *Disce mori*, a fifteenth-century manual of religious instruction addressed to "Dame Alice." The quotation indicates that some may have read *TC* as a warning against secular love.

72. Laird, Edgar. "Chaucer, Clanvowe, and Cupid." *ChauR* 44 (2010): 344–50. By taking into account the increasing degree of willful irrationality attributed to Cupid in Chaucer's *PF*, *KnT*, and *LGW* and in Clanvowe's *Boke of Cupid*, it becomes possible to view the writers' "god of Love [as] to some extent a collaborative creation."

73. Lerer, Seth. "Literary Histories." In Brian Cummings and James Simpson, eds. *Cultural Reformations: Medieval and Renaissance in Literary History* (*SAC* 34 [2012], no. 121), pp. 75–91. Lerer assesses the mid-sixteenth-century versions of *Truth* and *TC* in *Tottel's Miscellany* (among other texts) as evidence of Renaissance reception of medieval literary history.

74. ———. "Receptions: Medieval, Tudor, Modern." In Susanna Fein and David Raybin, eds. *Chaucer: Contemporary Approaches* (*SAC* 34 [2012], no. 125), pp. 83–95. Lerer comments on the recent study of Chaucer reception and exemplifies the "status of Chaucer's authority" in a letter of Alice Paston to her son, a version of *Truth* in *Tottel's Miscellany*, and an allusion to *KnT* in *The Two Noble Kinsmen*. Each context "modernizes" Chaucer's authority to suit an immediate purpose. Lerer includes a text of the two "Chaucerian" poems in *Tottel's Miscellany*.

75. Luft, Joanna, and Thomas Dilworth. "The Name Daisy: *The Great Gatsby* and Chaucer's Prologue to *The Legend of Good Women*." *F. Scott Fitzgerald Review* 8 (2010): 79–91. Rejects a previous attempt to link Fitzgerald's Daisy Fay and Alceste of *LGWP*, arguing instead that,

via imagery, Gatsby's love for Daisy in the novel resonates with the love of Chaucer's narrator for the daisy in the poem.

76. McCabe, Richard A., ed. *The Oxford Handbook of Edmund Spenser*. Oxford Handbooks of Literature. Oxford and New York: Oxford University Press, 2010. xxiii, 826 pp. 25 b&w illus. Covers a wide range of concerns in Spenser criticism, with forty-two individual essays arranged under five headings: Contexts, Works, Poetic Craft, Sources and Influence, and Reception. The handbook cites Chaucer and his works recurrently, with particular attention to Chaucerianism in Spenser's language and Spenser's emulation of his predecessor. In "Spenser's Language(s): Linguistic Theory and Poetic Diction" (pp. 367–84), Dorothy Stephens discusses Chaucer's linguistic influence. In "Spenser, Chaucer, and Medieval Romance" (pp. 553–72), Andrew King assesses how Spenser successfully bridges the "opposition" between English medieval romance and Chaucer's works. King focuses on *TC*, *SqT*, *MerT*, and the openendedness of *CT*.

77. Riddy, Felicity. "Late Medieval Literature in Scotland: Henryson, Dunbar, and Douglas." In Michael O'Neill, ed. *The Cambridge History of English Poetry* (*SAC* 34 [2012], no. 145), pp. 96–114. Riddy describes the literary accomplishments of Robert Henryson, William Dunbar, and Gavin Douglas as they together "created Older Scots as a literary language." Includes recurrent references to Chaucer and Chaucerianism in the works of these poets.

78. Rossiter, William. "'Disgraces the name and patronage of his master Chaucer': Echoes and Reflections in Lydgate's Courtly Poetry." In Kathleen A. Bishop, ed. *Standing in the Shadow of the Master? Chaucerian Influences and Interpretations* (*SAC* 34 [2012], no. 114), pp. 2–27. In his courtly verse, Lydgate elevates Chaucer's established topoi and discourse to bolster his own unique reformations and enhancements of Chaucerian style.

79. Santini, Monica. *The Impetus of Amateur Scholarship: Discussing and Editing Medieval Romances in Late-Eighteenth and Nineteenth-Century Britain*. Bern: Peter Lang, 2010. 255 pp. Tracing the revival of the romance genre, Santini describes in chronological order the work of amateur scholars, editors, and editorial societies that produced editions and commentary on Middle English romances between 1760 and 1860. Comments on the role of Chaucer's popularity in this revival and on his list of romances in *Th*.

80. Saunders, Corinne. "Epilogue: Afterlives of Medieval English

Poetry." In Corinne Saunders, ed. *A Companion to Medieval Poetry* (*SAC* 34 [2012], no. 157), pp. 647–60. Discusses the "living tradition" of Middle English poetry in later English culture, commenting on continuities, revivals, and imitations, with recurrent references to the status of Chaucer.

81. Spencer, Alice. "Osbern Bokenham Reads the 'Prologue' to the *Legend of Good Women*: The Life of St. Margaret." In Kathleen A. Bishop, ed. *Standing in the Shadow of the Master? Chaucerian Influences and Interpretations* (*SAC* 34 [2012], no. 114), pp. 160–203. Bokenham repeatedly refers to himself as an "auctor" as a way to extricate himself from the classicizing, conventional, and paternal shadow of Chaucer.

82. Sponsler, Claire. "A Response to Barrington." *American Literary History* 22 (2010): 831–37. Sponsler comments on the "appropriation theory" underlying Candace Barrington's analysis of a Chaucer-themed Mardi Gras pageant of 1914, raising broader questions about the ideology, methodology, and disciplinary implications of "American medievalism." See no. 57.

83. Sweet, W. H. E. "The Scottish Lydgateans." In Kathleen A. Bishop, ed. *Standing in the Shadow of the Master? Chaucerian Influences and Interpretations* (*SAC* 34 [2012], no. 114), pp. 28–45. Sweet examines works of William Dunbar and Robert Henryson as well as lesser-known texts to argue that, like Chaucer, Lydgate had significant influence on the development of literature in Scotland.

84. Vankeerbergen, Bernadette C. "Rhetoric, Truth, and Lydgate's 'Troy Book.'" *DAI* A70.10 (2010): n.p. Argues that Lydgate's allusions to *HF* are part of a larger effort to deny the accessibility of truth through language, which the author describes as a "Chaucerian poetics of ambiguity and skepticism."

85. Walker, Greg. "Folly." In Brian Cummings and James Simpson, eds. *Cultural Reformations: Medieval and Renaissance in Literary History* (*SAC* 34 [2012], no. 121), pp. 321–41. Includes comments on Chaucer's combination of jest and earnest as it was admired by Thomas Heywood and Thomas More.

86. Wiggins, Alison. "Frances Wolfreston's *Chaucer*." In Anne Lawrence-Mathers and Phillipa Hardman, eds. *Women and Writing, c.1340–c.1650: The Domestication of Print Culture*. [York]: York Medieval Press, 2010, pp. 77–89. Examines the readers' marks in an annotated copy of the 1550 Thynne edition of Chaucer's *Workes* (Folger STC 5074 Copy 2), identifying its century-long provenance (1578–1677) of female

ownership and commenting on how notes, bracketed passages, and underlinings show that it may have been used to promote female virtuous living.

See also nos. 4, 11, 114, 175, 190, 195, 236, 250, 319, 322.

Style and Versification

87. Foster, Michael. "The Myth of an Oral Style in Chaucer's Poetry." *MES* 18 (2010): 341–60. It is "anachronistic to assume" that Chaucer distinguished between the "reading and hearing of his literary works." His "style is best understood as a versatile adaptation of language to suit both silent and vocalized readings."

88. Johnston, Andrew James. "'Rum, Ram, Ruf': Chaucer and Linguistic Whig History." In Claudia Lange, Ursula Schaefer, and Göran Wolf, eds. *Linguistics, Ideology, and the Discourse of Linguistic Nationalism.* Frankfurt am Main: Peter Lang, 2010, pp. 37–51. Johnston scrutinizes Chaucer's comments on alliterative poetry in *ParsP*, interpreting them as evidence of a power struggle in England's evolving literary field. By presenting aesthetic difference as linguistic difference, Chaucer consciously presents alliterative poetry as provincial and old-fashioned and seeks to banish it from the literary scene.

89. Nakao, Yoshiyuki. "Chaucer's Ambiguity in Voice." In Osamu Imahayashi, Yoshiyuki Nakao, and Michiko Ogura, eds. *Aspects of the History of the English Language and Literature: Selected Papers Read at SHELL 2009, Hiroshima* (*SAC* 34 [2012], no. 131), pp. 143–57. Draws from *TC* examples of how voice contributes to ambiguity, considering how "suprasegmentals" and various phonetic and prosodic features contribute to voice.

90. Nicholson, Peter. "Irony v. Paradox in the *Confessio Amantis.*" In Elisabeth Dutton, with John Hines and R. F. Yeager, eds. *John Gower, Trilingual Poet: Language, Translation, and Tradition* (*SAC* 34 [2012], no. 122), pp. 206–16. Nicholson asserts that critics' "willingness to detect irony at every turn" is appropriate in Chaucer studies, but not in Gower studies, arguing that paradox is a recurrent and sustained mode of thought and expression in Gower's *Confessio.* Surveys examples of irony in Chaucer's works.

91. Nolan, Maura. "Style." In Brian Cummings and James Simpson, eds. *Cultural Reformations: Medieval and Renaissance in Literary History*

(*SAC* 34 [2012], no. 121), pp. 396–419. Nolan exemplifies the continuity of English versification through close metrical analyses of samples from Chaucer (*Truth*), Lydgate, and Wyatt. Each text "displays inherited forms at the very limits of their capacities."

92. Tani, Akinobu. "The Word Pairs in Chaucer's Verse in Comparison with Those in His Prose." In John Ole Askedal, Ian Roberts, and Tomonori Matsushita, eds. *Noam Chomsky and Language Descriptions*. Philadelphia: John Benjamins, 2010, pp. 149–68. Tani examines the word pairs or doublets in Fragment A of *CT* and those in Chaucer's prose texts. The pairs are used for rhyme and for generic and stylistic differentiation among verse texts.

93. Trim, Richard. *Metaphor Networks: The Comparative Evolution of Figurative Language*. New York: Palgrave Macmillan, 2007. xv, 231 pp. 44 b&w figs. Describes the historical evolution of figurative language, especially metaphors, identifying patterns of development. Metaphors depend on images in the past; new metaphors are created through linkage to core concepts or "underlying conceptual metaphors." Trim documents the legacy of English metaphors that pertain to love, focusing on Chaucer's works as a case study for comparing medieval and modern metaphors and for exploring the Latinate roots of English love metaphors.

94. Zarins, Kim. "Rich Words: Gower's *Rime Riche* in Dramatic Action." In Elisabeth Dutton, with John Hines and R. F. Yeager, eds. *John Gower, Trilingual Poet: Language, Translation, and Tradition* (*SAC* 34 [2012], no. 122), pp. 239–53. Zarins assesses Gower's and Chaucer's uses of *rime riche* ("in which rhyme patterns appear identical but diverge in meaning"), focusing on instances in which the device lends seriousness (or mock seriousness) in characters' dialogue. Appends a partial list of instances from *Confessio Amantis* and *CT*.

See also nos. 26, 51, 78, 103, 110, 256, 282, 299, 300, 317.

Language and Word Studies

95. Davidson, Mary Catherine. *Medievalism, Multilingualism, and Chaucer*. The New Middle Ages. New York: Palgrave Macmillan, 2010. 211 pp. In late medieval England, "code-switching" among English, French, and Latin was linked to literacy and social prestige, not to aberrant or nonconformist behavior; code-switching was a means to articu-

late social identity. Chaucer distanced his projects from attitudes of alleged "masculine" anglophone monolingualism. He viewed his Continental counterparts not as linguistic inferiors, but as writers to be emulated; English was linked strongly to orality and, thus, to dialectical *diversite*. Multilingualism constituted power. Code-switching into Latin and French gave Chaucer's language an authority not available in English alone. Davidson refers to *GP*, *NPT*, *PardT*, *WBT*, *SumT*, *FrT*, and *TC*, along with works by Gower and Langland.

96. Fujiwara, Yasuaki. "Expletive 'There' in Chaucer." *Studies in Languages and Cultures* [*Gengo Bunka Ronshu*] (Tsukuba University) 57 (2001): 1–14 (in Japanese). Examines the characteristics of Chaucer's usage of the expletive *there*.

97. Healey, Antonette diPaolo. " 'Heat' in Old English and in Chaucer's Creation of Metaphors of Love." In Osamu Imahayashi, Yoshiyuki Nakao, and Michiko Ogura, eds. *Aspects of the History of the English Language and Literature: Selected Papers Read at SHELL 2009, Hiroshima* (*SAC* 34 [2012], no. 131), pp. 3–18. The semantic field of "heat" includes emotional connotations in Old English, but Chaucer evokes new oxymoronic nuances when he uses it in Troilus's song, *TC* 1.400–420.

98. Horobin, Simon. "Middle English Language and Poetry." In Corinne Saunders, ed. *A Companion to Medieval Poetry* (*SAC* 34 [2012], no. 157), pp. 181–95. Comments on various aspects of dialect, diction, prestige, etc., in Middle English poetry, with many examples drawn from Chaucer's works.

99. ———. "Traditional English? Chaucerian Methods of Word-Formation." *NM* 110 (2009): 141–57. Horobin exemplifies how Chaucer used traditional methods of word formation to expand English vocabulary, creating new words and meaning by adding prefixes and suffixes, shifting grammatical function, and compounding words.

100. Jimura, Akiyuki. "Impersonal Constructions and Narrative Structure in Chaucer." In Osamu Imahayashi, Yoshiyuki Nakao, and Michiko Ogura, eds. *Aspects of the History of the English Language and Literature: Selected Papers Read at SHELL 2009, Hiroshima* (*SAC* 34 [2012], no. 131), pp. 93–100. Jimura cites instances of impersonal constructions in *TC* and *KnT* in which verbs of "occurrence or happening" (e.g., *befal*, *hap*) are used to present important events and to suggest inevitability.

101. Jucker, Andreas H. " 'In curteisie was set ful muchel hir lest': Politeness in Middle English." In Jonathan Culpeper and Dániel Z.

Kádár, eds. *Historical (Im)Politeness*. Linguistic Insights, no. 65. Bern and New York: Peter Lang, 2010, pp. 175–200. Traces developments in the politeness system between Old English and Early Modern English, focusing on Chaucer's uses of the term *curteisie*, his uses of the pronouns of address (*ye* and *thou*) in *MilT*, and cases of "discernment" politeness in fifteenth-century letter writing.

102. Kendrick, Laura. "Stress Tests and Quality Controls: The Medieval *Assay* as a Test of Character." *BAM* 77 (2010): 71–85. Explores testing in Chaucer's narratives, focusing on uses of the word *assay*.

103. Lancashire, Ian. *Forgetful Muses: Reading the Author in the Text*. Buffalo, N.Y.: University of Toronto Press, 2010. xii, 339 pp. b&w figs. and graphs. Explores literary composition as "cybertextuality," employing a fusion of cognitive theory, stylistic analysis, computer applications, and attribution studies. The goal is to uncover the compositional processes of writers by examining their verbal habits and their comments on authorship, including references to the muses and other remarks on literary creation. Lancashire examines the foul papers and stylistic habits of a wide range of poets and writers, medieval to modern. Discussion of Chaucer (pp. 116–33 and elsewhere) focuses on repeated phrases and on how patterns in repetition vary over the course of the composition of *CT*. Also comments on *HF*.

104. Murtaugh, Daniel M. "Chaucer's *As* and the Loose Fit of Meaning." *ChauR* 44 (2010): 461–70. When used in direct discourse, *as* often functions as a "discourse particle" in a manner similar to "the multivalent *like* that seasons the more youthful dialects of Modern English." Such words allow interlocutors to convey meanings while not completely committing to them.

105. Nykiel, Joanna. "Competence, Performance, and Extra Prepositions." *JEngL* 38 (2010): 143–66. Studies the occurrence of "extra" (doubled or mismatched) prepositions in Middle English relative and interrogative clauses and the persistence of the phenomenon in modern English. "Noncategorical" (gradient) constraints such as "preposition stranding" and "preposition pied-piping" derive from Middle English usage, and Nykiel argues for "lexicalist grammars" that are cognizant of these constraints. Cites *CT* and *Astr*.

106. Ohno, Hideshi. "The Impersonal and Personal Constructions in the Language of Chaucer." In Osamu Imahayashi, Yoshiyuki Nakao, and Michiko Ogura, eds. *Aspects of the History of the English Language and Literature: Selected Papers Read at SHELL 2009, Hiroshima (SAC 34*

[2012], no. 131), pp. 115–29. Tabulates features of impersonal usage in Chaucer, Gower, and Langland, using a variety of verbs and commenting on the conditions of usage.

107. Sawada, Mayumi. "Infinitival Complementation in Chaucer: The Case of *Command*." In Osamu Imahayashi, Yoshiyuki Nakao, and Michiko Ogura, eds. *Aspects of the History of the English Language and Literature: Selected Papers Read at SHELL 2009, Hiroshima* (*SAC* 34 [2012], no. 131), pp. 131–42. Tallies uses of *that* clauses and *to* clauses after the verb *command* in Chaucer's works, documenting their frequencies in various syntactic contexts.

108. Taylor, Karla. "Language in Use." In Susanna Fein and David Raybin, eds. *Chaucer: Contemporary Approaches* (*SAC* 34 [2012], no. 125), pp. 99–115. Taylor surveys the development of attention to language and linguistics in Chaucer studies, commenting on the usefulness of developments that enable increased attention to sociolinguistic uses rather than philological forms. She reads *RvT* as a work about the "social nature and uses of linguistic difference" and characterizes the Reeve (as opposed to the Miller) as a man caught in recalcitrant "linguistic localism." She observes in *Mel* the "emergence of a new civic discourse in English," focusing on its use of *deliberacioun* and *arbitracioun*.

109. Trobevšek Drobnak, Frančiška. "Distribution of Infinitive Markers in Chaucer's *Canterbury Tales*." *Linguistica* 50 (2010): 179–95. Tabulates and analyzes various combinations of Middle English infinitive markers—the *-e(n)* ending, the particle *to*, and the particle phrase *for to*—finding that they occur in no identifiable grammatical or semantic patterns of distribution in the first 1,000 lines of *CT*, here taken as representative of post-thirteenth-century English.

110. Windeatt, Barry. "Translating *Troilus and Criseyde*: Modernizing the Courtly Poetic." *Anglistik* 21.1 (2010): 37–48. Comments on translations/modernizations of *TC* from the seventeenth through the twentieth centuries. Considers modern problems with reproducing the nuances of Chaucer's courtly idiolect, particularly "courtly value words" such as *goodly, fresshe, wommanly*, and *manly* and the "tonal modulations" of, for example, *game* and *cheere* or *manere*.

See also nos. 21, 26, 37, 47, 209, 247, 257, 266, 272, 296, 301.

Background and General Criticism

111. Anlezark, Daniel. "Acquiring Wisdom: Teaching Texts and the Lore of the People." In Elaine Treharne and Greg Walker, with the

assistance of William Green, eds. *The Oxford Handbook of Medieval Literature in English* (*SAC* 34 [2012], no. 165), pp. 297–317. Explores differences between traditional "wisdom" literature and popular lore in Old and Middle English, discussing clashes between the "worlds of book learning and popular wisdom" in *CT*, especially in *WBP* and *MilT*.

112. Battles, Dominique. "The Chaucer Seminar: Rethinking the Long Research Paper." *SMART* 17.2 (2010): 101–12. Describes a series of six short assignments (three pages each) designed for a Chaucer class, intended to introduce students to the major methods and tools used by professional scholars. The assignments focus on diction analysis, tale/teller relations, reception history, historical context, source study, and adaptation of conventional scenes. Includes a working bibliography of major research tools.

113. Bayer, Gerd, and Ebbe Klitgård, eds. *Narrative Developments from Chaucer to Defoe.* Routledge Studies in Renaissance Literature and Culture, no. 11. New York: Routledge, 2010 [2011]. vi, 270 pp. Eleven essays by various authors and an introduction by the editors consider various aspects of narrative technique from Chaucer to Daniel Defoe. For four essays that pertain to Chaucer, see nos. 126, 219, 295, and 303.

114. Bishop, Kathleen A., ed. *Standing in the Shadow of the Master? Chaucerian Influences and Interpretations.* Newcastle upon Tyne: Cambridge Scholars, 2010. x, 317 pp. Thirteen essays by various authors, most of them concerned with the influence of Chaucer's work or his reception. See nos. 23, 44, 45, 68, 69, 78, 81, 83, 116, 190, 220, 322, and 323.

115. Blamires, Alcuin. "Individuality." In Elaine Treharne and Greg Walker, with the assistance of William Green, eds. *The Oxford Handbook of Medieval Literature in English* (*SAC* 34 [2012], no. 165), pp. 478–95. Discusses representations of individuality in medieval literature, exploring concepts of "singularity" and the Chaucerian notion of "condicioun." Comments on *BD*, *ClT*, and the descriptions of the pilgrims in *GP*, along with a range of medieval works.

116. Breuer, Heidi, and Jeff Schoneman. "So What? Making Chaucer Matter in the Undergraduate Classroom." In Kathleen A. Bishop, ed. *Standing in the Shadow of the Master? Chaucerian Influences and Interpretations* (*SAC* 34 [2012], no. 114), pp. 287–314. Teachers and students need to address explicitly the relevance of literary discourses to cultural practices—an approach best cultivated in a dialogic environment.

117. Bryant, Brantley L. *Geoffrey Chaucer Hath a Blog: Medieval Stud-*

ies and the New Media. The New Middle Ages. New York: Palgrave Macmillan, 2010. xiii, 197 pp. An eclectic collection of materials related to new-media play that focuses on Chaucer, including the following: a faux poem by "John Gower"; an introduction, by Bonnie Wheeler, to play and parody among medievalists at the conferences of the Medieval Institute; Bryant's brief history of his blog, "Geoffrey Chaucer Hath a Blog"; Jeffrey Jerome Cohen's description of the playful presence of medieval studies in the new media; and a "comic diary" by Robert W. Hanning of his own parodies, limericks, snipes, etc., written in playful response to academic seriousness. The bulk of the volume is an anthology of the "key 2006–2009 postings" from the Chaucer blog, slightly revised, plus a new expansion of an account of Chaucer's visit (with Richard II) to the United States.

118. Burger, Glenn. "Gender and Sexuality." In Susanna Fein and David Raybin, eds. *Chaucer: Contemporary Approaches* (*SAC* 34 [2012], no. 125), pp. 179–98. Burger characterizes second-wave feminism as a precursor of gay and lesbian studies, arguing that queer theory desires and explores the past in particularized rather than universalized ways, in part to "trouble Foucault's epistemic break between the medieval and the modern." Burger considers the current state(s) of feminist, queer, and transgender studies and imagines how "medievalist gender critics" can "remake the human" by the undoing of gender. Examples from Chaucer studies appear throughout.

119. Classen, Albrecht, and Marilyn Sandidge, eds. *Friendship in the Middle Ages and Early Modern Age: Explorations of a Fundamental Ethical Discourse*. New York: Walter de Gruyter, 2010. ix, 802 pp. Nineteen essays by various authors, an introduction by the editors, and a comprehensive index. Topics range from friendship in Augustine's *Confessions* to the Whitehall conference of 1655, with two essays that pertain to Chaucer; see nos. 196 and 237.

120. Corrie, Marilyn, ed. *A Concise Companion to Middle English Literature*. Blackwell Concise Companions to Literature and Culture. Malden, Mass.: Wiley-Blackwell, 2009. xii, 268 pp. Eleven essays by various authors, arranged under four headings: Key Contexts, The Production of Middle English Literature, Writing in Middle English/Writing in England, and Middle English Literature in the Post-Medieval World. The index lists more entries for Chaucer and his works than for any other topic.

121. Cummings, Brian, and James Simpson, eds. *Cultural Reforma-*

tions: Medieval and Renaissance in Literary History. Oxford Twenty-First Century Approaches to Literature. New York: Oxford University Press, 2010. xii, 689 pp. 5 b&w illus. Thirty-two essays by various individuals and the introduction by the editors exemplify the porous nature of the traditional boundary between medieval and Renaissance in literary history and demonstrate the interpenetration of literature and history. Topics range widely; references to Chaucer and his works occur frequently. Suggestions for further reading accompany each essay, and the volume includes an index. For nine essays that pertain to Chaucer, see nos. 58, 73, 85, 91, 162, 246, 252, 261, and 301.

122. Dutton, Elisabeth, with John Hines and R. F. Yeager, eds. *John Gower, Trilingual Poet: Language, Translation, and Tradition*. Westfield Medieval Studies, no. 3. Cambridge: D. S. Brewer, 2010. xii, 358 pp. Twenty-five essays by various authors and an introduction by Dutton, with a cumulative bibliography and index. The volume was inspired by the first international congress of the John Gower Society (2008). The essays range widely in Gower studies—manuscript study, source study, prosody, etc.—and Chaucer is cited recurrently. For five essays that pertain to Chaucer, see nos. 59, 90, 94, 217, and 286.

123. Epstein, Robert, and William Robins, eds. *Sacred and Profane in Chaucer and Late Medieval Literature: Essays in Honour of John V. Fleming*. Buffalo, N.Y.: University of Toronto Press, 2010. vi, 238 pp. Nine essays by various authors, an introduction by the editors, a commentary on Fleming's critical legacy by Steven Justice, and a bibliography of Fleming's publications. For five essays that pertain to Chaucer, see nos. 226, 243, 288, 306, and 315.

124. Eyler, Joshua R., ed. *Disability in the Middle Ages: Reconsiderations and Reverberations*. Burlington, Vt.: Ashgate, 2010. x, 235 pp. Fourteen essays by various authors on topics ranging from Old English and Icelandic sagas to early modern Spanish literature and Shakespeare's *Richard III*. The volume includes an introduction by the editor, an index, and a cumulative bibliography. For three essays that pertain to Chaucer, see nos. 66, 222, and 235.

125. Fein, Susanna, and David Raybin, eds. *Chaucer: Contemporary Approaches*. University Park: Pennsylvania State University Press, 2010. xv, 259 pp. Eleven essays by various authors designed for "those who want to explore how the works of Geoffrey Chaucer are now being approached." Arranged under four headings: Chaucer's Places, Chaucer's Audiences, Chaucer and Language, and Reenvisioning Chaucer. Sugges-

tions for further reading accompany each essay, and the volume includes a bibliography and an index. See nos. 35, 46–48, 53, 74, 108, 118, 133, 137, and 291.

126. Fludernik, Monika. "The Representation of Mind from Chaucer to Aphra Behn." In Gerd Bayer and Ebbe Klitgård, eds. *Narrative Developments from Chaucer to Defoe* (*SAC* 34 [2012], no. 113), pp. 40–59. Compares the ways narratives deal with interiority before and after the year 1500, noting an increase in the use of metaphorical language and allegories of the characters' emotions.

127. Friedman, John Block. *Brueghel's Heavy Dancers: Transgressive Clothing, Class, and Culture in the Late Middle Ages.* Medieval Studies. Syracuse, N.Y.: Syracuse University Press, 2010. xxv, 361 pp. 21 b&w illus. Studies the iconography of nonaristocratic, nonclerical dress in late medieval literature and art. Considers aspects of dress as they distinguished peasants and gentry in the Old French pastourelle and its descendant, the bergerie, and follows this legacy into more sharply satiric German mock pastourelles and social satires, influenced by fabliaux. Examines "transgressive" details of dress and physiognomy in Chaucer's *GP* description of the Miller, Alisoun of *MilT*, Symkyn of *RvT,* and the Squire's Yeoman of *GP*, focusing on indications of class, social aspiration, and urban/rural opposition.

128. Fumo, Jamie C. *The Legacy of Apollo: Antiquity, Authority, and Chaucerian Poetics.* Buffalo, N.Y., and Toronto: University of Toronto Press, 2010. xvi, 351 pp. Surveys the figure of Apollo in classical and medieval traditions, focusing on the figure in Chaucer's works as an embodiment of the poet's understandings of poetic authority. Chaucer "mythologized a new idea of authorship in English," escaping scholastic formulations of poetic authority and exploring the role of the poet as "*vates,* inspired vessel of truth," a "proto-humanist" outlook anchored in classical tradition. Chaucer's Apollo is more Ovidian than Virgilian, although Chaucer explores the latter version in *TC*. In Fragment 5 of *CT* (*SqT* and *FranT*), Apollo is a figure of poetic inspiration, conceived in a way that prompted Chaucer's descendants to regard him as such. In *ManT*, the depiction of Apollo implies that readers are responsible for shaping poetic authority.

129. Hanning, Robert W. *Serious Play: Desire and Authority in the Poetry of Ovid, Chaucer, and Ariosto.* New York: Columbia University Press, 2010. xviii, 286 pp. Considers "social and political crises that activate the comic poetry" of Ovid, Chaucer, and Ariosto. In particular,

chapter 2, "Chaucer: Dealing with the Authorities, Or, Twisting the Nose That Feeds You," addresses Chaucer's humor as it relates to desire and authority in *BD, TC, HF, PF, LGW*, and *CT*. Hanning emphasizes how "crises of desire and authority" in each work provide "ample opportunities for comic treatment of cultural and political issues of obvious importance to the poet" (125).

130. Heinzelman, Susan Sage. *Riding the Black Ram: Law, Literature, and Gender*. The Cultural Lives of Law. Stanford, Calif.: Stanford Law Books, 2010. xxv, 168 pp. Heinzelman examines the interdependencies of literary and legal discourses and the representations of women in them, seeking to define the development of the novel as a stage in the separation of the two discourses. She reads various French and English novels in this light and presents *MLT* and *WBT* as a pairing that anticipates the dynamic of legally affirmed normative behavior and reaction to it. The Man of Law seeks to replace unruly fantasy through law and hagiography, but the Wife responds by reinvesting romance with magic that is equated with the female body. The juxtaposition of the two *Tales* affirms that contrary narratives interact in ways that evoke ethical responses.

131. Imahayashi, Osamu, Yoshiyuki Nakao, and Michiko Ogura, eds. *Aspects of the History of the English Language and Literature: Selected Papers Read at SHELL 2009, Hiroshima*. Studies in Medieval English Language and Literature, no. 25. New York: Peter Lang, 2010. ix, 407 pp. Twenty-eight essays by various authors. For six essays that pertain to Chaucer, see nos. 89, 97, 100, 106, 107, and 256.

132. Jeffrey, David Lyle. "Courtly Love and Christian Marriage: Chrétien de Troyes, Chaucer, and Henry VIII." *C&L* 59 (2010): 515–30. Chrétien's *Erec and Enide* does not celebrate courtly love but provides a "model for rightly ordered desire." Chaucer highlights the "social and spiritual value" of marriage in *CT, PF, TC,* and various lyrics. Henry VIII's own theatrics, however, "strip the . . . literary conventions of their irony."

133. Justice, Steven. "Literary History." In Susanna Fein and David Raybin, eds. *Chaucer: Contemporary Approaches* (*SAC* 34 [2012], no. 125), pp. 199–214. Justice explores "historicism's liabilities" and their consequences for the prospects of an aesthetic "turn." Traces the interactions between historicism and "theory" in debunking formalism and comments on this process in medieval studies, particularly Chaucer studies. Calls for a "fully *literary* history," one attentive to "what is made and

received as 'the literary' in a given historical moment," anchored in a substantial "conception of poetic form," and capable of adjudicating between a specifically literary history and those histories that subordinate literature to politics, economics, or institutional change.

134. Katz, Stephen Andrew. "Intention and the Idea of the Literary in Chaucer." *DAI* A71.05 (2010): n.p. Examines Chaucer's declarations of *entente* and their uses in his works, concluding that Chaucer's deployment of the term compels the reader to interpret the texts as "intentional acts"—rather than an arrangement of "exemplary narratives"—thereby expanding the range of interpretation beyond mere "moral use."

135. Keil, Aphrodite M. "Incarnation Theology and Its Others: Female Embodiment in Fourteenth and Fifteenth Century English Literature." *DAI* A70.12 (2010): n.p. Discusses dream visions (including *HF* and *Pearl*) and dramas of the period to explore ideas of a "feminized" Christ in the medieval period, ultimately contending that any such feminization is problematic and "no simple affirmation of female bodies or female authority takes place."

136. Kelly, Henry Ansgar. *Law and Religion in Chaucer's England.* Collected Studies. Burlington, Vt.: Ashgate, 2010. xiv, 400 pp. Reprints twelve of Kelly's studies that pertain to Chaucer and his historical contexts, with an introduction, some addenda and corrigenda, and a cumulative index. The essays are reproduced in their original typefaces and with their original pagination. See nos. 218, 263, and 268.

137. Kendrick, Laura. "Humor in Perspective." In Susanna Fein and David Raybin, eds. *Chaucer: Contemporary Approaches* (*SAC* 34 [2012], no. 125), pp. 135–58. Commenting on the paucity of studies that directly address humor in Chaucer, Kendrick explores modern theories and medieval attitudes toward humor, especially as related to notions of tolerance. She examines instances in Chaucer, Deschamps, and medieval visual art where humor depends on "seeing and reading close-up," including examples from *CT*, especially *GP*.

138. Kerby-Fulton, Kathryn. "Authority, Constraint, and the Writing of the Medieval Self." In Elaine Treharne and Greg Walker, with the assistance of William Green, eds. *The Oxford Handbook of Medieval Literature in English* (*SAC* 34 [2012], no. 165), pp. 413–33. Kerby-Fulton looks at autobiography and "writing the self" in medieval literature, with particular focus on how and to what extent political con-

straint prompts expression of self. Draws examples from Chaucer, Langland, Christine de Pizan, Thomas Usk, and others.

139. Lavezzo, Kathy. "Complex Identities: Selves and Others." In Elaine Treharne and Greg Walker, with the assistance of William Green, eds. *The Oxford Handbook of Medieval Literature in English (SAC 34* [2012], no. 165), pp. 434–56. Lavezzo considers the "complexities of medieval identity formation by surveying the depiction of Jews and Saracens in English" between Bede and the late fifteenth century. Includes comments on *MLT* and its presentation of Britain as a medieval "global backwater," analogous to Syria in its relation to Rome.

140. Long, Lynne. "Medieval Literature Through the Lens of Translation Theory: Bridging the Interpretive Gap." *Translation Studies* 3.1 (2010): 61–77. Investigates whether modern translation theory can be usefully applied to the Middle Ages, when the *skopos* or "wider development of the literary culture" differed so widely from today's cultures. Long uses "*skopos*" theory and "polysystems" theory to explore reconstructing the purposes and audiences of "three of Chaucer's translation projects": *Bo, TC,* and *Astr.*

141. Luebering, J. E. *The 100 Most Influential Writers of All Time.* New York: Britannica Educational Publishing in association with Rosen Educational Services, 2010. 351 pp. Includes an introduction (pp. 58–61) to Chaucer and his works.

142. Matthews, David. "Chaucer's American Accent." *American Literary History* 22 (2010): 758–72. Matthews considers ways of distinguishing between "medieval studies" and "medievalism" (relating the latter to "antimodernism") and assesses how late nineteenth-century American study of Chaucer "problematizes" the terms. The article contrasts American and British involvement in the Chaucer Society and comments on how the recent "turn to affect" in Chaucer studies parallels earlier treatments of the poet. See no. 143.

143. Michelson, Bruce. "A Response to David Matthews." *American Literary History* 22 (2010): 773–80. Explores the intensity of America's involvement in the Chaucer Society discussed by Matthews (see no. 142), focusing on the rise of British national tourism and the Gothic Revival, as well as on American romantic notions of Chaucerian pastoralism and democracy.

144. Morgan, Gerald. *The Shaping of English Poetry: Essays on "Sir Gawain and the Green Knight," Langland, Chaucer, and Spenser.* New York: Peter Lang, 2010. xiii, 299 pp. Twelve essays by Morgan, reprinted to

clarify trends in the development of English literature. Four essays pertain to Chaucer: see *SAC* 1 (1978), no. 157; *SAC* 2 (1979), nos. 106 and 170; and *SAC* 5 (1982), no. 131.

145. O'Neill, Michael, ed. *The Cambridge History of English Poetry.* New York: Cambridge University Press, 2010. xvi; 1,100 pp. Fifty-three individual essays by various authors on topics ranging from Old English poetry to various movements, individual poets, and postmodern concerns. Arranged chronologically, with a cumulative bibliography and an index. For three essays that pertain to Chaucer, see nos. 77, 159, and 166. See also no. 382.

146. Oswald, Dana. " 'The lyf so short, the crafts so long to lerne': Reading Chaucer in Translation in the British Literature Survey Class." *SMART* 17.1 (2010): 95–118. Advocates the use of translation and translation exercises in teaching Chaucer's works in surveys of British literature. Criticizes major anthologies for promoting original-language study only and offers a syllabus, description of in-class activities, and discussion questions that pertain to *GP, WBP, MerT,* and *FranT.*

147. Patterson, Lee. *Acts of Recognition: Essays on Medieval Culture.* Notre Dame: University of Notre Dame Press, 2010. xii, 356 pp. Ten essays by Patterson on historical criticism, teaching medieval studies, Clanvowe, Hoccleve, Lydgate, Chaucer, Saint Francis, etc.; nine of the ten essays are reprinted. The one essay published here for the first time pertains to Chaucer; see no. 314.

148. Pearman, Tory Vandeventer. "Twinned Deviance: Women and Disability in Medieval Literature." *DAI* A70.07 (2010): n.p. Arguing that medieval thought links disability with the feminine, Pearman examines "medieval female disability" in works of Chaucer, Marie de France, Henryson, and Margery Kempe, among others.

149. ———. *Women and Disability in Medieval Literature.* The New Middle Ages. New York: Palgrave Macmillan, 2010. xiv, 206 pp. Theorizes how medieval medical and social discourses link the "categories of 'woman' and 'disabled,' " a linking anchored in the notion that women are defective men. Compares the notion of reproduction in *MerT* and *Dame Sirith*; punishment of women in *WBP* and Geoffrey de la Tour-Landry's *Book of the Knight*; enchantment and punishment in *Bisclavret, Sir Launfal,* and Henryson's *Testament of Cresseid*; and motherhood and disability in the *Book of Margery Kempe.*

150. Pearsall, Derek. "Postscript/Postlude/Afterword." In Jane Tolmie and M. J. Toswell, eds. *Laments for the Lost in Medieval Literature*

496

(*SAC* 34 [2012], no. 164), pp. 299–306. Summary commentary on the collection of essays, with remarks on maternal grief in *PrT*, *ClT*, *MLT*, and other works, especially Lydgate's *A Lamentacioun of Our Lady Maria*.

151. Perkins, Nicholas. "Writing, Authority, and Bureaucracy." In Elaine Treharne and Greg Walker, with the assistance of William Green, eds. *The Oxford Handbook of Medieval Literature in English* (*SAC* 34 [2012], no. 165), pp. 68–89. Explores how the affiliation of bureaucracy and writing developed in England, plus the impact of the association on notions of authority. Mentions several petitions and warrants pertaining to Chaucer and comments on *Purse* and *Pity* as petitions.

152. Phillips, Helen. "The Church in Chaucer." In Dee Dyas, ed. *The English Parish Church Through the Centuries: Daily Life and Spirituality, Art and Architecture, Literature and Music*. York: University of York; Nottingham: St. John's College, 2010, n.p. Interactive DVD. Describes key clerical figures in *CT* and exemplifies details of worship, parish social life, and the Church in daily life. Includes color illustrations and hypertext links to key terms and concepts.

153. ———. "Medieval Classical Romances: The Perils of Inheritance." In Rosalind Field, Phillipa Hardman, and Michelle Sweeney, eds. *Christianity and Romance in Medieval England*. Christianity and Culture: Issues in Teaching and Research. Cambridge: D. S. Brewer, 2010, pp. 3–25. Surveys the treatment of classical material in medieval romances (arranged by topic), exploring where and how the romance authors engage the status and validity of their pre-Christian material. Comments on *KnT* and *TC*.

154. Rentz, Ellen K. "Imagining the Parish: Parochial Space and Spiritual Community in Late Medieval England." *DAI* A71.02 (2010): n.p. Considers writers such as Chaucer, Robert Mannyng, John Mirk, and Langland in examining the medieval understanding of the parish and its associated individuals and phenomena. As a traditional center of religious practice, the parish was challenged by lay devotion, friars, hermits, and more.

155. Royer-Hemet, Catherine, ed. *Canterbury: A Medieval City*. Newcastle upon Tyne: Cambridge Scholars, 2010. ix, 230 pp. A collection of essays by various authors on the cultural history of Canterbury. Includes three essays that pertain to Chaucer; see nos. 172, 180, and 186.

156. Sauer, Michelle M., with an introduction by Harold Bloom. *Bloom's How to Write About Geoffrey Chaucer*. New York: Bloom's Literary Criticism, 2010. viii, 232 pp. Pedagogical introduction to Chaucer's

works, presented as advice for writing college-level essays (written by Sauer with Laurie A. Sterling, with a sample essay on male physiognomy in *GP* by Timothy Richards) and writing about Chaucer more particularly. Individual chapters summarize selected Chaucerian narratives and lyrics and identify themes, characters, historical contexts, genres, imagery, etc., accompanied by suggested topics for writing. The volume provides a bibliography for each chapter and includes a cumulative index. Works considered are *GP, KnT, MilT, RvT, WBPT, ClT, FranT, PardPT, PrT, NPT, TC*, and five complaints (*Pity, Lady, Mars, Venus*, and *Purse*).

157. Saunders, Corinne, ed. *A Companion to Medieval Poetry*. Blackwell Companions to Literature and Culture, no. 67. Malden, Mass.: Wiley-Blackwell, 2010. xvii, 683 pp. 6 b&w figs. Thirty-four essays by various authors, with an introduction and an epilogue by the editor, all on topics pertaining to English poetry from its origins through the fifteenth century. Each essay includes suggestions for further reading, and the volume has a cumulative index. References to Chaucer occur in many essays. Nine essays discuss Chaucer at length; see nos. 27, 32, 55, 61, 80, 98, 181, 289, and 299.

158. ———. *Magic and the Supernatural in Medieval English Romance*. Studies in Medieval Romance, no. 13. Cambridge: D. S. Brewer, 2010. viii, 304 pp. Saunders studies medieval understandings of "magic, enchantment, the demonic, marvel and miracle." Surveys these topics in biblical and classical precedents, focuses on a range of romances in Middle English, and provides an epilogue that looks toward the English Renaissance. Includes recurrent references to Chaucer, his romances, and his commentaries on magic and magicians, with sustained attention to *SqT* and *FranT*, which "make clear distinctions" between natural magic and "less acceptable practices."

159. Scase, Wendy. "Late Fourteenth-Century Poetry (Chaucer, Gower, Langland and Their Legacy)." In Michael O'Neill, ed. *The Cambridge History of English Poetry* (*SAC* 34 [2012], no. 145), pp. 43–62. Scase summarizes the Latin, French, and English traditions of poetry in late medieval England, describing how major poets of the era engaged these traditions and created a new legacy. Chaucer engaged tradition by posing as an "inadequate" poet, by enlivening his work colloquially, and by disparaging native English verse forms.

160. Tambling, Jeremy. *Allegory*. New Critical Idiom. London and New York: Routledge, 2010. viii, 192 pp. Examines allegory as a mode

in English and American literature (and art), surveying its roots in classical and medieval traditions, exploring its relations with other literary devices and forms (irony, personification, apostrophe, prosopopoeia, etc.), and examining several attempts to theorize the mode (Maureen Quilligan, Walter Benjamin, Paul de Man, etc.). Considers literary uses of allegory from Saint Paul to postmodernists, including discussion (pp. 52–55) of Chaucer's Pardoner as an adaptation of Jean de Meun's personification False Seeming.

161. Taylor, William Joseph. " 'That Country Beyond the Humber': The English North, Regionalism, and the Negotiation of Nation in Medieval English Literature." *DAI* A71.06 (2010): n.p. Taylor examines the role of the North as an "uncanny figure" in the development of English nationalism, as evidenced in the works of Bede, William of Malmesbury, the Robin Hood ballads, and *CT*.

162. Teskey, Gordon. "Literature." In Brian Cummings and James Simpson, eds. *Cultural Reformations: Medieval and Renaissance in Literary History* (*SAC* 34 [2012], no. 121), pp. 379–95. Teskey explores the development of "story-telling" into "literature" in English tradition, including comments on Chaucer's place in this development.

163. Tinkle, Theresa. *Gender and Power in Medieval Exegesis*. The New Middle Ages. New York: Palgrave Macmillan, 2010. [xvi], 196 pp. Despite its antifeminist core, medieval exegesis is not "universally misogynistic or patriarchal." Focusing on three historical moments—the age of Augustine, the twelfth century, and the age of Chaucer, including his fifteenth-century reception—Tinkle identifies instances from Jerome and Augustine forward in which "exegetes reject patriarchal power structures and invent their own subversive authority as feminine." *Gender and Power* incorporates expanded versions of two essays on Chaucer printed elsewhere: "Contested Authority: Jerome and the Wife of Bath on 1 Timothy 2" (*SAC* 34 [2012], no. 223) and "The Wife of Bath's Marginal Authority" (*SAC* 34 [2012], no. 224).

164. Tolmie, Jane, and M. J. Toswell, eds. *Laments for the Lost in Medieval Literature*. Medieval Texts and Cultures of Northern Europe, no. 19. Turnhout, Belgium: Brepols, 2010. xii, 306 pp. Fourteen essays by various authors, on topics ranging from the Psalms to *Beowulf* to Christine de Pizan, with recurrent attention to mothers and children and Marian lamentation. For three essays that pertain to Chaucer, see nos. 150, 208, and 229.

165. Treharne, Elaine, and Greg Walker, with the assistance of Wil-

liam Green, eds. *The Oxford Handbook of Medieval Literature in English*. New York: Oxford University Press, 2010. xiii, 774 pp. 7 b&w figs. Thirty-five essays by various authors, with a prologue by Treharne, an epilogue by Walker, and a cumulative index. The individual essays, each accompanied by a bibliography, are arranged thematically under seven thematic headings: Literary Production; Literary Consumption; Literature, Clerical and Lay; Literary Realities; Complex Identities; Literary Place, Space, and Time; and Literary Journeys. Recurrent references to Chaucer and occasional references to individual works. For seven essays that pertain to Chaucer, see nos. 29, 36, 111, 115, 138, 139, and 151.

166. Varnam, Laura. "Chaucer: *Troilus and Criseyde* and *The Canterbury Tales*." In Michael O'Neill, ed. *The Cambridge History of English Poetry* (*SAC* 34 [2012], no. 145), pp. 81–95. Varnam describes Chaucer's "legacy to English poetry as one of linguistic curiosity and a refusal of generic categorization." With *TC*, Chaucer "heralded a new era of narrative poetry" rich with philosophy and characterization; in *CT*, he "created a diversity of genre, character and language" not matched until Shakespeare.

167. Watson, Nicholas. "The Phantasmal Past: Time, History, and the Recombinative Imagination." *SAC* 32 (2010): 1–37. Proposes that historical thinking can be productively conceived of as recombinative fantasy rather than as empirical recollection. Uses several medieval examples of imaginative fantasy as exemplary models: Chaucer's House of Rumour in *HF*, Dante's Geryon in *Inferno* 16, John of Morigny's experimental envisioning in *Liber florum*, and Julian of Norwich's "hermeneutics of visionary suspicion" in *Revelation*. In these examples—and arguably in historical research—the phantasm is a "vehicle of the real"; it is potentially useful for helping to bridge the medieval/modern divide.

168. Williams, Jon Kenneth. "Languages of Kingship in Ricardian Britain." *DAI* A71.02 (2010): n.p. Through a close reading of various Ricardian texts, Williams examines the building of what appears to be a contemporary anti-Ricardian rhetoric. *Astr* implies loyalty to English monarchy, rather than personal loyalty to Richard; *KnT* and *Mel* offer a restrictive view of kingship; and *MkT* implies comparison between Richard II and the "heirless" Edward the Confessor.

169. Wolfe, Alexander Carlos. "In the Belly of the Tartar Beast: The Mongols and the Medieval English Culinary Imagination." *DAI* A70.12 (2010): n.p. Explores western medieval accounts of the Mongols in the context of historic antipathy between "agricultural" societies and their

"pastoral"/nomadic rivals. Includes comparative assessments of hunting practices (as seen in *BD*, *Gawain*, and *Parlement of the Thre Ages*), warfare, and cuisine.

The Canterbury Tales—General

170. Alias, Simona. "Converging of Traditions and Usability of the Short Story: Orality and Frame in the *Canterbury Tales*." *Studies in the History of the English Language, 2006–2009*. Osaka: Osaka Books, 2010, pp. 107–19. Also *Bulletin of the Japanese Association of the History of the English Language* n.v. (2009): 31–43. Examines the influence of the frame narrative tradition on *CT*, particularly on Chaucer's use of the *narratio brevis* genre.

171. Bowen, Kerri Ann. "Narrative Image: The Poetics of Patience from Dante to Shakespeare." *DAI* A71.06 (2010): n.p. Discusses *CT* as part of a larger consideration of patience—especially female patience— and notes that Chaucer often links patience with epistemological limits.

172. Cigman, Gloria. "Just Why Did They Go to Canterbury?" In Catherine Royer-Hemet, ed. *Canterbury: A Medieval City* (*SAC* 34 [2012], no. 155), pp. 127–36. Cigman examines the role and meaning of Canterbury and its cathedral in *CT*.

173. Francis, Christina. "'Maken Melodye': The Quality of Song in Chaucer's *Canterbury Tales*." In Georgiana Donavin and Anita Obermeier, eds. *Romance and Rhetoric: Essays in Honour of Dhira B. Mahoney*. Disputatio, no. 19. Turnhout, Belgium: Brepols, 2010, pp. 149–70. Contrasts human song and birdsong in *GP*, *NPT*, *MilT*, *PrT*, and *PF*: humans employ reason to understand and appreciate music, while birds sing purely for pleasure. Generally, the human voice is "an indicator of how Chaucer's characters misuse their voices to celebrate or pursue pleasure," and most of Chaucer's pilgrims are "inappropriate music makers."

174. Gómez Lara, Manuel José. "*Los Cuentos de Canterbury*: Risa, sexo, y sátira social en la edad media." *Cuadernos del CEMYR (Centro de Medievales y Renacentistas)* 16 (2008): 117–44. Studies the relationship between sex and laughter in *CT* both as a way of conveying a didactic purpose and as a manner of representing society and social relations— mostly across gender lines.

175. Ishino, Harumi. *Chōsā no shizen: Shigatsu no ame ga fureba* [*Chaucer's Nature*]. Kyoto: Shoraisha, 2009 (in Japanese). 234 pp. Considers

Chaucer's idea of nature in *CT*, assessing its relationship to Renaissance humanism, to scholarship and various arts, and to conceptions of the celestial world and natural science. Also gauges the influence of Chaucer's view of nature on Shakespeare and Spenser.

176. Jimura, Akiyuki. "Chaucer's Alcoholic Drink and *The Canterbury Tales*: With Particular Reference to Wine and Ale." In Noburo Harano, Hidemi Mizuda, Hiromichi Yamashiro, Akiyuki Jimura, and Yoshiyuki Nakao, eds. *Chuusei Yoroppa no shukuen* [Feasts in Medieval Europe]. Hiroshima: Keisuisha, 2010, pp. 145–73 (in Japanese). Study of wine and ale and *CT*.

177. Kane, George. "Poets and the Poetics of Sin [1989]." In Daniel Donoghue, James Simpson, and Nicholas Watson, eds. *The Morton W. Bloomfield Lectures, 1989–2005*. Kalamazoo: Medieval Institute Publications, Western Michigan University, 2010, pp. 1–19. The first of the Bloomfield lectures. Traces the impact of "hamartiology" (the study of sin and crisis) in Langland's *Piers Plowman* and Chaucer's *CT*, especially in *GP* and the fabliaux. Estates satire, penitential handbooks, and other examples of "awareness of sin" inform the poetics of both poets, evident in particular details and attitudes in their works.

178. Mattord, Carola Louise. "Lay Writers and the Politics of Theology in Medieval England from the Twelfth to Fifteenth Centuries." *DAI* A71.05 (2010): n.p. Suggests that Chaucer's *CT*, the *Lais* of Marie de France, and the *Book of Margery Kempe* include "theopolitical" ideas and thus are informed by the Church's influence on these ideas and on the notion of identity.

179. Meyer-Lee, Robert J. "Fragments IV and V of the *Canterbury Tales* Do Not Exist." *ChauR* 45 (2010): 1–31. The editorial break between *MerE* and *SqH* cannot be defended on the basis of manuscript evidence. The break has obscured an element of the "artistic design" of *CT*: a sequence of four tales whose tellers represent occupations held either by Chaucer or by his father. The thirty lines of *MerE* and *SqH* should be relabeled as *MerSqL*.

180. Sancery, Arlette. "Canterbury: The Cathedral Chaucer's Pilgrims Never Reached—or Did They?" In Catherine Royer-Hemet, ed. *Canterbury: A Medieval City* (*SAC* 34 [2012], no. 155), pp. 119–26. Regards the process of reading as the essential pilgrimage of *CT*, which obviates the need for an arrival at Canterbury. See also *SAC* 33 (2011), no. 104.

181. Saunders, Corinne. "Chaucer's *The Canterbury* Tales." In Co-

rinne Saunders, ed. *A Companion to Medieval Poetry* (*SAC* 34 [2012], no. 157), pp. 452–75. Introduces *CT* as the "epitome" of Chaucer's "literary experimentation," commenting on his social range, the unfinished nature of the work, and, especially, its generic variety—"romance, fabliau, beast-fable, saint's life, miracle story, sermon, [and] moral treatise." Explores instances in which Chaucer "presses genre to its limits" to investigate "story-telling itself."

182. Stengel, Paul Joseph. "A New Media Pilgrimage: Chaucer and the Multimodal Satire." In Mary T. Christel and Scott Sullivan, eds. *Lesson Plans for Developing Digital Literacies*. Urbana, Ill.: National Council of Teachers of English, 2010, pp. 253–62. This lesson plan focuses on Chaucer's *CT*. While initially requiring that students become familiar with Chaucer's rhetorical strategies, it also asks students to use these strategies to compose a "multimodal satire" of their own—one that focuses on high school culture and is created through various kinds of audio and video software. Although originally intended for high school students, the lesson plan can be adapted to other contexts.

183. Surber, Nida. *The Fierce Parade: Chaucer and the Encryption of Homosexuality in the "Canterbury Tales."* Geneva: Éditions Slatkine, 2010. 213 pp. Exploring details and multilingual and multidialectical puns and etymologies through a "Proustian lens," Surber discovers sustained attention to homosexuality in *CT*. Critical uncertainty about specific meaning in Chaucer enables a queer reading that grafts "the other logos of sexuality" onto the "tree of heterosexual discourse." Surber reads *GP*, the tales, and the links between the tales as indicative that the majority of the pilgrims are homosexual. These components of *CT* disclose Chaucer's Platonic embrace of homosexuality and celebration of the "first male trio of Gods of Eden, namely God, Adam and Eve." Surber appends a survey of attitudes toward homosexuality in the ancient world and medieval Church.

184. Yvernault, Martine. "Bonnes manières et dessous de table: *The Boke of Nurture* de John Russell." In Danielle Buschinger, ed. *Médiévales, 48*. Amiens: Presses du Centre d'Études Médiévales, Université de Picardie-Jules Verne, 2010, pp. 179–87. Comments on the relationship between narration and food in *CT*.

185. ———. "L'orient de Mandeville: Voyager par le texte." In Danielle Buschinger, ed. *Médiévales, 11–12*. Amiens: Presses du Centre d'Études Médiévales, Université de Picardie-Jules Verne, 2010, pp.

443–53. Includes introductory comments on displacement in Antiquity and the Middle Ages, specifically the meaning of travel in Chaucer.

186. ———. "Reading History in Enamel: The Journey of Thomas Becket's Experience from Canterbury to Limoges." In Catherine Royer-Hemet, ed. *Canterbury: A Medieval City* (*SAC* 34 [2012], no. 155), pp. 137–59. Analysis of Becket reliquaries made in Limoges, including commentary on the role of the city and its cathedral in Becket's experience and in *CT* (as an elusive destination).

187. Zedolik, John J., Jr. "The Transcendent Comedy of the *Canterbury Tales*: Harmony in 'Quyting,' Harmony in Fragmentation." *DAI* A71.04 (2010): n.p. Considers how "quyting" ("paying back or balancing") among the pilgrims enforces comic harmoniousness and balance in *CT*, despite the work's fragmentary structure. In addition, *CT* invites the reader to " 'quyt' the author."

See also nos. 6, 10, 13, 17, 29, 30, 33, 38, 40, 42, 43, 55, 76, 103, 105, 129, 132, 156, 161, 166, 227.

CT—The General Prologue

188. Scala, Elizabeth. "Yeoman Services: Chaucer's Knight, His Critics, and the Pleasures of Historicism." *ChauR* 45 (2010): 194–221. In striving to contextualize the portrait of the Yeoman in relation to real-world late medieval weaponry and hunting gear, critics overlook both the Yeoman's service as the "bearer" of aristocratic masculinity and the portrait's phallic humor. In doing so, they inevitably repeat the latter, even as they leave unacknowledged the "ardor" of "scholarly arduousness."

189. Tuma, George W., and Dinah Hazell, eds. " 'The Wicked Age': Middle English Complaint Literature in Translation." Special issue, *MedievalF* (2008): n.p. Second half of a two-part special edition of this electronic journal: an online collection of translations of Middle English texts. The first part translates ten Middle English romances, with introductions, notes, and commentary; this second part is an anthology of complaint literature that includes a variety of texts, arranged topically, with introductions, commentary, and notes. Includes a translation of Chaucer's *Sted*, and "Literature of the Estates," a discussion of *GP* as an example of estates satire (focusing on the Friar, the Man of Law, and the

Guildsmen), compared with Langland's *Piers Plowman* and Gower's *Vox clamantis*.

See also nos. 8, 95, 115, 127, 137, 146, 173, 177.

CT—The Knight and His Tale

190. Casey, Jim. "'What Things You Make of Us!': Amazons and Kinsmen in Chaucer and Shakespeare." In Kathleen A. Bishop, ed. *Standing in the Shadow of the Master? Chaucerian Influences and Interpretations* (*SAC* 34 [2012], no. 114), pp. 224–42. Explicitly influenced by *KnT*, Shakespeare's *Two Noble Kinsmen* adapts Chaucer's humor and creates a dark vision of the intersection of consumerism and sexuality.

191. Cerezo Moreno, Marta. "El canon literario y sus efectos sobre la construcción cultural de la violencia de género: Los casos de Chaucer y Shakespeare." In Ángeles de la Concha Muñoz, ed. *El sustrato cultural de la violencia de género: Literatura, arte, cine, y videojuegos*. Madrid: Síntesis, 2010, pp. 19–44. Analyzes how art—canonical literature, in particular—helps to construct, consolidate, and transmit patriarchal ideologies that support violence and female subjection. Assesses *KnT* as an example of how a masculine gaze affects female identity. Chaucer tones down the sexual allusions of his source, but not the sexual violence.

192. Kim, Hyonjin. "Chaucer's 'Wayke Ox': Rereading *The Knight's Tale*." *MES* 16.1 (2008): 77–111 (in Korean, with English abstract). Reads *KnT* as a "second prologue" to the whole *CT*, helping to "frame" the work with two prologues (*GP* and *KnT*) and two conclusions (*ParsT* and *Ret*). Analogously, the opening and closing weddings of *KnT* aim unsuccessfully to "overrule the chaotic world."

193. Lee, Dongchoon. "*The Knight's Tale*: Forms, Incongruities, and Chaucer's Intention." *MES* 16.1 (2008): 43–76 (in Korean, with English abstract). Distinguishes between Chaucer's voice and the Knight's voice in *KnT*, viewing the latter as a failed attempt to assert or express an orderly view, revealed as unreliable by means of incongruities in style and content.

194. Reiff, Raychel Haugrud. "Choosing *Thou* or *You* to Reveal Ideal Relationships in *The Knight's Tale*." *EMSt* 26 (2010): 69–84. Reiff examines uses of second-person-singular pronouns *thou* and *you* to indicate relationships among characters in *KnT*, particularly idealized chivalric relationships, Theseus's changing attitude toward the knights, the un-

faltering brotherhood between Palamon and Arcite, the courtly interactions of the gods, and the nobility's status before the gods.

195. Storm, Mel. "Rude Mechanicals and Minotaurs: Shakespeare and Chaucer Among the Mythographers." *Enarratio* 14 (2010, for 2007): 139–51. Storm surveys the debt to Chaucer's *KnT* in Shakespeare's *A Midsummer Night's Dream*, focusing on the works' mutual concern with hierarchy and order. In both works (and elsewhere in the authors' works), the figure of the Minotaur (parodied in Bottom's transformation) represents the counter-principles of disruptive lust and chaos. Storm also comments on Pasiphae in *WBP*.

196. Stretter, Robert. "Engendering Obligation: Sworn Brotherhood and Love Rivalry in Medieval English Romance." In Albrecht Classen and Marilyn Sandidge, eds. *Friendship in the Middle Ages and Early Modern Age: Explorations of a Fundamental Ethical Discourse* (*SAC* 34 [2012], no. 119), pp. 501–24. Stretter comments on various romances and includes discussion of how, in *KnT*, Palamon and Arcite's mutual love for Emily disrupts their sworn brotherhood, a powerful bond of obligation and friendship. Chaucer alters a long cultural and literary tradition of fidelity between sworn brothers by introducing the element of erotic love. The rupture between Palamon and Arcite may reflect cultural anxiety regarding "trouthe."

See also nos. 8, 49, 72, 74, 100, 153, 168, 188, 232, 266, 305.

CT—The Miller and His Tale

197. Beidler, Peter G. "It's Miller Time! Baba Brinkman's Rap Adaptation of the *Miller's Tale*." *LATCH* 3 (2010): 134–50. Commenting on how Brinkman's rap version of *MilT* "recast and reset" Chaucer's original, Beidler raises questions about the pedagogical and cultural value of the live performance, the audio recording, and the printed version. Includes (pp. 145–50) an interview with Brinkman concerning his goals and plans.

198. Evans, Robert C. "Social and Religious Taboos in Chaucer's *The Miller's Tale*." In Harold Bloom and Blake Hobby, eds. *The Taboo*. Bloom's Literary Themes. New York: Bloom's Literary Criticism, 2010, pp. 113–22. Tallies the "taboos" broken or flouted by the Miller and characters in *MilT*.

199. Heyworth, Gregory. "Ineloquent Ends: *Simplicitas*, Proctolalia,

and the Profane Vernacular in the *Miller's Tale*." *Speculum* 84 (2009): 956–83. 5 b&w figs. Aligns vernacularity with visual and audio profanity, observing occurrences in *MilPT* in which Chaucer "indulges in vernacular eschatology" and "moves to suppress it." Heyworth reads the window scene of *MilT* in light of medieval guides to prognostication by thunder ("brotology"), misericordes, and pilgrims' badges, exposing late medieval concerns with the oppositions between oral and literate, vernacular and Latinate, profane and sacred—oppositions that Chaucer "collapses" in his rehearsal of profanity and apology for it.

200. Morgan, Gerald. "Obscenity and Fastidiousness in *The Miller's Tale*." *ES* 91 (2010): 492–518. Chaucer's intentional contrasting of the language of the Knight and that of the Miller challenges his readers' openmindedness. The Miller's obscene language is cleverly applied and should on no account be censored from prudishness.

See also nos. 21, 101, 111, 127, 173, 201, 312.

CT—The Reeve and His Tale

201. Carella, Bryan. "The Social Aspirations and Priestly Pretense of Chaucer's Reeve." *Neophil* 94 (2010): 523–29. In his conduct and dress, the social-climbing Reeve associates himself with the clergy—an association that the Miller recognizes and ridicules unmercifully.

202. Sidhu, Nicole Nolan. "'To Late for to Crie': Female Desire, Fabliau Politics, and Classical Legend in Chaucer's *Reeve's Tale*." *Exemplaria* 21 (2009): 3–23. *RvT* "confronts the paradoxical status of women's desire" in medieval Christian and feudal systems. The *Tale*'s "significant divergences from the fabliau tradition" and several resemblances to the story of Theseus and Ariadne help undercut *KnT*; its obscenity is a "critique of aristocratic culture."

203. Taylor, Joseph. "Chaucer's Uncanny Regionalism: Rereading the North in *The Reeve's Tale*." *JEGP* 109 (2010): 468–89. In *RvT*, Chaucer's references to language, lore, and the North both explore uncanny (in the Freudian sense) political differences among regions and reveal notions of nation. The North or Northernism plays a small but significant role elsewhere in *CT,* particularly in *MLT.*

See also nos. 108, 127.

CT—The Cook and His Tale

See no. 67.

CT—The Man of Law and His Tale

204. Ashton, Gail. *Medieval English Romance in Context*. Texts and Contexts. New York: Continuum, 2010. viii, 163 pp. Outlines the literary and social contexts in which late medieval English romances were produced. Assesses a number of these romances and their "afterlives," exploring their gender affiliations, uses of symbols, concerns with familial and cultural origins, and recent critical approaches. Recurrent attention to *MLT* focuses on gender identity and postcolonial analysis.

205. Barlow, Gania. "A Thrifty Tale: Narrative Authority and the Competing Values of the *Man of Law's Tale*." *ChauR* 44 (2010): 397–420. Through its several nested narratorial performances, each of which includes its own disavowals and subtle appropriations of authority, *MLT* renegotiates the relative power of spiritual and secular domains to control the interpretation and transmission of texts.

206. Cawsey, Kathy. "Disorienting Orientalism: Finding Saracens in Strange Places in Late Medieval Manuscripts." *Exemplaria* 21 (2009): 380–97. Late medieval manuscript illuminations show Danes and other northern pagans with costumes and weapons that are emblematic of the Near East. Like *MLT* and Gower's Tale of Constance, these images indicate that the term *Saracen* included various non-Christian groups, evidence of a perspective that sees pagan threats on three fronts: pagan Norse, eastern Muslims, and the Moors and Arabs of Spain.

207. Cooper-Rompato, Christine F. *The Gift of Tongues: Women's Xenoglossia in the Later Middle Ages*. University Park: Pennsylvania State University Press, 2010. ix, 217 pp. Discusses (pp. 143–88) Chaucer's "great translation experiment" in *PrPT*, *MLT*, and *SqT*, arguing that Chaucer is "highly invested in the mechanics of miraculous and mundane translation" and that Custance is a "medieval example of a xenoglossic holy woman who possesses a complete mastery over Latinity." Translation is crucial to an understanding of "Chaucer's accomplishments as a vernacular writer and his contribution to Middle English literature."

208. Czarnowus, Anna. "Mary, Motherhood, and Theatricality in the Old Polish *Listen, Dear Brothers* and Chaucer's *Man of Law's Tale*." In

Jane Tolmie and M. J. Toswell, eds. *Laments for the Lost in Medieval Literature* (*SAC* 34 [2012], no. 164), pp. 129–47. Compares the "theatricality of imagery" in *MLT*, particularly in Constance's prayer to the Virgin (2.841–54), with the Polish Marian crucifixion lament "Listen, Dear Brothers." Includes an English translation of the Polish lyric.

209. Hsy, Jonathan H. "'Oure Occian': Littoral Language and the Constance Narratives of Chaucer and Boccaccio." In Paul Gifford and Tessa Hauswedell, eds. *Europe and Its Others: Essays on Interperception and Identity*. New York: Peter Lang, 2010, pp. 205–24. Hsy compares the ways *MLT* and Boccaccio's *Decameron* 5.2 present transnational diversity, especially through their depictions of "littoral language," i.e., Custance's and Gostanza's communications with people on the shores of foreign lands. Both works indicate the "provisionality of medieval conceptions of linguistic and cultural identity." Hsy comments on uses of the word *oure* in *MLT*.

210. Kader, David, and Michael Stanford, eds. *Poetry of the Law: From Chaucer to the Present*. Iowa City: University of Iowa Press, 2010. xxi, 200 pp. Includes the *GP* description of the Sergeant of the Law (lines 309–30) in an anthology of one hundred lyrics and poetic excerpts that pertain to lawyers and legal practice. Brief notes at the end of the work.

211. Morgan, Gerald. "Chaucer's Man of Law and the Argument for Providence." *RES* 61 (2010): 1–33. Skilled in the law and both learned and adept in poetry, the Man of Law crafts a tale of sin, free will, and providence. Although Custance is steadfast, her will is free and consequential, the foundation of true judgment. *MLT* proposes a concept of providence in a mutable world "as the idea of things ordained to an end pre-existing in the divine mind."

212. Nakley, Susan. "Sovereignty Matters: Anachronism, Chaucer's Britain, and England's Future's Past." *ChauR* 44 (2010): 368–96. The "temporal disorder" and "internationalism" of *MLT*—combined with its examination of competing familial and institutional loyalty—depict sovereignty as a redemptive governmental form capable of healing the ills of late medieval England, including "its language . . . and its institutions of marriage, Church, and law."

213. Stanbury, Sarah. "The *Man of Law's Tale* and Rome." *Exemplaria* 22 (2010): 119–37. For Chaucer, Rome is an ancient imperial capital, a goal of medieval pilgrimage, and a center of trade—trade in devotions, indulgences, and pardons that allies mercantilism and religion. Such a

Roman transaction also involves relics or monuments, and in *MLT* its most Christian "commodity" is Custance herself, the object of exchange, who becomes "an alternative to devotional images and relics."

214. Whitaker, Cord J. "Race and Conversion in Late Medieval England." *DAI* A70.12 (2010): n.p. Argues that racial differentiation—generally associated with the early modern period—was not necessarily secondary to religious distinctions in the late medieval period, using *MLT* and other texts as evidence.

215. Yager, Susan. "The BBC *Man of Law's Tale*: Faithful to the Tradition." *Literature and Belief* 27 (2007): 55–68. The BBC's 2003 adaptation of *MLT* updates Chaucer's *Tale*, incorporating plot, character names, and thematic elements such as faith, exile and return, trauma and healing, and time and repetition. Constance, a Nigerian refugee, finds love and fellowship in modern England but is wrongly accused of murder. Once exonerated, she is voluntarily deported, but her mother-in-law attempts to prevent her return to England.

See also nos. 46, 130, 139, 150, 203, 286, 292.

CT—The Wife of Bath and Her Tale

216. Field, P. J. C. "What Women Really Want: The Genesis of Chaucer's *Wife of Bath's Tale*." *Arthurian Literature* 27 (2010): 59–83. Reviews scholarship that discusses analogues of *WBT* and hypothesizes the nature and date of the archetype of these tales, focusing on the relative chronology of major motifs, shared and unshared. A hypothetical summary of the archetype—presented as a basis for gauging Chaucer's originality—concludes the work.

217. Gastle, Brian. "Gower's Business: Artistic Production of Cultural Capital and the Tale of Florent." In Elisabeth Dutton, with John Hines and R. F. Yeager, eds. *John Gower, Trilingual Poet: Language, Translation, and Tradition* (*SAC* 34 [2012], no. 122), pp. 182–95. All of the recensions of the Prologue to *Confessio Amantis*—especially the Ricardian recension—reflect Gower's economic concerns. His *Tale of Florent* also engages commercial concerns, particularly those of marital contracts, although to a lesser extent than does Chaucer's *WBT*.

218. Kelly, Henry Ansgar. "Medieval Laws and Views on Wife-Beating." In Kenneth Pennington, Stanley Chodorow, and Keith H. Kendall, eds. *Proceedings of the Tenth International Congress of Medieval*

Canon Law: Syracuse, New York, 13–18 August 1996. Monumenta Iuris Canonici, Series C: Subsidia, no. 2. Vatican City: Biblioteca Apostolica Vaticana, 2001, pp. 985–1001. Documents where wife beating was both allowed and forbidden in medieval canon and civil law, often presented in analogies to bishops' treatment of clerics and lords' treatment of slaves. Kelly comments on instances in *CT*, particularly in *WBP*. Reprinted in *SAC* 34 (2012), no. 136.

219. Klitgård, Ebbe. "The Encoding of Subjectivity in Chaucer's *The Wife of Bath's Tale* and *The Pardoner's Tale*." In Gerd Bayer and Ebbe Klitgård, eds. *Narrative Developments from Chaucer to Defoe* (*SAC* 34 [2012], no. 113), pp. 25–39. Testing the premise of A. C. Spearing's *Textual Subjectivity* (2005), Klitgård explores the dramatic monologues of the Wife of Bath and the Pardoner and uses of narrative personae.

220. Mruk, Karen. "Alice on the Couch: A 21st Century Psychoanalytic Interpretation of the Wife of Bath." In Kathleen A. Bishop, ed. *Standing in the Shadow of the Master? Chaucerian Influences and Interpretations* (*SAC* 34 [2012], no. 114), pp. 244–56. Mruk mines details and perspectives in the Wife of Bath materials to imagine the Wife as a real patient undergoing therapy.

221. Provost, Jeanne. "Illicit Country: The Loathly Lady and the Imaginary Foundations of Medieval English Land Law." *DAI* A71.05 (2010): n.p. Suggests that the "Loathly Lady" is an anthropomorphic representation of the land, linking human vagaries with the uncertain product of working any given land and underscoring the impossibility of human attempts to control and regulate the natural world.

222. Sayers, Edna Edith. "Experience, Authority, and the Mediation of Deafness: Chaucer's Wife of Bath." In Joshua R. Eyler, ed. *Disability in the Middle Ages: Reconsiderations and Reverberations* (*SAC* 34 [2012], no. 124), pp. 81–92. Sayers reviews commentary on the Wife of Bath's deafness; suggests that we treat it more literally than metaphorically; and posits that, through the deafened Wife, Chaucer "does not resolve the opposition between experience and authority, but rather forces its abandonment."

223. Tinkle, Theresa. "Contested Authority: Jerome and the Wife of Bath on 1 Timothy 2." *ChauR* 44 (2010): 268–93. Both Jerome and Chaucer follow Paul in deploying "provocative women" to dramatize contemporary controversies over who may interpret scripture. The Wife of Bath performs exegesis even as she effectively likens her husbands to "exegetes whose sins discredit their sermons"; however, her comedic

embodiment of the literary "unruly woman" neutralizes any threat to domestic and institutional hierarchies. See no. 163.

224. ———. "The Wife of Bath's Marginal Authority." *SAC* 32 (2010): 67–101. Surveys and assesses the manuscript glosses and notes to *WBP*, arguing that scribal commentary affirms the Wife's orthodoxy as an exegete. The glosses and notes in Oxford, New College 314 (Ne), and related manuscripts grant authority to her uses of scripture and "other learned discourses." The glosses in British Library Egerton 2864 (En³) reflect, perhaps, anxiety about female authority, but both sets of comments "grant her an authoritative grounding in canonical scripture and call attention to her lessons on marital sexuality." See no. 163.

See also nos. 49, 62, 67, 95, 111, 130, 146, 163, 195.

CT—The Friar and His Tale

225. Homar, Katie. "Chaucer's Novelized, Carnivalized Exemplum: A Bakhtinian Reading of the *Friar's Tale*." *ChauR* 45 (2010): 85–105. Through its "metafictional dialogue" between the teller and pilgrim narrator; its "inter-illumination" of genres, including anticlerical satire, oath making, and fabliau; and its depiction of a "carnival hell," *FrT* parodies and thus undermines the authority of the sermon exemplum.

See also no. 95.

CT—The Summoner and His Tale

226. Epstein, Robert. "Sacred Commerce: Chaucer, Friars, and the Spirit of Money." In Robert Epstein and William Robins, eds. *Sacred and Profane in Chaucer and Late Medieval Literature: Essays in Honour of John V. Fleming* (*SAC* 34 [2012], no. 123), pp. 129–45. Epstein argues for a nuanced understanding of money in *SumT*, reading its significations in light of the thirteenth-century Franciscan treatise *Sacrum commercium*, medieval commercial practice, and deliberations on quality and quantity among the "Oxford Calculators" of fourteenth-century Merton College. Focuses on the "long denouement" of *SumT* and its underlying concerns with spirituality.

227. Mahowald, Kyle. "'It may nat be': Chaucer, Derrida, and the Impossibility of the Gift." *SAC* 32 (2010): 129–50. Similar to gift giv-

ing as theorized by Jacques Derrida (in response to Marcel Mauss), the dividing of the fart in *SumT* is "an impossible" that prompts logical deliberation and logocentric reflection. Linked via punning, the giving of money in *SumT* is analogous to fart dividing, so the fart scene is an apt "coda" to the *Tale*. Both gifts-that-are-non-gifts align with the concerns of exchange, gifting, and language in *FranT*, occupatio in *SqT*, and the tale-telling contest of *CT*.

See also nos. 95, 262, 312.

CT—The Clerk and His Tale

228. Hejaiej, Mounira Monia. "The Motif of the Patient Wife in Muslim and Western Literature and Folklore." *CLCWeb: Comparative Literature and Culture* 12.1 (2010): n.p. Provides comparative analysis of the modern Tunisian tale "Sabra," an analogue of *ClT*, told by a woman to an exclusively female audience. Includes summary of and commentary on Chaucer's "ambivalent and ironic version," plus other medieval European analogues, exploring how context affects interpretation of the basic folkloric narrative.

229. Krug, Rebecca. "Natural Feeling and Unnatural Mothers: Herod the Great, *The Life of Saint Bridget*, and Chaucer's *Clerk's Tale*." In Jane Tolmie and M. J. Toswell, eds. *Laments for the Lost in Medieval Literature* (*SAC* 34 [2012], no. 164), pp. 225–41. Explores the depictions of grief over lost children in the Wakefield mystery play *Slaughter of the Innocents*; a Middle English life of Saint Bridget; and *ClT*. The depictions present grief as variously natural, unnatural, and a response to conflict; however, grief transforms the mother figure in each work.

230. Raybin, David. "Muslim Griselda: The Politics of Gender and Religion in Geoffrey Chaucer's *Clerk's Tale* and Pramoedya Ananta Toer's *The Girl from the Coast*." *Exemplaria* 21 (2009): 179–200. Raybin compares the work by the Indonesian novelist Toer with *ClT*. Both works involve a powerful man who marries a poor girl and who eventually dismisses her. Toer pays careful attention to the heroine's thoughts and feelings, while Chaucer largely obscures Griselda's feelings. Both works show how literature depicts the emotional life of "the oppressed female poor."

231. Yoon, Minwoo. "Griselda's Body and Labor in Chaucer's *Clerk's Tale*." *MES* 16.1 (2008): 113–41 (in Korean, with English abstract).

Griselda's body stands in contrast to translations that are imposed on it, a figure of resistance to male glossing. The constancy and efficacy of her labor make her "master" of her self—unlike Walter, who fails to achieve either self-recognition or consciousness of the "Other." However briefly, power translates to Griselda at the end of *CIT*.

See also nos. 54, 56, 102, 115, 150, 171, 232, 239.

CT—The Merchant and His Tale

232. Blamires, Alcuin. "May in January's Tree: Genealogical Configuration in the *Merchant's Tale*." *ChauR* 45 (2010): 106–17. Comments on the concern with propagating robust and pure lineages in numerous areas of medieval culture—including Chaucer's *CIT*, *KnT*, and *MerT* in particular. The denouement of the latter may be read as May's inserting herself into January's family tree, even as she foils his desire for "leveful" offspring by arranging "the prospect of offspring from a more attractive source."

233. Labère, Nelly. "De la généalogie sexuelle à la généalogie textuelle: L'obscenité du *Lidia*." In Anne Birberick, Russell J. Ganim, and Hugh G. A. Roberts, eds. *Obscenity*. EMF: Studies in Early Modern France, no. 14. Charlottesville, N.C.: Rookwood, 2010, pp. 41–57. Explores the nature and constitutive motifs of obscenity in the twelfth-century *Lidia*, Boccaccio's *Decameron* 7.9, *MerT*, and the fifteenth-century *Cent nouvelles nouvelles*.

234. Ladd, Roger A. *Antimercantilism in Late Medieval English Literature*. The New Middle Ages. New York: Palgrave Macmillan, 2010. [xi], 218 pp. Studies the development of mercantile practice in the late Middle Ages and depictions of merchants in English literature, from early satires to greater acceptability. Includes sections on merchants in Langland's *Piers Plowman*, Gower's *Mirour de l'omme*, *The Book of Margery Kempe*, the *Libelle of Englyshe Polycye*, *The Tale of Beryn*, the York cycle, and Chaucer's *CT*. Chapter 4, "The Deliberate Ambiguity of Chaucer's Anxious Merchants" (pp. 77–100), assesses Chaucer's concern with the "efficacy of satire" as he offers both pro- and antimercantile treatments in the *GP* description of the "elusive" Merchant, the "unmercantile" *MerT*, and *ShT*, where mercantilism is displaced to France. Through this variety, Ladd traces what "Chaucer requires from his readers."

235. Pearman, Tory Vandeventer. "'O Sweete Venym Queynte!':

Pregnancy and the Disabled Female Body in the *Merchant's Tale*." In Joshua R. Eyler, ed. *Disability in the Middle Ages: Reconsiderations and Reverberations* (*SAC* 34 [2012], no. 124), pp. 25–37. Explores a "gendered model of disability" in *MerT*, where the carnivalesque grotesqueness of May's performed pregnancy replaces January's blindness and impotence as a kind of disability.

See also nos. 21, 76, 146, 312, 321.

CT—The Squire and His Tale

236. Bedford, Ronald. "The Text Estranged: Topographies of Irony in Chaucer and Milton." In Philippa Kelly and L. E. Semler, eds. *Word and Self Estranged in English Texts, 1550–1660*. Burlington, Vt.: Ashgate, 2010, pp. 167–81. Bedford explores the development of the term *irony* and interpretive issues surrounding its use, focusing on Chaucer's use of irony as reflected in Milton's interpretations of *SqT*.

237. Schotland, Sara Deutch. "Talking Bird and Gentle Heart: Female Homosocial Bonding in Chaucer's *Squire's Tale*." In Albrecht Classen and Marilyn Sandidge, eds. *Friendship in the Middle Ages and Early Modern Age: Explorations of a Fundamental Ethical Discourse* (*SAC* 34 [2012], no. 119), pp. 525–41. Canacee's kindness toward the formel eagle shows Chaucer's sympathy for women and appreciation of female friendship. The formel, like other females in Chaucer, has been abused by men—and warns Canacee against them. In creating a painted mew for the falcon (an ekphrasis), Canacee expresses her pity and affection for the injured bird. Their friendship is brief but ideal, crossing apparently formidable borders.

See also nos. 49, 76, 128, 158, 188, 207, 227, 323.

CT—The Franklin and His Tale

238. Bugbee, John. "Solving Dorigen's Trilemma: Oath and *Law* in the Franklin's and Physician's Tales." *M&H* 36 (2010): 49–76. Dorigen in *FranT* has more than the two options of shame or death: she can also choose to break a bad law, even though the decision to let bad law stand "seems somehow, tragically, to have been taken long before the

characters became conscious of choosing." In *PhyT* as well as in *FranT*, characters respond to their situations in ways that legitimize bad law.

239. Fernández Rodríguez, Carmen María. "New Contexts for the Classics: Wanderers and Revolutionaries in the Tales of the Franklin and the Clerk." *SELIM* 13 (2005): 225–52. From a feminist perspective, Fernández Rodríguez compares *FranT* and *ClT* with Fanny Burney's *The Wanderer* (1814) and Maria Edgeworth's *The Modern Griselda* (1805). Dorigen's and Griselda's domestic constraints contrast the ones depicted by eighteenth- and nineteenth-century British female writers who lived surrounded by conduct books and the cult of sensibility.

240. Lee, B. S. "Apollo's Chariot and the Christian Subtext of *The Franklin's Tale.*" *Journal of Medieval Religious Cultures* 36 (2010): 47–67. Lee assesses *FranT* as a "sequel" to *SqT* that repudiates its magic, replaces its stasis with moral development in the idea of *gentilesse*, and provides a missing Christian subtext—a "Christmas miniature" that precedes the apparent disappearance of the rocks. The tales of Fragment 5 are also fused by references to Apollo, which Lee explains in light of Chaucer's *Mars*, his *ABC*, and the apocryphal "Flower and the Leaf."

241. Saunders, Corinne. "Subtle Crafts: Magic and Exploitation in Medieval English Romance." In Laura Ashe, Ivana Djordjević, and Judith Weiss, eds. *The Exploitations of Medieval Romance*. Cambridge: D. S. Brewer, 2010, pp. 108–24. The use of magic was exploitative and morally ambiguous; however, with the thirteenth-century rise of universities, attitudes shifted: through natural magic and great learning, one could harness natural powers. The "highly intellectual" *FranT* explores the power of natural (rather than demonic) magic to affect perception and exert a dangerous physical and mental control over others.

See also nos. 128, 146, 158, 227, 262.

CT—The Physician and His Tale

See no. 238.

CT—The Pardoner and His Tale

242. Abdalla, Laila. " 'My body to warente . . .': Linguistic Corporeality in Chaucer's Pardoner." In Jennifer C. Vaught, ed. *Rhetorics of Bodily Disease and Health in Medieval and Early Modern England*. Literary

and Scientific Cultures of Early Modernity. Burlington, Vt.: Ashgate, 2010, pp. 65–84. Considers *PardPT* in light of Augustinian semiotic theory. Focus on the body in the Pardoner's materials signals the need to attend to the objects of signs, and the quarrel with the Host "renders impotent" the Pardoner's nominalist "attack on signification." *PardPT* reconfigures the Sophist question of whether a false person can tell a good tale, placing responsibility on readers to attend to all available signs.

243. Camargo, Martin. "How (Not) to Preach: Thomas Waleys and Chaucer's Pardoner." In Robert Epstein and William Robins, eds. *Sacred and Profane in Chaucer and Late Medieval Literature: Essays in Honour of John V. Fleming* (*SAC* 34 [2012], no. 123), pp. 146–78. Camargo details how the Pardoner "pointedly rejects every tenet" of moral instruction found in Chapter 1 of Waleys's *De modo componendi sermones* and shows how the treatise discloses flaws in the Pardoner's rhetorical techniques. The Pardoner "may have been" self-deluded about his verbal prowess. The collection appends Camargo's translation of Chapter 1 of Waleys's treatise.

244. Middleton, Anne. "Commentary on an Unacknowledged Text: Chaucer's Debt to Langland." *YLS* 24 (2010): 113–37. Middleton reads the Pardoner materials as Chaucer's "formal and ideational" tribute to Langland's *Piers Plowman*—an embodiment of his appreciation of Langland's struggles with poetic self-representation, the gendered status of the poet, and the poetics of confession. Langland inspired the Pardoner and the penitential ending of *CT*.

245. Nickell, Joe. "The True Cross: Chaucer, Calvin, and the Relic Mongers." *Skeptical Inquirer* (http://www.csicop.org/si/) 34.6 (2010): n.p. Comments on brief selections from a translation of *PardT* as evidence that Chaucer accepts the validity of the True Cross even though he rejects the Pardoner's "fraudulent" practice. Discusses how John Calvin "took the matter several steps further" and asserts that there is no "credible evidence" that Saint Helena ever found the Cross.

246. Simpson, James. "Place." In Brian Cummings and James Simpson, eds. *Cultural Reformations: Medieval and Renaissance in Literary History* (*SAC* 34 [2012], no. 121), pp. 95–112. Compares what *PardT* and Erasmus's *Pilgrimage of Pure Devotion* reveal about the "locatability" and placelessness of the Church, exclusion from Church locations, and disgust associated with such exclusion.

See also nos. 95, 160, 219, 269.

CT—The Shipman and His Tale

See nos. 21, 47, 234.

CT—The Prioress and Her Tale

247. Barr, Helen. "Religious Practice in Chaucer's *Prioress's Tale*: Rabbit and/or Duck?" *SAC* 32 (2010): 39–65. Both *PrP* and *PrT* express "affective devotional piety," while simultaneously they are "swollen with reference to targets of Wycliffite polemic." As a result, their Marian generic affiliations and the "collocational patterns" of their diction can and do provoke distinctly orthodox and heterodox responses that are equally valid and probably sequentially evident to Chaucer's audience. Barr includes significant attention to liturgical concerns, the phrase "by rote" (in contrast to "in herte"), and the interpretive process of "inferencing."

248. Delany, Sheila. "The Jewish Connection: Chaucer and the Paris Jews, 1394." In David Gay and Stephen R. Reimer, eds. *Locating the Past/Discovering the Present: Perspectives on Religion, Culture, and Marginality*. Edmonton: University of Alberta Press, 2010, pp. 1–21. Delany explores the "imbrication" of life and art in *PrT* and the expulsion of Jews from France in 1394. She gauges Chaucer's contact with Jews and describes the conditions under which Jews lived in fourteenth-century France, specifically the results of the supposed abduction of Denis Machaut, a Jewish convert to Christianity. Delany identifies elements that *PrT* shares with history rather than what it shares with literary analogues.

249. Gayk, Shannon. " 'To wondre upon this thyng': Chaucer's *Prioress's Tale*." *Exemplaria* 22 (2010): 138–56. *PrT* depicts "the production and exigencies of wonder" in concert with the ambiguity and inscrutability of the miraculous. The abbot reestablishes the distinction between the animate and the inanimate by removing the mysterious "greyn," which does not "produce song" but instead "prolongs wonder." Medieval religious wonder, in turn, may provoke both passivity before what cannot be assimilated and "an active desire to assimilate and appropriate it."

250. Julius, Anthony. *Trials of the Diaspora: A History of Anti-Semitism in England*. Oxford and New York: Oxford University Press, 2010. lviii, 811 pp. Julius defines anti-Semitism and describes its history and poli-

tics in England. Literary anti-Semitism has "distinct tropes and themes, deployed without respect for genre boundaries." The "master trope" of "a well intentioned Christian place in peril by a sinister Jew or Jews" underlies *PrT* as well as Shakespeare's *Merchant of Venice*, Dickens's *Oliver Twist*, and many other works. Despite Chaucer's "humane and skeptical sentiments," *PrT* canonized the blood-libel legend and stands at the head of an authoritative tradition of its acceptance. See also no. 359.

251. Risden, E. L. "'A Revelation of Purgatory' and Chaucer's Prioress." *FCS* 35 (2010): 105–11. Assesses the Prioress in light of *A Revelation of Purgatory by an Unknown, Fifteenth-Century Woman Visionary* (1422), arguing that the later work provides evidence that Chaucer's character would have been found "culpable" for her worldliness.

252. Wallace, David. "Nuns." In Brian Cummings and James Simpson, eds. *Cultural Reformations: Medieval and Renaissance in Literary History* (*SAC* 34 [2012], no. 121), pp. 502–23. Wallace explores "degrees of enclosure" for nuns and surveys representations of nuns in medieval and Renaissance literature and art. Comments on Chaucer's depictions of the Prioress and the Second Nun: Chaucer "tells us much about one of his nuns and nothing about the other," an imbalance typical of the medieval representation of nuns.

See also nos. 150, 173, 207.

CT—The Tale of Sir Thopas

253. Brinkman, Baba. "Wrestling for the Ram: Competition and Feedback in *Sir Thopas* and *The Canterbury Tales*." *LATCH* 3 (2010): 107–33. Considers patronage and the developing status of the poet in the role of "court maker" in late medieval England, aligning the change with the influence of Italian culture. In his response to *Th*, the Host represents a courtly "negative feedback loop," probably reflects Chaucer's personal experiences as a young poet, and suggests Chaucer's awareness that his poetry is innovative and subject to audience response.

See also nos. 49, 53, 79, 321.

CT—The Tale of Melibee

254. Cannon, Christopher. "Proverbs and the Wisdom of Literature: *The Proverbs of Alfred* and Chaucer's *Tale of Melibee*." *Textual Practice* 24

(2010): 407–34. Explores medieval definitions and aesthetic responses to proverbs by examining *The Proverbs of Alfred* and *Mel*, exploring how each depends upon "acts of *recognition* that are produced by the repetition of well-worn truths." Both works are examples of "wisdom literature," which depends on an aesthetic sense alien to modern valorization of originality—one that satisfies by teaching us what we already know.

255. Jimura, Akiyuki. "Chaucer's Multiple Ways of Thinking: With Special Reference to Proverbial Expressions." In Shizuya Tara, Mayumi Sawada, and Larry Walker, eds. *Language and Beyond: Festschrift for Hiroshi Yonekura on the Occasion of His 65th Birthday*. Tokyo: Eichosha, 2007, pp. 265–83 (in Japanese). Discusses Chaucer's proverbial wisdom in *Mel*.

256. Tani, Akinobu. "Word Pairs or Doublets in Chaucer's *Tale of Melibee* and Their Variant Readings: A Preliminary Examination." In Osamu Imahayashi, Yoshiyuki Nakao, and Michiko Ogura, eds. *Aspects of the History of the English Language and Literature: Selected Papers Read at SHELL 2009, Hiroshima* (*SAC* 34 [2012], no. 131), pp. 101–13. Evidence from variants in manuscripts of *Mel* indicates that Chaucer's contemporaries accepted his use of doublets in "curial style." The variants reinforce affiliations between Hg and El and between Corpus Christi College 198 and Lansdowne 851, Cambridge; Caxton's reduction of doublets in his first edition may reflect his printing methods.

257. Taylor, Jamie. "Chaucer's *Tale of Melibee* and the Failure of Allegory." *Exemplaria* 21 (2009): 83–101. Considers *Mel* as an allegory of translation, proposing that Chaucer applies legal theory drawn from Henry de Bracton's *De legibus et consuetudinibus Angliae* to questions of ownership. In *MelP*, Chaucer uses "thyng" as a legal term pertaining to an author's use or ownership of an allegory.

See also nos. 108, 168, 270.

CT—The Monk and His Tale

258. Grimes, Jodi. "Knowing Fortune: The Limits of Boethian Knowledge in *The Monk's Tale*." *CarmP* 19 (2010): 49–68. *MkT* reflects Boethian epistemology and demonstrates the limits of human reason. The Monk presents Fortune as in Books 1 and 2 of the *Consolation*, but he lacks the faith necessary to understand the divine, while the mocking

Knight and Host misunderstand the *Tale*'s Boethian nature. Grimes contrasts the Monk with Troilus, who finds clear vision only in death.

See also nos. 54, 168, 314.

CT—The Nun's Priest and His Tale

259. Lindeboom, Wim. "Getting Out of Henry of Derby's Clutches: Richard II and the *Nun's Priest's Tale*." *Viator* 41.1 (2010): 276–300. Reads *NPT* as a political commentary, with Chaunticleer and Pertelote as Richard and Anne and the fox as Henry of Derby (later Henry IV), one of the appellants. Lindeboom comments on May 3, the dreams as Richard's anxieties, dating and astrological allusion in the poem, and the *Tale*'s relationship to *Le roman de Renart*.

260. Pietka, Rachel. "A Play of Opposites in the 'Nun's Priest's Tale.'" *Sigma Tau Delta Review* 7 (2010): 86–95. Through its "aversion to binary opposites," *NPT* promulgates "an inclusive perspective that avoids fixed interpretations" of notions of poverty, gender, free will, and authenticity.

261. Staley, Lynn. "Enclosed Spaces." In Brian Cummings and James Simpson, eds. *Cultural Reformations: Medieval and Renaissance in Literary History* (*SAC* 34 [2012], no. 121), pp. 113–33. Explores the trope of England as an idealized garden/island in imagery of homes in various medieval and Renaissance works, including *NPT*.

262. Travis, Peter W. *Disseminal Chaucer: Rereading "The Nun's Priest's Tale."* Notre Dame: University of Notre Dame Press, 2010. xi, 443 pp. Reads *NPT* as Chaucer's self-reflexive *ars poetica*, a Menippean parody of the complexities of engaging with language and literature. Through subtle play with the traditional liberal arts education, especially the trivium, *NPT* explores imitation, translation, and exemplification. It examines the nature of irony and metaphor, the relation of sound to meaning, the processes of time keeping and intellection, and the epistemology and ontology of truth and truth making. It challenges individual readers to achieve a "more sophisticated level of critical thinking." The volume includes close, extended analyses of the major cruces of *NPT* and comments at length on the Host, *FranT*, *SumT*, *PF*, *HF*, and *LGWP*. See also no. 401.

See also nos. 49, 95, 173.

CT—The Second Nun and Her Tale

263. Kelly, Henry Ansgar. "How Cecilia Came to Be a Saint and Patron (Matron?) of Music." In Blair Sullivan, ed. *The Echo of Music: Essays in Honor of Marie Louise Göllner*. Warren, Mich.: Harmonie Park Press, 2004, pp. 3–18. Kelly traces Cecilia's entry into hagiographic tradition and compares details of various versions of the saint's legend, including the original *passio* and the versions by Jacobus de Voragine, Chaucer (*SNT*), Osbern Bokenham, and John Dryden. Also tallies references to Cecilia in late medieval tradition and tracks the growth of her status as patron saint of music. Reprinted in *SAC* 34 (2012), no. 136.

See also nos. 252, 265.

CT—The Canon's Yeoman and His Tale

264. Pangilinan, Maria Cristina Santos. "Poetry and London Learning: Chaucer, Gower, Usk, Langland, and Hoccleve." *DAI* A70.10 (2010): n.p. Various Middle English authors succeeded in making London an urban, laicized intellectual center that balanced the clerical legacies of Cambridge and Oxford. These authors explored various academic disciplines (e.g., alchemy for Chaucer) in a manner accessible to the London audience.

265. Sisk, Jennifer L. "Religion, Alchemy, and Nostalgic Idealism in Fragment VIII of the *Canterbury Tales*." *SAC* 32 (2010): 151–77. Through its "nostalgic" recollection of an idealized "bygone era," *CYPT* "casts a shadow" on the reformist thinking of *SNT*. Like many advocates of ecclesiastical reform, the Nun idealizes the primitive Church, but the Canon's Yeoman's performance undercuts the idea that worldly decline can be reversed. Sisk clarifies late medieval notions of the primitive Church and attitudes toward alchemy.

CT—The Manciple and His Tale

266. Jones, Timothy S. *Outlawry in Medieval Literature*. The New Middle Ages. New York: Palgrave Macmillan, 2010. xiv, 221 pp. Studies the depiction and reception of historical and literary outlaws in England from the eleventh to the sixteenth century, focusing on how borders of various sorts—legal, ethnic, political, social, and religious—

define the outlaw identity. Jones comments on Palamon and Arcite as outlaws in *KnT* and on the use of the term *outlawe* in *ManT*.

267. Phillips, Helen. "Why Does Chaucer's Manciple Tell a Tale About a Crow?" *NMS* 54 (2010): 113–19. Phillips explores the proverbial and biblical background to *ManT*, identifying links between its plot and its teller, an untrustworthy servant. In popular tradition, crows were regarded as unfaithful servants and unreliable messengers, an association based on the raven that did not return to Noah. This idiom of the "corbie messenger" survives in Scots but is no longer widespread in Britain.

See also no. 128.

CT—The Parson and His Tale

268. Kelly, Henry Ansgar. "Penitential Theology and Law at the Turn of the Fifteenth Century." In Abigail Firey, ed. *A New History of Penance*. Brill's Companions to the Christian Tradition, no. 14. Leiden and Boston: Brill, 2008, pp. 239–317. Describes two late medieval penitential treatises—John Burough's *Pupilla oculi* (late fourteenth century) and William Lyndwood's *Provinciale* (early fifteenth century)—discussing their influence on Chaucer's understanding of the sacrament in *ParsT* and other works. Includes detailed summary/outlines of the two treatises (pp. 267–317). Reprinted in *SAC* 34 (2012), no. 136.

269. McCormack, Frances. "'Why sholde I sowen draf out of my fest?': Chaucer and the False Prophet Motif." In Eiléan Ní Chuilleanáin and John Flood, eds. *Heresy and Orthodoxy in Early English Literature, 1350–1680*. Dublin Studies in Medieval and Renaissance Literature, no. 3. Dublin: Four Courts Press, 2010, pp. 39–48. Ambiguous depictions of the Parson and Pardoner reflect contemporary debate regarding false prophets. The Pardoner's negligence, hypocrisy, and language suggest heresy, but he is not accused. The Parson is orthodox, but in his rejection of oaths, glosses, and fables seems a Lollard. The Parson's unwillingness to expound the Ten Commandments also suggests a fear of heresy charges, such as those leveled by the Shipman and the Host.

See also nos. 88, 244, 270.

CT—Chaucer's Retraction

270. Anastaplo, George. *The Christian Heritage: Problems and Prospects.* Lanham, Md.: Lexington Books, 2010. xvii, 446 pp. Twenty-six essays and thirteen appendices explore how Christianity underlies western attitudes. The section "Geoffrey Chaucer (1340–1400)" (pp. 67–75) reads *Ret* in light of *ParsT* and *Mel* as a mild account of misconduct in which Chaucer is guided more by prudence than by a sense of guilt.

271. O'Neill, Rosemary. "Accounting for Salvation in Middle English Literature." *DAI* A71.04 (2010): n.p. Discussing fiscal metaphors for the state of the soul in the Middle English period, O'Neill suggests that *Ret* is Chaucer's effort to escape "the imperatives of stewardship," evoking instead "a relationship of mutual intercession with his readers."

See also no. 244.

Anelida and Arcite

[No Entries]

A Treatise on the Astrolabe

272. Breen, Katharine. *Imagining an English Reading Public, 1150–1400.* Cambridge Studies in Medieval Literature, no. 79. Cambridge and New York: Cambridge University Press, 2010. x, 287 pp. 13 b&w illus. Describes late medieval efforts to "formulate vernacular languages that could stand in for Latin grammar as a first and paradigmatic *habitus,*" i.e., as a rule-based discipline of the mind that shapes cognition and moral action. Dante, the *Ormulum*, Matthew Paris, Wycliffite translators, and William Langland offer alternatives to the traditional Latin *habitus* and seek to contain the ways that their readers read, shaping and serving emergent, nontraditional reading populations. The volume concludes with an epilogue on *Astr*: Chaucer legitimates English as an alternative to Latin in "explicitly political terms"; he enjoins "the people of England to defer to their superiors and govern their inferiors," replacing the Latin *habitus* with an English courtly version. See also no. 333.

See also nos. 105, 140, 168.

Boece

273. Yoo, Inchol. "The Politics of Chaucer's *Boece*." *MES* 18 (2010): 361–84. Reads *Bo* as Chaucer's advice to young Richard on the subject of tyranny; later, *Bo* had "potential resonance" for opponents of Richard as king and may have served to support the usurpation of his crown.

See also nos. 37, 56, 140, 314.

The Book of the Duchess

274. Kao, Wan-Chuan. "Deployments of Whiteness: Affect, Materiality, and the Social in Late Medieval English Literature." *DAI* A71.04 (2010): n.p. Examines the use of whiteness in a variety of medieval works, arguing that being "white" is a mark not merely of ethnicity but also of Christianity, "beauty," and rank. Examples include mystery plays, *Pearl*, and *BD*.

See also nos. 47, 52, 115, 129, 169, 289, 291.

The Equatorie of the Planetis

[No Entries]

The House of Fame

275. Barr, Jessica. *Willing to Know God: Dreamers and Visionaries in the Later Middle Ages*. Columbus: Ohio State University Press, 2010. x, 262 pp. In Chapter 7, "Discrediting the Vision: *The House of Fame*" (pp. 184–207), Barr argues that *HF* portrays an active, unreliable visionary, one who unsuccessfully employs cognitive faculties to try to understand the contents of divinely granted vision. Chaucer, the self-conscious author, thereby highlights his own unreliability.

276. Bewernick, Hanne. *The Storyteller's Memory Palace: A Method of Interpretation Based on the Function of Memory Systems in Literature—Geoffrey Chaucer, William Langland, Salman Rushdie, Angela Carter, Thomas Pynchon, and Paul Auster*. European University Studies: Anglo-Saxon Language and Literature. New York: Peter Lang, 2010. 253 pp. Comments on *HF* and *TC* in Chapter 2, "Medieval Literature: Geoffrey Chaucer

and William Langland" (pp. 47–86). Compares the three buildings that the dreamer visits in *HF*—the temple in the desert, the palace of Fame, and the twirling house of Rumor—with the paradigms of imaginary buildings suggested in ancient and medieval memory systems. In *TC*, Chaucer uses a familiar topos: he compares the poet to a master builder who first makes a mental plan of an object before manifesting it in a physical sense.

277. Cañadas, Ivan. "The Shadow of Virgil and Augustus on Chaucer's *House of Fame*." *MES* 18.1 (2010): 57–79. Chaucer's depiction of the statues of Virgil and Ovid in *HF* comments ironically on Virgil's political support of Augustus Caesar and on Augustan notions of authority—evidence of Chaucer's skeptical attitude toward literary and political authority.

278. Coley, David K. " 'Withyn a temple ymad of glas': Glazing, Glossing, and Patronage in Chaucer's *House of Fame*." *ChauR* 45 (2010): 59–84. In *HF*, Chaucer's depictions of Venus's temple, the desert surrounding it, and the foundation of Fame's palace offer a vision of vernacular poetry that resembles glass. Like glass, such poetry is produced by transformation and translation of fragmentary materials; like stained-glass windows, it employs the strategies of narrative *amplificatio* while serving both to gloss and to memorialize.

279. Gertz, SunHee Kim. *Visual Power and Fame in René d'Anjou, Geoffrey Chaucer, and the Black Prince*. The New Middle Ages. New York: Palgrave Macmillan, 2010. xx, 227 pp. Gertz reads *HF* in light of modern semiotic theory (Maria Corti, Umberto Eco, and Roman Jakobson) and medieval traditions of *Fürstenspiegel* (mirror of princes), with particular attention to visual signs and codes. Contrasts Chaucer's techniques of "bringing the reader into a writerly position" with Anjou's uses of Arthurian topoi to claim fame for himself and with the performative efforts of Edward of Woodstock, the Black Prince, to claim fame. All three engagements with fame suggest that triggering the "quasi-platonic" idea of fame depends on tapping into popular awareness of common "trace narratives," even though, tellingly, Chaucer eschews familiar Arthurian motifs.

280. Godden, Richard Henry. "Fame's Untimeliness." *DAI* A70.07 (2010): n.p. Uses *HF*—along with Langland's *Piers Plowman*, *St. Erkenwald*, and *Sir Gawain and the Green Knight*—as evidence in a discussion of the medieval understanding of the memorialization process, suggest-

ing that fame "becomes emblematic" of the "ruptures that divide the past from the present."

281. Hernández Pérez, María Beatriz. "Housing Memory in the Late Medieval Literary Tradition: Chaucer's *House of Fame.*" *SELIM* 16 (2009): 103–20. Analyzes *HF* in light of Saint Augustine's understanding of memory, showing how Chaucer proposes a dialogue with history and literature of the past in which the author and the reader are recipients of a common legacy.

282. Olson, Mary. "Speaking Walls: Ekphrasis in Chaucer's *House of Fame.*" *Enarratio* 14 (2010, for 2007): 118–38. Surveys classical uses and techniques of ekphrasis and explores how Chaucer uses it in *HF* to comment on the shifting nature of communication. In descriptions of the House of Fame, the House of Rumor, and especially the House of Glass (Aeneas and Dido), visual renderings transform into different forms of communication; these transformations parallel the Eagle's concern with acoustics.

283. Powrie, Sarah. "Alan of Lille's *Anticlaudianus* as Intertext in Chaucer's *House of Fame.*" *ChauR* 44 (2010): 246–67. In playing on Alan's "theological epic" in *HF*, Chaucer projects a view of readerly interpretation as a key component of literary production, thus challenging the notions that poetry springs solely from inspiration and "that textual meaning could be securely sealed by an author."

284. Zarins, Kimberly. "Writing the Literary Zodiac: Division, Unity, and Power in John Gower's Poetics." *DAI* A70.10 (2010): n.p. As part of a discussion of Gower's trilingualism and his uses of history, science, and literature, Zarins contrasts the treatment of astronomy and literature in *HF* with Gower's "praise of science . . . for its own sake."

See also nos. 52, 58, 68, 84, 103, 129, 135, 167, 262, 289, 290, 291.

The Legend of Good Women

285. Bidard, Josselin. "Ovide, Chaucer, et Gower." In Danielle Buschinger, ed. *Médiévales, 11–12: L'antiquité dans la littérature et les beaux-arts.* Amiens: Presses du Centre d'Études Médiévales, Université de Picardie-Jules Verne, 2010, pp. 302–8. Focuses on Chaucer's uses of Ovid, specifically his use of the legend of Pyramus and Thisbe in *LGW*.

286. Bowers, John M. "Rival Poets: Gower's *Confessio* and Chaucer's *Legend of Good Women.*" In Elisabeth Dutton, with John Hines and R. F.

Yeager, eds. *John Gower, Trilingual Poet: Language, Translation, and Tradition* (*SAC* 34 [2012], no. 122), pp. 276–87. Bowers describes *LGW* as a "work-in-progress" of the 1390s and dates the G-prologue between 1392 and 1394, offering various comments to help justify these datings and explore their implications: *LGWP* emulates Gower's Ricardian prologue to *Confessio*, and Chaucer recurrently follows Gower in choosing plots; the Man of Law is a portrait of Gower; Pandarus is a version of Robert de Vere, friend of Richard II; Chaucer suffered an "inferiority complex" in the face of Gower's trilingualism and the success of *Piers Plowman* and the *Pearl*-poet; Gower was the cynosure of Lancastrian literary promotion in the early fifteenth century.

287. Fradenburg, L. O. Aranye. "Beauty and Boredom in *The Legend of Good Women*." *Exemplaria* 22 (2010): 65–83. Fradenburg begins with a brief psychoanalytic view of the aesthetic of enjoyment as the communication of affect. The article explores the image of Alceste/daisy in terms of psychological and philosophical intersubjectivity. The individual stories, however, are repetitive and deadening in a way that forecloses intersubjectivity and appreciation of beauty. Exchange, conceived here as the feminine, is oppressive, a "refusal of life."

288. Marvin, Julia. "The Suicide of the *Legend of Good Women*." In Robert Epstein and William Robins, eds. *Sacred and Profane in Chaucer and Late Medieval Literature: Essays in Honour of John V. Fleming* (*SAC* 34 [2012], no. 123), pp. 113–28. Marvin traces a pattern of concern with literary interpretation in *LGWP-F* and exemplifies that the pattern is also evident in "some of the legends themselves," particularly Dido's. The F-prologue and the tale assert bookish authority, question it, reject it, and then affirm the difficulty of resolving such contradictions.

289. Phillips, Helen. "Chaucer's Love Visions." In Corinne Saunders, ed. *A Companion to Medieval Poetry* (*SAC* 34 [2012], no. 157), pp. 414–34. Describes the nature and legacy of the dream-vision genre and assesses Chaucer's four dream poems (*BD*, *HF*, *PF*, and *LGW*), exploring the dynamics of courtliness and learning, experience and authority, endings and implications, and—especially—masculine and feminine. Comments on each of Chaucer's dream visions and reads *LGW* as an extension of his concerns in other poems, assessing details of his legends of Cleopatra, Dido, Philomela, Phyllis, and Hypermnestra.

290. Scott, Joanna. "Betraying Origins: The Many Faces of Aeneas in Medieval English Literature." *LATCH* 3 (2010): 64–84. In *HF*, Aeneas is a "possible love-traitor," while in *LGW* the "condemnation" is

much clearer. In the *Laud Troy Book*, he is a political traitor who is never presented as the founder of Rome. Such depictions of Aeneas reflect how the "threat—or promise—of treason was always lurking" in late medieval English consciousness.

291. Spearing, A. C. "Dream Poems." In Susanna Fein and David Raybin, eds. *Chaucer: Contemporary Approaches* (*SAC* 34 [2012], no. 125), pp. 169–78. Although Chaucer scholarship generally exaggerates the poet's learning, it seems to have missed his use of Huon de Méri's *Tornoiemenz* in *LGWP*. Scholarship also overemphasizes the visionary features of Chaucer's dream poems while underestimating the value of treating them as natural dreams, ripe with the "delicious unpredictability of their forward movement" that obviates thematic fatalism. Spearing invites explorations of dream poetry as a subgenre of the *dit*, expressive of life experienced in the first person.

292. Urban, Misty, with a foreword by Andrew Galloway. *Monstrous Women in Middle English Romance: Representations of Mysterious Female Power*. Lewiston, N.Y.: Edwin Mellen Press, 2010. ix, 277 pp. Explores treatments of monstrous women in Middle English romance, particularly Melusine, Medea, and Constance. Argues that Chaucer adapts the romance to critique the suffering, violent treatment, and "liminality" of women within the genre. Depicting Medea and Constance as neither monstrous nor violent and focusing on the violence or betrayal committed against them, Chaucer shows that the "good" woman of medieval romance is forced into one dimension and can exist only as a passive vessel acted upon by those around her.

See also nos. 52, 72, 81, 129, 262, 304.

The Parliament of Fowls

293. Klassen, Norm. "Suffering in the Service of Venus: The Sacred, the Sublime, and Chaucerian Joy in the Middle Part of the *Parliament of Fowls*." In Holly Faith Nelson, Lynn R. Szabo, and Jens Zimmermann, eds. *Through a Glass Darkly: Suffering, the Sacred, and the Sublime in Literature and Theory*. [Waterloo, Ont.]: Wilfrid Laurier University Press, 2010, pp. 39–53. Without a shift in tone, Chaucer both appreciates and censures the fruitless love depicted in the Temple of Venus in *PF*. By fusing "joy and judgment," he evokes paradoxically the "deeper joy" of beauty. Revised version of "Surprised by Joy: Chaucer's Tonal

Achievement in *Parliament of Fowls*, 92–294." In Michel Desjardins and Harold Remus, eds. *Tradition and Formation: Claiming an Inheritance: Essays in Honour of Peter C. Erb*. Kitchener, Ont.: Pandora Press, 2008, pp. 213–28.

294. Musgrave, Thea. *Sing to Celebrate Summer (2010): For Tenor, Harp, and Optional Audience Participation*. Commissioned by the Buck Hill–Skytop Music Festival. London: Novello, [2010]. 11pp. Musical score for a normalized-spelling version of the closing song of *PF* (lines 680–92). Performance notes suggest harp effects and ways to involve audience participation.

295. Quinn, William. "Chaucer's *Parliament of Fowls* and His Pre-Text of Narration." In Gerd Bayer and Ebbe Klitgård, eds. *Narrative Developments from Chaucer to Defoe* (*SAC* 34 [2012], no. 113), pp. 79–96. Considers how editorial and critical assumptions have retroactively made the manuscript records of *PF* conform to postprint expectations about narrative poetry.

See also nos. 72, 129, 132, 135, 173, 262, 289, 291.

The Romaunt of the Rose

296. Iyeiri, Yoko. "Negation in Fragments A, B, and C of the Hunter Manuscript of *The Romaunt of the Rose*." In Merja Kytö, John Scahill, and Harumi Tanabe, eds. *Language Change and Variation from Old English to Late Modern English: A Festschrift for Minoji Akimoto*. New York: Peter Lang, 2010, pp. 79–101. Iyeiri analyzes the "various forms of negation" in the fragments of *Rom*, commenting on their implications for attribution. Fragment C is more like B than like the Chaucerian A in many of its forms of negation; hence, it is unlikely to be by Chaucer.

See also nos. 24, 56.

Troilus and Criseyde

297. Arner, Timothy D. "Chaucer's Second Hector: The Triumphs of Diomede and the Possibility of Epic in *Troilus and Criseyde*." *MÆ* 79.1 (2010): 68–89. In *TC*, Diomede, rather than Troilus, functions as the second Hector, and Diomede is the only hero who escapes the cycle of Theban and Trojan violence. At a dangerous time in English history,

Chaucer desires a healing ideology for England; his turn from epic and history to romance parallels problems with political discourse in the Ricardian era.

298. Beal, Rebecca S. "What Chaucer Did to an *Orazion* in the *Filostrato*: Calkas's Speech as Deliberative Oratory." *ChauR* 44 (2010): 440–60. Rubrics in *Filostrato* manuscripts label Calkas's bid to trade a prisoner for his daughter as an "oratory." Chaucer's version of the speech fulfills the formal requirements of a speech arguing "for a particular course of action" and in so doing demonstrates that a rhetorician, unlike a prophet, "can revise the past as he acts to change the future."

299. Blamires, Alcuin. "Chaucer's *Troilus and Criseyde*." In Corinne Saunders, ed. *A Companion to Medieval Poetry* (*SAC* 34 [2012], no. 157), pp. 335–51. Blamires introduces *TC* as Chaucer's "longest finished poem," commenting on sources, fusion of genres, suppleness of verse form and diction, the characters' sympathies, and the poem's "emotional trajectory."

300. Boynton, Owen. "The *Trouthe/Routhe* Rhyme in Chaucer's *Troilus and Criseyde*." *ChauR* 45 (2010): 222–39. The "complex" *trouthe/routhe* rhyme tracks the stages in the lovers' relationship: from its beginnings, when Troilus's *trouthe* is pledged for Criseyde's *routhe*; to its consummation, when mutual compassion assures reciprocal honesty and fidelity; to its breakup, when the two rhyme words—along with Criseyde—are put back into circulation in "the world of intrigue, bargaining, and manipulation."

301. Butterfield, Ardis. "National Histories." In Brian Cummings and James Simpson, eds. *Cultural Reformations: Medieval and Renaissance in Literary History* (*SAC* 34 [2012], no. 121), pp. 33–54. Comments on Chaucer's address to his book at the end of *TC* as an example of the poet's awareness of linguistic and cultural diversity.

302. Cartlidge, Neil. "Criseyde's Absent Friends." *ChauR* 44 (2010): 227–45. Chaucer's evocation of contrasting senses of *frend* sharpens his depiction of Criseyde's precarious state in Troy. Lacking advisers, and thus dangerously dependent on Pandarus and Troilus, she also belongs to a network of relationships devoted solely to "an ideal of sociability" and therefore possesses a dangerous independence.

303. ———. "Narrative and Gossip in Chaucer's *Troilus and Criseyde*." In Gerd Bayer and Ebbe Klitgård, eds. *Narrative Developments from Chaucer to Defoe* (*SAC* 34 [2012], no. 113), pp. 221–34. Cartlidge

investigates gossip as mundane, trivial speech in *TC*, in contrast to the more dangerous tradition of damaging speech invoked by Pandarus.

304. Coleman, Joyce. "Where Chaucer Got His Pulpit: Audience and Intervisuality in the *Troilus and Criseyde* Frontispiece." *SAC* 32 (2010): 103–28. 8 b&w illus. Argues that the frontispiece to *TC* in Cambridge, Corpus Christi College 61, was modeled on the scene in which Genius addresses Nature in the *Roman de la Rose*. Focuses on the "lower register" of the frontispiece, arguing that it depicts Chaucer as a Lancastrian version of "Richard's poet," situating him within the "late medieval culture of love." The scene is appropriate to the concerns with sex and love in *TC* and consistent with the depiction of Richard as the God of Love in *LGWP*.

305. Cook, Alexander. " 'O swete harm so queynte': Loving Pagan Antiquity in *Troilus and Criseyde* and the *Knight's Tale*." *ES* 91 (2010): 26–41. In *TC* and *KnT*, Chaucer "revises Augustinian and Boethian formulations of *contemptus mundi*, pointing out that any ethical system which seeks to address the topic of earthly desires must also address the human subject's endless appetite for desire as such." The article also deals with risqué aspects of medieval interest in pagan lore.

306. Fumo, Jamie C. "The Ends of Love: (Meta)physical Desire in Chaucer's *Troilus and Criseyde*." In Robert Epstein and William Robins, eds. *Sacred and Profane in Chaucer and Late Medieval Literature: Essays in Honour of John V. Fleming* (*SAC* 34 [2012], no. 123), pp. 68–90. Fumo reads Criseyde as someone "who does not believe in love" and perhaps "does not believe at all," a representation of fourteenth-century epistemological concerns "reanimated in the context of a Petrarchan psychology of enamourment." Criseyde's comments on love, in contrast to Troilus's, demonstrate that her view is essentially skeptical, perhaps atheistic.

307. Ganim, John. "Cosmopolitanism and Medievalism." *Exemplaria* 22 (2010): 5–27. Explores international cultural exchange and openness in the Middle Ages, commenting on scenarios of medieval cosmopolitanism in three modern fictions: Youssef Chahine's film *Destiny*, Tariq Ali's novel *Shadows of the Pomegranate Tree*, and Milorad Pavić's metafictional *Dictionary of the Khazars*. Finding both cosmopolitanism and anti-cosmopolitanism in *TC*, Ganim distinguishes between cosmopolitanism and worldliness in the character of Pandarus. He also comments on works by John Gower and on *Mandeville's Travels*.

308. Garrison, John. "One Mind, One Heart, One Purse: Integrat-

ing Friendship Traditions and the Case of *Troilus and Criseyde.*" *M&H* 36 (2010): 25–47. The friendship between Troilus and Pandarus synthesizes Cicero's "pure friendship" with "potential for mutual gain," emblematized in Troilus's offer to procure any woman Pandarus wants. Portraying friendship in economic terms, *TC* reveals more *cupiditas* than *caritas*. Garrison includes evidence from Aelred's *De spirituali amicitia* and Alfonsi's *Disciplina clericalis*.

309. Helmbold, Anita. *Understanding the Manuscript Frontispiece to Corpus Christi College MS 61: The Political Landscape of a Lancastrian Portrait.* Lewiston, N.Y.: Edwin Mellen Press, 2010. v, 450 pp. Considers the frontispiece to *TC* found in Corpus Christi College MS 61 (which depicts Chaucer addressing a court audience, particularly the court of Richard II). The frontispiece shows that literature was delivered orally (by "prelection") and received aurally in Chaucer's time and much later. Helmbold assesses in this light modern misreadings of Chaucer as a poet to be read silently, Lydgate's aurality, the status of *TC* and the manuscript in the court of Henry V, and the "persistence" of aurality in literary reception through the nineteenth century.

310. Ingham, Patricia Clare. "Chaucer's Haunted Aesthetics: Mimesis and Trauma in *Troilus and Criseyde.*" *CE* 72.3 (2010): 226–47. Ingham uses Freud's meditations on Tasso's knight Tancred as a model for how literary texts mediate between the repetitive and the representational aspects of trauma. Chaucer's *TC* resonates with trauma in the work's historical context, in the abandonment of Criseyde by Calchas and the trafficking of women, and in its depiction of Pandarus's transfer of "wo" to Troilus. The allusions to Procne and Philomela in the poem problematize the voicing of trauma.

311. Knowles, James Robert. "Love, Labor, Liturgy: Languages of Service in Late Medieval England." *DAI* A70.12 (2010): n.p. Knowles views deployments of the medieval concept of "service" (which encompassed an elaborate network of interpersonal and institutional relationships) in Langland, Julian of Norwich, and *TC*.

312. Mieszkowski, Gretchen. "Chaucerian Comedy: *Troilus and Criseyde.*" In Albrecht Classen, ed. *Laughter in the Middle Ages and Early Modern Times: Epistemology of a Fundamental Human Behavior, Its Meaning, and Consequences.* Fundamentals of Medieval and Early Modern Culture, no. 5. Berlin and New York: Walter de Gruyter, 2010, pp. 457–80. Mieszkowski contrasts the situational comedy of *TC* and the structural comedic techniques of *MilT*, *MerT*, and *SumT*. Chaucer generates "all

the comedy" of *TC* by means of Pandarus, whose comic counterpoint compels readers to reconceptualize love without obviating the romantic view. In the poem, love is both comic and transcendent.

313. Palmer, James M. "When *Remedia Amoris* Fails: Chaucer's Literary-Medical Exploration of Determinism, Materialism, and Free Will in *Troilus and Criseyde*." In Marcelline Block and Angela Laflen, eds. *Gender Scripts in Medicine and Narrative*. Newcastle upon Tyne: Cambridge Scholars, 2010, pp. 292–312. Investigates Pandarus's attempts to cure Troilus's lovesickness, physically and psychologically, in *TC*. Pandarus's failure to effect a cure indicates that Chaucer rejects determinism and endorses free will, showing that Christian morals are incompatible with materialist cures for lovesickness.

314. Patterson, Lee. "Genre and Source in *Troilus and Criseyde*." In Lee Patterson. *Acts of Recognition: Essays on Medieval Culture* (*SAC* 34 [2012], no. 147), pp. 198–214. Considers Chaucer's understanding of "tragedy" in *Bo*, *MkT*, and *TC*, tracing this understanding to Dante's use of the term in his *Inferno*, where it is affiliated with history. In *TC*, Chaucer chose to emulate Boccaccio's *Filostrato* because doing so allowed him to explain an "original catastrophe [the fall of Troy] by exploring the origins of a catastrophic love affair." Chaucer found, however, that such an explanation cannot be sustained.

315. Robins, William. "Troilus in the Gutter." In Robert Epstein and William Robins, eds. *Sacred and Profane in Chaucer and Late Medieval Literature: Essays in Honour of John V. Fleming* (*SAC* 34 [2012], no. 123), pp. 91–112. Reads "goter, by a pryve wente" (*TC* 3.787) literally—a passageway that passes a latrine—and comments on the poetic functions of Troilus's approaching Criseyde's bedroom by this means. The passage characterizes Pandarus's house as up to date and aligns Troilus with sexual idolatry.

See also nos. 32, 54, 65, 66, 69, 71, 73, 76, 89, 95, 97, 100, 110, 128, 129, 132, 140, 153, 156, 166, 258, 276, 286.

Lyrics and Short Poems

316. Johanson, Paula. *Early British Poetry: "Words That Burn."* Poetry Rocks! Series. Berkeley Heights, N.J.: Enslow, 2010. 160 pp. Color illus. Introductory commentary on British poetry from Anglo-Saxon poetry to the works of John Keats, focusing on canonical works and

writers. Chapter 2 (pp. 21–30) summarizes Chaucer's life and describes his iambic meter, explicating *Truth* (original and translation) and commenting on *Adam* and *MercB*.

See also nos. 132, 156, 294.

An ABC

See no. 240.

Adam Scriveyn

See no. 316.

A Complaint to His Lady

See no. 156.

The Complaint of Chaucer to His Purse

317. Matthews, David. *Writing to the King: Nation, Kingship, and Literature in England, 1250–1350*. Cambridge Studies in Medieval Literature, no. 77. Cambridge: Cambridge University Press, 2010. xv, 221 pp. Matthews explores the English rhetorical device of writing about political topics as if the author were writing directly to the king, even though these works were intended for a wider audience. This device flourished in the late thirteenth and early fourteenth centuries, so it predates Chaucer. However, Chaucer, Gower, and others explored this literary strategy during the reign of Richard II in works such as Chaucer's *Purse*.

318. Scattergood, John. *Occasions for Writing: Essays on Medieval and Renaissance Literature, Politics, and Society*. Portland, Ore.: Four Courts Press, 2010. 272 pp. 14 b&w figs. Twelve essays by Scattergood, five here published for the first time. Chaucer is cited in several of the reprinted essays, one of which is an extended analysis of *Purse*: "London and Money: Chaucer's *Complaint to His Purse*" (see *SAC* 30 [2008], no. 301).

See also nos. 151, 156.

The Complaint of Mars

See nos. 156, 240.

The Complaint of Venus

See no. 156.

The Complaint unto Pity

See nos. 151, 156.

Lak of Stedfastnesse

See no. 189.

Merciles Beaute

See no. 316.

Truth

See nos. 73, 74, 91, 316.

Chaucerian Apocrypha

319. Marshall, Simone Celine. *The Anonymous Text: The 500-Year History of "The Assembly of Ladies."* New York: Peter Lang, 2011. vii, 211 pp. Questions why *The Assembly of Ladies* has been in print for so long and explores the role of its anonymity in its publishing history. Addresses its attribution to Chaucer, affiliations with the corpus of his works, and surmises about female authorship of *The Assembly*.

320. Murphy, Donna N. *"The Cobbler of Canterbury* and Robert Greene." *N&Q* 255 (2010): 349–52. Given the numerous verbal parallels between Greene's work and *The Cobbler of Canterbury* (an avowed imitation of *CT*, published anonymously in 1590), it would seem that Greene "fibbed" when, in a separate publication, he "informed the spirits of Geffrey Chaucer and John Gower" that he was not the author of *The Cobbler of Canterbury*.

321. Ortego, James N., II. "Seeking the Medieval in Shakespeare: The Order of the Garter and the Topos of Derisive Chivalry." *FCS* 35 (2010): 80–104. Reviews several late medieval texts to demonstrate the "devolution of knighthood" before Shakespeare's time. Comments on the *GP* description of the Knight, on *MerT*, and on *Th*.

322. Spencer, Alice. "'To walke aboute the mase, in certeynte, / As a woman that nothing rought': The Maze Motif and Feminine Imagination in *The Assembly of Ladies*." In Kathleen A. Bishop, ed. *Standing in the Shadow of the Master? Chaucerian Influences and Interpretations* (*SAC* 34 [2012], no. 114), pp. 204–23. The anonymous author of *The Assembly of Ladies* counterdefines herself against a clearly Chaucerian courtly tradition by allying herself with a distinctly feminine textuality that is opposed to a traditional masculine hermeneutics.

323. Symons, Dana. "Not Just 'Chaucer's England' Anymore: Reassessing John Clanvowe's *Boke of Cupide*." In Kathleen A. Bishop, ed. *Standing in the Shadow of the Master? Chaucerian Influences and Interpretations* (*SAC* 34 [2012], no. 114), pp. 123–59. Also named *The Cuckoo and the Nightingale*, *Boke of Cupide* was once considered one of Chaucer's great poems until it fell into obscurity when it was removed from the canon. The essay considers stylistic similarities to Chaucer's dream visions, the implications of the work's critical history, and its parallels with the themes of courtly language, use of the vernacular, and truth telling in *SqT*.

See also nos. 11, 39, 62, 67, 234, 240.

Book Reviews

324. Alexander, Michael. *Medievalism: The Middle Ages in Modern England* (*SAC* 31 [2009], no. 48). Rev. Julie Pridmore, *JBSt* 49 (2010): 681–82.

325. Allen, Valerie. *On Farting: Language and Laughter in the Middle Ages* (*SAC* 33 [2011], no. 130). Rev. Bettina Bildhauer, *SAC* 32 (2010): 386–89.

326. Andrew, Malcolm. *The Palgrave Literary Dictionary of Chaucer* (*SAC* 30 [2008], no. 3). Rev. Julia Boffey, *N&Q* 255 (2010): 123–24.

327. Ashton, Gail, and Louise Sylvester, eds. *Teaching Chaucer* (*SAC* 31 [2009], no. 82). Rev. Stephen F. Evans, *SMART* 17.2 (2010): 149–59.

328. Astell, Ann W., and J. A. Jackson, eds. *Levinas and Medieval Literature: The "Difficult Reading" of English and Rabbinic Texts* (*SAC* 33 [2011], no. 59). Rev. David Williams, *JEGP* 109 (2010): 515–17.

329. Barrington, Candace. *American Chaucers* (*SAC* 31 [2009], no. 50). Rev. Thomas Prendergast, *SAC* 32 (2010): 393–95.

330. Blamires, Alcuin. *Chaucer, Ethics, and Gender* (*SAC* 30 [2008], no. 105). Rev. Andrew James Johnston, *Anglia* 127 (2010): 336–41.

331. Bliss, Jane. *Naming and Namelessness in Medieval Romance* (*SAC* 32 [2010], no. 99). Rev. Laurence de Looze, *JEGP* 109 (2010): 397–99.

332. Bowers, John M. *Chaucer and Langland: The Antagonistic Tradition* (*SAC* 31 [2009], no. 37). Rev. Matthew Giancarlo, *Speculum* 84 (2009): 404–5; Andrew James Johnston, *Anglia* 127 (2010): 336–41.

333. Breen, Katharine. *Imagining an English Reading Public, 1150–1400* (*SAC* 34 [2012], no. 272). Rev. Mary C. Flannery, *TLS*, March 4, 2011, pp. 26–27.

334. Burrow, J. A. *The Poetry of Praise* (*SAC* 32 [2010], no. 63). Rev. Jim Rhodes, *Speculum* 84 (2009): 1017–19.

335. Butterfield, Ardis. *The Familiar Enemy: Chaucer, Language, and Nation in the Hundred Years War* (*SAC* 33 [2011], no. 51). Rev. Joanna Bellis, *Marginalia* 11 (2010): 64–66; Helen Cooper, *London Review of Books*, October 7, 2010, pp. 9–11; David A. Fein, *French Studies* 64 (2010): 476–77; Ad Putter, *TLS*, July 9, 2010, p. 11.

336. Cannon, Christopher. *Middle English Literature: A Cultural History* (*SAC* 32 [2010], no. 105). Rev. Robert M. Stein, *Speculum* 85 (2010): 654–55.

337. Cole, Andrew. *Literature and Heresy in the Age of Chaucer* (*SAC* 32 [2010], no. 107). Rev. Henry Ansgar Kelly, *Speculum* 85 (2010): 123–24; Derrick Pitard, *JEGP* 109 (2010): 401–3.

338. Condren, Edward L. *Chaucer from Prentice to Poet: The Metaphor of Love in Dream Visions and "Troilus and Criseyde"* (*SAC* 32 [2010], no. 299). Rev. Michael Foster, *JEGP* 109 (2010): 130–32; Alexander Gabrivsky, *Marginalia* 11 (2010): 67–68; Kathryn McKinley, *Speculum* 85 (2010): 143–45; A. V. C. Schmidt, *MÆ* 79.2 (2010): 325–27.

339. Connolly, Margaret, and Linne R. Mooney, eds. *Design and Distribution of Late Medieval Manuscripts in England* (*SAC* 32 [2010], no. 32). Rev. Michael Calabrese, *TMR* 10.03.07, n.p.; Michael P. Kuczynski, *JEGP* 109 (2010): 546–48; Oliver Pickering, *SAC* 32 (2010): 402–5.

340. Crépin, André, et al., trans., with collaboration by Ann Wéry.

Geoffrey Chaucer: "Les contes de Canterbury" et autres œuvres (*SAC* 34 [2012], no. 12). Rev. Leo Carruthers, *La quinzaine littéraire* 1017 (2010): 17–18.

341. Dane, Joseph A. *Abstractions of Evidence in the Study of Manuscripts and Early Printed Books* (*SAC* 33 [2011], no. 188). Rev. Orietta Da Rold, *SAC* 32 (2010): 405–8; Germaine Warkentin, *Library*, 7th ser., 11 (2010): 481–83.

342. Desmond, Marilynn. *Ovid's Art and the Wife of Bath: The Ethics of Erotic Violence* (*SAC* 30 [2008], no. 199). Rev. John M. Fyler, *MP* 107 (2010): E20–E23.

343. Driver, Martha W., and Sid Ray, eds. *Shakespeare and the Middle Ages: Essays on the Performance and Adaptation of the Plays with Medieval Sources or Settings* (*SAC* 33 [2011], no. 39). Rev. Andrew B. R. Elliott, *Arthuriana* 20.4 (2010): 103–4; Susan C. Frye, *Arthuriana* 20.4 (2010): 104–5.

344. Echard, Siân. *Printing the Middle Ages* (*SAC* 32 [2010], no. 20). Rev. Helen Brookman, *Marginalia* 11 (2010): 70–72; David Matthews, *Arthuriana* 20.2 (2010): 140–41; Scott Swara, *PBSA* 104 (2010): 383–86.

345. Fyler, John M. *Language and the Declining World in Chaucer, Dante, and Jean de Meun* (*SAC* 31 [2009], no. 101). Rev. Stephen G. Nichols, *CLS* 47.1 (2010): 120–24.

346. Galloway, Andrew, and R. F. Yeager, eds. *Through a Classical Eye: Transcultural and Transhistorical Visions in Medieval English, Italian, and Latin Literature in Honour of Winthrop Wetherbee* (*SAC* 33 [2011], no. 69). Rev. Alessandra Petrina, *TMR* 10.03.05, n.p.; John O. Ward, *SAC* 32 (2010): 408–11.

347. Giancarlo, Matthew. *Parliament and Literature in Late Medieval England* (*SAC* 31 [2009], no. 103). Rev. Ralph Hanna, *Speculum* 85 (2010): 143–45.

348. Goodall, Peter, ed. *Chaucer's "Monk's Tale" and "Nun's Priest's Tale": An Annotated Bibliography, 1900–2000* (*SAC* 33 [2011], no. 3). Rev. Dosia Reichardt, *Parergon* 27.2 (2010): 279–80; Amanda Walling, *TMR* 10.02.04, n.p.

349. Gray, Douglas. *Later Medieval English Literature* (*SAC* 32 [2010], no. 53). Rev. Derek Pearsall, *JEGP* 109 (2010): 244–46.

350. Gust, Geoffrey W. *Constructing Chaucer: Author and Autofiction in the Critical Tradition* (*SAC* 33 [2011], no. 73). Rev. Steve Ellis, *SAC* 32 (2010): 411–14.

351. Hagedorn, Suzanne C. *Abandoned Women: Rewriting the Classics*

in Dante, Boccaccio, and Chaucer (*SAC* 28 [2006], no. 35). Rev. Rebeca Cubas Peña, *SELIM* 13 (2005): 269–74.

352. Hazell, Dinah. *Poverty in Late Middle English Literature* (*SAC* 33 [2011], no. 75). Rev. Elizabeth Harper, *TMR* 10.05.16, n.p.

353. Heffernan, Carol Falvo. *Comedy in Chaucer and Boccaccio* (*SAC* 33 [2011], no. 25). Rev. K. P. Clarke, *RES* 61 (2010): 631–32; Robert R. Edwards, *Speculum* 85 (2010): 970–71; William T. Rossiter, *SAC* 32 (2010): 414–17.

354. Heyworth, Gregory. *Desiring Bodies: Ovidian Romance and the Cult of Form* (*SAC* 33 [2011], no. 110). Rev. Michael Calabrese, *SAC* 32 (2010): 417–20; Diana Glenn, *Parergon* 27.2 (2010): 133–35; Heather Sottong, *Comitatus* 41 (2010): 261–64.

355. Hill, T. E. *"She, This in Blak": Vision, Truth, and Will in Geoffrey Chaucer's "Troilus and Criseyde"* (*SAC* 30 [2008], no. 281). Rev. Kathryn L. Lynch, *Speculum* 84 (2009): 731–33; Tison Pugh, *SAC* 32 (2010): 424–26.

356. Holton, Amanda. *The Sources of Chaucer's Poetics* (*SAC* 32 [2010], no. 68). Rev. John M. Ganim, *TMR* 10.04.06, n.p.

357. Howes, Laura L., ed. *Place, Space, and Landscape in Medieval Narrative* (*SAC* 31 [2009], no. 112). Rev. Robert W. Barrett Jr., *SAC* 32 (2010): 429–32.

358. Johnston, Andrew James. *Performing the Middle Ages from "Beowulf" to "Othello"* (*SAC* 32 [2010], no. 179). Rev. Michael R. Near, *JEGP* 109 (2010): 413–15; Margaret Pappano, *SAC* 32 (2010): 432–35; Edward Wheatley, *Speculum* 85 (2010): 692–94.

359. Julius, Anthony. *Trials of the Diaspora: A History of Anti-Semitism in England* (*SAC* 34 [2012], no. 250). Rev. James Shapiro, http://www.f-t.com [*Financial Times*], February 20, 2010, n.p.

360. Keith, Alison, and Stephen Rupp, eds. *Metamorphosis: The Changing Face of Ovid in Medieval and Early Modern Europe* (*SAC* 31 [2009], no. 208). Rev. Luciana Cuppo, *SCJ* 61 (2010): 539–41; Craig Kallendorf, *JEGP* 109 (2010): 124–25.

361. Kelen, Sarah A. *Langland's Early Modern Identities* (*SAC* 34 [2012], no. 11). Rev. Lawrence Warner, *SAC* 32 (2010): 435–38.

362. Keller, Wolfram R. *Selves and Nations: The Troy Story from Sicily to England in the Middle Ages* (*SAC* 32 [2010], no. 310). Rev. C. David Benson, *Speculum* 85 (2010): 154–55.

363. Knapp, Peggy A. *Chaucerian Aesthetics* (*SAC* 32 [2010], no.

121). Rev. Warren Ginsberg, *Speculum* 84 (2009): 1070–72; Maura Nolan, *SAC* 32 (2010): 438–41.

364. Kolve, V. A. *Telling Images: Chaucer and the Imagery of Narrative II* (*SAC* 33 [2011], no. 142). Rev. Robert Boenig, *M&H* 36 (2010): 166–69; Richard K. Emmerson, *SAC* 32 (2010): 441–45; John M. Ganim, *RES* 61 (2010): 460–62.

365. Kowaleski, Maryanne, and P. J. P. Goldberg, eds. *Medieval Domesticity: Home, Housing, and Household in Medieval England* (*SAC* 33 [2011], no. 79). Rev. Ruth Mazo Karras, *JBSt* 49 (2010): 145–47; Cristina Stancioiu, *Comitatus* 41 (2010): 273–76.

366. Kuskin, William. *Symbolic Caxton: Literary Culture and Print Capitalism* (*SAC* 32 [2010], no. 24). Rev. Julia Boffey, *Speculum* 85 (2010): 698–99.

367. Lavezzo, Kathy. *Angels on the Edge of the World: Geography, Literature, and the English Community, 1000–1534* (*SAC* 30 [2008], no. 192). Rev. Peter Larkin, *MP* 107 (2009): 167–72.

368. Léglu, Catherine E., and Stephen J. Milner, eds. *The Erotics of Consolation: Desire and Distance in the Late Middle Ages* (*SAC* 32 [2010], no. 124). Rev. George McClure, *MLR* 105 (2010): 502–4; L. M. C. Westin, *SCJ* 61 (2010): 940–41.

369. Lightsey, Scott. *Manmade Marvels in Medieval Culture and Literature* (*SAC* 31 [2009], no. 118). Rev. Sarah Stanbury, *Speculum* 84 (2009): 1076–78.

370. Lipton, Emma. *Affections of the Mind: The Politics of Sacramental Marriage in Late Medieval English Literature* (*SAC* 31 [2009], no. 240). Rev. Rebecca Krug, *Speculum* 84 (2009): 180–81.

371. Little, Katherine C. *Confession and Resistance: Defining the Self in Late Medieval England* (*SAC* 30 [2008], no. 245). Rev. Sarah Stanbury, *MP* 107 (2009): 177–80.

372. Mann, Jill. *From Aesop to Reynard: Beast Literature in Medieval Britain* (*SAC* 33 [2011], no. 82). Rev. Susan Crane, *SAC* 32 (2010): 445–48; Luuk Houwen, *TMR* 10.09.20, n.p.; James Wade, *TLS*, March 26, 2010, pp. 30–31.

373. Masciandaro, Nicola. *The Voice of the Hammer: The Meaning of Work in Middle English Literature* (*SAC* 31 [2009], no. 121). Rev. Andrew Cole, *Speculum* 84 (2009): 469–71; Gregory M. Sadlek, *MP* 108 (2010): E85–E90.

374. McCormack, Frances. *Chaucer and the Culture of Dissent: The Lollard Context and Subtext of the "Parson's Tale"* (*SAC* 31 [2009], no. 274).

Rev. Richard Newhauser, *JEGP* 109 (2010): 132–34; Derrick Pitard, *Speculum* 84 (2009): 1085–87.

375. McMullan, Gordon, and David Matthews, eds. *Reading the Medieval in Early Modern England* (*SAC* 31 [2009], no. 56). Rev. Theresa Tinkle, *Speculum* 84 (2009): 471–73.

376. Mieszkowski, Gretchen. *Medieval Go-Betweens and Chaucer's Pandarus* (*SAC* 30 [2008], no. 285). Rev. Peter G. Beidler, *MP* 107 (2010): E13–E17.

377. Minnis, Alastair. *Fallible Authors: Chaucer's Pardoner and Wife of Bath* (*SAC* 32 [2010], no. 247). Rev. Neil Cartlidge, *MÆ* 79.1 (2010): 138–39; David Lawton, *Speculum* 84 (2009): 758–60; Stephen R. Reimer, *SHARP News* 19.4 (2010): 8–9.

378. ———. *Translations of Authority in Medieval English Literature: Valuing the Vernacular* (*SAC* 33 [2011], no. 154). Rev. Mishtooni Bose, *SAC* 32 (2010): 451–54; James Simpson, *N&Q* 255 (2010): 578–80.

379. Morrison, Susan Signe. *Excrement in the Late Middle Ages: Sacred Filth and Chaucer's Fecopoetics* (*SAC* 32 [2010], no. 152). Rev. Bettina Bildhauer, *SAC* 32 (2010): 386–89; Michael Calabrese, *Speculum* 85 (2010): 440–41.

380. Neal, Derek G. *The Masculine Self in Late Medieval England* (*SAC* 32 [2010], no. 129). Rev. Christopher Fletcher, *EHR* 125 (2010): 970–71; Katherine J. Lewis, *Speculum* 85 (2010): 1005–6; Tison Pugh, *SCJ* 61 (2010): 1267–68.

381. Norris, Ralph. *Malory's Library: The Sources of the "Morte Darthur"* (*SAC* 32 [2010], no. 58). Rev. Edward Donald Kennedy, *JEGP* 109 (2010): 251–53.

382. O'Neill, Michael, ed. *The Cambridge History of English Poetry* (*SAC* 34 [2012], no. 145). Rev. Clive Wilmer, *TLS*, March 11, 2011, pp. 8–9.

383. Perry, Curtis, and John Watkins, eds. *Shakespeare and the Middle Ages* (*SAC* 33 [2011], no. 34). Rev. Elizabeth Scala, *TMR* 10.05.21, n.p.

384. Pugh, Tison. *Sexuality and Its Queer Discontents in Middle English Literature* (*SAC* 32 [2010], no. 132). Rev. Nicole Nolan Sidhu, *Speculum* 85 (2010): 186–87; Diane Watt, *GLQ: A Journal of Lesbian and Gay Studies* 16 (2010): 451–64.

385. ———, and Marcia Smith Marzec, eds. *Men and Masculinities in Chaucer's "Troilus and Criseyde"* (*SAC* 32 [2010], no. 319). Rev. Maud Burnett McInerney, *JEGP* 109 (2010): 405–7.

386. Purdie, Rhiannon. *Anglicising Romance: Tail-Rhyme and Genre in*

Medieval English Literature (*SAC* 32 [2010], no. 265). Rev. Mark C. Amodio, *Speculum* 85 (2010): 1014–15.

387. Quinn, Esther Casier. *Geoffrey Chaucer and the Poetics of Disguise* (*SAC* 32 [2010], no. 133). Rev. K. P. Clarke, *SAC* 32 (2010): 454–57; David Raybin, *Speculum* 84 (2009): 766–68.

388. Radulescu, Raluca L., and Cory James Rushton, eds. *A Companion to Medieval Popular Romance* (*SAC* 33 [2011], no. 165). Rev. Laura Ashe, *SAC* 32 (2010): 457–59; Amanda Hopkins, *Arthuriana* 20.4 (2010): 106–7; David Klausner, *TMR* 10.03.22, n.p.

389. Rayner, Samantha. *Images of Kingship in Chaucer and His Ricardian Contemporaries* (*SAC* 32 [2010], no. 135). Rev. María Bullón-Fernández, *Speculum* 85 (2010): 187–89; Shannon Gayk, *Journal of Medieval Religious Cultures* 36 (2010): 259–62; Elliot Kendall, *SAC* 32 (2010): 460–62.

390. Rice, Nicole R. *Lay Piety and Religious Discipline in Middle English Literature* (*SAC* 32 [2010], no. 252). Rev. Virginia Blanton, *Speculum* 85 (2010): 1017–19; Mary C. Erler, *SAC* 32 (2010): 462–65.

391. Rigby, Stephen H., ed. *A Companion to Britain in the Later Middle Ages* (*SAC* 33 [2011], no. 85). Rev. A. J. Pollard, *Speculum* 85 (2010): 1019–20.

392. Sanok, Catherine. *Her Life Historical: Exemplarity and Female Saints' Lives in Late Medieval England* (*SAC* 31 [2009], no. 298). Rev. Sarah Salih, *MP* 108 (2010): E15–E17.

393. Scala, Elizabeth, and Sylvia Federico, eds. *The Post-Historical Middle Ages* (*SAC* 33 [2011], no. 88). Rev. Kathleen Davis, *TMR* 10.04.14, n.p.; Paul Strohm, *Postmedieval: A Journal of Medieval Cultural Studies* 1 (2010): 380–91.

394. Scanlon, Larry, ed. *The Cambridge Companion to Medieval English Literature, 1100–1500* (*SAC* 33 [2011], no. 89). Rev. Karen Gross, *SAC* 32 (2010): 465–69.

395. Scase, Wendy. *Literature and Complaint in England, 1272–1553* (*SAC* 31 [2009], no. 127). Rev. Julia Boffey, *N&Q* 255 (2010): 122–23; Russell A. Peck, *Speculum* 85 (2010): 461–62; John Watts, *EHR* 125 (2010): 690–91.

396. Schibanoff, Susan. *Chaucer's Queer Poetics: Rereading the Dream Trio* (*SAC* 30 [2008], no. 145). Rev. Tison Pugh, *MP* 107 (2009): 175–77.

397. Schoff, Rebecca L. *Reformations: Three Medieval Authors in Manu-*

script and Movable Type (*SAC* 31 [2009], no. 128). Rev. Thomas Prendergast, *Speculum* 84 (2009): 1109–11.

398. Summit, Jennifer. *Memory's Library: Medieval Books in Early Modern England* (*SAC* 32 [2010], no. 28). Rev. Gordon McMullen, *JBSt* 49 (2010): 148–50.

399. Sylvester, Louise M. *Medieval Romance and the Construction of Heterosexuality* (*SAC* 32 [2010], no. 142). Rev. Anne Laskaya, *Speculum* 84 (2009): 1114–15.

400. Thomas, Alfred. *A Blessed Shore: England and Bohemia from Chaucer to Shakespeare* (*SAC* 31 [2009], no. 137). Rev. Peter Brown, *ShakS* 38 (2010): 279–83.

401. Travis, Peter W. *Disseminal Chaucer: Rereading "The Nun's Priest's Tale"* (*SAC* 34 [2012], no. 262). Rev. Martin Camargo, *RES* 61 (2010): 807–8; Theresa Tinkle, *TMR* 10.09.21, n.p.

402. Woods, William F. *Chaucerian Spaces: Spatial Poetics in Chaucer's Opening Tales* (*SAC* 32 [2010], no. 160). Rev. Louise M. Bishop, *Speculum* 84 (2009): 1122–23; Laura Varnam, *MÆ* 79.1 (2010): 137–38; Susan Yager, *JEGP* 109 (2010): 403–5.

403. Zieman, Katherine. *Singing the New Song: Literacy and Liturgy in Late Medieval England* (*SAC* 32 [2010], no. 263). Rev. Brandon Alakas, *EHR* 125 (2010): 404–6; Alexandra Barrett, *JEGP* 109 (2010): 248–50; Jay Diehl, *Journal of Medieval Religious Cultures* 36 (2010): 136–39; Sherry L. Reames, *Speculum* 84 (2009): 791–93.

Author Index—Bibliography

INDEX